BLUE GUIDE

SICILY

ELLEN GRADY

EDITORIAL CONSULTANT: MICHAEL METCALFE

SOMERSET · LONDON

CONTENTS

PRACTICAL INFORMATION

MAPS & PLANS

Ninth edition 2017

Published by Blue Guides Limited, a Somerset Books Company
Winchester House, Deane Gate Avenue, Taunton, Somerset TA1 2UH
www.blueguides.com
'Blue Guide' is a registered trademark.

ISBN 978-1-905131-74-7

A CIP catalogue record of this book is available from the British Library.

Distributed in the United States of America by
W.W. Norton & Company, Inc.
500 Fifth Avenue, New York, NY 10110.

The author and publisher have made reasonable efforts to ensure the accuracy of all
the information in *Blue Guide Sicily*; however, they can accept no responsibility for any
loss, injury or inconvenience sustained by any traveller as a result of information or
advice contained in the guide.

Statement of editorial independence: Blue Guides, their authors and editors,
are prohibited from accepting any payment from any restaurant, hotel, gallery or other
establishment for its inclusion in this guide, or for a more favourable mention than
would otherwise have been made.

Every effort has been made to contact the copyright owners of material reproduced in this
guide. We would be pleased to hear from any copyright owners we have been unable to reach.

Your views on this book would be much appreciated. We welcome not only specific
comments, suggestions or corrections, but any more general views you may have: how
this book enhanced your visit, how it could have been more helpful. Blue Guides authors
and editorial and production team work hard to bring you what we hope are the best-
researched and best-presented cultural guide books in the English language. Please
write to us by email (editorial@blueguides.com), via the comments page on our website
(www.blueguides.com) or at the address given above. We will be happy to acknowledge
useful contributions in the next edition, and to offer a free copy of one of our titles.

Series editor: Annabel Barber
Maps: Dimap Bt. Floor plans: Imre Bába
Architectural line drawings: Michael Mansell RIBA & Gabriella Juhász
All maps, plans and drawings © Blue Guides.
All images © Blue Guides except p. 131 (©istockphoto.com/V1V1),
p. 149 (©istockphoto.com/photovideostock), p. 291 (Wikicommons/Davide Mauro), p. 247
(©istockphoto.com/Giovanni Rinaldi), p. 417 (©istockphoto.com/DomenicoPellegriti),
p. 447 (©istockphoto.com/sal61); pp. 87, 351, 399 (James Howells) and pp. 57, 159, 251, 306,
323, 473 (grateful thanks to Giacomo Mazza, Diana Mazza and Ellen Grady).
Cover: Monreale cathedral, by Michael Mansell RIBA & Gabriella Juhász © Blue Guides.
All material prepared for press by Anikó Kuzmich.

Ellen Grady wishes to thank the Touring Club Italiano. Also Signoretta Alliata, Marta Anelli, Grazia Barbagallo Mazza, Beatrice Basile, Fabio Bonaccorsi, Salvo Buffa, Rosario Cassaro, Laura Cassataro, Enzo Castagna, Claudio Castiglione, Tony D'Aiello, Franco D'Angelo, Primo David, Emily Felis, Damiano Ferraro, Michele Gallo, Italo Giordano, Maria Costanza Lentini, Francesco Lisciotto, Tania Lo Cicero, Diana and Giacomo Mazza, Nigel McGilchrist, Franco Purpura, Nicola Santamaria, Antonio Scalisi, Francesca Spadafora, Sebastiano Tusa, Maria Grazia Vanaria, the Whitaker Foundation and Roger Wilson, and to Gaetano Maurizio Pantano, for his *Megaliti di Sicilia* (Edizioni Fotocolor). Very special thanks to Giuseppe Leonardi, who saved her life so she could finish the book, and to Annabel Barber, her patient editor. For comments on the previous edition, thanks to Per-Erik Skramstad and William Cole.

Printed in Hungary by Dürer Nyomda Kft., Gyula.

Ellen Grady (author) is a writer, interpreter and tour guide. She has lived most of her life in Italy and her interests and expertise range from art, archaeology and history to birdwatching and the study of local cuisine. She is the author of the last four editions of *Blue Guide Sicily*. She has also written *Blue Guide The Marche & San Marino* and is contributor to the latest edition of *Blue Guide Italy Food Companion*.

Dr Michael Metcalfe (editorial consultant) lived in Sicily for many years, during which time he taught at the University of Catania and the Mediterranean Centre for Arts and Sciences in Syracuse. He is currently Academic Director at the Syracuse Academy. A specialist in ancient history and Greek epigraphy, he has taken part in several archaeological projects in Sicily, Greece and Turkey and is preparing the first complete database of archaeological collections in Sicily for publication with the I.Sicily project of Oxford University. He organises and leads cultural and archaeological tours in Italy, Greece and Turkey for Peter Sommer Travels, for whom he has created a series of tours of southern Italy and Sicily. He is also co-editor of *Blue Guide Greece the Aegean Islands*.

Charles Freeman (contributor) is a freelance academic historian who has travelled widely in the Mediterranean and written extensively on Classical culture. The third edition of his *Egypt, Greece and Rome* (Oxford, 2014) is widely used as an introduction to the ancient Mediterranean and is complemented by his *Sites of Antiquity, 50 Sites that Explain the Classical World* (Blue Guides, 2009). His programme of study tours includes Sicily and he has contributed material to many Blue Guides.

Historical Sketch

by Charles Freeman and Ellen Grady

Sicily lies at the crossroads of the Mediterranean. The Italian mainland is very close, separated by the narrow Straits of Messina, while the coast of North Africa is only some 250km away, a day's sailing in good conditions. Anyone passing across the Mediterranean would be likely to make landfall in Sicily, which historically gave it immense strategic value. The island's fertility also attracted settlement, with the result that periods of prosperity were interspersed with violent conflict over resources. Sicily today is a palimpsest of earlier civilisations, their remains jostling alongside each other against the backdrop of extraordinary natural beauty.

There are traces of human settlement from the Palaeolithic age (35,000–9000 BC), with the Upper Palaeolithic (18,000–9000) especially rich in sites. These show a population able to exploit a variety of habitats along with the development of burial rituals, decorative artefacts, mostly in stone, and cave art. The art is concentrated in a group of caves on Levanzo and around Monte Pellegrino in the northwest of the island, with the focus mainly on animals, predominantly horses, oxen and deer. In the Mesolithic period (9000–6000 BC) there was more exploitation of the sea, with the result that some communities became settled on the coast. However, it was red deer which were the main source of food and hides: their bones make up 70 percent of remains on some sites. Settled agriculture, which in Sicily dates from c. 6000–5500 BC, appears to have been an imported change. The remains of corn, sheep and goats are found for the first time in this period. Pottery, known as Stentinello ware, from a Neolithic site near Syracuse, has impressed or incised decoration and from about 5500 is painted, copying styles from Italy. A particularly important trade until about 2500 was in obsidian from the Aeolian island of Lipari, a volcanic stone which can be easily cut and shaped to make tools.

The first extensive contact with the wider Mediterranean comes in the Mycenaean age (1600–1150 BC). The Mycenaean strongholds were in the Greek Peloponnese and their chieftains were successful traders, whose presence in Sicily reached its height in about 1400 BC. This is the first time that Sicily can be placed within a far-flung trading complex, with evidence of routes which stretched as far east as Rhodes and Cyprus. A harbour site such as Thapsos, near modern Syracuse, certainly grew prosperous on trade. Mycenaean civilisation disintegrated after 1200, and Sicily, like many other parts of the Mediterranean, retreated into isolation. The island's primary contact for the next three centuries was with Italy.

SICANS, SICELS, AUSONIANS AND ELYMIANS

Greek historians provide some details of the inhabitants of Sicily before the 8th century. Thucydides, writing in the 5th century BC, speaks of a native people of Sicily known as the Sicans, who were pushed into the southern and western parts of the island by newcomers from Italy, the Sicels (hence 'Sicilia'), who settled in the eastern region. Thucydides gives a date for the 'invasion' of some three centuries before the first Greek settlement (i.e. about 1050), but other Greek sources suggest it was much earlier, well before the Trojan War, so perhaps 1300–1250. There is some archaeological and linguistic evidence to support the arrival of newcomers from Italy in the 13th century BC, with another group known as the Ausonians, named after their mythical founder Auson, arriving from central Italy perhaps in the 11th century. A third people, the Elymians, whom Thucydides tells us were refugees from Troy, are recorded as having settled in the west of Sicily.

PHOENICIANS AND GREEKS

In the 8th century Mediterranean trade began to revive. The Phoenicians, the biblical Canaanites, from the ancient cities of the Levantine coast, are normally seen as the pioneers, probing into the western Mediterranean in search of metals with which to pay their overlords, the Assyrians. They gave confidence to the Greeks who began following the same routes. Naxos was the first Sicilian landfall for those aiming to sail round the toe of Italy from the east and it was here that settlers from Chalcis in Euboea established a base in 734. A small fertile valley gave them the means to settle and the native population appears to have been dispersed. This became the usual practice as a mass of other Greek migrants followed the Chalcidians. The Corinthians settled the best harbour of the coast, Syracuse, the very next year, while Euboeans who had earlier settled at Cumae on the west coast of Italy, then took over the harbour at Zancle (later Messina) to protect their route to Italy. So quite quickly the better harbours were taken and settlements founded. Excavations at Megara Hyblaea show how temples and an agora (a market place) on a native Greek model were planned into the early settlement. With the best sites on the east coast taken, Greeks moved along the southern coast of Sicily to found Gela (688) and Akragas (Agrigento; 580). The Sicel communities were broken up, their populations dispersed or absorbed. The Greek colonisation of Sicily was so successful that grain was soon being exported back to Greece and across to Italy and Africa. Pottery from Athens, Sparta and Corinth is found on Sicilian sites and coinage appears quite early, in the last half of the 6th century. Settlements developed into cities with large temples and other public buildings. (Selinunte and Akragas have particularly impressive ruins) They sent competitors to the Olympic games and, with plenty of fertile pasture for horses, were especially successful in chariot racing. The famous bronze charioteer at Delphi commemorates the victory of Polyzelis of Gela in the Pythian Games of 478 BC.

Yet there was trouble brewing. The Phoenicians had established their own settlements, notably Carthage on the coast of north Africa, and in Spain, which was rich in metal resources, and it was inevitable that there would be settlements on Sicily itself. At first these were no more than staging posts concentrated in the west.

Coins from the Agrigento Gold Hoard (*see p. 209*). All 52 coins have the helmeted head of Mars on the obverse and the eagle of Jupiter on the reverse, with the god's thunderbolt and the inscription ROMA.

The most successful Phoenician site was Motya, a small island off the west coast (modern Mozia). It was close to Carthage, defensible (with a perimeter wall 2500m) and enjoyed good relationships with the native Elymian population. The earliest occupation dates from the late 8th century BC but by the 7th century there is evidence of industrial activity, in iron and dyes, and the population may have reached 16,000 in the 6th century. It was now that the Persian empire absorbed the Phoenician cities of the Levant, and gradually the western settlements developed their own independent empire under the control of Carthage.

THE CARTHAGINIANS

Conflict between Carthaginians and Greeks was perhaps inevitable. The first clashes were over sites outside Sicily as the Carthaginians tried to exclude outsiders from the western Mediterranean. In 514 BC, a Spartan, Doreius, attempted to challenge Carthage's growing power by making a Greek settlement within Carthaginian territory in Sicily, but he was driven out. The Greek cities began mobilising themselves in resistance. It became increasingly common for strong leaders, so-called tyrants, to emerge as rulers of the Greeks. One such was Gelon of Gela (491–477), who decided to make Syracuse his capital by transferring half his own city's population there. In 480 he won a spectacular victory at Himera, which led to the Carthaginians being subdued for the next 70 years. In 453 the Greeks then faced another threat, from a Hellenised Sicel, Ducetius. His Sicel League defeated several Greek cities until he was overcome in 451.

In 431 a major war broke out between Athens and Sparta, the Peloponnesian War. One of Sparta's allies, Corinth, still had close ties with its colony Syracuse, and the wealth of Sicily made it an important prize. The Athenians saw their chance to exploit local tensions, allying themselves with the city of Segesta which built a spectacular temple to impress the Athenians to gain support against their rival, Selinunte. Athens sent a major expedition to the island but the size of the fleet aroused suspicions in Syracuse. Suspecting that Athenian ambitions encompassed more than just tiny Selinunte, the Syracusans called on Spartan military expertise and Corinthian naval support and destroyed the Athenian fleet. The historian Thucydides has left a harrowing account of the debacle, with the few Athenian survivors being herded off to work in Syracuse's stone quarries. However, Syracuse was also weakened. The Carthaginians saw their chance of taking revenge for Himera, and in 405 moved from their western enclave to capture Akragas and Gela. It was this crisis which saw the emergence of Syracuse's most successful tyrant, Dionysius I (see p. 368).

On Dionysius' death, his son Dionysius II became the new ruler of Syracuse. He was a failure. Despite a visit from the Athenian philosopher Plato to school him in the art of good government, the empire collapsed into anarchy. The smaller Greek cities broke away under their own tyrants, who fought among themselves as well as against the Carthaginians. Things became so desperate that the Syracusans sent back to their mother city Corinth to ask for help in restoring order. The man sent was Timoleon. He deposed Dionysius II in 344, but then had to face a siege of Syracuse by a resurgent Carthaginian empire. Only an outbreak of plague saved the city from capture. Timoleon finally defeated the Carthaginians at the Crimissus River in 341. He regained control of the smaller Greek cities, and brought about a short lived but significant period of prosperity. On his death, however, anarchy returned as different groups fought each other for power over Greek Sicily. This was the pattern for the next 70 years. A war leader would emerge, have a few years of success, and then be killed or lose control. So one Agathocles came to power as 'general with full powers' in Syracuse in 319 and took on the Carthaginians in a campaign which included an expedition to Africa itself but which ended in his defeat both there and in Sicily. He was forced to sue for peace and was assassinated in 289. One of his few achievements had been to marry a stepdaughter of the new Greek ruler of Egypt, Ptolemy I, and by doing so, bring Sicily into the wider Hellenistic world. From now on Sicilian tyrants tended to ape their colleagues in the eastern Mediterranean by taking on the trappings of kingship, including a cult of the ruler, courts and a royal family. The most influential legacy of Agathocles was largely unexpected. His mercenary force from Italy, the so-called Mamertines (in their native language 'sons of the war god Mamers', the Oscan equivalent of Mars), exploited the anarchy after his death to seize the city of Messana (later Messina), the former Greek city of Zancle, and use it as a base for plundering northeastern Sicily. A new tyrant of Syracuse, Hieron II, who like Agathocles presented himself as royalty, defeated them in 265, whereupon the Mamertines called on the Carthaginians for help. The Carthaginians did send a small garrison but the next year the Mamertines went further and appealed to Italy's most successful military power, the city of Rome. It was to be a decision which would change history.

THE ROMANS

The Romans decided to launch an expedition to Sicily. The threat of Roman incursion brought the Carthaginians and Hieron into alliance against them but the Romans defeated their united forces, whereupon Hieron sought an alliance with Rome. It was granted and Hieron became one of the most successful of the Sicilian tyrant-kings. By supplying the Roman armies with grain, he was able to keep his kingdom and status intact and was able to stand by and watch the protracted and debilitating war which Rome waged against the Carthaginians (the First Punic War 264–241 BC).

One of Rome's first successes in Sicily was the capture of Akragas, which had been held by a Carthaginian garrison. However, it became clear that Rome—then without a navy—could never defeat Carthage unless it acquired one. There are few better examples of Rome's resilience than the story of how she became a naval power and, despite many setbacks and some major defeats, finally crushed the Carthaginians in a naval victory off the Aegadian islands in 241 (in 2010, *rostra*, battering rams from ships sunk in the battle were dredged up from the seabed). Carthaginian control of western Sicily, which had lasted many centuries, was brought to an end. The Carthaginians were still not finally defeated, however. In 218 a brilliant leader emerged: Hannibal. Seeking revenge on Rome, he invaded Italy from Spain. Then, in 215, Hieron II of Syracuse died. Syracuse was still an independent state: not wanting to fall under Roman control, she appealed to Carthage for support. Realising how crucially important it would be to regain Sicily as a base for supplies, Hannibal granted it and sent troops. The Roman counter-attack was swift, and they captured Syracuse in 212 (their victory retarded by the brilliant defence techniques masterminded by the great scientist Archimedes). The Roman general Marcellus freighted such rich booty back in triumph to Rome that Roman conservatives talked of the corruption of their city by the decadence of the Greek East.

Sicily, 'the nurse at whose breast the Roman people is fed' as Cicero was to put it, proved to be vital to Rome for a steady supply of grain to the growing city and the Roman armies. Also an important strategic base, it was Rome's first overseas province and was ruled through a praetor, an elected magistrate with military powers. Hieron had instituted a tax in grain and it was comparatively easy for the Romans to divert this to themselves. Sicily would prove to be a well-behaved province: administration was light and cities were given a high degree of independence. By the 2nd century BC there was once again great prosperity on the island. Though the old hilltop cities went into decline, it was because their inhabitants were moving down to take advantage of the new security and opportunities for grain production on lower land. Estates grew large and slaves were brought in *en masse* from Rome's new conquests in the East. Their treatment by the new owners appears to have been brutal, however, and between c. 135–132 and c. 104–100, there were major slave revolts (*see p. 271*) which took hard fighting to suppress. Oppression of a very different kind came at the hands of corrupt governors, the most notorious of whom was Verres (73–71; *see p. 205*). Archaeology suggests that nonetheless the underlying prosperity of the province continued without interruption.

The island could not escape the civil wars which tore Rome apart in the second half of the 1st century BC. When Julius Caesar confronted the ageing general Pompey in Italy in 49, he won over Sicily by promising the Sicilians 'Latin rights', privileges which in earlier times had been given to favoured cities (and which gave access to full Roman citizenship). In the short term it worked (Pompey was defeated in 48) but after Caesar's own assassination in 44, the son of Pompey, Sextus, seized Sicily and withheld the grain supply from Rome. The Sicilians unwisely collaborated with him and when Caesar's great-nephew, Octavian, retook the island, he dealt ruthlessly with any city which did not immediately surrender. The entire population of one, Tauromenium

Hispano-Moresque lustreware dish of the 15th century. Now part of the collection of Palazzo Abatellis in Palermo.

(Taormina), was deported and others lost their Latin rights. Octavian (known, from 27 BC, as Augustus, and the first Roman emperor) established several colonies of former Roman soldiers in the province, to enforce better control, and took large tracts of land as imperial estates.

As the Roman empire expanded, the importance of Sicily as a source of grain was diminished and Egypt and the North African provinces became major suppliers. A 1st-century AD mosaic of corn-growing provinces in Ostia, the port of the city of Rome, shows symbols of Sicily alongside those of Egypt, Africa and Spain. No legions needed to be stationed on the island and there is only one isolated reference to banditry, in the 260s. Mount Etna and Syracuse have occasional mentions as tourist attractions. Sicilians seem to have played little part in imperial administrations, but the archaeological evidence is of general prosperity: well-endowed towns with theatres, baths and aqueducts. One source even lists two Sicilian towns, Catania and Syracuse, as thirteenth and fourteenth in a list of celebrated cities of the empire, while the villa at Piazza Armerina shows just how sophisticated life was for the elite in the 4th century.

THE BYZANTINES AND ARABS

Life continued on an even keel until the Western empire began to disintegrate in the 5th century. In AD 429, the Vandals under their leader Gaiseric took North Africa and began raiding the prosperous coastal towns of Sicily. In 486 he was finally able to take control of the whole island, which he sold eight years later to Odoacer, ruler of Italy following the deposition of the last Western emperor. In 535, a counter-attack by the Eastern, now Byzantine, empire, under its general Belisarius, ended with Sicily becoming part of the empire itself. By now Sicily was heavily Christianised and papal estates had succeeded the older imperial ones. More letters survive from Pope Gregory the Great (590–604) about his Sicilian estates than about all the others put together.

With time, however, the island's economy, based only on silk and wheat, began to decline and the population dramatically decreased due to poor farming methods and

Above and opposite: Three faces of Christ Pantocrator from the Norman churches of Sicily.
Left to right: Palermo (Cappella Palatina), Monreale, Cefalù.

bouts of famine. The Byzantine governor Euphemius called on the Arabs, who landed at Mazara del Vallo in AD 827. Within 50 years they had taken over governance of the whole island and were to prove far-sighted and intelligent rulers. They brought with them skilled craftsmen, both Jewish and Muslim. Jewish Berbers from Morocco settled in Syracuse, where they became acclaimed weavers. In Piazza Armerina and Messina their goldsmiths became renowned in the art of making wire from gold mixed with a little copper, which was exported for making filigree jewellery. Arab farmers revolutionised agriculture by introducing terracing, irrigation and water-storage tanks. They planted new crops, including rice, cotton, sugar-cane, pistachios, apricots, peaches and citrus fruits, as well as roses and jasmine for the perfume industry, indigo, and groves of mulberry trees to feed silk-worms. The island was divided into three administrative districts: Val Demone, Val di Mazara and Val di Noto, each governed by a *cadi*, who reported to an emir in Palermo. Numerous settlers came from North Africa and Spain to swell the population. By the 10th century Sicily was one of the most prosperous regions of Europe, and Palermo was a great centre of scholarship and art, rivalling Cordoba and Cairo for the number of mosques, gardens and fountains. The Arabs called this country *Balad es-Siqilliah*, 'Land of the Sicels'.

THE NORMANS

The Normans probably set their sights on Sicily around 1035, but like the Arabs they had to wait for the right moment, and theirs too would prove to be an extremely long-drawn-out conquest. The Normans' greatest strength was in their mercenary troops, the most respected and feared in Europe. Their moment came in 1060, when the *cadi* Ibn at-Thumnah of Catania fell foul of Ibn al-Hawwas of Agrigento. He summoned the armies of Robert Guiscard and Roger de Hauteville to fight for him; they won that battle, the *cadi* was killed, and the Normans hung onto their spoils. Not only this; they

kept fighting. In the same year Roger took Messina; by 1091 the whole island was under his control.

Despite their ruthlessness in battle, the Normans proved willing to adapt to the many cultural traditions which already existed on the island and different religions and customs were respected. The first Sicilian Parliament met at Mazara del Vallo in 1097. Count Roger was never crowned king, although he is usually known as Roger I of Sicily. In 1099 Pope Urban II named him great-count of Calabria and Sicily, and apostolic legate. This prerogative was to prove of fundamental importance for the future of Sicily, because it meant that the ruler had the right to name the prelates in his territory—in practice, total power. When his son Roger II was crowned in 1130, it was his own archbishop who performed the ceremony, not the pope. Roger II was probably the wealthiest ruler in Europe and his court in Palermo the most opulent. Meanwhile Messina flourished as a supply base for the Crusaders. Roger was succeeded by his son William I (the Bad; d. 1166), who was in turn succeeded by his son William II (the Good; d. 1189), whose wife was Joan Plantagenet, daughter of Henry II of England and Eleanor of Aquitaine.

Norman domination, with its architecture showing a strongly oriental influence, has left many magnificent buildings, of which the churches are its most celebrated achievement today. The interiors of Cefalù and Monreale cathedrals and of the Cappella Palatina in Palermo all have exquisite mosaic decoration.

THE SWABIANS, ANGEVINS, ARAGONESE AND BOURBONS

The Norman dynasty did not last long; in 1194 the crown was claimed by Emperor Henry VI of Swabia in the name of his wife Constance (daughter of Roger II), and the last of the Hautevilles were put to death. Henry died young and was succeeded in 1198 by his baby son Frederick II of Hohenstaufen, 'Stupor Mundi' (*see p. 34*), whose reign marks the passage between the Middle Ages and modern times. His court in Palermo was famous for its splendour and learning. Unlike his predecessors, Frederick did not endow monasteries or build cathedrals; he devoted his building energies to creating a line of fortifications running from Germany to southern Italy and Sicily. Castles dominated the cities and fortresses were erected at strategic points inland. The Swabian line ended with the beheading of Frederick's young grandson Conradin in 1268 by the forces of Charles of Anjou.

Charles of Anjou, brother of Louis IX of France, had the backing of the (French) pope and was invested with the crown of Sicily and Naples, thus beginning the hated rule of the Angevins. The famous revolt of 1282, known as the Sicilian Vespers (*see p. 75*), brought an end to that unhappy period, and the Sicilians called Peter of Aragon, renowned for his sense of justice and good government, to be their king. He accepted, on condition that after his death Sicily and Aragon would be ruled as separate kingdoms. This did not come to pass, and in the course of time Sicily lost her independence and became a province of Aragon and then of Spain as a whole, to be ruled by a series of viceroys for the Spanish and then the Bourbon kings. One of these kings, Alfonso the Magnanimous, founded the University of Catania in 1434, the first in Sicily. Rebellions, famine, unrest and epidemics mark the 15th century, and in 1492 when Muslims and Jews were expelled from Spain's dominions by Ferdinand and Isabella, they were expelled from Sicily too (which had been home to a quarter of all Jews in the Italian peninsula) and the Inquisition was set up in Palermo.

Architecture and painting in the early 15th century were much influenced by Catalan masters, as can be seen from the south porch of the cathedral and at Palazzo Abatellis in Palermo. Matteo Carnelivari was the most important architect working in Palermo at this time. The Renaissance sculptor Francesco Laurana came to work in Palermo in the middle of the 15th century. Another influential sculptor in the second half of the same century was Domenico Gagini; his style was continued into the following century by his son Antonello and his vast progeny. The most famous artist of the late 15th century is Antonello da Messina, whose introduction of the technique of oil painting, which he had probably learned in the Netherlands, dramatically altered the history of Western art.

THE COUNTER-REFORMATION AND BAROQUE

Because of its position on the Straits, Messina was in closer contact with the mainland than other towns in Sicily, and during the 16th century artists from Florence and Rome often travelled there. Sculptors were particularly welcome, as civic administrations endeavoured to beautify their towns with flamboyant 'urban furniture'. When the young monk Giovanni Angelo Montorsoli arrived from Florence in 1547, he introduced Tuscan Mannerism with his Orion fountain (*see p. 448*), a work which proved immensely influential. This was the period of the Counter-Reformation, when lavish churches and convents were being erected all over the island in response to the Protestant threat. It was also an age of increased insecurity, as Turkish pirates continually harried ships and coasts. The brilliant victory of the Christians over the Muslims of Mohammed Ali at Lepanto in 1571 did little to solve this particular

Head of a boy by Antonello Gagini, part of the collection
of Palazzo Abatellis in Palermo.

problem; and in the interior of the island brigands and bandits were making life difficult for farmers and travellers.

From the mid-17th century to the end of the 18th numerous splendid Baroque churches were erected in Palermo, many of them by the local architect Giacomo Amato, the interiors lavishly decorated with coloured marble, mosaic inlay and stuccoes. Giacomo Serpotta was a great master of this art, while Pietro Novelli of Monreale was the most outstanding of the 17th century Sicilian painters. But it is in eastern Sicily where we find the finest examples of the so-called Sicilian Baroque (*see* *p. 321*). An eruption of Mount Etna in 1669, followed by the earthquake of 1693, meant that first Catania, and then most of the other towns, had to be completely rebuilt. Beauty emerged defiantly from tragedy. Architects, sculptors, master-masons, stucco-moulders, wood-carvers and painters were suddenly in great demand, and their art flourished.

In 1713, after the Treaty of Utrecht which concluded the War of the Spanish Succession, Spanish rule in Sicily ended. The island was assigned first to Savoy, then to Austria, and finally to the Bourbons of Naples, who would hold it as part of the Kingdom of the Two Sicilies until 1860.

REVOLUTION AND UNIFICATION

When Napoleon failed to invade Sicily in 1806, the British took control for a short time, and established a constitution (though it never received sufficient backing to be effective). Disaffection with the Bourbons, whose inept rule had left so many Sicilians impoverished and disenfranchised, led to revolution in 1848. Though the rebels were savagely crushed, the revolutionary spirit refused to die, and in 1860 Garibaldi led an attack against the Bourbons which paved the way for Italian Unification. Unification worked better for the north of Italy than it did for Sicily, who found the rule of the Piedmontese statesman Camillo Cavour unsympathetic and felt that northern Italian cities were being favoured over southern. What is certain is that the economic position of Sicily remained a long way behind that of the rest of Italy. The collapse of the sulphur industry coupled with a blight that attacked the silkworms making it impossible form them to spin cocoons, and the phylloxera outbreak which destroyed the vineyards, led to the emigration of almost a million and a half Sicilians (almost half the population at the time) to the Americas and to Australia, between 1895 and 1910.

THE TWENTIETH CENTURY

Despite economic hardship, the early 20th century was the golden age of Art Nouveau. The inspired work of Ernesto Basile and Francesco Fichera made this style fashionable throughout Sicily: as a centre of Art Nouveau architecture, Palermo is surpassed in Italy only by Turin and Milan. The carefree, wealthy middle class of Palermo, orbiting around the Florio financial empire, flitted from their beautiful new homes to one lovely theatre after another and to the fashionable bathing resort of Mondello, in a city which had only one hospital (and a rather forbidding one at that) and where thousands of people were living in extreme poverty, in crowded slums hidden behind the attractive main streets.

After the disastrous earthquake which hit Messina in December 1908, the economy of the whole island suffered. Rebuilding was by no means complete when the Second World War broke out. The geographical position of Sicily meant that the Allies chose the island for their first important attack on Hitler in Europe, Operation Husky in 1943. In 1944 civil war broke out on the island, with many islanders calling for independence. The statute for autonomous government was approved by Rome in 1946 and the first modern Sicilian parliament was elected in 1947. No economic miracle has been performed however, and even now thousands of Sicilians are still forced to emigrate in search of work. For the visitor, however, Sicily is still a land of marvels.

THE MAFIA

The Mafia probably began as a kind of insurance policy against the insensitive governments of the 18th and 19th centuries, providing immediate justice for those who had been wronged. A senior person was chosen in each community to solve controversies; he was paid in kind and his decisions were final; everything about the system was protected by closely-guarded secrecy (*omertà*), which even torture or death could not break. The method was certainly favoured by the aristocracy of the island, who saw it as a way of maintaining control over the people through the offices of much-feared local agents. Shopkeepers, farmers and craftsmen were invited to make regular 'offerings', or provide free services to these individuals to be sure of protection and to avert dire consequences. It became an ingrained custom, known as *mafia* (a Piedmontese word) only after the Unification of Italy in 1860; on the island it has always been known as *Cosa Nostra*, 'Our Thing'.

After the Second World War, thanks to the collusion between politics and the Mafia, the phenomenon grew much worse. Giovanni Falcone, the magistrate who investigated the Mafia and was assassinated in 1992, estimated that there were more than 5,000 'men of honour' in Sicily, chosen after a rigorous selection process. He saw them as true professionals of crime, who obeyed strict rules. Through the rigid 'protection' system they have controlled Sicilian business transactions for many years.

In the 1980s a number of people in key positions, including magistrates, journalists, trade unionists, politicians and members of the police force who stood up to the Mafia, were killed by the organisation. A sentence passed in 1987, at the end of the largest trial ever held against the Mafia (the evidence for which had been collected by Giovanni Falcone), condemned hundreds of people for crimes connected with the organisation. But this victory was soon overshadowed when the anti-Mafia 'pool' of judges, created by Antonino Caponnetto in 1983 and led by Giovanni Falcone, disintegrated because of internal conflicts and a belief on the part of Falcone that his fight against the racket was being obstructed from above. In 1992 this courageous Sicilian, who had raised the hopes of so many Italians, was assassinated with his wife and bodyguards on the motorway not far from Palermo. Just three months later his friend and fellow magistrate Paolo Borsellino was also murdered, outside his mother's house in Palermo. Then, in Florence a bomb exploded in the heart of the old city, in Via dei Georgofili. These events were seen by many as cynical attempts to force the government into making prison conditions easier for condemned Mafia affiliates; the response from Rome was to send in the army.

However, since 1992 the whole question of the power of the Mafia has been placed on a different level. 1992, the year of the assassinations of Falcone and Borsellino, was also the year of *Tangentopoli*, or 'Clean Hands', when the link between corrupt politicians, kick-backs and extortion was finally brought to light in Milan. Many well-known political figures could not survive the scandal.

In 1993 the arrest of Totò Riina, the acknowledged *capo dei capi*, after more than 20 years 'in hiding' in Palermo, closely followed by the capture of Nitto Santapaola, local boss of Catania, and more recently by that of Bernardo Provenzano (he had been 'in hiding' for over 40 years, isolated in a derelict farm cottage, living on a diet of ricotta and wild greens), was greeted—with some scepticism—as a step in the right direction. In 1997 many bosses were convicted (and most were sentenced to life imprisonment) for their part in the murder of Falcone. Meanwhile, a group of stalwart magistrates in Palermo and Caltanissetta continues the struggle against the power of the Mafia; in spite of meagre resources they never give up.

PALAZZO ABATELLIS
Francesco Laurana's bust of Eleonora of Aragon (1475).

Palermo

T he city of Palermo (*map p. 574, B1*), capital of the Sicilian region, stands on a bay at the foot of Monte Pellegrino, a headland described by Goethe as the loveliest he had ever seen. During the early Middle Ages it was a prosperous and beautiful city, filled with fountains and gardens, a seat of culture and knowledge. It still preserves some of the great Arab-Norman buildings erected between the 9th and 12th centuries, as well as numerous Baroque churches and oratories of more recent date. It is the fifth largest city in Italy, a busy port, home to a diverse population of c. 660,000 and it enjoys a superb climate. The great 17th-century musicians and composers Francesco, Alessandro and Domenico Scarlatti were born here.

Sea levels were higher in antiquity and the original Phoenician settlement, established in the 8th century BC, was on a promontory bounded by two rivers. During the Arab period this was the site of the heavily fortified inner city, *al-Kasr*. As the waters receded, a lower city grew up nearer the port, *al-Halisah* (today's Kalsa), site of the emir's palace. The Normans chose the inner city as their base and transformed the Arab castle into their royal palace. The street leading from it to the cathedral was paved in marble and provided with porticoes, as the king, the royal family and the court would proceed on foot from one building to another. This street became known as the Cassaro (pron. CASsaro; from the Latin *castrum* and the Arabic *kasr*). By the mid-16th century the rivers had silted up and the harbour was much reduced in its proportions. From this time onward the plan of Palermo would hinge on two main thoroughfares: the Cassaro (today's Corso Vittorio Emanuele), extended to the east in 1565 and prolonged to the sea in 1581; and Via Maqueda (laid out c. 1600), running roughly parallel with the coast. These bisect one another at the Quattro Canti, neatly dividing the city into four quarters.

In the 19th and 20th centuries the city expanded northwards, from Piazza Verdi along the Viale della Libertà, and spreading far beyond its original boundaries. In the Jewish Quarter (Giudecca), roughly corresponding to the area just south of Sant'Agostino, you will notice that the street signs are written in Italian, Arabic and Hebrew, underlining the cosmopolitan character of old Palermo.

The Salinas Archaeological Museum, the Regional Art Gallery in Palazzo Abatellis, the Diocesan Museum and the Gallery of Modern Art all contain outstanding collections, while the Arab-Norman churches and palaces are memorable for their pure architecture and splendid mosaics. The famous street markets should not be missed.

TEN THINGS TO DO IN PALERMO

La Martorana, the Cathedral, Palazzo dei Normanni and the Cappella Palatina, the Archaeological Museum, Palazzo Abatellis and Villa Whitaker Malfitano are the must-see sights of Palermo. Here are ten others, less well-known.

1. A friendly jostle, elbow-to-elbow, for the breakfast ritual at the Bar Massaro (*Via Basile 24, near the main University on Viale delle Scienze; beyond map 5*).
2. Pay your respects to Rosalia, patron saint of the city, in her cave home near the top of Mt Pellegrino (*map p. 71*). Elegant in her dress of gold, she sleeps, while you marvel at the collection of ex-votos.
3. Palermo's insouciant blend of sacred and profane can be experienced by a stroll through the raucous Ballarò street market, with its colourful mountains of fish, fruit and vegetables; step into the Casa Professa and blink at the equally voluptuous Baroque splendour (*map 15*). A similar contrast is found by walking through the Capo stalls, laden with produce, and then popping into the church of the Immacolata (*map 10*).
4. Browse for curios in Piazza Peranni (*map 10*), and don't be afraid to haggle.
5. If in season, don't miss an opera at the Teatro Massimo (*map 11*).
6. Lunch should consist of an *arancina bomba* at the Bar Touring at Via Lincoln 18 (*map 16*), followed by a healthy constitutional in the Villa Giulia park, which is conveniently opposite, and the Botanical Gardens close by.
7. Find time for a surprising puppet show at Mimmo Cuticchio's little theatre in Via Bara dell'Olivella (*map 11*) and watch those wooden paladins spring to life—and fight to the death.
8. Among the marvels of the Loggia, in Via Valverde (*map 11*), the most astonishing is the Oratory of Santa Cita, with its exuberant stuccoes by Serpotta, justly described as the 'Birth and Death of Baroque'.
9. Of all the gardens of Palermo, that of San Giovanni degli Eremiti (*map 14*) is the most romantic.
10. In the evening, try some Palermo-style street food *'nni Francu u vastiddaru* (*Corso Vittorio Emanuele 102; map 12*), where the eclectic Franco prepares delectable sandwiches using chick-pea fritters, octopus, lamb intestines, beef spleen and ricotta, as his forebears have been doing since the founding of the city.

The *Spatola*, or Scabbard fish, shining silver and thin as a steel blade, commonly seen for sale in Sicilian markets.

HISTORY OF PALERMO

Traces of Palaeolithic settlements have been found in grottoes on Mt Pellegrino. The great fertility of the Conca d'Oro, the plain behind the bay, has supported the inhabitants of Palermo throughout her history. A Phoenician colony was founded here c. 750 BC and was known to the Greeks as Panormos ('all harbour', in other words a safe anchorage). It became an important Carthaginian centre, hotly disputed during the First Punic War and not finally acquired by Rome until 254 BC. It became a *municipium*, and after 20 BC, a flourishing *colonia*. After the invasions of the Vandals and Ostrogoths it was conquered for the Byzantine emperors in 535 and remained in their possession until 831, when the Arabs captured it after a prolonged resistance. Under Muslim rule it was made capital of an emirate (and named *al-Madinah*: 'the city'), rivalling Cordoba and Cairo in oriental splendour as 'the city of a thousand mosques'; its luxuriant gardens and fountains enchanted travellers. It became an important trading-post and cosmopolitan centre where Christians and Jews were tolerated.

Taken by Robert Guiscard and his younger brother Roger de Hauteville (later Count of Sicily) in 1072, it again enjoyed prosperity under Roger's son King Roger II (1130–54) and became the centre of trade between Europe and Asia. Under the brilliant reign of Emperor Frederick II of Hohenstaufen (1198–1250) the city became famous throughout Europe for its learning and magnificence.

The famous rebellion of the Sicilian Vespers (*see p. 75*) put an end to the misrule of Charles of Anjou in 1282. During the increasingly tyrannical Spanish domination which followed, the city gradually declined. Under the terms of the Treaty of Utrecht (1713) Sicily was allotted to Vittorio Amedeo of Savoy, who was, however, forced to exchange it for Sardinia (1718), ceding Sicily to the Neapolitan Bourbons. Under their rule the island fared little better, though Ferdinand IV was forced to establish his court at Palermo in 1799 during the French occupation of Naples, and during the 18th century Palermo was the largest town in Italy after Naples. The island was granted a temporary constitution in 1811 while under British protection. The city rebelled against misgovernment in 1820 (when Sir Richard Church was relieved of his governorship), 1848, and in April 1860. On 27th May 1860 Garibaldi and the 'Thousand' made a triumphant entry into the city.

Much of the centre of Palermo was badly damaged during air raids during the Second World War. After the war the Mafia took advantage of the confusion and much illegal building took place, both in the city and in the Conca d'Oro, its hinterland. Extensive and careful renovation is now going ahead.

AROUND THE QUATTRO CANTI

The centre of the old city is the crossroads known as the **Quattro Canti** (*map 11*), at the central intersection of Corso Vittorio Emanuele and Via Maqueda. The central space is named Piazza Vigliena after the Duke of Vigliena, Spanish viceroy in 1611, but it is

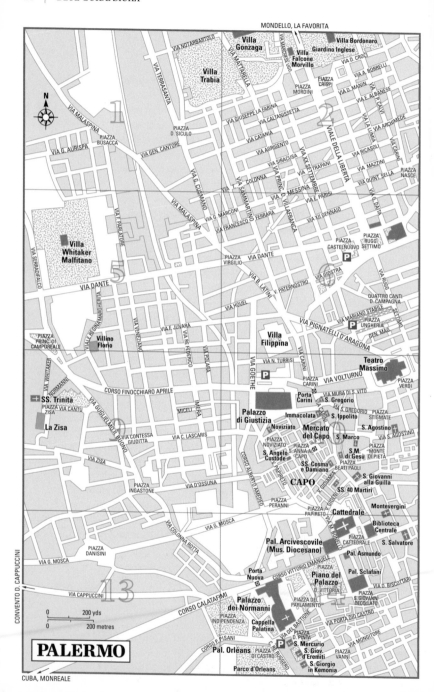

PALERMO

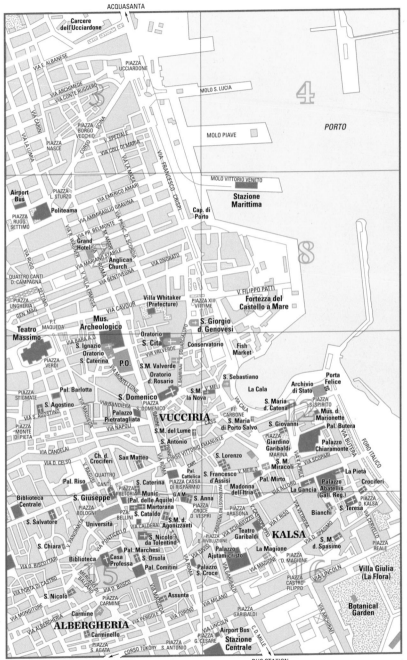

QUATTRO CANTI
South corner of the 'Teatro del Sole', with Santa Cristina and Charles V.

now often called Teatro del Sole, 'Theatre of the Sun', because during the course of a day the sun illuminates each of the four corners in turn. The decorative façades at each corner bear fountains with statues of the Four Seasons, four Spanish kings of Sicily, and the four patron saints of Palermo, Cristina, Ninfa, Oliva and Agata. Looking down Corso Vittorio Emanuele, you will see the Porta Nuova in one direction (southwest) and the sea in the other (northeast) beyond Porta Felice. From Via Maqueda, there is a vista of the hills surrounding the Conca d'Oro.

PIAZZA PRETORIA

A few steps along Via Maqueda to the southeast, Piazza Pretoria (*map 11*) is almost entirely occupied by a **High Renaissance fountain** (1554–5), designed by Francesco Camilliani, and later (1573) assembled and enlarged here by his son Camillo and Michelangelo Naccherino. The rivalry between Palermo and Messina, both of which through the centuries have struggled to emerge as the foremost city on the island, can be read in the history of this fountain. Messina was the first to supply its citizens with water from a nearby river by means of a modern aqueduct in 1547. A beautiful fountain, designed by a follower of Michelangelo, was commissioned to celebrate the event, and situated beside the cathedral. The Senate of Palermo, loth to be outdone, then purchased the enormous fountain which Camilliani had originally designed for the gardens of the Tuscan villa of Peter of Toledo, father-in-law by his daughter Eleonora to Cosimo de' Medici. Vasari was a great admirer of the fountain, which introduced the High Renaissance Mannerist style to Palermo. Occupying almost the whole of the piazza, the great basin is decorated with some 50 statues of monsters, harpies, sirens and tritons. Also copied from Messina was the idea of representing the four rivers, in this case the Oreto, Papireto, Kemonia and Gabriele, and instead of Orion, the figure on the summit was made to represent the Genius of Palermo (*see below*). Unfortunately for the city government, the nude or semi-clad white Carrara marble sculptures from Florence did not win the approval of the pious citizens of Palermo, who dubbed the new arrival the 'Fontana della Vergogna', or Fountain of Shame.

Palazzo delle Aquile, named after the eagles which decorate its exterior, but sometimes also referred to as Palazzo Pretorio, is the Town Hall (*open Mon–Sat 8–7.30, Sun 8–1; T: 091 740 2280, www.palazzodelleaquile.org*). Sadly in need of repair, especially inside, it was built in 1470, enlarged in the 16th century, and over-restored in 1874. The façade is surmounted by a 17th-century statue of Santa Rosalia. This was formerly the seat of the Senate, which governed the city from the 14th century until 1816, senators being nominated from the local aristocracy. In the atrium is a Baroque portal by Paolo Amato and a Roman funerary monument with statues of a husband and wife. At the foot of the 19th-century staircase stands part of a 16th-century **fountain of the *Genius of Palermo***, one of eight allegorical statues in the city with the figure of a young king with an old face, personifying Civic Rule, entangled in a serpent biting his chest, representing Wisdom, sometimes with a dog at his feet, for Loyalty, or a lion, for Strength, and an eagle on his shoulder, representing the Empire. On the first floor, the assembly room, which has a 16th-century painted wooden ceiling, is covered with numerous inscriptions relating to events which have taken place there. The other rooms, including that of the mayor, were decorated in 1870 by Giuseppe Damiani Almeyda and contain mementoes of Garibaldi and Napoleon.

The east side of the piazza is closed by the flank and dome of the 16th-century church of **Santa Caterina** (*officially open daily 10–6; T: 338 451 2011 or 338 722 8775*). The interior, especially the choir, is an elaborate example of Sicilian Baroque, with striking effects of early 18th-century sculptural decoration and marble veneering. In the right transept is a marble statue of St Catherine by Antonello Gagini (1534). The frescoes in the cupola are by Vito D'Anna (1751).

A 16th-century palace on the north side of the square, **Palazzo Bonocore**, houses the Patrimonio Immateriale Culturale della Sicilia (*open Mon–Fri 10–1.30 & 2.30–6; last tickets 30mins before closing; T: 091 697 0520*). This is an unusual, spectacular museum dedicated to Sicily's intangible cultural heritage, with a series of galleries illustrating by means of huge video-walls the activities which make the island unique. The cultivation of wheat and of Zibibbo grapes, the puppet theatre, ceramics, tuna fishing, saints' days and food are the main subjects.

SAN GIUSEPPE DEI TEATINI

Map 11–15. Open summer Mon–Sat 7.30–11 & 6–8; winter Mon–Sat 7.30–12 & 5.30–8. No visits on Sun, holidays or during services. T: 091 331239.

The upper church, built by Giacomo Besio of Genoa, was the scene of two popular assemblies called by Giuseppe d'Alessi during the revolt of 1647 against the Spanish governors. In the lavish Baroque interior, in addition to the 14 monolithic columns in the nave, eight colossal columns of grey marble support the well-proportioned central dome. The frescoes of the nave roof are copies of the originals by Filippo Tancredi; those in the dome are by Borremans; the stuccoes are outstandingly good. The two large angels holding the stoups on either side of the entrance are by Marabitti. In the fourth south chapel, with handsome marble decoration, is a statue of the Madonna by the Gagini school, while in the south transept, beneath the altarpiece (*St Andrew of Avellino* by Sebastiano Conca), is a charming frieze of child musicians, and the altar has a bas-relief of a *Madonna amidst Angels*, both by Federico Siragusa (1800). In the choir vault are fine reliefs, with full-length figures by Procopio Serpotta. In the chapels flanking the choir are (right) a Crucifix by Fra' Umile da Petralia and (left) reliefs by Filippo Pennino, and an 18th-century statue of St Joseph. In the north transept, above an altar of marble mosaic (probably late 17th century), is a painting of *St Cajetan* (Gaetano) by Pietro Novelli. St Cajetan (1480–1547) founded the strict Theatine congregation in response to a perceived lack of monastic spirit among the clergy.

Next to the church is the former convent of the Theatines, now occupied by the **university**. The small geological museum founded here in the early 19th century by the Theatine Giorgio Gemmellaro is now at Corso Tüköry 131 (*beyond map 15; Museo Geologico; open Mon–Fri 9–1 & 3–5, Sat 9–1, closed Sun and holidays, last tickets 30mins before closing; bookshop; T: 091 238 64665*). It houses a collection of fossils (including some of the dwarf elephants that lived in Sicily during the Pleistocene), local rocks, and a woman's skeleton, known as Thea, from the Upper Palaeolithic era.

LA MARTORANA & SAN CATALDO

Adjoining Piazza Pretoria is Piazza Bellini (*map 15*), dominated by the colonnaded campanile of La Martorana and the three little red domes of San Cataldo, raised above part of the east wall of the Roman city and surrounded by trees; it is fitting that these two beautiful churches, founded by George of Antioch and Maio of Bari, two of Norman Sicily's greatest statesmen, should survive together in the centre of the city.

LA MARTORANA

La Martorana or Santa Maria dell'Ammiraglio (*open 9–12, Wed and Fri also 3–6; T: 091 616 1692; joint ticket with San Cataldo; part of the Circuito Arte Sacra, see p. 77*) was founded in 1143 by George of Antioch, a Syrian of the Greek Orthodox faith who became admiral and chancellor for Roger II. It was presented in 1433 to a Benedictine convent founded in the 12th century by Eloisa Martorana, wife of Goffredo de Martorana. The Sicilian Parliament met here after the Sicilian Vespers. Since 1935 it has shared cathedral status with San Demetrio in Piana degli Albanesi, a small town of Albanian origin, and holds services according to the Greek Orthodox rite. Outside, the Norman structure survives on the north and south sides, although a Baroque façade was added in 1588 to the north side when the Norman narthex was demolished and the atrium covered.

The present entrance is beneath the 12th-century **campanile**, which survived the alterations (only its red dome is missing). Inside, the central Greek-cross plan of the tiny original church can still be detected, despite the Baroque alterations at the west end and the lengthening of the chancel in 1683.

The original mosaic decoration remains on and around the **central cupola (1)**. The mosaics, probably by Greek craftsmen from Constantinople, were completed between 1143 and 1151: Christ and four Archangels are depicted in the dome and, in Arabic lettering, a quotation from a Byzantine hymn; around the drum are Prophets and the Evangelists; on the triumphal arch, the *Annunciation*; in the **south apse (2)** St Anne (with orange trees below her) and in the **north apse (3)** St Joachim (with date palms), the parents of the Virgin; and in the side vaults, the Apostles, saints, the *Nativity* and the *Dormition of the Virgin*.

The **Baroque-style chapel (4)** in the central apse was frescoed by Antonino Grano. Above the lapis lazuli tabernacle is a fine altarpiece of the *Ascension* (1533) by Vincenzo da Pavia. It was painted shortly after Vincenzo returned from Rome to Sicily with Polidoro da Caravaggio. The balustrades in front of the apses and the mosaic floor, with its delicate designs in tones of pink and blue, are also Norman.

At the west end are two further original mosaic panels (restored; set in Baroque frames) from the destroyed portico: on the north side, a tortoise-like *George of Antioch at the Feet of the Virgin* (5), and, on the south side, *King Roger Crowned by Christ* (6), a rare portrait of Roger II of Sicily. The Baroque vault frescoes illustrating episodes from the life of St Benedict, using brilliant, harmonious colours, were carried out by Willem Borremans (1714), his first work in Sicily, with the collaboration here

LA MARTORANA

- Norman
- Norman (destroyed)
- Baroque

1 Central cupola (*Christ and the Archangels*)
2 South apse (*St Anne*)
3 North apse (*St Joachim*)
4 Baroque chapel
5 *George of Antioch at the Feet of the Virgin*
6 *King Roger Crowned by Christ*
7 Arab door

West end

Campanile (entrance)

and there of Olivio Sozzi and Gaetano Lazzara. Along the side walls are gilded bronze grilles which allowed the Benedictine nuns, a cloistered order, to follow Mass without being seen. In the embrasure of the south portal is a 12th-century **carved wooden door (7)**, of Arab workmanship.

Southeast of the church some arches survive of the cloister of the 12th-century **Casa Martorana**, the Benedictine convent founded by Eloisa Martorana. The convent has disappeared, but the marzipan fruits which used to be made by the nuns here, immortalised by the name *frutti di martorana* and one of Sicily's most famous products, are still produced by numerous confectioners all over the island. Next to the church, a small operetta theatre, **Teatro Bellini** (1726; restructured in 1820) was being restored at the time of writing.

SAN CATALDO

In the courtyard, opposite the campanile of La Martorana, is the church of **San Cataldo** (*map 15; open 9.30–12.30 & 3–6; T: 091 611 8168; joint ticket with La Martorana; part of the Circuito Arte Sacra, see p. 77*). It was founded by Maio of Bari, William I's chancellor, but because of his murder in 1160 the interior was never decorated. After 1787 it served as a post office and was restored in 1885. The fine exterior has blind arcading round the windows and crenellations at the top of the wall. Three small red domes with little windows rise in the centre. The simple plan of the interior has three aisles ending in apses and three domes high up above the central aisle. The beautiful old capitals are all different. The original mosaic floor and lattice windows survive. Today the church belongs to the Knights of the Order of the Holy Sepulchre, whose coat of arms illuminates the central apse window.

ALONG CORSO VITTORIO EMANUELE TO THE CATHEDRAL

Corso Vittorio Emanuele (*map 12–14*), the main street of the city, has had several names in the past. The Arabs called it *Tarek el-Kasr*, the 'Way to the Castle', and from this derives the popular name *'u Cassaro*. The Spanish named it Via Toledo, in honour of one of their viceroys.

On the left after Quattro Canti (heading away from the port) the Corso passes the decrepit but handsome **Piazza Bologni**, with a statue of Charles V by Scipione Li Volsi (1630). The statue is the butt of local jokes about the meaning of the emperor's outstretched hand, suggesting for example that he is indicating the height of the city's tide of litter. To the right is the ample prospect of **Palazzo Alliata di Villafranca** (Giovanni Battista Vaccarini), now belonging to the Church (*open Sat and Sun 10–5; to request visit on other days, T: 324 071 5043; part of the Circuito Arte Sacra, see p. 77*). A long sequence of beautiful salons, with ceilings decorated by the Serpotta family, and important paintings, including works by Matthias Stom and a remarkable *Crucifixion* by Van Dyck. The fumoir, or gentlemen's smoking-room, is entirely lined with leather to absorb the cigar smoke; it is the largest of its kind in Europe.

From the far end of the piazza, beside the neglected Palazzo Ugo delle Favare with its attractive balconies, a detour down the interesting old **Via Panormita** on the right (*map 15*) takes in the Piazzetta Speciale, where the Palazzo Speciale has an 18th-century staircase in its pretty courtyard and there is a small café. Further on is **Piazza Santa Chiara** where the church, with a splendid interior, is often used for concerts. Numerous African immigrants have settled in this part of the city. Via dei Biscottari continues, with a view left down Via Benfratelli to the 14th-century tower of San Nicolò, and passes under a massive arch to emerge in Piazza San Giovanni Decollato beside the impressive **Palazzo Sclafani** (*map 14*), built by Matteo Sclafani in 1330. Part of the original façade has attractive lava-stone decoration around the windows. The fine 14th-century portal has sculptures by Bonaiuto da Pisa, who probably came to Palermo with traders from his native city. Opposite is the **ruined church of San Giovanni Decollato**, with a huge Morton Bay fig tree growing through its façade.

PIAZZA BOLOGNI TO PIAZZA DELLA CATTEDRALE

Facing Piazza Bologni, across the Corso, is the façade of **Palazzo Riso** (1784), the grandest of all the buildings designed by the pre-eminent Neoclassical architect

Giuseppe Venanzio Marvuglia, now the seat of the **Museo d'Arte Contemporanea della Sicilia** (*open Tues, Wed, Sun 10–8, Thur, Fri, Sat 10–midnight, closed Mon; last tickets 30mins before closing; bookshop and café; no lift; T: 091 320532, www. palazzoriso.it*). The permanent collection consists of paintings and sculptures by Sicilian artists from 1950 to the present day, together with works made by Italian and international artists while in Sicily.

Further west along the Corso (no. 395) is the church of **San Salvatore** (*map 14; open 10–6, closed Tues; dome visitable 11–12 & 4–5; T: 091 323392*), built in 1682 by Paolo Amato on a preceding Norman church and abbey where, according to legend, the daughter of Roger II, Constance de Hauteville, was abbess when on 27th January 1186 she was forced to renounce her vows and marry Henry VI, son of Barbarossa, for reasons of political expediency. Even the pope (Urban III) refused to officiate at the union of this unlikely pair, who were wedded in Milan by the patriarch of Aquileia, promptly excommunicated for his defiance of papal wishes. Bombed during the Second World War, the oval interior with its marvellous stuccoes by Serpotta was well restored in 1969 by Franco Minissi. The views from the dome are superb.

On the opposite side of the Corso, the narrow Via Montevergini leads to the church of **Montevergini** (*closed*) with a lovely façade by Andrea Palma and a little campanile with an onion-shaped dome decorated with early 18th-century tiles, beside an 18th-century loggia for the nuns. After deconsecration in 1866 it became a school for artisans, then the seat of the Fascist party, and was later used (until 1955) as a law court. The trial of Gaspare Pisciotta, who in 1950 murdered his brother-in-law, the famous bandit Salvatore Giuliano, took place here.

Further along the Corso (no. 429) is the prestigious regional library, **Biblioteca Centrale della Regione Siciliana** (*open Mon–Fri 8.30–7; T: 091 707 7606*), which occupies the former Jesuit college and is entered by the portal of the adjacent church of Santa Maria della Grotta. It owns over 500,000 volumes and many ancient manuscripts (particularly of the 15th and 16th centuries). Just beyond is **Piazza della Cattedrale**, with the elaborate flank of the cathedral on the opposite side of a garden enclosed by a balustrade bearing statues of saints.

THE CATHEDRAL

Map 14. Open Mon–Sat 7–7, Sun and holidays 8–1 & 4–7. No visits during services. Treasury, crypt and royal tombs open Mon–Sat 9–5.30, royal tombs also open Sun and holidays 10–12.30. Roofs open 10–5. Sometimes evening visits 9pm–midnight. T: 329 397 7513 or 091 334373, www.cattedrale.palermo.it.

The cathedral is dedicated to the Assumption of the Virgin. It is a building of many styles, not too skilfully blended, but remains a striking edifice with golden-coloured stone and sharp contrasts of light and shade. The present church, on the site of an older basilica which did duty as a mosque in the 9th century, was founded in 1185 by Walter of the Mill, an Englishman who came to Sicily as tutor to the young William II and later became archbishop of Palermo, known locally as Gualterio Offamiglio. Acting on behalf of the pope, and with considerable funds at his disposal, Walter intended this cathedral to be a political statement of the extent of his power within the kingdom of Sicily. William II, who wanted to maintain his independence from the papacy, met this challenge by creating a new archbishopric and a new cathedral at Monreale, endowing it with vast numbers of rich farms and wealthy villages. Walter died, however, before his cathedral was finished.

EXTERIOR OF THE CATHEDRAL

Work on the fabric continued for many centuries, and in the 15th century much of the exterior acquired a Catalan Gothic style. The incongruous dome was added by Ferdinando Fuga in 1781–1801. The façade, turned towards the southwest on Via Matteo Bonello, is a fine example of local Gothic craftsmanship (13th–14th centuries). The doorway dates from 1352. Two powerful Gothic arches span the road to a Norman tower, transformed into the campanile in the 19th century. The east end, with three intricately-decorated apses and two towers matching those at the west end, is almost entirely original 12th-century work. The usual entrance is from the garden (with its statue of St Rosalia) through the great south porch, a splendid Catalan Gothic work by Antonio Gambara (1426). In the tympanum there is a delicate relief of the Redeemer between the Archangel Gabriel and Mary. Beneath is a frieze of saints in relief. The remarkable painted intarsia decoration above the three arches, which probably dates from 1296, was recently discovered. It represents the Tree of Life in a complicated geometric composition showing Islamic influence. The twelve roundels are decorated with a great variety of symbolic animals, including fish, cockerels, serpents, crabs, mice, camels, lions, wolves, bears, peacocks, dragons, doves and owls, as well as fruit and flowers and human figures. Intended to be 'read' from left to right, the last roundel seems to represent the sun with the head of Christ in the centre. Beneath the porch, the column on the left, probably preserved from the earlier mosque, is inscribed with a passage from the Koran. The fine wooden doors are by Francesco Miranda (1432).

INTERIOR OF THE CATHEDRAL

The interior is relatively plain, 18th-century restoration having removed the majority of the decorative artwork. However, there is much to see.

Royal tombs

The first two chapels of the south aisle enclose six royal tombs. In front on the left is the porphyry sarcophagus of **Frederick II of Hohenstaufen (1)** (d. 1250), Holy Roman Emperor and King of Sicily. Frederick's dearly loved first wife, **Constance of Aragon (2)** (d. 1222), lies in the white Roman sarcophagus against the west wall, with a frieze showing a lion hunt. The tomb on the right **(3)** is of **Henry VI** (d. 1197), Holy Roman Emperor, son of Frederick Barbarossa and father of Frederick II of Hohenstaufen. Behind, beneath mosaic canopies, are the tombs of the first king of Sicily, **Roger II (4)** (d. 1154), who was crowned in this cathedral in 1130, and his daughter **Constance de Hauteville (5)** (d. 1198; *see overleaf*). Later Aragonese burials are, on the left, **Duke William of Athens (6)** (d. 1338), son of Frederick II of Aragon, and (in Frederick II's sarcophagus) Peter II (d. 1342), King of Sicily. The smooth porphyry sarcophagi are almost certainly Imperial Roman in workmanship, because the Egyptian quarries of this type of stone were already exhausted in the Middle Ages. It is not known how they found their way to Palermo.

STUPOR MUNDI

'The wonder of the world' is what his contemporaries called Frederick II of Hohenstaufen, for his many skills, ranging from languages (he could speak six), mathematics, astronomy, astrology, music, literature (he was the founder of the 'Sicilian School' which flourished at his court in Palermo), the building of castles, hunting (his fundamental text on falconry, *De arti venandi cum avibus*, is in the Vatican Library), to the fine arts of diplomacy. He was born quite by chance in Jesi, in the Marche, on 26th December 1194, because his mother, Constance de Hauteville, was travelling from Milan to Sicily to join her husband. She chose to give birth in the main square, under a canopy, so that the matrons of Jesi could witness the fact that the baby was really hers; gossip and speculation were rife; there was even a prophecy that the Antichrist was about to be born. Nine years earlier, Constance, as the last Norman princess of Sicily, had been brought out of a cloistered convent in Palermo in order to marry the unpleasant, dissolute Henry VI of Swabia, eleven years her junior. Now she was 40, and this was her first child. Henry and Constance died soon after, so Frederick was brought up in Palermo, running free through the streets of the city, undoubtedly acquiring many of those accomplishments which would later stand him in good stead. Last of the medieval monarchs, first of the modern rulers, Frederick spent all his life trying to unite the Holy Roman Empire to the rich Kingdom of Sicily: unfortunately for him, the Papal States stood—both literally and metaphorically— between him and success. He remains a colourful and fascinating figure in the history of Europe, defiant of the pope, even excommunicated, yet leader of the most successful and least bloody Crusade; the founder of modern diplomacy; and the first to draw up laws defending the rights of women and for the protection of wildlife.

Nave and south side

In the nave are **statues of saints** from a high reredos (25m) by Antonello Gagini and his family, who worked on it for over 64 years. Known as the Tribuna, this masterpiece was dismantled arbitrarily in the 18th century. Now models of the work, and some fragments of it, are on view in the Diocesan Museum. The canopied **stoup (7)** is attributed to Domenico Gagini. The other **stoup (8)**, damaged but of fine workmanship, is by his school.

In the fourth south chapel is an **altarpiece by Pietro Novelli (9)**; notice also, in the sixth chapel **(10) reliquary urns of saints of Palermo** and, used as an altar frontal, the tomb slab of St Cosmas, a Sicilian bishop martyred in 1160; the seventh chapel **(11)** has a fine marble inlaid altar (1713).

The **meridian line** on the floor **(12)**, 22m long, was made by Father Giuseppe Piazzi, priest, mathematician and astronomer, in 1801. The light coming through the tiny hole in the dome on the right at midday, indicates the zodiac sign for the time of year.

In the south transept **(13)** there is an altarpiece by Giuseppe Velasco and, above the altar, a bas-relief of the *Dormition of the Virgin* by Antonello Gagini (1535).

In the **Chapel of St Rosalia (14)** is a 17th-century silver coffer containing the relics of the saint (*see p. 73*); the reliefs on the walls are 19th-century.

The choir and north side

The east end of the **choir (15)** has a *Resurrection of Christ* on the altar, high reliefs, and (in niches), statues of the Apostles, all fragments of Antonello Gagini's reredos. The choir stalls date from 1466.

The chapel left of the choir **(16)** houses a large domed ciborium in lapis lazuli (1663) and the funerary monument of Bishop Sanseverino (1793).

In the north transept **(17)**, at the foot of an early 14th-century wooden Crucifix

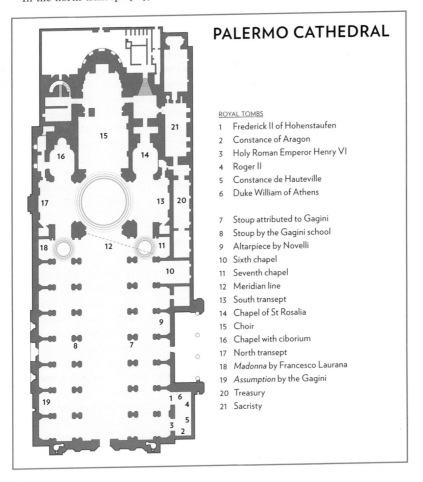

PALERMO CATHEDRAL

ROYAL TOMBS
1   Frederick II of Hohenstaufen
2   Constance of Aragon
3   Holy Roman Emperor Henry VI
4   Roger II
5   Constance de Hauteville
6   Duke William of Athens

7   Stoup attributed to Gagini
8   Stoup by the Gagini school
9   Altarpiece by Novelli
10 Sixth chapel
11 Seventh chapel
12 Meridian line
13 South transept
14 Chapel of St Rosalia
15 Choir
16 Chapel with ciborium
17 North transept
18 *Madonna* by Francesco Laurana
19 *Assumption* by the Gagini
20 Treasury
21 Sacristy

donated by Manfredi Chiaramonte, are marble statues of mourners by Gaspare Serpotta and Gaspare Guercio. On the altar are fine reliefs with scenes of the Passion by Fazio and Vincenzo Gagini.

In the seventh north chapel **(18)** there is a statue of the Madonna by Francesco Laurana and his school. The second north chapel **(19)** has an *Assumption* and three reliefs by the Gagini, also once part of the high altar.

Treasury, sacristy, crypt and roofs

The **treasury (20)** contains the extraordinary crown of Constance of Aragon (first wife of Frederick II), made by local craftsmen c. 1210, in fine gold filigree set with semi-precious stones, and found in her tomb in the 18th century. Also displayed here are the contents of some of the other royal tombs, 18th- and 19th-century copes, chalices and altar frontals.

Beyond the treasury is the **sacristy (21)**, which has two fine portals by Vincenzo Gagini (1568), and the entrance to the **crypt**, where 23 tombs are preserved, many of them Roman sarcophagi (all of them numbered and labelled in Italian). The tomb (no. 12) of Archbishop Giovanni Paternò (d. 1511) has a very fine effigy by Antonello Gagini, whose patron he was, resting on a Greek sarcophagus. The tomb (no. 16) of the founder of the cathedral, Archbishop Walter of the Mill (d. 1190), has a beautiful red, green and gold mosaic border. No. 7 is a large Roman sarcophagus with a scene of the coronation of a poet with the nine Muses and Apollo. The tomb of Frederick of Antioch (d. 1305), no. 9, has a Gothic effigy of the warrior semi-recumbent, with his helmet at his feet and sword by his side.

Recently made accessible to the public, the **roofs** (*tetti*) offer incomparable views (especially at night, but not for vertigo sufferers), and allow a greater understanding of the gradual metamorphosis of Palermo, from its early beginnings on this spot to the present day.

MUSEO DIOCESANO

Map 14. Open Tues–Sun 9.30–1.30, Sat 10–6, closed Mon. Bookshop, T: 091 607 7111, www.museodiocesanopa.it. Part of the Circuito Arte Sacra (see p. 77).

Across Via Matteo Bonello, the Palazzo Arcivescovile (Archbishop's Palace), with a portal of 1460 which survived the 18th-century rebuilding, houses the Museo Diocesano. Here a large and important collection of marble and mosaic fragments from the cathedral and other churches destroyed during the Second World War, together with splendid paintings dating from the 11th–18th centuries, are displayed to the best advantage.

On the ground floor are 15th-century frescoes, a 12th-century mosaic from the cathedral, and Vincenzo da Pavia's *St Conus the Hermit and St Anthony Abbot* (1550). In the basement the museum's superb collection of sculpture is displayed, with several examples by the Gagini family as well as works in stucco. On the ground floor again, in the north wing, 16th- and 17th-century paintings chart the development from

Mannerism to *Caravaggismo*, with one room entirely dedicated to Pietro Novelli. On the first floor are 13 galleries, including the Alcova del Cardinale (cardinal's bedroom); Sala Azzurra (Blue Room) decorated with 19th-century chinoiseries; Sala Verde (Green Room) once used by the nuns of St Clare, with a beautiful floor painted with flowers. Perhaps the crowning glory of the museum is the Cappella Borremans, with a series of joyful, colourful religious allegories of the childhood of Christ, painted as frescoes on every available surface; commissioned from Willem Borremans by Archbishop Matteo Basile in 1733.

On the other side of Via Bonello is the **Loggia dell'Incoronazione**, erected in the 16th–17th centuries using columns and capitals from an older structure. It takes its name from the tradition that the kings used to show themselves to the people here after their coronation. Behind is the **Cappella dell'Incoronata**, a Norman building partly destroyed in 1860. Opposite the cathedral square, at Via Pietro Novelli 3, is **Palazzo Asmundo** (*open Tues–Sat 10–1.30, last tickets 30mins before closing, cafeteria open April–Sept; T: 335 668 7798, www.palazzoasmundo.it*). Built in 1615, it contains beautifully frescoed salons (by Gioacchino Martorana, 1764) that give an insight into the lives of the Sicilian nobility. The *Wunderkammer* collections include paintings, wooden trousseau-chests, coins, postcards, old maps, watercolours, French and Neapolitan porcelain, majolica tiles and a unique set of census bricks inscribed with details of the donor, they were walled into churches, convents and other institutions.

PIAZZA VITTORIA, PORTA NUOVA AND LA SPECOLA

Piazza Vittoria, or Piano del Palazzo (*map 14*), is occupied by Villa Bonanno, a public garden thick with trees, some of which were unfortunately killed by palm weevil, accidentally introduced into Sicily in the 1990s. At the centre of the old city and in front of the Palazzo dei Normanni, the piazza has been used throughout Palermo's history for public celebrations. Partially protected by a roof are some remains of three **Roman houses** (*open 9–5.30 winter, 9–6.30 summer, Sun and holidays 9.30–1.30*), the only buildings of this period so far found in the city, one a substantial villa with mosaics including the *Hunt of Alexander*, possibly copied from an original work by Philoxenos of Eritrea, a Greek painter of the 4th century BC. It is comparable with the famous mosaic of the Battle of Alexander and Darius in the House of the Faun in Pompeii. Building A is of a later date, probably 2nd century BC.

The garden adjoins **Piazza del Parlamento**, with a monument to Philip V of Bourbon, at the foot of the Palazzo dei Normanni. Spanning the Corso is the **Porta Nuova**, a triumphal gateway with a conical top celebrating Charles V's Tunisian victory (1535). At the north end of the long façade (1616) of Palazzo dei Normanni is the massive Torre Pisana, which houses the **Museo della Specola** (*entrance at Piazza del Parlamento 1, guided visits only Mon–Fri at 9 and 10.30, Sat 9, 10.15, 11.30; no lift; to book visit, T: 091 233247, www.astropa.unipa.it*), with the instruments used by Father Giuseppe Piazzi, the first director of the astronomical observatory founded here in 1786, including his famous Ramsden Circle, 1.5m in diameter, by means of which he discovered the first dwarf planet, Ceres, in 1801. You will also find three telescopes which belonged to the great-grandfather of Giuseppe Tomasi di Lampedusa, a keen amateur astronomer. The view over Palermo from the tower is exceptional.

PALAZZO DEI NORMANNI & CAPPELLA PALATINA

Map 14. Chapel and palace open Mon, Fri, Sat 8.15–5.40 (last tickets 5), Sun and holidays 8.15–1 (last tickets 12.15). Chapel also open Tues, Wed and Thur, same times. Closed 25 Dec and 1 Jan. T: 091 626 2833, www.federicosecondo.org. The visitors' entrance is at the back, from Piazza Indipendenza, reached by steps down from the south side of the façade to the busy Via del Bastione, which skirts the great wall of the building.

HISTORY OF THE PALAZZO DEI NORMANNI

Palazzo dei Normanni, or Palazzo Reale, stands in the highest part of the old city. The meandering palace, with its myriad rooms, corridors and subterranean chambers, is a real labyrinth, as old as Palermo itself, and over the centuries has followed the fortunes of the city at its feet while emirs, dukes, princes, kings and viceroys have added to its fabric at whim, enlarging and embellishing; here a tower or a treasury, there an elegant courtyard, a chapel or a sumptuous ballroom. Thought to have been built originally by the Arabs, recent surveys show that they merely consolidated and enlarged a Phoenician fortress, the key point of the fortifications of the first settlement. Since then it has always been the headquarters of the rulers of the island, and here the splendid courts of Roger II and Frederick II held sway over much of Europe and the Mediterranean. Roger II opened a workshop where Arab weavers and embroiderers made cloth for the royal garments; his magnificent robe of red silk and gold can still be seen in Vienna's Schatzkammer. The main façade of the palace was added by the Spanish. Since 1947 the palace has been the seat of the Regional Assembly.

From the ticket office a ramp leads to the entrance. Here a monumental **staircase** (**A**; 1735) leads up to a loggia overlooking a fine **courtyard** (**B**; 1600). Set into the wall of the loggia, behind glass, is a **section of pillar** (**C**) with an inscription in Greek, Latin and Arabic, relating to a water-clock built for Roger II in 1142, probably in Fez, Morocco.

CAPPELLA PALATINA

Open as palace, but closed 8.30–9 every day, Sun and holidays 9.45–11.15 for Mass, and for weddings. No visits during services. NB: Binoculars are useful to view the painted ceiling.

Beneath a portico of seven columns (six of which are of Egyptian granite) with modern

CAPPELLA PALATINA
Alabaster portrait of Roger II on the Paschal candlestick.

mosaics, is the side entrance to the Cappella Palatina **(D)**, a jewel of Arab-Norman art commenced by Roger II in 1130 and consecrated ten years later. The interior is famous for its mosaics, among the finest of their kind in the world. The mosaics were commissioned by Roger II to follow a carefully-planned design intended to celebrate his monarchy, and the subjects seem to have been chosen with particular reference to the Holy Spirit and the theology of light. *Ego eimai to phos tou kosmou*; *Ego Sum Lux Mundi* (I am the light of the world) is the message in Greek and Latin shown by the figure of Christ Pantocrator in the central apse. In fact, although much space is dedicated to Sts Peter and Paul and the life of Christ, no mention is made of their martyrdom and humiliation, the Passion and Crucifixion; the stories instead culminate with their triumph. There were 50 windows (later blocked) designed to illuminate at all times of the day the stories told on the walls. The earliest and finest mosaics are in the east part of the chapel and are thought to have been the work of Byzantine Greeks. Here their splendour is increased by the use of silver as well as gold tesserae. The light changes constantly in the chapel: if you have the opportunity to visit it more than once, try to come at different times of day.

A small aisled basilica in form, with a raised choir and a cupola above the central bay, the chapel demonstrates the perfection of this style of architecture. Every detail of the decoration is exquisite. The ten antique columns of the nave are of granite and cipollino marble. The unique **ceiling** (dated 1143) is of Fatimid workmanship, with splendid *muqarnas* in carved and painted cedarwood from Lebanon, in rich and varied designs. There are no saints and angels here, but musicians and dancing-girls, banquets at court with servants pouring wine for the guests, warriors and hunters, picnics under the trees (later ecclesiastical authorities added haloes to the figures in order to transform the decoration into a representation of a Christian paradise) and eight-pointed stars with borders of Kufic script. The ambo and **paschal candlestick (i)** are good examples of the richest Norman marble decoration. The figure wearing a crown supporting Christ at eye level on the candlestick is a rare portrait of Roger II. The floor and dadoes are made of white marble inlaid with red, green and gold patterns, all different, combining in a delightful harmony of colour and design with the glittering mosaics on a gold ground above. Here too the finest available materials were used: red porphyry and green serpentine alternate with rare stones from all over the known world.

On the **triumphal arch (ii)** separating nave and chancel, the *Annunciation* is depicted. In the **sanctuary cupola (iii)** is *Christ Surrounded by Angels and Archangels*; on the drum, David, Solomon, Zachariah and St John the Baptist; in the niches, the Evangelists. Above the **south apse (iv)** is the *Nativity* above St Paul and on the **south wall**, *Joseph's Dream* and the *Flight into Egypt*; *Baptism*, *Transfiguration*, and the *Raising of Lazarus* and *Entry into Jerusalem*. On the lower part of the **north wall (v) (vi)**, five bishops of the Greek Church (among the best preserved mosaic figures in the building). Above the **north apse** are a *Madonna and Child* and St John the Baptist above St Peter. In the **main apse (vi)** is the solemn, stern *Christ Pantocrator* above a late 18th-century mosaic of the Virgin.

The **mosaics in the nave** were probably the last to be carried out, under William I (r. 1154–66); they illustrate the Book of Genesis, in two tiers of scenes between the clerestory windows and in the spandrels of the arches. The cycle begins in the upper tier of the right wall nearest to the sanctuary, showing the first seven days of the Creation up to the Creation of Eve. The sequence continues in the upper tier of the left wall (beginning at the entrance end) with the *Fall* up to the *Building of the Ark* (striking in its similarity to a Viking longship). The lower tier of the right wall (from the apse end) illustrates the *Flood* up to the *Hospitality of Lot*, and continues in the lower tier of the left wall (entrance end) with the *Destruction of Sodom* and continues up to *Jacob's Dream* and *Jacob Wrestling with the Angel*, which is the last scene in the sequence (nearest to the sanctuary).

In the **aisles** are scenes from the lives of Sts Peter and Paul, also executed after the mosaics in the apse part of the church, possibly by local artists. The sequence begins at the apse end of the south aisle with *Saul leaving Jerusalem for Damascus* and the last scene in this aisle shows *St Peter's Escape from Prison*. The cycle continues at the entrance end of the north aisle with *Sts Peter and John Healing the Lame Man at the Temple Gate*, and the last scene in this aisle, nearest to the sanctuary, shows the *Fall of Simon Magus*.

Above the recomposed Norman throne on a dais at the entrance end is a 15th-century mosaic of ***Christ Enthroned Between Sts Peter and Paul* (vii)**. The original **narthex (viii)**, now the baptistery with a mosaic font, has two beautifully carved mosaic doorways with bronze doors. One of these doors leads to the **Treasury**, with a superb collection of rare medieval coffers and small boxes in ivory, ebony, gold and silver; chalices, monstrances and reliquaries; a seal from Mesopotamia, and a parchment attesting the consecration of the chapel in 1140.

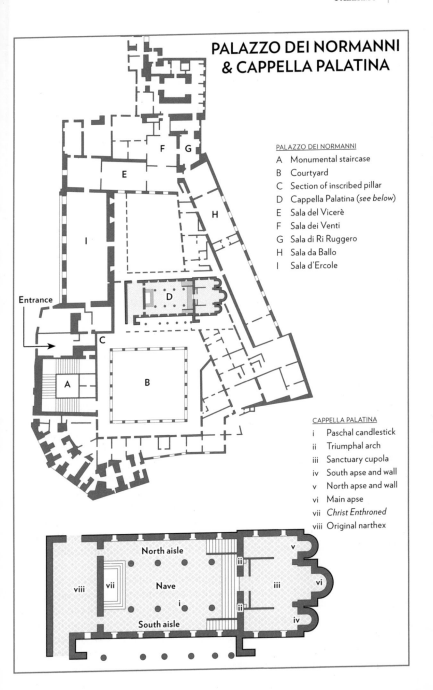

PALAZZO DEI NORMANNI & CAPPELLA PALATINA

PALAZZO DEI NORMANNI

A Monumental staircase
B Courtyard
C Section of inscribed pillar
D Cappella Palatina (*see below*)
E Sala del Vicerè
F Sala dei Venti
G Sala di Ri Ruggero
H Sala da Ballo
I Sala d'Ercole

CAPPELLA PALATINA

i Paschal candlestick
ii Triumphal arch
iii Sanctuary cupola
iv South apse and wall
v North apse and wall
vi Main apse
vii *Christ Enthroned*
viii Original narthex

Entrance

THE ROYAL APARTMENTS

The staircase leads up to the top floor of the palace and the former royal apartments, largely decorated in the 19th century. The **Sala dei Vicerè (E)** has a series of portraits of viceroys from 1754 to 1837. The **Sala dei Venti (F)** at the top of the Torre Joaria (from the Arabic *al-johara*, the pearl, meaning the heart of the building), gets its Italian name (Tower of the Winds) from the weather-vane in the roof. It preserves part of its Norman construction, with four columns. The most interesting room, leading off the Sala dei Venti, is the so-called **Sala di Re Ruggero (G)**, generally considered to have been commissioned by Roger II, though the delightful mosaics of centaurs, birds, palm trees, lions and leopards are usually dated to the reign of William I (d. 1166). They are the only surviving secular mosaics of this period in Europe, contemporary with much of the Cappella Palatina decoration. On the ceiling is a mosaic with the Swabian eagle clutching a hare, added by Frederick of Hohenstaufen. The lower parts of the walls with marble and mosaic decoration and the floor all survive intact. The **Sala da Ballo (H)** (ballroom) has a fine view over the piazza to the sea.

Other parts of the palace are not shown when in use (*usually Tues, Wed, Thur; ask at the ticket office*), including the Sala del Parlamento, or **Sala d'Ercole (I)**, decorated by Giuseppe Velasco, where the Regional Assembly meets. There is no access to the vaulted armoury, treasure-chamber and dungeons, surviving from the Norman period.

ENVIRONS OF PALAZZO DEI NORMANNI

Across Corso Re Ruggero is **Palazzo d'Orleans** (*map 14*), now the seat of the president of the Sicilian Region. This was the residence of the exiled Louis-Philippe d'Orléans (1773–1850), eldest son of the Duc d'Orléans and the last king of France, at the time of his marriage in 1809 to Marie-Amélie, daughter of Ferdinand IV of the Two Sicilies. Their son Ferdinand-Philippe (1810–42) was born here in the following year. The beautiful gardens, Parco d'Orleans, recently much enlarged and full of birds, were laid out in 1797 (*open Mon–Fri 9.30–1 & 3–5, Sun and holidays 9.30–1; T: 091 707 5038*).

In Piazza della Pinta (or Cortile di San Giovanni Eremiti) is the little **Oratorio di San Mercurio** (*map 14; open 10–6; T: 091 611 8168 or 091 607 7215; part of the Circuito Arte Sacra, see p. 77*), also known as the Oratorio della Compagnia della Madonna della Consolazione (1572). Recently restored, the stucco decoration in the interior was carried out in 1678 by a young Giacomo Serpotta, probably his first commissioned work. The project was completed much later by his son Procopio. The hand of the master can already be recognised in the moulding of the masks and shields over the two entrance doors, while the interior—in Giacomo's preferred white stucco—has a host of playful cherubs and angels cavorting happily everywhere, especially around the doors and the windows. The splendid majolica tiled floor (1715) is unique in Palermo.

SAN GIOVANNI DEGLI EREMITI

The church of San Giovanni degli Eremiti (*map 14; open Mon–Sat 9–6.30, Sun and holidays 9–1.30; T: 091 651 5019*), symbol of the city and perhaps the most romantic building of Norman Palermo thanks to its small, carefully-tended and luxuriant garden. It was built by Roger II in 1132–48 and has now been deconsecrated. Paths lead up through the beautiful groves, with palm trees, cactus and flowering jasmine, overshadowed by five charming red domes, the tallest one crowning the campanile of the little church. In the bare interior, the nave is surmounted by two domes divided by an arch (pierced by a window). At the east end are three apses and three smaller domes, the one on the left part of the campanile.

To the right is an older structure, probably a mosque, consisting of a rectangular hall with cross vaulting and once divided by a row of pillars. Adjoining this (seen from the right of the entrance to the church) is a portico of five arches, whose inner wall is now the right wall of the church, and an open courtyard. The little cloister of the late 13th century has twin columns bearing pointed arches which surround a delightfully peaceful part of the garden.

THE ALBERGHERIA DISTRICT

This district derives its name from *albergaria*, a place where the Normans gave accommodation to refugees and exiles, and used as such also by Frederick of Hohenstaufen. It was a depressed and insanitary place, inhabited by humble artisans and labourers. Badly damaged during the bombardments of the Second World War, many streets are still awaiting repair. Before 1492 a large part of the district was the Jewish quarter.

CASA PROFESSA

The church of the Gesù (*map 15; open Mon–Sat 6.30–1 & 4–7, Sun and holidays 6.30–12.30 & 5–6.30; T: 091 580655*), otherwise known as Casa Professa, was the first church to be erected in Sicily by the Jesuits (1564–1633). The sturdy tower (with a Catalan window) of the 15th-century Palazzo Marchesi, in Piazza dei Santissimi 40 Martiri, forms the base of its campanile. Perhaps the palace was built on an old synagogue, because during recent restoration works in the cellars an intact Jewish mikveh for ritual ablutions was found, one of the largest yet discovered in Europe and still with its spring of fresh water,.

The splendid interior of Casa Professa was decorated in the 17th and 18th centuries with colourful inlaid marble (it is a masterpiece of the *marmi mischi* technique) and sculptures (especially good in the nave chapels, 1665–91; the lovely 18th-century Andronico organ is out of order, although fortunately intact). The entrance wall inside has very fine 18th-century sculptural decoration. The second south chapel has paintings of two saints (St Philip of Argirò and St Paul the Hermit) by Pietro Novelli, and the fourth chapel has a statue of the *Madonna* by the Gagini school. The presbytery also has remarkably good marble decoration. Also accessible is the crypt and the charming Oratorio del Sabato.

Beside the church is the fine Baroque atrium of the Casa Professa, the Jesuit convent, now partly occupied by the town library, **Biblioteca Civica** (*open Mon–Fri*

9–1.45, Tues, Wed, Thur also 2.45–5.45), founded in 1760. It has over 330,000 volumes, and more than 1,000 incunabula and manuscripts.

AROUND PIAZZA BALLARÒ

Piazza Ballarò is the scene of the noisy, colourful daily market known since the Arab period as the **Mercato di Ballarò** (*map 15*; from the Arabic *suq al-Bahlara*, when Bahlara was a village near Monreale where the merchants lived, and the fruit and vegetables were brought into town through the nearby Porta Sant'Agata. Beyond, the church tower of **San Nicolò** can be seen, once part of the 14th-century town fortifications, also used for transmitting messages. In its day it was probably the highest tower in the city (*Via Nunzio Nasi 18; to request a visit T: 329 876 5958, www. terradamare.org*).

Via Ballarò continues left through the market to Piazza del Carmine, with more stalls, above which towers the fantastic dome of the church of the **Carmine Maggiore** (*open 8.45–10.45; no visits during Mass, wait in the cloister; T: 091 651 2018*) with its telamones and colourful majolica tiles (rebuilt 1681). The sumptuous Latin-cross interior, a central nave and two side aisles divided by columns, contains on the first south altar a painting of *St Andrew Corsini* by Pietro Novelli; on the fourth, a statue of St Catherine by Antonello Gagini; and on the fifth, a Madonna by the Gagini school. The altars in the transepts are by Giuseppe and Giacomo Serpotta (1683–4) and the paintings (in the sanctuary) by Tommaso de Vigilia (late 15th century). From the north aisle you can reach the charming 14th-century cloister. Since 1219 the church preserves a thorn from the crown of Jesus, shown to the faithful on the Fridays of Lent and 3rd May. The door to the left of the passage to the cloister leads to the sacristy, with a 14th-century wooden Crucifix.

Behind the church is **Via delle Mosche**, where Giuseppe Balsamo is thought to have been born in 1743. Under the assumed title of Count Cagliostro, he travelled all over Europe professing skills as a physician and alchemist until sentenced to life imprisonment by the Inquisition in 1795.

Via Musco and Via Mugnosi lead to the **Oratorio del Carminello** (*open for Mass Sun and holidays at 10.30, T: 329 295 0170*) at Via Porta Sant'Agata 5, built in 1605 and richly decorated with stuccoes at the end of the 17th century and the beginning of the 18th by the Serpotta family. Until the early 1990s the crypt underneath was used as a burial-place for the Carmelite brethren.

ALONG VIA MAQUEDA

Palazzo Comitini, on the corner of Via del Bosco and Via Maqueda (*map 15; open Mon–Fri, guided tours hourly 9.30, 10.30, 11.30, 12.30; Tues, Wed, Thur also 3.30 & 4; T: 091 662 8260*) by Nicolò Palma (1771), is the seat of the province of Palermo. The 18th-century Rococo interior has lovely frescoed ceilings, Murano chandeliers, floors of Vietri tiles and decorative mirrors; particularly significant is the Sala Martorana. On the opposite side of Via Maqueda (to the right) is the long façade (mid-18th century) of Palazzo Santa Croce. Just beyond is the **Assunta**, a convent-church built in 1625–8 through the generosity of the Moncada family. The small interior is glowing white, richly decorated in the 18th century with stuccoes by Giacomo Serpotta (perhaps assisted by his son Procopio) at the very height of his skill—notice in particular the high altar and the angels. The lovely swirling vault frescoes are by Filippo Tancredi, the altarpieces by Borremans; that on the high altar is by Giuseppe Patricolo. The inlaid marble floor dates from 1638.

Returning towards the Quattro Canti Via Maqueda passes, next to Palazzo Comitini, the church of **Sant'Orsola dei Negri** (*open Mon–Fri 7.30–11, Sun and holidays 9.30–11, closed Sat; T: 091 616 2321*), built in 1662 for the religious confraternity of the Negri, so called because of their black cassocks. The interior was redecorated in the late 18th century. The two last chapels on either side of the nave contain stuccoes by Giacomo Serpotta (1692), and (in the left chapel) an altarpiece of *St Jerome* by a Zoppo di Gangi. The wonderful vault fresco shows the *Glory of St Ursula*. A fine painting of the *Madonna and Child* (as *Salvator Mundi*) by Pietro Novelli is kept in the sacristy; it is sometimes possible to visit the underlying crypt, also decorated by Giacomo Serpotta.

Further on, on the opposite side of the road, is the church of **San Nicolò da Tolentino** (*open Tues–Sat 9–12 & 4–7, Sun and holidays 8.30–12, Mon afternoons only 4–7; T: 091 616 3013*), in the centre of a district where Jews lived freely from the 9th century onwards. However, Ferdinand of Spain expelled them from the city in 1492 and the synagogue here was destroyed and replaced by this church in 1609. The two altarpieces in the transepts are by Pietro Novelli. The convent houses the city archives.

Just beyond, **Via dei Calderai**, the picturesque 'Street of the Tinkers', diverges right from Via Roma. It leads to Via Giovanni da Procida where the church of Santa Maria degli Agonizzanti is situated, which belonged to a confraternity tasked with praying for the deliverance of the souls of those who had died before obtaining absolution.

EAST OF QUATTRO CANTI TO PIAZZA MARINA

East of the Quattro Canti, Corso Vittorio Emanuele leads towards the sea. A short way along on the left is the sturdy Baroque church of **San Matteo** (*open Mon–Sat 10.30–1.30 & 4–6.30, Sun only for Mass; T: 335 749 0960*). It was begun in 1633 by Mariano Smiriglio and the façade is enlivened by chiaroscuro effects. The interior contains lovely bas-relief stucco work by Giacomo Serpotta and vault frescoes by Vito D'Anna (1754). On the fourth south altar is the *Presentation in the Temple* by Pietro Novelli (1647) and on the fourth north altar the *Marriage of the Virgin* (also painted by Novelli in 1647; these were probably his last two works, before he was killed during the revolt of that year against the Spanish).

SAN FRANCESCO D'ASSISI AND SAN LORENZO

Beyond Via Roma, the narrow Via Paternostro (with numerous shops where luggage is sold or repaired) curves right towards the attractive piazza in front of the 13th-century church of **San Francesco d'Assisi** (*map 12; open Mon–Sat 7–11.30 & 4–6, Sun 7–1 & 4–6.30; T: 091 616 2819 or 091 582370*). The façade has a beautiful portal with three friezes of zigzag ornamentation (1302) and a lovely rose window. The church was damaged by an earthquake in 1823 and again during air raids in 1943, after which it was restored. The Franciscan nave of 1255–77 is flanked by beautiful chapels added in the 14th–15th centuries. Eight statues by Giacomo Serpotta (1723) decorate the inside portal and nave. Above the door is a fine sculpted arch of 1465. In the second south chapel there is an altarpiece of *St George and the Dragon* in high relief and carved roundels by Antonello Gagini (1526); in the third chapel is a *Madonna* attributed to Antonino Gagini flanked by 15th-century statues of saints. The Gothic fourth chapel contains a beautiful 15th-century *Madonna* by a Catalan sculptor and the sarcophagus of Elisabetta Omodei (1498) attributed to Domenico Gagini. Beyond the side door and another Gothic chapel is the sixth chapel, with three bas-reliefs by Ignazio Marabitti (including the altar frontal). The seventh chapel has interesting 14th-century lava-stone decoration on the arches. The chapel to the right of the sanctuary has a fine polychrome marble intarsia decoration (17th–18th century; carefully restored after war damage). The eight figures of Sicilian saints are by Giovanni Battista Ragusa (1717). The altarpiece of the *Immacolata* in mosaic is to a design by Vito D'Anna and below is an elaborate marble altar frontal. The sanctuary has fine 16th-century carved and inlaid choir stalls. The chapel to the left of the sanctuary has intricate marble decoration and an 18th-century wooden statue of St Francis. The eighth north chapel once had a bust of St John in polychrome terracotta, attributed to Antonello Gagini. It has been replaced by a cast (the original is in the Museo Diocesano; *see p. 36*). The four statuettes of the *Virtues* are attributed to Pietro da Bonitate. By the door into the sacristy there is a tomb-effigy of the young warrior Antonio Speciale by Domenico Gagini (1477) with a touching inscription above it (son of the governor of Sicily Pietro Speciale, he had died on the day before his wedding). The fifth chapel has a 14th-century portal with zigzag ornamentation and remains of early frescoes. The arch of the fourth chapel, the Cappella Mastrantonio, is a superb piece by Francesco Laurana and Pietro da Bonitate (1468), the earliest important Renaissance work in Sicily. On the left wall of the chapel, the *Madonna and Saints* has been attributed to Vincenzo da Pavia. In the second chapel a highly venerated silver statue of the Immaculate Virgin (1647) is hidden by a curtain, and the remains of a fresco of St Francis is on the left wall. In the first chapel (light on the right), with a fine 16th-century portal, is a *Madonna and Child with St John*, by Domenico Gagini (with a beautiful base), and a relief of the Madonna.

To the left of the church is the late 16th-century **Oratorio di San Lorenzo** (*entrance at Via Immacolatella 5; open daily 10–6; T: 091 611 8168; part of the Circuito Arte Sacra, see p. 77*). The interior, designed by Giacomo Amato, is decorated with stuccoes illustrating the lives of St Lawrence and St Francis, a master work by Giacomo Serpotta (1699–1707). Ten symbolic statues, eight vivacious little reliefs, and the *Martyrdom of St Lawrence* situated above the door, the whole encircled by a throng of plump cherubs, make up a well-balanced and animated composition. The modelling of the male figures above the windows is especially skilful. The altarpiece of the *Nativity*, by Caravaggio (1609; his last known work, painted for this church), was stolen in 1969 and has never been recovered. It has been replaced by a carefully-made digital copy.

PALAZZO MIRTO

At Via Merlo 2, an 18th-century gateway leads into **Palazzo Mirto** (*map 12; open Tues–Sat 9–6, Sun 9–1, Mon closed; possible combined ticket with Palazzo Abatellis and Oratorio Bianchi; T: 091 616 4751*). The main façade on Via Lungarini, with a double row of balconies, dates from 1793. The residence of the Lanza-Filangeri family since the early 17th century, it was donated by them, together with its contents, to the Sicilian Region in 1982. The well-kept interior is interesting as a typical example of a princely residence in Palermo, with 18th- and 19th-century decorations, including a little 'Chinese' room with a leather floor. The contents include furniture (mostly 18th and 19th century), Capodimonte porcelain and Murano glass.

Beyond, opposite Palazzo Rostagno, is the Renaissance church of **Santa Maria dei Miracoli** (1547), with a votive ship in its interior. The church was once on the harbour front and its loggia was used by merchants (now a small theatre, the Teatro Libero).

PIAZZA MARINA & LA CALA

Santa Maria dei Miracoli overlooks **Piazza Marina** (*map 12*), once a shallow inlet of the sea. Here 16th-century Aragonese weddings and victories were celebrated by jousting. Later, in the proximity of two prisons (the Vicaria and that of the Inquisition), public executions were held here: condemned prisoners were burned alive or hung, drawn and quartered. The centre is occupied by the Giardino Garibaldi, with fine palms and enormous old Morton Bay figs, *Ficus magnoloides*, one of which, before recent pruning, was the largest tree in Europe; they are now home to a colourful and garrulous colony of ring-necked parakeets.

On the corner by the Corso is the church of **San Giovanni dei Napoletani** (1526–1617; *open Tues–Fri 10–12 & 5–7, Sat 10–12*), built by the merchants from Naples who lived in this area. The elegant interior has stucco work by Procopio Serpotta, a magnificent 17th-century organ by Raffaele La Valle, a choir loft decorated with 15 panels, perhaps the work of Vincenzo da Pavia, and a *St John the Baptist* by a Zoppo di Gangi.

In the corner of the square and Corso Vittorio Emanuele is the outstanding **Fontana del Garraffo** (Paolo Amato, 1698), a sumptuous piece of Baroque street furnishing surrounded by a garden. The slender little figure on the top represents *Abundance Chasing Away the Hydra*.

PALAZZO CHIARAMONTE AND THE MUSEO DELL'INQUISIZIONE

At the seaward end of Piazza Marina is **Palazzo Chiaramonte** (*open Mon–Fri 9–6.30, Sat and Sun 10–5; T: 091 238 93788*), known as Lo Steri (i.e. *hosterium*, or fortified palace), begun in 1307 by the powerful Chiaramonte family on a Norman glass factory, and finished in 1380. The exterior, though deprived of its battlements, retains several of its original windows. Warned by her spies, Queen Blanche of Navarre in 1412 fled from the palace in the middle of the night, in order to escape her would-be wooer,

Cabrera. In 1535 Charles V convened the Sicilian parliament here, ~ame the palace of the Spanish viceroys. From 1601–1782 it was the ~. ine Inquisition; some graffiti, restored and displayed in the Sala delle Armi, provide a fascinating historical record of the persecutions. Occupied by the law courts from 1799 until 1972, the building was restored in 1984 by the university to serve as the rectorate. The Sala Magna has a wooden ceiling painted by Simone da Corleone and Cecco di Naro (1377–80), illustrating 32 different episodes of chivalry, courtly love and legend. Also on display is Renato Guttuso's most famous painting, the *Vucciria*, illustrating shoppers and merchandise in the sensual confusion of the daily food market, which he donated to the university in 1974.

In the notorious Inquisition prison next door, the **Carcere dei Penitenziati** (*same ticket*), people accused of heresy or witchcraft underwent atrocious torture, as commanded by Torquemada. One of them was a friar from Racalmuto, Diego La Matina (his story is told by Leonardo Sciascia in *Morte dell'Inquisitore*), who in 1656, during a particularly gruelling interrogation, managed to kill his inquisitor with his handcuffs. After that he was tied to a chair for months before being burnt at the stake, while his tormentor was proposed to the Vatican as a saint and martyr. The old prison now houses the **Museo dell'Inquisizione**, dedicated to Diego La Matina. The labyrinth of cells where thousands of 'heretics' were imprisoned has been restored. The fascinating graffiti (some in English and German) and the drawings which entirely covered the walls of the cells, first discovered in the 19th century and covered up again, have also now been painstakingly brought to light by the removal of many accretions of paint and plaster.

THE CASSARO MORTO

The lower end of the Corso, the Cassaro Morto, was virtually destroyed by bombing raids in 1943; the **Fontana del Cavallo Marino**, with a seahorse by Ignazio Marabitti, is now surrounded by a garden. The reconstructed **Porta Felice** (1582–1637) has no arch between the two monumental pillars to allow the passage of the tall *vara* (float) on the feast day of St Rosalia. The long 17th-century façade of Palazzo Butera stands above the terraced *Mura delle Cattive*, or 'Wall of the Bad Women'. The name may refer to a time when women caught in adultery were exposed to public ridicule. Alternatively, it may refer to the widows who, for reasons of decorum, could not take their *passeggiata* with other ladies along the Foro Italico, so they passed the time here in malicious gossip. The busy, broad **Foro Italico**, which runs outside the walls, offers a splendid view of Mt Pellegrino, and a large public park has been created on the seafront.

MUSEO DELLE MARIONETTE

At Piazzetta Antonio Pasqualino 5 (a turning off Via Butera, *map 12*) is the Museo Internazionale delle Marionette Antonio Pasqualino (*open Mon–Sat 9–1 & 2.30–6.30, closed Sun and holidays; T: 091 328060, www.museomarionettepalermo.it*), founded in 1975. There is a well-displayed collection of puppets, from Sicily and around the world.

OPRA DEI PUPI

Sicily has long been famous for its puppet theatres, known as the *opra dei pupi*. In the 19th century, at the height of their popularity, the most important puppet theatres on the island were in Palermo, Trapani, Syracuse, Caltagirone, Acireale and Catania. In the 1960s, puppet theatres languished and many closed down, but recently there has been a revival of this traditional entertainment. The puppets, which vary in size from Palermo (small, with jointed knees) to Catania (large, even 30kg, stiff legs), are made of wood, with shiny armour. The puppeteer, who stands on a wooden platform just above the stage, manoeuvres them by using quite heavy iron bars. However cumbersome they may look offstage, they immediately come to life when brought into the scene, and swagger into position with great panache. The plays focus on chivalric episodes in the lives of the paladins of Charlemagne's court, portrayed through the various heroic deeds of Orlando, Rinaldo, Astolfo and others who challenge the Saracens. The key moment in every play is the battle, enacted in the traditional style, with much foot stamping, blood spurting, heads rolling, corpses piling up on both sides of the stage (Christians on one side, Muslims on the other), even the occasional dragon or wizard putting in an appearance. Garibaldi is also a source of inspiration for the *pupari*, as is King Arthur of the Round Table. The Sicilian puppet theatre has been declared a UNESCO Masterpiece of Intangible Heritage.

SANTA MARIA DELLA CATENA

On the opposite side of the Corso is the late 15th-century church of **Santa Maria della Catena** (*open Mon–Sat 10–6, Sun 2–6; T: 091 611 8168; ; part of the Circuito Arte Sacra, see p. 77*), probably by Matteo Carnelivari (1502–34). The name *catena* (chain) refers to the chain that used to close the old port: it stretched from this bank across the harbour to Castello a Mare. There is also a legend that three innocent people were condemned in 1391 and as custom demanded, were sent to spend the night in this church in prayer; as they prayed their chains dropped from them and they were spared. A flight of steps leads up to the three-arched porch, which, with its two corner-pilasters, provides an ingenious combination of Gothic and Renaissance styles. The delicate carving of the three doorways is attributed to Vincenzo Gagini. The elegant interior has been beautifully restored. In the first south chapel, under a 16th-century canopy, is a lovely 14th-century fresco of the *Madonna and Child,* discovered in the 1980s. The four statues are by the Gagini school. In the second chapel is a late 15th-century relief of the *Madonna and Child with Angels* from the church of San Nicolò alla Calza. In a chapel with a 16th-century relief are frescoes by Olivio Sozzi. The sanctuary is particularly beautiful with elaborate Gothic decoration and double columns.

LA CALA

The deeply curving inlet of La Cala, now a small yachting harbour surrounded by a promenade, is all that remains of the Phoenician port which once extended far into the old town. On fine days it is pleasant to sit out with a drink and a snack at the bar beside the old fish market. Just beyond there are visible sections of the old harbour wall, and you can wander among the ruins of the old Castello a Mare fortress (*see p. 61*).

PALAZZO ABATELLIS (GALLERIA REGIONALE)

Map 12. Via Alloro 4. Open Tues–Fri 9–5.30; Sat, Sun and holidays 9–1; closed Mon. Possible combined ticket with Palazzo Mirto and Oratorio dei Bianchi. Bookshop and café. T: 091 623 0000.

Via Alloro, a narrow medieval street with some old palaces, leads east from Piazza Aragona (*map 16*). On the left is the church of the **Madonna dell'Itria dei Cocchieri** (*open Sat 3.30–6, Sun for Mass at 11, T: 091 616 5848*), once the seat of the confraternity of coachmen. Built in 1596, it has a crypt with 18th-century frescoes. Further up on the right is the church of **La Gancia** (*see p. 53*) and then Palazzo Abatellis.

HISTORY OF THE PALACE

Palazzo Abatellis was designed in 1490–95 by Matteo Carnelivari, Nicolò Grisafi and several other architects and master-builders for Francesco Abatellis, appointed 'master-pilot' (or admiral) of Sicily by the Spaniards, in a style combining elements of the Renaissance with Late Catalan Gothic. The façade is unusual and interesting, especially the square portal, formed of slender carved stone poles tied together by writhing serpents to form a trellis. Above it is the coat of arms of Francesco Abatellis: a griffon wearing a coronet. Although he married twice, Abatellis died without issue, so he left the palace to the Benedictine nuns, who later passed it to the Dominican order, which held it from 1526 until 1943, when it was damaged by bombs. It had been much altered internally and was freely restored in 1954 as the home of the Galleria Regionale della Sicilia. This is a superb collection of sculpture and paintings, well documented and beautifully arranged, and recently much enlarged.

The 16th-century monastery church of the Portulano, used by the Dominican nuns, is also open to the public, after having been completely cleared, showing to advantage its beautiful architecture and an altarpiece by Vincenzo da Pavia of *Christ at the Column*, together with other works by the same artist. This gallery is used for temporary exhibitions.

Ground floor

The ground-floor rooms, opening off the courtyard, are devoted principally to sculpture. Steps to the left of the main entrance lead up to a loggia with Islamic lapidary fragments. The arrangement of the collection beyond is largely chronological. In the first room are window- and door-frames from the Martorana convent, now demolished, which stood next to the church of the same name; they are remarkable for the typical 12th-century carvings of geometric designs.

The former chapel is dominated by a famous large fresco of the ***Triumph of Death***, detached from Palazzo Sclafani. Dating from c. 1449, it is of uncertain attribution, thought by some scholars to be a Sicilian work and by others to be by Pisanello or his school. Death is portrayed as an archer on a spectral horse, killing with is arrows the

PALAZZO ABATELLIS
Detail of the *Triumph of Death* (1449).

contented and successful (a king, prelates and fine ladies), while the unhappy, sick and aged (left), among whom are the painter and a pupil, pray in vain for release. The painting has provided inspiration for several artists, among them Picasso (*Guernica*).

A corridor containing **Islamic majolica lustreware**, known as *loza dorada*, includes a magnificent pale ivory and gold-coloured vase of Hispano-Moresque type (13th–14th century) from a church in Mazara del Vallo, thought to come from Malaga, and three splendid dishes manufactured in Manises (15th century).

Francesco Laurana's masterpiece, his **bust of Eleonora of Aragon** (1475), is beautifully displayed. Eleonora, daughter of Ferdinand I of Naples, married Ercole d'Este, Duke of Ferrara, gave him three children and presided over a particularly rich period in that city's history. The next room is devoted to the **Gagini family**: particularly notable are a marble statuette of the *Madonna and Child*, the *Madonna del Buon Riposo* (1528) and the head of a young boy, all by Antonello Gagini.

The final room contains architectural fragments by the Gagini and their school, including the capitals from the church of the Annunziata in Palermo, destroyed by a bombing raid in 1943; some painted panels of typical medieval *drôleries* from the church of Sant'Agostino in Trapani; and fragments from a ceiling in Palazzo Chiaramonte in Palermo, painted by Cecco di Naro and Simone da Corleone in 1377–80 with scenes from the Bible and of knightly chivalry.

First floor

The first floor contains the Picture Gallery (Pinacoteca), with its representative series of Sicilian paintings, most of which are from churches and convents of Palermo, including 13th–14th-century works still in the Byzantine manner, and later works showing the influence of various schools (Umbrian, Sienese, Catalan, and Flemish).

The earliest works include a delicate Byzantine mosaic of the Madonna and a painted 13th-century Crucifix. A series of panel paintings illustrates the arrival in Sicily of works from Tuscany and Liguria, thanks to commercial ties linking Palermo with Pisa and Genoa in the 14th century. Paintings of the late 14th and early 15th centuries from Tuscany and Liguria include a splendid polyptych by an unknown master from Siena, the *Madonna Enthroned between Sts Catherine of Alexandria, Paul, Peter and Dominic*, together with other triptychs and polyptychs by Sicilian masters, including several *Coronations of the Virgin* by the same unknown artist, and works by the Master of the Trapani Polyptych.

A large gallery is dominated by two splendid early 15th-century wooden **Crucifixes** painted in tempera on both sides, one by the Master of Galatina and the other by Pietro Ruzzolone. On the walls are detached frescoes by Tommaso de Vigilia, and the magnificent Gothic-style Corleone Polyptych, still intact with its original wooden panelling, from the monastery of San Salvatore in Corleone.

Precious works by Antonello da Messina are the stunning little panel painting universally considered to be his masterpiece, the *Virgin Annunciate* (1474), and *Sts Gregory, Augustine and Jerome*, parts of a polyptych probably painted in 1473. Other late 15th-century paintings and frescoes include works by Tommaso de Vigilia, a Crucifix by Pietro Ruzzolone and works by Riccardo Quartararo, notably *Sts Peter and Paul* (1494) and a *Coronation of the Virgin*. Notice the rich, dark colours used by Quartararo, and his sense of balanced design; behind the array of saints and martyrs, the bright wings of the angels indicate God on high, looking down from his mandorla in the sky.

A later mandorla, of the 16th century, has Antonello Crescenzio's *Assumption of the Virgin*. Other 16th-century works include Andrea da Salerno's *Sts John the Baptist and John the Evangelist* and Antonello Crescenzio's copy (1538) of Raphael's *Spasimo* (*see p. 55*). There are also several 15th- and 16th-century Flemish works, most notably, by Mabuse, the **Lanza Triptych** (after 1511), a portable devotional work with the *Virgin and Child between Sts Catherine and Dorothy* (on the outside, *Adam and Eve*), a painting of extraordinary detail and a superb example of its kind.

There follow Mannerist-style paintings by the Tuscan-Roman school of the 16th century and more works by Vincenzo da Pavia, dating from after his Roman sojourn, where he was strongly influenced by Polidoro da Caravaggio.

In the tiny **Quadreria**, which leads through to the new wing, paintings are hung in the old-fashioned way, crowding the walls under a painted wooden ceiling, among abundant decorative elements in carved and inlaid wood. Religious subjects, landscapes, still lifes, interiors and portraits, mostly from the aristocratic homes of Sicily, are displayed in a fascinating sequence. There are also carved 18th-century crib figures.

New Wing

The new wing displays works on two floors. The first-floor Sala Verde (Green Room) was designed to show to advantage the huge canvases of Sicilian late Mannerist art. During the Counter-Reformation, large, lavish altarpieces were much in demand for churches and convents. The highlight of the collection, however, is a glittering monstrance in gold, silver-gilt, enamel and diamonds known as the *Sfera d'Oro* (Golden Sphere), a masterpiece by the silversmith Leonardo Montalbano, who was commissioned to make it in 1640 by Anna Graffeo, duchess of Majno, forced to enter a convent after the death of her husband and sons. She gave the craftsman all her jewellery to use as his materials. Stolen from the museum in 1870, it was recovered in 300 pieces, because the thieves had smashed it for the gold and precious stones. It proved impossible to repair until recently, when the parts were joined using a laser, the first time the technique was used in this way.

The second-floor Sala Rossa is dedicated to the works of artists influenced by Caravaggio, including Pietro Novelli, Van Dyck, Andrea Vaccaro, Cesare Fracanzano, Matthias Stom, Luca Giordano, Mattia Preti and Agostino Scilla.

THE KALSA DISTRICT

LA GANCIA

Map 12. Via Alloro 27. Open April–Oct Mon–Sat 9.30–1.30, Nov–March Sat only. Sun and holidays 10–12.30. No visits during services. If closed, try asking at the Franciscan convent next door.

The church of La Gancia has a fine exterior is of the 15th century. In the interior, the wooden ceiling and organ (no longer in use) date from the transformation begun in 1672. In the second south chapel are Antonello Crescenzio's *Madonna with Sts Catherine and Agatha* (signed and dated 1528) and a *Holy Family* attributed to Pietro Novelli; in the fourth chapel: Antonello Gagini's (attributed) seated *Madonna* (the head of the Christ Child is modern); in the fifth and sixth chapels are inlaid marble panels with scenes of the *Flight into Egypt* and outside is a pulpit made up of fragments of sculpture by the Gagini. The chapel to the right of the choir has fine marble decoration and stuccoes by Giacomo Serpotta. On the choir piers are two delicately carved *Annunciations* attributed to Antonello Gagini. In the chapel to the left of the choir are more stuccoes by Serpotta and a *Marriage of the Virgin* by Vincenzo da Pavia. North transept: on the wall (high up), *St Francis* by a Zoppo di Gangi. North aisle: in the sixth chapel are two beautiful reliefs by Antonello Gagini; in the third chapel, Pietro Novelli's *St Peter of Alcantara*, and in the second, Vincenzo da Pavia's *Nativity*.

The adjoining **convent** is famous in the annals of the revolution of 4th April 1860 against Neapolitan rule. The convent bell gave the signal to the insurgents; Francesco Riso, their leader, was mortally wounded, 13 were captured and shot while two hid for five days in the vaults of the church under the corpses of their companions, before escaping through the *Buca della Salvezza*, a hole they dug through the wall next to Palazzo Abatellis, while three housewives pretended to quarrel in order to distract the Bourbon troops.

Abutting Palazzo Abatellis is the church of **Santa Maria della Pietà** (*map 12; open 10–12 & 4–6; no visits during services; T: 091 616 5266*), with a splendid Baroque façade by Giacomo Amato (1678–84), intended by the architect as the pair with Santa Teresa (*see below*); the two churches are among his finest works. The interior is a particularly striking example of local Baroque architecture. The delightful vestibule has stuccoes by Procopio Serpotta and frescoes by Borremans: it supports a splendid nuns' choir. Four choir-screens in gilded wood decorate the nave. The fresco in the vault is by Antonino Grano (1708). The first south altar has a painting of *Dominican Saints* by Antonio and Francesco Manno, and the second, a *Madonna of the Rosary* by Olivio Sozzi. The high altar has a tabernacle in lapis lazuli. The third north altar has a *Pietà* (in the beautiful original frame) by Vincenzo da Pavia and the second, *St Dominic* by Olivio Sozzi.

PIAZZA DELLA KALSA

From La Pietà, Via Torremuzza leads south to the heart of the Quartiere della Kalsa, an area that was almost flattened by 1943 bombing raids and has only recently been restored. **Piazza della Kalsa** (from the Arabic *el-Halisa*, 'the Elect', where the emir had his residence; *map 16*) was one of the oldest parts of the city, fortified by the Arabs in 938, with its own walls and defensive castle. Here is the superb façade (1686–1706) of the church of **Santa Teresa alla Kalsa** (*open 7.30–11 & 3–7, Sun morning closes at 12; T: 091 617 1658*) by Giacomo Amato. In the interior, the first south chapel contains Giovanni Odazzi's *Holy Family* (1720) and the second has Ignazio Marabitti's marble *Crucifixion* (1780–1). The high altarpiece is by Gaspare Serenario (1746) and the two

statues of female saints in the sanctuary are by Giacomo S
altarpiece is by Sebastiano Conca and the second is by Willen

Almost opposite Santa Teresa is the **ex-church of the (**
also by Amato, now an exhibition venue. Tucked away in
behind Santa Teresa, in Piazzetta dei Bianchi, is the statel
dei Bianchi (*open Tues–Sun 9–1; possible joint ticket wiṭ₁ ₁ ₐₗₐᵤ₋₋*
Palazzo Mirto; T: 091 617 3080). It incorporates the Chiesa della Vittoria, built over
one of the gates of the Kalsa citadel and named after a vision of the Virgin Mary that
is said to have appeared to Robert Guiscard, spurring him on to victorious conquest.
The ground floor displays sculptures rescued from churches in the neighbourhood
destroyed by the 1943 bombs, and the first floor, reached by a magnificent staircase,
is used for exhibitions. The duty of the confraternity that had its seat here, called
the 'Bianchi' because of their white robes, was to comfort condemned criminals and
obtain repentance before their deaths.

SANTA MARIA DELLO SPASIMO
*Map 16. Open Nov–March 9.30–5.30, April–Oct 9.30–6.30. Closed Mon. T: 091 616
1486.*
The former church and convent of Santa Maria dello Spasimo have been restored as
a cultural centre. Founded in 1509, the complex was never completed, as the area was
taken over by the Spanish viceroy in a plan to strengthen the city's defences. In 1573
the convent was sold to the Senate and the church was used as a theatre after 1582, and
again at the end of the 17th century. Part of the convent became an isolation hospital
for plague victims in 1624, and in the 19th and 20th centuries it was used as a general
hospital. Over the centuries the buildings have been adapted as warehouses, a deposit
for snow, and as storage for the débris after the bombardments of the Second World
War. After the hospital was finally closed in 1986, restoration work began.

Beyond the 16th-century cloister is the church (roofless except for the beautiful
Gothic apse vault), which has been made safe, leaving a few trees growing in the
nave. In 1516 Raphael was commissioned to paint for this church an altarpiece of
Jesus Falling Beneath the Cross. It came to be known as *Lo Spasimo di Sicilia*. After an
adventurous journey, during which, according to Vasari, the painting was lost at sea
in a shipwreck, but subsequently discovered on the shore near Genoa, it was finally
installed here in 1520, the year Raphael died. The Spanish viceroy presented it to
Philip IV of Spain in 1661 and it is now in the Prado in Madrid. Several copies were
made of the painting (one made by Antonello Crescenzio in 1538 can be seen in Palazzo
Abatellis), and some experts believe that the original may now be in the Prefecture of
Catania, because a switch was accidentally made at some unknown date. The original
frame is by Antonello Gagini.

VILLA GIULIA AND THE BOTANICAL GARDEN
The Kalsa district is bordered to the south by Via Lincoln, across which is **Villa
Giulia** (*open Nov–Feb 9–5, March–Oct 8–8*) or La Flora, a delightful garden laid out
in 1777, with beautiful trees and flowers, much admired by Goethe. In the centre are

...es in the Pompeian style, and a sundial fountain; towards the sea is a statue _Genius of Palermo_ by Marabitti. The **Botanical Garden** (_open Nov–Feb 9–5, and March 9–6, Sept and April 9–7, May–Aug 9–8; closed principal holidays; last tickets 30mins before closing; bookshop; T: 091 238 91236_), adjoining the Villa and entered through the side gate, is one of the loveliest in Europe. The entrance pavilion was built in Doric style in 1789 by Léon Dufourny; Venanzio Marvuglia worked on the decoration and added the side wings. The garden was laid out by the botanist Filippo Parlatore, who was born in Palermo. Opened to the public in 1795, it has ficus trees, bamboo, palms, lotus trees, bananas, frangipane, and many other plants from all over the world, a lovely circular lily pond, and the Serra Carolina, a beautiful 19th-century greenhouse. The exotic character of the garden is enhanced by a colony of ring-necked parakeets, nesting in the hollow trunks of the poplar trees along the avenues.

PIAZZA MAGIONE AND PALAZZO AJUTAMICRISTO

In the centre of **Piazza Magione** (_map 16_), between two agaves, is a small memorial plaque to Giovanni Falcone, who was born in this district in 1939. It was set up by the city of Palermo in 1995, 'in gratitude and admiration' for this courageous magistrate, assassinated by the Mafia in 1992. At the beginning of Via Castrofilippo is the little **Teatro Garibaldi** (_T: 091 611 8246_), built in 1861 on what was the garden of the Magione and visited by Garibaldi himself in 1862. Also on this side of the piazza is the fine Norman apse of the **church of La Magione** (_open Mon–Sat 9–7, Sun and holidays 9–1 in winter, 9–7 in summer; last tickets 30mins before closing; T: 091 617 0596; part of the Circuito Arte Sacra, see p. 77_), which stands in majestic isolation, painstakingly restored after the 1943 bombing raids. A precious example of Arab-Norman architecture, it was founded for the Cistercians by Matteo d'Aiello before 1151 as the church of the Trinity, but transferred to the Teutonic knights in 1193 by Emperor Henry VI as their mansion, from which it takes its name. The interesting façade has three handsome and very unusual doorways. The beautiful tall interior has a fine apse decorated with twelve small columns. Above the 14th-century stone altar hangs a painted Crucifix. The contents include statues of Christ and also the _Madonna and Child_ by the Gagini school, a 15th-century marble triptych, and a tabernacle of 1528. The custodian will show you the charming little Cistercian cloister of c. 1190 around a garden; one walk with twin columns and carved capitals survives. A room off the cloister contains a detached 15th-century fresco of the _Crucifixion_ with its sinopia. Outside is a delightful garden and a monumental 17th-century gateway on Via Magione.

Via Magione leads to **Via Garibaldi**, typical of Palermo, a dilapidated street with some handsome palaces and opulent balconies. Here at no. 23 is **Palazzo Ajutamicristo** (now also a B&B; _see p. 77_), built by Matteo Carnelivari in 1490, with Catalan Gothic elements. It is still a private home. Charles V was entertained here on his return from Tunis in 1535. Part of the palace (entered from a doorway a little further along the street, without a number) now houses a sculpture gallery, the **Museo di Sculture** (_open Mon–Sat and 1st Sun of month 9–1.30, Tues and Sat late closing at 6.30; T: 091 707 1404_). Statues, reliefs and fragments, salvaged from demolished churches and museum storerooms, are assembled together to illustrate the art of carving stone. Among the highlights are

MUSEO DI SCULTURE
Portrait bust of the satirical poet Giovanni Meli by Valerio Villareale (c. 1838).

the funerary stelae of Giambattista and Elisabetta Mellerio (1814) by Canova, which were purchased by the Region in 1978 to prevent them being sold abroad; a remarkably expressive portrait bust by Domenico Gagini (1468) of Pietro Speciale, a praetor of the city who had commissioned several important works from Gagini, helping to build their reputation. On the first floor are the famous Art Nouveau decorative mosaics from the façade of the Morello bakery in the Capo market.

Via Garibaldi and its continuation south, Corso dei Mille, mark the route followed by Garibaldi on his entry into the city. At the end is **Piazza della Rivoluzione**, scene of the outbreak of the 1848 rebellion, inspired by Giuseppe La Masa and mercilessly crushed by Bourbon troops; even today people use the expression *un quarantotto*, a 'forty-eight', to mean a total disaster. A fountain here portrays the *Genius of Palermo* (*see p. 27*).

GALLERIA DI ARTE MODERNA
Piazza della Croce dei Vespri (*map 15–16*) is named after the graves of many French victims of the Sicilian Vespers, marked in 1737 by a Cross. Two sides of the piazza are occupied by the fine 18th-century **Palazzo Valguarnera-Ganci**, still owned by the family. Visconti used the sumptuous *Salone degli Specchi* as the setting for the scene of the great ball in his film *The Leopard*, based on the novel by Giuseppe Tomasi di Lampedusa. Nearby is the church of **Sant'Anna**, with a fine Baroque façade begun in 1726 by Giovanni Biagio Amico, with sculptures by Giacomo Pennino and Ignazio Marabitti, on designs by Giacomo Serpotta. The interior dates from 1606–36, with frescoes in the south transept by Filippo Tancredi.

The enormous former convent next door now houses the splendid **Galleria di Arte Moderna E. Restivo (GAM)** (*map 15; open Tues–Sun 9.30–6.30; last tickets 1hr before closing; café, restaurant and bookshop; wheelchairs available; T: 091 843 1605, www.gampalermo.it*), with 19th- and 20th-century works, mostly by artists from Sicily and southern Italy, and well worth a visit. Particularly memorable are the sections dedicated to Michele Catti (splendidly mournful scenes of Palermo in the rain), Francesco Lojacono (some beautiful landscapes), Antonino Leto and Ettore De Maria Bergler. There are representative works by Palermo artists of the 20th century (Renato Guttuso, Pippo Rizzo) and some good pieces by well-known names of the Italian Novecento (Sironi, Campigli and Casorati). The displays frequently change in order to bring works out of storage, but keep an eye open for outstanding paintings by Onofrio Tomaselli (*I Carusi*, his famous canvas of child sulphur miners), Domenico Morelli and Antonio Mancini, the huge canvas by Corrado Cagli on the landing between the first and the second floor, portraits by Boldini and sculptures by Trentacoste.

SAN DOMENICO, THE VUCCIRIA & LA LOGGIA

The church of **Sant'Antonio Abate** at Via Roma 203/a (*map 11*) occupies the highest point of the eastern part of the old city. The 14th-century campanile, which once used to summon the citizens to assembly, was lowered in height at the end of the 16th century, and the church reconstructed after the earthquake of 1823 in the medieval style of the original. Opposite the church, at no. 258, is Palermo's drama theatre, **Teatro Biondo** (*www.teatrobiondo.it*). Beside the church, steps lead down into the maze of small streets around Piazza Caracciolo and Piazza Garraffello, the scene of a daily market known as the **Vucciria**, once of the most colourful sights in the city, now more popular in the evenings as a gathering-place. In Piazza Garraffello is Palazzo Lo Mazzarino, where the father of the famous Cardinal Mazarin was born in 1576. The market extends along Via dei Cassari passing the 18th-century church of Santa Maria del Lume, designed by Salvatore Marvuglia. From Piazza Garraffello Via Materassai leads to Piazza San Giacomo La Marina and the 16th-century church of **Santa Maria la Nova** (*open 9–11.30; T: 091 326597*) with a Catalan Gothic porch (the neo-Gothic upper storey was added in the 19th century). The fine interior contains stuccoes in the presbytery and 18th-century paintings.

Close by, towards the sea, you can see the well-sited late Renaissance façade of **San Sebastiano** (*closed*). Inside are stuccoes by Giacomo Serpotta (1692).

SAN DOMENICO

In the centre of Piazza San Domenico (*map 11*) rises the column of the Immaculate Virgin by Giovanni d'Amico (1724–7). The large **church of San Domenico** (*open Tues–Fri 8–1.30, Sat and Sun 8.30–1 & 5–7*), rebuilt in 1640, has an imposing façade of 1726 in grey and golden brown. Since the middle of the last century the church has served as a burial place for illustrious Sicilians. In the third south chapel is a very fine statue of St Joseph by Antonino Gagini. The sixth chapel has a painting of *St Vincent Ferrer* by Giuseppe Velasquez (1787). The beautiful altarpiece of *St Dominic* in the south transept is by Filippo Paladini, and on the left wall there is a monument to Giovanni Ramondetta by Giacomo Serpotta and Gerardo Scudo (1691). In the chapel to the right of the sanctuary is a fine bas-relief of St Catherine attributed to Antonello

Gagini, a Neoclassical monument by Benedetto de Lisi (1864), a small *Pietà* in high relief by Antonello Gagini and a pretty little stoup. One of the organs dates from 1781; beneath the one on the right is a small funerary stele (1848) of the poet Giuseppina Turrisi Colonna by Valerio Villareale. The sanctuary has 18th-century choir stalls. The chapel to the left of the sanctuary has Gaginesque reliefs and the tomb of Ruggero Settimo (1778–1863), who convened the Sicilian parliament in this church in 1848. On either side of the altarpiece by Vincenzo da Pavia in the north transept, are funerary monuments by Ignazio Marabitti. A bust of the painter Pietro Novelli is in the north aisle. In the fourth chapel is an altarpiece of *St Raymond*, using his cloak as a sail, attributed to Filippo Paladini, while in the third chapel is a statue of St Catherine by Antonello Gagini (1527), with reliefs on the base, and on the right, a statue of St Barbara by his school. The second chapel has a terracotta statue of St Catherine of Siena, and the first an altarpiece by Andrea Carreca da Trapani. The fragmentary 14th-century cloister, which was part of the first church built on this site by the Dominicans, can only be visited by prior arrangement (*T: 091 589172 from 9–12*).

Next to the church is a small but well-arranged museum dedicated to the Unification of Italy, the **Museo del Risorgimento** (*open Mon–Fri 10–12, T: 091 582774, www. storiapatria.it*), with documents and memorabilia relating to this dramatic period in the history of Palermo. You will find Garibaldi's favourite chair, his crutches, cigar, swords and slippers. Portraits and marble busts portray protagonists of the 1848 rebellion and the anti-Bourbon battles of 1860 which would result in Italy becoming one nation, 'from Trento to Pantelleria', as Garibaldi expressed it.

LA LOGGIA AND ITS CHURCHES

NB: The ticket office for the two oratories of La Loggia is at Via Valverde 1, next to the church of Santa Cita. Same opening times for both, including the churches: Mon–Sat 9–6. T: 091 332779, www.ilgeniodipalermo.com.

The district known as La Loggia is so named because the merchants and bankers of Genoa had their booth (*loggia*) here. Today there are still many jewellery shops in the area. Via Bambinai continues as Via Squarcialupo, the large church on the left being **Santa Cita** or Santa Zita (*map 11*). It was first built, together with a hospital, in the early 14th century by a merchant from Lucca, who dedicated it to St Zita, patron saint of domestic servants, who is buried in his native city). In the 16th century the Dominicans, who had acquired the church, allowed wealthy families to bury their dead here, thus ensuring an income for their convent and permitting the creation of the lavish funerary chapels. The church was rebuilt in 1586–1603 and badly bombed in 1943. Today the interior contains fine but war-damaged sculptures by Antonello Gagini (1517–27). In the apse behind the altar is a marble tabernacle surrounded by a magnificent arch, both superbly carved. The splendid altarpiece is a panel painting by Filippo Paladini of *St Agnes of Montepulciano* (1603). In the second chapel to the left of the choir is the sarcophagus of Antonio Scirotta, also by Gagini; and more sculptures by the same artist are in the second chapel (Platamone) to the right of the choir. The Chapel of the Rosary has refined polychrome marble decoration (1696–1722) and sculpted reliefs by Gioacchino Vitaliano. The crypt of the Lanza family, under the chapel, is also open to the public; it has an altarpiece of inlaid marble and a sculpture by Giorgio da Milano.

Adjoining the left side of the church is the **Oratorio del Rosario di Santa Cita** (*T: 091 785 3181*), reconstructed in the early 17th century, approached through a little garden and loggia. The stucco decoration of the interior is one of Giacomo Serpotta's masterpieces: between 1685 and 1688 he worked on the nave and in 1717 on the apse. On the entrance wall is an elaborate representation of the *Battle of Lepanto*, which commemorates the victory over the Turks in which the Christian fleet was protected by the Madonna of the Rosary (the Confraternity of the Rosary had been founded just before the battle in 1571). On the two side walls are New Testament scenes in high relief representing the 15 Mysteries of the Rosary between numerous seated allegorical statues. The decorative frames and stucco drapes are supported by hundreds of mischievous cherubs, for which Serpotta used the street urchins of Palermo as models. The altarpiece of the *Madonna of the Rosary* (1702) is by Carlo Maratta. The ebony benches with mother-of-pearl inlay are of 1702, while the beautiful inlaid marble floor is decorated with eight-pointed stars, symbol of the Madonna.

In Via Bambinai is the **Oratorio del Rosario di San Domenico** (*part of the Circuito Arte Sacra; see p. 77*). The interior is dominated by the masterful blue-and-red altarpiece by Van Dyck, representing the *Virgin of the Rosary with St Dominic and the Patronesses of Palermo*. The artist painted it in Genoa in 1628, having left Palermo because of the plague. The wall paintings of the *Mysteries* are by Novelli (who was particularly influenced by Van Dyck), Lo Verde, Stom, Luca Giordano and Borremans. Giacomo Serpotta's graceful stuccoes (1720), elegant society ladies representing various virtues, display amazing skill. The black and white ceramic floor is also well preserved.

In the handsome Piazza Cavalieri di Malta, the church of **Santa Maria di Valverde** was built in 1635 by Mariano Smiriglio. It has a grey marble side portal, and a campanile rebuilt in 1723. The sumptuous Baroque interior (1694–1716), decorated with polychrome inlaid marble, was designed by Paolo Amato and Andrea Palma. On the high altar is an 18th-century wooden statue of the *Madonna of the Rosary* and a fine canvas of the *Madonna of Carmel*, painted for this church by Pietro Novelli in 1642. The Virgin and Child are pictured holding the sacred scapular of the Carmelite Order; to the left, St Teresa of Avila is about to receive from a cherub the emblematic burning arrow of her calling. The vault fresco and those on the walls of the choir are by Antonino Grano, while the large one over the choir is by Olivio Sozzi (1750). Of the four highly elaborate altars, the most important is that of St Lucy (*see p. 358*), for whom there was a strong cult in Palermo. The beautifully solemn and dignified 15th-century statue of the saint is by an anonymous sculptor.

Nearly opposite Santa Cita is the fine 14th-century doorway of the **Conservatorio di Musica**. Close by is the isolated 15th-century church of **San Giorgio dei Genovesi** (*map 7–8*), restructured for the Genoese merchants by Giorgio di Faccio in 1576–91 and intended to be an indication of their wealth and influence (at the time they were the most powerful bankers and merchants in Sicily and the Kingdom of Naples). It has a sturdy Renaissance façade with a restored portal; the interior is also in the purest Renaissance style. Marble tomb slabs (17th and 18th centuries) cover the floor of the nave. There are paintings by Luca Giordano (*Madonna of the Rosary*), Bernardo Castello, Filippo Paladini (*St Luke Painting the Madonna*) and Palma Giovane (*Martyrdom of St George* and *Baptism of Christ*).

Beyond lies **Piazza delle Tredici Vittime**, where an obelisk commemorates 13 republicans shot by the Bourbons on 14th April 1860. A huge steel stele, 30m high, was set up here in 1989 to commemorate victims of the struggle against the Mafia. A fence protects an archaeological park with excavations of 10th-century Arab buildings and part of the Norman fortifications of the city (restored in the 16th century), known as **Castello a Mare** (*map 8; open Tues–Sat 9–7, Sun, Mon and holidays 9–1*).

In Via Cavour, on the other side of Piazza Tredici Vittime, is **Villa Whitaker** (1885; *map 7*), surrounded by a garden. This was one of two properties in Palermo owned by the Whitaker brothers.

AROUND SANT'IGNAZIO

In front of Piazza San Domenico, across Via Roma, the narrow Via Monteleone leads up behind the remarkable Art Deco **Post Office** (1933) to, at no. 50, the 17th–18th-century **Oratorio di Santa Caterina d'Alessandria** (*open Tues–Sun 9.30–1 & 3–6; T: 333 850 6187*). The oratory, owned by the Knights of the Order of the Holy Sepulchre since 1946, has recently undergone careful restoration. The interior has fine stuccoes by Procopio Serpotta (1719–26), including a series of statues symbolising Science and Knowledge. On the altar is the *Martyrdom of St Catherine* by Giuseppe Salerno, the Zoppo di Gangi, and on the west wall, a *Madonna and Child* by Vincenzo da Pavia, above a bench inlaid with ivory and mother of pearl. The vault fresco portraying the *Triumph of St Catherine* was carried out by Antonino Grano and his son Paolo. The polychrome marble floor dates from 1730.

The church of **Sant'Ignazio all'Olivella** (*map 11; open Mon, Tues, Thur and Sat 7–10 & 5–8, Wed 7–8am & 5–8pm, Sun 9–1; T: 091 586867*), begun in 1598, has a fine 17th-century façade. The beautiful interior has a barrel vault designed by Venanzio Marvuglia (1772) with frescoes by Antonino Manno (1790). In the first south chapel is Filippo Paladini's *St Mary of Egypt*; the second chapel has beautiful 17th-century inlaid marble decorations. In the south transept is an altarpiece by Filippo Paladini. The painting of the *Trinity* over the main altar is by Sebastiano Conca, and in the sanctuary are two statues by Ignazio Marabitti. In the left transept is an interesting altarpiece, of unusual design, of the *Martyrdom of St Ignatius* by Filippo Paladini (1613).

In the north aisle, the fifth chapel was sumptuously decorated in 1622 and has an altarpiece of *St Philip Neri* by Sebastiano Conca (1740) and two statues by Giovanni Battista Ragusa. The third chapel is also elaborately decorated with polychrome marble and semi-precious stones and an altar frontal in relief. The small fresco of the *Pietà* in the vault is by Pietro Novelli, who also painted the altarpiece of the *Archangel Gabriel* in the first chapel.

The narrow **Via Bara all'Olivella**, in front of the museum and the church of Sant' Ignazio, is one of the liveliest streets in Palermo, with craft shops, cafés, traditional restaurants and a puppet theatre. It leads to Piazza Verdi and the Teatro Massimo, from where Via Maqueda leads back to the Quattro Canti.

MUSEO ARCHEOLOGICO REGIONALE SALINAS

Map 7–11. Open Tues–Fri 9.30–7, Sat–Sun 9.30–1. Café and bookshop. T: 091 611 6807. NB: Closed since 2009, the museum was still undergoing reorganisation at the time of writing. Parts of the museum remain open, especially for exhibitions, until the work is complete. The description below covers the main highlights, which may be rearranged once the museum finally reopens.

Adjoining the church of Sant'Ignazio is the 17th-century former monastery of the Philippine order, now the seat of the Museo Archeologico Regionale Salinas, one of the finest museums in Italy, illustrating the history of western Sicily from prehistoric times to the Roman era. The museum was founded in the early 19th century by the university, and moved to this present site in 1866. During that time it acquired various material, including the important Casuccini collection, the most representative display of Etruscan antiquities outside Tuscany. It also houses finds from excavations in the western part of the island, notably those of Selinunte.

Ground floor

Small Cloister: An introductory display illustrates the history of the building and the story of the collections. In the centre of the courtyard is a 16th-century fountain with a triton, from the Palazzo dei Normanni. Under the colonnade is a display dedicated to the art of writing, with inscribed stones and Punic sculpture, including two Phoenician sarcophagi of the 5th century BC found near Palermo, and the ***Pietra di Palermo***, a slab of black diorite with a hieroglyphic inscription listing 700 years of Egyptian kings, with the major events of their reigns; for example recording the delivery of 40 shiploads of cedarwood to the pharaoh Snefru (c. 2700 BC). It has proved invaluable in dating ancient Egyptian history; two pieces from the same stele are in the museum of Cairo, and one is in the Petrie Collection at London University.

Large Cloister: In the niches of the arcades are Roman sculptures: *Zeus Enthroned*, a pseudo-acrolithic statue of the 4th century BC from Solunto, and a colossal statue of the emperor Claudius, in a similar pose. Here also are an interesting funerary stele with three portrait busts (40–30 BC) and an interesting Egyptian statue in black basalt fished from the Marsala lagoon. Of particular interest are the statues found by Robert Fagan (1761–1816) at Tindari.

Selinunte Galleries: The famous **metopes from Selinunte** are the most important treasures of the museum. These sculpted panels once decorated the friezes of some of the temples there and they show the development in the skill of the local sculptors from the early 6th to the end of the 5th centuries BC. On either side of the entrance are three delicate female heads and fragmentary reliefs from Temple E. Beneath the windows are six small Archaic metopes, sculptured in low relief, from Temple Y or the Temple of the Small Metopes, an early 6th-century temple whose exact location is unknown. These fragments were discovered reused in a later defensive wall. They represent the Rape of Europa, a winged sphinx, the Delphic triad, Herakles and the Cretan Bull, Demeter and Persephone in their quadriga, and Demeter, Persephone and Hecate. On one wall is a reconstruction, incorporating original fragments, of a frieze and cornice with three triglyphs and three stunning Archaic metopes from Temple C (early 6th century), representing Apollo on a quadriga; Perseus, protected by Athena, beheading the Gorgon; and Herakles punishing the Cercopes, thieves who had attempted to steal his weapons. Also on this wall are parts of two metopes from Temple F, with scenes from the gigantomachia (5th century BC). Four splendid Classical metopes from Temple E (early 5th century) show Herakles fighting an Amazon, the marriage of Zeus and Hera, the punishment of Actaeon, who is attacked by dogs in the presence of Artemis, and Athena overcoming a Titan.

A gallery is dedicated to the architecture of the temples, while another section is devoted to finds from the vast necropoleis of Selinunte. There are displays with finds from the sanctuaries, such as that of Demeter Malophoros. Another display contains material from the villages built among the ruins after 409 BC, including Byzantine objects and the remains of an Arab village, abandoned perhaps because of an earthquake or because of an outbreak of malaria, to which the area was prone.

Third Courtyard: Recently cleared and provided with a glass roof, this contains the splendid cornice of lion-head water spouts from the Temple of Victory at Himera (5th century BC), discovered by Pirro Marconi in 1929–30.

First floor (reached from the Small Cloister)

Here you will find the Casuccini collection of **Etruscan antiquities** from Chiusi. Particularly interesting are the urns and tombs in high relief, a number of panels with delicately carved bas-reliefs (many with traces of painting), and a magnificent oinochoe of bucchero ware (6th century BC) portraying the story of Perseus and Medusa.

An interesting display shows the 19th-century collection of Baron Astuto di Filangeri, consisting of archaeological material together with 'fakes', frequently produced at the time.

Sculpture donated by the Bourbon kings includes the *Satyr Filling a Drinking Cup*, a Roman copy from Villa Sora at Torre del Greco of a Praxitelean original. Further items displayed here are a portrait bust of Aristotle (a Roman copy of an original by Lysippus of c. 330 BC) and the very fine *Hercules Fighting a Stag*, a Roman copy of a 3rd-century BC original which decorated a fountain in the House of Sallust at Pompeii.

Among the large **Roman bronzes** is the *Ram of Syracuse*, a superb sculpture dating from the 3rd century BC, probably modelled on an original by Lysippus and formerly one of a pair. Until 1448 they were above the portal of the Castello Maniace in Syracuse. By the 18th century they were in Palermo. The second ram was destroyed in 1848 by a cannon shot.

A large space is taken up by **Roman floor mosaics** (1st century BC–4th century AD), mostly from Piazza Vittoria in Palermo. Another section is devoted to objects found underwater.

These include anchors of stone, lead and terracotta, amphorae dating from Phoenician to Byzantine times, and a Greek 5th-century BC kylix, fished from the sea off Termine Imerese.

Also on the first floor is the tiny chapel (*may be open on request*) used by those who were too infirm to go to the church next door. Here too is the Salinas library, consisting of 25,000 volumes on archaeology, numismatics, art and ancient history. Two reading rooms are available.

Second floor

Finds from **Marsala** (Lilybaeum) are represented by floor mosaics and painted funeral stelae. There is a considerable amount of material from **Solunto**, including wall paintings.

There is also some splendid **pottery**, including Attic black-figure vases (580–460 BC). Among the white-ground lekythoi is one showing the sacrifice of Iphigenia, signed by Douris. Red-figure vases are also displayed, including a hydra with the *Judgement of Paris*, and a bell krater with Dionysiac scenes.

The collection of **prehistoric and Early Bronze Age material** comes mainly from northwest Sicily. Here are displayed casts of the fine incised drawings (Upper Palaeolithic) of masked figures and animals from Cave B at Addaura (*see p. 73*). Nearby are the bones of elephants, rhinoceros and hippopotami found in Via Villafranca, in the so-called Grotta dei Giganti, Cave of the Giants.

SANT'AGOSTINO & THE CAPO DISTRICT

From the Quattro Canti, Via Maqueda runs gradually uphill to the north, passing the Capo quarter (*map 10*), a large bombed site whose ruined buildings were cleared in 1981. Plans for this district, which is owned by the Church, are uncertain.

THE MERCATO DEL CAPO AND ITS DISTRICT

The **Mercato del Capo** is a street market for cloth, clothes and household goods and, in Via Porta Carini, fish, fruit and vegetables. Also in Via Porta Carini is the church of **Sant'Ippolito Martire** (1583; *open Mon–Sat 8–11.30, Sun and holidays 8–12; T: 091 328430*), with a façade of 1728. A chapel off the south aisle contains numerous ex-votos, and in the north aisle is a damaged 14th-century Byzantine fresco of the

Madonna. The 18th-century paintings include the high altarpiece of the *Martyrdom of St Hippolytus* by Gaspare Serenario. Opposite is the church of the **Immacolata Concezione** (*open Mon–Sat 9–12; T: 327 453 2153*) built in 1612. The interior, one of the most beautiful in the city, was elaborately decorated during the 17th century with paintings, sculptures, singing galleries, inlaid marble altars, and a sumptuous organ. On the gilded stucco ceiling is a fresco by Olivio Sozzi. At the end of the street is the **Porta Carini**, the only one of the three gateways to have survived at the northern limit of the old city (although even this was reconstructed in 1782).

From the crossroads of the Mercato del Capo, Via Cappuccinella continues through the food market and Piazza Sant'Anna al Capo in a very rundown area of the city. Via Matteo Bonello and Via del Noviziato lead to the church of the **Noviziato dei Gesuiti**, St Stanislaus Kostka (*open Mon–Fri 8.50–12 & 4–6, Sun and holidays 9–12, closed Sat; T: 091 662 2430*), in the area behind the law courts. Built in 1591, the interior preserves some fine 18th-century stuccoes and inlaid marble decoration, as well as an effigy of St Stanislaus by Giacomo Pennino (1725).

In the other direction, Via Matteo Bonello leads to the picturesque church of **Sant'Angelo Custode** (on the corner of Via dei Carrettieri), preceded by an outside stair. It dates from the early 18th century. To the west is the wide and busy Via Papireto across which is Piazza Peranni, where Palermo's famous **flea market** for antiques and bric-à-brac, the Mercato delle Pulci, is held.

Via Carrettieri returns down to the Mercato del Capo in Via Beati Paoli, which leads right to **Piazza Beati Paoli**, named after a much-feared secret society which operated in this area in the 17th century. The church of **Santi Cosma e Damiano** was built after the plague of 1575 and that of **Santa Maria di Gesù** was founded in 1660 (it contains a large 18th-century vault fresco). Via Beati Paoli continues past the church of San Giovanni alla Guilla, rebuilt in 1669 and badly damaged in the Second World War. On the right, Vicolo Tortorici leads into Piazza Santi 40 Martiri with the **church of Santi Quaranta Martiri alla Guilla** (*open Sun 9–1, or on request, T: 339 158 8692 or 329 397 7513*), founded by some Pisan nobles in 1605 and rebuilt in 1725. It contains splendid frescoes by Willem Borremans. The word *guilla* derives from the Arabic *wadi*, or river, since the church was built on the banks of the River Papireto.

SANT'AGOSTINO

Open Mon–Sat 7–12 & 4–6; Sun and holidays 7.30–1. T: 091 584632.

Beyond the market to the east, hidden by traders' stalls, is the church of Sant'Agostino. The unusual tall side portal is attributed to Domenico Gagini. The beautiful façade, on Via Maestri dell'Acqua, has a late 13th-century portal decorated with lava-stone mosaic and a 14th-century rose window.

The interior, consisting of a single massive nave, was decorated with gilded stuccoes by Giacomo Serpotta and assistants from 1711, with numerous cherubs, statues and lunettes over the side altars. The first south altar has a panel painting by Simon de Worbrecht (16th century) of *Blessed William of Aquitaine*; the second altar, a 17th-century *Flight into Egypt*; the fourth altar, by Antonino Grano (17th century), *St Nicholas of Tolentino*; beyond the passage of the right entrance is the chapel of the

Madonna del Soccorso, with a bas-relief of the *Eternal Father*. Left of the high altar is the Chapel of the Crucifix, with a precious 17th-century reliquary. The fourth north altar has a painting by Giuseppe Salerno (Zoppo di Gangi) of *St Thomas of Villanova* and stories from his life. To the left of the second altar is a monument to Francesco Medici, with his bust (1774; surmounted by a cockerel) by Ignazio Marabitti. The 16th-century cloister, with tall pulvins above its capitals, surrounds a little garden. The fine Gothic entrance to the chapter house was exposed here in 1962 and restored.

THE NINETEENTH-CENTURY CITY

Piazza Verdi (*map 11*), laid out at the end of the 19th century, is now one of the central squares of the city. It is dominated by the opera house, **Teatro Massimo** (*open 9.30–6, last tour 5.30; no visits during rehearsals; to book tour, T: 091 605 3267, www. teatromassimo.it*), a huge Corinthian-style structure by Giovanni Battista and his son Ernesto Basile (1875–97). Among the historic late 19th-century opera theatres in Europe, its stage is exceeded in size only by those of the Paris and the Vienna operas. It was inaugurated in 1897 with Verdi's *Falstaff*. In the piazza in front of the theatre are two decorative little kiosks which used to be the ticket offices, also designed by Basile.

Opposite the theatre is Via Bara dell'Olivella (*map 11*), where at no. 2 is **Palazzo Branciforte** (*open March–Oct 9.30–7.30, Nov–Feb 9.30–2.30; closed Sun; last tickets 1hr before closing; guided tours only; café, restaurant and bookshop; T: 091 888 7767 or 091 765 7621, www.palazzobranciforte.it*). The old palace, magnificently restored by Gae Aulenti, houses the Fondazione Mormino collections of the Banco di Sicilia. There is well labelled (also in English) archaeological material from excavations financed by the bank, including a large collection of ancient Greek pottery from sites throughout western Sicily, exhibited in a deliberately old-fashioned style. The cases arranged along the centre of the room contain some of the most interesting pieces. There is also a collection of Sicilian pottery of the 15th–19th centuries. On the main floor are the numismatic and philatelic collections (that representing the Kingdom of the Two Sicilies is unique in the world), and the historic library, with over 30,000 volumes. The library gives access to the so-called Monte di Santa Rosalia, an outstanding example of 19th-century wooden architecture. You will also find a permanent display of 109 marionettes from the Cuticchio brothers' Opra dei Pupi (*see p. 49*).

From Piazza Verdi, Via Maqueda continues north by **Via Ruggero Settimo** (*map 7*), named after the president of a short-lived independent Sicily in 1848, proclaimed in defiance of the Bourbons. The street is lined with clothes shops as far as the enormous double Piazza Ruggero Settimo and Piazza Castelnuovo (*map 6*), home to the **Politeama Garibaldi**. This 'Pompeian' structure (1874, Giuseppe Damiani Almeyda) is crowned by a bronze quadriga by Mario Rutelli and is now used mostly for concerts, although originally designed to accommodate the circus.

Via Dante (*map 6*) leads west out of Piazza Castelnuovo. Once very fashionable, there are several delightful Art Nouveau houses along its length, and it ends by the parks of Villa Serradifalco and Villa Whitaker Malfitano (*see p. 70*). To the east, in Via Roma (*map 7*), is the **Grand Hotel et des Palmes** (formerly Palazzo Ingham). Wagner stayed here in 1882 with his family and completed *Parsifal*. The building was modified in 1907 by Ernesto Basile. Close by (opposite) is the **Anglican church** of the Holy Cross (*open Wed 10–12*), commissioned by Pip Whitaker in 1872, an example of Victorian Arts and Crafts in the heart of Palermo. **Viale della Libertà** (*map 2*), a wide avenue laid out in 1860, with trees and attractive Art Nouveau houses, leads north. Beyond the two squares Mordini and Crispi, the road narrows. On the left it passes a garden named after the magistrate Giovanni Falcone and his wife Francesca Morvillo, both assassinated by the Mafia in 1992 (*see p. 18*).

Opposite is the larger **Giardino Inglese** (*open 8–sunset*), a sadly neglected 19th-century public garden. It is bordered on the far side by Via Generale Dalla Chiesa which commemorates General Carlo Alberto Dalla Chiesa, prefect of the province and a *carabiniere*, who was assassinated by the Mafia here in 1982 (plaque), along with his wife and chauffeur, after just five months in office.

Further east towards the sea is the **Ucciardone** (*map 3*), built as a prison by the Bourbons in 1837–60 and now a maximum security jail, near the modern port. On the north side of the port, at Via dell'Arsenale 142, is the **Museo del Mare** (*Environs map; open Tues–Sun 9.30–1, T: 091 361309 or 335 610 2379*), in the old Bourbon arsenal, restored after damage in Second World War bombing raids on the port. It has an interesting collection relating to fishing, engines and shipbuilding, with historical photos, model ships, cannons and a display on the history of the port and the local tuna-fishing industries.

VILLA TRABIA TO PIAZZA VITTORIO VENETO

West of Viale Libertà is **Villa Trabia** (*map 1*), seat of the Lanza di Trabia family, an elegant 18th-century building (now used as a public library), with beautiful gardens open to the public (*open 8–sunset, entrance from Via Salinas 3: T: 091 7405943*).

Across Via Notarbartolo, Viale della Libertà passes (left; no. 52) **Villa Zito**, the art gallery of the Fondazione Banco di Sicilia (*Environs map; open Tues, Thur, Sat and Sun 4–8, Wed and Fri 10–2; T: 091 778 2180*), which on three floors displays paintings, prints, maps and watercolours from the 17th–20th centuries. Ground floor: 20th-century works by Mario Schifano, Renato Guttuso (including a remarkable *Eruzione dell'Etna*, painted during the 1983 eruption) and a section devoted to paintings by the Futurist artist from Corleone, Pippo Rizzo. First floor: works by Mattia Preti, Luca Giordano, Salvator Rosa and many others; 19th-century Sicilian artists are represented by Francesco Lojacono, Antonino Leto, Michele Catti, and Ettore De Maria Bergler (a splendid group of pictures donated by his heirs). Second floor: 19th-century, mainly Italian, artists are displayed here, including De Nittis, Boldini, Ottone Rosai, Carlo Carrà, Fausto Pirandello, Mario Sironi and De Pisis. The collection of maps is particularly important.

Viale della Libertà ends in the circular **Piazza Vittorio Veneto**, with its marble *Nike* monument to Liberty. From here Via d'Artigliera (right) leads shortly to Piazza dei Leoni at the south entrance (c. 4km from the Quattro Canti) to La Favorita park (*described on p. 72*).

LA ZISA & THE WEST OF TOWN

The palace of La Zisa (*map 9; open Tues–Sun and holidays 9–1.15 & 2–6.15, Mon mornings only; T: 091 652 0269*) takes its name from the Arabic *al-aziz*, meaning magnificent. It is the most important secular monument of Arab-Norman architecture to survive in Sicily, and is purely Islamic in inspiration. La Zisa was one of a group of palaces built by the Norman kings in their private park of Genoard (used as a hunting reserve) on the outskirts of Palermo. It was begun by William I c. 1164–5 and completed by his son. The palace is known to have been used by Frederick II, but it was already in disrepair in the late 13th century. It was fortified by the Chiaramontes in the 14th century. By the 16th century it was in a ruined state and was drastically reconstructed by the Spanish Sandoval family, who owned it from 1635 to 1806. It was expropriated by the Sicilian government in 1955, but then abandoned until part of the upper floors collapsed in 1971. After years of neglect, a remarkable restoration programme was begun in 1974 and it was finally opened to the public in 1990. The structure had to be consolidated throughout, but the astonishing architecture has been preserved. As a finishing touch, the magnificent gardens were imaginatively re-created, with lily ponds, fountains and walks, but unfortunately they were then totally neglected and are now ruined.

Exterior of La Zisa

The fine exterior has a symmetrical design, although the double-light windows on the upper floors were all destroyed in the 17th century by the Sandoval family, who set up their coat of arms on the façade and altered the portico. In King William's day the sandstone was faced with plaster decorated in a red and white design. The small pond outside, formerly part of the gardens, collected the water from the fountain in the ground-floor hall, which was fed by a nearby Roman aqueduct. A damaged inscription in Kufic letters at the top of the east façade has not yet been deciphered.

Interior of La Zisa

The beautiful interior is on three floors. The exceptionally thick outer walls (1.9m on the ground floor), the original small windows and a system of air vents kept the palace protected from the extremes of hot and cold. The rooms were all vaulted: the square rooms with cross vaults and the oblong rooms with barrel vaults. Amphorae were used in the vault construction to take the weight of the foundations of the floors above. Some of the vaults have had to be reconstructed in reinforced concrete. The floors (very few of the originals remain) were of tiles laid in a herring-bone pattern, except for the ground-floor hall which was in marble. The miniature *muqarnas* which decorate niches in some of the rooms, and the recesses of many of the windows, are borrowed from Arab architecture.

On the ground floor are explanatory plans and a display illustrating the history of the building. A model in Plexiglass shows the parts where it had to be reconstructed and where iron girders have been inserted to reinforce the building. The small chambers here were originally service rooms or for the use of court dignitaries. The splendid

LA ZISA

central hall, used for entertainments, has niches with stalactite vaults. Around the walls runs a mosaic frieze which expands into three ornamental circles in the central recess.

The Norman mosaics (which recall those in King Roger's Room in Palazzo dei Normanni) show Byzantine, Islamic and even Frankish influences. A fountain gushed from the opening surmounted by the imperial eagle in mosaic and flowed down a runnel towards the entrance to be collected in the fish pond outside. A majolica floor survives here and the faded frescoes were added in the 17th century. The little columns have beautiful capitals. On the inner side of the entrance arch is a damaged 12th-century inscription in large stucco letters.

Two symmetrical staircases (replaced by modern iron stairways) led up to the first floor. Here the living-rooms are connected by a corridor along the west front. Numerous fine vaults survive, and a series of air vents. Medieval Egyptian objects, including metalwork, ceramics and wooden lattice-work window screens, are displayed in some of the rooms, as well as amphorae found in the vaulting. On the top floor is a remarkable central hall with columns and water channels which was originally an open atrium surrounded by loggias, used in the summer. The small rooms on either side were probably a harem.

AROUND LA ZISA

To the north of the Zisa, on the corner of Via Whitaker, is a church which incorporates the **Norman chapel of the SS. Trinità**, built at the same time as the palace (*part of the Circuito Arte Sacra; see p. 77*). At the south edge of Piazza Zisa is the 17th-century church of the **Annunziata**, with Sandoval family monuments.

VILLA WHITAKER MALFITANO AND VILLINO FLORIO

From La Zisa, Via Whitaker and Via Serradifalco lead north to **Villa Whitaker Malfitano** (*map 5; open 9–3, closed Sun and holidays, guided visits only; T: 091 682 0522*) at Via Dante 167. Built for Pip and Tina Whitaker by Ignazio Greco in 1887, the house became the centre of English society in Palermo at the beginning of the 20th century. The Whitakers were visited by Edward VII in 1907 and by George V and Queen Mary in 1925. Pip Whitaker, descendant of the famous Marsala wine merchants (*see p. 163*), was owner and excavator of Mozia and the house was left by his daughter to the Joseph Whitaker Foundation in 1971. The furnishings, Sicilian, French and English, are superb. It is surrounded by a magnificent park of rare trees and plants collected by the owners, an orangery and an orchid nursery.

To the south of Villa Whitaker Malfitano, at Viale Regina Margherita 38, is the **Villino Florio** (*open Tues–Sat and 1st Sun of month 9–1; T: 091 702 5471*), one of Ernesto Basile's best works (1889), perfectly Art Nouveau in style and furnished by Ducrot. It has been carefully restored after a fire in 1962, and may become a museum.

CONVENTO DEI CAPPUCCINI

South of La Zisa, at Via Cappuccini 1, is the **Convento dei Cappuccini** (*beyond map 13 and Environs map; open 9–1 & 3–6, Sun and holidays mornings only; bookshop; T: 091 652 7389 or 329 415 0462*), famous for its catacombs. Here, the bodies of priests and friars, aristocrats and wealthy citizens—adults as well as children—were dried by the Capuchins, dressed in their best finery, and hung up along the underground passages. The practice continued until 1881, after which date only two further embalmings took place. There are still more than 2,000 bodies here, including that of one of the exceptions, Rosalia Lombardo, a little girl who died in 1920 and was embalmed by Alfredo Salafia. He died immediately afterwards and was thought to have taken the secret of her perfect conservation to his tomb—until in 2010 the manuscript in which he described his technique was discovered and published. Among the famous people buried in the **cemetery behind the monastery** is Giuseppe Tomasi di Lampedusa, in the family vault.

OUTSKIRTS OF PALERMO

THE PUNIC NECROPOLIS AND LA CUBA

Outside Porta Nuova (*map 14*), Corso Calatafimi begins, which leads to Monreale. On the left is a huge charitable institute built in 1735–8 by Cosimo Agretta; the church façade (1772–6) is by Marvuglia. On the corner is a fountain of 1630, the only one to survive of the many which once lined the road. Opposite is the vast **Albergo dei Poveri**, an intimidating building (1746–72) by Orazio Furetto, built as the Poor House, recently restored and now used for exhibitions. Beyond it is a series of barracks including (on the left, c. 1km from Porta Nuova) the Caserma Tüköry (no. 100), where excavations since 1989 have revealed part of a huge **Punic necropolis** (*entrance*

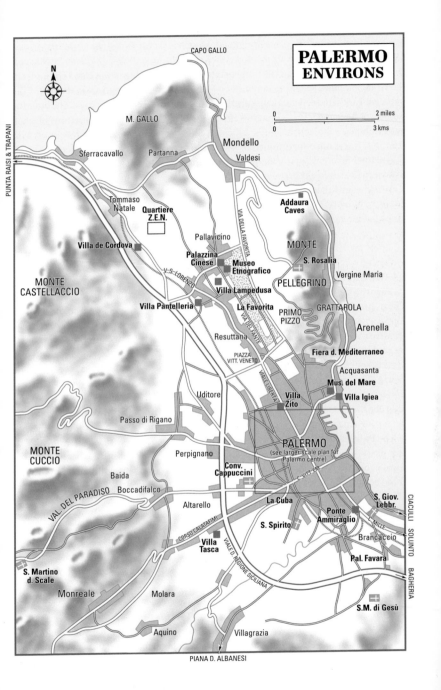

from La Cuba), with tombs dating from the 6th century BC. Here, separated from the barracks by a wall with a charming modern mural, is **La Cuba** (*Environs map; open Mon–Sat 9–6.30, 1st Sun of month 9–1, closed holidays; T: 091 590299*), a Norman palace built by William II (1180) in imitation of La Zisa. The name Cuba comes from the Arabic *kubbeh*, meaning dome. A copy of the Arabic inscription at the top of the outer wall and a model of La Cuba are displayed in a restored stable block. The building is now roofless and a few trees grow inside the walls. In one part are remains of a hall with miniature stalactite vaults, delicate reliefs, and a small cupola decorated with stuccoes. It was once surrounded by water, today replaced by a little garden.

Still further along Corso Calatafimi, opposite a department store and behind no. 575, a short road leads right to the remains of the now derelict 17th-century Villa Di Napoli. Here is the entrance to the **Cubula** (*closed*), a little pavilion with its characteristic red dome, built by William I. Once surrounded by a fishpond, it is the only survivor of the many pavilions which used to decorate his private park here.

THE NORTHERN OUTSKIRTS AND MONTE PELLEGRINO

LA FAVORITA

La Favorita's extensive area of woods and gardens lies at the foot of Monte Pellegrino. The public park (nearly 3km long) is crossed by a one-way road system and contains a hippodrome and other sports facilities. Just beyond Piazza Niscemi (c. 7km from the Quattro Canti) is Porta dei Leoni, the main entrance to the **Parco della Favorita**, an estate bought by Ferdinand of Bourbon in 1799 and laid out by him according to the taste of the times, adapting a dainty villa in Viale Duca degli Abruzzi as his and Queen Maria Carolina's residence from 1799–1802 during their enforced exile from Naples under Napoleon. The estate was only officially named 'La Favorita' in 1814, when the king contracted a morganatic marriage with the beautiful widow Lucia Migliaccio, his 'favourite' since 1812.

The **Palazzina Cinese** (*open Tues–Sat 9–6 and 1st Sun of month 9–1; T 091 707 1411*) is a pastel-coloured building, Chinese-inspired in every detail, re-designed for the royal couple by Venanzio Marvuglia. It consists of a basement with the ballroom and three floors terminating in a pagoda. The first floor, with its walls covered with painted silk, a triumph of *trompe l'oeil*, was used for receptions. The dining-table is provided with a central mechanism connecting it to the kitchen below, so dishes could be sent up and down as necessary, avoiding the presence of servants. The bathroom has a large oval tub of marble sunk into the floor. On the second floor is the king's bedroom, with a baldachin supported by eight white marble pillars, while Maria Carolina's Neoclassical bedroom is on the third floor together with two guest rooms, one in Turkish style and the other recalling Pompeii.

Next door to the Palazzina Cinese, in a pretty cottage once used as the servants' quarters, is the **Museo Etnografico Siciliano Pitrè** (*open 9–1, closed Mon; T: 091 740 9008*), founded in 1909 by Giuseppe Pitrè. The rich collection illustrates Sicilian life through its customs, traditions and popular arts. On display are painted carts and two state carriages, a puppet theatre, household utensils, objects pertaining to magic and religion, costumes, musical instruments, implements used by shepherds, fishermen and peasants. Very interesting is the section dedicated to bread and pastries made for festive occasions, and children's toys.

MONTE PELLEGRINO

Between the Mondello road and the sea is Monte Pellegrino (606m), described by Goethe as the most beautiful headland in the world: it rises sharply on all sides except the south. The rock, in places covered with trees and cacti, has a remarkable golden colour. Almost certainly the ancient *Heirkte*, the headland was occupied by Hamilcar Barca in the First Punic War and defended for three years (247–244 BC) against the Romans. The Arabs called it *Jebel Grin*, hence the modern name Pellegrino; however, the Peregrine falcon, *Falco pellegrino* in Italian, still nests on the headland. In the **Addaura Caves** (*no access*) on the northern slopes, prehistoric rock carvings were discovered in 1952. The incised human and animal figures date from the Upper Palaeolithic period: they include an exceptionally interesting scene of uncertain significance with 17 human figures, some with animal masks, who appear to be carrying out a cruel ritual or dance. Plaster casts of the carvings can be seen in the Salinas Archaeological Museum (*see p. 64*). Recent exploration of several caves in this area have revealed imprints of hands in red ochre, also dating to the Upper Palaeolithic.

SANTUARIO DI SANTA ROSALIA

The most direct approach to Mt Pellegrino from Palermo is from Piazza Generale Cascino, near the fair and exhibition ground (Fiera del Mediterraneo). From here Via Pietro Bonanno ascends to the Sanctuary of Santa Rosalia, crossing and recrossing the shorter footpath used by those making the annual pilgrimage on 3rd–4th September (often barefoot or on their knees). A flight of steps zigzags up the Scala Vecchia (17th century) between the Primo Pizzo (344m; left) and the Pizzo Grattarola (276m). The terrace of the rosy-pink Castello Utveggio (built as a hotel in 1932, now used as a conference centre), provides the best view of Palermo.

A small group of buildings marks the sanctuary, at 428m, a cavern converted into a chapel in 1625 (*open summer 7.30–7.30, winter 7.30–6.30; T: 091 540326*). It contains a statue of the saint by Gregorio Tedeschi and a bas-relief of her coronation by Nunzio La Mattina. The water trickling down the walls is held to be miraculous and is carefully captured by Futuristic-looking metal conduits. The outer part of the cave is filled with an extraordinary variety of ex-votos.

Rosalia, daughter of Duke Sinibald and niece of William II, lived here as a hermit until her death in 1166. She is supposed to have appeared to a hunter on Mt Pellegrino in 1624 to show him the cave where her remains were, since she had never received a Christian burial. When found, her relics were carried in procession through Palermo and a terrible plague, then raging in the town, miraculously ceased. She was declared patron saint of Palermo and the annual procession in her honour (14th–15th July), with a tall and elaborate float drawn through the streets by oxen, became a famous spectacle.

A steep road on the farther side of the adjoining convent climbs up to the summit, from which there is a wonderful panorama extending from Ustica and the Aeolian Islands to Etna. Another road from the sanctuary leads to a colossal 19th-century statue of St Rosalia by Benedetto de Lisi, high on the cliff edge.

MONDELLO

From the north end of the Parco della Favorita, a road runs through the suburb of Pallavicino and beneath the western slope of Mt Pellegrino, finally reaching the shore and the numerous elegant little seaside villas of Mondello, a sandy beach extending for 2km from Mt Pellegrino to Mt Gallo. This noted bathing resort was created by Donna Franca Florio for the amusement of her guests. The opulent Art Nouveau-style pier (1910) with a restaurant which overhangs the water, was originally the bathing establishment from which society ladies could discreetly lower themselves into the sea. The surrounding garden city was laid out between 1892–1910. At the north end is the old fishing-village of Mondello with a medieval tower. To the south is Valdesi, from where Lungomare Cristoforo Colombo returns towards the centre of Palermo following the rocky coast at the foot of Mt Pellegrino. Inland from Mondello is Partanna, and above the promontory, the dramatically beautiful Capo Gallo (527m) rises vertically from the sea (now a nature reserve).

THE FLORIO FAMILY

If Palermo in the 1890s was a capital city of the Belle Epoque, and if Mondello was one of the world's most fashionable bathing resorts, credit is certainly due to the Florio family. In 1893, when Ignazio Florio married Donna Franca Jacona di San Giuliano, the most beautiful and fascinating woman in Sicily, he owned the Aegadian Islands with the tuna fisheries, the Marsala wine company, and a large fleet of merchant ships. In 1906 his nephew Vincenzo launched the Targa Florio, a motor race on the hair-raising roads of the Madonie Mountains, which still takes place today (for veteran cars only; *www.girodisicilia.com*). Donna Franca's home in Palermo became a magnet for poets, artists, royalty and heads of state, while her Cartier jewellery was envied by Britain's Queen Mary. The length of her string of pearls (seven metres) gave rise to the malicious tall tale that for every infidelity, Ignazio Florio gave his wife a pearl. Bankruptcy eventually induced Donna Franca to sell her pearls. Although not untouched by personal tragedy, the Florios glittered on the social horizon of Palermo until well into the 1920s.

THE SOUTHERN DISTRICTS

SANTO SPIRITO AND THE SICILIAN VESPERS

From the station Corso Tüköry (*map 15*) leads west to Porta Sant'Agata (follow the signs for Policlinico/Ospedale). Here Via del Vespro forks left; beyond the Policlinico and just across the railway are the flower stalls and stonemasons' yards outside the cemetery of Sant'Orsola, in the midst of which is the **church of Santo Spirito** or dei Vespri (*Environs map; open 8–1.30; T: 091 422691*), a fine Norman building (1173–8) founded by Walter of the Mill (*see p. 32*). It has an attractive exterior with arches and bands of lava stone and lattice-work windows. The interior has a painted wooden ceiling and a painted wooden 15th-century Crucifix.

On 31st March 1282, at the hour of vespers, a French soldier offended a young Sicilian bride in front of this church by shoving his hands down her bodice, ostensibly to see whether she was carrying a dagger on her husband's behalf (Sicilians had been forbidden to carry weapons): her husband retaliated by strangling the soldier and the crowd immediately showed their sympathy by killing the other French soldiers present. Their action sparked off a rebellion against the Angevin overlords and by the next morning some 2,000 Frenchmen had been killed. The revolt spread to the rest of the island and in the following centuries the 'Sicilian Vespers' came to symbolise the pride of the Sicilians and their struggle for independence from foreign rule. The revolt also had important consequences for the course of European history, as from this time onwards the political power of Charles of Anjou, who had the support of the papacy, dwindled and he lost his ambition to create an empire.

SAN GIOVANNI DEI LEBBROSI AND CIACULLI

From Porta Garibaldi near the station, **Corso dei Mille** (*map 16*) leads south to the Oreto; this ancient thoroughfare was used by Garibaldi and his men when they entered the city in 1860. Just across the river is the **Ponte dell'Ammiraglio**, a fine bridge built by George of Antioch in 1113, and extremely well preserved. Since the river has been diverted it is now surrounded by a derelict garden and busy roads. Here the first skirmish between the *garibaldini* and Bourbon troops took place on 27th May 1860. On the left of the Corso, hidden behind crumbling edifices (and now approached from Via Salvatore Cappello 38), is **San Giovanni dei Lebbrosi** (*Environs map; open Mon–Sat 9–11 & 4–7, Sun and holidays 7.30–12.30; T: 091 475024*), one of the oldest Norman churches in Sicily, said to have been founded by Roger I in 1071. In 1150 Roger II added a leper hospital to the complex, which gave it the present name. Next to the church are the scant remains of an Arab castle.

A short way beyond is Piazza Scaffa. Via Brancaccio leads south through its unattractive suburb. Via Conte Federico continues to the **Castello del Maredolce** or Favara (*entrance from Vicolo Castellaccio; open Mon–Sat 9–1.30, Tues and Sat 9–6; T: 333 153 1785*), which although almost totally engulfed by apartment blocks has been miraculously saved and partly restored. The palace, once surrounded on three sides by an artificial lake, was built as a pleasure palace by Emir Jafar in the late 10th century, restored by Roger II, then used in the 12th century as a prison and in the 13th century as a barracks; after serving as a hospice of the Teutonic Knights, in the 18th century it was relegated to the status of farm warehouses and its form almost was completely obliterated by illegal constructions and demolitions. Valiant work has been done on gardens and lake (where the water has already begun to flow again) in order to create a large public park, including the Baroque church of San Ciro at the foot of Monte Grifone and the so-called Grotta dei Giganti (*at present inaccessible*).

A road leads from here to the suburb of **Ciaculli**, where a large estate once owned by the Mafia boss Michele Greco was confiscated by the state and is now farmed by a group of young people; the area is famed for its late-ripening tangerines, *mandarino* *tardivo di Ciaculli*, a Slow Food niche product. Greco, known as *il Papa* (the Pope), was found guilty of some 100 murders and died in prison. The vegetation and landscape of the park is typical of the Conca d'Oro which once surrounded Palermo.

PRACTICAL INFORMATION

GETTING AROUND

• **By air:** Falcone Borsellino airport is at Punta Raisi, 35km west of Palermo (*www.gesap.it*). Prestia e Comandè (*www.prestiaecomande.it*) runs daily coach services every 30mins from the airport to the central railway station at Piazza Giulio Cesare (*map 15–16*), with stops along Viale della Libertà (*map 2*) and at the Politeama (*map 7*). The service operates from 4am–10.30pm (Palermo–Airport) and 5am–12.15am (Airport–Palermo); journey time 50 mins; tickets can be bought on the bus, at the ticket office or online. Companies offering a minibus-share service can also be found at the airport: when enough passengers have congregated, the bus sets off, dropping passengers on request. The fare is shared. There is also the hourly Trinacria Express/Metro (*www.palermoweb.com/metropa/*) train connection to the central station (4.55am–8.09pm from Palermo and from 5.54am–10.5pm from the airport), journey time 55mins. Taxis are expensive.

• **By car:** Parking is difficult in the centre of Palermo. Much of the centre is ZTL (Limited Traffic Area), or for pedestrians only. Pay car parks (with parking attendant) are near Piazza Castelnuovo (*map 6*), the station and Via

Stabile (*map 6–7*). Elsewhere there are blue-line areas, for which scratch-and-show tickets are purchased at vending machines (placed at strategic intervals along the street; keep plenty of change for these) and then displayed inside the windscreen. If you want to stay longer, you can leave two or three tickets at once. If your car is illegally parked and towed away, telephone the AMAT (*T: 091 350262 or 091 674 2021*), or ask a taxi driver to help.

• **By public transport**
NB: for up-to-date information on Palermo's public transport, see www.amat.pa.it.

City buses tend to be overcrowded, infrequent and very slow because of the traffic. Tickets must be purchased at tobacconists or newsagents and stamped at automatic machines on board. There are two excellent mini-bus circular services, both of which penetrate some of the narrower streets and pass many of the city's most important monuments.

Mini-buses
Linea Gialla (yellow): railway station—Corso dei Mille—Orto Botanico—Kalsa—Via Alloro (Regional Art Gallery in Palazzo Abatellis) —Via Maqueda—Ballarò—Corso Tüköry—Santo Spirito—Via Oreto—railway station.
Linea Rossa (red): Via Alloro (Regional

Art Gallery in Palazzo Abatellis) — Quattro Canti—Cassaro (Corso Vittorio Emanuele) —Cathedral—Via Papireto—Via Sant'Agostino—Via Maqueda—Vucciria—Cala—Piazza Marina—Via Alloro (Palazzo Abatellis).

Bus 389 from Piazza Indipendenza in Palermo (*map 14; every 20–30mins*) to Monreale.

Hop On-Hop Off City-Sightseeing Bus is an unmistakable red bus starting from Piazza Castelnuovo (Politeama; *map 6*), following two routes 'A' and 'B' (*www.palermo.city-sightseeing.it*).

Tram Palermo has four tram lines, running from 6am–9pm. The routes are designed as a commuter service for the densely inhabited suburbs, and as yet do not go to the centre. Maps will be found on *www.amat.pa.it*, click TRAM.

Metropolitana Palermo's metro (recently taken over by Trenitalia, *www.trenitalia.it*) is still under construction in some stretches, but when complete will connect the city to the airport in the west and to Bagheria and Altavilla Milicia in the east.

CIRCUITO ARTE SACRA

The 'Sacred Art Circuit' is a group of Palermo monuments for which a combined ticket is available. Once you have visited one of them, keep the ticket, which will allow you a discount when visiting the other sites. The sites are as follows: the cathedral, Santa Maria della Catena, Oratorio di San Lorenzo, Oratorio del Rosario di San Domenico and Santa Cita, Oratorio di San Mercurio, La Martorana, San Cataldo, Cloister of the Magione, Palazzo Alliata di Villafranca, Church of the Santissima Trinità and the Diocesan Museum at Monreale.

WHERE TO STAY

€€€ **Centrale Palace**. Once a prestigious 19th-century hotel, now a little old-fashioned and faded but still a gracious and atmospheric place to stay. Courteous staff, rooftop terrace, 104 spacious rooms (quieter at the back away from the Via Maqueda, with wonderful views from the top floor), good restaurant, good breakfasts, garage parking. *Corso Vittorio Emanuele 327, T: 091 8539, www.eurostarscentralepalace. com. Map 15.*

€€€ **Grand Hotel et des Palmes**. Richard Wagner's favourite, this was formerly Palazzo Ingham, transformed into a hotel in 1874. 172 rooms and suites, some are better than others. Good restaurant, popular with

politicians. *Via Roma 398, T: 091 6028111, www.grandhotel-et-des-palmes. com. Map 7.*

€€€ **Grand Hotel Piazza Borsa**. In medieval Palermo, three old palaces have been transformed into a comfortable hotel with 127 rooms and suites, restaurant, fitness centre. *Via dei Cartari 18, T: 091 320075, www. piazzaborsa.it. Map 11.*

€€€ **Mercure Palermo Excelsior**. Belle-Epoque atmosphere, central position, 119 quiet rooms, excellent service and good restaurant. *Via Marchese Ugo 3, T: 091 790 9001, www. excelsior-palermo.com. Map 2.*

€€€ **Palazzo Ajutamicristo**. This splendid palace, designed by Carnelivari, is still the family home of the Calefati di Canalotti barons, offering

B&B accommodation in 2 delightfully old-fashioned rooms. Memorable breakfasts on the loggia overlooking the verdant courtyards. *Via Garibaldi 23, T: 091 6161894, www.palazzoajutamicristo.it. Map 16.*

€€€ **Palazzo Alliata di Pietratagliata**. ■ 15th-century palace in one of the oldest streets of Palermo, still the family home of Princess Signoretta Alliata di Pietratagliata, offering accommodation in a luxurious self-catering apartment (sleeps 4, five nights minimum stay, breakfast provisions provided). Ask the princess to show you the marvellous 18th-century Murano chandelier, composed of 2,500 elements. Like a frothy confection of spun sugar, it is the largest ever made by the Ca' Rezzonico company. *Via Bandiera 14, T: 347 526 4276, www.palazzoalliata.it. Map 11.*

€€€ **Principe di Villafranca**. Small, refined hotel, central position in the new city; good restaurant, cosy library and lounge with open fireplace, garage and fitness centre. 32 elegant bedrooms, fine bed-linen. *Via Turrisi Colonna 4, T: 091 611 8523, www.principedivillafranca.it. Map 2.*

€€€ **Villa Igiea**. A beautiful Art Nouveau building at Acquasanta, 3km north of the city. Built as a sanatorium by Donna Franca Florio (*see p. 74*), it never functioned as such. With the help of Ernesto Basile she pragmatically transformed it into a luxurious hotel for her friends (inaugurated on 19th December 1900). The old dining-room (Sala Basile; ask to see it) is a masterpiece, with walls painted with opulent murals by Ernest De Maria Bergler, and matching Ducrot furniture. Luxurious cushiony salons abound; a peaceful refuge over the years for the rich and famous, besides many crowned heads. 122 rooms and suites, park, access to the sea, tennis, fitness centre, beauty salon, restaurants and pool. *Salita Belmonte 43, T: 091 631 2111, www.villa-igiea.com. Map p. 71.*

€€ **La Dimora del Genio**. Unusual B&B full of character, 4 rooms with frescoed ceilings, in the heart of Palermo. Very good breakfasts (the owner loves cooking). *Via Garibaldi 58, T: 091 616 6981 or 347 658 7664, www.ladimoradelgenio.it. Map 16.*

€€ **Massimo Plaza**. Elegant little hotel on the central traffic-free Via Maqueda, in front of the Opera House, with 11 comfortable modern rooms, popular with singers and musicians. No restaurant, breakfast is served in the room. *Via Maqueda 437, T: 091 325657, www.massimoplazahotel.com. Map 11.*

€€ **Porta Felice**. 33 rooms and a good fitness centre with Turkish bath and sauna, in an 18th-century palace close to the medieval quarter. Breakfast is served on the terrace. *Via Butera 45, T: 091 617 5678, www.hotelportafelice.it. Map 12.*

€€ **Quinto Canto**. Charming small hotel, good central position, with 21 rooms, restaurant, fitness centre with Turkish bath. *Corso Vittorio Emanuele 310, T: 091 584913, www.quintocantohotel.com. Map 11.*

€ **Chez Jasmine**. ■ Book early for this peaceful nook, a quiet self-contained split-level apartment (stairs) with its own shady leafy rooftop terrace, tucked behind the church of Santa Maria della Pietà, just behind Palazzo Abatellis. Mary will provide you with everything you need for breakfast, plus her expert help and advice for getting by in Palermo. *Vicolo dei Nassaiuoli 15, T: 091 616 4268 or 338 632 5192, www.*

chezjasmine.biz. Map 12.

€ **Joli**. Comfortable family-run hotel, central position, 30 spacious rooms, good value for money. *Via Michele Amari 11, T: 091 611 1765/6, www. hoteljoli.com. Map 7.*

€ **Orientale**. Close to the railway station, quite a find, this little family-run hotel occupies part of the huge 18th-century palace built for Prince Alessandro Filangieri di Cutò, and has been a hotel since 1890. 22 quaint, large rooms, most with private bathrooms and air conditioning. No restaurant. *Via Maqueda 26, T: 091 616 5727, www. albergoorientale.191.it. Map 15.*

€ **Posta**. Historic hotel in the centre, opposite the Post Office, much favoured in the past by actors and singers on tour. 30 rooms and good service, run by the same family for over 100 years. *Via Gagini 77, T: 091 587338, www. hotelpostapalermo.it. Map 11.*

WHERE TO EAT

€€€ **Castello a Mare**. Lovely location for this elegant restaurant, where well-known chef Natale Giunta creates superb dishes, joy for the eye and the palate, using exclusively Sicilian ingredients. Not to be missed, especially if you can eat outside. Also Sunday brunch. *Via Filippo Patti 2, T: 345 074 3095. Map 8.*

€€€ **Osteria dei Vespri**. Under Palazzo Ganci, where Visconti filmed the ballroom scenes of *The Leopard*, a tavern where you can sample exciting dishes prepared with Sicilian products. Extensive wine list including most Sicilian and Italian wines. From April–Oct, gourmet menu; from Nov–March very good *osteria* menu. Closed Sun.

Piazza Croce dei Vespri 6, T: 091 617 1631. Map 15–16.

€€ **Buatta**. In what was a luggage shop, you can sample typical Palermo food, prepared in the traditional way and presented to advantage. Try the *anelletti al forno*, little pasta rings in a rich sauce baked in the oven. Good desserts. All the ingredients are organic and come from local sources. *Corso Vittorio Emanuele 176, T: 091 322378. Map 11.*

€€ **Maestro del Brodo**. One of the oldest restaurants in town, famous for beef stew with saffron—still excellent, but nowadays people flock here for the imaginative seafood dishes too. Sorbet or *cannolo* for dessert. Closed Mon. *Via Pannieri 7 (Vucciria), T: 091 329523. Map 11.*

€€ **Piccolo Napoli**. This historic *trattoria*, run by the same family since 1951, is a lunchtime venue for Palermitans in the know; certainly worth a journey for those who appreciate well presented cooked or raw fish. Try the spaghetti with cuttlefish ink. Good list of Sicilian wines. Open for lunch; Thur, Fri and Sat also dinner. Closed Sun and Aug. *Piazzetta Mulino a Vento 4 (off Via dello Speziale), T: 091 320431, www.trattoriapiccolonapoli.it. Map 3.*

€€ **Sapori Perduti**. A marvellously restored old citrus-fruit warehouse is the setting for this restaurant offering dishes prepared exclusively with local products and according to tradition, with the occasional innovative fillip. Local wines. Don't miss the *gelo di mellone*, watermelon jelly, a Palermitan dessert of Arab origin. Closed Sun. *Via Principe di Belmonte 32, T: 091 327387. Map 7.*

€ **Bisso Bistrot**. ■ Once a well-known bookshop, this tiny bistrot is a brave new venture for the owners of the Santandrea restaurant (Vucciria), forced to close because of the Mafia. Friendly, casual atmosphere, traditional delicious Palermo fare, all prepared from local organic produce, accompanied by good house wines. Open Mon–Sat 9–11pm, always crowded so be prepared to wait in line (you can't book). *Via Maqueda 172 (Quattro Canti), T: 328 131 4595. Map 11.*

€ **Calamida**. Overlooking the harbour of La Cala. Good for wine and nibbles or a full lunch, especially on a fine day. *Via Cala, T: 091 777 3368, www.calamida.it. Map 12.*

€ **Il Bar**. Roof terrace on top of the La Rinascente department store overlooking Piazza San Domenico. A great place for a cocktail as the sun sets. There's an Obicà restaurant attached so you can eat as well (Obicà is a chain known for its buffalo mozzarella). *Piazza San Domenico 18, T: 091 601 7861, www.obica.com. Map 11.*

€ **Nino 'u Ballerino**. ■ One of the most famous *meusari* of Palermo, who serves his snacks and sandwiches with the speed and the grace of a dancer, as his family has been doing since 1802. Street food at its best, not to be missed. Open evenings 6–10. *Corso Finocchiaro Aprile 76. Map 9.*

€ **Le Tre Sorelle**. Historic *trattoria* (opened in 1888), still offers simple traditional Palermo food, such as *pasta con le sarde* (macaroni with sardines and wild fennel), or *macco di fave* (broad-bean potage), using fresh ingredients from the Capo market close by. Sicilian wines. Closed Sun. *Via Volturno 110 (Politeama), T: 091 585960. Map 10.*

LOCAL SPECIALITIES

Il Laboratorio Italiano (*Via Principe di Villafranca 42/a; map 6*), is a good address for Sicilian pottery. **Domus Artis** (*Via Nino Basile 6, near Casa Professa; map 15*) is where Luigi Arini still makes exquisite religious articles using wax, silver and coral, as established by a Vatican ruling in 1566 which indicated the materials, colours and symbolism that artists and craftsmen could use. **Pasticceria Cappello** (*Via Colonna Rotta 68; map 13*) is famed for prize-winning cakes; the delectable *torta sette veli*, a glossy black confection with 7 layers of chocolate, was invented here. **Scimone** (*Via Imera 8, corner of Via Miceli; map 9*), also sells good confectionery, ask for *dita d'apostolo* (Apostle's finger pastries), made with sponge-cake and fresh ricotta. **I Peccatucci di Mamma Andrea** (*Via Principe di Scordia 67, www.mammaandrea.it; map 7*) for home-made chocolates, pralines, jams and liqueurs. **Massaro** (*Via Basile 24; beyond map 15*) for superb breakfast pastries, perhaps the best in town. Near the Ballarò market is **Terranova** (*Via Albergheria 87; map 15*), manufacturers of unique carob sweets since 1890, still prepared to the same recipe. Similar to barley sugar, they have a more intense flavour as well as healthful effects on the system. If you want to stock up on cheese and olive oil, the best shop is **Garofalo** (*Corso Finocchiaro Aprile 129; map 9*), which opened in 1948.

There are **silversmiths** at Piazza Meli (behind San Domenico; *map 11*), **coppersmiths** near Ponte dell'Ammiraglio, and tinkers in Via Calderai (*map 15*).

The picturesque **Via Bara all'Olivella** (*map 11*) is a hive of activity, where many craftsmen can be found (but don't eat in the *trattorie*). At no. 40, Antonio Cuticchio makes **marionettes** for his brother Mimmo, celebrated *puparu*, who has his puppet theatres close by (*at nos 52 and 95; plays usually on Sat–Sun at 6.30; T: 091 323400, www. figlidartecuticchio.com*). At no. 60 is the **Laboratorio Artigianale**, toy-makers offering rocking-horses, model trains and dolls of wood or *papier-mâché*, while at no. 74 you will find **La Coppola Storta** (the Twisted Cap; a reference to the way Mafia members don their headgear; *www.lacoppolastorta.it*), where young people sell the cloth caps of various materials that they manufacture in a large building confiscated from the Mafia by the magistrates. At no. 64 is a nice shop, **Ceramica d'Arte**, with pottery from Caltagirone.

The **street markets** of Palermo are justly famous, and should not be missed even by the most hurried visitor. The stalls are set up in the morning around 8 and stay open all day until around 7.30. The biggest are: **Vucciria** (*Piazza Caracciolo; map 11*), for produce (especially fish), although now sadly in decline; **Ballarò** (*Piazza Ballarò; map 15*), for produce and household goods; **Capo** (*Via Sant'Agostino; map 10*), for fruit and vegetables, clothes, cloth and shoes; **Papireto** (*Piazza Peranni; map 10*), for antiques and bric-à-brac, usually called *Mercato delle Pulci*, flea market. **Lattarini** (*Piazza Cassa di Risparmio, Via Roma; map 11*) takes its name from the Arabic *suq al-attarin*, perfume market, but nowadays they sell cloth, ropes, knitting yarn, underwear, boots and army surplus gear. Another food market opens in the afternoon and evening in Corso Scinà (*map 3*). The new **San Lorenzo** (*open 9–10pm; Via San Lorenzo 288, near Palazzina Cinese; Environs map*) is the latest market, elegant and spacious because it occupies huge old citrus warehouses, and even has a garden; you will find local organic produce, cheese, bread, ice cream, books, wine and street food. A weekly **antique market** is held on Sun morning in Piazza Marina (*map 12*).

FESTIVALS AND EVENTS

10–15 July, *Fistinu di Santa Rosalia*, with celebrations including theatre performances, concerts, fireworks and a street procession with the statue of St Rosalia on a huge cart drawn by oxen. 3–4 Sept, pilgrimage (with a torchlight procession) to the shrine of St Rosalia on Mt Pellegrino. Nov–Dec, *Festival di Morgana*, annual meeting at the Pasqualino Puppet Museum of the puppeteers of Sicily, with plays, music, and exhibitions (*www. festivaldimorgana.it*).

The Territory of Palermo

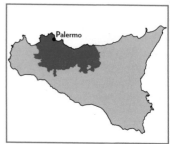

Palermo's former province occupies an area in the northwest, geologically the oldest part of Sicily, with serrated, spectacular mountains of Dolomitic limestone, fertile valleys and a beautiful coastline. The area contains many small towns, some of great historical importance such as Piana degli Albanesi, Castelbuono, Caccamo (with Sicily's largest castle) and Cefalù, while others are noted for their architecture; the opulent 18th-century villas of Bagheria, for example, are renowned. The Arab-Norman buildings of Cefalù and Monreale are now UNESCO World Heritage Sites.

MONREALE

On the slopes of Mt Caputo behind Palermo, overlooking the Conca d'Oro, Monreale (*map p. 574, B1 and Environs map*) is the site of one of the most superb churches in the world and certainly the most important Norman building in Sicily, with extensive 12th-century mosaics.

THE CATHEDRAL

Open 8.30–12.45 & 2.30–5, Sun and holidays 8–10 & 2.30–5.30. No entry during services. T: 091 640 4413. Tickets for roof terrace, Cappella Roano and north transept are available at the Diocesan Museum.

The town of Monreale grew up around William II's great duomo. One of the architectural wonders of the Middle Ages, it was begun c. 1174 and already near to completion by 1182. The cathedral was dedicated to the Madonna and called Santa Maria la Nuova, alluding to a new archbishopric created in her honour. It was the last of the Norman churches built in Sicily, as much for political as for religious motives, an immensely impressive structure high on the hill above Palermo.

The west façade, facing Piazza Guglielmo, is flanked by two square towers (one incomplete) linked by an 18th-century marble porch. The fine portal has a beautiful bronze door signed by Bonanno da Pisa (1186). The usual entrance is beneath the portico along the north side, facing Piazza Vittorio Emanuele with its Triton fountain by Mario Rutelli. The portico was built in 1547–69 by Gian Domenico and Fazio Gagini, and is complete with benches. The entrance portal has a mosaic frieze and a wonderful bronze door by Barisano da Trani (1179).

CONSTRUCTION OF THE CATHEDRAL

William II needed to create a new archbishopric and ensure the sympathy of its new incumbent in order to counterbalance the power of his former tutor, the English archbishop of Palermo, Walter of the Mill, who was supported by the papacy. By handing over the cathedral to the Cluniac Benedictines, the king made a clever move: the abbot was automatically an archbishop in rank and his appointment needed no further approval, either from the pope or from the clerics in Sicily, and the French monks had no sympathy for Walter or for the Vatican. The king justified the enormous expenditure of this project by telling of a dream he had while sleeping under a carob tree during a hunting expedition. The Madonna appeared to him and told him to dig under the tree and use the treasure he would find there to build her a great church. The mosaics were made with pure gold. Hundreds of the finest craftsmen from Constantinople were employed at great expense to expedite the work. The monolithic granite columns that separate the nave from the aisles are from a temple or temples of the Roman era. The slender marble columns in the cloisters are also Roman in origin, believed by some scholars to have been brought here by the Benedictine monks from the sunken city of *Baia*, near Naples. There they may once have formed the portico of a villa: some, especially on the east side, show traces of having spent years under the sea, the marble bored in places by a type of mussel, the sea-date (*Lithophaga mytiloides*). Baia, being subject to a volcanic phenomenon which causes the area to rise and sink alternately, may have been easily accessible at the time of the cloister's construction.

Interior of the cathedral

The interior (102m by 40m), remarkably simple in design but glittering with golden and coloured mosaics covering a surface of over 6400 square metres, gives an immediate impression of majesty and splendour. The concept is similar to the Cappella Palatina in Palermo but the design is carried out on a much greater scale. Beyond the rectangular crossing, surmounted by a high lantern, with shallow transepts, is a deep presbytery with three apses, recalling the plan of Cluniac abbey churches. The stilted arches in the nave are carried on 18 slender columns with composite capitals, of Roman origin and all of granite except the first on the south side, which is of cipollino marble. The ceiling of the nave was restored after a fire in 1811, and then again in the 1980s when the 19th-century timber proved to be full of termites; that of the choir bears the stamp of Arab workmanship.

MONREALE
Detail of St Eustace from the north door of the cathedral by Barisano da Trani (1179).

The mosaics

The magnificent series of mosaics tell in pictures the stories of the Old and New Testaments (binoculars are useful to see the details, particularly of those higher up). It is not known whether only Greek, or local craftsmen trained by Byzantine artists, were involved in this remarkable project, and the exact date of its completion is uncertain (though it is thought to have been around 1182). The large scenes chosen to illustrate the theme of Christ's Ascension and the Assumption of the Virgin fit an overall scheme designed to celebrate the Norman monarchy and to emphasise its affinity with Jerusalem. Under the rich decoration of the upper walls runs an elegant marble and mosaic dado in Arab style.

Nave: Above the arcade the Genesis cycle begins in a double tier, starting with the upper row at the eastern end of the south side with the Creation and continuing round the western wall and along the northern side to end (on the lower tier) with *Jacob's Dream* and *Jacob Wrestling with the Angel.*

Crossing and transepts: The story of Christ is illustrated from the *Nativity* to the *Passion.* The piers in the transept are covered on all sides with tiers of saints.

Aisles: The Ministry of Christ.

Presbytery: On either side are scenes from the lives of Sts Peter and Paul, whose figures are represented in the side apses. In the main apse is the mighty half-length figure of Christ Pantocrator, with a solemn and rather severe expression. Below is the enthroned Madonna, with angels and apostles, and lower still, on either side of the east window, figures of saints including Thomas Becket, made within ten years of his martyrdom; Henry II of England, Becket's nemesis, was William II's father-in-law. Above the original royal throne (left) *William II Receives* *the Crown from Christ*; above the episcopal throne (right) *William Offers the Cathedral to the Virgin*. The floor of marble mosaic dates in its present form from 1559, but that of the transepts is the original 12th-century paving.

Transepts: The **south transept** contains the porphyry sarcophagus of William I (**1**; d. 1166) and that of William II (**2**; d. 1190) in white marble (1575). Here too is the **Cappella di San Benedetto** (**3**; 1569), with a relief of the saint by Marabitti (1760), and the entrance to the Diocesan Museum (**4**; *see overleaf*).

In the **north transept** (*admission from Diocesan Museum*) conserves the tombs (**5**) of Margaret, Roger and Henry, the wife and sons of William I, and an inscription (**6**) recording the resting-place (1270) of the body of

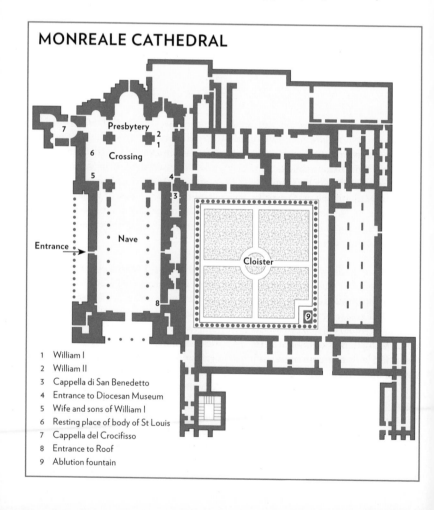

MONREALE CATHEDRAL

1 William I
2 William II
3 Cappella di San Benedetto
4 Entrance to Diocesan Museum
5 Wife and sons of William I
6 Resting place of body of St Louis
7 Cappella del Crocifisso
8 Entrance to Roof
9 Ablution fountain

MONREALE
Adam and Eve covering their nakedness: detail of a column in the cloister.

St Louis when on its way back from Tunis; his heart remains buried here. Also accessed with a ticket from the Diocesan Museum are the **Cappella del Crocifisso (7)** and the Treasury.

In the southwest corner of the nave is the **entrance to the roof (8**; *admission fee*), from where there are wide views of the Conca d'Oro and the coast. Stairs (180 steps) and walkways lead above the cloisters and round the apses.

The cloister

The lovely Chiostro dei Benedettini (*open Mon–Sat 9–6.30, Sun & holidays 9–1, T: 091 640 4403*) is a masterpiece of 12th-century art, with Arab-Norman arches borne by 228 twin columns (curiously narrow for the arches they bear; it is possible that a last-minute adaptation to the plans was made by the architects in order to allow for the use of these salvaged columns). All have carved Romanesque capitals, of which very few are alike. Many of the columns are also decorated with mosaics or reliefs. They are the work of five master craftsmen, each of whom made some of the capitals, assisted by several apprentices, but only one capital is signed. A prolific confusion prevails of birds, animals, monsters, plants and people, representing a variety of scenes, both mythological and religious, with Christian symbolism and even the sacrifice of a bull to Mithras. The monks grew fruit trees in the enclosure (or *hortus conclusus*): trees symbolising Paradise—date-palms, olives, figs and pomegranates. In the southwest corner, a column carved like a stylised palm tree in a little enclosure of its own forms a charming fountain **(9)**, used by the monks to wash their hands before entering the refectory; the symbolism of the various elements here alludes to the rite of baptism.

THE DIOCESAN MUSEUM

Open Oct–March Tues, Thur, Sat 9.15–15.15; April–Sept Tues–Sat 9.15–6.30, Sun 2.30–6.30. Closed Mon. T: 091 641 9001, www.museodiocesanomonreale.it.

Situated in the old seminary next to the Archbishop's Palace at Via dell'Arcivescovado 2, the Museo Diocesano displays many exceptional works of art and also gives the opportunity of admiring the cathedral, both inside and out, from some unexpected angles. Housed on three floors, the collection of religious art dates from the 13th–19th centuries and consists of paintings, embroidered silk vestments, tapestries, articles in gold, silver and coral, and sculptures in wood, terracotta and stone.

Ground floor: The entrance corridor, flanked by a series of stone sculptures, including the so-called sarcophagus of William, leads into the San Placido gallery with a view of the cloister from the far end. Dominating the gallery is a large tapestry representing the *Dream of William*, the symbol of the museum, showing William II asleep under the carob tree while cherubs play with the gold coins he will use to build this great church. On the walls are showcases designed to recall the side altars of a church, each one displaying an altarpiece of various types, for example the delicate ceramic *Madonna and Child* by Andrea della Robbia. Chronological order is not followed here, because this room was the only one large enough to hold some of the huge 17th- and 18th-century altarpieces, such as the *Last Supper* by Giuseppe Patania.

First floor: There are two galleries on this floor, both offering splendid views over the Gulf of Palermo. **Room 1**, from where you can also see the interior of the cathedral and the mosaics, is dedicated to the earliest works of art, which go back to the Norman period. Of particular interest is the *Madonna Hodegetria* icon, where the Madonna, wearing a blue dress (humanity) and a purple robe (divinity), is gently supporting the tiny, red-robed (the colour of the Passion) Child, who is offering His mother a rose (sweetness and thorns) with His right hand, and holding a scroll (I am the Light of the World) in His left. From this room you reach the richly-decorated, *horror-vacui* Baroque **Cappella del Crocifisso** (Cappella Roano) inside the cathedral, commissioned by Archbishop Juan Roano in the late 17th century and designed by Angelo Italia. The Spanish prelate intended this to be his own funerary monument, displaying all the works of art he had commissioned in the space he intended for them. The superb wooden Crucifix on the altar was William II's personal gift to the archbishop. The floor design represents the prophet Jonah being swallowed by the whale, a symbol of resurrection (the whale spat him out three days later). Also noteworthy are the painted stucco altarpiece of *St Mary of the Woods* and Vito D'Anna's impressive *Madonna*. The chapel gives access to a small inner room, the **Treasury**, which contains a valuable collection of reliquaries.

Room 2, from where this is a good view of the exterior of the apses with their intarsia decoration, displays works of the 16th and 17th centuries and is dominated by Pietro Novelli's masterpiece, the *Guardian Angel*. The

Archangel Raphael, with swan's wings and attired in swirling silk robes of saffron and scarlet, is showing Heaven to his charge, a little boy dressed in dark green. The arms of the angel divide the canvas diagonally, from the face of a cherub in the upper left corner to that of the child in the lower right.

Second floor: On the second floor are two large intercommunicating galleries. The first is dedicated to a private collection donated by Salvatore Renda Pitti. Part of the room, which looks out over the cloister, displays a series of priestly robes and religious objects commissioned by the archbishops over the centuries, accompanied by explanatory panels. The second gallery, housed in a room with a beautiful barrel-vaulted, coffered ceiling commissioned by Archbishop Domenico Gaspare Lancia di Brolo in the late 19th century, displays an interesting selection of the more recent works of art. A separate section here shows items of popular devotion, such as ex-votos and humble carvings and paintings.

MONREALE TOWN

The square outside the cathedral's west end, **Piazza Guglielmo II**, boasts a small pizzeria (an acceptable if unadventurous lunch option) and, flanking its long side, the restored 18th-century Town Hall, which occupies a former convent. A passageway leads past the post office into a public garden and playground occupying the convent buildings. Behind it, with fine views, is the **Belvedere**, on the site of William II's royal gardens. Also entered from the square is the **Galleria d'Arte Moderna Sciortino** (*open daily 9–1, sometimes (not Sat) also 3–6; T: 091 656 4655*), a rich collection donated to the town of paintings, drawings, sculptures and ceramics by contemporary artists, including Greco, Guttuso, Pirandello, De Chirico, De Pisis, Schifano, Morandi, and an *Adoration of the Shepherds* by Matthias Stom. There is also an alternative entrance to the cathedral cloister (which can sometimes be used if the cathedral itself is closed).

Behind the adjacent square, Piazza Vittorio Emanuele, in Via del Arcivescovado, you can see the splendid **apses at the back of the cathedral**, decorated with interlacing arches of limestone and lava stone. Here too are some arches and windows of Palazzo Reale, the old Norman palace.

The little town once possessed some fine Baroque churches but many today are in a state of disrepair and are usually closed. One of the most attractive is the old Jesuit **Chiesa del Sacro Cuore** (1554–1742) in Via Palermo, recently entrusted to the Order of Teutonic Knights of Sicily, who have restored it. The presbytery and walls are pleasingly decorated with pastel-coloured frescoes and stucco mouldings, while the three paintings are by an unknown 18th-century artist. That on the high altar represents the *Sacred Heart of Jesus*; over the south altar is *St Francis Xavier* and over the north altar is *St Ignatius Loyola*, both Jesuit saints.

The **Chiesa della Collegiata**, in Via Umberto I, has a large panel of majolica tiles on the external wall of the apse, showing the *Crucifixion* with Monreale in the background; it is probably the work of Giuseppe Mariani (early 18th century).

The main street of the little town is Via Roma, which winds gradually uphill. At no. 48 (Piazzetta Vaglica) is the 18th-century **Collegio di Maria** (a religious boarding-school for girls), its façade designed a century later by Giovanni Battista Basile, next to its little church, the **Santissima Trinità** (1763; *open daily 10–4; T: 091 640 4401*). The church is octagonal, with an elegant interior surmounted by a large dome, decorated with an eight-pointed star, the symbol of the Madonna.

There is a fine view from the 19th-century church of **Madonna delle Croci**, high above Monreale.

SAN MARTINO DELLE SCALE

The road between Monreale and San Martino delle Scale ascends to Portella San Martino. Here a path climbs up through a pinewood to (c. 20mins) the **Castellaccio** (766m; *open Sat and Sun 9–2*), the southwestern summit of Mt Cuccio and a splendid viewpoint. The castle was originally a fortified monastery built by William II as a hospice for the convent of Monreale. It then passed to the Benedictines. Towards the end of the 18th century it was abandoned and fell into ruin; Guy de Maupassant, in his search for Sicilian brigands, was told that this had once been their hideout. In 1899 it was purchased by the Club Alpino Siciliano.

San Martino delle Scale (500m) is a hill resort in pinewoods. The huge Benedictine **Abbey of San Martino** (*open 9–12.30 & 4–6.30, Sun and holidays 8.30–11.30 & 5–6.30; T: 091 418104, www.abbaziadisanmartino.it*), possibly founded by St Gregory the Great in the 6th century, was destroyed by the Arabs in 820, rebuilt after 1347 by Archbishop Emanuele Spinola and the Benedictine Angelo Sisinio, and enlarged c. 1762 by Venanzio Marvuglia. It is now occupied by the Abadir, a fine arts academy and restoration laboratory. The church, dating from 1561–95 (with part of the 14th-century masonry in the north wall) contains choir stalls (1591–7) carved by Nunzio Ferraro and Giovanbattista Vigilante from Naples. *St Benedict* and the *Madonna with Sts Benedict and Scholastica* are both by Pietro Novelli. Six altarpieces here are by a Zoppo di Gangi (a particularly interesting one shows the *Seven Archangels*, each with his symbol: Uriel (a lamp, Light and Fire); Michael (a sword, Justice); Gabriel (a lily sceptre, Messenger); Jehudiel (a crown, Prizes and Pestilences); Raphael (a child, Healer and Guardian); above them, on a cloud, are blue-dressed Barachiel (a book, Blessings) and, dressed in red, Sealtiel (a vase of flowers, Grace). There is also a *St Martin* by Filippo Paladini. The sacristy contains vestments of the 16th–18th centuries, paintings attributed to Annibale Carracci and Guercino, and a fine reliquary. The carved doorway into the claustral part of the convent dates from the 15th century and nearby is a stoup dated 1396.

At the foot of the bell-tower is a statuary group of *St Martin and the Beggar* by Marabitti. A statue (1728) of St Benedict, by Giuseppe Pampillonia, surmounts the fountain in the main cloister (1612; altered and enlarged in the 18th century). The Oreto fountain is by Marabitti (1784). The refectory ceiling (*Daniel in the Lions' Den*) was frescoed by Pietro Novelli. A small museum shows paintings, Church silver, embroidered altar-cloths and vestments, and coral. A gallery of paintings on the subject of St Benedict, *Nel nome di Benedetto*, occupies the former library.

BAGHERIA & ITS HEADLAND

BAGHERIA

Bagheria (*map p. 574, B1*) is a country town famous for its 18th-century Baroque villas set amidst lemon groves and vineyards. It was the birthplace of the artist Renato Guttuso and also of the Oscar-winning film-maker Giuseppe Tornatore, author and director of *Cinema Paradiso* (1989). Beset for many years by uncontrolled post-war building, which encroached on the gardens and parks of the villas, the town now scarcely lives up to the old saying: *Baaria, sciuri ppi la via*, ('in Bagheria flowers grow on the streets'). Many of the villas are neglected. Only three of them, Villa Cattolica (brown signs), Villa Palagonia and Villa Sant'Isidoro De Cordova at Aspra, are now usually open to visitors.

The conspicuous Villa Cattolica, a fine building of c. 1737, houses the **Museo Guttuso** (*open 10–7, closed Mon; T: 091 943902*), which has a large collection of paintings by Renato Guttuso and other contemporary artists. Guttuso's bright blue marble tomb by Giacomo Manzù is in the garden. Near the villa, beyond a railway crossing (right), is the start of the long Corso Butera, which passes the lovely Palazzo Inguaggiato attributed to Andrea Giganti (1770) before reaching the piazza in front of the 18th-century **Chiesa Madre** (*open 7.30–12 & 4.30–8, T: 091 963750*); the frescoes were carried out by Guttuso in 1923. Villa Butera is visible at the far end of the Corso, built in 1658 by Giuseppe Branciforte (façade of 1769).

In front of the Chiesa Madre is the beginning of Corso Umberto, which ends at Piazza Garibaldi beside (left) a garden gate (guarded by two monsters) of **Villa Palagonia** (*open April–Oct 9–1 & 4–7, Nov–March 9–1 & 3.30–5.30; T: 091 932088*). The garden, as well as the vestibule and hall on the first floor, are open. The beautiful building was erected in 1705 by Francesco Gravina, Prince of Palagonia (and his architect Tommaso Maria Napoli). His eccentric grandson Ferdinando Gravina Alliata lived in rooms decorated in a bizarre fashion, including the hall with its ceiling covered with mirrors set at strange angles (now very damaged) and its walls encased in marble with busts of ladies and gentlemen. The oval vestibule has frescoes of four labours of Hercules. The villa is famous for the grotesque statues of monsters, dwarves and strange animals set up on the garden wall by Ferdinando. At the time these carved figures were not to everyone's taste; when Goethe visited the villa in 1787 he was appalled by them. Opposite is the entrance gate to the avenue which leads up to Villa Valguarnera (*sadly not visible from here and closed to the public*). Built by Tommaso Napoli c. 1713–37, this is the handsomest of the Bagheria villas, with statues above the parapet by Marabitti.

At Via Cherubini 12 is a modern art museum, **Museo Osservatorio dell'Arte Contemporanea in Sicilia** (*open Tues–Sat 5–8.30; closed Sun, Mon and holidays; T: 091 968020, www.museum-bagheria.it*) dedicated to modern and contemporary Sicilian artists including Consagra, Fiume, Guttuso and Caruso. Off Via IV Novembre is **Villa Trabia** (mid-18th century), perhaps by Nicolò Palma, with a façade of 1890. It is surrounded by a neglected park. Near the railway station is the early 18th-century **Villa Cutò**, and a little further on is **Villa San Cataldo**, which received a neo-Gothic facelift in the early 19th century. The frescoed salons of the 18th-century Villa Certosa, close to the motorway exit in Via Dietro La Certosa, house a poignant museum dedicated to toys and wax figures, the **Museo del Giocattolo e delle Cere Pietro Piraino** (*open Tues–Sun 9–1; T: 091 967569 or 366 593 2714, www.museodelgiocattolo. org*), including a remarkably complete collection of French clockwork figures, made in the 19th century by the Gaultier brothers.

ASPRA

On the coast below Bagheria is the picturesque, jumbled fishing village of Aspra, where the 18th-century **Villa Sant'Isidoro De Cordova** is situated (*entrance from Viale dei Cipressi; open daily May–Sept 10–1 & 4–7, Oct–April 10–1 & 3–6; last tickets 30mins before closing; T: 091 6360389, www.villasantisidorodecordova.it*). After the recent death of the last owner, her heirs decided to transform this magnificent house into a museum. It is surrounded by a large garden, part of the farmland where olives, wheat, lemons, peaches and grapes were grown; the last marquis exported lemons, wine and olive oil to Britain and Germany. The furniture, pictures and personal effects are miraculously intact; sections are devoted to family photographs, toys, clothes and farm equipment. There is also an extensive library. Among the paintings are two which have never before been shown in public; both are signed by the artists: *David with the Head of Goliath* by Pietro Novelli, and *The Martyrdom of St Sebastian* by Jusepe de Ribera.

Close to Villa Sant'Isidoro, at Via Cotogni 1 (Piazza Verdone), is the **Museo dell'Acciuga** of Anchovy Museum (*call to request visit, possible daily 9.30–12.30 & 4.30–6.30; the museum incorporates the 'Fish Shop' stocking anchovy products, souvenirs and soft drinks; T: 091 928192*). It houses a particularly complete display of old photographs, fishing equipment, material relating to canning techniques and other curiosities collected by the brothers Girolamo and Michelangelo Balistreri, anchovy fishermen. This activity is still the backbone of the economy at Aspra, where a thriving fish market opens very early in the morning. In Piazza Monsignor Cipolla stands the parish church, **Santa Maria Addolorata** (*no visits during Mass*), frescoed by Renato Guttuso when still a boy.

SOLUNTO

Map p. 574, B1. Open summer 9–7, winter 9–5; Sun and holidays 9–1. T: 338 784 5140. Necropolis shown on request.

The solitary ruins of Solunto are in a beautiful position on the slopes of Mt Catalfano (374m) overlooking the sea and close to Santa Flavia. The ancient town of *Solus* is thought to have replaced a Phoenician settlement in the vicinity of the same name (perhaps at Cozzo Cannita where traces of walls have been found), which was destroyed in 397 BC by Dionysius of Syracuse. Solus was built in the 4th century BC on an interesting grid plan similar to the urban layout of some Hellenistic sites in Asia Minor. It fell to the Romans, who named it *Soluntum*, in 254 BC and had been abandoned by the beginning of the 3rd century AD. It was discovered in 1825 and much of the site still remains to be excavated.

The entrance is through Padiglione A of the Antiquarium, an introduction to the site with plans and descriptions, illustrated by Hellenistic capitals, statues and architectural fragments. A Roman road, beside terraces of prickly pear, mounts the side of the hill past **Via delle Terme** (with the remains of baths) and curves round to the right into the wide **Via dell'Agora**. This, the main street, traverses the town to the cliff edge overlooking the sea; it is crossed at regular intervals by side streets with considerable remains of houses on the hillside above. The early section is beautifully paved in brick. On the stepped Via Cavallari (named after the 19th-century excavator

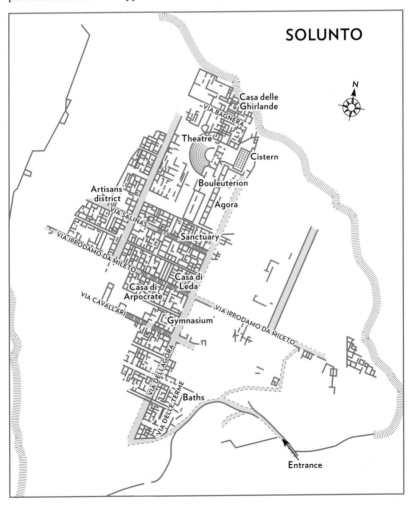

SOLUNTO
Fragment of Roman wall-painting from the Casa delle Ghirlande.

here) are some columns and the architrave of the so-called **Gymnasium** (restored in 1866), in fact a large private house.

The next stepped road, Via Ippodamo da Mileto (named after the 5th-century BC town planner Hippodamus of Miletus who was noted for the grid pattern he used for his cities; he has no other connection to Solunto), links the main hill to another small hill towards the sea. Here on the slope to the left is the so-called **Casa di Leda** on three levels: above four small shops on Via dell'Agora is an oblong cistern and courtyard with a fountain, off which are rooms with mosaic and tiled floors and traces of red wall-paintings. Further up Via Ippodamo da Mileto stand the remains of other interesting houses, including the **Casa di Arpocrate**, with a well-preserved mosaic pavement.

Back on Via dell'Agora, beyond a large sanctuary (on the corner of Via Salinas), the road widens out into the large **agora** with brick paving in front of nine rectangular exedrae along the back wall, thought to have been used as shelters for the public. On the hillside above are traces of the **theatre** and a small bouleuterion probably used for council meetings. The hillside higher up may have been the site of the acropolis. Via dell'Agora next passes a huge public **cistern**, still filled with water, part of a complex system of storage tanks (many vestiges of which are still visible), made necessary by the lack of spring water in the area.

At the farthest edge of the site, on the edge of the cliff looking towards Cape Zafferano, in Via Bagnera, are the remains of a small Roman villa, the **Casa delle Ghirlande**, in which mosaics and some fine fragments of wall-painting were found. The view along the coast towards Cefalù, of the Aeolian Islands and Etna, is magnificent. In the foreground are the medieval castle of Solanto and the bay of Fondachello with the villas of Casteldaccia amid luxuriant vegetation on the slopes behind.

Before leaving the site you pass through Padiglione B of the Antiquarium, a small **museum** displaying archaeological finds, descriptions of funerary practices, arts and crafts of ancient Solunto, and finally, objects pertaining to the city, recovered from the seabed off Porticello.

At the foot of Mt Catalfano a few lemon groves survive but the area is becoming increasingly developed with holiday homes. **Cape Zafferano** is an isolated crag of dolomitic limestone, of great geological interest. On the cape grow dwarf palms and (flowering in the spring) wild orchids, and on the sandy beach at its foot the loggerhead turtle sometimes nests.

TERMINI IMERESE & HIMERA

Termini Imerese *(map p. 574, C2)*, consisting of an upper and lower town, is built on the slopes of a hill and has a commercial port. *Thermae Himerenses* received its name from the two neighbouring Greek cities of *Thermae* and *Himera*. After the sack of Himera in 409 BC by the Carthaginians *(see p. 99)*, the inhabitants of the destroyed city were resettled in Thermae. In 307 BC it was ruled by Agathocles (361–289 BC), a native of the town and the most ferocious of the Greek tyrants of Syracuse. Its most prosperous period followed the Roman conquest. The thermal mineral waters were praised by Pindar. Outside the town are conspicuous remains of a Roman aqueduct built in the 2nd century AD to bring water from a spring 7km away and in the lower town, on the site of the Roman baths, the Grand Hotel delle Terme, begun in 1890 on a design by Giuseppe Damiani Almeyda. In the upper town there is a spacious main square with an old-fashioned men's club.

EXPLORING TERMINI IMERESE

The 17th-century **duomo** *(open 9–12 & 3.30–8.30; T: 091 814 1291)*, dedicated to St Nicholas, has a façade dating from 1912. The four statues of saints are copies of the originals, now removed inside. Beneath the tower (right) is a fragment of a Roman cornice. The interior, with huge columns and capitals, contains sculptures by Giuliano Mancino and Bartolomeo Berrettaro, including a statue of the Madonna over the main altar, bas-reliefs, and the four statues of saints (1504–6) from the façade. The chapel also has two 17th-century funerary monuments. On the third north altar is a Crucifix, painted on both sides, by Pietro Ruzzolone (1484). In the chapel to the left of the choir are reliefs by Ignazio Marabitti and Federico Siragusa. On the fourth south altar is a marble oval relief of *Our Lady of the Bridge* by Marabitti. The duomo houses a small museum of sacred art *(to request visit, T: 368 778 1258)*, including items of gold and jewellery donated to the Madonna as ex-votos. From the belvedere behind the duomo there is a good view of the coast and the port.

The **Palazzo Comunale** (Town Hall), also built in the 17th century, is approached by an outside staircase. Just out of the piazza, in Via Marco Tullio Cicerone, is the important, well-displayed **Museo Civico Baldassare Romano** (*open Tues–Sat 9–1 & 4–6.30, Sun and holidays 9–1; T: 091 812 28550*), founded in 1873. On the ground floor are prehistoric finds from Termini, vases from Himera, coins, Roman capitals, sculptures, inscriptions and glassware. The last room contains Arab-Norman material and a Renaissance doorway. On the first floor is a chapel frescoed in the 15th century by Nicolò da Pettineo, paintings (16th–19th centuries), a natural history collection and the plaster gallery of the local sculptor Filippo Sgarlata. The museum incorporates the little church of **Santa Maria della Misericordia** (1600), entirely decorated with stuccoes of the Serpotta school, with a beautiful triptych (*Madonna with Sts John and Michael*) ascribed to Gaspare da Pesaro (1453). There is also a garden containing architectural fragments.

In Via Mazzini, which leads out of Piazza Duomo, is the church of **Santa Croce al Monte** containing 16th- and 17th-century Sicilian paintings. Viale Iannelli leads west from Piazza Duomo to the 14th-century **church of Santa Caterina**, with 15th-century frescoes illustrating the life of the saint, probably by the local artists Nicolò and Giacomo Graffeo; they have been beautifully restored.

In Villa Palmeri, the **public gardens** laid out in 1845, are remains of a Roman public building known as the **Curia**, dating from the 2nd century AD. From the gardens Via dell'Anfiteatro leads to the sparse ruins of the **Roman amphitheatre** (1st century AD).

CACCAMO

Caccamo (pron. CAKkamo; *map p. 574, C2*) is a little town of ancient origin in a fine position above olive groves. There is a tradition that the Carthaginians took refuge here after their defeat at Himera in 480 BC, after their general Hamilcar had committed suicide by throwing himself into the sacred flames lit for battlefield sacrifices after his army had been defeated.

The impressive 12th-century **castle** (*open 9–1 & 3–7, closed Mon; T: 091 810 3207 or 091 814 252*), the largest in Sicily, stands at the entrance to the town. It was one of the major Norman strongholds on the island, and, never captured, remained the residence of the dukes of Caccamo until the 20th century. Here in 1160 Matthew Bonellus organised a revolt of the barons against William I (the Bad); after the failure of the rebellion, Bonellus was captured and taken to Palermo, where he was hamstrung, blinded and imprisoned. The castle was enlarged by the Chiaramontes in the 14th century, and was sold to the region of Sicily in 1963 by the De Spuches family. The main tower was 70m high but toppled in an earthquake in the 19th century. The empty interior has been heavily restored.

From the main road (Corso Umberto), steps and narrow streets lead down to **Piazza Duomo**, an attractive and unusual square on two levels, with a marvellous view over the valley. Above the raised terrace, with a balustrade decorated with four statues of the town's patron saints, is the 17th-century **Monte di Pietà** (the former pawnbrokers', now housing the tourist office and exhibitions) flanked by the façades of two churches. The one on the right is dedicated to the Souls in Purgatory and contains charming gilded stuccoes in the sanctuary. The custodian will show the crypt below, also beautifully decorated with stuccoes and containing the crumbling, fully-clothed mummified corpses of past inhabitants.

The duomo

The Duomo di San Giorgio Martire has a fine 17th-century façade. Founded in 1090, it was altered in 1477 and 1614. Above the door is a lovely relief (1660) of St George by Gaspare Guercio. The tall campanile was built above a 14th-century tower of the castle.

In the interior St George features in numerous fine works of art, notably in a 15th-century triptych in the right aisle. In the south transept, the architrave of the sacristy door has delicate carvings of the Madonna and Child with angels and Sts Peter and Paul, attributed to Francesco Laurana. The roundels of the *Annunciation* and relief of the *Madonna and Child* are by the Gagini school. The rich treasury and sacristy are also shown on request. They contain 16th–19th-century Church silver, vestments, and Flemish paintings. In the chapel to the right of the sanctuary is a *Madonna and Child* by the Gagini school. By the main altar is an unusual font (1466) with four large heads, perhaps representing the Evangelists. In the sanctuary are two polychrome wooden statues: *St John the Baptist* by Antonino Siragusa (1532) and *St Lucy* (16th century). An exquisite silver processional statuette of St Rosalia is also kept here. On the main altar are three very fine alabaster carvings (16th–18th century).

In the north transept are two painted terracotta sculptures: a *Madonna and Child* by the Gagini school and a *Pietà* group by the early 15th-century Sienese school. The altar here has 16th- and 17th-century reliquary busts and an early 18th-century Neoclassical carved and gilded altar frontal. In the north aisle an altar decorated with inlaid marble has a 14th-century painted Crucifix, and the first altarpiece, depicting the *Miracle of St Isidore*, is a stunning painting by Matthias Stom (1641). A sedan chair and armour belonging to the De Spuches family are also kept in this aisle.

Other churches of Caccamo

There are good views of the castle from the old streets behind the duomo. In the other direction, Via Cartagine leads to the deconsecrated church of San Francesco and, beyond, the church of the **Santissima Annunziata**, its Baroque façade flanked by two earlier towers. Inside is a carved 16th-century organ case, and the sanctuary has stuccoes by the Serpotta school. The church of **San Benedetto alla Badia** ((1615; *open Tues–Sun 9–1; reduced ticket price by showing that for Caccamo Castle*) was attached to a former Benedictine convent. The charming interior has a splendid majolica floor in the nave and choir, once attributed to Nicolò Sarzana but now thought to date from before 1701. There are also fine wrought-iron grilles. The two graceful female figures in stucco on either side of the sanctuary are by the school of Serpotta.

Santa Maria degli Angeli (1497; *ring at the convent*) has a fine relief of the *Madonna and Child* over the door. Inside, its original wooden trussed ceiling is preserved (with 15th-century paintings of Dominican saints) and a statue of the Madonna by Antonello Gagini.

ALIA AND ROCCAPALUMBA

Some 30km southeast of Caccamo, **Alia** (*map p. 574, C2–C3*) is a remote town founded by the Arabs, surrounded by spectacular hills and wheat-fields. Later, under Spanish rule, it became the seat of the Santa Croce barons, who built their palace next to the church of Madonna delle Grazie (1639). At the time of writing the economy was depressed and the once-flourishing town was suffering from depopulation. Well-kept and picturesque nevertheless, Alia has a large ethno-anthropological collection housed in the old Casa Pittà in Via San Giuseppe (*open Mon–Sat 9–1 & 3.30–6.30, Sun 10–2 & 3.30–6.30; T: 091 821 9528*).

Not far from the town (4km), in a dramatic isolated sandstone outcrop, is a group of caves called **Grotte di Gurfa** (*request visit at Tourist Office, Via Santa Croce 10, closed Mon; T: 091 821 9528*), carved out by hand in ancient times and successively used as dwellings. The caves include a mysterious tholos, 16m high. Some scholars date the complex to the Copper Age, about 5,000 years ago, when it would have been either a sanctuary to a divinity or a burial site. An inscription in Phoenician has been discovered close to the entrance of one of the caves. Other scholars refute these claims, saying that the caves are no older than Norman and that the 'Phoenician inscription' is simply a series of accidental scratches in the soft rock. A Palaeo-Christian carving has also been discovered here.

ROCCAPALUMBA

The town of Roccapalumba (*map p. 574, C2*), on the west side of the River Torto, was founded in 1630 by the Ansalone family at the foot of an enormous, isolated rock—the Rock of the Doves—which is the meaning of the name. The settlement must be much older, because the **sanctuary church of the Madonna della Luce**, partly built into the rock, is one of the oldest Norman churches of the territory, dating back to the 11th century. The prodigious image of the Madonna inside the church is said to have appeared suddenly to protect some travellers assailed by bandits as they were going through the pass. Roccapalumba is known as the *Paese delle Stelle*, the 'Village of Stars', because the clear air and low light pollution allow good observation of the stars at all times of year. The **Parco Astronomico** at Borgo Regalgioffoli (*request visit at the Pro Loco, Via Ospizio 36, T: 091 821 5207, www.ce-s-a-r.it*) has two observatories and a planetarium.

HIMERA

Near a large industrial area occupying the low coastal plain east of Termini Imerese is the site of Himera (*map p. 574, C2*), close to the Buonfornello motorway exit (*if coming from the Palermo direction, take the exit for Catania and the Buonfornello exit appears nearly immediately*) and on the bank of the River Grande (or Imera Settentrionale), but very poorly signposted. On the right of the road, just across the busy railway line, are the remains of a temple. Above the road is a conspicuous modern museum, below the site of the ancient city.

HISTORY OF HIMERA

This was a colony of *Zancle* (Messina), founded in 648 BC near the mouth of the Himera river and at the head of the valley which provided access to the interior of the island. It was the westernmost Greek colony on the north coast of Sicily, and the probable birthplace of the lyric poet Stesichorus (born c. 630 BC), famed in antiquity for his innovative treatment of traditional myths. In 480 BC Terillus, the exiled tyrant of Himera, called on the Carthaginians to help him against his enemies, resulting in a great battle outside the city between the Carthaginians and the combined armies of Agrigento and Syracuse, reported by Herodotus as one reason why the Sicilians couldn't aid their fellow Greeks during the great Persian invasion. The Greek alliance won a decisive victory. The Carthaginian leader Hamilcar (not to be confused with Hannibal's father) reportedly spent the battle attempting to seek favourable omens from his religious sacrifices, then threw himself into a sacrificial fire on the battlefield and was burnt to nothing when he saw that the battle had been lost.

In the last decade of the 5th century the Carthaginians returned in force, and in 409 BC Himera bore the brunt of an attack which almost destroyed Greek power in Sicily and ushered in a new age of tyrants of Syracuse. This time, Greek collective defence failed utterly and Diodorus Siculus describes the heroic and desperate defence of Himera. Eventually the Greeks tried to evacuate the city, but lacked enough ships. Half the population was evacuated while the remainder fought on, scanning the horizon for their salvation, but after a few days, when the evacuation fleet finally came into view, the defences were breached and the Carthaginians poured in, bringing slaughter and enslavement on a huge scale to the city, which never recovered. The fugitive survivors founded the new city of *Thermae* (now Termini Imerese) to the west (*see p. 95*).

The site

The remains of Himera (*open Tues–Sat 9–5.30, until 6.30 in summer, 1st Sun of month 9–1.30; T: 091 814 0128*) occupy two areas, divided by the main road. On the north side of the road are the ruins of a **Doric temple**, probably built around 470 BC. It measured 22m by 55m, with 14 columns at the sides and six in front. The cella had a pronaos and opisthodomos in antis. This is the only surviving building of a sanctuary probably dedicated to Athena. It is still known as the Temple of Victory, although some scholars no longer believe it was built to celebrate the victory of 480 BC over the Carthaginians. In any case it seems to have been burnt and destroyed by the Carthaginians in 409 BC. Only the crepidoma and lower part of the columns and part of the cella walls survive. In the Middle Ages the site was built over and it was only rediscovered in 1823 and excavated by Pirro Marconi in 1929–30, when the splendid lion-head water spouts from the cornice were taken to the archaeological museum in Palermo.

In 2008 work on the railway line brought to light the **western necropolis** (*no access*), with over 9,500 intact tombs dating from the mid-7th to the end of the 5th century BC. Hundreds of burials were of new-born children, who had been placed in jars together with their terracotta feeding-bottles. The Greek warriors who took part in the epic battles of 480 and 409 BC were buried in collective tombs containing up to 59 bodies, all young men killed with lances. A particularly interesting detail is that in many cases they were buried together with their horses. An antiquarium, recently opened in renovated buildings next to the temple, displays some of the finds from this necropolis.

Off the main road, just beyond, a byroad (south; *signposted*) leads up to the areas of the city excavated since 1963. The **Antiquarium** has good plans and site descriptions. The first section displays finds from the temples in the sacred area on the hilltop, including a votive deposit with fragments of metopes. The second section has material from the city and necropoleis. There is also a third section devoted to finds from recent excavations in the surrounding territory, including Cefalù and Caltavuturo. The highlight of the collection is the gold libation bowl from Caltavuturo, a phiale-mesomphalos or offering-dish with a central depression (the *omphalos* or 'belly button') allowing it to be balanced on the hand without fingers touching the rim. This rare example weighs 982.4g and is made of solid gold, with *repoussé* ornamentation of four concentric circles of honey bees, acorns, lotus blossoms and beech nuts on a ground of gold granules, with vine tendrils and bunches of grapes on the smooth central omphalos. A Greek inscription has enabled scholars to date the vessel to the late 4th/early 3rd century BC. It is very similar to another dish in the Metropolitan Museum, to the point that they could have been made by the same craftsman, but the other dish is inscribed in Phoenician.

Just above the museum are more excavations. Steps continue up to a plateau overlooking the plain towards the sea. The path follows an ancient street bordered on either side by partially excavated houses. On the plateau, in the area known as Quartiere Nord, is the **Area Sacra** with a temenos enclosing the bases of an altar and four temples (7th–5th centuries BC). There are also traces of houses from the Archaic period here. The view extends along the coast as far as Solunto. In the other direction you can see the village of Gratteri, nestling in the Madonie Mountains.

CEFALÙ

Cefalù (*map p. 574, C1–D1*), with its stunning Norman cathedral and ruins of an ancient acropolis on the rock above the city, is a very picturesque small town with a lovely beach. The old town is still medieval in character, with many enticing shops, restaurants and cafés along its well-kept streets.

Founded at the end of the 5th or early 4th century BC, the ancient *Kephaloidion* was named from the head-like shape of the rock which towers above it (*kephalos* = head in Greek). In 307 BC it was taken by Agathocles of Syracuse. In 857 it was conquered by the Arabs and in 1131 Roger II rebuilt it and constructed the magnificent cathedral, which became head of a powerful bishopric. In the 1920s the occultist Aleister Crowley lived near Cefalù, transforming a cottage into the Temple of Thelema ('Do as thou wilt, shall

CEFALÙ CATHEDRAL

be thy creed') and scandalising the locals to the point where he was arrested, found guilty of immoral behaviour and expelled from Italy.

EXPLORING CEFALÙ

At the beginning of **Corso Ruggero**, the main street of the town, is Piazza Garibaldi (*map 6*), where the old men sit out on benches and pass the time of day. On the right is the sandstone façade of Maria Santissima della Catena (1780; *closed*) preceded by a high portico with three statues. On the right of the façade are a few large blocks from the old walls (late 5th century BC) on the site of Porta Terra, the main entrance to the old town. The Corso continues past (right) Vicolo dei Saraceni (signposted for the Tempio di Diana; *see p. 107*) and then runs slightly downhill. On the left are a series of nine picturesque, straight, parallel streets which lead downhill to Via Vittorio Emanuele, with a view of the sea beyond. They possibly reflect the grid plan of the ancient city. On the corner of the Corso and Via Amendola is the **Osterio Magno**, once King Roger's palace and now used for exhibitions, with a fine 13th-century triple window high up on its façade and (in Via Amendola) windows decorated with black lava stone.

The Corso continues past the little piazza in front of the 15th-century **church of the Purgatorio** (or Santo Stefano Protomartire; up steps; *map 2*). Inside (immediately on the right as you enter) is the tomb of Baron Mandralisca (*see p. 104*).

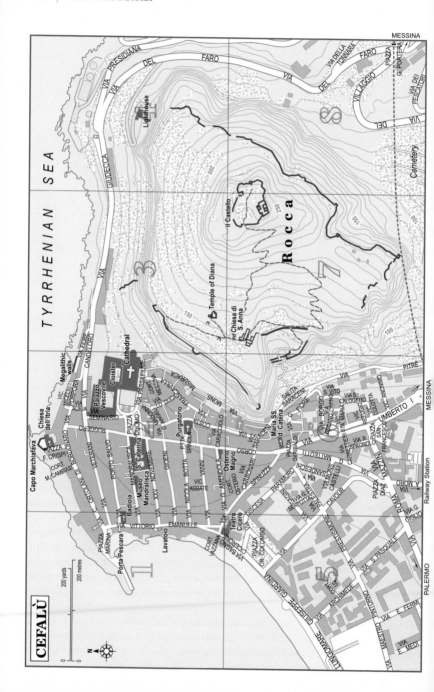

THE CATHEDRAL

Map 2. Open April–Sept Mon–Sat 9–6.30, Sun and holidays 9–12.30; Oct–March 8.30–6. Cloister daily 10–1 & 3–6. T: 338 817 5498, www.cattedraledicefalu.com.

Further along the Corso on the right, the piazza planted with palm trees leads up to the splendid **cattedrale**, a UNESCO World Heritage Site. The setting is dramatic, with the formidable rock rising immediately behind it and the small town at its feet. Begun by Roger II in 1131 and intended as his burial place, it was still unfinished at the time of his death in 1154. His successors lost interest in the project and it was not consecrated until 1267; Frederick II of Hohenstaufen even removed the royal porphyry tombs—officially for safety—and took them to Palermo, but to carry out this scandalous act he waited until the bishop was away on a mission in the East. Excavations during restoration work have revealed Roman remains on this site. The church is preceded by a raised terrace, part of the original Norman design, surrounded by a balustrade with statues. The soaring façade is flanked by two massive, subtly different bell-towers with fine windows. Above the narthex built by Ambrogio da Como in 1471 is a double row of blind arcades. The beautiful exterior of the south side and transept are visible from Via Passafiume.

Interior of the cathedral

The basilican interior has 16 ancient columns with Roman capitals, probably from the Temple of Diana (*see p. 107*), supporting Arab-Norman arches. The open timber roof of the nave bears traces of painting (1263). The contemporary stained-glass clerestory windows are the work of Michele Canzoneri and represent episodes from the Old and New Testaments. In the sanctuary is a 15th-century painted Crucifix attributed to Tommaso de Vigilia.

The apse is decorated with exquisite **mosaics**—the best preserved and the earliest of their kind in Sicily—on a background of dusky gold, symbolic of divinity. They were carried out for Roger II in a careful decorative scheme, reflecting Byzantine models but much more free and spontaneous than anything seen before from those workshops. The king probably intended them to line the whole interior of the building. They are thought to be the work of Greek craftsmen summoned from Constantinople by Roger himself. In the conch is the splendid colossal figure of **Christ Pantocrator** holding an open book with the Greek and Latin biblical text from John 8:12 ('I am the Light of the World: he that followeth me shall not walk in darkness'), a masterpiece.

On the curved apse wall below are three tiers of figures: the Virgin in prayer between four archangels (dressed as Byzantine dignitaries and holding loaves of bread symbolising Salvation); and in the two lower registers the Apostles, quite informal in their stance, as if we had suddenly interrupted their conversation. In the vault of the presbytery are angels and seraphim and on the walls below are (left) prophets, deacon-martyrs and Latin bishop-saints, and (right) prophets, warrior-saints and Greek patriarchs and theologians. An inscription beneath the window states that the mosaics of the apse were completed in 1148. The soft folds of the robes, the gentle expressions, the marvellous texture and subtle colour of the angels' wings, are certainly the work of very accomplished artists.

The south aisle and transepts were stripped of their Baroque decoration in the 1970s, in order to restore the building as far as possible to its Norman aspect. As a result, one of the twin world-famous 16th-century organs by Raffaele La Valle was lost without trace, perhaps stolen on commission. Such drastic intervention has been the subject of much heated discussion, but the achieved effect of light and space is breathtaking. On the pier between the sanctuary and the chapel to its left, in a niche, is a statue of the annunciatory angel (on the opposite pier is the Virgin Annunciate). In the chapel itself is an elaborate 18th-century silver altar. In the south chapel is a statue of the Madonna by Antonello Gagini, in honey-coloured stone.

The cloister

An alley leads along the north side of the church to the entrance to the cloister (*open Mon–Sat 10–1, last tickets 12.45*), the first of its kind to be built in Sicily. The closed quadrangle (now rectangular) was intended to favour meditation, while the garden in the centre was a *hortus conclusus*, where the monks would have cultivated medicinal herbs, vegetables and the four trees representing paradise, fig, pomegranate, olive and palm. The four quadrants of the garden, starting midway along the south side and heading east, represented Genesis, then the Song of Songs, followed by the Gospels and the Apocalypse. The ablution fountain which would have stood in the corner of the Gospel quadrant, is awaiting restoration. Though damaged, two sides remain of a portico of twin columns with shafts fashioned to represent the four elements (smooth = Earth; zigzag = water; twisted = Fire; octagonal = Air). The carved capitals support pointed Arab-Norman arches. The capitals originally numbered 70. Those that survive include Noah's Ark (no. 5 in the Genesis quadrant). It is thought that the same stonemasons also worked on the cloister in Monreale.

PIAZZA DUOMO

In Piazza Duomo is Palazzo Maria, with medieval traces, and the 17th-century Oratorio del Santissimo Sacramento beside the Neoclassical Palazzo Legambi. Opposite is the Palazzo Vescovile (1793), next to the 17th-century seminary with a hanging garden. Opposite the cathedral is the former monastery of **Santa Caterina**, extensively restored as the Town Hall a few years ago by the architect Gae Aulenti. Its huge, centrally-planned former church is now used for exhibitions.

MUSEO MANDRALISCA

Map 2. Open 9–7, Aug 9am–11pm. T: 0921 421547, www.fondazionemandralisca.it.
The cellars of this former palace, containing huge terracotta jars for storing oil, can be seen from the street, Via Mandralisca. Enrico Pirajno, Baron Mandralisca (1809–64) once lived here and he left his remarkable collection to the city as a museum (now run by a private foundation). The baron was a member of the first Italian parliament and he took a special interest in archaeology (participating in excavations on Lipari and near Cefalù) and natural history. He also endowed a local school.

On the ground floor is a mosaic from Cefalù (1st century BC). On the first floor is a famous vase from Lipari showing a vendor of tuna fish (4th century BC); a numismatic collection dating from the Greek period up to the 19th century, with about 400 pieces, particularly notable for its coins from Lipari, Cefalù and Syracuse; and a collection of paintings. The highlight here, in a separate small room, is the famous *Portrait of a Man* by **Antonello da Messina** (c. 1465–72), the jewel of the collection and one of the most striking portraits of the Italian Renaissance. Mandralisca apparently bought this small painting from a pharmacy in Lipari, where he discovered it in use as part of a cupboard door. The sitter, with his enigmatic smile, has never been identified. The influence of the Flemish school is evident in this exquisite work, here displayed to great advantage. Recently discovered in the cellars of the museum and carefully restored and displayed alongside, is another masterpiece, *St John the Baptist* by Giovanni Antonio Sogliani, perhaps purchased by Mandralisca during a visit to Florence in 1861. Notice the subtle colouring, the gentle expression of the saint, the clever depiction of his red silk mantle in this painting, which almost certainly formed part of a much larger work. The Crucifix is cut off at the top and the saint's left hand is not entirely visible.

Also in the collection is a 2nd-century BC sarcophagus in the form of an Ionic temple. Other rooms hold Mandralisca's remarkable collection of some 20,000 shells; archaeological material including Italiot vases from Lipari (320–300 BC) and a well-preserved kylix; miscellaneous objects including a 19th-century dinner service, arms, reliquaries, paintings (*Madonna and Child* attributed to Antonello da Saliba) and an ornithological collection. Mandralisca's important library, which has been expanded, is also accessible. There is a small bookshop on the ground floor.

THE PORT AND LAVATOIO

At the end of Corso Ruggero, Via Porpora (*map 2*) leads right to a restored square tower in a gap between the houses. Outside the tiny postern gate, a fine stretch of **megalithic walls** (5th century BC) built onto the rock can be seen. In the other direction Via Bordonaro leads past (right) Piazza Francesco Crispi with the Chiesa dell'Itria. Modern steps lead up to a 17th-century bastion (Capo Marchiafava) where a 14th-century fountain has been placed (good view). Via Bordonaro itself continues down towards the sea and ends beside a terrace overlooking the little port, with picturesque old houses on the seafront.

From here Via Vittorio Emanuele leads back past the old church of the **Badiola** (12th–17th centuries), with characteristic jointed terracotta drainpipes on its flank. It stands opposite its convent (the old portal survives on the corner of Via Porto Salvo). Opposite is the 16th-century **Porta Pescara**, a series of arches through which you can reach the beach. At the bottom is a display of fishermen's tackle and nets. Further along Via Vittorio Emanuele, on the right, wide steps curving down past a few trees lead to the **Lavatoio**, a picturesque medieval wash-house, where a spring of slightly salty water (the tears of Daphnis; *see below*) was converted into a laundry by the Arabs and was still in daily use until quite recently. At the south end of Via Vittorio Emanuele, in Via Spinuzza, is the early 19th-century opera house, **Teatro Cicero**, with 204 seats (*T: 0921 925011*), recently restored. Very pretty, the vault painting by Rosario Spagnolo (1889) represents three of the Muses: Euterpe (Music), Terpsichore (Dance) and

CEFALÙ
View over the old town from the Rocca ramparts.

Thalia (Comedy).In the 1930s it was used as a cinema and during the Second World War it was the headquarters of the German garrison.

THE ROCCA

From Corso Ruggero and Vicolo dei Saraceni (*map 6*), steps and a path lead up (in c. 1hr) to the Rocca (*fee*), the summit (278m) of which commands a wonderful view. According to legend, the rock is the head of the shepherd Daphnis. He so loved the nymph Nomia that he promised to be faithful to her, on pain of being blinded. Chimaera then enticed him into the woods, gave him wine and seduced him. Nomia accordingly blinded him, and Hermes, on the orders of Hera, to whom Nomia was dear, turned him into stone. His bitter tears at his folly are said to form the spring that supplies the Lavatoio. On the west of the hillside is the so-called **Temple of Diana**, with walls made out of huge polygonal blocks and a carved architrave over the entrance. It was probably a sacred edifice built in the 5th–4th century BC over an earlier cistern. Stretches of **castellated walls** can also be seen here (excellent views down over the old town) as well as numerous cisterns. Further up, at the very top of the hill, are vague traces of the original **castle**.

THE MADONIE MOUNTAINS

The Madonie Mountains (*map p. 574, C2–D2*) lie between the Imera Settentrionale river to the west and the Pollina to the east. The Pizzo Carbonara (1979m) is the second highest mountain on the island (after Etna). The area of some 40,000 hectares is protected as a nature reserve known as the Parco Naturale Regionale delle Madonie. The vegetation in the upland plains and mountains includes beech, enormous holly trees (some 14m high and centuries old), manna ash (manna is still extracted from the bark in the Pollina and Castelbuono area), chestnuts, oaks, poplars, ilexes, cork oaks and ancient olives. A rare species of fir, *Abies nebrodensis*, only found here and distinguished by the terminal twigs on the branches which form a neat cross, was saved from extinction in 1969. Apart from these extensive woods the landscape has spectacular rock formations, pastureland where sheep and cattle are grazed, and small hill towns of great interest. For more information on the flora and fauna of the Madonie, visit the museum in Castelbuono (*see overleaf*).

GIBILMANNA

The sanctuary of Gibilmanna (*map p. 574, D2*) is in a beautiful position looking towards the sea, on the slopes of the Pizzo Sant'Angelo (1081m), with woods of olives, cork oaks, pines and chestnuts. The name is derived from the Arabic *jebel*, meaning mountain, and manna, which was extracted from the manna ash trees in the locality and used for medicinal purposes. There was a **sanctuary** here founded by the Benedictines in the 6th century; in 1535 it became a Capuchin convent and it is still a famous centre of pilgrimage. The sanctuary (*open Mon–Fri 9–7, Sat–Sun 8–9*), rebuilt in the 17th century, has been altered many times and its external appearance dates from the 20th century. The exquisitely carved altarpiece was made by the Gagini family.

The **Museum of the Franciscan Presence in Sicily** (*open April–Sept 9.30–12.30 & 3.30–7, Oct–March 9–1 & 3–5; tickets at the sanctuary library*) preserves works of art from convents and churches in this area of the island. These include 16th–18th-century paintings, church vestments, statuettes (in wax and wood), ex-votos, a rare early 18th-century wooden organ with cane pipes, and an ethnographic collection illustrating monastic life. It is also possible to visit the catacombs.

GRATTERI

A little hill town facing west, Gratteri (*map p. 574, C2*) provides a fine distant view along the coast. The churches (*often closed*) are the 19th-century Nuova Matrice, containing four thorns from the Crown of Jesus and a fragment of the True Cross, and the Matrice Vecchia, dedicated to the Archangel Michael, built in the 14th century. It has a separate bell-tower with seven bronze bells, one of them dated 1390. Beautiful crochet work is still made here by the women.

ISNELLO

Isnello (*map p. 574, C2–D2*) is a photogenic little town built along a long rock which gives the town its name, the Rocca dell'Asinello (Rock of the Little Donkey), with the ruins of the castle at one end. Although very small, it was wealthy in the past, thanks to its industries: its glass, leather, bell-founding and wood carving were renowned, and its craftsmen carried out beautiful work in local churches.

Dedicated to St Nicholas, the **Chiesa Madre** (*T: 0921 62008*) has 16th-century frescoes by Antonino Ferraro, 17th-century stuccoes by Giuseppe Li Volsi, and a carved wooden choir and organ loft dating from the early 17th century; the organ is dated 1615. A marble ciborium is attributed to Domenico Gagini (1492). The *Deposition* is by Giuseppe Salerno, Zoppo di Gangi. The little church of **San Michele** (14th–18th centuries) has a rare painted wooden ceiling, a wooden Crucifix by Fra' Umile da Petralia over the south altar, a painting of the *Forty Martyrs*, perhaps by Giuseppe Salerno, and a 15th-century fresco of *St Leonard*.

In Piazza dei Caduti is the church of the Rosario, which contains a painting of the *Madonna of the Rosary* attributed to Simon de Worbrecht. The church of the **Annunziata** (*T: 347 073 5252*) contains a *Nativity* by Giuseppe Salerno. The organ is by Antonino La Valle (1635).

Steps lead up from the piazza by the Chiesa Madre to the church of **Santa Maria Maggiore** (late 14th century) near the ruins of the castle and beneath a rock called the Grotta Grande. It dominates the village, with its pretty cusped bell-tower. The charming interior has a decorative organ loft over the entrance. A late 15th- or early 16th-century Crucifix, unusual in its iconography and painted on both sides (*Crucifixion* on one side and *Resurrection* on the other), hangs from the centre of the nave ceiling. Above the main altar is a *Madonna and Child* of the Gagini school (1547). There is also a charming little statue of the Madonna as a baby, lovingly preserved in a glass case.

Recently inaugurated on Mt Mufara (1865m), south of Isnello, is the **Parco Astronomico delle Madonie**, or PAM, an astronomical and astrophysical station with several telescopes and a planetarium (*www.galhassin.it*). This mountain was chosen because of its ideal climatic conditions and low light interference.

COLLESANO

The spectacular little medieval town of Collesano (*map p. 574, C2*) has several interesting churches including the **Chiesa Madre** (Basilica San Pietro), which contains a painted Crucifix of 1555, an **organ** dated 1627 by Antonino La Valle, a fine carved tabernacle of 1489 by Domenico Gagini, and a *Madonna with Angels* by Giuseppe Salerno. The frescoes (1624) are the work of Gaspare Vazano, a Zoppo di Gangi. In **Santa Maria la Vecchia** (1140) is a statue of the *Madonna* by Antonello Gagini. At Corso Vittorio Emanuele 3 is the informative **Museo Targa Florio** (*open 9.30–12.30 & 3.30–7, closed Mon and Thur afternoons; T: 0921 664684, www.museotargaflorio.it*), dedicated to the oldest motor race in the world (*see p. 74*). The pottery made in Collesano is unusual and interesting, both in terms of the shapes of the vases and the colours used.

CASTELBUONO

An ancient town of warm rose-coloured stone and mellow old brick, whose rooftops are animated by jackdaws and swifts, Castelbuono (*map p. 574, D2*) basks at the foot of its spectacular castle, in a fold of hills covered with forests of manna ash and chestnuts. Of Byzantine origin, it became the seat of the Ventimiglia princes of Geraci in the 14th century, and the medieval structure of the centre is still intact. The streets are so narrow that donkeys are used to collect garbage, door-to-door.

The Matrice Vecchia and the castle

The main road leads up past a 16th-century fountain, with bas-reliefs and a statue of Venus, to Piazza Margherita, which has another 16th-century fountain. Here the **Matrice Vecchia** of 1350 is preceded by a loggia. It contains a marble ciborium attributed to Giorgio da Milano (late 15th century), a huge polyptych on the high altar attributed to Pietro Ruzzolone, and statues and frescoes of the 16th century. The crypt has frescoes of the Passion of Christ. Also in the piazza is a building owned by the Ventimiglia family in the 14th–16th centuries and used as a prison from the 18th century up to 1965. Exhibitions are now held here and it houses a local tourist office.

The ancient street continues uphill past the Town Hall to the **castle** (*open 9–1 & 3.30–7, closed Mon; T: 0921 671211*), built by the Ventimiglia family in 1316 and exceptionally well restored. Off the courtyard is the Cappella di Sant'Anna, or Cappella Palatina (c. 1683), profusely decorated white stucco cherubs on a gold ground attributed to Giuseppe Serpotta (brother of Giacomo). Behind the altar in a 16th-century silver reliquary urn is a skull venerated as that of St Anne, mother of the Virgin. The castle also houses the Civic Art Gallery (contemporary artists) and a small museum of country life and the extraction of manna. From the terrace behind the castle there is a good view of the Madonie mountains and the little hill town of Geraci Siculo.

The Matrice Nuova and San Francesco

From the Matrice Vecchia a road (signposted) leads up to a piazza with palm trees and a memorial surrounded by cannon used in the First World War. Here is the **Matrice Nuova**, begun in the early 17th century and rebuilt in 1830. It contains a painted Crucifix attributed to Pietro Ruzzolone. Another road leads up from the right of the Matrice Nuova to the church of **San Francesco**, which has a pretty white and gold interior decorated in the 18th century, with an organ and monks' choir above the entrance. It also has decorative chandeliers and charming little confessionals dating from 1910. Off the right side of the sanctuary, entered through a lovely late 15th-century doorway carved by the school of Laurana, is a pretty octagonal chapel with twisted columns. Here are the tombs of the Ventimiglia family, including one dated 1543 and one 1687. According to local lore, this chapel is linked to the castle by a secret passage. The two 15th-century frescoes were detached from the Franciscan convent, whose attractive 18th-century cloister is entered between two marble columns left of the church façade.

Museo Minà Palumbo

At Via Roma 52 the former convent of Santa Venera now houses the Museo Minà Palumbo (*open 9–1 & 3–7; T: 0921 671895, www.museominapalumbo.it*). It is named after the naturalist Francesco Minà Palumbo, a native of Castelbuono. His collections, which he carefully catalogued, provide a fascinating documentation of the Madonie. The exhibits include fossils, minerals, archaeological finds (including prehistoric material), examples of glass produced here from the late 16th–18th centuries, and examples of paper produced in the town between 1822 and 1846. There is also an interesting display illustrating the extraction of manna (used as a mild laxative, especially for babies, and also as a sweetener in cakes) from the trunks of manna ash trees. Castelbuono and Pollina are the only places in the world where manna is still produced.

SCLAFAGNI BAGNI AND CALTAVUTURO

Sclafani Bagni (pron. SCLAfani BANyi; *map p. 574, C2*) is a small, remote fortress-village on a precipitous crag with superb views. The name derives from *Aesculapii fanum*, a place sacred to Asklepios, the god of healing. The medieval town gate bears the coat of arms of the Sclafani (Matteo Sclafani, count of the town in 1330, constructed its defences). Higher up, the Chiesa Madre or **Santa Maria Assunta** (*to request visit call priest T: 347 073 5252, normally possible Mon, Wed, Fri 2–6*) contains a splendid Greek marble sarcophagus with Bacchic scenes, thought to come from Himera; statues of the Madonna and St Peter by the school of Gagini, an organ by Antonino La Valle (1615) and a processional statue of the Ecce Homo, made of *mistura*, the work of Fra' Umile da Petralia. Above, steps lead up to the scant remains of the Norman castle, with an excellent view.

In the lower part of the town is the church of **San Giacomo** on the edge of the hillside, with charming stuccoes in the interior (albeit in very poor condition). The church of **San Filippo** contains a worn but pretty tiled floor, a 17th-century wooden processional Crucifix in a tabernacle, and two curious statues of waxed canvas (1901), much venerated locally.

CALTAVUTURO

Caltavuturo means 'Rock of the Vulture', and its ancient fortress on a crag was of great strategic importance from the earliest times, bringing considerable fortune; the accidental discovery in 1980 of a gold libation bowl (now in the Antiquarium of Himera; *see p. 100*) bears witness to this. Together with Sclafani, Caltavuturo protected Himera against attacks from the interior. It was also an important fortress to the Arabs but by the 16th century it had lost its importance, mainly because of its inaccessibility, and the population moved down to a lower, more comfortable position. The site of the old settlement, the rocky area to the north, is known as Terravecchia. During World War Two it was a German base, and suffered heavy bombing in 1943.

Today the town is very picturesque, with many streets either narrow and cobbled or steeply stepped. Via Dante leads into the tiny Piazza Madre Chiesa, with the church of **SS Pietro e Paolo**, the Chiesa Madre, built in 1582. Inside there is a sad-faced *Madonna della Neve* by Francesco Laurana, in white marble, interesting for the unusual ringleted hair-style and the masterful rendering of the folds of the Virgin's mantle. Also in this church is the case (unfortunately the pipes are missing) of a rare organ by Raffaele La Valle.

In Terravecchia, on a terrace below Via Alfieri, looking out over the landscape, is the **Chiesa del Casale** or Santissimo Salvatore (12th century), the oldest church in Caltavuturo. It also served as a watch-tower. **I Mannari**, on the steep mountainside here, are a series of tiny gardens and sheep-pens, each surrounded by a low stone wall and united by stairs; here and there are tiny cottages. They give an idea of how difficult life was for the farmers on these inhospitable crags.

POLIZZI GENEROSA

Beautifully positioned at the head of the Imera valley, Polizzi Generosa (*map p. 574, C2–D2*) is a delightful little town which received the sobriquet 'Generosa' from Frederick II in 1234. It once boasted 76 churches within its walls and many of them now belong to local confraternities (who have the keys).

SANTA MARIA MAGGIORE

On Via Roma, near the north edge of town, stands the Chiesa Madre of Santa Maria Maggiore. Under its charming 16th-century south porch, two very worn statues of St Peter and St Paul flank the Renaissance doorway, beside which a Gothic portal has been exposed. In the south aisle is a painting of the *Nativity* by Giuseppe Salerno. At the end of the aisle, closed by a grille, is a chapel with some particularly fine sculptures, including reliefs by the Berrettaro family and the (recomposed) sarcophagus of Beato Gandolfo da Binasco by Domenico Gagini. The Blessed Gandolfo was a Franciscan who preached in Polizzi in 1260 and is now the town's patron saint. In the sanctuary, but very high up, is a precious large **Flemish triptych** (some scholars have suggested that it might be partly the work of Rogier van der Weyden). The central panel shows the *Madonna and Child with Angel Musicians* and the side panels *St Catherine* and *St Barbara*. It is one of the loveliest paintings in Sicily, painted on Flemish oak and still in its original frame.

Opposite the Chiesa Madre is the little church of **San Gandolfo la Povera** (1622), with a high altarpiece of the Blessed Gandolfo by Giuseppe Salerno.

ON AND AROUND PIAZZA CASTELLO

Via Roma continues up to Piazza Castello, where the former church of San Francesco, founded in 1303, is now used as an events space. On the left are the (extremely scanty) ruins of the so-called castle of Queen Blanche of Navarre (11th century) and a walled garden where two fir trees belonging to the rare indigenous species *Abies nebrodensis* survive. Also in the square is a little museum of the Madonie, **Museo Ambientalistico Madonita—MAM** (*open Mon–Fri 8.30–2 & 3.30–6.30, Sat–Sun 9.30–12.30 & 4–7; T: 0921 641811, www.mam.pa.it*) with exhibits on local natural history (especially rocks and fossils).

Below San Francesco on Via Carlo V is the **Badia Vecchia** or church of Santa Margherita, a 15th-century foundation for Benedictine nuns. It has delicate white and gold stucco decoration and, particularly noteworthy, a beautiful wrought-iron grille enclosing the nuns' choir. At the corner of Via Carlo V and Vicolo di Chiara is the little church of San Nicolò de Franchis (*locked*), founded in 1167 by Peter of Toulouse, with a belfry above its entrance portal.

On Via Itria, which skirts the north edge of town, is the little church of **San Pancrazio dei Greci**, which contains a painting by one of the Zoppi di Gangi. From the terrace there is an impressive view of the mountains. Next to the church are the remains of the circular **Torre di Leo**, named after a family who purchased it in 1240.

Parallel to Via Itria is the main street, Via Garibaldi, with the centrally-planned church of San Girolamo by Angelo Italia. Next to it is the **former Collegio dei Gesuiti** (*open Oct–March Tues, Thur, Sat, Sun 10–1; April–Sept Tues–Sun 10–1, Sat–Sun also 3–6.30; T: 0921 551613*), a large building now occupied by the Town Hall, civic library and a museum in four sections: archaeological finds from the area; ancient books; ancient toys; school through the years. The fine interior courtyard has loggias on two levels and a single balcony on the top storey. In the morning visitors are allowed up to the top storey where an open balcony has a fine view over the rooftops (and the ruined church of the Commenda below the town to the south).

Via Garibaldi continues past a flight of steps (right) which lead up to the large Palazzo Carpinello with a long, low façade, and ends at the wide, open **Piazza Santissima Trinità**, which has a magnificent panorama: the Palermo–Catania motorway is reduced to a winding stream in the distant valley below, while to the east rise the Madonie Mountains. Facing the square at the end of Via Garibaldi is the ancient church of Santa Maria Lo Piano, seat of the Teutonic Knights, with a curious triple belfry.

From the south tip of Piazza Santissima Trinità, take Vicolo Garofalo to the junction with Via Vinciguerra. On the corner to your right you will see the bell-tower of **Sant'Antonio Abate**, formerly a mosque. It contains paintings by Giuseppe Salerno.

PETRALIA SOTTANA AND SOPRANA

Petralia Sottana (*map p. 574, D2*) sits on a hillside enclosed by the mountains. On the attractive Corso Paolo Agliata, at no. 100, is the **Museo Civico Antonio Collisani** (*open Mon–Fri 8.30–2 & 3.30–6.30, Sat–Sun and holidays 9.30–12.30 & 4–7; T: 0921 641811*), with well displayed archaeological material from across Sicily spanning the Neolithic to the Roman period. There is a comprehensive display on the Grotta del Vecchiuzzo (which Collisani rediscovered). Corso Agliata terminates in Piazza Umberto (with a view of the Imera Valley). The **Chiesa Madre**, which has a lovely bell-tower, was rebuilt in the 17th century. It contains a fine sculpted altarpiece of 1501 and a 17th-century statue of the *Madonna and Child*. In Via Monastero is the church and convent of the **Santissima Trinità**, with a marble altarpiece by Gian Domenico Gagini (1542). The women of the village still weave brightly coloured rag rugs called *pezzane* or *frazzate*.

PETRALIA SOPRANA

Occupying a beautiful position on a hillside (1147m) above pinewoods, Petralia Soprana (*map p. 574, D2*) is an interesting and well-preserved little town, and the highest in the province. The ancient *Petra*, which surrendered to Rome in 254 BC and grew wealthy as a grain provider to that city, might have been located here. The Romans built an aqueduct, parts of the pillars of which survive. Petralia prospered also under the Arab domination, when it was known as *Batraliah*. In 1062 it passed into the hands of Count Roger. During the 19th and early 20th centuries, salt mines were at the base of the economy; one of them is still in use (*see below*).

In the central **Piazza del Popolo** is a large war memorial and the neo-Gothic Town Hall (1896). With the Town Hall behind you, take **Via Generale Medici**, which leads up past (left) the façade of San Giovanni Evangelista (1770; *closed*) to a crossroads (Piazza Ruggero Settimo). Look right to see the very worn portal of the 18th-century Oratorio delle Anime del Purgatorio. To the left you will see a bust commemorating Fra' Umile da Petralia, the local sculptor famous for his Crucifixes (they adorn many churches in Sicily). A short way further up is Piazza dei Quattro Cannoli with a pretty 18th-century fountain, at the time the only source of water for the inhabitants.

Beyond on the right a sign points two ways: left to the 18th-century domed circular church of **San Salvatore**, built on the site of a Norman church which was possibly built on the site of a mosque by order of Count Roger; and right to the **Chiesa Madre di SS Pietro e Paolo**. Consecrated in 1497, it has a delightful 18th-century portico. At one end is a squat tower and at the other is the 15th-century campanile with a two-light window in which two quaint statues of St Peter and St Paul have been placed. The gilded and white stucco decoration in the interior was carried out in 1859. On the north side the first altar has a fine painted statue of the *Madonna and Child* and the fourth a marble statue of the *Madonna*. The fifth has a high relief of the *Pietà* with symbols of the Passion by Giuliano Mancino. In the chapel to the left of the sanctuary is an 18th-century gilded wooden altarpiece by Pietro Bencivinni. The realistic Crucifix in the south aisle was the first of the 33 carved by Fra' Umile (c. 1624). The polychrome statues of St Peter and St Paul are by the local sculptor Gaetano Franzese (1764), and the large painting of their martyrdom is by Vincenzo Riolo. On the fifth south altar is a beautiful *Deposition*, attributed since its recent restoration to Pietro Novelli.

From the other side of Piazza del Popolo, Via Loreto leads uphill past a pretty courtyard, several handsome palaces and the 16th-century church of San Michele. The street ends in the piazza (paved with cobblestones) in front of the attractive church of **Santa Maria di Loreto**. The façade of 1750 is by local sculptors, and the two little spires on either side are decorated with coloured stones. It is preceded by a wrought-iron gate of 1881. The beautiful **interior** has a carved altarpiece attributed to Gian Domenico Gagini (with a *Madonna* attributed to Giacomo Mancini). It also contains paintings by Vincenzo Riolo, 18th–19th-century statues, and a fine sacristy of 1783. On the right a lane (Via Belvedere) leads out under an arch to a terrace beside the apse of the church, with an excellent vista which extends as far as Etna on a clear day. Below the town here are some remains of the Roman aqueduct.

On the east side of town is the church of **San Teodoro**, founded by Count Roger and rebuilt in 1759. An interesting 12th-century sarcophagus decorated with animal carvings was discovered here in 1991.

The **Italkali salt mine** at Petralia Soprana lies some 5km to the east of the town, approached either from the SS120 or from a road (signposted) between the two Petralias. It houses the Museo d'Arte Contemporanea Sotto Sale, an interesting collection of salt sculptures, the work of artists taking part in a biennial exhibition (*museum open Sat only; request a visit a few days ahead, T: 331 185 6868*).

GANGI

East of the Petralias, a few kilometres east of the boundary of the Madonie park, is Gangi (1011m; *map p. 574, D2*), a little town perched on a ridge in the middle of mountainous countryside. In 2014 it won the title of 'Most Beautiful Village in Italy'. The town's medieval origins can still be appreciated in the street plan. At the top of the hill is the Palazzo Bongiorno, now the Town Hall, formerly the seat of the wealthiest family in the region, decorated with 18th-century frescoes by Gaspare Fumagalli. The town was the birthplace of two painters known as Zoppo di Gangi (the Cripple of Gangi): Gaspare Vazano and Giuseppe Salerno. Salerno's *Last Judgement* was painted after the artist saw Michelangelo's work of the same name in the Sistine Chapel, and is an interesting reworking of it. It hangs in the church of **San Nicolò**, which also houses three thorns from the Crown of Christ. In the crypt are the mummified bodies of 60 priests of the 18th century; they are unique among the mummies of Sicily because their faces were covered with wax masks (*crypt open Sat– Sun mornings; to request a visit on other days, also with an English-speaking guide, call the Tourist Office, T: 0921 501471*). In Piazza Valguarnera is the **castle**, built in the 14th century by the

Ventimiglia family. In the right wing is a beautiful Renaissance chapel attributed to the Gaginis (early 16th century), unfortunately closed. There is also a sizeable **Museo Civico** in Palazzo Sgadari, at Corso Vitale 54 (*open Tues–Sun 9–1 & 3–7.30; T: 0921 689907*). The collection has archaeological finds, paintings, books, coins and weapons.

THE WEST OF THE PROVINCE

PIANA DEGLI ALBANESI

In Piana degli Albanesi (*map p. 574, B2*), the most interesting of the 15th-century Albanian colonies in Sicily, the inhabitants still use their native tongue, are Catholics of the Byzantine-Greek rite, and wear traditional costume for weddings and important festivals. Garibaldi planned the tactics that led to the capture of Palermo from here. Piana is known for its excellent bread, cheeses and huge *cannoli di ricotta*.

In the handsome main street, Via Giorgio Kastriota, is the cathedral of **San Demetrio** of 1498 (*usually open 10–12.30*). On the west wall is a 19th-century painting of St Nicholas by Andrea d'Antoni. On the north wall is a small Byzantine *Madonna and Child*. The statues are attributed to Nicola Bagnasco, and the damaged apse frescoes are by Pietro Novelli. The iconostasis was decorated with paintings in 1975.

The main street leads uphill to the piazza beside the church of the Madonna Odigitria (1607), on a design by Pietro Novelli. Just out of the square is the church of **San Giorgio**, the oldest in the town, built in 1495. Inside, on the south side, is a mosaic by the local artist Tanina Cuccia (1984) and a painting of St Philip Neri by Giuseppe Patania. The iconostasis has 20th-century paintings. On the north side is a fresco of St Anthony Abbot by Antonio Novelli and a charming equestrian statue of St George, fully armed. Other churches of interest include **San Vito** (18th century, with statues) and **Santissima Annunziata** (1624; with a fresco by Pietro Novelli).

At Via Guzzetta 11, the old Oratorio San Filippo Neri is now a library, cultural centre and the delightful **Museo Civico Nicola Barbato** (*open Tues–Sun 9.30–1, Tues and Thur also 3–7; T: 091 857 5668*), with interesting sections displaying traditional costumes and 18th-century jewellery worn by the women of Piana.

A few kilometres south of the town is **Portella della Ginestra**, where there is a memorial to the peasants massacred here while celebrating a traditional May Day festival in 1947. Eleven people were killed and 59 wounded by outlaws led by Salvatore Giuliano from Montelepre. This was later understood as an attempt by right-wing activists, in collusion with the Mafia, to combat Communism and advocate independence for the island (both the right wing and the separatists had just lost votes in the local elections).

Southeast of the town is the **lake of Piana degli Albanesi**, a reservoir formed in 1923 by an impressive dam between Mt Kumeta (1200m) and Mt Maganoce (900m) across the River Belice, now a nature reserve (Oasi di Piana degli Albanesi), a good place to observe migrating duck.

MONTE JATO

West of Piana is **San Giuseppe Jato** (pron. YAto; *map p. 574, A2*). Excavations on Mt Jato have unearthed remains of the ancient city of *Iaitas*, which flourished from the 4th century BC until it was destroyed by Frederick II in the 13th century. The area has 21 marked trails, of various levels of difficulty, for trekkers and ramblers, using for the most part ancient and medieval paths and bridle-tracks, which had all but disappeared from sight and from memory. The trails offer unforgettable glimpses of historic remains, wildlife, and the lovely countryside of the area. Descriptions of the walks and maps are available from the local tourist offices (*or see www.vallejato.it/sentieri-naturalistici*).

From the village of San Cipirello, a road leads up through lovely countryside to the **archaeological area** on the hill (*open Tues-Sat 9–4, last tickets 2½hrs before closing; Sun and holidays 9–1, last tickets 2hrs before closing*) and the farmhouse containing the **Antiquarium** (*open Tues–Sat 9–6, Sun and holidays 9–1; T: 091 8577943 or 338 785 2632*). An interesting collection of finds from the site is displayed here. The highlights are four stone telamones (two satyrs and two maenads) from the theatre, and a collection of coins found among the ruins. From the entrance gate it is a walk of about 20mins to the top of the hill (852m) with the theatre (late 4th century BC, reconstructed in the 1st century AD), which could seat 4,500 (Classical drama performances are given in summer). There is also a temple of Aphrodite (c. 550 BC) and a large villa that had two floors with a peristyle and 25 rooms. The agora has also been partially uncovered. There are splendid views from this isolated spot.

PARTINICO AND MONTELEPRE

Partinico (*map p. 574, A1*) is an agricultural town associated with the name of Danilo Dolci (1924–97), a philanthropist from Trieste who dedicated his life to opposing the Mafia using non-violent methods. In Piazza Duomo is a fountain of 1716 in front of the Baroque cathedral of the Santissima Annunziata, soaring above its flight of steps. From the cathedral, Corso dei Mille leads past a Neoclassical bandstand (1875) to the 17th-century church of San Leonardo, with works by the school of Novelli. Opposite is the church of the Carmine (1634).

The hill town of **Montelepre** is a maze of steep and narrow streets gravitating around the massive square Torre Ventimiglia, built to house a defensive garrison by the archbishop of Monreale in 1429, when he acquired the surrounding land and wanted to protect it from bandits who stole his crops. Appreciating the security offered by the tower, numerous peasants came and built their homes as close as possible to its walls. The resulting village was called Montelepre, 'Mountain of the Hare'. Today it is associated with the name of Salvatore Giuliano. During the war he used his mule to carry black-market flour to the village; when apprehended, he shot a *carabiniere*. He reigned over a large part of the province for seven years before he was murdered here in 1950 by his brother-in-law, Gaspare Pisciotta, at the age of 27. His body was shown to the press in a courtyard in Castelvetrano with the story that he had been tracked down and killed there by the Carabinieri. He remained a mythical figure in the imagination of many Sicilians until 1960, when his connection with the Mafia and local police was revealed, as well as his presumed part in the massacre of peasants at Portella della Ginestra (*see above*).

CARINI, TERRASINI AND THE ISOLA DELLE FEMMINE

A lovely town that gives its name to the gulf here, **Carini** (*map p. 574, A1*) is dominated by the splendid Castello La Grua Talamanca (*Via Termitana 2; open summer 9–1 & 3–8, winter 9–1 & 3–7; Tourist Office T: 091 881 5666*), whose visible remains are of the 16th century, though it is likely that it has much older origins. The castle is remembered for the tragic story of Laura Lanza, Baronissa di Carini, who in 1563 was murdered by her father when he believed she had a lover.

Close to shore here is an eye-catching rock with a lonely watchtower, **Isola delle Femmine** ('Island of the Women'; *map p. 574, A1*). It is a haven for seabirds and is protected as a nature reserve. The name probably derives from *Eufemio*, the Byzantine governor, but according to legend this was the spot where women of Palermo were brought when caught in adultery. In spite of its small size, it can be seen from a large part of the province.

Beyond the airport at Punta Raisi and Mt Pecoraro is the spectacular Gulf of Castellammare, which stretches away to Capo San Vito, the mountains behind providing a striking backdrop. It is a popular area for holiday homes and the countryside is beautiful, with olive and citrus groves. **Terrasini** (*map p. 574, A1*) is a holiday resort with a particularly good museum on Lungomare Peppino Impastato, the **Museo Civico Palazzo d'Aumale** (*open Mon, Sun and holidays 9–1, Tues–Sat 9–7, Aug–Sept late closing every day 10pm; T: 091 881 0989*), with an archaeological section consisting of objects found in and around shipwrecks (with explanations of how the ships were built, how the amphorae were stacked on board, etc.), fishing techniques and ex-votos. On the first floor is an excellent natural history section, including geology and palaeontology, with a collection of fossils. The museum also displays an exceptionally complete collection of hand-painted Sicilian carts.

THE SOUTH OF THE PROVINCE

BELMONTE MEZZAGNO TO FICUZZA

Between Bagheria and Piana degli Albanesi, **Belmonte Mezzagno** (*map p. 574, B1*), founded in 1752, has a scenographic church built in 1776, and dominates the valley of the Eleuterio (the ancient *Eleutheros*) below; densely inhabited but with some surviving persimmon plantations. Above the plain soars the **castle of Misilmeri**, which takes its name from the Arabic *Menzil el-Emir* (dwelling of the Emir; *open daily 9–1 & 3–7*). Here in 1068 Count Roger de Hauteville defeated a large Muslim army, paving the way for the Norman domination of Sicily.

The town of **Marineo** (*map p. 574, B2*) surrounds an extraordinary rocky outcrop called the Montagnola, the first thing you see when you arrive. The Castello Beccadelli Bologna, at its foot, was built as the residence of the aristocratic Bologna family by

Matteo Carnelivari in 1559 (six years after the founding of the town). It houses the Museo Regionale della Valle dell'Eleuterio (*open winter 9–6.30, summer 9–7.30, Sun and holidays 9–1; T: 091 872 6491*), and besides offering stupendous views over the Eleuterio Valley, has an interesting archaeological collection of objects found in digs in the surrounding area.

Further south, **Ficuzza** is a village dominated by the Palazzina Reale (*open winter 9–12 & 1.30–3, summer 9–12.30 & 2.30–6, closed Mon; T: 091 846 0108*), a handsome building in sandstone with numerous chimneys and two clocks, now used by the Azienda Forestale. It was built by Venanzio Marvuglia in 1803 as a hunting lodge for the Bourbons. Behind it is the **Bosco della Ficuzza**, once the king's chase and now a nature reserve, a splendid forest of oak, chestnut and ilex. Although once much larger, it still covers some 4,000 hectares and is among the most extensive wooded areas of its kind left on the island. Several rough roads and paths run through it, although much of it is fenced off for protection. Above the forest rises the Rocca Busambra (1613m), a huge spur of calcareous rock which dominates the plain for many kilometres around. Above the sheer rockface, its summit provides pastureland. Numerous birds nest here, including the golden eagle. The Gorgo del Drago, the source of the River Frattina, is a lush green oasis, with a gorge and a waterfall running through yellow and red rocks.

CEFALÀ DIANA TO CASTRONOVO DI SICILIA

The town of **Cefalà Diana** (*map p. 574, B2*) has a unique Islamic bath-house, the Bagni di Cefalà (*open Mon–Sat 8.30–1.30, Thur and Sat 8.30–7, 1st Sun of month 8.30–1.30; T: 091 829 1551*), which dates back to the 10th–11th centuries and is considered the most interesting Arab building to survive on the island. The baths have a splendid barrel vault and a pretty arch with two capitals and columns at one end. The water bubbles up here at 38°C and the spring and its course are protected as a nature reserve. On a frieze of tufa around the top of the outside wall runs a Kufic inscription ('Of our lord prince the Emir two admirable baths') which has virtually disappeared. The 13th-century castle is prominent on a rocky outcrop to the south, and very photogenic with its crenellated battlements.

Ciminna, further east, has a number of interesting churches including the Chiesa Madre with 17th-century stuccoes by Scipione and Francesco Li Volsi and a painting of *St John the Baptist* by the architect Paolo Amato, who was born here. The village was famously used as a location in Visconti's film *The Leopard* (1963).

The little hill town of **Mezzojuso** (*Menzil el-Jusuf*, 'Village of Joseph') has Arab origins. Settled by Albanians in the 15th century, it has two mother churches, side by side in the main square. The church of the Annunziata follows the Latin rite while that of San Nicola holds Greek Orthodox services. The Basilian monks of the convent behind the church specialise in the art of restoring ancient books.

Vicari, above the fertile valley of the River San Leonardo, has a wonderfully romantic ruined castle, probably built by the Arabs, with views of extraordinary beauty. Count Roger wintered here after the battles of 1077.

Lercara Friddi (*map p. 574, B3*), founded in 1605, with its attractive crumbling 18th-century churches, was once important for its sulphur mines. When the sulphur economy collapsed at the end of the 19th century, a thousand families emigrated to Venezuela and the USA, practically depopulating the town. In his compilation of Sicilian reflections, *Words are Stones*, Carlo Levi describes the mines and their working conditions here during a strike in 1951. In the town centre is a monument to Frank Sinatra, whose family originated here.

On the southern border of the province, on a hill overlooking the River Platani, is **Castronovo di Sicilia** (*map p. 574, B3*), once a town of strategic importance but now in decline. Much reforestation has been taking place here in the last few years; the inhabitants are farmers and raise milk-cows: the *tuma persa* cheese made here, a Slow Food niche product, has a superb flavour, as does the bread. Many of the churches contain 18th-century stuccoes by Antonio Messina, and the 15th-century Chiesa Madre has works by the Gagini family.

Some way further to the east at **Regaleali** (*map p. 574, C3*) is the famous wine estate of the Tasca d'Almerita family (best reached from Vallelunga in the province of Caltanissetta). The cellars are open to the public on request a day or so before (*open 10–11.30 & 3–6; T: 0921 544011*) and wine can be purchased.

PRIZZI TO CONTESSA ENTELLINA

The medieval town of **Prizzi** (*map p. 574, B3*) stands near a lake formed by damming the River Sosio, beneath curious outcrops of rock. Many of the old houses in the centre have been painted with bright murals. Excavations on the Montagna dei Cavalli in the vicinity have revealed 4th–3rd century BC remains, possibly the ancient city of *Hippana*, destroyed by the Romans during the First Punic War. The finds, and more besides, can be seen in the Museo Hippana at Corso Umberto 14 (*open Tues–Fri 9–1, Sat 4-8, Sun 10–1; T: 091 834 4379*).

The little town of **Palazzo Adriano** is a late 15th-century Albanian colony with its main monuments in Piazza Umberto; it became world-famous when Giuseppe Tornatore used it as the location for his Oscar-winning film *Cinema Paradiso* (1989).

Bisacquino (*map p. 574, A3–B3*) was once an Arab citadel, then a medieval fortress-town, and is now an agricultural centre renowned for cheese and onions. 'Moth-soft Besacquino [sic]' wrote Lawrence Durrell in his *Sicilian Carousel*, an apt description of this gentle place where time stands still. Yet the inhabitants know all about the passage of time: church clocks were still made here until recently, and can be found throughout Italy. There is a Museo dell'Orologio da Torre (*to request visit, T: 0918 351239*), a museum of tower clocks, at Corso Umberto 76, where the last craftsman worked. The bell-tower (1591) of the church of San Francesco d'Assisi is rare because of its triangular shape; it is one of only two in Europe. The film director Frank Capra (1897–1991), who won six Oscars, was born in Bisacquino.

Contessa Entellina (*map p. 574, A3*) is a charming mountain village that takes its first name from the Countess Caterina Cardona di Chiusa (who gave asylum to Albanian refugees in 1450; there is still a numerous Arbëreshe community here) and its surname from Entella (a town of the Elymians which lies to the northwest in a spectacular position on a high, isolated rock). On the extensive plateau, excavations of the ancient city, ravaged in the past by *tombaroli* (clandestine diggers), are in progress.

So far the fortifications, part of the medieval fortress, and a building of 4th–3rd century BC have been identified. The necropoleis lay at the foot of the hill. The archaeological area is always open. The Antiquarium, small but interesting, is at Via I Maggio 1 (*open Tues, Thur, Sat, Sun 9–12 & 3.30–6.30; T: 091 835 5556*). Unique in Sicily is the section dedicated to finds from the Muslim cemetery.

CORLEONE

Corleone (*map p. 574, B2*) is a picturesque town of Arab origin nestled in the hillside, now surrounded by anonymous modern buildings. In recent years it has been notorious for its powerful Mafia gang, whose boss Totò Riina ruled Cosa Nostra for many years until his arrest in 1993, after more than 20 years 'in hiding' in Palermo.

A Lombard colony was established here by Frederick II in 1237. Traces of Corleone's importance as a medieval town can be seen in the old centre, which preserves some fine palace doorways in its narrow streets, and numerous churches (over 100, because every important family felt the need for a personal church). The **Chiesa Madre** (*if closed, ring at the inconspicuous north door, approached from the road on the left of the outside steps through a gate*) contains some interesting wooden statues (16th–17th centuries), wooden choir stalls by Giovanni Battista Li Volsi, and paintings (on the transept altars) by Fra' Felice da Sambuca and (first north chapel) Tommaso de Vigilia (*Adoration of the Magi*).

The **public gardens**, laid out in 1820, are well kept and the **Museo Civico Pippo Rizzo** (*open 9.30–1 & 3.30–7.30, closed Sun afternoon; T: 091 846 3918*), which houses an interesting archaeological collection, is in Palazzo Provenzano; on display is the only Roman milestone yet found in Sicily, from the ancient consular road linking *Panormus* to *Agrigentum* (Palermo–Agrigento).

THE ISLAND OF USTICA

Ustica, with some 1,400 inhabitants, lies a little over 50km northwest of Palermo (*map p. 574*). It is a small fertile island (just over 8.6km square), all that remains of an ancient volcano more than a million years old. The colours of Ustica are memorable; Antonio Gramsci, the prominent Communist who was held prisoner here, remembered the 'impressive rainbows, and the extraordinary colours of the sea and the sky'. Ustica's highest hills rise to c. 240m above sea level. The island was once covered with trees but few woods remain, the landscape now dotted with wheatfields, vineyards, almond groves and orchards, with hedges of prickly pear. Capers and lentils are also produced. Ustica has interesting migratory birdlife, including the peregrine falcon, kestrels, storks, herons, razorbills and cormorants. The rocky shoreline has many grottoes; it is particularly remarkable for its numerous fish— grouper abound, as well as hake, red mullet, prawns, shrimps, lobsters and (in spring) swordfish—and for its seabed, hosting a great variety of seaweed, including the rare *laminaria*. In 1986 the first marine reserve in the Mediterranean was established around the island's coast, bringing renewed prosperity to the island. The reserve has now been extended to include the whole island. There is no source of water on Ustica apart from some of the caves, such as the Blue Grotto, but there is now a desalination plant. The pleasant little village above the port of Cala Santa Maria is well kept, and only crowded in the summer months. One road encircles the island, and mule tracks, ideal for trekking, wind through the interior.

HISTORY OF USTICA

The name Ustica, from the Latin *ustum* (burnt), derives from the colour of its black volcanic rock. It was inhabited in prehistoric times and in the Roman era. The Greeks called it *Osteodes*, (the place of bones), in reference to the 6,000 mercenaries abandoned here by the Carthaginians when they rebelled after a pay dispute at the time of the wars with Syracuse. Attacks of Barbary pirates defeated all attempts to colonise it in the Middle Ages. It remained deserted for many centuries until in 1762 it was repopulated from the Aeolian Islands and Naples by the Bourbons because of its strategic location on the trade route between Naples and Palermo. At the time three towers were constructed to defend the island.

The island was used as a place of exile and as a prison until 1961: Carlo and Nello Rosselli and Antonio Gramsci were held here as political prisoners under the Fascist regime. In September 1943 Italian and British officers met in secret on the island to discuss details of Italy's change of sides.

CALA SANTA MARIA AND THE EAST

In the centre of the bay, close to the water's edge, in an old fishermen's warehouse, is the **Aquarium** of the marine reserve with a series of huge tanks, showing marine life at various depths. The little village above the port of Cala Santa Maria was laid out on geometric lines by the Bourbons in the 18th century. A road winds up to Piazza Umberto (also reached by steps from the port). To the right of the church, Via Calvaria leads uphill to the Via Crucis, where on the left a path continues up to the **Rocca della Falconiera**, a defensive tower now used for exhibitions (the fort is also reached by car along a narrow road paved with pebbles). The tower is on the site of a 3rd-century BC settlement, also inhabited in Roman times. It has been excavated on three levels; the most conspicuous remains include a staircase and some 30 cisterns used to collect rainwater, and a number of tombs. On the ridge overlooking the harbour, in Largo Gran Guardia, is the former Bourbon prison known as Il Fosso (The Ditch), which now houses the **Museo Archeologico** (*open Aug every evening 6–9; other times call to request visit, T: 091 844 9237 or check for updates on www.visitustica.it*). Archaeological material from the island, including Bronze Age objects from the village at Faraglioni (*see below*) and underwater finds, are well displayed. The museum visit can be concluded by descending a ladder (prisoners were thrown through a trapdoor) into the gloomy solitary-confinement cell, the 'Ditch'.

There are marvellous views above the **lighthouse** which marks the eastern tip of the island and the rocky point known as the **Punta Omo Morto**, a nesting place for numerous birds. To the southwest of the lighthouse a necropolis of the 5th–6th centuries AD has been identified.

On the other side of the village stands the **Torre Santa Maria**, another Bourbon tower. Near it are remains of a 16th-century Benedictine convent and interesting old houses known as the *centro storico*, with stables built around courtyards, some of them carefully restored as homes by the local inhabitants.

THE NORTH AND WEST

On the northern tip of the island, at **Faraglioni**, excavations begun in 1974 unearthed a large prehistoric village (14th–13th centuries BC), probably settled from the Aeolian Islands, with some 300 houses built in stone. The defensive walls are among the best fortifications of this period to have been discovered in Italy.

On the west coast, between Cala Sidoti and Caletta, is the central zone of the **Riserva Naturale Marina** (*Information Centre in Piazza Umberto, T: 091 844 8124, www.ampustica.it*), a protected area marked by red buoys where fishing is prohibited and boats have to keep offshore. Swimming is allowed only at the extreme northern and southern ends of the reserve (*limited access*). Above the bay is the Bourbon **Torre dello Spalmatore**, with fine vaulted rooms, owned by the marine reserve and used as a library and conference centre. Just to the south is the lighthouse at Punta Cavazzi. A buoy in the sea here marks an underwater archaeological itinerary for skin-divers where a number of finds from various wrecks have been left *in situ*. Ustica is much visited by divers and the marine reserve collaborates with the fishermen who live on the island to arrange boat trips for visitors. Underwater tours are organised and the waters are particularly rich in hidden caves and slopes.

PRACTICAL INFORMATION

GETTING AROUND

• **By air:** For information about Palermo airport, see p. 76.
• **By rail:** For timetables of all state railway services connecting Palermo, Agrigento, Messina, Trapani, Catania, Caltanissetta and Enna, see the website (*www.trenitalia.it*). Bagheria and Santa Flavia–Solunto, Termini Imerese, and Cefalù are on the main Palermo–Messina line. The nearest station to Alia is Roccapalumba (5km from both towns).

• **By bus:** *NB: Palermo's intercity bus station is in Piazzetta Cairoli, on Corso dei Mille, c. 500m from the railway station (beyond map 16). When calling for information, make sure to ask for the departure point.*
AST (*www.aziendasicilianatrasporti.it*) runs services from Palermo (Viale delle Scienze) to Bagheria, Burgio, Carini, Castelbuono, Cefalà Diana, Corleone,

Isnello, Lercara Friddi, Monreale, Montelepre, Montevago, Palazzo Adriano, Partanna, Partinico, Prizzi, San Cipirello, Solunto, Termini Imerese, and Vicari.

Cuffaro (*www.cuffaro.info*) from Via Balsamo (Palermo railway station) to Agrigento, Canicattì, Comitini, Favara and Racalmuto.

Interbus/Segesta (*www.interbus.it*) to Syracuse (3hrs 15mins) and Trapani (approx. 2hrs). Buses leave Palermo from Via Balsamo and arrive at Piazzetta Cairoli.

Russo Autoservizi (*www. russoautoservizi.it*) from Palermo (Piazzetta Cairoli) to Balestrate, Buseto Palizzolo, Castellammare del Golfo, Cinisi, Custonaci, San Vito Lo Capo, Scopello, Terrasini, Valderice.

SAIS Autolinee (*www.saisautolinee. it*) to a number of destinations on the island including Caltagirone, Caltanissetta, Catania, Catania Airport (2hrs 30mins), Enna, Gela, Messina, Pergusa and Piazza Armerina.

Salemi Autolinee (*www. autoservizisalemi.it*) to Campobello di Mazara, Castelvetrano, Marsala and Mazara del Vallo.

• **By sea:** Siremar (*www.siremar.it*) runs ferries and hydrofoils to Ustica. Liberty Lines (*www.libertylines.it*) has hydrofoils connecting Palermo to Ustica (90mins) and to the Aeolian Islands. Boats for the Aeolian Islands also leave from Cefalù in the summer. Ustica office: Piazza Capitano Di Bartolo (*T: 091 844 9002*).

WHERE TO STAY

BAGHERIA/ASPRA (*map p. 574, B1*)
€€€ **Villa Valguarnera**. The most

imposing of the Bagheria villas, the home of the Duke of Salaparuta, where Dolce and Gabbana have their publicity film shoots. Offers accommodation in 3 self-catering apartments. Car park. In summer also restaurant with fixed-menu service. *Via Gramsci 27, T: 091 777 7816, www.villavalguarnera.com.*

€€ **Centrale Bagheria**. 14 rooms in a recently restructured palace in the city centre. Restaurant. *Via Greco 5, T: 091 934023, www.hotelcentrale.biz.*

€ **Da Franco il Conte**. Friendly, modern establishment with 13 rooms, garage, good restaurant, Count Franco is quite a character. *Via Vallone de Spuches 29, T: 091 966815, www.dafrancoilconte.it.*

€ **Villa Scaduto Residence**. Just outside the fishing village of Aspra, at the foot of Bagheria, restored house with 13 rooms, garden, wine bar and car park. *Corso Baldassare Scaduto 9, T: 091 931320, www.villascadutoresidence.it.*

CASTELBUONO (*map p. 574, C3*)
€€ **Relais Santa Anastasia**. Hotel in a renovated Benedictine abbey surrounded by its own extensive vineyards. Good restaurant, good wine, superb views, nice rooms. Great base for exploring the surrounding area. *Contrada Santa Anastasia. T: 0921 672233, abbaziasantanastasia.com.*

CEFALÙ (*map p. 574, C1–D1*)
€€€ **Alberi del Paradiso**. Quiet eco-friendly hotel, hillside position, lovely garden with small pool and a spa in the ancient water-mill. 55 comfortable modern rooms and good restaurant, shuttle service to Cefalù town centre and private beach. *Via dei Mulini 18, T: 0921 423900, www.alberidelparadiso.it. Beyond map 5.*

€€ **La Plumeria**. Restored palace in the town centre, 10 beautiful rooms, friendly staff, good restaurant. *Corso Ruggero 185, T: 0921 925897, www. laplumeriahotel.it. Map 2.*

€€ **Villa Gaia**. Close to seafront and medieval centre, friendly hotel with 12 rooms and suites, breakfast on the terrace. *Via Maestro Pintorno 101, T: 0921 420992, www.villagaiahotel.it. Map 5.*

CORLEONE (*map p. 574, B2*)

€€ **Casa Mia**. Vineyard on the hillside close to town, producing famous Principe di Corleone wines. 5 quiet and comfortable rooms, restaurant, pool with whirlpool, children's playground, tennis, mini-golf. *Contrada Malvello, T: 091 846 2922 or 328 6029088, www. agriturismo-casamia.com.*

FICUZZA (*map p. 574, B2*)

€ **L'Antica Stazione**. What was once the railway station is now a delightful place to stay, with 8 comfortable rooms decorated by local artists, a good place for naturalists and hikers. The restaurant has an excellent reputation. *T: 091 846 0000, www. anticastazionedificuzza.com.*

ISNELLO (*Map p. 574, C2*)

€€€ **Fattoria Mongerrate Baucina**. Historic farm in the Madonie Park, surrounded by woods, in a good position for touring in the area being midway between Isnello and Collesano. Offers 5 comfortably furnished self-contained apartments (breakfast ingredients from the farm provided). Pool, car park. *Contrada Mongerrate 1, T: 0921 662687 or 340 009 9014, www. fattoriamongerrate.eu.*

MONDELLO (*map p. 574, B1*)

€€ **Villa Esperia**. Attractive Art Nouveau building close to the beach; 22 comfortable bedrooms, garden and good restaurant. *Via Margherita di Savoia 53, Valdesi, T: 091 684 0717, www. hotelvillaesperia.it.*

€ **Il Banano**. B&B in 19th-century villa with bright rooms, garden. Close to beach and main square; airport transfer on request, pets welcome. Minimum 2 nights. *Via Stesicoro 3, T: 091 672 6112 or 328 410 8554, www.ilbanano.com.*

MONREALE

€€ **Hootel** [sic] **Duomo**. ■ B&B situated in front of the cathedral with 3 comfortable rooms. Stairs. Massimiliano is a helpful host. *Via Guglielmo II 2, T: 340 914 4133 or 320 906 426, www. hootelduomomonreale.it.*

MONTELEPRE (*map p. 574, A1*)

€€ **Il Castello di Giuliano**. Modern castle owned by Giuliano's nephew in a panoramic position on the outskirts of this village, still nostalgic for the legendary bandit (*see p. 116*). 23 spacious rooms, good restaurant, especially for pizza in the evenings. Local wines. *Via Magistrato Pietro Merra 1, T: 091 894 1006, www.castellodigiuliano.it.*

PALAZZO ADRIANO (*map p. 574, B3*)

€€ **Casale Borgia Resort**. Old country house 2km from the centre, 10 comfortable rooms (all different), indoor heated pool and fitness centre, delicious food including dishes of the Arbëreshe tradition (the town was founded by Albanian refugees in the 15th century). Pets welcome. *Contrada Favara di Borgia, T: 091 834 8774 or 338 927 4201, www.casaleborgia.it.*

PIANA DEGLI ALBANESI (*map p. 574, B2*)

€ **Masseria Rossella**. Eighteenth-century country villa surrounded by olive groves, with 9 rooms, frescoed ceilings, pool and private chapel, close to the Ficuzza woods and the Rocca Busambra. Organic vegetable garden, restaurant providing vegan or vegetarian dishes on request. *Contrada Rossella, T: 091 846 0012 or 366 469 3129, www.masseria-rossella.com.*

POLIZZI GENEROSA (*map p. 574, C2–D2*)

€€ **Antico Feudo San Giorgio**. A 19th-century farmhouse within the Madonie Park, producing organic wheat, olive oil, wine and vegetables. Accommodation in rooms or apartments, large pool, good restaurant. *Contrada San Giorgio, T: 0921 642613 or 0921 600690, www.feudosangiorgio.it.*

SANTA FLAVIA-PORTICELLO (*map p. 574, B1*)

€€ **Donna Concetta**. Small hotel in a lovely old building overlooking the fishing harbour of Porticello, once belonging to Luigi Pirandello's uncle; all 14 rooms are dedicated to a work by the playwright. Fitness/beauty centre and restaurant. *Via Roma 113, T: 091 939 0060, www.donnaconcetta.com.*

SCLAFANI BAGNI (*map p. 574, C2*)

€€ **Case di Cardellino**. Farm with panoramic views of Piano Battaglia, with 10 lovely rooms in the converted medieval grain silos. Fitness centre, pool. Marvellous home cooking. *Contrada Cardellino, T: 0921 541825, www.lecasedicardellino.it.*

USTICA (*map p. 574*)

€€ **Diana**. Odd round yellow building, panoramic, with 36 comfortable rooms, set in a large park with 2 pools. Good restaurant. *Contrada San Paolo, T: 091 844 9109, www.hoteldiana-ustica.com.*

€€ **Clelia**. Welcoming little hotel with 26 rooms, no restaurant, close to the central square. *Via Sindaco 29, T: 091 844 9039, www.hotelclelia.it.*

€ **Hibiscus**. For a quiet holiday, this farm producing lentils and wine offers self-catering accommodation in 4 air-conditioned cottages immersed in vegetation. There is a restaurant 10mins' walk away. *Località Tramontana, T: 091 844 9179, www.agriturismohibiscus.com.*

WHERE TO EAT

BAGHERIA (*map p. 574, B1*)

€€€ **I Pupi**. Elegant little Michelin-starred restaurant offering beautiful and creative dishes; excellent wine cellar. Booking advisable. Closed June–Sept Sun and Mon lunchtime; Oct–May Sun evening and Mon. *Viale del Cavaliere 59, T: 091 902579.*

€€ **Don Ciccio**. ■ A popular, reasonably-priced family-run *trattoria*, born as a tavern in 1943. No menu, tablecloths or *antipasti*; the traditional starter is a hard-boiled egg with a glass of *zibibbo*. Allow yourself to be guided through the range of fish or meat dishes; when in season, excellent tuna with mint, peas and tomato sauce, or tasty choices from the charcoal grill such as stuffed squid, lamb chops, local sausages, all accompanied by their own wines. Home-made pasta very good. Fantastic, happy atmosphere, worth a detour. Closed Wed, Sun, public holidays and Aug. Don Ciccio also has comfortable rooms close by, with garden and pool. *Viale del Cavaliere 87, T: 091 932442.*

CASTELBUONO (*map p. 574, D2*)

€€€ **Nangalarruni**. ■ Renowned in this part of the world, people come a long way to feast on wild fungi, delicious grills, home-made desserts, accompanied by the best wines. Closed Wed. *Via delle Confraternite 5, T: 0921 671228.*

CASTELLANA SICULA (*map p. 574, D2–D3*)

€€ **Natura in Tavola**. Long-lost recipes of the Sicilian tradition are prepared here, including *capretto a' sciusciarieddu* (kid with vegetables and eggs), wild fungi and herbs from the countryside, and sometimes even *'u cunigghiu*, a preparation consisting of vegetables with anchovies, tuna and dried cod. *Via Battisti 7, T: 0921 642880.*

CEFALÙ (*map p. 574, C1–D1*)

€€€ **La Brace**. An elegant restaurant with a vaguely exotic atmosphere; booking advisable. Grilled meat or delicious fish, very good Sicilian wine list. Closed Mon and lunchtime Tues. *Via XXV Novembre 10, T: 0921 423570. Map 2.*

€€€ **Cortile Pepe**. Attached to the Plumeria hotel. Small, cosy restaurant with a tiny outdoor courtyard serving inventive, skilfully prepared dishes using local ingredients. *Corso Ruggero/ Cortile Pepe 2. T: 0921 421630 or 327 259 5873. Map 2.*

€€ **Ostaria del Duomo**. Overlooking the cathedral, reliable repertoire of Sicilian food, good wines. *Via Seminario 5, T: 0921 421838. Map 2.*

€ **Rossorubino**. Enoteca and delicatessen where you can taste an excellent range of Sicilian wines. *Via Bordonaro 16. T: 0921 423340. Map 2.*

MONDELLO (*map p. 574, B1*)

€€€ **Bye Bye Blues**. The owner, Patrizia, is a Michelin-starred chef and is always inventive. Fish dishes are a speciality but the vegetable *antipasti* are magnificent too. Superb desserts. Good wine list and they make their own liqueurs. Closed Mon. *Via del Garofalo 23, T: 091 684 1415.*

MONREALE (*map p. 574, B1*)

€€ **Bricco and Bracco**. A restaurant for carnivores. No pasta, everything is based on meat, including some unusual cuts and local specialities, all expertly cooked and served. Red wines only, from the best Sicilian vineyards. Closed Mon. *Via Benedetto D'Acquisto 13, T: 091 641 7773.*

€ **Taverna del Pavone**. A short distance from the cathedral, tiny informal *trattoria* which serves good pasta, and delicious home-made almond parfait with hot chocolate sauce. Closed Mon. *Vicolo Pensato 18, T: 091 640 6209.*

POLIZZI GENEROSA (*map p. 574, D2*)

€€ **'U Bagghiu**. Traditional mountain fare, including wild asparagus and fungi when in season, accompanied by local wines. Closed Tues evening. *Via Gagliardo 3, T: 0921 551111.*

SAN CIPIRELLO (*map p. 574, A2*)

€ **Apud Iatum**. Fantastic *antipasti*, home-made pasta dishes, good desserts, also pizzeria in the evenings. Closed Mon. *Corso Trento 49, T: 091 857 6188.*

SAN GIUSEPPE JATO (*map p. 574, A2*)

€€ **Da Totò**. Home-made tagliatelle, delicious desserts; also pizzeria in the evenings. Closed Fri evening. *Via Vittorio Emanuele 251, T: 091 857 3344 or 338 776 3391.*

TERRASINI (*map p. 574, A1*)

€€€ **Il Bavaglino**. Tiny, elegant restaurant (booking advisable) with a garden, the realm of Michelin-starred chef Giuseppe Costa. Traditional dishes with an innovative twist, often using unusual ingredients; good wine cellar. Closed Tues. *Via Benedetto Saputo 20, T: 091 868 2285.*

USTICA (*map p. 574*)

€€€ **Faraglione**. Lovely restaurant on the harbour, ideal for dinner; fresh fish dishes, or a wide choice of pizzas. Open June–Sept. *Via Pio La Torre, T: 091 684 1020 or 339 861 4930.*

€€ **Schiticchio**. Close to the Town Hall, a *trattoria* offering an exciting array of dishes prepared with fresh local fish and vegetables. Sicilian wines. Open every day in summer. *Via Tre Mulini, T: 091 844 9662.*

€€ **Giulia**. Booking essential. The restaurant (also an excellent hotel) is small and very famous. The chef specialises in *cernia* (grouper), either marinated in lemon or cooked with breadcrumbs, tomato, olive oil, lemon and garlic. Closed winter. *Via San Francesco 16, T: 091 844 9007.*

LOCAL SPECIALITIES

ALIA **Bar Centrale** (*Via Garibaldi 32*), has *scattate*, biscuits made of almonds and cinnamon, unique to Alia.

BAGHERIA **Bar Ester**, in the centre (*Via Palagonia 113*), is famous for ice cream and exquisite *cannoli di ricotta*, while at **Don Gino** (*Via Dante 66*) they make truly excellent espresso coffee. You will find award-winning ice cream at **Dolce Gelato** (*Via Alcide de Gasperi 21*) .

BISACQUINO Crunchy biscuits, called *pane nero*, are made from roughly chopped and toasted almonds. Find them at the **Caffè Presioso** (*Piazza Triona 23*).

CASTELBUONO The **Fiasconaro brothers** (*Piazza Margherita 10, www.fiasconaro.com*) produce nougat, liqueurs and a very particular cake called *mannetto*, a light-textured sponge iced with manna in various flavours; served warm, it is the ideal accompaniment for tea or hot chocolate. It keeps for weeks, so you can take it home. They also prepare their award-winning Milanese *panettone*, using sourdough brought back from Lombardy

by their grandfather 60 years ago. In October 2007 Fiasconaro products were among the foodstuffs provided for the astronauts on the *Discovery*. Another confection unique to Castelbuono is *testa di turco*, a kind of blancmange with a layer of flaky pastry in the middle, sprinkled with chocolate and cinnamon; also chocolate-covered roasted almonds.

CASTELLANA SICULA This village in the heart of the Madonie Mountains is famous for the sourdough bread baked at the **Forno Librizzi** (*Corso Mazzini 17*), and also for the exquisite hand-made chocolates filled with almond or pistachio paste sold by **Pasticceria Ferruzza** (*Corso Mazzini 141*).

CEFALÙ **Anchovies**, in olive oil with capers or chillies, are prepared by the fishermen of Cefalù. You will easily find them. **Ciccio** (*Lungomare Giardina 21, www.ciccioshoes.it; map 5*) makes sports shoes to measure; he made his name by making shoes for Formula 1 racing drivers such as Nicki Lauda and Jacky Ickx. In his atelier on Via XXV Novembre (*map 2*), **Roberto Giacchino** makes sculptures from cypress and olive, as well as olive tree roots.

MONREALE As might be expected, there is an excellent school for mosaics in the town, where young people learn the art. Examples can be purchased in Piazza Guglielmo II or at the **Laboratorio del Mosaico Cangemi** (*Via Torres 28*). Monreale pottery is also attractive; here they specialise in applying brightly-coloured glazed trimmings to earthenware vases. **Elisa Messina** is a talented craftswoman (*Via Torres 16, www.elisamessina.it*). Excellent Monreale sourdough bread can be found at **Antica Forno Tusa**, founded in 1908 (*Via Odigitria 39, open*

daily 8.30–2.30, Sat also 5–8).
PIANA DEGLI ALBANESI Extrabar (*Piazza Vittorio Emanuele 4*) is the place to come for the celebrated enormous *cannoli di ricotta*, but they make delicious ice cream and *granita* too.
Lucito (*Via Costantini 3*) is a goldsmith specialising in replicas of antique Sicilian jewellery.
POLIZZI GENEROSA The speciality of the local confectioners is a pie made with fresh cheese, sugar, candied pumpkin, chocolate and cinnamon, called *sfoglio*. The classic address is **Pasticceria Al Castello** (*Piazza Castello 10, closed Wed*), or try **L'Orlando** (*Via Cardinale Rampolla 1*).
SAN GIUSEPPE JATO Monreale DOC Merlot is produced here, on the **Feotto dello Jato estate** (*Contrada Feotto, T: 346 105 6393 or 334 664 3770, www. todarowinery.com*).
SCLAFANI BAGNI For the DOC wines for which this area is so famous, you can visit the **Tasca d'Almerita estate**, Tenuta Regaleali in Contrada Regaleali (*map p. 574, C3; call to request visit, closed Sat, Sun and holidays, T: 0921 544011, www.tascadalmerita.it*). It is also listed as one of Italy's most beautiful gardens (*www.grandigiardini.it*).
USTICA Ustica's historic coffee-house is the **Bar Centrale** (*Piazza Umberto 8*), a popular meeting-place, justly famous for its fruit *granita*.

FESTIVALS AND EVENTS

BISACQUINO Good Friday, evening procession which slowly weaves its way through the streets, singing the Passion of Christ in Sicilian, after the symbolic Crucifixion in the church of the Calvario.

CACCAMO Palm Sunday morning, *'U Signuruzzu a cavaddu*, little boys chosen for their good behaviour and small size, mime the entry of Jesus (on a small donkey) and the Apostles into Jerusalem.
CASTELBUONO 24 June, feast of the patron St John the Baptist, with nocturnal banqueting on boiled potatoes and broad beans.
CEFALÙ 14 Aug, an evening procession of fishing boats, lit up with lanterns, goes from the harbour to Punta Kalura and back for the *Madonna della Luce*. Sept, Sherbet festival, dedicated to ice cream, *granita* and sorbets (*www. sherbethfestival.it*).
COLLESANO Good Friday, *Festa della Casazza*, when the Passion of Christ is re-enacted (*www.collesano.org*).
GANGI Palm Sunday, solemn Procession of the Confraternities, white-robed worshippers accompanied by drummers, visiting all the churches of the town (*www.pasquainsicilia.it*).
GERACI SICULO Aug, the *Giostra dei Ventimiglia*, with jousting, pageants, music, dancing, medieval cookery demonstrations, to celebrate the triumphant times of Giovanni Ventimiglia (*www.siciliainfesta.com*).
GIBILMANNA 1st Sunday in Sept, pilgrimage.
GRATTERI On the first Thur after Corpus Domini (June), *'A Tuccata di Lupi*, a very ancient ceremony, takes place with much beating of drums. It goes back to the time when the young men used to go hunting wolves on that day. 8–9 Sept, feast of the patron St James (Giacomo) (*www.gratteri.org*).
ISNELLO 5–7 Sept, feast of the patron St Nicholas. 29 June, broad bean and boiled potato feast. 1 May, pancake feast

(*www.siciliainfesta.com*).

MEZZOJUSO Last Sun before Lent, *Il Mastro di Campo*, when the town inhabitants enact the story of Count Cabrera who, madly in love, tries to make away with Queen Blanche of Navarre. Cannons are fired, biscuits are thrown into the crowd, Garibaldi's soldiers intervene, then the actors offer wine, cheese and barbecued sausages to everybody (*www.prolocomezzojuso.it*).

MONREALE Nov, *Settimana Musica Sacra*, a week dedicated to sacred music, performed in the cathedral.

PIANA DEGLI ALBANESI Easter celebrations are very special here. On Good Friday and Easter Sunday women wear gorgeous traditional dress, ancient Albanian hymns are sung in the cathedral, there are readings from the Gospel in seven languages, then a colourful procession takes place, and the traditional red eggs are distributed (*www.pasquainsicilia.it*).

POLIZZI GENEROSA End of Aug, hazelnut fair with parades of Sicilian carts and folk music (*www.siciliainfesta. com*). 3rd Sun in Sept, feast of St Gandulph. 26 Dec, festivities when a huge bonfire is lit in front of the ruined church of La Commenda (*www. polizzigenerosa.it*).

PRIZZI Easter Sun, *L'Abballu dei Diavoli*, or Dance of the Devils. In the morning, Death, dressed in yellow, and the Devils, dressed in red and wearing metal masks, race through the streets trying to capture souls to send to Hell (the nearby inn). In the afternoon the Madonna meets her Son Jesus, and they and the Angels, who fight with swords, defeat the Devils and Good triumphs over Evil once again.

SCLAFANI BAGNI Last Sun in June, procession of the *Ecce Homo* (*www. siciliainfesta.com*).

TERRASINI Easter Sat and Sun, '*A festa di li Schietti* is probably of pagan origin and means 'the feast of the bachelors'. A young man who wants to prove his strength has to lift an orange tree weighing about 50kg with one hand, then parade it around the town on his shoulders until he reaches the home of the girl he admires, when the orange tree is raised again. If she is suitably impressed with his strength, she may decide to marry him (*www. prolocoterrasini.it*).

USTICA June–July, *Rassegna Internazionale di Attività Subacquee* dedicated to underwater activities, with meetings, competitions and diving.

Trapani

Trapani (pron: TRApani), the most important city on the west coast of the island, is the capital of a region where the wide, open landscapes, full of light reflected off the sea, are picked out in white, straggling, flat-roofed villages; very North African in atmosphere. Selinunte and Segesta, two of Sicily's most exciting archaeological areas, are in this part of the island, as are the fascinating old cities of Erice, Mazara del Vallo, Marsala and Alcamo, and the beautiful offshore islands of

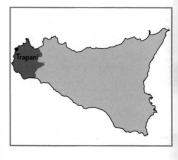

Pantelleria, close to Tunisia, and the Aegadians: Favignana, Levanzo and Marettimo. The ancient industry of extracting salt from seawater evaporated in salt pans is still an important part of the local economy and produces a quality of salt that matches the best in the world; the salt-pans of Trapani and Marsala are a UNESCO World Heritage Site. Local coral is still worked in Trapani and Sciacca. Other local products include excellent olive oil guaranteed by the DOP label, olives, cheese and black bread, but the place of honour goes to the fine DOC wines, including the various Marsalas, the acclaimed Bianco d'Alcamo, and those from Pantelleria; the province of Trapani, in fact, contains more than half of the vineyards of Sicily, and after Bordeaux, is the second largest wine-producing district in Europe.

TRAPANI

The city of Trapani (*map p. 575, B1*) lies below the headland of Mt San Giuliano, with the Aegadian Islands close offshore. The old city occupies a scimitar-shaped promontory between the open sea to the north and the port and salt marshes to the south, although from inland the town is approached through extensive modern suburbs laid out on a regular chessboard pattern. The elegant shops in the traffic-free old town have inviting window displays and the Corso is lined with interesting monumental buildings. The collection of decorative arts in the Pepoli Museum is one of the best on the island and is particularly famous for its works in coral.

TRAPANI
View across the salt pans.

HISTORY OF TRAPANI

Drepana or *Drepanon*, meaning 'scythe' (legend has it that the goddess Demeter dropped her scythe into the sea while distractedly searching for her daughter Persephone, and it became the promontory of Trapani), was the earliest recorded settlement here, when it was the port of *Eryx* (modern Erice). It was raised to the status of a Carthaginian city when Hamilcar Barca brought down part of the population of Eryx in 260 BC, but was captured for the Romans by Catulus only 19 years later, in 241 BC.

Trapani acquired strategic importance as the maritime crossroads between Tunis, Anjou and Aragon in the 13th century. In 1270 King Theodore of Navarre died in Trapani of typhoid, contracted near Tunis while he was returning from the Crusades, and here on the 'Scoglio del Malconsiglio', a rock at the extreme end of the cape, John of Procida is supposed to have plotted the Sicilian Vespers with his confederates. Edward I of England, who also landed at Trapani on his return from the Crusades in 1272, received the news of his accession to the throne here. The city was particularly favoured by Peter of Aragon, who landed at Trapani as the saviour of Sicily in 1282 after the Sicilian Vespers, and also by Charles V. After passing a relatively prosperous time under the Spanish Bourbons, the Bourbons of Naples were decidedly unpopular, and Trapani took part in the 1848 rebellion with such fervour that the city was awarded the silver medal for valour after Unification. The city was heavily bombed during World War Two.

EXPLORING TRAPANI

PIAZZA VITTORIO VENETO AND VIA GARIBALDI

In the large Piazza Vittorio Emanuele (*map 3–4*), laid out in the mid-19th century, is a monument (1882) to King Vittorio Emanuele II by Giovanni Dupré, one of his last works. From here Viale Regina Margherita skirts the north side of Villa Margherita, a charming garden laid out in the late 19th century, to **Piazza Vittorio Veneto** (*map 3*), the administrative centre of the city, with early 20th-century buildings including the elegant Art Deco post office (1924). Close by is the Castello di Terra, a castle of ancient origin reconstructed during the centuries and converted into a barracks in the 19th century. The outer walls now surround the modern police station (Questura). Streets to the north give access to the seafront, with a good view of the old town on the promontory.

Via Garibaldi leads towards the old centre past the 18th-century Palazzo Fardella Fontana, with an elaborate window above its portal, and the 18th-century Palazzo Riccio di Morana, decorated with stuccoes. The 17th-century church of **Santa Maria dell'Itria** has a façade completed in 1745. On the main altar is a work in wood and *papier mâché* representing the Holy Family by Andrea Tipa. Beyond is the 19th-century red-brick Palazzo Staiti opposite the 18th-century Palazzo Milo.

Also on Via Garibaldi is the church of the **Carminello** (*or San Giuseppe; open 9.30–1*

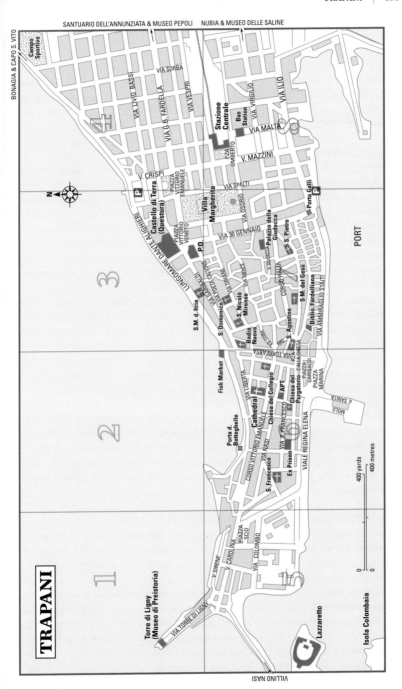

SANTUARIO DELL'ANNUNZIATA & MUSEO PEPOLI   NUBIA & MUSEO DELLE SALINE

BONAGIA & CAPO S. VITO

TRAPANI

Torre di Ligny
(Museo di Preistoria)

Lazzaretto

Isola Colombaia

VILLINO NASI

PORT

0   400 yards
0   400 metres

& 4–8; *may be closed for repairs*), with an 18th-century portal with twisted columns. It was built in 1699 on the spot where the Byzantine general Belisarius in AD 536 founded one of three churches in Trapani for the Basilian monks that accompanied him; the others stood where now we find San Nicolò Mirense and the Badia Nuova. The statue in the apse, of *Joseph and the Young Christ Child* (1789), is a charming sculpture by Antonio Nolfo (an earlier version of the statue, used for processions, is kept in the sacristy). A wooden Crucifix in the church is attributed to Giacomo Tartaglio.

SAN DOMENICO AND SAN NICOLÒ

The Salita San Domenico (with steps and cobbled paving) leads up to the church of **San Domenico** (*map 7; open 9–12*), with a blind 14th-century rose window. The interior contains a remarkable wooden Crucifix (thought to date from the 13th century) in an 18th-century chapel by Giovanni Biagio Amico in the north aisle. The sanctuary preserves the sarcophagus of Manfred, son of Frederick III of Aragon, who died still a child when he fell from his horse. Recent repairs brought to light fresco fragments of the 14th and 15th centuries. The Baroque frames, pulpit and organ (in good condition) bear witness to the wealth of the city in the 18th century, thanks to the importance of its salt and fishing industries.

Nearby, downhill to the south, in Via Barone Sieri Pepoli, is the church of **San Nicolò Mirense**. One of the oldest churches in the city (local legend holds that it stands on the site of a temple of Poseidon), it was rebuilt by the Chiaramonte family in the 14th century and enlarged in 1749 by Giovanni Biagio Amico. Inside, over the main altar, is a marble triptych (1560) carved by Antonello and Vincenzo Gagini, and in the left transept a striking sculptural group of *Christ Between the Two Thieves*, a realistic 18th-century work in wood and *papier mâché* by a local sculptor.

Via delle Arti and Via della Badia lead back to Via Garibaldi and the **Badia Nuova** (or Santa Maria del Soccorso). It has a fine single-nave interior decorated in pink and grey marble and a Baroque nuns' gallery; the marble intarsia floor is 17th century. The *Madonna of the Rosary* over the main altar is by Willem Borremans. To the right is a statuary group by local 18th-century sculptor Cristoforo Milanti of *Our Lady of Succour*, wielding a club to defend two children. The altar to the right of this has a painting of *St Dominic* by Pietro Novelli.

VIA TORREARSA AND THE OLD JEWISH DISTRICT

From the Badia, Via Torrearsa leads right, past the 16th-century **church of the Carmine**, with a fine exterior with tall pilasters and a high cornice, to the seafront passing an attractive market building (1874; *map 6*). There is a fountain with a statue of Venus in the piazza.

Via Torrearsa leads in the other direction to **Palazzo Senatorio**, used as municipal offices, built in 1672, which has an unusual façade with statues on the upper part. Left of Palazzo Senatorio stands the 13th-century **Porta Oscura**, the only surviving medieval gate of the original four which gave access to the walled city, each surmounted by a watch-tower and said to go back to the time of Carthaginian rule. In 1596 the tower was provided with an astronomical clock with two quadrants, representing 'Sun' and

'Moon', which give the time of the day, the equinox and the phases of the moon. The hole in the 'Moon' quadrant represents the planet Earth.

South of Palazzo Senatorio, Via Sant'Agostino leads east from Via Torrearsa to the restored church of **Sant'Agostino** (*map 7*), with its 14th-century portal and intricate rose window (containing symbolic references to the three monotheistic religions), now used for exhibitions of religious art. The church, almost completely destroyed during the bombing raids of World War Two, was built for the Knights Templar by Roger II in 1118, close to their hospice for the assistance of Crusaders or pilgrims to Jerusalem. After a fire in 1425, the ceiling was replaced with an unusual series of painted wooden panels representing grotesque figures and allegories. The surviving ones are now partly in the local Pepoli Museum and partly in the Palazzo Abatellis gallery in Palermo.

The **Saturn fountain** here (a reference to the mythical foundation of the city by that god) is on the site of a 14th-century fountain. Nearby, at Largo San Giacomo 18, is the **Biblioteca Fardelliana** (*open Mon-Fri 9–1.30 & 3–7.30, Sat 9–1; T: 0923 21506 or 0923 21540*), the prestigious civic library of the province, housed in the former church of San Giacomo, with a fine Mannerist façade. Opened to the public in 1830, it contains many important manuscripts, a collection of etchings, and some 118,000 volumes. Ask to see the Sala Fardella; its marble columns were brought here from the old church of St Roch, and in their turn they come from the great mosque of Arab Trapani. Originating in Tunis, they bear inscriptions from the Koran.

In the rebuilt district of San Pietro, back towards Villa Margherita, in Via Elisabetta, is **Santa Maria del Gesù** (*map 7; open only for Mass Tues-Fri 5.30pm, Sat and days preceding holidays 6pm, Sun 11.30am; closed Mon*), a church with a transitional 16th-century façade and a Renaissance south doorway in Catalan Gothic style bearing an *Annunciation*. The luminous golden interior, with a truss-beam roof, contains a decorative niche with a very beautiful *Madonna and Child* surrounded by angels in enamelled terracotta by Andrea della Robbia, under a marble baldachin by Antonello Gagini.

Further east in the former Jewish district, is the unusual **Palazzo della Giudecca**, usually called 'Lo Spedaletto', with an embossed tower, rusticated walls and 16th-century windows recalling the highly decorated plateresque style of Castile.

ALONG CORSO VITTORIO EMANUELE

The broad, handsome Corso Vittorio Emanuele (*map 6*) leads west from Via Torrearsa towards the end of the promontory. On the right is the **Chiesa del Collegio dei Gesuiti** (*open 9–12 & 4–7*), built c. 1614–40 and designed by Natale Masuccio. The Baroque façade was added later. Recent repairs have revealed an admirable marble icon of the Madonna. Ask to see the magnificent old wooden cupboards in the sacristy.

Beyond the monumental former Collegio dei Gesuiti (now a school), preceded by a portico, is the **Cathedral of San Lorenzo** (*open 9–12 & 4–7*), built by Giovanni Biagio Amico in 1743. On the fourth south altar is a *Crucifixion* attributed to the local 17th-century artist Giacomo Lo Verde, a follower of Pietro Novelli. On the second north altar is a painting of *St George* by Andrea Carreca and on the fourth, a fine *Deposition* showing Flemish influence.

In front of the cathedral, Via Giglio leads to the **church of the Purgatorio** (*open 9–12 & 4–7*), with statues of the Twelve Apostles on the façade. This is where the figures of the *Misteri*, statuary groups made of *mistura*: (wood, cloth, *papier mâché* and glue), are kept in between the Good Friday processions. The church has a fine tiled dome and elaborate façade by Giovanni Biagio Amico.

Nearby in Via San Francesco is a 17th-century **ex-prison house**, with four caryatids on its façade, and, further along, on the opposite side of the street, the **church of the Immacolatella**, with a delightful apse by Giovanni Biagio Amico (1732). At the end of the street, the green-domed church of **San Francesco** (13th–17th centuries) can be seen, next to a beautiful doorway. In the single-nave interior are statues representing the Cardinal Virtues, and on the left wall is a curious 17th-century tombstone dedicated to the 'death of the nation of Armenia', with a bilingual inscription.

The Corso continues past (left) the 18th-century **Palazzo Berardo Ferro**, which has an inviting courtyard, and then **Palazzo Alessandro Ferro** (1775), decorated with a clock and busts in medallions. Beyond on the right is the little **Porta delle Botteghelle** (13th century); outside can be seen the defensive fortifications which protected the town from the sea.

THE TORRE DI LIGNY HEADLAND

The promontory ends at the **Torre di Ligny** (*map 1*), a fortress built in 1671 by the Spanish viceroy. It has been well restored to house the Museo Civico (*open May–Sept 10.30–12.30 & 5–7.30, Oct–April 10.30–12.30 & 4–6.30, closed Mon, Sun and holiday mornings; T: 338 724 4970*), with a section devoted to submarine archaeology displaying amphorae and two bronze helmets of 241 BC, probably lost at sea during the First Punic War. There is a spectacular panorama from the roof. From beside it there is a view across the bay to the small **Isola Colombaia** (*map 5*), whose castle was once the main defence of the port and the base for the Romans' siege operations in 241 BC. An excellent example of military architecture, the first fortress on the spot was, according to legend, built by the surviving Trojans when they arrived here with Aeneas, but Diodorus Siculus tells of a castle built by Hamilcar Barca in 260 BC. Under the Arabs the castle was restored and used as a lighthouse, and the Normans strengthened it. In 1320 Frederick III of Aragon added the beautiful octagonal tower, and in 1714 the lantern was added by Giovanni Biagio Amico. It was first used as a prison in 1821, for rebellious Sicilians who were claiming independence, and later for common criminals, until 1965 when it was abandoned.

SANTUARIO DELL'ANNUNZIATA

Inland, in the modern part of town, at Via Conte Agostino Pepoli 179, is the Santuario dell'Annunziata (*c. 4km from the centre; beyond map 4; bus nos 1, 10 and 11; open 7–12, 4–8; T: 0923 539184, www.madonnaditrapani.org*). A church on this site has belonged to the Carmelite Order since the 13th century, when they arrived here as refugees from Mt Carmel in the Holy Land. The present structure dates from the early 14th century, rebuilt in 1760. Little remains of the 14th-century church except the west front with a rose window which overlooks a garden. The bell-tower dates from 1650.

The unusual grey and white interior was redesigned in the 18th century by Giovanni Biagio Amico. Off the south aisle is the beautiful Cappella dei Pescatori (the fishermen's chapel), built in 1481, perhaps an adaptation of an earlier chapel. On the left of the presbytery is the Cappella dei Marinai (the seamen's chapel), another attractive chapel built in the 16th century in a mixture of styles. From the sanctuary, which has a lovely apse, two elegant 16th-century doorways lead into the Cappella della Madonna; here another arch, with sculptures by Antonino Gagini (1531–7) and a bronze gate of 1591 by Giuliano Musarra, gives access to the inner sanctuary containing a highly-venerated 14th-century statue of the *Madonna and Child*, known as the **Madonna di Trapani**, a very fine work by Nino Pisano or his workshop. Below the statue is a tiny silver model of Trapani by the 17th-century silversmith Vincenzo Bonaiuto, who also made the silver statue in the Chapel of Albert of Trapani, to the right of the Cappella della Madonna.

MUSEO PEPOLI

Beyond map 4. Entrance to the right of the Santuario church façade. Open Mon–Sat 9–5.30, Sun and holidays 9–12.30; last tickets 30mins before closing. T: 0923 553269.
The Museo Regionale Pepoli, housed in the former Carmelite convent, holds a municipal collection formed in 1827; a group of Neapolitan paintings which belonged to General Giovanni Battista Fardella; and a large fine- and applied-art collection donated by Count Agostino Pepoli in 1906. The exhibits are beautifully arranged and well labelled. The entrance is through the paved 16th–17th-century cloisters, with palm trees.

Two rooms on the ground floor contain architectural fragments and a wooden ceiling salvaged from a chapel, along with a sculpted 16th-century portal by Bartolomeo Berrettaro, a stoup of 1486 from the Santuario dell'Annunziata, and works by the Gagini, notably a figure of *St James the Great* (1522) by Antonello Gagini.

The first floor is devoted to the museum's collections of paintings and decorative arts, the archaeological collection and the Arab art section. Paintings range from Roberto di Oderisio's *Pietà* (c. 1380), the early 15th-century Master of Trapani's polyptych *Madonna and Child with Saints* (from the church of Sant'Antonio Abate) and *St Francis Receiving the Stigmata* attributed to Titian, to a portrait of the politician Nunzio Nasi (c. 1902) by Giacomo Balla. Displays of wooden figurines by Giovanni Matera illustrate the *Massacre of the Innocents* in 16 tableaux.

The superb collection of decorative arts, the work of local craftsmen from the 17th–19th centuries, includes scenes of the *Adoration of the Magi* and *Nativity* by Andrea Tipa in wax, alabaster and coral; a late 17th-century salt cellar; magnificent 18th–19th-century Sicilian coral jewellery and a 17th-century chalice. Particularly important are the charming crib figures (the best by Giovanni Matera) and Nativity scenes. Elaborate 17th-century objects in red coral—a skill for which Trapani is particularly famous— include a *Crucifixion* and a candelabrum.

The archaeological collection has been prepared for display, but at the time of writing had yet to be opened to the public. Arabic art includes textiles, majolica, lamps, glassware and funerary inscriptions (10th–12th centuries). At the top of the stairs, in the first corridor, are majolica-tiled floors, including one with a splendid scene of tuna fishing (the Mattanza; *see p. 182*). The small prints and drawings collection here includes works by the printmakers Stefano Della Bella and Jacques Callot. The flag of *Il Lombardo*, the ship sailed by Garibaldi and the 'Thousand', is owned by the museum.

THE SALT PANS OF TRAPANI

The *saline* or salt pans of Trapani can be seen from the secondary road which runs from the port to Marsala. A number of windmills survive, turning Archimedes screws in order to raise the seawater from one pan to the next in spring, and to grind the salt in summer. Much of the area is now a nature reserve run by the WWF (Riserva Naturale delle Saline di Trapani e Paceco: *T: 0923 867700 or 327 562 1529, www. salineditrapani.it*), and flamingoes, avocets (symbol of the reserve) and black-winged stilts nest here. At Nubia, on the coast c. 5km south of Trapani (*map p. 575, B2*), is the **Museo del Sale** (*open March–Oct 9.30–7, winter on request; T: 0923 867061 or 320 657 5455*). Here an old wooden mill is now used to illustrate the ancient salt-extracting industry, started here by the Phoenicians and still working a number of pans between Trapani and Marsala. Mounds of salt, protected by tiles, are a common sight in the area, the salt being exported all over the world. The wind and sun here favour evaporation, while the seawater has a naturally high level of salinity. From February to March seawater is pumped by the windmills from a canal into the salt pans. The water level is gradually decreased, encouraging the evaporation process and the water assumes a reddish colour as the mineral content becomes more concentrated. The harvest begins in July, before total evaporation, avoiding the deposit of harmful minerals; the salt is then raked from the pans into mounds to dry.

ERICE

Erice (*map p. 575, B1*) is a medieval walled town perched on top of Mt San Giuliano (751m), an isolated limestone spur high above the sea. It can be reached in ten minutes by cableway from Trapani. The number of permanent residents has now dropped to about 300, and many of the houses are occupied only in the summer months by people from Trapani or Palermo who come here to escape the heat: the number of inhabitants in August rises to about 5,000. By far the most populous part of Erice is at the foot of the hill, close to Trapani. The locals call their town *'u Munti*, the mountain. It is often shrouded in a mist, known as *il velo di Venere* (the veil of Venus), and it can be very chilly here, the steep cobbled streets deserted and slippery—even snowy in winter—which contributes to the feeling of isolation. The perfect triangular shape of the town makes it difficult to find one's bearings, despite the fact that it is so small. The view to the north of the pyramid-shaped Mt Cofano, one of the most beautiful promontories on the coast of Sicily, is exceptional. To the southwest there is another memorable view of Trapani and the Aegadian Islands and, on a clear day, Cape Bon in Tunisia can be seen, and looking east, even Mount Etna.

The grey stone houses of Erice (mostly dating from the 14th–17th centuries), hidden behind high walls, and the beautiful cobbled streets, give the town an austere aspect.

But behind the walls are many charming courtyards, some of which have little gardens. There are no fewer than 60 churches in the town, testifying to the once large population.

HISTORY OF ERICE

Eryx, an Elymian city said to have been founded by Aeneas and his surviving Trojans, was famous all over the Mediterranean for its magnificent temple to the goddess of fertility. This splendid site, naturally defended and visible for miles around, was a noted landmark for navigators from Africa and was an important sanctuary from at least the period of Phoenician dominance. The Phoenician goddess worshipped here was Astarte. Later, under the Romans, the temple was dedicated to the cult of Venus Erycina. It is said that the numerous flocks of pigeons that roosted here and which were thought to be the goddess' pets, would disappear each year for a period of nine days to accompany the goddess on a brief visit to her shrine at Sicca Veneria (in northwest Tunisia). Her return would be signalled by the arrival of a sole rose-coloured pigeon that was soon followed by all the others.

In 415 BC the inhabitants of nearby Segesta took the visiting Athenian ambassadors to see the rich treasury of the temple, which convinced Athens to take their side against Selinunte and Syracuse (the Segestans were pretending to be wealthier than they actually were, and thus capable of financing the expedition), a decision which led to the fatal Athenian attack on Syracuse in the same year and their consequent defeat (*see p. 344*). Captured by Pyrrhus in 278 BC, the site was destroyed in 260 by Hamilcar Barca. The Roman consul Lucius Junius Pullus took the hill in 248 and was besieged by Hamilcar, who was himself blockaded by another Roman army until the Carthaginians were defeated by the Romans, led by Catulus.

The cult of the goddess reached its maximum splendour under the Romans and the sanctuary was restored for the last time by Tiberius and Claudius. The Arabs called the mountain Jebel Hamid, while Count Roger—who had seen St Julian in a dream while besieging it—changed it to Monte San Giuliano, a name it kept until 1934. The city thrived in the 18th century (with a population of around 12,000) and there were many religious communities. The town is now known for its Ettore Majorana Cultural Centre, founded by the local physicist Antonino Zichichi in 1963.

THE MATRICE

The entrance to the town is by **Porta Trapani** (*map 3*), beyond which Via Vittorio Emanuele climbs steeply uphill. Just to the left is the **Matrice** (Assunta; *the church and its campanile form part of the MEMS Erice la Montagna del Signore, a 'museo diffuso' involving the whole town. Historical collections of various types are displayed in several of the previously closed churches; a combined ticket, on sale at the sites, is available to visit them all. Open March 10–2, April, May, June 10–6, July–Aug 10–8, Sept 10–7, Nov–Dec 10–12; closed Jan–Feb; T: 0923 869123*). The rose window over the porch, similar to that of the church of St Augustine in Trapani and perhaps from the same workshop, is

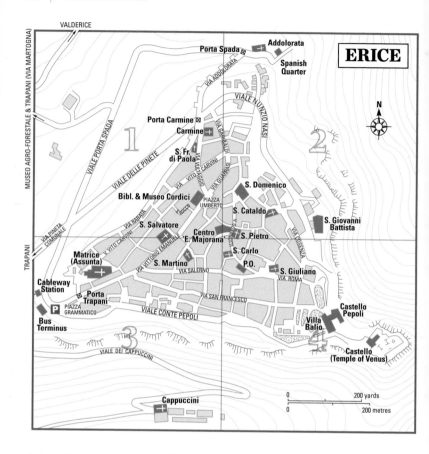

ERICE

of a beautiful design featuring columns borne on interlaced arches which weave in and out of each other in an abstract design which recalls Islamic architecture. The porch itself was added later, in 1426. The splendid detached campanile (28m) was built as an Aragonese watch-tower c. 1315 by Frederick III, several years before the foundation of the church. The interior received its impressive neo-Gothic form, with an elaborate cream-coloured vault, in 1852, after the collapse of the roof. The apse is filled with a huge marble altarpiece (1513) by Giuliano Mancino. In the sanctuary, through a small round opening on the left wall, a fresco fragment of an angel can be seen, the only part of the 15th-century decoration to have survived. The north chapels display gold and silverware, monstrances and reliquaries, the treasures from Erice's many churches, along with vestments and altar-cloths. Also on view here is a copy of the 16th-century painting of the *Madonna of Custonaci* (the venerated patron of Erice); the original is now on display in the sanctuary of Custonaci on the coast. In a south chapel is a marble *Madonna* (1469) by Domenico Gagini, with a finely-carved base. Outside, on the south wall, there are nine iron crosses said to come from the Temple of Venus (*see p. 143*).

VIA VITTORIO EMANUELE AND THE POLO MUSEALE CORDICI

Via Vittorio Emanuele leads steeply uphill past several old shopfronts and characteristic courtyards. At a fork Via Vittorio Emanuele continues left past the ruined Gothic church and monastery of the **Santissimo Salvatore** (*open as the Matrice; see above*). Perhaps the oldest religious institution in the town, it was originally a Chiaramonte palace which in 1290 was given to the Benedictine nuns, who were all wealthy aristocrats. Not much of the monastery is accessible, apart from the huge kitchens where every day they baked bread for the poor and dainty sweets for the rich, especially at Eastertime. Close by is a lovely old narrow street which leads downhill (and has a distant view of the sea). To the right Via Bonaventura Provenzano ends at a house with a Baroque doorway and window near the church of **San Martino** (*map 3; open as the Matrice; see above*), with another Baroque portal, and an interesting collection of wooden carvings in the interior.

Just before reaching Piazza Umberto, beside a charming café in a 19th-century palace, a flight of steps leads down left to the monumental doorway with four columns of San Rocco (*closed*) and the **Polo Museale Cordici**. The museum (*map 1; open Nov–March Sat, Sun and holidays 10–4; April–May 10–6; June–14 July 10–7; 15 July–14 Sept 10–8; 15 Sept–Oct 10–7; other days on request; T: 366 671 2832 at least 24hrs before; www.fondazioneericearte.org*) is named after the local historian Antonino Cordici (1586–1666). The collection is arranged thematically in a series of rooms on two floors, and includes archaeological material, weaponry (mid-18th–mid-20th century), decorative arts, paintings, sculpture and contemporary art. The highlight of the collection is a beautiful relief of the *Annunciation* by Antonello Gagini, one of his finest works (1525).

PIAZZA UMBERTO AND VIA VULTAGGIO

The central **Piazza Umberto** (*map 1*) is the only large open space in the town. An elegant *palazzo* is now used by a bank and a long 19th-century building houses the Town Hall. The library in this building was founded in 1867 with material from the suppressed convents of the city. It now has c. 20,000 volumes. Close by is the tiny opera house, Teatro Gebel el Hamid (*T: 0923 869189*).

Via Guarrasi leads north out of the piazza and immediately on the left, a stepped street (Via Argentieri) leads down across Via Carvini into Via Vultaggio, which continues to wind down past the 17th-century church of **San Francesco di Paola** (*open 10–12.30*), with a Classical façade. The beautiful interior was restored in 1954 by an American benefactor. It has white stucco decoration in very low relief on the walls and the barrel vault, a worn tiled floor in the sanctuary, fine woodwork, and popular votive statues.

Lower down on the right is the 14th-century Palazzo Militari, with Gothic traces, next to the Gothic church of the Carmine (*closed*). The nearby **Porta Carmine** has a worn, headless statue of Albert of Trapani, a patron saint of Erice, in a niche on its outer face.

THE TOWN WALLS

The magnificent walls, which stretch from Porta Spada (*map 2*) to Porta Trapani (*map 3*), protected the only side of the town which has no natural defences: on all the other sides the sheer rockface made Erice one of the most impregnable fortresses on the island. The walls are constructed on huge blocks of rough stone which probably date from the Elymian period (c. 1200 BC), above which the square blocks added by the Carthaginians can be seen. The masonry in the upper parts, with stones of smaller dimension, date from the 6th century BC. The defences were strengthened in the Roman era and in the Middle Ages, and six postern gates and 16 medieval towers survive. Inside the gate the stepped **Via Addolorata** leads down past a well-preserved stretch of the walls, with a distant view ahead of Mt Cofano, to the church of the Addolorata (or Sant' Orsola), surrounded by a little garden.

In this remote and picturesque corner of the town is the Norman **Porta Spada** (*map 2*), where the Jewish cemetery was situated. Outside Porta Spada is the so-called **Spanish Quarter** (Quartiere Spagnolo), a desolate group of buildings on a spur, intended by the Spanish to be the barracks for their troops in the 17th century, and for some reason never finished. Local people say the place is haunted by Birrittu Russu or 'Red Cap', the phantom of a soldier hanged for murder. He has been spotted over the centuries in various parts of the city, but especially in the Spanish quarter—and it is easy to believe it on damp, foggy winter nights. Near the gate a fierce battle was fought during the Sicilian Vespers, hence the name Porta Spada, meaning 'Gate of the Sword'. At the time of writing it was announced that a coffee bar will be opened here soon, in the hope of chasing away any evil spirits.

From **Porta Carmine** (*map 1*) Via Rabatà leads back to Porta Trapani following the walls where there are a number of postern gates. Tiny narrow alleyways, designed to provide shelter from the wind, lead up left to Via Carvini and Piazza Umberto.

ON AND AROUND PIAZZA SAN DOMENICO

On Piazza San Domenico, the former church of **San Domenico**, with a Classical porch (*map 2*), has been restored as a lecture hall for the Ettore Majorana Centre (*see below*). From the right side of the church, Via San Cataldo leads downhill (and right) past a neo-Gothic electricity tower to the bare façade of **San Cataldo** (*open summer 10–1*), on the edge of the old town. It was founded before 1339 and rebuilt in 1740–86. It contains a stoup of 1474 by the workshop of Domenico Gagini.

Further downhill and to the right is the deconsecrated church of **San Giovanni Battista** (*open as the Matrice; see p. 139*) on the cliff edge, with a 15th-century dome whose shape recalls Arab architecture, and an ancient side doorway. It contains a collection of marble and stucco statues from the closed churches of Erice, including a *St John the Evangelist* by Antonello Gagini and a *St John the Baptist* by Antonino Gagini.

From Piazza San Domenico, Via Guarnotti leads up right to the church of **San Pietro** (*open summer 10–1*), with an 18th-century portal. Beside it is an arch over the road and on the right (at no. 26) a convent has been restored as the headquarters of the **Ettore Majorana International Centre for Scientific Culture**. Founded in 1963, this has become a well-known centre of learning where courses and seminars are held for scientists from all over the world.

Via Guarnotti continues past the former convent and orphanage next to the bare façade of **San Carlo** (*map 4; open 10–12.30*). It has a pretty majolica floor and on a side altar there is a statue of *Our Lady of Succour* with a tiny relief of *St Michael Archangel* on the base. The nuns' choirs are protected with carved wooden screens.

On the right is the Post Office and downhill on the left is a pleasant raised piazza with the statue of Albert of Trapani in front of the deconsecrated church of **San Giuliano**, with an elegant 18th-century campanile. This church (*open as the Matrice; see p. 139*) now holds the statues of the *Misteri*, which are taken in procession through the streets of Erice on Good Friday, and the wax figurines once made by the nuns.

THE CULT OF VENUS IN ERICE

The Temple of Venus in Eryx was highly regarded by the Phoenicians as well as by the Greeks, who considered it to be one of the most important temples of Aphrodite in the Mediterranean. This status allowed the city to maintain a privileged position on the island while it was being contested by the Carthaginians and the Greeks between the 6th and 3rd centuries BC. Thanks to a quirk of mythological fortune, the people of Eryx were also able to build an important relationship with the rising power of Rome, which was of even greater benefit to them in the long run. Aeneas, one of the key figures in Roman mythology, was a son of Venus, and the story was told that he had visited the temple at Eryx on his way to the Italian peninsula. This myth led, in 215 BC, to a temple of Venus Erycina being dedicated on the Roman Capitol. The Roman governors of Sicily greatly honoured the temple in Eryx and funnelled tax contributions from some of the other cities of Sicily into its coffers. Thanks to the mythological kinship link, the Roman emperor Tiberius was persuaded to pay for the later restoration of the temple.

As at the Carthaginian temple of Astarte at Sicca Veneria, sacred prostitution was also practised at this temple in Erice. In his *Geography*, Strabo writes that the temple had previously been full of female temple slaves or hierodules, who had been dedicated by many people, both residents and foreigners, in fulfilment of vows, but that this had ceased to be the case at the time that he was writing (c. AD 17–23). Neither Strabo nor any other ancient source gives particulars of the situation at Erice but this has not prevented persistent rumour: that the girls were initiated at the age of 12 or 13 after being trained in the art of lovemaking; that they retired at 21, rich and were much sought-after as wives; that visitors to the temple were expected to leave gifts for the girls in exchange for the sexual act, during which it was believed they assumed the guise of the goddess herself; and that the girls were fed on large quantities of milk and honey to make them pleasantly fat. It is also said that they seldom conceived, perhaps because they were made to drink a concoction of hemlock and parsley root specially prepared by the priests.

VILLA BALIO AND THE CASTELLO DI VENERE

Villa Balio (*map 4*) is a delightful public garden with wonderful views, laid out in 1870 by Count Agostino Pepoli on the summit of the hill. It has a monumental entrance with a double staircase on Via San Francesco. Above is the **Castello Pepoli** (*privately owned; no admission*), a Norman castle reconstructed in 1875–85 by Count Pepoli, with a 15th-century tower restored in 1973. The marvellous panorama from the terrace on the left encompasses Mt Cofano, the coast, and San Giovanni Battista on the side of the hill. Below, among the trees, you can see the abandoned neo-Gothic **Torretta**, also built by Count Pepoli.

A ramp leads down from the gardens beside the castle to Viale Conte Pepoli, on the southern edge of the hill, which continues left, ending at the 17th-century steps up to the **Castello di Venere** (*open as the Polo Museale Cordici, see p. 141; T: 346 577 3550*). Above the entrance to the castle is the coat of arms of Charles V and a Gothic window. In the disappointing interior, the ruined Norman walls surround the sacred area which was once the site of the famous Temple of Venus (*see overleaf*), many fragments of which are embedded in the castle masonry. A few very worn fluted Roman column drums can be seen here as well as the so-called Pozzo di Venere, once thought to be a ceremonial pool but more probably a silo or water cistern. The view is breathtaking, extending to Mount Etna, Enna and Caltabellotta.

BAGLIO SAN MATTEO (MUSEO AGRO-FORESTALE)

On the hillside below the town is the interesting Museo Agro-Forestale (*open Mon–Sat 8–2, Sun 10–6*). It is reached from the Raganzili road. About 3km below Erice a signposted turn leads in c. 500m to the gates of the estate, run by the Azienda Forestale. A rough road (c. 1km) continues to the museum in the lovely old Baglio di San Matteo, arranged in rooms around the courtyard. The exhibits include wine- and olive presses, farm carts, saddle and tack, agricultural implements and household objects. There is also a natural history section. The beautifully kept farm of c. 500 hectares, where San Fratello horses and Pantelleria asses are raised, may also be visited. It occupies a spectacular site with fine views towards Capo San Vito, and the vegetation includes fruit trees, dwarf palms, cypresses and forest trees.

THE NORTH COAST

North along the coast from Trapani, at the foot of Mt San Giuliano, is **San Cusumano** (*map p. 575, B1*) where a salt-pan windmill (now a hotel) can be seen. Ships are alerted to the low-lying islands offshore here by a lighthouse. Pizzolungo is the spot where, according to Virgil, Aeneas came ashore, welcomed by King Acestes of Eryx, and where his father Anchises died, obliging Aeneas to bury him here (an event commemorated by a white column). At **Bonagia** the picturesque tuna fishery has been restored as the Tonnara di Bonagia hotel. Beside the little fishing harbour are hundreds of rusting anchors and an impressive tall tower.

Just inland, **Custonaci** has a lovely old sanctuary-church (*open 9–12 & 4–7; T: 0923 971113*), a frequent pilgrimage destination because of the venerated 16th-century panel-painting of the *Madonna of Custonaci*, said to be particularly generous with miracles and hotly contested in the past by Erice. The economy, once based on agriculture, is now supported by a number of stone quarries, where the beautiful red marble called *perlato di Custonaci* is extracted. On the outskirts, a road (signposted

'Grotte Mangiapane') leads past an old quarry to the enormous **Grotta di Scurati** (*map p. 575, B1*) at the foot of Mt Cofano. The cave contains a hamlet, now no longer inhabited. On either side of the paved street are little houses with courtyards, bread ovens and workshops, and high above, the vault of the cave serves as a second roof. The village comes to life at Christmas, in a very successful venture called *Presepe Vivente*, or 'Living Crib' (*see p. 196*), when local people demonstrate the various trades and crafts of the area in the old houses.

Surrounded by barren hills, **Castelluzzo** has a picturesque sloping main street with one-storey houses, and outside the town are groves of almonds and olive trees on the plain, which descends to the seashore. There is a fine view of the lovely headland of Mt Cofano, with Erice in the distance. **Mount Cofano** (659m), a perfect pyramid in shape, is now a nature reserve run by the Azienda Forestale; apart from its sheer beauty, it is interesting for the abundant spring wildflowers, several of which are endemic. On the main road stands the little 16th-century domed church called the **Cubola di Santa Crescenzia**, derived from Arab models.

SAN VITO LO CAPO

At the tip of the headland, San Vito Lo Capo (*map p. 575, B1*) is a seaside resort with gorgeous beaches of pale velvety sand, among the most beautiful in Italy, which are regularly awarded the EU Blue Banners for quality. Laid out on a regular plan in the 18th–19th centuries, the houses are bright with geraniums and bougainvilleas.

In **Piazza Santuario**, the heart of the town, the unusual sanctuary-church (*open 8–8; July, Aug, Sept closes at midnight*) is a square fortress first built by the Byzantines and later fortified by Arabs, Normans and Spaniards in turn, incorporating the ancient 4th-century chapel dedicated to the patron saint Vitus, martyred under Diocletian. In 2003 the crypt was brought to light, with a 5th-century baptismal font. Part of the building is used as a museum (*open summer only, 5.30pm–7.30pm & 9.30pm–11.30pm; T: 0923 972327*) for the collection of ex-votos and other material donated by worshippers from all over the world, and the robes said to have been worn by the saint. From the roof there is a glorious view over the bay. On the eastern side of the lovely promontory of Mt Monaco is a disused tuna fishery overlooking the Gulf of Castellammare.

A deserted road (signposted 'Calampiso') continues high above the shore across bare hills through a North African landscape, with dwarf palm trees and giant carobs, where broom and wildflowers blossom in spring, to the secondary northern entrance to the Zingaro Nature Reserve (*see below*).

CASTELLAMMARE DEL GOLFO

Cradled by mountains, Castellammare del Golfo (*map p. 575, C1*) lies on the bay, a jumble of small houses in pink, cream, yellow and orange. The fishing fleet is still active here, and the town has not yet been entirely won over to tourism. The charm of the place has attracted many second-homeowners from northern Italy, drawn by the different pace of life, to enjoy summer evenings watching the sun drop behind the mountain and the fishermen sitting on the quay preparing the *conzu*, the bait for the night's fishing, while tempting cooking aromas waft from open doorways.

The town was originally founded by the Elymians as the harbour for the city of Segesta. The 18th-century **Chiesa Madre** houses a life-size majolica statue of *Our Lady of Succour*, patron saint of the town, in the act of threatening its enemies with her distaff, balancing the Christ Child on her left arm. The statue has been attributed to the 16th-century Della Robbia workshop in Tuscany. The castle, built by the Saracens in the 9th century and then enlarged by the Normans and later by the Swabians, is now the seat of the civic museum, **Polo Museale** (*open Mon–Sat 9–1 & 3.30–7.30; T: 0924 30217*), with several sections: one is dedicated to life in the area and the close ties of the inhabitants with the sea, displaying antique clothes, furniture, tools, pots and pans, and equipment for fishing and making wine and olive oil; another displays archaeological material, and an interesting private collection (*open Tues–Sat 10–1 & 4–7*) describes the activity of the water mills. A local fisherman has created a fascinating little museum in Via Mascagni 1, the **Museo del Mare 'Uzzaredru'** (the name given to the local fishing-boat; *open on request, T: 335 653 6077*), with his collection of nets, ropes, lamps used on the boats to attract the fish, hooks and other equipment. The old tuna warehouses on the seafront are very attractive; some of these, too, are being restored and turned into summer homes and hotels.

SCOPELLO

A byroad follows the coast north of Castellammare for Scopello (*map p. 575, C1*). Paths lead down to Cala Bianca, Cala Rossa and Baia Guidaloca, beautiful bays on the rocky coast where the sea is particularly clear. **Baia Guidaloca** is locally claimed to be the spot where Nausicaa found the shipwrecked Odysseus and led him back to her father's court.

Scopello itself is a tiny picturesque village. From the little piazza, with its large drinking-trough, an archway leads into the old paved courtyard of an 18th-century *baglio*, with a few trees surrounded by one-storey houses, a number of them now used as cafés or restaurants.

Just beyond the village is the **Tonnara di Scopello**, an important tuna fishery from the 13th century up to the middle of the last century, now available for accommodation (*see p. 189*). It is easily visible on the sea below the road, beside fantastically-shaped rocks on which ruined defence towers are situated. The buildings have been beautifully preserved. A footpath leads down to the seafront, where hundreds of anchors are piled up beside the picturesque old buildings. The sea is very clear in the small cove, where feral cats teach their kittens the art of survival.

THE ZINGARO NATURE RESERVE

The coast road soon ends at the main southern entrance to the Riserva Naturale dello Zingaro (*map p. 575, C1; open mid-Oct–mid-March 8–4; mid-March–mid-Oct 7–7.30; T: 0924 35108, www.riservazingaro.it*), a beautiful nature reserve, the first to be instituted in Sicily (6th May 1981), with 7km of unspoilt coastline that can be explored on foot along marked paths. There are also several beaches where you can swim. Dwarf palms, Mediterranean maquis, ilex, carob, olive and cork oak flourish here amid wheat fields and meadows. No motorised transport of any kind is allowed inside the park;

the keepers use mules to carry out their work. Traditional farming methods are also preserved: durum wheat is sown and reaped by hand, and threshed by mules, before being ground into flour at the old mill inside the reserve.

The museum, about 500m from the Scopello entrance, illustrates the life of the peasants who once lived in the area, and also traditional fishing methods. The Grotta dell'Uzzo, also in the reserve (about 5km from the Scopello entrance), was inhabited in the Palaeolithic era and is now home to six different species of bat. Among the birds, nesting species include Bonelli's eagle, peregrine falcon, and the Sicilian form of the rock partridge; among the mammals are fox, rabbit, porcupine and the garden dormouse. An important part of the reserve consists of the coastal waters, where no fishing is allowed. There is another entrance to the park on its northern border, approached by the road from San Vito lo Capo (*see above*), but visitors are encouraged to use the Scopello access.

SEGESTA

The temple and theatre of Segesta (*map p. 575, C2*) are two of the most magnificently sited Classical monuments in the world. From the old road, the view of the Doric temple, on a bare hillside in deserted country amid the rolling hills west of the Gaggera river, has been admired by travellers for centuries. The theatre is on a second, higher hill to the east. The surrounding countryside is beautiful, with extensive vineyards, tiny olive trees and old farmhouses or *bagli*, and it is peaceful, despite the proximity of the motorway.

HISTORY OF SEGESTA

Segesta, also originally known as Egesta, was the principal city of the Elymians, one of the pre-Greek populations of Sicily. According to legend, the survivors of the Trojan war were led here by Aeneas. The city was rapidly Hellenised, and was continually at war with Selinunte from 580 BC, seeking an alliance with Athens in 426 BC. After the destruction of Selinunte in 409 BC, Segesta became a subject-ally of Carthage, and was saved by Himilco (397 BC) from the attacks of Dionysius of Syracuse. In 307 BC, however, Agathocles sacked the city and slaughtered most of the male population before selling the surviving women and children into slavery and changing the city's name to Dikaiopolis ('Just City'). Diodorus Siculus (*20.71*) says that he murdered most of the population in a single day, and fired a few of the richest from catapults. The city resumed its old name under the protection of Carthage, but treacherously murdered the Carthaginian garrison during the First Punic War, after which it became the first city in Sicily to announce allegiance to Rome. The city's fortunes declined during the Arab period, and by the late 13th century it was abandoned.

THE SITE

Open 9–1hr before sunset, last tickets 1hr before closing (afternoon times can differ when the theatre is in use for shows; if in doubt call ahead); T: 0924 952356; shuttle bus tickets (c. every 30mins) to the theatre can be purchased at the bar (bookshop and toilets).

The ancient city which covered the slopes of Mt Barbaro has been extensively excavated, but the location of the necropolis has not yet been identified. Sporadic excavations have taken place since the end of the 18th century, when the temple was first restored. The theatre was brought to light in 1822. An important sanctuary at the foot of Mt Barbaro was discovered in 1950 and the entire area has been declared an archaeological park.

THE TEMPLE

The temple is situated on a low hill (304m above sea level) on the edge of a deep ravine formed by the Pispisa torrent, across which is a hillside covered with pinewoods. One of the grandest extant monuments of Doric architecture, it is peripteral and hexastyle, with 36 columns (c. 9m high, 2m wide at base) on a stylobate 58m by 23m. The high entablature and the pediments are intact. Its apparently perfectly straight lines are in fact curvatures; the corner columns are slightly thicker than the others, and lean a little towards the centre. All the columns bulge very slightly in the middle (entasis); the stylobate and the entablature are convex, by a matter of millimetres. All was carefully calculated to avoid the optical illusion which, if the lines were perfectly straight, would make them appear distorted when seen from a distance. It was almost certainly an unfinished building, as the columns have not been fluted and the bosses used for shifting the blocks of stone have not been removed. Although it was long thought that the builders had never intended for there to be a cella, archaeologists working on the site in the 1980s discovered that the foundations had been prepared to support one, and its eventual absence is yet another indication that the site was abandoned before it was completed. It can be dated to the later years of the 5th century BC. The building is inhabited by a colony of jackdaws, their garrulous call adding to the mystery of the site.

THE ROUTE TO THE THEATRE

A road leads up to the theatre from the car park. At the foot of the hill, conspicuous excavations of part of the **walls** (and gate) of the ancient city can be seen. Yellow signs mark various excavations including an upper line of walls (2nd century BC) and a **cave dwelling** (re-used in Roman times; protected by a wooden roof). The road ends in an open square now used by the shuttle bus to drop off and pick up passengers, but which was in the ancient world the **agora** (and later forum) of ancient Segesta. Recent work has revealed traces of the once-beautiful and monumental buildings that lined it to the north and west, including a stoa that was over 70m long, fronted by statue bases and small monuments. These structures were built in the 2nd century BC and were abandoned at the beginning of the 3rd century AD. A few information panels provide wonderful reconstruction drawings of how this area would once have looked. A **bouleuterion** has been uncovered to the west of the agora. A path continues towards

SEGESTA
View of the temple.

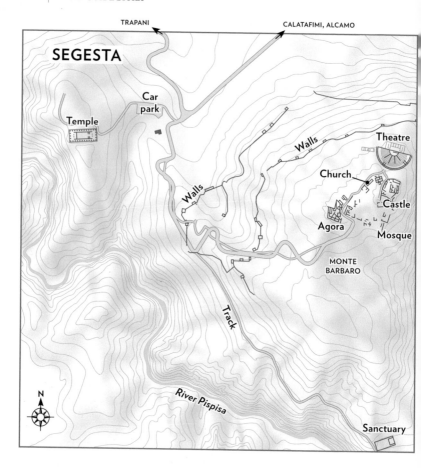

the theatre with a superb view of the temple below. On the right is an enclosure with a **ruined church** (12th–15th centuries). On the summit of the hill are the remains of a 12th–13th-century **castle** and, on the opposite side of the hill, a 12th-century **mosque** (destroyed by the owners of the castle in the 13th century).

THE THEATRE

The theatre occupies a spectacular position near the summit of Mt Barbaro (415m), facing the Gulf of Castellammare beyond Mt Inici (1064m) while more ranges of high mountains rise to the east. It was built in the mid-3rd century BC or possibly earlier. With a diameter of 63m it could hold 3,200 spectators. The exterior of the cavea was supported by a high polygonal wall, which is particularly well preserved at the two sides. Beneath the cavea a grotto with Late Bronze Age finds was discovered in 1927 by the archaeologist Pirro Marconi. Classical drama productions are presented here in summer.

THE SANCTUARY
In Contrada Mango at the foot of Mt Barbaro, to the east near the River Gaggera, is a large Archaic sanctuary (not fully excavated), of great importance, thought to date from the 7th century BC. The temenos measures 83m by 47m. A huge deposit of pottery sherds dumped from the town on the hill above has also come to light here.

CALATAFIMI SEGESTA

The nearest town to the ancient site is Calatafimi Segesta (*map p. 575, C2*), frequently visited by the writer Samuel Butler between 1893 and 1900. He identified in this corner of Sicily all the places described in Homer's Odyssey, and in *The Authoress of the Odyssey* he reveals his belief that the epic was really written by a woman, Nausicaa.

Southwest of the town (signposted 'Pianto Romano', off the SS 113) an obelisk on top of a steep terraced hill commemorates Garibaldi's unexpected victory there on 15th May 1860 against the Bourbon troops, far superior numerically and in terms of the military preparation of their men. A cypress avenue leads to the monument by Ernesto Basile (1892) on which Garibaldi's words on reaching the hill after his disembarkation from Marsala are inscribed: '*Qui si fa l'Italia o si muore*' ('Here we will create Italy or die'). There are spectacular panoramic views from the hilltop.

ALCAMO

At the eastern extremity of the province of Trapani is the agricultural town of Alcamo (*map p. 575, C2*), with numerous fine 18th-century churches. Founded at the end of the 10th century, it derives its name from the Arabic *manzil al-qamah*, perhaps meaning the 'farm of bitter cucumbers'. It was the birthplace of the 13th-century poet Cielo or Ciullo, short for Michele, one of the earliest exponents of the Sicilian School (*see p. 153*), and a forefather of Italian literature. The town has a strongly Arab flavour in its regular plan, with many attractive cobbled streets.

ON AND AROUND CORSO VI APRILE
In Piazza Bagolino the terrace offers an ample panorama of the plain stretching towards the sea. Beyond the 16th-century Porta Palermo, Corso VI Aprile leads into the town. On the left is the church of **San Francesco d'Assisi**, founded in 1348 and rebuilt in 1716. It contains a beautiful marble altarpiece attributed to Giacomo Gagini (1568), statues of St Mark and Mary Magdalene by Antonello Gagini and a 17th-century painting of the *Immaculate Virgin* by Giuseppe Carrera.

The Corso continues past the former church of **San Tommaso** (c. 1450) with a carved Gothic portal. Opposite, next to a convent, is the church of **Santi Cosma e Damiano** (*usually closed*), a domed centrally-planned building of c. 1721 by Giuseppe Mariani. It contains two stucco statues, *Justice* and *Charity*, by Giacomo Serpotta, and two altarpieces by Willem Borremans of the *Immaculate Virgin* and the *Madonna*

Presenting the Christ Child to St Clare. The interior is among the finest examples of Baroque architecture in Sicily.

. The Corso crosses Via Rossotti, with a view left of the castle and right of San Salvatore. The **Castello dei Conti di Modica** (*open Mon–Fri 9–1; T: 0924 22915*) was built c. 1350, on a rhomboid plan with four towers. For many years it was used as the local prison. Now it has been lovingly restored and is the seat of the Civic Historical Library and the Oenological Museum dedicated to the prize-winning Bianco d'Alcamo, one of Sicily's 23 DOC wines. Not far from the castle, tucked away in this part of town, is the **Torre De Ballis** (1495), one of the few surviving tower-houses in Sicily. It is now a private home with no public access.

The Corso continues past the former church of the **Madonna del Soccorso** (15th century) with a portal attributed to Bartolomeo Berrettaro, to the **Chiesa Madre**. Founded in 1332, it was rebuilt in 1669 by Angelo Italia, with a fine dome. In the interior are columns of red marble quarried on Mt Bonifato. The frescoes in the vault, cupola and apse are by Willem Borremans. In the tiny first south chapel is a triptych by Antonello Gagini (1519), showing the *Madonna with Sts Philip and James*, and the *Dormition of the Virgin* in the predella; in the second are two late 16th-century sarcophagi belonging to members of the De Ballis family; their portraits are by Filippo Paladini. In the fourth there is the *Crucifix of Abundance*, carved by Antonello Gagini in 1523, his only work in *mistura* to survive. In the large chapel to the right of the choir are two marvellous Gothic arches and a beautiful fresco fragment of the *Pentecost* (1430). The silver reliquary contains a Holy Thorn from the crown of Christ, given to the city of Alcamo by Charles V in 1535. In the chapel to the left of the main altar is a wooden statue of the Madonna (1721). Known as *Our Lady of Miracles*, she is the patron saint of Alcamo and is carried in procession through the streets in June. On the altar of the north transept, the statue of St Peter is by Giacomo Gagini (1556); the mummified body under the altar is that of St Vincent Martyr. The sacristy (beyond the wooden door in the north aisle) has carvings attributed to Bartolomeo Berrettaro. In the third north chapel there is a high relief of the *Transition of the Virgin* by Antonello Gagini and a marble statue of the *Madonna and Child* (1730) by Giuseppe Marino.

MUSEO DELLA BASILICA SANTA MARIA ASSUNTA
The long-abandoned oratory of the Holy Sacrament next to the Chiesa Madre, built in 1718, now houses the Diocesan Museum, the Museo della Basilica Santa Maria Assunta (*entrance from Piazza IV Novembre 4; open Mon–Sat 10–12.30, Tues and Thur also 4.30–7.30, closed Sun; T: 0924 21578*), a rich array of paintings, vestments, codices and statues dating from the early 15th–19th centuries, mostly of a religious character, admirably displayed and illuminated. Arranged in chronological order, the works were collected by the high priest Monsignor Vincenzo Regina during his period in office, from 1944–91. Among the highlights are the *Madonna of the Graces with Sts Vitus and Bartholomew* (1612) by Gaspare Vazano, the Zoppo di Gangi, with Palermo and its mountains in the background; a sensitive portrait of Baron Felice Pastore (1840) by Giuseppe Patania, and an equally revealing portrait of the high priest Benedetto Mangione (1793), by Giuseppe Renda. A rarity is the collection of *cerniglia*, discs of glass and gold enclosing small

items of jewellery, precious stones or coral, dedicated as ex-votos to the miraculous Madonna of this church. Not to be missed is the lovely statue in nut-brown alabaster of the *Madonna and Child*, by an unknown 16th-century artist, brought here from the church of the Rosario. The serene Madonna, enveloped in a heavy mantle picked out in gold and blue, is offering a pomegranate (symbol of humanity and also of the Passion) to her vivacious Child; gold-winged cherubim decorate the plinth.

CIULLO D'ALCAMO AND THE SICILIAN SCHOOL

The group of poets writing for the court in Palermo of the Holy Roman Emperor Frederick II, in the first half of the 13th century, were first identified as the 'Sicilian School' by Dante. He regarded his own work as an attempt to transcend their achievements, which included the adaptation of Provençal forms, largely lyrical celebrations of courtly love, into the local vernacular. One of their number, Jacopo da Lentini, is generally credited with inventing the sonnet, later perfected by Petrarch, with his *Io m'aggio posto in core* (I have a place in my heart...). Little is known about the life of Ciullo d'Alcamo, but his work *Contrasto Amoroso*, probably written c. 1230, was cited by Dante in *De Vulgari Eloquentia*. Frederick II's court would have exercised a severe restraining influence on the Sicilian School's' subject matter, something which Ciullo is believed to have subverted with his bright and earthy parody of the School's conventions. His poem begins *Rosa fresca aulentissima* (Sweetest smelling fresh rose...) and tells of a young man's illicit seduction of a high-born lady, displaying such intimate acquaintance with life at court that some authorities have suggested that Ciullo was the *nom de plume* of a senior member of the nobility, close to the emperor himself. Other scholars maintain that Ciullo was never in fact a part of the Sicilian School, although his work provided inspiration for its members.

PIAZZA CIULLO AND ENVIRONS

The Corso continues to the elegantly curved Piazza Ciullo, at the centre of town, which was the medieval market place. On the corner is the **church of Sant'Oliva**, built by Giovanni Biagio Amico in 1724. It was restored in 1990 after a fire destroyed the 18th-century frescoes and stuccoes in the nave vault. The interior has altars beautifully decorated with marble. In the fourth south chapel is a statue of the titular saint by Antonello Gagini (1511). One of the four patron saints of Palermo, Oliva (9th century) was 13 when she was kidnapped in Palermo and carried off to Tunis, where, somehow having avoided the sultan's harem, she lived in a cave healing the sick, performing miracles and converting many Muslims to Christianity. Arrested, she was tortured and beheaded. Respected by the Muslims, the great mosque of Tunis is dedicated to her. The high altarpiece is by Pietro Novelli and on the left wall is a 16th-century marble tabernacle. On the left side are 18th-century statues and a marble group of the *Annunciation* (1545) by Antonino and Giacomo Gagini. Piazza Ciullo is dominated by the magnificent **Collegiate Church** (1684–1767) containing 18th-century stuccoes and altarpieces. On Sunday mornings a large proportion of the population—the wine farmers and their families, the women elegantly dressed, the men wearing black serge jackets and cloth caps—tends to congregate in front of this church.

Corso VI Aprile continues from Piazza Ciullo past 18th-century and Neoclassical palaces to the church of **Santi Paolo e Bartolomeo** (1689) with a splendid interior decorated by Vincenzo and Gabriele Messina and Antonino Grano. The oval *Madonna del Miele* (Our Lady of Honey), so called because she is shown with a honeycomb symbolising her sweetness, dates from the late 14th or early 15th century.

In Via Amendola, the road leading out of the square to the north, opposite the church of Sant'Oliva, is the **church of the Rosario** (San Domenico) which contains a fresco attributed to Tommaso de Vigilia. Beyond the castle and the large Piazza della Repubblica is the church of **Santa Maria del Gesù** (1762). Beneath the portico is a portal attributed to Bartolomeo Berrettaro (1507). The church also contains a 16th-century altarpiece, the *Madonna and Saints with the Counts of Modica*, and a statue of the *Madonna and Child* attributed to Bartolomeo Berrettaro or Giuliano Mancino. The cloister of the adjoining convent is especially beautiful.

In Via Caruso is the church of **San Francesco di Paola**, rebuilt in 1699 by Giovanni Biagio Amico. The elegant interior has eight statues modelled in stucco by Giacomo Serpotta, commissioned in 1724, and an altarpiece of *St Benedict* by Pietro Novelli. The church is only open for services, but it is possible to ask for admission at the Benedictine convent next door.

ENVIRONS OF ALCAMO

On **Monte Bonifato** (825m), south of the town, in a pinewood, a ruined Norman castle of the Ventimiglia is situated, with the chapel of the Madonna dell'Alto (superb view). The medieval Fontanazza here is a huge reservoir or thermal edifice dating from the 14th century. Most of the mountain is a nature reserve (Riserva Bosco di Alcamo).

To the north, between the town and the sea, the spectacular castle on a spur known as **Calatubo** (*no access*) adequately protected Alcamo on that vulnerable side; probably Byzantine, the fortress was rebuilt and renamed by the Arabs in the 9th century. Close to the railway station is a spa, **Stabilimento Termale Gorga**, where in a beautiful setting, water from hot springs flows into a pool prepared, according to Diodorus Siculus, by the local nymphs for Hercules 'to refresh his body'.

THE WEST COAST

The west coast of Sicily from Trapani to Mazara del Vallo is flat, with many salt marshes, which have given rise to one of the oldest salt-extracting industries in the world. Between Trapani and Marsala they are now protected, in part because of the interesting birdlife, and also as important sites of industrial archaeology. The coastal plain is dotted with white cube-shaped houses, palms and Norfolk Island pines. Beyond Marsala the plain is densely cultivated with olives, low vineyards and gardens of tomatoes, melons and cantaloupes, stretching as far as colourful Mazara del Vallo, an important fishing port.

Four privately-owned islands lie close offshore in the beautiful shallow lagoon of **Lo Stagnone** (*map p. 575, B2*), which has an average depth of just over one metre and is abundant in fish. Isola Longa is the largest, while the smallest is Isola Scola, site of an ancient academy where Cicero is said to have taught Oratory. The only island fully accessible to visitors is San Pantaleo, the site of ancient Motya (Mozia in Italian).

On the edge of the lagoon at Ragattisi (*signposted from the coastal road*), there are several jetties from which boats ferry visitors to Mozia. Near the main jetty is an old salt mill, now a museum with a small hotel, **Saline Ettore e Infersa** (*open April–Oct 9–8.30, winter on request; T: 0923 733003, www.salineettoreinfersa.com*). The various phases of obtaining salt from seawater are explained, and a film illustrates the method of production; canoes may be rented for exploring the lagoon, and of course you can buy some salt. There are splendid views of the islands from the water's edge, and on the far right the mountain of Erice is prominent beyond salt pans, windmills and piles of salt.

MOZIA

Open Nov–March 9–3, closed Thur; April–Oct 9.30–6.30; T: 0923 712598. Boats to the island are operated by Arini e Pugliese (T: 347 779 0218, 347 343 0329). The ruins are unenclosed and a single ticket payable at a kiosk on the path up from the arrival jetty provides access to the island and the museum.

The island of San Pantaleo was owned from 1888 by Joseph (Pip) Whitaker (1850–1936), a distinguished ornithologist and amateur archaeologist, and member of the famous family of Marsala wine merchants. The low vineyards here still produce an excellent wine: seven hectares of vines originally planted by Pip Whitaker are now cared for by the Tasca d'Almerita winery. Background music is provided by the cicadas. The entire island is an oasis of luxuriant vegetation, a sanctuary for birds, with sweet-smelling plants, palm trees and pinewoods. Whitaker began excavations around 1913. Since the death of his daughter Delia in 1971, the island has been the property of the Fondazione Whitaker (*Via Dante 167, Palermo; T: 091 682 0522, www.fondazionewhitaker.it*).

VILLA WHITAKER AND ZONA E

The boat docks near a stretch of the fortifications of the Punic city, from which a path leads to the crenellated **Villa Whitaker**, founded as a museum in 1925. Some of the display cases brought at that time from Edinburgh and Belfast are still in use. The material on display comes from the excavations at Mozia, Lilybaeum and Birgi, carried out by Whitaker and later by the Italian government. It includes Phoenician ceramics, the earliest dating from the 8th century BC, and Greek ware including proto-Corinthian and Corinthian vases, and Attic black- and red-figure vases. Other finds from the island include Phoenician glass, alabaster and jewellery, and a large collection of arrow heads and missiles from the Greek siege.

Among the sculptural fragments is an extraordinarily vivid metope from the North Gate showing two lions attacking a bull, distinctly Mycenaean in style (late 7th or early 6th century BC) and a marble krater with bas-reliefs (Augustan period). The expressive statue of a young man in a finely-pleated linen tunic, *Il Giovane di Mozia*, known in English as the *Motya Charioteer* (*see p. 159*), was found at Cappiddazzu on the northeast side of the island in 1979 and is given pride of place in the collection.

Nearby is a small building used up until the 1970s for wine-making. During reconstruction work in 1995 remains of houses (called **Zona E**), dating from the 7th–4th centuries BC, were found beneath the pavement: the excavations can now be viewed from a walkway.

HISTORY OF MOTYA

Motya was founded in the mid-8th century BC by the Phoenicians as a commercial base and industrial area (the name means 'mills'). By the mid-6th century BC the island was entirely surrounded by defensive walls, 2400m long and over 2m thick. Over time it came under the sway of Carthage (another Punic city, near modern-day Tunis), to whom it looked for protection. In his determination to remove Carthaginian influence from Sicily, Dionysius I of Syracuse marched a large Greek army, formed partly of mercenaries, across Sicily to besiege Motya in 397 BC. During the fierce battle that ensued, his army built moles out across the lagoon, toward the island of Motya, so that he could bring his siege machines right up to the city walls. He drew the ships of the fleet that had accompanied him onto the shore and prepared for the battle ahead. When a Carthaginian fleet arrived, they thought that they had trapped the Greek ships in the shallow water, but Dionysius ordered his vessels to be dragged over a narrow isthmus using log rollers, and launched them into the open sea where they defeated the Carthaginians. Now that there was no prospect of reinforcement arriving from overseas, the people of Motya prepared to fight to the bitter end, and the Greeks began the attack. Using battering rams, catapults and siege towers six storeys high, they wore away at the defenders who fought back with flaming missiles and desperate courage. The Greeks finally broke into the city, but were forced to fight building by building, street by street, taking heavy losses, until they finally burst through the last defences and flooded into the undefended parts of the city. Slaughtering everyone they met, the Greek soldiers plundered whatever they could lay their hands on, and only a few inhabitants survived to be sold into slavery. Some Greeks who were found to have fought on the side of the Motyans were crucified, and the island was left in ruins. When the Carthaginians returned, they saw no point in refounding a city here, and moved their attention south to Lilybaeum (modern Marsala), where they created a new city as their headquarters on the island.

THE EXCAVATIONS

In front of the museum a path leads towards the lagoon to the **House of the Mosaics**, surrounded by a fence and rich vegetation, with bases of columns and pebble mosaics showing a panther attacking a bull and a griffin chasing a deer, among other designs (4th–3rd centuries BC). A longer path (c. 400m) leads from the custodian's house across the southern part of the island to the waterfront at the southeast corner, beside

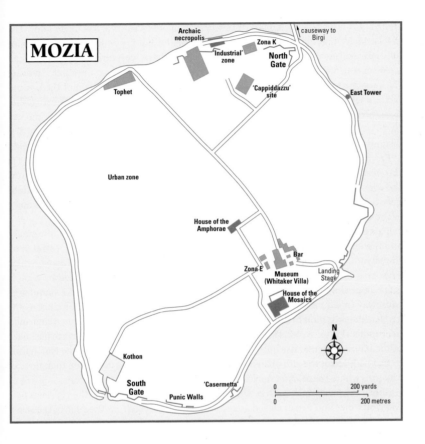

the Kothon and the South Gate. An open excavation area roughly half way along this path, on the right-hand side, is all that has so far been discovered of the **ancient acropolis** of Motya. Excavations carried out in the 1980s and '90s suggest that this was the first part of the island to be inhabited, and more recent work has revealed two large houses of the 5th century BC (La Casa del Sacello Domestico and La Casa del Corno di Conchiglia) which were destroyed by a terrible fire during the siege of 397 BC. The path that branches off to the right here leads through fields of vines to the west coast and the Tophet (*see below*).

The **Kothon** is a small basin (50m by 40m) within the walls, with a channel leading to the sea, long thought to have been a repair yard for boats. Recent excavations have, however, brought to light a large temple on the east side of the pool, with a portico facing the water. The pool (its four corners correspond to the cardinal points) was drained and cleaned, revealing that it was originally fed by a natural spring, which also provided water to a sacred well inside the temple, found to have been one of the oldest buildings on the island, going back to the mid-8th century BC and rebuilt after

Dionysius's attack. The channel connecting the pool to the sea was made later. The cult—which evidently required much water—and the divinity or divinities worshipped here are still mysterious, but inside the temple there were originally two upright stelae and an obelisk. Viewing the night sky at the winter equinox, the stones indicate the constellation of Orion, Baal for the Phoenicians, while the portal of the temple, facing south-southwest, at the spring equinox frames the same divinity, often together with the planet Venus, the Phoenician Astarte. Some scholars believe this temple was particularly sacred to the inhabitants because it represented the spot where they first disembarked, finding abundant fresh water, and therefore the benevolence of the gods.

From here you can retrace your steps to the acropolis and take the path directly to the western coast. Alternatively, another path leads back towards the museum along the edge of the south shore past an enclosure near a stand of pine trees. Excavations here have unearthed a building that was probably used for military purposes, known as the **Casermetta**.

This path continues along the water's edge below the villa, passing the landing stage and the impressive fortifications (late 6th century BC), the best-preserved stretch on the island, along the eastern shore, reaching (after 400m) the **East Tower**, which preserves its flight of steps. Beyond some recent excavations (protected by a roof) is the imposing **North Gate**, with a triple line of defences. It defended a submerged causeway (meant to be invisible from land, but perfectly practicable for a horse and cart), which was built in the late 6th century BC to link the island to the mainland and a necropolis at Birgi. Several kilometres long, just wide enough for two carts to pass each other, it was in regular use until the 1950s. A path leads inland through the North Gate to **Cappiddazzu**, the site of an important sanctuary, perhaps dedicated to Astarte or Melqart, where the *Motya Charioteer* was found.

Above the level of the path is a building with mosaic remains. To the right is a field with low vines and two enclosed areas, the farthest of which, on the edge of the sea, is the **Archaic necropolis** with tombs dating from the 8th–6th centuries BC. Nearby a fence surrounds an 'industrial area', known as **Zona K**, with interesting kilns, similar in design to some found in Syria and Palestine.

Further along the west coast is the **Tophet**, a Punic sacrificial burial-ground dedicated to the god Baal Hammon and his wife Tanit, where children, possibly the male first-born, were sacrificed. The sanctuary consisted of a large urnfield and an adjacent shrine and sacred well, and seems to have been in use from shortly after Motya was founded. Rebuilt on a more monumental scale in the mid-6th century BC, it was destroyed in 397 but was rebuilt shortly afterwards and continued in use for some time. Excavations here have produced cinerary urns, votive terracotta masks and stelae (some with human figures), on display in the Whitaker Museum.

From the Tophet a path leads round the western shore to the Kothon and South Gate (after c. 700m). The **West Gate** stood near a military fort, the largest building so far discovered on the island. An alternative path, marked by low olive trees, leads back through a vineyard in the centre of the island towards the museum (c. 400m). It passes (right) an enclosure with remains of the **House of the Amphorae**, so-called because a huge deposit of amphorae was found here.

MOZIA
Detail of the famous statue discovered at the site in 1979.

THE MOTYA 'CHARIOTEER'

This remarkable marble statue was found lying on its back, buried beneath a pile of rubble and earth that had been hurriedly erected as an interior line of defence by the people of Motya in 397 BC. The head had been broken off the body by the great weight of debris above it, but the missing arms, feet and metal decoration (indicated by the holes on the chest) suggest that it had already been damaged elsewhere (perhaps by Greek missiles being fired over the city walls) before being used in this temporary barricade. In the stance of a victor, with left hand on hip, the pose of the statue exudes the subject's confidence in his youth, beauty and power. The masterful carving of the tight-fitting tunic, which enhances every part of his finely-toned body while preserving just a little of his modesty, creates a vivid sensuality. After much heated debate, art historians and archaeologists are now almost entirely in agreement that it represents a charioteer victorious in one of the great Panhellenic games of the ancient Greek world, who would have been holding his symbol of victory above his head in his right hand. Although clearly the work of a master sculptor, it is uncertain who this was, and it can only be tentatively dated to the first half of the 5th century BC. Another theory, however, insists that the statue represents Melqart, the Phoenician equivalent of Herakles, and that he would have had a lion's pelt partly covering his head, with its legs knotted and pinned to the chest. For the denizens of Motya, it would have been a cult statue and the lifelike features make it datable to the mid-5th century BC.

CHILD SACRIFICE AMONG THE CARTHAGINIANS

The Tophet is infamous for being the location where the Punic peoples occasionally sacrificed their own children to the gods. Over the years, many people have refused to accept that this actually happened, electing to blame the Greek and Roman authors who report it for concocting the slur in order to justify the costly wars that they fought against the Punic populations, and Carthage in particular. However, recent groundbreaking work by a European team of researchers appears to have proved beyond doubt that child sacrifice was indeed carried out here, and that it did not simply rely on the use of already dying or dead infants. Drawing together the literary, archaeological, osteological and epigraphical evidence, it is clear that some members of the Punic societies did kill their own young children, to fulfil a promise that had already been made to the gods in return for divine favours. Due to the costly ritual that it involved, this practice was probably restricted to the wealthier members of society and the numbers sacrificed would have been relatively small. This nevertheless makes it no less horrifying when we contemplate such an idea today.

MARSALA

Marsala (*map p. 575, B2*) is a pleasant town with a neat city centre and an attractive open seafront on Capo Boeo, the site of the Carthaginian city of Lilybaeum. The town gives its name to a famous dessert wine still produced here in large quantities from the vineyards along the coast.

HISTORY OF MARSALA

Lilybaeum, founded by the Carthaginians in 396 BC, became their strongest bulwark in Sicily after the sack of Motya in 397 BC. It succumbed to the Romans only after a siege of ten years (250–241 BC). During the Second Punic War, Scipio (later to be named Africanus) set sail from Lilybaeum on his way to defeat Hannibal near Carthage at the Battle of Zama (202 BC). As the seat of the Roman governor of Sicily, the city reached the zenith of its importance. Cicero, made quaestor here in 75 BC, called it '*civitas splendidissima*'. In 47 BC Julius Caesar also pitched camp here on his way to Africa. A *municipium* during the Augustan age, it was later raised to the status of *colonia*. It kept its importance as an avenue of communication with Africa during the Saracen dominion under the name *Marsa Alí*, Harbour of Ali, but declined after 1574 when Don Juan of Austria (illegitimate son of Charles V) almost completely blocked its port to protect it from Barbary pirates. The famous Marsala wine trade dates from the late 18th century (*see p. 163*). Garibaldi and the 'Thousand' landed here on 11th May 1860, being unobtrusively assisted by two British warships which had officially been assigned to protect the wine merchants. In 1943, Marsala was heavily damaged by Allied air attacks during preparations for Operation Husky.

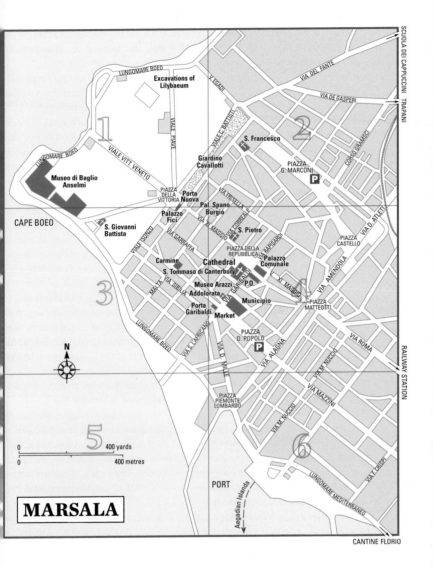

MARSALA

PORTA GARIBALDI TO THE CATHEDRAL

The centre of town is entered from the port and southwest by the monumental **Porta Garibaldi** (*map 3–4*), formerly the Porta di Mare, reconstructed in 1685. On the left is the church of the **Addolorata**, with a fine circular domed 18th-century interior. In the apse is a cypress-wood statue (1790) of the Madonna wearing a black cloak. Opposite, municipal offices occupy a restored 16th-century military building, behind which is the market square. Via Garibaldi continues to the central **Piazza della Repubblica** with the idiosyncratic Palazzo Comunale (Town Hall), which has original lamps on its upper storey. Opposite, on Via XI Maggio, is a wall and dome of the 17th-century church of **San Giuseppe**, with a lovely interior and a fine organ.

The **cathedral** (*map 4*) has a Baroque front completed in 1957. The first church on this site was built in 1176–82 and dedicated to St Thomas Becket, because the columns of various kinds of marble used in the building were recuperated from a shipwreck, and were intended for a church under construction in England, dedicated to the new saint (Thomas had been canonised in 1173). The renovated cathedral, begun in 1607 and completed in 1717, was ruined when the dome collapsed in 1893, and was partly rebuilt in the 20th century. The interior contains some important 17th-century paintings and sculptures. In the first south chapel there is an unusual statue of the *Assunta* and two reliefs on the side wall, all by Antonino Gagini. The delicately-carved tomb slab dates from 1556. In the second chapel there is a 15th-century statue of the Madonna, and a tomb with the effigy, attributed to Domenico Gagini, of Antonio Grignano (d. 1475) who fought with honour in the wars of King Alfonso. In the third chapel is an elaborate statue of the *Madonna dell'Itria* (Our Lady the Protector of Wayfarers, derived from the Byzantine Hodegetria type, usually depicting the infant Christ standing as an indication of the Way) and the tomb of Giulio Alazzaro with an amusing effigy, both by Antonino Gagini. The fifth chapel has a 15th-century Crucifix and an expressive, popular statue of the Virgin in mourning. In the south transept is a striking altarpiece of the *Presentation in the Temple* by Antonello or Mariano Riccio, and the tomb of Antonio Lombardo, who donated the tapestries to the cathedral (now in the Tapestry Museum; *see below*). In the chapel to the right of the sanctuary is an unusual statue of the Madonna wielding a distaff, attributed to Giuliano Mancino, and a tomb with an effigy of Antonio Liotta (d. 1512), also attributed to Mancino. On either side of the sanctuary are two statues, one of St Vincent Ferrer attributed to Giacomo Gagini and one of St Thomas the Apostle by Antonello Gagini. In the apse is a 17th-century painting of the *Martyrdom of St Thomas* in the original frame. In the chapel to the left of the sanctuary is a beautiful gilded marble altarpiece of the *Passion* begun in 1518 by Bartolomeo Berrettaro and finished by Antonello Gagini (1532; four of the panels have been set into the walls). On the north side, in the sixth chapel is a charming polychrome wooden statue of *Our Lady of Carmel*, and in the second chapel is another wooden statue (1593) of the Madonna, and two frescoed ex-votos with scenes of Marsala.

Behind the cathedral, at Via Giuseppe Garraffa 57, is the small **Tapestry Museum** (Museo degli Arazzi; *open Tues–Sat 9–1 & 4–6, Sun 9–1; T: 0923 712903*), displaying eight precious tapestries given to the cathedral in 1589 by Antonio Lombardo, archbishop of Messina, born in Marsala and buried in the cathedral. He became ambassador to Spain and the very fine tapestries, depicting the Capture of Jerusalem and made in Brussels between 1530 and 1550, are known to have come from the palace of Philip II in Madrid. They are displayed on three floors, in specially darkened rooms.

THE MUSEUMS OF SAN PIETRO AND THE CARMINE

The 15th-century convent of **San Pietro** (*map 4; open Tues–Sun 9–1 & 4–8; closed Mon, T: 0923 718741*), in Via Correale, with a massive pointed tower, is now used as the town library, cultural centre and Civic Museum. It has sections on the archaeology of ancient Lilybaeum, the exploits of Giuseppe Garibaldi, and popular traditions.

Just off Via Malta, in Piazza Carmine, the former church and convent of the **Carmine** (*map 3*) houses the municipal archives and an interesting contemporary art gallery (*open Tues–Sun 10–1 & 6–8; T: 0923 713822*), with paintings by 20th-century Italian masters such as Alberto Sughi, Bruno Caruso, Corrado Cagli, Fausto Pirandello, Giacomo Baragli, Franco Gentilini, and the mythopoeic painter and sculptor Mirko. The detached campanile was designed by Giovanni Biagio Amico. The former convent was founded in the late 14th century and has an 18th-century cloister.

Back on Via XI Maggio, just before Porta Nuova (on Piazza della Vittoria), is the façade (left) of **Palazzo Fici**, with a tall palm tree in its delightful Baroque courtyard. Opposite is the 19th–20th-century Palazzo Spanò Burgio (no. 15). Outside the gate is the entrance (right) to the **Giardino Cavallotti** (*map 1–2*), lovely public gardens with huge ficus trees, magnolias and ornamental Norfolk Island pines.

MARSALA WINE

The wine trade was founded by John Woodhouse in 1773 when he made the first shipment of local white wine to Liverpool, conserving it on its month-long journey by adding alcohol. In 1798, after the Battle of the Nile, Nelson placed a large order of Marsala for his fleet. In 1806 Benjamin Ingham also took up trading in Marsala with great success; in 1812 he summoned his nephew Joseph Whitaker from Yorkshire, and soon they were exporting the wine to North America. Production on an even grander scale was undertaken by Vincenzo Florio (d. 1868), an able businessman. In 1929 the establishments of Woodhouse, Ingham Whitaker and Florio were taken over by Cinzano, and merged under the name of Florio. The house of Florio continues to flourish along with many other companies, including Pellegrino and Donnafugata. Pellegrino dates from 1880, when Paolo Pellegrino founded the winery and dedicated his life to the wine.

Marsala is stored in huge *bagli*, fortified farmhouses. The name derives from the Latin *balium* or *vallum*, being a group of buildings forming a square or a rectangle around a central courtyard, with one entrance, sometimes lavishly decorated, in the front wall. In the courtyard there is often a well-head above the rainwater cistern. On entering, the house immediately in front is that of the owner, usually with a private chapel to one side. Other buildings house the farm workers, the wine or olive presses and the stables.

MUSEO DI BAGLIO ANSELMI AND THE EXCAVATIONS OF LILYBAEUM

Between Piazza della Vittoria and the seafront extends **Capo Boeo** (*map 1*), an open area with lawns and trees. Some picturesque old *bagli* on the seafront are still used as warehouses for wine. Others have been converted into restaurants and one of them, on the tip of the promontory, houses the **Museo Regionale Archeologico Baglio Anselmi** (*closed for major restoration work at the time of writing but scheduled to be open Tues–Sat 9–7.30, Sun, Mon and holidays 9–1.30, last tickets 1hr before closing; T: 0923 952535*). A small collection of some of the key pieces has been put on display in one of the wings of the building, accessible through a temporary ticket office on Viale Vittorio Veneto. When it reopens, this museum will display finds from the Marsala area, in particular Motya and Lilybaeum itself. The highlights of the collection will undoubtedly be the beautiful carved and painted inscriptions from the Lilybaeum cemeteries, a marble Aphrodite known as the *Afrodite Callipige* ('of the firm buttocks'), recently discovered near the church of San Giovanni Battista, and the well-preserved remains of a Punic ship discovered by Honor Frost in 1971 off Isola Longa in the Stagnone lagoon.

The **excavations of Lilybaeum**, in the area known as the Insula Romana, now form an archaeological park (*open as Museo Archeologico*). In a well-restored house are diagrams of the site, which includes a sumptuous Roman villa (surrounded by a fence and covered for protection) dating from the 3rd century AD, which was built over in the Arab period. Around the impluvium are four mosaics of wild beasts attacking each other (thought to represent circus animals), probably the work of African craftsmen. There are remains of baths and other rooms with mosaics, including a head of Medusa, the symbol of Trinacria and the Four Seasons. Nearby are more recent excavations including part of the walls, a necropolis and a Roman road. The **hypogeum of Crispia Salvia** (*request visit at Museo Archeologico*), with painted walls, where the Roman lady Crispia Salvia was buried in the 2nd century AD has also been discovered. The remains of a sanctuary dedicated to Isis are not yet open to the public.

At the edge of the site is the church of **San Giovanni Battista** (*map 3; request visit at museum a few days in advance, T: 0923 952535*), covering the so-called Grotto of the Sibyl, with a spring of water which later became an early Christian baptistery. There are still faint traces of 5th-century frescoes.

> ## THE SIBYL OF LILYBAEUM
>
> Prophetesses or sibyls were popularly believed to be able to speak for the gods, and hence foretell the future. Apollo was especially generous in this respect, and is often referred to as the 'far-seeing one'. There were several places where these oracles could be consulted, such as Delphi or Cumae, but the Sibyl of Lilybaeum had a particularly good reputation for accuracy. The person requiring the information would enter the grotto where the priestess lived and put their question; she would then bathe his face and her own with water from the little pool. The pair would then take turns in sipping wine from a golden cup, after which the sibyl would enter a trance-like state and read the future in the dregs of wine remaining. The custom died out when Sicily became a province of Rome in the 3rd century BC.

THE FLORIO WINERY (STABILIMENTO FLORIO)

Behind the harbour front of the port, in **Piazza Piemonte Lombardo** (*map 6*), is the base of a monument by Ettore Ximenes commemorating the landing of the Thousand. It was destroyed in the Second World War. The coast road from here, Lungomare Mediterraneo, passes a number of dilapidated old *bagli*, their entrances guarded by round towers, until you come to the **Cantine Florio** (*Via Vincenzo Florio 1, beyond map 6; tour and wine-tasting Mon–Fri 9–6, Sat 9–1; booking required; T: 0923 781111,* *www.duca.it*). The monumental buildings designed by Basile surround an inner courtyard planted with trees. Visitors are shown the historic cellars and invited to taste the wine. In the small museum a letter is preserved from Nelson, Duke of Bronte to John Woodhouse in 1800 with an order for Marsala for his fleet.

The Neoclassical villa built by Benjamin Ingham can be seen a little further along the waterfront.

MAZARA DEL VALLO

Mazara del Vallo (*map p. 575, B3*), at the mouth of the Mazaro, is the most important fishing town in Italy, with a large population of Tunisians who work on the farms and in the fishing fleet. Animated and attractive, with elegant shops and graceful squares, Mazara is one of the liveliest towns in western Sicily. Built in golden tufa, with a colourful waterfront and busy canal-port, it has a distinctly Arab flavour. The harbour, at the mouth of the river, is normally filled with the fishing fleet during the day, except on Saturdays. This is the more picturesque part of the city, together with the Kasbah district around Via Porta Palermo and Via Bagno.

HISTORY OF MAZARA DEL VALLO

Mazara, once a Phoenician trading-post, became an emporium of Selinunte and fell with it in 409 BC. It was held by the Carthaginians until 210 BC when it came under Roman rule. Here in AD 827 the Arabs, called in by the governor Euphemius to assist in his pretensions to the imperial purple, gained their first foothold on the island. There followed the most important period in the town's history, when it became the capital of the Val di Mazara, one of the three administrative districts into which the Arabs divided Sicily. It was captured by Count Roger in 1075; and it was here in 1097 that the Sicilian parliament, one of the oldest in the world, was convened for the first time.

THE CATHEDRAL, DIOCESAN MUSEUM AND MUSEO ORNITOLOGICO

The cathedral was founded in 1093 and rebuilt in 1690–4. Above the main door, which faces the sea, is a 16th-century sculpture of Count Roger on horseback. The interior contains a *Transfiguration* in the apse by Antonello Gagini (finished by his son Antonino in 1537). The statues of St Bartholomew and St Ignatius are by Ignazio Marabitti. In the south aisle is a sculpted portal by Bartolomeo Berrettaro. In the vestibule of the chapter house are two Roman sarcophagi. Off the north aisle is a chapel with a 13th-century painted Cross, and in the chapel of the Madonna del Soccorso is a Byzantine fresco (in a niche) of *Christ Pantocrator*.

Between the cathedral and the seafront is a public garden with huge trees, on the site of the Norman castle, one ruined wall of which faces the busy Piazza Mokarta at the end of the main Corso Umberto.

On the left side of the cathedral is the 18th-century **Piazza della Repubblica**, the heart of the city, with a statue of St Vitus Martyr by Marabitti (1771) under shady trees. The handsome Seminario dei Chierici (1710) stands on the south side, with a double portico; it houses the **Diocesan Museum** (*open Tues–Sat 10- 12.30, Fri and Sat also 4.30–6.30; entrance from Via dell'Orologio 3 to the south*) which contains the tomb (1495) of Bishop Giovanni Montaperto, who ordered the construction of the cathedral in Agrigento, by Domenico Gagini, as well as paintings, vestments and Church silver, including a processional Crucifix from Salemi dated 1386, by a Pisan artist. Also on display is the carriage belonging to another bishop, Antonio Salomone. The highlights of the museum are the tiny pink marble statue of *Christus dolens* (an 18th-century ex-voto) and a stunning silver monstrance, glittering with diamonds, pearls, amethysts, emeralds, garnets and topaz; probably made using the jewellery of a noble lady on entering a convent.

The Palazzo Vescovile, on the north side of the square, houses the **Museo Ornitologico** (*open daily 9–1 & 3–8; T: 347 554 3002*), a collection of 373 stuffed birds, some of them extremely rare, and a few mammals, prepared with great skill by a local taxidermist in the 1920s.

MUSEO DEL SATIRO DANZANTE

On the west side of Piazza della Repubblica, Via XX Settembre leads to Piazza Plebiscito, with the two 16th-century churches of the Carmine and Sant'Egidio. That of Sant'Egidio now houses the **Museo del Satiro Danzante** (*open 9–7.15; T: 0923 933917*). In 1998 some local fishermen found a bronze statue of a satyr caught in their nets, while fishing in the Strait of Sicily (between Sicily and Tunisia). For a moment, while they were hauling up the catch, they thought it was a seaman who had fallen overboard and was clinging to the ropes, but an arm broke off and fell into the depths. A year earlier, the same crew had found a bronze leg. By returning to the same area a few weeks later they found a bronze elephant's foot, perhaps from the same statuary group; in spite of much searching, they never found the missing arms and the other leg. It has been suggested that the satyr could be Dionysus himself: he is shown with his body twisted in a dance of drunken ecstasy, his head thrown back, with wild hair and pointed ears. A little larger than life size, the statue is made of bronze about 7mm thick. The weight, including the stand, is about 140kg. Judging from other works of art on the same subject (statues, reliefs, cameos), the satyr would have been carrying an empty wine cup in his left hand and a long rattle in his right. A panther skin would have been thrown over his left arm with its legs and tail flailing, and this, plus his donkey tail behind him, would have increased the effect of his frenzied whirling. A tentative date for it can be set between 404 and 280 BC. One authority has declared that the statue could even be the work of Praxiteles.

Close by is the church of Sant'Ignazio (*closed*) and the Collegio dei Gesuiti (1675–86), which now houses the municipal library and archives, and the **Museo Civico** (*open daily 8.30–2 & 3.30–6.30*) which has Roman finds from the area and two interesting sculpted elephants which once bore the columns outside the west porch of the Norman cathedral. Many drawings by the local sculptor Pietro Consagra are displayed here. Also close to Piazza Plebiscito is Via Carmine, where at no. 17 is the newly-restored opera house, **Teatro Garibaldi** (1849; *open Mon–Sat 8.30–1.30*). All in wood, this exquisite little theatre has only 100 seats. The boxes are decorated with scenes from Sicilian folklore.

SANTA CATERINA, SAN MICHELE ARCANGELO, MIRABILIA URBIS AND AMPHOREUS

Via San Giuseppe leads from Piazza della Repubblica to the church of **Santa Caterina**, decorated in 1797 by Giuseppe Testa, with a statue of the saint by Antonello Gagini (1524).

Leading northwest from Piazza della Repubblica is Via Garibaldi; Via Itria or Via Pino are turnings on the right to Piazza Santa Veneranda and Via San Michele, where at no. 5 is the very attractive church of **San Michele Arcangelo**. The golden sandstone façade, picked out in white stucco, is of 1702, and the oriental-style bell-tower with its rounded cusp was added in 1771, but the church with its monastery was first built in the early 12th century by George of Antioch, Roger II's Greek admiral, for Basilian Greek Orthodox monks, on the edge of the Jewish quarter, near the synagogue. The Rococo interior glitters with polished marble, frescoes and gilded stucco. There are 20 stucco statues of the Virtues by Bartolomeo Sanseverino. The statue in cypress wood and silver is of the patron saint, Vitus Martyr. The vault fresco, *The Archangel Michael Triumphing over Satan*, together with other paintings in the church, were carried out by the local artist Tommaso Sciacca. The superb majolica floor, glowing with colourful flowers, garlands and figures, was made by craftsmen of a Trapani workshop in the early 18th century. In the sacristy is a rare 15th-century painted Crucifix in *mistura*, certainly of Sicilian workmanship, showing Christ as *Christus dolens*. The monastery soon passed to the Benedictine nuns and became one of the wealthiest and most powerful in western Sicily, and a boarding school for noble girls, many of whom came from Palermo. Now only seven nuns remain, but they still bake the unique local pastries (*see p. 195*).

Via Garibaldi continues northwest to Piazza Chinea and Via San Bartolomeo, on the fringe of the teeming **Kasbah district** with its tiny alleys and courtyards. Here is the deconsecrated church of San Bartolomeo (1601), which now houses the archaeological museum, **Mirabilia Urbis** (*open Mon–Sat 8.30–1.30*). The collection consists of finds from the Neolithic and Bronze Age settlement of Roccazzo, to the south of the city, together with Corinthian ceramics (note the exquisite skyphos) and Attic ware.

The narrow Via San Giovanni runs north–south, parallel to the Lungomazaro Caito. Here the deconsecrated church of San Carlo Borromeo houses **Amphoreus** (*open Mon–Sat 8.30–1.30*), a display of objects brought to the surface by the fishermen in their nets, especially from areas in the Strait of Sicily (between Sicily and Tunisia) where the sea is treacherously shallow, and through the centuries many ships have sunk. Arranged as if washed up on a deserted sandy beach, there are amphorae from all over the Mediterranean, used for transporting various liquids or foodstuffs, and a large number of anchors, mostly Roman. During sea battles the crew would often throw the anchor overboard, in order to gain speed. Items of tableware and cooking pots from the galleys complete the interesting collection.

TWO ARAB-NORMAN CHURCHES

On the left bank of the Mazaro, near the mouth, stands the elegant little Arab-Norman church of **San Nicolò Regale**, cube-like, of golden stone, with a domed roof, three apses, and rounded crenellations. Built in the early 12th century when Mazara was the seat of the Sicilian Parliament and the first bishopric of the island, it replaced a Palaeo-Christian basilica; during repairs some fragments of the mosaic floor were discovered.

The similar church of the **Madonna dell'Alto** (or delle Giummare, dwarf palms) was erected in 1103 by Juliet (sometimes known as Judith), daughter of Count Roger, to celebrate her father's victory over the Muslims. It is 2km east of the town, on a rocky knoll, and is approached by a long, much worn and overgrown stone stairway.

SELINUNTE

One of the most impressive Classical sites in Sicily because it was never subsequently re-developed, the extensive ruins (270ha) of the ancient city of Selinunte (Selinous in Greek, Selinus in Latin) are in a superb position overlooking the sea (*map p. 575, C3*). On the coast nearby, the simple fishing village of Marinella has been developed as a small resort. The beautiful coast to the east, around the mouth of the River Belice (and as far as Porto Palo), with its sand dunes, is preserved as a nature reserve (Riserva Naturale Foce del Fiume Belice; *T: 0923 806111*). The ancient town with its acropolis occupied a raised terrace between the River Selinon, or Modione, and the marshy depression now called Gorgo di Cottone or Galici, and possessed a harbour at the mouth of each valley. An important group of temples lay to the east of this site, and a necropolis to the north. The sandy soil is overgrown with wild celery, lentiscus, mandrake, acanthus and capers. The site has been enclosed, and is now the largest archaeological park in Europe.

THE ARCHAEOLOGICAL PARK

Open 9–1hr before sunset. Park entrances at Marinella or Triscina. Last tickets 1hr before closing. T: 0924 46277. The same ticket allows access to the Cave di Cusa (see p. 174). A visit, best started early in the morning, takes at least three or four hours, to include the three quite widely separated areas of the site: the East Hill temples; the Acropolis; and the Sanctuary of Demeter Malophoros. At the time of writing the Efebo di Selinunte (see p. 176) was on temporary display in a room on the Acropolis. A separate ticket gives access to it and to the Museo Civico in Castelvetrano, where the Efebo will eventually return.

Selinunte was a colony of Megara Hyblaea, perhaps founded as early as c. 650 BC. It takes its name from the wild celery, *Apium graveolens* (Greek, *selinon*), which still grows here in abundance, and which appears on its coins. The colony's most

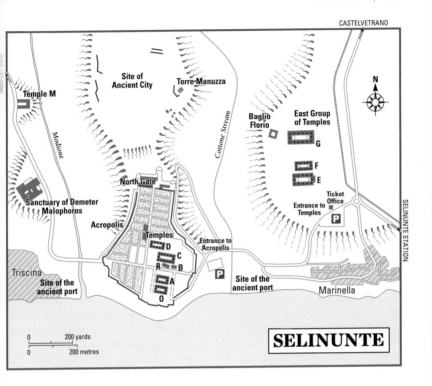

prosperous period was the 5th century BC, when the great temples were built and the city was laid out on a rectangular plan. After the Battle of Himera in 480 BC Selinunte took part with Syracuse in an alliance against Carthage, and in 409 BC the Carthaginians, summoned to the help of Segesta, the mortal enemy of Selinunte, sent an army of 100,000 under Hannibal, son of Gisco, which captured Selinunte before the allied troops of Akragas and Syracuse could arrive. The city, which fell in only nine days, was sacked and destroyed, and its inhabitants sold as slaves. A later settlement, led by Hermocrates, a Syracusan exile, was dispersed by Carthage in 250 BC, and the population resettled at Lilybaeum. It is thought, however, that the utter destruction of every building, scarcely a single column being left upright, could also have been due to earthquakes. In fact, around and under the columns of Temple C are the ruins of a Byzantine settlement, and a later, Arab village called Rahal al-Asnaan, or 'village of the columns', which must have been destroyed by an earthquake in the Middle Ages.

A bronze statue (Phoenician, 12th–11th centuries BC) of Reshef (kept in the Archaeological Museum in Palermo), found in the vicinity, might suggest that the Phoenicians traded here before the foundation of Carthage.

The site was rediscovered in the 16th century by Tommaso Fazello; but systematic excavations were begun only in 1822–3 by the Englishmen William Harris and Samuel Angell, after a fruitless dig had been made in 1809–10 by Robert Fagan, British consul-general in Sicily. Harris and Angell found the famous metopes of temples C and E, but Harris died of malaria, contracted while excavating here, and Angell was killed by bandits on a successive visit.

The majority of the temples are distinguished by letters as their dedications are still under discussion. Some of them had sculptured metopes, a rarity in Sicily, many of which are now in the archaeological museum of Palermo. Most of the temples were peripteral and hexastyle. The measurements given in the following descriptions refer to the temple stylobates. Many architectural fragments bear remains of stucco, and throughout the site are underground cisterns, built to collect rainwater. Beside most of the temples are sacrificial altars.

THE EAST HILL

The East Hill shows the ruins of three large temples. Behind the ticket office is a large modern dyke that isolates them from the village of Marinella.

Temple E: A Doric building of 490–480 BC, measuring 67.7m by 25.3m, and probably dedicated to Hera. It had beautiful sculpted metopes, four of which were discovered in 1831 and are now in Palermo's archaeological museum. Toppled by an earthquake, its columns were re-erected in 1958.

Temple F: The oldest on this hill (c. 560–540 BC), possibly dedicated to Aphrodite and almost completely ruined. It once had a double row of columns in front and 14 at the sides. Part of one column rises above others which are now only a few metres high.

Temple G: Probably dedicated to Zeus. Octastyle in form, it is the second largest (110m by 50m) Sicilian temple after the Olympieion at Agrigento. The columnar arrangement (8 by 17) is the same as that of the Parthenon on the Athenian Acropolis. Laid out in the 6th century and left incomplete (with unfluted columns) in 409 BC, when the city was destroyed, it is now an impressive pile of overgrown ruins. One column still stands, locally known as '*u fusu d'a vecchia* ('the old lady's distaff'). The columns, over 16m high with a base diameter of 3.4m, were built up of drums, each weighing c. 100 tons, from the quarries at Cusa (*see p. 174*), where some blocks destined for the site can still be seen. The cella, preceded by a pronaos of four columns, had a central colonnaded way, open to the sky, leading to the shrine of the divinity. The fallen capitals give some idea of the colossal scale of the building and the crepidoma is in itself a marvel of monumental construction.

THE ACROPOLIS

From the first car park a road continues downhill across the Gorgo di Cottone (site of one of the ancient harbours) and up to the Acropolis, where there is a second car park (*see plan on p. 169*). From here a path continues up between the sea and massive double walls, in which five towers and four gates have been located, dating from c. 307–306 BC. On the clifftop is an old farmhouse, the Casa del Viandante, one room of which (at the

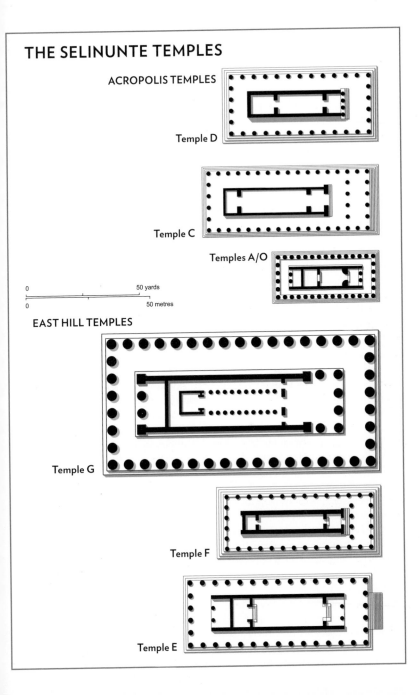

THE SELINUNTE TEMPLES

ACROPOLIS TEMPLES

Temple D

Temple C

Temples A/O

0   50 yards

0   50 metres

EAST HILL TEMPLES

Temple G

Temple F

Temple E

time of writing) displays the *Ephebe of Selinunte* (*separate ticket required, purchasable at the ticket office: see p. 168 for ticket details; see p. 176 for details of the statue*).

Temples O and A: Only the stylobate of Temple O remains; the superstructure has disappeared. Next to it is the stylobate of Temple A with some fluted drums. The cella was one step higher than the pronaos and the adyton one higher still. Between the cella and pronaos two spiral staircases led to the roof. Fragmentary ruins of a monumental entrance exist to the east. Temples A and O, both built in 490–480 BC and identical in form and dimension (40m by 16m; 36 columns), were the latest and probably the most perfect of the Selinuntine temples. In front of Temple O a sacred area has been excavated, thought to date from after the destruction of the city in 409 BC.

Temple C: The ruins of the Acropolis are crossed by two principal streets at right angles, with lesser streets running parallel in a grid pattern. To the north are the remains of the great Temple C, on the highest point of the knoll, and the most conspicuous monument on the Acropolis. It measured 63.7m by 24m and dates from the early 6th century, when it would have replaced a more simple megaron. Probably dedicated to Apollo, it was once adorned with metopes found here in 1823, now in the Palermo archaeological museum. In order to accommodate the sacrificial altar, the temenos was artificially extended some way eastwards, supported by monumental steps. The colossal columns (6 by 17), some of which were monolithic, are nearly 2m in diameter at the base, except for the corner-columns which are even

thicker; they fell during an earthquake in the Middle Ages, burying a Byzantine village that had grown up in the 5th century (a Crucifix and a Christian bronze lamp were found here) and a later Arab village. The north colonnade, now the temple's most salient feature, was re-erected in 1925–7. Part of the sacrificial altar remains.

To the south of the temple is a megaron (17.6m by 5.5m), dating from 580–570 BC. In the east corner of the temenos a stoa has been excavated which was probably built at the same time as the acropolis walls (late 6th century).

Temple B: To the southeast is the small shrine known as Temple B, a prostyle aediculum with pronaos and cella; recent archaeological work suggests that it was dedicated to Demeter. The path leads left, following the east–west thoroughfare of the city, passing in front of the pronaos of Temple A. Near a solitary ancient ilex tree is a crude mosaic floor depicting an image of the Punic goddess, Tanit.

Temple D: The wide main northern thoroughfare of the city (the North Gate can be seen at its end) leads away from the sea, past the stylobate of Temple D (570–554 BC), probably dedicated to Athena, which stands beside the road: it carried 34 columns, measures 56m by 24m, and was the second temple to be built on the Acropolis. Some of its blocks still have their bosses. Beyond, by a small pine tree, is a row of modest constructions thought to have been shops, each with two rooms, a courtyard, and stairs up to the living quarters on the first floor. Nearby are the foundations of the Temple of the Small Metopes, named after the six small metopes found here, now in Palermo. It had a simple cella and adytum and measured 15.2m by 5.4m.

Temple R: Ongoing excavations in this temple, almost certainly dedicated to Demeter, have revealed fascinating insights into the history of the city. At the lowest levels, the archaeologists have discovered the remains of a temple that is the earliest so far found at Selinunte, and is also one of the very earliest Greek temples in the entire Western Mediterranean. This was superseded by a later Archaic temple, in which a figurine of Demeter was found, and in turn by a Classical temple that was violently destroyed, presumably by the Carthaginians in 409 BC, at which point a robber trench was dug into the floor of the adyton so that the foundation treasure could be plundered. Temple R was reconsecrated when Selinunte was briefly resettled in the Hellenistic period.

North Gate: Just before the North Gate there is a good view east of Temple E on its hill. The North Gate itself, one of the main gates of the city, is well preserved. Beyond is a sophisticated defence system once thought to date from the time of Hermocrates, but probably constructed by Agathocles in 307–306 BC. The fortifications include three semicircular towers, and a second line of walls c. 5m outside the earlier ones which were reinforced after their destruction by Hannibal in 409 BC using material from the acropolis, including capitals. The imposing remains are explained in a diagram at the site.

THE ANCIENT CITY

A sandy path continues through the low vegetation to a recent excavation, near an old farmhouse, where the remains of a small industrial area have been found, dedicated to the manufacture of terracotta votive offerings. The city was orientated north–south and recent research has suggested it may originally have extended beyond the perimeter wall to the north, and into the valleys of the Cottone and Modione rivers. Another area of the city farther north, on the sand-covered hill of Manuzza, may have had a slightly different orientation. Further north was a necropolis (probably on the site of a prehistoric burial-place).

SANCTUARY OF DEMETER MALOPHOROS AND THE NECROPOLIS

Outside the North Gate, to the west, can be seen the excavations on the right bank of the Modione. These can most easily be reached by the rough road (c. 1km, used by the custodians) which branches off from the main crossroads near Temple C. Here the interesting Sanctuary of Demeter Malophoros, the 'Bearer of Fruits', consists of a sacred area enclosed by walls. It is now approached by a monumental entrance (late 5th century) and portico. In the centre is a huge sacrificial altar and beyond, the temple (a megaron), thought to have been built c. 560 BC, with a Doric cornice. Nearby are the scant remains of two other sacred precincts, one of them dedicated to Zeus Meilichios with two altars, where numerous stelae carved with a male and female head were discovered. More than 5,000 terracotta figurines have been found in the vicinity. Another temple is being excavated to the south.

Near a spring, some 200m north, a sacred edifice has recently been excavated and called Temple M. This may, in fact, be an altar or a monumental fountain of the 6th century BC. The necropolis proper extends for some kilometres to the west: several tombs and heaps of bones are still visible behind the modern holiday village of Triscina, but at least another two burial-grounds have been located besides this one.

VINCENZO TUSA

That we can visit Selinunte today and appreciate the beauty and wealth of the great city, its temples and the elegant design of its residential areas, is due to Vincenzo Tusa (1925–2009), for many years superintendent of monuments for Palermo and Trapani. In 1983 he fought a tremendous battle to save the archaeological site. Firstly, the people of the nearby towns wanted to build holiday bungalows on the beach. Added to this the Mafia, represented by the notorious brothers Nino and Ignazio Salvo, had plans to build a hotel and 40 holiday condominiums on the East Hill. Meanwhile tomb-raiders were digging every night, completely undisturbed. But Tusa was tenacious and found solutions. He obtained a permit from Rome enabling him to hire the raiders to work for him, within the law. Being a farmer himself, he found a way to convince the 76 smallholders who husbanded the land of the advantages of expropriation. They could continue to grow their crops (as they still do today) and at the same time achieve something that would stand their community in good stead. There is no record of the arguments he used to persuade the Salvo brothers. He probably exhausted their patience, even though, as he revealed later, they offered him 'a luxurious Mercedes, all the women I wanted on a silver dish, and royalties from the hotels for the rest of my life'. He then planned a huge dyke covered with vegetation to enclose the east side of the park, hiding Marinella from view for those inside the area (when the people of Marinella protested that they could no longer see the temples from their bungalows, Tusa lowered the dyke a fraction). The effect of the dyke, with its three entrances each framing a different temple, is completely successful and once inside, it is like being in another world. Tusa received a number of death threats but never lost his nerve, enlisting help from journalists, teachers, intellectuals and show-business personalities in order to convince the local people of the enormous treasure they were running the risk of losing.

THE CUSA QUARRIES

Off the road between Selinunte and Castelvetrano a country road (signposted) leads through extensive olive groves and vineyards to **Campobello di Mazara** (*map p. 575, C3*), a wine-producing centre. From Campobello a road (signposted) leads south towards Tre Fontane on the coast. At a crossroads by the Baglio Ingham, a right turn continues past a disused sewage plant to end at the **Cave di Cusa** (*open 9–1hr before sunset, winter Sundays 9–1; same ticket as Selinunte*), the ancient quarries used for building the Selinunte temples.

The quarries have not been worked since the destruction of Selinunte in 409 BC and no excavations have ever been carried out here. Ancient olive trees grow among the peaceful ruins, and the beautiful site, inhabited by birds, is surrounded by olive and orange groves and vineyards. Only some 120m wide, the quarries extend for 2km, unenclosed, unannounced and often, especially in winter, utterly deserted and romantic. The various different processes of quarrying can be studied here, from the first incisions in the rock to the empty spaces left by the removal of the completed drums for columns. One block, still attached to the rock, seems to have been intended for a capital. Around each column carved out of the rock, a space of c. 50cm allowed room for the stonemason to work. Four drums stand close together, carved along the whole of their length and apparently waiting simply to be detached at their bases. The large cylindrical masses of stone (c. 3m by 2m) were probably intended for Temple G. It is thought that wooden frames were constructed around the columns and that they were transported to Selinunte, about 18km away, on wheels of solid wood strengthened by iron bands and pulled by oxen.

CASTELVETRANO

Castelvetrano (*map p. 575, C3*) is a farming community in the centre of a wine- and oil-producing area. The olive trees are very small, the fruits being gathered by hand for preserving or for making oil, among the finest in Sicily; the local bread is particularly good, too, and is a Slow Food Foundation niche product. To the south the view falls away across the cultivated plain towards the sea and the ruins of Selinunte. The simple architecture of many of the houses, with internal courtyards, is interesting, although the town was damaged in the Belice earthquake of 1968. The body of the bandit Salvatore Giuliano was 'found' here in 1950.

THE TOWN CENTRE

In the centre of town is the cramped and oddly-shaped Piazza Garibaldi, which is planted with trees. The **duomo** (*usually entered by the side door in Piazza Umberto*) is a 16th-century church with an unusual, ornately decorated portal. The central roof beam has preserved its painted decoration. Two triumphal arches are bedecked with white stuccoes of cherubs, garlands and angels, by Antonino Ferraro and Gaspare Serpotta (who also carved the four saints in the nave). In the presbytery there is gilded decoration by Antonino Ferraro and an *Assumption* (1619) by his son Orazio Ferraro. The chapel to the right of the sanctuary has a 16th-century wooden Crucifix. The chapel to the left of the sanctuary has a marble Gaginesque statue and, on the wall, a painting attributed to Pietro Novelli. Off the north aisle, the Cappella della Maddalena has fine decoration, especially in the dome, by Tommaso Ferraro. The detached campanile dates from the 16th century.

On the corner of Piazza Umberto is an elaborate **fountain** (1615) by the Neapolitan sculptor Orazio Nigrone, with a statue of a nymph. The church of the **Purgatorio**, which has a decorative 18th-century façade (now used for concerts), and the Neoclassical **Teatro Selinus** (1870; Giuseppe Patricolo) are also both in the piazza.

The little opera house, with 350 seats, looks like a miniature Doric temple, with four columns in front; in the entrance is a marble sculpture of *Children at Play* by Mario Rutelli.

From the top of Via Garibaldi, Via Fra' Pantaleo leads downhill southeast to **Piazza Regina Margherita**, where there is a little public garden and two churches. **San Domenico**, which has a plain façade, contains a riot of 16th-century Baroque terracotta figures, coloured and stuccoed, by Antonino Ferraro, who included his self-portrait in the choir, and unusual funerary monuments, the richly-decorated tombs of the family of Don Carlos of Aragona, the first prince of Castelvetrano and later Governor of Milan, who had commissioned Ferraro's meticulous work. On another side of the piazza is the 16th-century church of **San Giovanni Battista**, with an elaborate façade and a green cupola. The interesting interior contains a remarkable statue of St John the Baptist by Antonello Gagini (1522) and three 17th-century paintings.

MUSEO CIVICO SELINUNTINO

Open 9–1 & 3–6.30; 4– in summer; Sun and holidays mornings only. Ticket at the time of writing allowed access to the Efebo exhibit at Selinunte (see p. 172). T: 0924 909605.
Via Garibaldi continues downhill southeastwards past Via Francesco la Croce, on the corner of which is Palazzo de Majo, housing the Museo Civico Selinuntino. The chief exhibit is the bronze statuette known as the ***Ephebe of Selinunte*** (5th century BC), stolen from the Town Hall in 1962 (the mayor used it as a coat stand) and subsequently recovered in 1968. It was restored and displayed in the archaeological museum of Palermo for many years, before returning here (though at the time of writing it was on temporary display at Selinunte; check before visiting). Found by a nine-year-old boy at Selinunte in 1882, it is thought to be a locally-produced work of c. 480–460 BC, made using the lost-wax method. The collection also includes the ***Lamina plumbea***, a 5th-century BC transcription of a sacred law on a thin sheet of lead, from the archives of one of the Selinunte temples. It is the largest of its kind in existence and was recently returned from the Paul Getty Museum in Malibu, to whom it had been sold by clandestine diggers. Among the other finds from Selinunte are a red-figure krater with four satyrs (470–460 BC), Corinthian ware, terracottas, coins, and a two-headed stele from the sanctuary of Demeter Malophoros. The tawny alabaster statue of the *Madonna and Child* by Francesco Laurana and his workshop (c. 1460) comes from the ruined church of the Annunziata. Also here are three Roman rostra, found on the seabed off Levanzo in 2015. These objects are testimony to the great victory of Catulus in the fierce battle of the Aegadians during the First Punic War in 241 BC, when the Romans routed the Carthaginian fleet. The tourist office is on the first floor, over the museum.

SANTISSIMA TRINITÀ DI DELIA

This lovely church (*map p. 575, C3*), about 3km west of Castelvetrano, is reached by taking Via Pietro Colletta downhill from Piazza Umberto and continuing straight ahead (signposted 'Trinità di Delia'). After c. 1km, at a fork, the road (unsignposted) continues left past a gravel works and straight on (signposted 'Lago di Trinità'). It passes a small eucalyptus wood and then follows the white wall of the farm, which incorporates the church. The key is kept at the modern house on the right. The chapel, dating from the 11th–12th centuries, is a very fine building derived from Arab and Byzantine models. It was beautifully restored in 1880 and contains 19th-century family tombs. The crypt beneath is entered by an outside staircase. In the churchyard in a little wood is a romantic tombstone by Benedetto Civiletti, erected by the Saporito family. Beneath the hill is the beautiful reservoir of Lago della Trinità.

THE BELICE VALLEY

The Belice is one of Sicily's most important rivers. Once known as the *Hypsas*, it is formed by the union of the Belice Destro (the ancient *Crimissus*) from the mountains of Piana degli Albanesi, and the Belice Sinistro, or River Frattina, from Rocca Busambra. The two rivers meet near Poggioreale, forming the boundary between the provinces of Trapani and Agrigento. The Belice Valley, east of Castelvetrano, together with the parallel Mazaro, Modione and Carboj valleys, lie upon natural fault lines in the earth's crust, and earthquakes are therefore to be expected: that of 15th January 1968, although only 6.1 on the Richter scale, was exceptionally destructive and the inhabitants are still recovering from the impact. At least 370 people died and some 70,000 people were made homeless; reconstruction was long, slow and fraught with scandal, and is still not complete.

GIBELLINA

The town of Gibellina (*map p. 575, C2*) was the worst affected by the earthquake. It stood below a ridge of sulphur-bearing hills and was abandoned completely after its destruction. The new town, relocated some 20km to the west, occupies a badly-chosen position that becomes unpleasantly hot in summer. Several of Italy's most prominent artists and sculptors provided the new town with works of art, some of which were clumsily made and are now already dilapidated. In 1994 the new church collapsed without warning. Little thought was given to town planning; the new houses have no balconies where people can put a pot of basil or a few geraniums, and the streets have no porticoes and only a few trees to provide protection from the relentless sun.

At the entrance to Gibellina is the **Porta** (1980), a five-pointed star designed by Pietro Consagra, who dedicated much of his artistic activity to the reconstruction of the town. In the central Viale Segesta is the **Museo Civico di Arte Contemporanea** (*open 9–1 & 4–7; closed Sun, Mon and holidays; T: 0924 67428*), which displays the models for the monuments of the new city and paintings by Renato Guttuso, Fausto Pirandello, Mario Schifano and many others.

The ruins of the old town, **Rovine di Gibellina**, were covered with 13 hectares of cement as a work of art by the Tuscan artist Alberto Burri; on the death of the artist in 1995, the project was still unfinished. After years of neglect the work has now been repaired and provided with a car park. Undoubtedly it is a masterpiece of Land Art.

During the summer, open-air theatrical performances called *Orestiadi* are held here; for the first production, in 1983, the sculptor Arnaldo Pomodoro made items of scenery in wood and fibreglass, decorated with gold leaf. These have recently been restored and are shown in a special museum called the **Museo delle Trame Mediterranee** (*open 9–1 & 3–6, closed Mon; T: 0924 67844, www.orestiadi.it*), in an old wheat farm known as Baglio Di Stefano, c. 2km from Gibellina. It houses a collection of local Elymian and Greek archaeological material and there is also an ethnographical section, with costumes, jewellery from the Maghreb, and more than a hundred 14th-century majolica dishes from Spain. The gallery displays an exceptionally fine collection of works donated to Gibellina by contemporary Italian artists such as Scialoja, Consagra, the Pomodoro brothers and Schifano.

SANTA NINFA AND POGGIOREALE

Even though the 1968 earthquake caused the collapse of a large majority of its houses, **Santa Ninfa** (*map p. 575, C2*) was rebuilt where it stood; it was a good choice. In Piazza Aldo Moro, near the public library, is the Museo Cordio (*open weekdays 9–1, www.museocordio.net*), dedicated to the genial local artist Nino Cordio (1937–2000) and displaying a selection of his opus. His etchings are notable, as are his poignant little bronze statuettes. Near the town is a cave with splendid stalactites and 'cave pearls', and a necropolis of the Elymians, called Grotta di Santa Ninfa, protected as a nature reserve (*Visitor's Centre, Castello Rampinzeri, open Tues, Thur, Sat, Sun and holidays, T: 329 862 0473/5; they will provide a guide; www.legambienteriserve.it*).

On the eastern border of the province is the old town of **Poggioreale**, also destroyed in the earthquake and later rebuilt. To the east of it, excavations in 1970 revealed part of an ancient city and a necropolis (with 7th- and 6th-century BC tombs). **Salaparuta** (*map p. 575, C3*), famous for its vineyards belonging to the Corvo family, was abandoned after the earthquake and a new town partially reconstructed.

PARTANNA

Partanna (*map p. 575, C3*) is an agricultural centre which was also badly damaged. The stunning Castello Grifeo (*open Oct–April 9.30–12.30 & 3.30–6.30, May–Sept 9.30–12.30 & 4.30–8, closed Mon; T: 0924 923970, www.grifeo.it*), a castle built by Count Roger in 1076 and rebuilt in the 17th century, houses the Museo della Preistoria, displaying prehistoric artefacts discovered in the Belice Valley, including a remarkable collection of primitive vases in the style of Naro. The highlight is a skull with a large hole at the back, cut using a stone blade, perhaps for medical or magical reasons, an operation which the patient survived for some years. Under the castle are numerous tunnels carved into the rock, not yet fully explored. In the courtyard is a damaged coat of arms sculpted by Francesco Laurana, who visited here in 1468. The Chiesa Madre has been partially reconstructed after being almost totally destroyed in the earthquake. It contains stuccoes by Vincenzo Messina, an organ by Paolo Amato, and a statue of the Madonna by the workshop of Francesco Laurana. Nearby in the Parco Archeologico di Contrada Stretta are numerous rock-hewn tombs, caves, and trenches for collecting water for irrigation, which have revealed the presence of a group of

Bronze Age people who lived here c. 5,000 years ago. Objects discovered during the excavations (including the skull) are in the museum of Castello Grifeo (*see above*).

SALEMI

Salemi (*map p. 575, C2*) is probably the site of *Halicyae*, a town of the ancient Sicans or Elymians and later an important Arab city. The town's layout is clearly Arab in character. When Ferdinand of Aragon signed the famous edict on 31st March 1492 banishing Muslims and Jews from Sicily, Salemi was one of the few places to offer them refuge. The town was badly damaged in the 1968 earthquake, when the Chiesa Madre and the Capuchin Monastery were destroyed.

The steep and slippery Via Garibaldi leads up to Piazza Alicia and the impressive golden 13th-century **castle** (*open 10–1 & 4–7, closed Mon*), with fine vaulted rooms and three towers, two square and one round, from which on 14th May 1860 Garibaldi raised the three-coloured banner, proclaiming Salemi to be capital of Italy, a privilege it maintained for only three days. The church of the **Collegio** (in Via D'Aguirre, near the summit of the hill), with its twisted Baroque columns either side of the entrance, became the new Chiesa Madre (among the various works of art, note the beautiful 18th-century organ) while the enormous Collegio itself, the Jesuit monastery, was restored to house the town's museums. The **Palazzo dei Musei** (*open 10–1 & 4–7, closed Mon, T: 0924 982376*), contains paintings and sculptures attributed to Domenico and Antonello Gagini and Francesco Laurana, brought here after the earthquake of 1968 from damaged churches, and an archaeological section with material excavated at Salemi, Mokarta and Monte Polizzo. The Museo del Risorgimento is dedicated to the Sicilian phase of the Unification of Italy, with memorabilia of Garibaldi's time in Sicily in 1860. A third section, subject of much polemical discussion, is the Museo della Mafia 'Leonardo Sciascia'. The contents of some displays are extremely unpleasant: a series of eight small cabins gives a vision of progressively intensifying moments of horror, showing the effect of the criminal organisation on society. Other works of art on the subject, including sculptures and paintings, are displayed in the gallery.

Close to the Collegio is Largo IV Novembre, with the **Civic Library** containing over 50,000 volumes, and the **Museo del Pane** at the oratory of San Bartolomeo (*open 10–1 & 4–7, closed Mon*), which houses a display of the decorative loaves baked for the feasts of St Blaise and St Joseph, for which Salemi is famous.

Continuing down the stairs at the end of Via D'Aguirre, you reach **Piazza della Dittatura** and the Town Hall. On the right is the charming Rabato district, and the church of **Sant'Agostino** (*open 10–1 & 4–7, closed Mon*), with a permanent exhibition of diocesan gold and silverware.

On the northern outskirts of the town is the early Christian **basilica of San Miceli**, discovered in 1893. It had a central nave and two side aisles, divided by two rows of five pilasters, and three layers of mosaic floors, one on top of the other. Unfortunately the mosaics were badly damaged by local peasants searching for buried treasure at the moment of the discovery. All they found were bones, because the little church had been used as a burial ground between the 4th and the 7th centuries AD, with a total of 58 graves.

THE AEGADIAN ISLANDS

The Aegadian Islands, Favignana, Levanzo and Marettimo (*map p. 575*), lie 15km–30km off the west coast of Sicily. They are reached by boat and hydrofoil services from Trapani or Marsala. The inhabitants, famed as skilled fishermen, are now turning to tourism to earn a living. The varied birdlife includes migratory species in spring and autumn and the islands now form a marine nature reserve, the largest of its kind in Italy. The waters around the islands are popular with divers, and those between Favignana and Marsala are also of great interest to marine archaeologists because of the many sea battles fought here. These islands were the ancient Aegades or Aegates. In the mid-16th century the islands were given to the Genoese Camillo Pallavicini, from whom they were purchased in 1874 by the Florio, a family from Calabria, who settled in Palermo (*see p. 74*) and became important entrepreneurs on the west coast of Sicily.

FAVIGNANA

Favignana, 17km southwest of Trapani, is the largest island of the group and is mostly flat with a rather bare landscape, used mainly as pastureland. The best swimming is at the rocky bay of Cala Rossa, on the north coast; there are more crowded sandy beaches on the south coast between Grotta Pergiata and Punta Longa, where there is a tiny harbour and fishing village. In the eastern part of the island are numerous disused tufa quarries (the soft white tufa found here is an excellent building material). The small quarries are now mostly used as orchards, although one quarry still operates, supplying the local market, and some have been transformed into hotels. Near the cemetery, several wells with huge wooden water wheels of Arab origin survive, once used for irrigation. At Punta Marsala there is a view of Marsala and (on the left) the low, green island of Mozia. The prettiest part of the island is to the west beyond Mt Santa Caterina, where a Norman castle once used as a prison and now abandoned, can be reached in about 1hr on foot.

THE TOWN

The little medieval town, where most of the inhabitants live, and where all the shops are located, was refounded in 1637 by the Pallavicini family. It has a peaceful, rather run-down atmosphere, with a number of the cube-like houses half-restored, half-built, or for sale. The passenger boats and hydrofoils dock at the picturesque harbour, filled with fishing vessels. Palazzo Florio, a large Art Nouveau palace near the port, was built in 1876 for Ignazio Florio by Giuseppe Damiani Almeyda. It is now used as a police headquarters. Nearby is a smaller 19th-century palace, now the Town Hall, with a statue of Ignazio Florio in front of it. The **Stabilimento Florio delle Tonnare di Favignana e delle Formiche** (*open summer only 10–1.30 & 5–11.30, last tickets 30mins before closing; T: 324 563 1991*) is an enormous old tuna-canning facility built in 1859 by Giulio Drago for the Pallavicini, and beautifully restored. It used to be among the most important in the Mediterranean, processing 10,000 tuna a year. The bluefin tuna (*Thunnus thynnus*), renowned for its excellent quality, is no longer caught here, to give the fish (on the verge of extinction) the chance to recuperate. Before the cannery was built the fish were salted, hung up by the tail, then cut in pieces to be smoked, cooked or preserved in oil. Every piece of the fish was used: the skin was used as sandpaper; the tail and fins became brooms; some bones were used to make tools; and other parts either boiled to make glue or fishmeal. The industry thrived and in 1874 Drago ceded his contract to the Florio, who ran this factory until 1937. By 1977 it had closed down owing to competition from Atlantic tuna (yellowfin). The buildings, a splendid example of industrial archaeology, now house a theatre, an auditorium, and the **Archaeological Museum** (*guided tours only; several tours during the course of the day*). This last now hosts an impressive display of material from the Battle of the Aegadian Islands, the naval struggle that ended the First Punic War (*see below*), with anchors, helmets and amphorae, as well as eight rostra (prow rams), seven of which are Roman, bearing inscriptions with the names of the noble families who provided them, and one Carthaginian, with a dedication to Baal. Other galleries are dedicated to the tuna fishing industry in all its aspects, from the moment of the *mattanza* (*see overleaf*) to the sealing of the tin cans, while two rooms display intriguing and often dramatic black and white photos from the famous Magnum agency, founded in 1947 by Robert Capa, Henri Cartier-Bresson, David Seymour, George Rodger and William Vandivert.

Via Vittorio Emanuele, the main street of town, leads to **Piazza Matrice** where there is the main church with a green dome, near the tourist office.

THE BATTLE OF THE AEGADIAN ISLANDS

Rome and Carthage fought the First Punic War between 264 and 241 BC, mainly in Sicily. Possibly one of the most costly and devastating conflicts in human history, it was one of the key factors in Rome's eventual rise to dominance over the central and western Mediterranean. The decisive moment in the war came on 10th March 241 BC, when an enormous Carthaginian fleet, carrying supplies for their besieged garrisons in western Sicily, was attacked off the Aegadian Islands by a well-drilled Roman fleet under the command of the proconsul Gaius Lutatius Catulus. The Roman ships had been cleared for action and were therefore much more manoeuvrable than the heavily-laden Carthaginian vessels. In the ensuing battle the Carthaginians were rapidly overwhelmed and only half their fleet managed to escape. The magnitude of this defeat led the Carthaginians to seek peace negotiations, and the war was finally over.

Since 2004, an international team of underwater archaeologists has discovered 13 bronze rams (rostra) on the seabed off Levanzo. Eleven had been raised at the time of writing and, together with some helmets, amphorae, metal objects, other pottery and another two rams that had been found previously by fishermen, they provide vivid evidence of this pivotal naval battle. Most of these finds are now on display in the archaeological museum on Favignana but there is also an excellent series of information panels about the battle at the Cordici Museum in Erice (see p. 141).

LA MATTANZA

Tuna fishing has historically been an important part of life on these islands, as this scene from a red-figure krater shows (in the Mandralisca museum in Cefalù).

In the deep channel between Levanzo and Favignana the method of tuna fishing known as *La Mattanza* was practised in spring since prehistory. A series of net traps formed a corridor leading to a square pen called the *camera della morte* (death chamber), which was activated under the instructions of the head fisherman, or *rais*. The wind called the Favonio, which brings the fish here for spawning, starts to blow at the end of May or in early June; choosing the right moment for fishing was all important. The females, already fertilised by the males, escaped the trap because they swim deep down, about 20m below the surface, while the males are much closer to the surface. When there were around 100 fish in the pen the area was encircled by boats, with that belonging to the rais in the centre, and the nets were slowly hauled in, accompanied by the ancient haunting chants of the fishermen, called *cialome*: 'aja mola, aja mola, aja mola e iamuninni...Gesù Cristu cu' li Santi...nianzò...nianzò...', to maintain the correct rhythm. It was very hard work; one fish caught in 1974 weighed 600kg. Tuna tend to dive when in danger so that during this operation they often collided with one another and hit their heads: by the time the net reached the surface (the whole operation took about an hour) many of them were wounded and stunned. They were then harpooned and pulled into the boats. The sea ran red with blood; it was a horrid but fascinating spectacle which had changed little since the Bronze Age. The catch drastically declined in recent years, due in part to modern fishing techniques and to over-exploitation caused by the high prices offered by Far Eastern markets. Sicily once had many tuna fisheries: they have all closed now because the bluefin tuna is in danger of extinction and its capture is no longer permitted.

LEVANZO

Levanzo (pron: LEvanzo), 15km from Trapani, has no natural springs, and virtually no cars. The ancient *Phorbantia* or Pliny's *Bucinna*, its austere, windbeaten landscape is set in a transparent sea of turquoise and cobalt blue. The island is particularly interesting for botanists: many of the plants are endemic. It is also famous for its caves, notably the Grotta del Genovese, which has the most interesting prehistoric wall-art in Italy, discovered by chance in 1950. The cave paintings, comparable with those at Lascaux in France or Altamira in Spain, date from the Neolithic period; the primitive paint is made of animal fat, ochre and charcoal; fish and people are represented. The stunning incised drawings of bison and deer date from the Upper Palaeolithic period, when the island was still joined to Sicily. A track leads across the island from the port to the cave, which can also be reached by boat. Visits (jeep or boat) must be booked in advance (*the excursion lasts c. 2hrs; departures at 10.30 and 2.30; T: 0923 924032, 339 741 8800, www.grottadelgenovese.it*).

A capsized Roman cargo ship was recently located close to the island, with its cargo of garum amphorae still intact. In Roman times, Levanzo was noted for the production of garum, a fish sauce much appreciated by connoisseurs.

MARETTIMO

Marettimo (pron: MaRETtimo), once known as *Hiera* or *Hieromesus* (sacred place), is the most isolated of the Aegadian Islands, 38km from Trapani, and immersed in a transparent deep blue sea. Only 16km square, wild, beautiful and mountainous, it is rich in natural springs and grottoes, and is the best preserved of the three islands, mainly because it was once a notorious pirate stronghold, which discouraged settlers. There are many birds, especially during the migratory season, and the nesting species include Bonelli's eagle, peregrine falcon, kestrel, lesser kestrel, buzzard, black wheatear, as well as many interesting sea birds including the stormy petrel, gannet and Cory's shearwater. In the interior of the island there are even boars and mouflons. The island is cared for by the Azienda Forestale and there are well-signposted tracks to the various points of interest. With a charming little Moorish-style village, there are no roads, no cars and no hotels. Samuel Butler suggested that this was the island described in the story of the Cyclops in Homer's *Odyssey*, the islets of Le Formiche being the rocks hurled by Polyphemus at Odysseus. A rewarding and spectacular hike leads to the ruins of the ancient castle called Castello Saraceno at Punta Troia. Some Roman ruins and a small Palaeo-Christian church can also be found. Boat trips around the island and its sea caves can be arranged at the harbour. At the end of the 19th century many islanders from Marettimo found their way to Monterey in California, where they established a successful canned fish enterprise, immortalised by John Steinbeck in his *Cannery Row* (1945).

PANTELLERIA

Far away to the southwest, about 110km from the Sicilian mainland (and only 67km from Tunisia) lies Pantelleria (83 square kilometres, population 8,000), the largest of Sicily's offshore islands. The wild scenery includes volcanic phenomena such as hot springs (the last eruption was in 1891). The central conical peak rises to a height of 836m. Tiny capers, figs, olives and sweet grapes called Zibibbo are cultivated in spite of strong winds, little rain and no underground springs, and the island is especially famous for its wines, Moscato di Pantelleria and Moscato passito. In fact, most of the mountainsides are terraced, with tiny gardens descending to the sea, each with its dry-stone wall to protect the crops from the wind. The cube-shaped black stone cottages, with domed whitewashed roofs, called *dammusi*, are of Arab origin. The inhabitants of Pantelleria are farmers rather than fishermen, showing considerable patience and fortitude in caring for their plants in the difficult, windswept volcanic terrain. Sufficient water is provided for the cultivations thanks to the lava-stone walls built around the plants to protect them from the wind; humidity condenses during the night onto the cold stone, and then gradually seeps through the porous rock until it reaches the roots of the plants. This simple, ancient method has now received UNESCO recognition.

HISTORY OF PANTELLERIA

The island was the legendary home of Calypso, the nymph who was able to distract Odysseus from his travels for seven years. Archaeological evidence has shown that the island was inhabited in the Neolithic era, when the obsidian on the southern shores would have been particularly useful. At Mursia 58 prehistoric tombs, known as *sesi*, were discovered by Paolo Orsi in the 19th century. These large domed tumuli were built in blocks of lava in the 17th century BC and were probably founded in order to exploit the deposits of obsidian, the volcanic glass used for making knives. Only 27 have survived, notably the Sese Grande, the others having either fallen into ruin or been engulfed by new buildings. Several of them still contained human remains, buried in the foetal position, with their personal possessions close by. Recent excavations revealed a square stone hut in which a cloth bag with some items of bronze jewellery with glass beads was found, perhaps from Egypt or Syria.

Later the island was home to a Phoenician settlement called *Hiranin*, meaning 'place of the birds'. The Greeks called it *Cossyra*, meaning 'small one', a name it maintained under the Romans, who took it in 217 BC. The Arabs gave it the name it still bears, *Bint er-rhia*, or 'daughter of the wind'. After conquest by Count Roger in 1123 it remained a Sicilian possession. During the Second World War it was used as a base for harrying Allied convoys. The island was once used as a place of exile for political prisoners. It is now popular with the rich and famous: Gerard Depardieu, Sting and Giorgio Armani, among others, own properties on the island.

Now protected as a National Park (decision which fortuitously came just months after arsonists hoping to win development permits had set fire to forests), Pantelleria is also particularly attractive to lovers of the sea. There are no beaches, but swimming from the rocks is very pleasant, because the water is clean and clear. Dolphins are common, and the nun seal is once again occasionally being spotted, after many years of absence from Italian waters. It is a good place for birdwatching too, especially during the migratory passage, when herons, cranes, flamingoes, geese and ducks can be seen. During the summer the hoopoe is resident, as is the cattle egret, the Tunisian chaffinch and the blue rock thrush. Among the mammals, the wildcat is still present. The Pantelleria ass is a kind of donkey native to the island, where it has been used since the 1st century BC. It is large (the size of a pony), sure-footed and very strong, with a smooth, shiny black pelt. It became extinct some years ago because islanders were no longer using them (the last one slipped into the sea and drowned). However, forestry technicians at the San Matteo stud farm at Erice have been able to recreate the animal by taking genes from donkeys throughout Italy which had the Pantelleria ass in their ancestry. It took them 17 years, but now these donkeys can be seen carrying tourists on treks around the volcanoes. Of Pantelleria's 597 plant species, 13 are endemic.

EXPLORING PANTELLERIA

The port of Pantelleria was completely rebuilt after the Second World War; the little houses around the harbour go back to the 1950s and are not renowned for their architectural elegance. The oldest building is the forbidding **Castello Barbacane** (*open winter Mon, Wed, Thur, Sat 9.15–1.30 & 4.30–7.30; Tues, Fri 10.30–1.30 & 4.30–7.30; Sun 9.15–1.30; summer every day 6pm–midnight; T: 0923 695035 Tourist Office*), first built by the Arabs, when it was surrounded by water and entered by a drawbridge; successive dominations each altered the castle to adapt it to their particular needs; it was used as a prison until 1975 and now it is planned to situate the museum of Pantelleria within its walls. The Roman sculptures found at Cossyra, an exceptional series of three finely-carved Roman heads, are kept here. The custodian will show you them on request. Two of the heads, a portrait of Julius Caesar and another of Antonia the Younger, daughter of Mark Anthony, sister-in-law to Tiberius and mother of Claudius, are of Paros marble and were found in a cistern, where apparently they had been placed with care; the third (also found in a cistern) is a stunningly realistic portrait of Titus, son of Vespasian. The finds are evidence of the vitality of Cossyra in the 1st–2nd centuries AD. In another recent exceptional find, close to shore at Cala Tramontana on the east coast, 3,418 Carthaginian bronze coins, minted between 264 and 241 BC, were found scattered on the seabed. On one side the coins show Tanit crowned with wheat and on the other a horse's head. In all probability the money was intended to pay the soldiers taking part in the First Punic War.

Among the villages of the island, **Scauri** is high on the edge of a cliff, with a spectacular view down to its little fishing harbour. **Nicà** is a fishing village, on a narrow inlet, while the inland village of **Rekhale**, close by, is still intact, with the typical stone cottages and tiny, luxuriant gardens. Spectacular views can be had at **Saltalavecchia** and the ancient landing-place of **Balata dei Turchi**, both on the south coast. The most famous viewpoint is at **Punta dell'Arco**, where there is good swimming and the rock formations look like the head and the trunk of an elephant extending into the sea. **Gadir** is another fishing village, where the sea is easily accessible even for inexperienced swimmers.

The **extinct volcanoes** in the middle of the island, Montagna Grande (836m) and Monte Gibele (700m) offer rewarding treks through vineyards and pinewoods; the wobbly song-flight of the fan-tailed warbler can be observed, and the Algerian form of the bluetit can also be spotted. The old volcanic cones are called *cuddie*. The beautiful inland crater-lake of **Bagno dell'Acqua** (Lago di Venere, the Lake of Venus) is about 6km from the port. It is fed by a hot-water spring and is 500m in diameter and 2m above sea level.

PRACTICAL INFORMATION

GETTING AROUND

• **By air:** Daily flights from several mainland Italian airports to Vincenzo Florio Airport at Birgi, equidistant from Trapani and Marsala (*www.airgest. it, www.aeroportotrapani.com*). Buses connect the airport to Trapani, Marsala, Mazara del Vallo and Palermo. Flights to Pantelleria from Trapani are run year round by Alitalia (*www.alitalia.it*), and from Rome and Bergamo June–Sept by Blu Express (*www.blu-express.com*). Ryanair (*www.ryanair.com*) connects several mainland cities to Pantelleria from April–Oct.

• **By sea:** For up-to-date information on ferry and hydrofoil schedules, consult *www.traghetti.com*.

To Pantelleria (*NB: When sailing to Pantelleria, always check beforehand that the ferry will be leaving: high seas are common.*) Siremar Compagnia delle Isole (*www.siremar.it*) runs ferries from Trapani daily except Sat (7hrs 30mins). Traghetti delle Isole (*www. traghettidelleisole.it*) runs ferries 5 days a week in summer and 3 in winter. Hydrofoils are operated by Liberty Lines (*www.libertylines.it*).

To the Aegadian Islands: Siremar (*www.siremar.it*) runs 4 daily ferries to Favignana and Levanzo, c. 50mins; and to Marettimo twice weekly, 3hrs, from Molo della Sanità. Hydrofoils (more expensive) run by Siremar (*www. siremar.it*) leave from Molo Dogana; those run by Liberty Lines (*www. libertylines.it*) leave from the Banchina Dogana, Via Ammiraglio Staiti, several times a day in summer: services also for

Ustica. Liberty Lines also run hydrofoils from Marsala to the Aegadian Islands.

Siremar ticket offices: In Trapani: Agenzia Sanges, Stazione Marittima, Molo Sanità; on Favignana: Compagnia delle Egadi, Molo San Leonardo; on Levanzo: Caterina Campo, Via Calvario 29; on Marettimo: Francesco Torrente, Piazza Umberto 2; On Pantelleria: Agenzia Rizzo, Via Borgo Italia 22.

Traghetti delle Isole ticket offices: In Trapani: Agenzia Egatour, Via Ammiraglio Staiti 13; On Pantelleria: Adriano Minardi, Via Borgo Italia 15.

Liberty Lines ticket offices: In Trapani: Banchina Dogana, Via Ammiraglio Staiti; In Marsala: Molo Porto Marsala, Piazza Piemonte Lombardo; on Favignana: Molo San Leonardo; on Levanzo: Porto di Levanzo; on Marettimo: Corso Umberto 15; on Pantelleria: Via Borgo Italia 5.

• **By train:** The central railway station in Trapani is in Piazza Umberto, with services to Palermo, Marsala (c. 40mins), Mazara del Vallo (c. 1hr) and Castelvetrano (c. 2–3hrs). Trains stop at Ragattisi, the nearest station for the boat to Mozia (about a 1km walk from the station). Segesta is on the Palermo–Trapani line (infrequent services) but the station is a 20-min walk from the site (*www.trenitalia.it*).

• **By bus:** For up-to-date bus schedules consult www.orarioautobus.it.

ATM (*www.atmtrapani.it*) runs services within the city of Trapani, to the port, the salt pans and also to the cableway station for Erice.

AST (*www.aziendasicilianatrasporti. it*) runs to Trapani Birgi Airport, also

Bonagia, Campobello di Mazara, Castellammare, Castelvetrano, Custonaci, Erice, Gibellina, Marsala, Mazara del Vallo, Messina, Palermo, Partanna, Salemi, San Vito Lo Capo, Sciacca,and Selinunte.

Lumia (*www.autolineelumia.it*) connects Trapani to Agrigento, Burgio, Caltabellotta, Menfi, Montallegro, Montevago, Porto Empedocle, Realmonte, Ribera, Santa Margherita di Belice, Sambuca, Sciacca, Siculiana and Villafranca Sicula. Also Marsala to Mazara del Vallo and Agrigento.

Marsala Travel Bus (*www.marsalatravelbus.it*) runs services connecting all the villages of Pantelleria and the airport.

Salemi (*www.autoservizisalemi.it*) connects Marsala to Campobello, Castelvetrano, Palermo, Salemi and Trapani Birgi Airport.

Segesta (*www.interbus.it*) runs inter-city services from Piazza Malta in Trapani to/from Palermo and Palermo Airport.

There are buses from Castelvetrano to Selinunte (the stop is a 5-min walk from the entrance).

• **By cableway:** A cablecar (*funivia*) connects Trapani (corner of the SP 31 Trapani–Erice road and Via Capua, Casa Santa, *www.funiviaerice.it*) and Erice in just over 10mins (*Tues–Fri 9.10–9, Sat and public holidays 9.30–midnight, Sun 9.40–9.30, closed Jan–mid-March and every Mon for maintenance*).

WHERE TO STAY

ALCAMO (*map p. 575, C2*)
€€€ **Centrale**. Restored *palazzo* where Goethe once stayed, with 32 rooms, good restaurant and car park, centrally situated; rooms can be noisy. *Via Amendola 24, T: 0924 507845, www. hotelcentrale.sicilia.it.*

€ **Terme Gorga**. Simple little hotel and spa down by the railway station, between Alcamo and Segesta, with 11 comfortable rooms, no restaurant. Swimming pool open all year, with water from the nearby thermal springs. *Contrada Gorga, west of Alcamo and the A29, T: 0924 23842, www.termegorga. com.*

€€ **La Battigia**. On the beach (completely deserted in winter), with 26 rooms, pool, good restaurant. Small pets welcome. *Lungomare La Battigia, T: 0924 597259, www.labattigia.it.*

CALATAFIMI SEGESTA (*map p. 575, C2*)
€ **Mille Pini**. Small hotel with 10 rooms in the pinewoods just out of town, good value for money, with a restaurant. 5km from Segesta. *Belvedere Francesco Vivana 4, T: 0924 951260, www. hotelmillepini.com.*

CASTELLAMMARE DEL GOLFO (*map p. 575, C1*)
€€€ **Cetarium**. On the harbour, a beautifully restored tuna fishery; 26 bright, comfortable but rather small rooms, excellent restaurant. *Via Zangara 45, T: 0924 533401, www. hotelcetarium.it.*

€€ **Al Madarig**. ■ Close to the castle and the old city, with 38 rooms, car park, nice breakfasts but no restaurant. *Piazza Petrolo 7, T: 0924 33533, www. almadarig.com.*

€ **Cala Marina**. Attractive and practical little hotel, on the harbour, in a converted warehouse. Environmentally sensitive management. 14 rooms, no restaurant, car park. They can organise boat trips and diving. *Via Zangara 1, T:*

0924 531841, www.hotelcalamarina.it.
€ **Locanda Scirocco**. Unusual hotel with 12 comfortable rooms distributed among two buildings in the old city centre. Good breakfasts, no restaurant, but an excellent wine bar offering opportunities to taste local products. Airport/port shuttle on request, boat trips organised. *Corso Garibaldi 117, T: 0924 30010, www.locandascirocco.it.*

CASTELVETRANO (*map p. 575, C3*)
€€ **Althea Palace**. Practical new structure surrounded by olive groves and vineyards, 2km southeast of town centre, close to the Castelvetrano–Selinunte bus stop. 42 very comfortable spacious rooms, good restaurant and car park. *Via Caduti di Nassiriya, T: 0924 904873, www.altheapalacehotel.it.*
€ **Villa Mimosa**. ■ About halfway between Castelvetrano and Selinunte, in the countryside. Very attractive self-catering rooms, garden full of dogs and cats, pergola and veranda. The home of Jackie Sirimanne, a sommelier and expert on wine and olive oil, a charming and helpful person. Breakfast is provided. *Contrada La Rocchetta, T: 0924 44583 or 338 138 7388, www.villamimosasicily.com.*

CUSTONACI (*map p. 575, B1*)
€€€ **Villa Zina Park**. New hotel with 89 rooms and suites, small fitness centre, tennis, bowls, huge pool, good restaurant. *Via Viterbo 20, east of the centre, T: 0923 973937, www.villazina.it.*
€ **Cala Buguto**. Tiny hotel in an old farmhouse not far from the cave which encloses the hamlet of Scurati, with 9 small rooms and a restaurant serving delicious food. *Via D1 23, Contrada Scurati, T: 0923 973953 or 347 925 6864, www.calabuguto.it.*

ERICE (*map p. 575, B1*)
€€ **Elimo**. Small and comfortable with 21 rooms, on the main street, with a rooftop terrace and lovely little courtyard garden; nice restaurant. *Via Vittorio Emanuele 75, T: 0923 869377, www.hotelelimo.it. Map 3.*
€€ **Moderno**. Fascinating old hotel with 40 rooms; very good restaurant, part of the Buon Ricordo chain. *Via Vittorio Emanuele 63, T: 0923 869300, www.hotelmodernoerice.it. Map 3.*

MARSALA (*map p. 575, B2*)
€€€ **Baglio Oneto**. ■ 18th-century wine farm with lots of atmosphere, 5km southeast of Ragattisi (Mozia), the hotel has 49 charming rooms, garden, pool, and a good restaurant. *Contrada Baronazzo Amafi 8, T: 0923 746222, www.bagliooneto.it.*
€€€ **Stella d'Italia**. Built in 1873, Marsala's first hotel overlooks the cathedral. 35 delightful rooms, no restaurant but good breakfasts. Part of the Best Western chain. *Via Rapisardi 7, T: 0923 761889, www.hotelstelladitalia.it. Map 4.*
€€€ **Grand Hotel Palace**. The core of this hotel is a 19th-century English-style mansion, once the home of Charles Gordon, manager of the Florio winery. More recent extensions to the building give it 55 rooms and suites (choose the 'Antica Dimora'). Garden, pool, car park, good restaurants. *Lungomare Mediterraneo 57, T: 0923 719492, www.grandhotelpalace.eu. Map 6.*
€€ **Carmine**. A 17th-century monastery transformed into a modern, comfortable hotel, with 28 welcoming rooms, all different, and a garden. *Piazza Carmine 16, T: 0923 711907, www.hotelcarmine.it. Map 3.*

€€ **La Finestra sul Sale**. Three comfortable rooms in an old salt mill, right in front of the island of Mozia, north of Marsala, on the coast. Perfect for artists and photographers. *Saline Ettore e Infersa, Contrada Ettore Infersa 55, T: 0923 194 1509, www. salineettoreinfersa.com.*

MAZARA DEL VALLO (*map p. 575, B3*)
€€€ **Giardino di Costanza**. Situated among palms, olive groves and orchards, with 91 rooms and suites (2 with penthouse pool); fitness centre and spa, enormous pool and private beach. However, it is a long way from town. *Via Salemi km 7, T: 0923 675000, www. giardinodicostanza.it.*

€€€ **Visir Resort**. Comfortable hotel 2km from the centre of Mazara, a short walk from the sandy beach of Tonnarella, with 27 luxurious rooms and suites, restaurant, cosy bar, huge pool, fitness and beauty centre. *Via del Mare 211, Tonnarella, T: 0923 653738, www. visirresort.it.*

€€ **Mahara**. Once the winery of the English Hopps family, now an elegant hotel just out of town, offering 81 comfortable rooms and suites, good restaurant, garden, fitness centre. Many special offers. *Lungomare San Vito 3, T: 0923 673800, www.maharahotel.it.*

€ **City Centre B&B**. Situated on the first floor of the old railway station, 4 small but comfortable rooms, good breakfasts, ample parking. *Piazza De Gasperi 13, T: 0923 931686 or 345 328 6464, www.bbcitycentre.it.*

SAN VITO LO CAPO (*map p. 575, B1*)
€€€ **Capo San Vito**. Right on the beach, garden, good restaurant for candlelit dinners on the terrace, modern design in the rooms, small fitness centre, car park.

Via San Vito 1, T: 0923 972122, www. caposanvito.it.

€€€ **Riva del Sole**. In a good position close to the sea and to the town centre, small family-run hotel with 13 bright rooms and private beach, very good breakfasts. *Via Generale Arimondi 11, T: 0923 972629, www.hotelrivadelsole.it.*

€€ **Piccolo Mondo**. Small family-run hotel with 13 comfortable rooms, close to the beach, good breakfasts. *Via Nino Bixio 7, T: 0923 972032 or 338 483 2601, www.hotelpiccolomondosanvitolocapo.it.*

€ **Baglio Cusenza**. Comfortable B&B on the main street, 300m from the beach, with three spacious rooms; nice breakfasts. *Via Savoia 220 (corner of Via Foritano), T: 0923 972427 or 320 375 7439, www.bagliocusenza.it.*

SCOPELLO (*map p. 575, C1*)
€€€ **Tonnara di Scopello**. Exclusively self-catering accommodation in the three houses comprising the tuna fishery, each with kitchen and bathroom, no TV, telephone or wifi. Diving and sailing opportunities. Expensive. Open year round; one week minimum stay in summer. *Tonnara di Scopello, T: 339 307 1970, www.tonnaradiscopello.com.*

€ **Casale Corcella**. Panoramic B&B in an old stone house with 5 comfortable rooms, 1km inland (west) from Scopello and 2km from the Zingaro reserve. *Contrada Scardina, T: 368 365 4482 for info, to book see www.casalecorcella.com.*

SELINUNTE/MARINELLA (*map p. 575, C3*)
€€€ **Admeto**. In a lovely position overlooking the harbour and a short walk from the temples, modern hotel with comfortable rooms, good restaurant. *Via Palinuro 3, T: 0924 46796, www.hoteladmeto.it.*

€€ **Alceste**. Small hotel, a little dated, but with considerable charm; 30 rooms, good restaurant. Walking distance from the archaeological park. Closed Nov–March. *Via Alceste 21, T: 0924 46184, www.hotelalceste.it.*

TRAPANI (*map p. 575, B1*)

€€ **Vittoria**. Central position, 76 spacious rooms (some can be noisy), no restaurant but good breakfasts. *Via Francesco Crispi 4, T: 0923 873044, www.hotelvittoriatrapani.it. Map 4.*

€€ **Ai Lumi**. Ten minutes from the station, in the old quarter, lovely award-winning B&B in an 18th-century *palazzo* with flowery patio, 4 rooms, also self-catering apartments, restaurant. Very good breakfasts. *Corso Vittorio Emanuele 71, T: 0923 540922, www.ailumi.it. Map 6.*

€ **Maccotta**. In the old city, small guest house with 20 comfortable rooms and friendly owners, airport transfer on request, no restaurant. *Via degli Argentieri 4, T: 0923 28418, www.albergomaccotta.it. Map 7.*

ENVIRONS OF TRAPANI

€€€ **Relais Antiche Saline**. Beautifully restored *baglio* in the salt marshes at Nubia, 18 rooms, pool, fitness centre; good restaurant, the Trattoria del Sale. Ideal for birdwatchers, artists and photographers. *Via Giuseppe Verdi, Nubia. T: 0923 868042, www.relaisantichesaline.it.*

€€ **Case Colomba**. ■ In lovely countryside at Buseto Palizzolo, midway between Trapani and Castellammare, a comfortable environmentally-friendly B&B in an old farmhouse, with 10 spacious rooms, good breakfasts, pool; kind and knowledgeable owners. Open Easter–Oct. *Via Pietro Toselli 183, T: 0923 852729 or 347 211 6470, www.*

casecolomba.it.

€ **Duca di Castelmonte**. A comfortable old olive farm, close to Trapani, with 15 rooms and self-catering apartments; good home cooking. 2 nights minimum stay. *Via Salvatore Motisi 11, Contrada Xitta, T: 0923 526139, www.ducadicastelmonte.it.*

WHERE TO STAY ON THE ISLANDS

FAVIGNANA

€€€ **Dimora dell'Olivastro**. Nineteenth-century villa in the centre of the island, with 6 modern rooms, each with a terrace or patio, some with splendid views over Marettimo. *Via Seppi Torrente 3, Contrada Strusceri, T: 0923 921179 or 338 435 4484, www.dimoradellolivastro.it.*

€€€ **Cave Bianche**. Modern design in a low-environmental-impact hotel situated in a tufa quarry. Beautiful rooms with stone walls and floors, wooden furniture made by local craftsmen. Pool, good breakfasts. *Strada Comunale Fanfalo, T: 0923 925451, www.cavebianchehotel.it.*

€€ **Aegusa**. Delightful little hotel, central, with 28 rooms in two old buildings, very welcoming, excellent restaurant in the patio. *Via Garibaldi 11 (at the port), T: 0923 921638, www.aegusahotel.it.*

€€ **Egadi**. The oldest hotel on Favignana, recently beautifully restored, with 11 cool and relaxing rooms. Book well in advance. Renowned restaurant. Closed winter. *Via Cristoforo Colombo 17, T: 0923 921232, www.albergoegadi.it.*

LEVANZO

€€ **La Plaza Residence**. Seven self-catering apartments, each accommodating four people, in the village, open year round. *Salita Poste, T: 0923 194 1526, 335 671 8308 or 340 235 5949, www.levanzoresidence.com.*

€ **Paradiso**. Very simple hotel in front of the port, with good seafood restaurant. Closed winter. *Via Lungomare 8, T: 0923 924080, www.albergoparadiso.eu.*

MARETTIMO

There are no hotels on Marettimo, but rooms can be rented in private houses. The fishermen will meet you on the quay offering this kind of accommodation. They are not touts: absolutely trustworthy.

€ **Marettimo Residence**. Offers 42 charming self-catering apartments in cottages for stays of one week or more, garden, pool, pets welcome, very helpful hosts. *Via Telegrafo 3, Località Spatarello, T: 0923 923202, www. marettimoresidence.com.*

€ **B&B Scala Vecchio**. Comfortable B&B with 2 rooms, good position, terrace. *Via San Giuseppe 9, T: 329 785 7713, www.bebscalovecchio.it.*

€ **La Perla**. Guest house overlooking the old harbour, simple, 29 very clean rooms, panoramic rooftop terrace. Breakfast not provided; steep stairs, no credit cards. *Via Scalo Vecchio 13, T: 0923 923206, 333 278 2602 or 333 651 2618, www.marettimolaperla.it.*

PANTELLERIA

NB: Hotels on Pantelleria usually require bookings on a weekly basis only. A car is useful; available to rent at the port or the airport.

€€€ **Santa Teresa Resort**. 20 self-catering *dammusi* among the vineyards in the interior of the island; car advisable; small pets welcome. Three small pools, golf practice course. Open end April–end Sept. *Sibà Monastero Alto, T: 0923 916389 or 348 085 3013, www.santateresa.it.*

€€€ **Relais Gli Euterpini**. Quiet and exclusive, on the west side, close to the easily accessible sea, 10 secluded *dammusi* surrounded by pine trees and gardens, breakfast included in summer. Small pets welcome. *Strada Perimetrale 122, T: 0923 918070, www.euterpini.it.*

€€€ **Zubebi Resort**. ■ Hilltop position overlooking the port for this Oriental-style resort, with 8 beautifully restored and furnished *dammusi*. Pool, fitness centre, open-air restaurant under the palms, car park; airport/port shuttle included. *Contrada Zubebi, T: 0923 913653, www.zubebi.com.*

€€€ **Le Case di Gloria**. Facing southwest, for glorious sunsets, close to the sea and to the village of Scauri, 8 *dammusi* set in luxuriant vegetation, one with private pool; another pool in the garden. Pets welcome. *Contrada Penna, T: 339 755 1824 or 328 277 0934, www. dammusidigloria.it.*

€€ **Mediterraneo**. City-centre hotel in front of the port, with 39 functional rooms and a good penthouse restaurant. Airport shuttle on request. *Lungomare Borgo Italia 71, T: 0923 912114 or 0923 911299, www.vacanzeapantelleria.com.*

WHERE TO EAT

BONAGIA (*map p. 575, B1*)

€€ **Sirena di Sansica**. On the sea front, famous old family-run restaurant renowned for *busiate all'aragosta* (pasta cooked in lobster broth), tuna and shellfish. Short but well-chosen wine list. Closed Tues. *Lungomare Bonagia 45, T: 0923 573176.*

CASTELLAMMARE DEL GOLFO (*map p. 575, C1*)

€€€ **Ristorante del Golfo**. Fresh anchovies or tuna in *agrodolce* (sweet-sour sauce), home-made *busiate* (macaroni) with fresh sardines and wild fennel, sometimes *macco di fave* (broad-bean potage), fried baby squid; leave room for the *cassatelle*, little pies filled with lemon-scented ricotta. Closed all day Tues in winter, open Tues evening in summer. *Via Segesta 153, T: 0924 30257.*

€€ **Al Burgo**. Well presented, imaginative food, prepared with marvellous fish or meat and local vegetables. Good wine list. Closed Mon lunchtime. *Via Malta 19, T: 0924 531882.*

CASTELVETRANO (*map p. 575, C3*)

€ **Da Giovanni**. ■ Superb home-style cooking, using local vegetables, fish and meat to perfection. Closed Sun. *Via Milazzo 38, T: 0924 89053.*

ERICE (*map p. 575, B1*)

€€ **Monte San Giuliano**. Refined restaurant offering carefully prepared seafood and marvellous *busiati*, home-made macaroni; finish your meal with an assortment of the local pastries. Good wine list. Closed Mon. *Vicolo San Rocco 7, T: 0923 869595. Map 1.*

€€ **Osteria di Venere**. In the deconsecrated church of the Blessed Alberto, a welcoming *trattoria* offering seafood, meat and vegetable dishes. Closed Wed. *Via Roma 6, T: 0923 869362. Map 4.*

€€ **La Pentolaccia**. The best cous cous in Erice, fast service. Closed Tues. *Via Guarnotti 17, T: 0923 86909. Map 2–4.*

€ **Caffè San Rocco**. Welcoming bar and restaurant, crowded with scientists from the nearby Majorana centre. Great atmosphere. Closed Wed. *Via Guarnotti 23, T: 0923 869337. Map 2–4.*

MARSALA (*map p. 575, B2*)

€€ **Portico Blu**. Central, restaurant serving very fresh fish, delicious pasta dishes. Local wines. *Via Mario Nuccio 118, T: 0923 719840 or 338 589 4765. Map 6.*

€ **Natura a Tavola**. Ideal for light lunch or dinner, this is a wine bar where you will find delicious snacks (smoked fish, cheese and salami board, *arancini*), and also taste all the best local wines, liqueurs and preserves; they will ship on request. Closed when it rains. *Via Garibaldi 2, T: 329 3774701. Map 4.*

MAZARA DEL VALLO (*map p. 575, B3*)

€€€ **La Bettola**. Central position for this little restaurant, very good local fare and wines. Start with a dish of crudités from the sea: scampi, tuna, swordfish, shrimps, Greater amberjack and sea-perch. Two special desserts, sponge cake with organic ricotta cream, toasted almonds and chocolate, or almond parfait. Closed Wed. *Via Maccagnone 32, T: 0923 946422.*

€€ **Alla Kasbah**. In the heart of the old city, intriguing little restaurant offering Tunisian and Sicilian cuisine, cous cous prepared with fish, vegetables or meat. Closed Mon in winter. *Via Itria 10, T: 0923 906126.*

€ **Da Giacomo**. ■ The nondescript exterior hides a super little *trattoria*, for abundant dishes of pasta, tasty vegetable or seafood *antipasti*, fried fish, spit-roasted chicken and expertly cooked roast potatoes. Also take-away. *Via Salemi 23, T: 0923 933874.*

SANTA NINFA (*map p. 575, C2*)

€€ **Al Colle Verde**. Pina and Lucrezia will serve you all the best local dishes, including home-made pasta, *cinghiale* (boar), *lumache* (snails, when in season), and tripe. Good assortment of wines. Closed Wed. *Via Carducci 36, T: 0924 62377.*

SAN VITO LO CAPO (*map p. 575, B1*)
€€€ Al Ritrovo. In Castelluzzo, just south of town, the restaurant of a small hotel where the chef prepares superb seafood *antipasto*, cous cous, and memorable tuna in an almond crust. Closed winter. *Via Cristoforo Colombo 314, Castelluzzo, T: 0923 975656.*

€€€ Syràh. Refined little restaurant on the main street, excellent and well-presented *antipasti* and pasta dishes; ask for roast tattler squid (*totano*) for your main course. Booking advisable. *Via Savoia 5, T: 0923 972028 or 347 136 7315.*

€€ Casa del Cous Cous. The delightful restaurant of Enzo Battaglia, son of a fisherman, who tackles whatever he does with passion. He prepares the very best cous cous with fish or meat and vegetables, accompanied by Sicilian wines, and rounded off with a glass of Tunisian tea. Closed Tues lunchtime and winter. *Via Principe Tommaso 8, T: 0923 621488 or 349 407 0990.*

€€ Gnà Sara. Cous cous, home-made pasta, fresh fish, served in a congenial little trattoria/pizzeria. Closed Mon. *Via Duca degli Abruzzi 8, T: 0923 972100.*

SELINUNTE (*map p. 575, C3*)
€ Lido Zabbara da Jojò. ■ This legendary beach bar opened in 1969. Lunch here is delightful, with an ample buffet; fresh salads, grilled sausage or steaks, local home-made bread. Summer only; swimming facilities. *Via Pigafetta (on the beach under the Acropolis), T: 0924 46194.*

TRAPANI (*map p. 575, B1*)
€€€ Caupona. Small restaurant offering an imaginative cuisine, using the excellent local ingredients to advantage. Very good *antipasti*; don't miss the *polpette di seppia*, cuttlefish rissoles.

Closed Tues and Feb. *Via San Francesco d'Assisi 32 (Piazza Purgatorio), T: 0923 546618 or 340 342 1335. Map 6.*

€€ Antichi Sapori. An old fishermen's tavern is now a tiny restaurant serving fresh fish straight from the Aegadian Islands. Tasty cous cous and *zuppa d'aragosta*, lobster soup. Home-made desserts. Booking essential. Closed Tues. *Corso Vittorio Emanuele 191, T: 0923 22866 or 334 371 4599. Map 6.*

€€ Cantina Siciliana. This *trattoria* in the old Jewish ghetto opened in 1958 and is recommended by the Slow Food organisation. Try owner-chef Pino's *bruschette con uova di tonno* (croutons with tuna roe) as a starter, or some of his imaginative fish salads, perhaps followed by seafood cous cous, then *cassatelle di ricotta*, an irresistible dessert. Sicilian wines. Closed Wed in winter. Next door there is a well-stocked wine shop run by the same management. *Via Giudecca 36, T: 0923 28673. Map 7.*

€€ Taverna Paradiso. Good cous cous, even with squid ink (*nero di seppia*), or try the *busiate* (macaroni) with Trapani pesto: crushed raw tomato, garlic, basil and almonds. Closed Sun. *Lungomare Dante Alighieri 22, T: 0923 22303 or 348 807 0025. Map 3.*

WHERE TO EAT ON THE ISLANDS

NB: Restaurant prices here are considerably higher than on the mainland.

FAVIGNANA
€€ Amici del Mare. On the port, you can eat outside in a peaceful atmosphere, deliciously fresh seafood, good wine list. Closed Feb and Wed

in winter. *Piazza Marina 6, T: 0923 922596.*

LEVANZO

€€ **Paradiso**. Simple little *trattoria*, abundant portions of tasty food, prepared by chef Mimmo with the freshest fish and aromatic herbs from the island, and served on a shady veranda overlooking the harbour. Closed winter. *Via Lungomare 8, T: 0923 924080.*

MARETTIMO

€€ **Il Veliero**. ■ Meals served on the terrace; try Peppe's legendary *zuppa d'aragosta*, lobster soup in which he cooks spaghetti; the *pasta al pesto di Trapani*, made with raw tomato, is also good. Best to book the lobster soup and the table by the sea. *Corso Umberto 22, T: 0923 923274.*

€ **Il Pirata**. By the old harbour, serves appetising seafood risotto, lobster soup, and grilled fish. Also rooms to rent. *Via Scalo Vecchio 27, T: 0923 923027 or 333 303 0545.*

€ **Il Timone**. Signora Maria prepares home-made pasta and cous cous; the *antipasti* of seafood crudités and her delicate *cassata siciliana* for dessert are memorable. Closed Sat and Sun. *Via Mazzini 30, T: 0923 923142.*

PANTELLERIA

€€€ **Al Tramonto**. In a beautiful setting, try *ravioli amari* (the local ravioli, filled with ricotta cheese and mint), spicy cous cous, slow-cooked rabbit, tuna tartare; lovely fresh fruit desserts. Closed winter. *Località Penna 12, Scauri Basso, T: 349 537 2065.*

€€€ **Franco Castiglione**. Elegant restaurant serving excellent *antipasti*; the spaghetti with *ammogghiu*, the local raw pesto, is exceptional; chef Franco also prepares good fish soup,

and a delicious dessert called *baci*, crispy pastry layered with sweet creamy ricotta. Closed Wed and winter. *Lungomare Borgo Italia 81, T: 0923 911448.*

€€ **Il Cappero**. Among the best restaurants on Pantelleria, unfortunately no tables outside; delicious tuna dishes; pizza in the evenings; crowded on Sat. *Via Roma 33, T: 0923 912601.*

€€ **La Pergola**. Large restaurant with garden and car park; try the local salad or very good pizza. Closed Tues. *Contrada Suvaky 111, T: 0923 918420.*

LOCAL SPECIALITIES

ALCAMO The **Bar 900** (*Corso VI Aprile 105*) opened in 1937 and is still the best coffee-house in town. Excellent DOC Bianco d'Alcamo wine is produced by **Rapitalà** (*Contrada Rapitalà, Camporeale, www.rapitala.it*), on the gentle hills behind Alcamo.

CALATAFIMI SEGESTA The family-run **Ceuso farm** (*Contrada Vivignato, T: 0924 22836, www.ceuso.it*) produces good red wines.

CASTELVETRANO There are several bakeries which make the local sourdough loaves. The bread is a characteristic coffee-brown colour, with a delicious flavour, and it keeps well. Try **Rizzo** (*Via Garibaldi 85, opposite the museum*), or **Pierino Fratelli** (*Via Garibaldi 169*).

ERICE The pastries made here are unique in Sicily, and were once made by the nuns of the many convents in the town. Go to **Pasticceria Grammatico** ■ (*Via Vittorio Emanuele 14, www. mariagrammatico.it; map 3*) for Maria Grammatico's confectionery. She is one of the most accomplished pastry-cooks in Sicily. Ask for *brutti ma buoni* almond cookies, or *genovesi*, tiny shortcrust-pastry pies filled with confectioner's custard, served warm and fragrant. The women of Erice also weave the bright cotton rugs called *frazzate* and sell colourful pottery: try **Signora Amico** (*Via Guarrasi 5; map 1–2*), or **Pina Parisi** (*Via Conte Pepoli 55; map 3*).

LEVANZO The *cannoli di ricotta* are excellent everywhere; they are freshly prepared every day with milk from the goats which roam the island. The **Panetteria di Levanzo** (*Via Pietre Varate 5, going towards lighthouse*) is the bakery and nerve centre of the village, where Signora Olimpia (who is also an artist) makes delicious currant biscuits.

MARSALA There are several good places for buying DOC wines, and if you call the wineries first they will show you around the cellars. **Cantine Florio** (*Via Vincenzo Florio 1, T: 0923 781111; beyond map 6*), has a long tradition of excellence: their Marsala Vergine Baglio Florio is wonderful. Also **Carlo Pellegrino** (*Via del Fante 39, T: 0923 719911; map 2*); try the Soleras or the Fine Ruby. **Enoteca La Ruota** (*Via Scipione l'Africano 39; map 3*) and **Enoteca Luminario** (*Lungomare Boeo 34/a; map 3*) are near the Museo Baglio Anselmi. **Cantine Mothia** is a small winery on the outskirts of Marsala (*Via Giovanni Falcone 22, T: 0923 737295; beyond map 2*), producing exceptionally good wines. The **Bottega del Sale** (*Saline Ettore e Infersa*) has a wide selection of local salt, also cosmetics and jewellery made using the crystals. Always crowded, **Enzo e Nino** (*Via XI Maggio 130; map 4*) is the historic coffee-house of Marsala. Try the home-made ice cream or the little ricotta pies called *spagnolette*, or their famous chicken focaccia.

MAZARA DEL VALLO There are only seven Benedictine nuns remaining at the **Monastero di San Michele Arcangelo** (*Piazza San Michele 5; T: 0923 942491*), baking delectable sweets to the same secret recipes since 1600 and passed through to customers in the wheel. Choose from an assortment of *croccanti* (crunchies), *cassatelle ai fichi* (with dried figs), *savoiardi* (delicate biscuits to dunk into hot chocolate), *pasta reale* (marzipan) and *muccunetti*, little pies of almond paste with a sweet pumpkin filling. The **Pasticceria Lamia** (*Via Val di Mazara 44*) also has a good reputation for local pastries. Ask for their *muccunate* and *mazaresi al pistacchio*. **Pietro Rocca** (*Via Marsala 29*) is another skilled confectioner; his specialities with ricotta are particularly inviting. Mazara is also famed for its bread, which had to be skilfully made to provide an edible resource for the fishermen heading out to sea for a week at a time: try **Panificio San Pietro** (*Via San Pietro 24*), or **Panificio Roccaforte** (*Corso Vittorio Veneto 149*).

PANTELLERIA Local wines are made using a high proportion of white Zibibbo grapes; although they are usually considered to be dessert wines, they work as aperitifs when drunk icy cold. The DOC kinds to look out for are Moscato di Pantelleria, a sweet, strong wine, best drunk chilled, perfect with cheese, and Moscato Passito di Pantelleria, made with grapes which have been allowed to shrivel in the sun before pressing. Excellent moscato or passito from the **Minardi vineyards** (*Strada Panoramica, www.viniminardi.*

it), planted in 1940, or the costly Ben Ryé, from the **Donnafugata estates** (*Khamma, T: 0923 915649, www. donnafugata.it, call for appointment*) have won international acclaim. **Salvatore Murana** (*Khamma, T: 0923 915231*) produces excellent quality wines, described as 'liquid poetry'. Famous home-made ice cream and granita can be found near the port at the **Gelateria Katia** (*Via Borgo Italia 84*). **SALEMI** The town is famed for its decorative loaves of **bread**, baked to celebrate the feasts of St Blaise (3 Feb) and St Joseph (19 March); they are also sold, and the proceeds go to charity. Prices are high, and can exceed 50 euros for one small, albeit very intricate, loaf. All the women of the town take part in the baking, which begins about ten days before the feasts. Award-winning DOP olive oil of the Cerasuola variety is produced by **Società Agricola Alicos** (*Via Cremona 21,www.alicos.it*); they prepare very nice gift boxes including honey, jam or gourmet sauces.

TRAPANI Platimiro Fiorenza (*Via Osorio 36, behind Villa Margherita; map 7*) is one of the few coral craftsmen remaining in Trapani. He makes exquisite jewellery, using silver and coral. **Saverio D'Angelo** (*Via Della Cuba 19; map 7*) is an old-fashioned shop specialising in antique coral jewellery. Ice cream here has a unique fluffy consistency and delightful flavours: try *croccantino* or *gelsomino*; award-winning ice cream will be found at **Gino** (*Piazza Generale Dalla Chiesa 4; map 6*). Trapani is also famous for jasmine-flavour granita, though it is not really made with the flowers at all; the aroma is given by the root of a wild parsnip called *scorsonera* (salsify), once used by

herbalists as a cure for the plague and snakebite. The best address is **Liparoti** (*Viale delle Sirene 21; map 5*).

FESTIVALS AND EVENTS

ALCAMO 20–21 June, Feast of the patron saint, Our Lady of Miracles, with a heartfelt procession in traditional dress.

CASTELLAMMARE DEL GOLFO 19–21 Aug, Feast of the patron saint, Our Lady of Succour, with two sunset processions: the first of boats escorting the statue around the harbour, and the second on land, when the effigy is carried through the streets by the townsfolk singing the Rosary in Sicilian dialect.

CASTELVETRANO Easter Sun morning, the Aurora festival is celebrated with a traditional procession and an enactment of the meeting of the Madonna with her risen Son. Mid-May, the *Corteo Storico di Santa Rita*, two days of celebrations for St Rita of Cascia, who has a devoted following in Castelvetrano, with parades in medieval costume, sword-dancers, jugglers, flag-tossers, medieval musicians and falconers.

CUSTONACI Christmas, the 'Living Crib' takes place in the cave of Scurati, involving 300 villagers who illustrate local crafts and trades. It is very famous and attracts large numbers; it is a good idea to get your tickets online (*T: 340 143 2291, www. presepeviventedicustonaci.it*).

ERICE Good Friday, procession of the *Misteri*. July–Aug, *Estate Ericina*, festival of music and art. Last Wed in Aug, Feast of Our Lady of Custonaci, the patron saint, with a magnificent procession organised by the women, who wear medieval dress. December, Christmas markets and *La Zampogna d'Oro*, international bagpipes and folk music competition.

GIBELLINA Aug–Sept, *Orestiadi* with plays, concerts and ballet, among the ruins of the old town (*T: 0924 67844, www.orestiadi.it*).

MARSALA Maundy Thursday procession representing the Via Crucis. The little girls dressed as Veronica are particularly impressive, as traditionally they must wear all the family jewels.

MAZARA DEL VALLO Late Aug, *'U Fistinu di San Vitu*, celebrations for St Vitus, during which the fishermen pull a cart with his statue through the streets (*www.comune.mazaradelvallo.tp.it*).

SAN VITO LO CAPO May, International Kite Festival, when kite-flyers from all over the world demonstrate their skills on San Vito's splendid beach (*www.festivalaquiloni. it*). 13–15 June, the patron St Vitus is celebrated, culminating with firework displays, a procession, and a competition among the fishermen who try to walk along a slippery pole suspended over the water to get a flag at the far end. Sept, International Cous Cous Fest, with cooks from all over the world competing for the coveted award (*T: 0923 974300, www.couscousfest.it*).

TRAPANI Good Friday, procession of the *Misteri*, groups of life-size figures made in the 17th–18th centuries by local artists. Each group represents an episode in the Passion of Christ, and is carried by the representatives of the 20 corporations, or *mestieri*—hence the name. The procession starts at 3pm and continues all night long, passing through the narrow streets, never decreasing in emotional intensity (*www.processionemisteritp.it; www. francescogenovese.net*). 2nd Sun after Easter, spectacular procession and fireworks for *Santu Patri*, the feast of San Francesco da Paola. July, *Luglio Musicale*, opera in the gorgeous setting of the public gardens, Villa Margherita (*www.lugliomusicale.it*).

AGRIGENTO
The Temple of Concord.

Agrigento

Once a prosperous ancient Greek city, Agrigento (*map p. 571, C3*) presents a remarkable series of Doric temples of the 5th century BC. On a higher ridge, the site of the ancient acropolis, stands the medieval and modern town, overlooking a valley which stretches towards the sea.

HISTORY OF AGRIGENTO

Agrigento, the *Akragas* of the Greeks and the *Agrigentum* of the Romans, claims Daedalus as its legendary founder, but seems almost certainly to have originated in 580 BC as a colony of Gela. An early ruler was the tyrant Phalaris. The 6th–5th-century BC poet Pindar described Akragas as 'the fairest city of mortals', and some of its citizens were renowned for their wealth—a certain Gellias, during a storm, offered hospitality, new clothes and stabling to a group of 500 horsemen heading for Gela. Akragas was the birthplace of the philosopher Empedocles and his follower Akron.

In 406 BC the Carthaginians captured the city after an eight-month siege, burnt it, and sold the inhabitants as slaves. Timoleon defeated the Carthaginians (340) and rebuilt the city but it was taken by the Romans in 261 and again in 210, and remained in their possession until the fall of the Empire. It fell to the Arabs in AD 828, who cultivated cotton, sugar cane and mulberries for the silk industry: trade flourished so much that the old port (now San Leone) at the mouth of the River Akragas was abandoned in favour of the larger, deeper harbour at Porto Empedocle. Count Roger's Normans arrived in 1087 and took the city after a pitiless siege of 116 days, depriving the inhabitants of any kind of food, to the point that they resorted to cannibalism. But after the surrender the city was rebuilt, and the bishopric was founded.

The present town was long known as Girgenti, deriving from *Kerkent*, an Arabic corruption of the Roman *Agrigentum*, meaning 'People of the Fields'. The name Girgenti was abandoned in 1927 on the orders of Mussolini.

THE VALLEY OF THE TEMPLES
& THE ANCIENT CITY

The ancient city, encircled by a wall, occupied the angle between the rivers *Hypsas* and *Akragas* (now the rivers Sant'Anna and San Biagio) which meet near the coast to flow into the sea. The temples should, if possible, be seen at several different times of the day, especially in the early morning, at sunset, and at night when floodlit. In early spring, when the almond trees are in bloom, they are particularly beautiful. Butterflies are in the valley in abundance. The archaeological park with its temples is a UNESCO World Heritage Site.

The temples of Hera, Concord and Herakles are open daily 8.30–7; the Temple of Zeus and Sanctuary of the Chthonic Divinities are open 9–7; last tickets 6.30. From 15 July–18 Sept all temples open also evenings: Mon–Fri 7.30–10, out by 11; Sat, Sun and holidays 7.30–11, out by midnight; T: 0922 621657. Tickets available at the upper entrance by the Temple of Hera or at the lower entrance by Gate 5 (where there is also a bookshop, café and stalls selling local products). One ticket allows entry to all the temples or a combined ticket is available for temples, museum and the Kolymbethra Garden.

At least a whole day should be allowed as the site covers a large area (ancient Akragas and its temples measured 4.5km by 3km). There are car parks near both the entrances and by the museum. Those with less time should not miss the museum, the temples on the Via Sacra (it is about a 30-min walk from the Temple of Hera to the Temple of Herakles) and the Temple of Zeus. Shuttle buses are available between the two entrances to the park. Several sites, such as the Casa Pace, the Pezzino Necropolis or San Biagio are only opened by prior request. For information on access to these, T: 0922 621618.

TEMPLE OF HERA

The upper entrance leads directly to the much ruined but picturesque Temple of Hera, also called the temple of Juno Lacinia (Hera to the Greeks), from a confusion with a temple dedicated to Hera on the Lacinian promontory at Crotone in Calabria. It resembles the Temple of Concord in form but is slightly smaller and older (c. 450 BC). The stylobate, on a massive level platform, measures 38m by 16.8m. Of its 34 columns (6 by 13), 6.4m high with a base-diameter of 1.3m, nine have fallen. Traces of a fire (which probably occurred in 406) are still visible. The work of the Roman restorers was ruined by an earthquake. To the east is the sacrificial altar, to the west an ancient cistern.

Looking west there is a good view of the outer face of the wall of Akragas, in some places carved out of the natural rock, clinging to the brow of the hill. Nearby are the scant remains of Gate Three (one of the ancient city gates), and outside the city walls, an ancient roadway used for transporting the stones for the temples: the deep wheel-ruts can still be seen.

The **Via Sacra** (*closed to cars, unless a request for disabled access has been made in advance*) traverses the temple ridge. Between the temples of Hera and Concord it leads through beautiful countryside, with groves of almonds and ancient olive trees, and runs parallel to the ancient city walls, the inner face of which contains many Byzantine tomb recesses. On the right, about halfway between the two temples, is a café with toilets. There is a view on the right of the cemetery of Agrigento, to the right of which San Biagio can be seen beside a clump of trees. On the skyline, radio masts mark the Rupe Atenea.

THE PALAEO-CHRISTIAN ANTIQUARIUM AND GROTTA FRAGAPANE

A little gate to the right, about 100m before the Temple of Concord, gives access to the Casa Pace, an old building restored to house the **Palaeo-Christian Antiquarium** (*request visit in advance, entrance to the Grotta Fragapane can be requested at the same time, T: 0922 621618*). The exhibits illustrate the history of the three early Christian churches so far found in Agrigento: one outside the walls at the eastern edge of the temple ridge; one built inside the Temple of Concord; and one excavated beside the Villa Athena hotel. Finds include a finely-carved sarcophagus (5th century AD), left unfinished. Upstairs are photographs and plans of the Palaeo-Christian necropoleis excavated in the area.

A path leads through olive groves from the Casa Pace up to a **Palaeo-Christian necropolis** with tombs cut into the rock, and the entrance to the extensive **Grotta Fragapane** catacombs with subterranean passages extending below the road (*only opened by prior request, see above*), rejoining the Via Sacra by the Villa Aurea. In the field nearby are two tholos tombs thought to date from the 5th century BC.

TEMPLE OF CONCORD

The Temple of Concord at Agrigento is the second-best preserved of all Greek temples after that dedicated to Hephaistos in Athens, which it recalls in its majestic symmetry and rich golden colour. The name Concord occurs in a Latin inscription found here, but has no real connection with the temple, which has not as yet been firmly attributed to any particular divinity (although there is a tradition among the inhabitants of Agrigento that the temple should be visited by a husband and wife on their wedding day to ensure a future free from marital strife).

The building, which probably dates from about 430 BC and was only slightly damaged by the Carthaginians, stands on a stylobate above a crepidoma of three steps and is peripteral hexastyle in plan. Its 34 Doric columns are 6.8m high including the capitals, with a diameter of 1.4m at the base, each column with 20 grooves. The intercolumniations of the façades become narrower towards the sides (to accommodate the corner metopes); this is one of the earliest instances in Sicily of this refinement in temple design. The roof was made of slabs of coloured marble, provided with lion-head water-spouts. The cella has a pronaos and an opisthodomos, both distyle in antis. From the east end of the cella two spiral staircases mount to the architrave. The complete entablature survives at both ends.

The excellent state of preservation of the temple is explained by the fact that it was converted into a church (placing the entrance on the west side, as usual in Christian churches, and preceded by a stairway) dedicated to Sts Peter and Paul by San Gregorio

Map labels:

200m

260m

VIA IMERA

Seminario

Duomo

PZA BIBIRRIA

VIA SOTTO BIBIRRIA

VIA GIOENI

S. Giorgio

PZA D. MINZONI

VIA DEL DUOMO

Biblioteca Lucchesiana

VIA DELLE MURA

S. Caterina

S. Maria d. Greci

VIA S. GIROLAMO

VIA GARIBALDI

S. Giacomo

Munic.

VIA MATTEOTTI

Purgatorio

P.O.

VIA BAC. BAC.

VIA ATENEA

VIA FODERA

Museo Civico

S. Spirito

PIAZZA FRATELLI ROSSELLI

VIA DANTE

VIALE NENNI

PZA PIRANDELLO

PIAZZA RAVANUSELLA

Biblioteca

V. PIRANDELLO

PIAZZALE ALDO MORO

VIA GIOENI

VIA S. VITO

P

PZA SINATRA

S. Giuseppe

VIA EMPEDOCLE

Stazione Centrale

180m

VIA ACRONE

PIAZZA MARCONI

VIA CALLICRATIDE

VIA MANZONI

VIA ESSENETO

VIALE D. VITTORIA

VIA CRISPI

Pezzino Necropolis

5

6

Gate 9

140m

Gate 8

Stadium

100m

Gate 7

VIA MORANDI

PORTO EMPEDOCLE

80m

9

River Hypsas (Sant'Anna)

Gate 6

10

Museo Archeologico (Ekklesiasterion)

VILLASETA

PORTO EMPEDOCLE

100m

Oratory of Phalaris

100m

N

13

SS115

Temple of Hephaistos

Kolymbethra Garden

14

Posto di Ristoro

Sanctuary of the Chthonic Divinities

Temple of Olympian Zeus

Temple of Herakles

Gate 5

Porta Aurea (Gate 4)

Tomb of Theron

Lower Entrance

P

SS115

CONTRADA BENNICI

S. LEONE

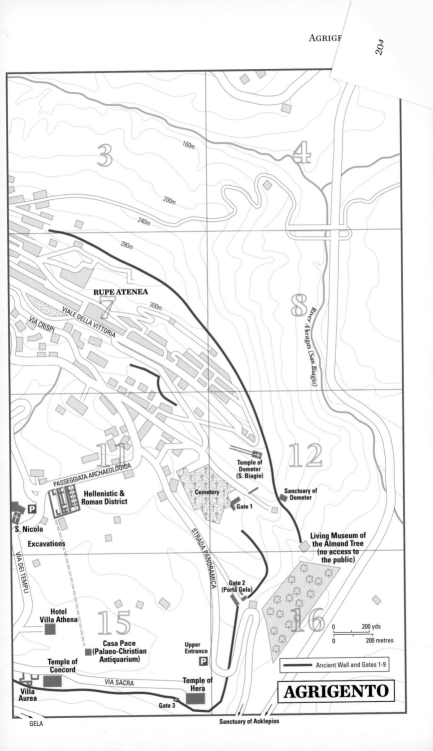

AGRIGENTO

AGRIGENTO
The inscription found near the Temple of Concord which led scholars
to attribute (almost certainly wrongly) its dedication.

delle Rape ('St Gregory of the Turnips'), bishop of Agrigento, in the late 6th century. The building was restored as a temple in the 18th century, but the arches of the nave remain in the cella walls. The material of this and of the other temples is the local, easily-eroded sandstone, formerly protected by stucco, which has now almost completely disappeared. The stucco would have been painted white, with triglyphs and metopes picked out in blue and red. Today the stone is burnt by the sun to a rich tawny gold.

THE VILLA AUREA

Beyond the Temple of Concord is the Villa Aurea, surrounded by a luxuriant garden that contains tombs and underground cisterns.

Visible from the road, in the forecourt, is a memorial bust set up in 1984 of Captain Alexander Hardcastle. This eccentric Englishman arrived as a tourist aged 49 in 1921, was captivated by Agrigento, repaired the villa and lived here with his brother Henry until his death in 1933. The captain provided substantial funds to restore and excavate the ancient city, supporting the work of the archaeologist Pirro Marconi. He also took an interest in the modern city, providing an aqueduct from there to the temple valley. In gratitude, the Italian government awarded him the important honorary title of *Commendatore della Corona d'Italia* and the Home Office allowed him to wear the insignia. The Wall Street crash of 1929 caused his bank to fail and he found himself bankrupt; unable to sell the villa, he lost his mind and was taken to the local lunatic asylum, where he died. The villa is now used for cultural events.

TEMPLE OF HERAKLES

On the left, towards the end of the Via Sacra, is a footbridge above a deep street of tombs carved into the rock which leads to the Temple of Herakles, a heap of ruins showing traces of fire, with nine upright columns, eight of them re-erected in 1922–3 thanks to Captain Alexander Hardcastle (*see above*). To the left of the bridge, on a flat expanse of rock, are a few blocks from the altar of the temple.

This is probably the oldest visible temple of Akragas (built c. 500 BC). Peripteral hexastyle in plan, its 38 columns (6 by 15) were 9.9m high and 2m in diameter. It had a cella with pronaos and opisthodomos, both distyle in antis. The cella was later altered and three cult spaces were created at the rear. A damaged statue of Asklepios was found in the southern chamber. The marble *Warrior of Agrigento*, now the symbol of the Archeological Museum, which was found nearby, could have come from the pediment. The attribution of this temple to Herakles is due to a reference in Cicero's *Verrine Orations* (*II: 4.43*) and is not certain. If it is the temple referred to by Cicero then in ancient times it was famed for its cult statue, which Verres (see below) attempted to steal. It also contained a painting by Zeuxis, one of the most famous artists of the ancient world, of Herakles strangling the serpents.

VERRES THE ART THIEF

In 73 BC the Roman politician Caius Verres was made praetor (governor) of Sicily. Cicero relates that no sooner was he installed in the governor's palace at Syracuse than he began pillaging works of art to adorn it. At first, he requisitioned beautiful objects from private homes, but later he stole from temples: a statue of Ceres from Catania, the gold and ivory doors of the Temple of Athena at Syracuse, together with paintings and the effigy of the goddess, whose face and hands are said to have been of gold. In Akragas, the magnificent bronze statue of Apollo, signed by Myron, was again stolen from the Temple of Asklepios (it had once before been carried away by the Carthaginians, in 406 BC, and returned by Scipio in 146). Verres sent a group of soldiers to steal the statue of Herakles from the temple at Akragas at dawn one day, but word of the raid got out and the soldiers were overpowered by furious citizens. Cicero, who had been called by the Sicilians in 71 BC to plead their cause in front of the senate, described the statue as the most beautiful work of art he had ever seen, and the effect of Verres on the island as more devastating than war. The case launched Cicero's political career but Verres was only nominally punished: he went into voluntary exile at Marseilles, where he died in 43 BC. The stolen artworks were never recovered.

TEMPLE OF OLYMPIAN ZEUS

From the Temple of Herakles a footbridge crosses the road to the vast and complex ruins of the altar and temple of Olympian Zeus or Olympieion, thought to have been begun by the Carthaginian prisoners taken at Himera in 480 BC, and left unfinished in 406. Temporarily transformed into a fortress in 255 BC, it was the last refuge for the inhabitants and the Roman garrison during a Carthaginian siege. Its destruction, partly due to earthquakes, was completed by quarrying in the 18th century, much of the stone going into the harbour mole of Porto Empedocle.

This huge Doric temple (110.1m by 52.7m, virtually a double square), is the largest Doric temple known and is unique in form among Greek temples. The major architectural elements were composed of multiple individual blocks (each capital was composed of three blocks) and then covered in stucco. It is heptastyle and pseudoperipteral, i.e. the seven columns at each end and the 14 on each side were engaged in the walls, being rounded externally and presenting a square face towards the interior. In between the semi-columns, 16.7m high and 4m thick at the base, were 38 colossal telamones set on the outer wall; their exact arrangement is still under discussion. In the east pediment a Gigantomachia was represented, and in the west pediment the capture of Troy. The cella was divided into three aisles, separated by square pillars, and was almost certainly roofless.

Little remains in position except the stereobate, but this alone is sufficient to convey an impression of the immensity of the monument. Part of the north wall survives (note the outer face), and the foundations of the aisle pillars. To the east are the foundations of the huge ceremonial altar. All over the stereobate are collapsed stones, amid which lies a copy of a giant (7.6m high), one of the telamones (the original 19th-century reconstruction is displayed in the archaeological museum), and a partly-reconstructed original. The U-shaped incision visible on many stones is believed to have facilitated their being raised by ropes. Near the southeastern corner, below one of the colossal fallen capitals, is a small Archaic temple with a cella divided by piers, flanked by another partly-reconstructed telamon.

THE LOWER AGORA

A path from the northeastern corner of the altar of the Temple of Zeus leads through an orange grove to the lower agora and gymnasium. The remains of the lower agora are poorly preserved and difficult to understand, while the gymnasium, probably built in the Hellenistic period, consists of a long portico (a xystus or covered track) in which the bench now located in the inner courtyard of the archaeological museum was discovered. In the Roman Imperial period, perhaps in the 2nd century AD, a circular structure (nearly 22m in diameter) of unknown function, with column bases in its interior, flanked by two enormous rectangular rooms (12m by 37m), was built over the portico.

BETWEEN THE TEMPLE OF ZEUS AND GATE 5

To the west of the Temple of Zeus is a wide area of remains from a densely-occupied section of the city. Three 5m-wide north–south roads (the easternmost of which is practically buried under the fallen elements of the Temple of Zeus) divide two blocks of houses dating to the end of the 6th century BC and rebuilt in the Hellenistic period after the Carthaginian destruction. Immediately to the west, between the blocks of houses and Gate 5, are the traces of an L-shaped portico enclosing a complex sanctuary founded in the middle of the 6th century BC. The first phase consisted of a non-peripteral temple with pronaos, cella and adyton located right by the walls, surrounded by a paved square, and faced to the north by a rectangular building, perhaps a meeting

AGRIGENTO
Head of a telamon from the Temple of Zeus.

room. In the second phase, between the 6th and 5th centuries BC, the area was lavishly renovated: a monumental altar and a propylon were built, a new pavement was laid in the square, and a sacred grove was planted. In the third and final phase, dating to the Hellenistic period, the buildings (which had been destroyed by the Carthaginians) were levelled, new paving was laid, another altar was constructed, a sacred tholos and the L-shaped portico were built. The identity of the divinity worshipped in this sanctuary is as yet unknown.

The road that borders the northern extent of this sacred area and the adjacent housing blocks runs in through Gate 5 and crosses the entire city to exit again at Gate 2. The carriageway from Gate 5 is obstructed by masonry; it was probably a double gate defended by a large rectangular tower to the west and two smaller towers on either side of the entrance. The path leads down from here through a tunnel under the walls to the lower ticket booth and car park.

SANCTUARY OF THE CHTHONIC DIVINITIES

To the west of Gate 5 are various shrines that together formed the **Sanctuary of the Chthonic Divinities** (the gods of the earth as opposed to the gods of Olympus). The shrines were entirely enclosed by a precinct wall, a portion of which is visible on the west side. The misnamed **Temple of Castor and Pollux**, the Dioscuri, is here. The four columns bearing a portion of the architrave, which have been used as a picturesque symbol of Classical Sicily, are a reconstruction of 1836 now known to incorporate elements from more than one building on this site. The traces of stucco are original.

Superimposed ruins show the existence of shrines dedicated to the cult of the earth gods as early as the 7th century BC. The structures on the north side, notably the pair of altars, one circular with a central hole and one square, date from this period. To the south of these are the remains of two unfinished 6th-century temples; the third is that formerly ascribed to Castor and Pollux, which was probably to the same plan as the Temple of Concord. A fourth temple was built just to the south, in Hellenistic or Roman times. Many of the fallen column-drums belong to the last temple and the well-preserved altar east of the platform.

THE KOLYMBETHRA GARDEN

Map 14. Open Feb, Nov and Dec 10–2, March, April and Oct 9.30–5.30, May, June and Sept 9.30–6.30, July–Aug 9.30–7.30. Closed Jan and during the Almond Blossom Festival. T: 335 122 9042.

Beyond the house on the southern side of the terrace is a recently excavated area on the spur of the hill with a few poorly preserved structures, some of which were the bases for statues of the Chthonic divinities. The area was probably used for cultic songs and dances. From here two columns of the Temple of Hephaistos (*see p. 214*) can be seen, across a little valley verdant with orange trees. This is the Kolymbethra Garden, originally an artificial lake dug by Theron's Carthaginian prisoners taken at Himera in 480 BC (*kolymbethra* in ancient Greek means 'pool'). The Aqueduct of Phaiax (*see p. 215*), the 5th-century BC channel carved into the rock which brought water to feed the lake, is still functioning. Intended for use as a reservoir and a source of fish, ancient sources describe this as a place of great beauty with swans, ducks and many other birds. After a relatively short time, probably little more than a century, the lake was filled in, perhaps because of water-borne diseases caused by lack of maintenance of the hydraulic systems, and it became a fertile garden where the Arabs cultivated oranges. Abandoned for centuries, it has been restored by the FAI, the Italian conservation agency, who are caring for it. From the garden it is easy to cross the railway line to reach the remains of the Temple of Hephaistos.

THE ARCHAEOLOGICAL MUSEUM

Open Tues–Sat 9–7; Sun, Mon and holidays 9–1. T: 0922 401565.

The exceptional archaeological museum, Museo Regionale Archeologico Pietro Griffo, is located in a sector of the ancient city that was always of prime importance. In the Archaic and Classical period it was the location for a series of sanctuaries. In the rebuilt city of the 4th century BC, it became the upper agora and was furnished with important civic buildings such as the bouleuterion and ekklesiasterion, which remained in use until the late 2nd/early 1st century BC when, under Roman control, the area was remodelled in a process that is not as yet fully understood. The museum is entered from the main road (Passeggiata Archeologica), about 1km uphill from the Posto di Ristoro. It is spaciously arranged in a 1960s building designed by Franco Minissi, approached past the ekklesiasterion (*see p. 211*) and through a garden and the 14th-century cloisters of the convent attached to the church of San Nicola. In the cloisters is a long stone bench carrying an inscription to Herakles and Hermes found in the gymnasium by the lower agora.

Ground-floor level

The first rooms display Early and Late Bronze Age material from sites near Agrigento, including a small Mycenaean amphora (probably found at Porto Empedocle) and painted vases. There are also prehistoric objects found in Agrigento beneath the Classical area and objects from Gela (6th–7th centuries BC), including Corinthian and

Rhodian ware (note the head of a bull), and Licata (votive statuettes; late 4th-century BC). A small dish shows the three-legged symbol of Sicily, the Trinacria or Triskeles, one of its earliest known depictions (7th century BC).

There is a superb collections of vases, including a group of outstanding **Attic vases** from the mid-6th–early 3rd centuries BC. Black- and red-figure kraters from the 4th–3rd centuries BC include a lekythos with Nike sacrificing (460–450 BC) and kraters depicting Dionysiac scenes (c. 440 BC) and Perseus and Andromeda in polychrome on a white ground (a rare example of c. 430 BC); a stamnos (440–430 BC) shows a sacrifice to Apollo; a small red-figured krater with a bull being led to sacrifice, and several kraters and stamnoi with banqueting scenes (some by the Lugano Painter, c. 400 BC). At the end of the hall is a fine marble sculpture of a soldier, known as the *Warrior of Agrigento* (c. 480 BC), that may have adorned part of the pediment of the temple of Herakles. The remarkable large amphora with four gods and a quadriga is by the Dikaios Painter (6th century BC).

Architectonic fragments including a remarkable variety of lion-head water-spouts from various buildings (including the Temple of Herakles and the Temple of Demeter).

Statuettes and heads in terracotta include female votive statues; the mask of a black African of the 6th/5th century BC; a head of Athena with a helmet (c. 490 BC); head of a kouros (500 BC). The highlight is the terracotta **head of Persephone** (5th century BC), showing her with a firm chin and a strong nose; the statuette was modelled by hand (you can still vaguely see the fingerprints of the craftsman) and not made using a mould. On the end wall are delicate bas-relief friezes, including some showing the telamones. Beyond the steps which descend to the lower level, a case on the balcony displays the head of a kouros (c. 540 BC) and a female bust (end of the 6th century BC). Other cases here contain finds from the area near the Temple of Herakles, including architectonic fragments in terracotta.

Lower level

The main space on the sunken lower level is devoted to **finds from the Temple of Zeus**. Here the remarkable telamon (7.6m high) is displayed, which was recomposed from fragments in the 19th century; along the wall are three colossal telamon heads of three different types. The blocks of stone were originally covered with plaster. Plans and models, including a superb one in cork, suggest possible reconstructions of the temple, and the disputed position of the telamones.

A room off to the side on this level displays fragments of wall paintings and mosaics from the Roman district. Another is dedicated to the coin collection. The highlight is the **Agrigento Gold Hoard**, 52 Roman gold coins found near the bouleuterion that were buried during the Second Punic War and never recovered, presumably because the owner had died in the war.

Ground-floor level, north side

Some fine statuary is displayed here, including the 5th-century BC *Ephebe of Agrigento*, a marble statue of a young man, found in a cistern near the Temple of Demeter. It is thought to represent an athlete from Agrigento victorious in various

AGRIGENTO
Kneeling Aphrodite (2nd–1st centuries BC).

events at the Olympic Games. Also here is a lovely fragment of a **kneeling statue of Aphrodite** (2nd–1st centuries BC) and a male torso (2nd–3rd centuries BC) and three portrait busts.

The visit continues into a corridor overlooking a garden, where inscriptions and eipgraphs are displayed, including the **Concordia inscription** found near the temple which now erroneously bears that name, and terracotta 'sulphur' tiles used to stamp bricks of sulphur with the name of their owner/producer. They are, naturally, inscribed in reverse.

Next come finds from various necropoleis, notably that at Contrada Pezzino (*see p. 214*). The miniature vases were found in children's tombs. At the end of the room is the fine alabaster sarcophagus of a child, with poignant childhood scenes (the deceased shown as a newborn at bathtime, and in his own mini-chariot towed by a tame sheep) ended by illness and death, a Hellenistic work of the 2nd century BC, was found near Agrigento. Nearby is another Roman sarcophagus.

There is an introductory display of prehistoric material and finds from Sciacca, including a burnt terracotta statuette from the Piano Vento necropolis that may represent a divinity.

Objects from the province of Agrigento include finds from the Grotto dell'Acqua Fitusa and from Sant'Angelo Muxaro. The pieces of ochre are thought to have been used to colour vases. There is material from Herakleia Minoa and Greek and Roman helmets; busts from Licata; also bronze cooking utensils. In this final part of the museum, displayed on its own, is a single magnificent **red-figure krater from Gela** (5th century BC) by the Niobid Painter. In perfect condition, it displays an episode from the Trojan War: the battle with the Amazons on one side, and on the other Achilles falling in love with Penthesilea, Queen of the Amazons, even as he strikes her to death.

Finds from Montagna di Marzo include a charming red-figure cup with an owl and from Caltanissetta is another fine red-figure krater of 450–440 BC showing horsemen.

THE AREA AROUND THE MUSEUM (UPPER AGORA)

The area to the south of the museum is dominated by the so-called **Oratory of Phalaris**, a Roman prostyle building in antis which was transformed into a Gothic chapel, hence the windows in the cella. This temple was partly constructed over the Hellenistic **ekklesiasterion**, which was capable of accommodating 3,000 citizens for assemblies), which was levelled to create a terrace on which the temple was placed. The foundations on view held the tiered seats which would have risen up in the shape of a curved theatre. A path with a footbridge circles the temple and the ekklesiasterion, crossing an area with remains of late Hellenistic houses, and mosaics from Imperial Roman buildings.

The early 13th-century **church of San Nicola** (*open 9–1hr before sunset*) has a curious façade made up of a Gothic doorway in strong relief between antae with a Doric cornice (the material probably came from a Roman edifice nearby). The architecture of the interior, reconstructed in 1322, and altered in 1426, is interesting. In the second south chapel there is a magnificent sarcophagus of white Parian marble, which with great delicacy and purity of style portrays four episodes in the story of Hippolytus and Phaedra, son and second wife of Theseus. Phaedra fell in love with Hippolytus, who ignored her desperate pleas and the love-letter she sent with her maid. She blamed her suffering on an attempted rape by her step-son, who was killed when Theseus cursed him. The sarcophagus could be a Greek work of c. 450 BC or a later Roman copy of the original, and was much admired by travellers of the past, especially Goethe. The front panel shows Hippolytus with his male companions and their horses and dogs, about to leave for the hunt, ignoring the maid who attempts to give him her mistress's letter. The right-hand end panel shows Phaedra in despair, while the unfinished scene on the left-hand panel shows Theseus falling from his chariot and trampled to death by his horses, terrified by Poseidon's bull emerging from the sea. The scenes are completed by a delicate frieze at the top and bottom. The rear panel is also unfinished, possibly because the sarcophagus was placed in the corner of a building. The church also contains a venerated wooden Crucifix, a statue of the *Madonna and Child* by the Gagini school and an unusual stoup supported by a grey marble hand, bearing two dates (1529 and 1685). From the terrace there is a wonderful view of the Valley of the Temples.

In 2016, while working on the area of the **upper agora**, archaeologists stumbled upon what some hope may be the long-lost theatre of Agrigento, on the steep rocky slope across the modern road from San Nicola. At the time of writing no firm identification of the structure had been made, though its size appears to be considerably larger than originally conjectured.

THE AREA TO THE NORTH OF THE MUSEUM

A path leads from the north of the museum, near the exit to the car park, to a viewing area overlooking extensive excavations. Two interesting structures have been found

here. To the east was a **bouleuterion**, used for the meetings of the *boulé*, a politica
ruling body. It could hold some 300 people, who probably stood; the narrow divisiona
rows are carved into the rock. The Romans transformed it into an odeon. The second
important building was a **sanctuary** built in the Augustan period and modified in the
2nd century AD, comprising a temple and a triporticus probably dedicated to Isis.

OTHER SITES OF THE ANCIENT CITY

THE HELLENISTIC AND ROMAN DISTRICT

On the opposite side of the Via dei Templi, directly to the east of the archaeologica
museum, is the entrance (behind a fence) to an enclosure with the conspicuous
remains of the Hellenistic and Roman district of the city (*map 11; open 9–1hr before
sunset, closed Sun and holidays*). Here an area of c. 120m square has been excavated
exposing four cardines, running north and south, with their complex of buildings
sloping downwards from east to west in a series of terraces. The district was first
developed towards the end of the 6th century BC and was destroyed and rebuilt
through the years, its civic life lasting probably to the 4th or 5th century AD. The
drainage system is elaborate, and traces of stairs show that buildings were of more
than one storey. The size of the houses varied greatly, but it is clear that this was one
of the wealthiest districts in the city. Houses, of sandstone blocks, were built around
a peristyle, or with an atrium containing a sunken tank to collect rainwater; many o
their rooms have good floors (the best, which include the Casa della Gazzella and the
Casa del Maestro Astrattista, are covered for protection).

SAN BIAGIO AND THE SANCTUARY OF DEMETER

From Viale Crispi a road to the left crosses a main road and continues to the **cemetery**
(*map 11–12*). Captain Alexander Hardcastle, who was responsible for excavating the
ancient walls here, was buried in this cemetery beside a 'window' in the wall, cut
purposely so he could enjoy the view over the Valley of the Temples for eternity. A
gate on the left (signposted) is officially open at the same time as the temples but it
is often locked (*best to request a visit a day or so before; T: 0922 621618*). Beyond it an
unsurfaced road (c. 200m) leads (on foot) to the edge of the cliff.

On the hillside above is **San Biagio**. This Norman church was built on the cella of a
small temple (peripteral hexastyle in plan, with a double cella distyle in antis), begun
after the victory at Himera in 480 and possibly dedicated to Demeter and Persephone.
The pronaos and stylobate of the temple protrude beyond the apse of the church. To
the north are two large round altars, one of which was a *bothros* or sacred well, in which
hundreds of votive statuettes were found. The temple was approached by the ancient
track with deep wheel ruts, still clearly visible, mounting the side of the hill. On the
rockface a marble plaque records Captain Hardcastle's excavations.

On the edge of the cliff, the line of the ancient city walls can clearly be seen running
from the Rupe Atenea, above San Biagio, to the Temple of Hera; beyond, the view
extends along the temple ridge and to the sea. Just outside the walls and below the
cliff edge is the entrance gate to the **rock sanctuary of Demeter**, reached by long,

steep flights of steps (20th century) built into the rockface, which lead down through a delightful garden. Beside two natural caverns in the rock (in which numerous votive busts and statues dating from the 5th–4th centuries BC were found) is a tunnel which carries a terracotta aqueduct from a spring far inside the hill. In front is a complex series of cisterns on different levels and remains of what may have been a monumental fountain. The sanctuary was formerly thought to antedate the foundation of the city by some two centuries, but many scholars now believe it was constructed in the 5th century BC.

Another unsurfaced road (signposted) leads along the wall of the cemetery to (200m) an interesting wedge-shaped bastion built to guard this vulnerable spot where a valley interrupts the natural defence line. To the north is Gate One.

The Rupe Atenea (351m), a rocky hill, was part of the acropolis of Akragas. It is reached by a road which runs beyond the hospital, but as it is now military property the ruins of a large ancient building found here are inaccessible.

SANCTUARY OF ASKLEPIOS

The Strada Panoramica leads south from Via dei Templi, passing near Porta Gela (Gate Two; *no access*) and continues past the car park and ticket booth at the upper entrance to the Valley of the Temples, near the Temple of Hera. The road curves down to a roundabout that is crossed by the SS 115. The first exit to the right (the SS 115 heading west) runs beneath the temple ridge and walls, past a park of four hectares, designated to protect some 300 varieties of almond tree, of the 522 known to exist. This **Living Museum of the Almond Tree** (*map 12; no public access*) is run jointly by the local administration and the University of Palermo.

An unsurfaced road on the left (signposted) leads through an almond grove to a farm beside the little **Sanctuary of Asklepios** on the bank of the River San Biagio, near a medicinal spring. The site is enclosed (*beyond map 16; only opened by prior request*). There is a Doric temple in antis with a pronaos, cella and false opisthodomos. In spite of its much smaller size, it shows the advanced techniques of construction associated with the (contemporary) Parthenon. The stairway is preserved between the cella and pronaos. Asklepios was the god of medicine and the temple and its precincts would have been a clinic for the sick; rooms for this purpose have been discovered in porticoes to the north and west of the temple. Other structures include a pair of altars and a monumental fountain and studied have shown that the area around the buildings was planted with olives and oaks, examples of which have been replanted. This is the temple mentioned by Polybius in his account of the siege of 262–261, when it was used as a Roman base. It once contained a famous bronze statue of Apollo by Myron, signed by the artist in letters of silver on the right thigh, and looted by Verres in 72 BC (*see p. 205*).

TOMB OF THERON

Continuing along the SS 115, the area to the north between the road and the temple ridge comprises a huge Roman cemetery (1st century BC–5th century AD). Just before the roundabout, on the right, is a Roman mausoleum misnamed the **Tomb**

of Theron (*map 14*), a two-storey edifice with a Doric entablature and Ionic corner columns that would probably have supported an obelisk. According to local legend, it is the place where Theron buried his favourite horse, which had won several Olympic competitions.

TEMPLE OF HEPHAISTOS

The SS 115 continues across the roundabout and passes (200m on the left) the car park and ticket office at Gate 5. A little further ahead (c. 300m), just before a bridge at the bottom of a little valley, an unsurfaced road (not signposted) forks right. Follow it as far as the high railway viaduct. Here, steps (signposted) lead up past agaves and aloes to the Temple of Hephaistos (the Roman Vulcan; *map 14*), beyond an orchard of contorted almond trees and beside an old farmhouse. The temple, hexastyle and peripteral, was built c. 430 BC and two of its columns remain upright. The cella was constructed in part over a small Archaic temple of the early 6th century. A marble stone beneath the stylobate on the south side records excavations here in 1928–9 by Alexander Hardcastle.

From here the irregular line of walls leading up to Monte Camico and the old part of modern Agrigento is pierced by Gates 6, 7, 8 and 9.

THE PEZZINO NECROPOLIS

Map 5. Accessed from Via Dante. Turn right at the signpost for 'Il Rustichello', keep to the right, go through a tunnel, keep to the left and after a short while during which the track runs parallel to the main road—they are separated by a wire fence—it leads through the middle of the excavated part of the necropolis: the track is extremely rough, so proceed with caution or, better yet, walk from just before or just after the tunnel. The necropolis is only opened by prior request but most parts can be seen from behind the fences.

The enormous Pezzino Necropolis extends to the west of Gates 6 and 7. The visible section is beneath the viaduct of Via Morandi. Dating from the 6th–4th centuries BC, it was the largest necropolis at the time in Akragas and probably one of the richest. Unfortunately, tomb robbers ransacked much of it before the archaeologists began work here. The uncovered area is only a tiny section of the entire necropolis and the continuous undulations in the surrounding fields give some idea of its original extent. The tombs were separated by roads and there is evidence that the burials were grouped together on the basis of family ties.

EXPLORING AGRIGENTO TOWN

The oldest part of Agrigento town occupies the summit of Monte Camico (326m), the acropolis of the Greek city. Its modern suburbs extend along the ridge to the east below the Rupe Atenea and the city is also expanding down the hillsides to the north and south. Three connected squares divide the centre; the area to the west contains the old city.

SANTO SPIRITO AND THE MUSEO CIVICO

Via Atenea, the long main street of the old town (*map 2*), leads west from Piazzale Aldo Moro. Just out of the square to the right is **Palazzo Celauro**, where Goethe stayed while on his Grand Tour of the island. It is now a B&B (*see p. 238*). Via Porcello (right) and the stepped Salita Santo Spirito lead steeply up to the abbey church of **Santo Spirito** (*T: 0922 20664*), founded c. 1290 for Cistercian nuns. The nuns still make delectable sweets which may be purchased close by (*see p. 243*). The church façade has a Gothic portal surmounted by a rose window; inside are lovely stuccoes (c. 1693–5) by Giacomo Serpotta and his school. The statue of the *Madonna Enthroned* is by the workshop of Domenico Gagini.

Part of the convent houses part of the **Museo Civico** (*open Mon–Sat 9–12.30, Tues and Thur also 3–6.30, closed Sun and holidays; T: 0922 401450*), approached through a pretty cloister and up a modern flight of stairs. The two *Wunderkammer* rooms on the top floor contain a confused assemblage of tools, musical instruments, *papier mâché* toys, baskets, kitchenware and Christmas cribs of ivory, coral and mother-of-pearl. On the first floor below, archaeological material and remains of frescoes are displayed. Steps lead down to the beautiful Stanza della Badessa, the Abbess's Room, in a tower, where the highlight is a magnificent early 15th-century painted Crucifix showing the Trees of Good and Evil, the first with a pelican, the second with a serpent. The dormitory has fine vaulting and an exhibition of sculptures. On the ground floor is a chapel with a Gothic vault. The chapter house (now used for weddings) is also shown.

TOWARDS THE DUOMO

The unfinished façade of Santa Rosalia stands beside the church of the **Purgatorio** or San Lorenzo (*map 2*), containing elegant statues of the *Virtues* by Serpotta. The lion to the left of the church sleeps above the locked entrance to a huge labyrinth of underground water-channels and reservoirs, built by the Greek architect Phaiax in the 5th century BC, part of which is visible in the Kolymbethra Garden (*see p. 208*). Beyond the neo-Gothic Chamber of Commerce the street widens at the undistinguished Piazza Nicola Gallo, once the centre of the old city. Beyond the church of San Giuseppe, at the top of the rise, Via Atenea descends to **Piazza Pirandello** (*map 1*; formerly Piazza del Municipio). On the right is the Baroque façade of San Domenico; while occupying the former convent of St Philip Neri (mid-18th century) are the Town Hall (Municipio) and the fine 500-seat Teatro Pirandello opera house (Ernesto Basile, inaugurated on 24 April 1880; *open Mon–Fri 9.30–12.30 & 3.30–6.30; T: 0922 590360*). Another part of this huge convent, entered from Via Atenea 270, houses the civic art gallery, **Pinacoteca Palazzo dei Filippini** (*open Mon–Sat 9–1 & 3.30–6.30; T: 0922 590140*), displaying works by Vincenzo da Pavia and Pietro Novelli, together with paintings by modern artists such as Francesco Lojacono and Ettore De Maria Bergler.

To the right of San Giuseppe, Via Bac Bac leads to the stepped Via Saponara (signposted for Santa Maria dei Greci). From here it is a steep climb up the Salita Gubernatis and Salita Santa Maria dei Greci to (*right; inconspicuous entrance*) **Santa Maria dei Greci** (*open 10–1 & 3.30–6; Mass 8.30*), preceded by a charming little courtyard with a palm tree and a cypress. This small basilica was built with antique materials, on the site of a

Doric temple, perhaps of Athena or Zeus, possibly begun by Theron in the 5th century BC. The interior preserves fragments of charming 14th-century frescoes, and the wood and glass floor provides views of the foundation blocks of the cella of the temple and also, near the church altar, a 15th-century Capuchin crypt used for mummification (the bodies were placed upright in the seats and the fluids drained into the hole in the centre of the room). Several of the temple columns are visible inside the church, and in a passage below the north aisle (*entered from the churchyard; unlocked by the custodian on request*) are the stumps of six fluted columns on a c. 20m stretch of the stylobate.

THE DUOMO

The alleys on the north side of the church of Santa Maria dei Greci join Via Duomo. A magnificent old staircase leads to the duomo (*map 1; may be partly closed for repairs; T: 320 314 6599, www.cattedraleagrigento.com*). Dedicated to the Norman St Gerland, first bishop of Agrigento, it was consecrated in 1099 and rebuilt in the 14th century. The unfinished campanile (to the southwest; it is possible to climb it) has Gothic windows revealing a mixture of Arab-Norman and Catalan influences and was partly constructed using stones from the lower city. Inside, a single round arch divides the nave in two: at the entrance the tall polygonal piers support an open painted roof of 1518; in the sanctuary is a coffered ceiling of 1603 decorated with the two-headed eagle of the House of Aragon. At the end of the south aisle is the Chapel of St Gerland (who refounded the see after the Arab defeat), with a lovely 17th-century silver reliquary by Michele Ricca. Opposite, in the north aisle is the tomb of the merchant Gaspare de Marino, by Andrea Mancino and Giovanni Gagini (1492), and other Baroque funerary monuments and fragments of 15th-century frescoes. A curious acoustic phenomenon (*il portavoce*) permits a person standing beneath the cornice of the apse to hear every word spoken even in a low voice near the main doorway, though this does not work in reverse.

The extensive façade of the **Biblioteca Lucchesiana** (*open Wed–Fri 9–1, Wed also 3–5.30; T: 0922 22217*) lines Via Duomo. This fine building (*entrance at no. 94*) was founded in 1765 as a public library by the bishop of Agrigento. Its treasures number 40,000 volumes (including Arab MSS still housed in the original presses). Forming part of the building is the archbishop's palace, housing (at no. 100) the **Museo Diocesano MUDIA** (*open April–Oct Tues–Sat 10–7, Sun 10–1.30 & 3.30–7; Nov–March Tues–Sun 10–1.30; closed Mon; T: 0922 490040 or 327 754 9152*), with well-displayed cathedral treasures from the 12th–19th centuries, including some rarities.

ENVIRONS OF AGRIGENTO

The province of Agrigento, which after the collapse of its famous sulphur industry became one of the poorest districts in Italy, is now reaping the benefits from tourism and the export of high-quality agricultural produce: wine, oranges, wild strawberries, olive oil and vegetables. The area has also become an important international centre for the study of almond trees.

PORTO EMPEDOCLE (VIGATA) AND KAOS

Porto Empedocle (*map p. 571, C2*) takes its name from the philosopher Empedocles (c. 495–430 BC), the most famous native of ancient Akragas. For Empedocles, cosmic history was a cyclical process of union and division under the alternating influences of love and strife and the four immutable Elements, earth, air, fire and water. Little survives from his writings but it is clear that his work influenced Aristotle and he is also said to have been a renowned physician who composed in both prose and verse.

In 2003 the city, wishing to assert a new-found vocation for tourism (it boasts wide sandy beaches, good cuisine and delicious ice cream, but also a rather unpleasant cement factory, while a huge offshore re-gassification plant is planned), officially also assumed the name Vigata, in honour of locally-born Andrea Camilleri (*see below*), who names it thus in his novels. You will find a bronze statue of his fictional police chief Salvo Montalbano midway along the main street, Via Roma, leaning against a lamp-post. Close by, the little 19th-century opera house, Teatro Empedocle, has been restored.

The harbour is the point of departure for the remote Pelagian Islands: Lampedusa, Linosa and Lampione (*described on p. 235*). On the inner quay, built using stone from the temples of Agrigento between 1749 and 1763, is a massive tower built by Charles V, which will become a regional museum dedicated to the sea in all its aspects, **Museo Regionale del Mare** (*open 9–1 & 4–8*); for now it displays a collection of cannons. Close to the tower is a bronze monument to Empedocles by the American sculptor Greg Wyatt. Around the central statue of the philosopher are four smaller figures, representing Earth, Water, Air and Fire.

Just outside Porto Empedocle is **Kaos**, Luigi Pirandello's birthplace, now a delightful small museum (*open 9–7, closed Sun except 1st of the month and closed the following Mon; T: 0922 511826*), with books, manuscripts, paintings and photographs. Under a wind-blown pine, the ashes of the dramatist and novelist were finally buried according to his wishes, beneath a 'rough rock in the countryside of Girgenti'.

TWO WRITERS FROM AGRIGENTO: PIRANDELLO AND CAMILLERI

Luigi Pirandello (1867–1936) was the son of a sulphur-dealer in Girgenti. He became famous as a playwright in 1921 with the first performance of *Sei personaggi in cerca d'autore* (*Six Characters in Search of an Author*), which caused a scandal in Rome. Quickly produced in Milan, Paris, London and Berlin, it was much admired by G.B. Shaw and was followed the next year by the equally successful *Henry IV*, dealing with themes of illusion, insanity and reality. From 1925, with the backing of Mussolini, Pirandello established and directed the Art Theatre. His short three-hander *The Man with a Flower in his Mouth* was the first-ever broadcast TV drama, being used by the BBC for test transmission in 1930. Four years later he was awarded the Nobel Prize for literature. In his writings Pirandello conveys an idea of man suffering from solitude, disillusioned by his ideals. With a strong element of irony he suggests that his characters frequently reveal the necessity of 'wearing a mask', and this has been credited with inspiring the Theatre of the Absurd. Pirandello wrote some 40 plays, six novels, many novellas and hundreds of short stories, many of which are still in print, and was widely acclaimed in his lifetime: one of his most famous novels is *Il Fu Mattia*

Pascal (*The Late Mattia Pascal*), published in 1904, but it is as a playwright and short-story writer that his genius fully emerged. Much against his own wishes ('When I am dead, do not clothe me. Wrap me naked in a sheet... Burn me'), the Fascist government gave him a full state funeral.

Andrea Camilleri (b. 1925), currently Italy's best-selling author, is also the most translated of Italian writers, with a keen readership in 37 countries. The difficult task of rendering his mix of Sicilian and Italian has been tackled with enthusiasm and imagination by his translators, doubtless contributing to his worldwide success. Episodes in recent Sicilian history are made all the more credible by Camilleri's deft character descriptions and his understanding of human nature, but it was the fortunate invention of Chief Inspector Salvo Montalbano that brought him fame. Montalbano's unorthodox investigations into the crimes of his district are often hindered by his superiors, but are always successful thanks to his stubbornness and intuition. No traditional hero, Montalbano has plenty of human failings with which we can identify.

SCIACCA

Sciacca (*map p. 571, B2*), thought to be the oldest spa in existence, has been known since Greek times, when it may have been the thermae of Selinunte. It took the name Sciacca after the Arab domination (9th–11th centuries AD): the town rises in front of a white limestone cliff that looks rather like an iceberg when seen from the sea, and the name probably derives from the Arabic *as-saqqah*, meaning ice. It has an important and picturesque fishing harbour, where every day about 5,000 tons of fish are disembarked, most of it for processing, and there is a renowned boat-building tradition. Along the tiny streets of the fishermen's district, both men and women sit in front of their doors to clean sardines and anchovies ready for salting. A local ceramics industry flourished here in the 16th and 17th centuries and there are several artisans' workshops in the town. The colours and patterns are quite different from those seen elsewhere in Sicily; often the bright floral designs or human figures stand out against a black or dark blue background.

PORTA SAN SALVATORE

The centre of town is reached from the west, close by the fortified Porta San Salvatore (1581), a fine work in sandstone by local masons. Beside it in Piazza Carmine is the arresting façade of the **Carmine**, with a half-finished Neoclassical lower part and an asymmetrical 13th-century rose window. The dome, with green tiles, dates from 1807. The church contains a beautiful *Transition of the Virgin*, the last work of Vincenzo da Pavia, completed by another artist in 1572.

A short way up Via Geradi (left) is the **Steripinto**, a small fortified palace in the Catalan Gothic style. It has an interesting façade with diamond-shaped stone facing, erected in 1501, and is now the symbol of Sciacca. Opposite the Carmine, on the other side of Via Incisa, is the north portal of the church of **Santa Margherita**, sculpted in 1468 by Francesco Laurana and his workshop. The church (*open 9–1 & 4–8, closed*

Mon) originally built by Eleonora of Aragon in 1342 for the Knights Templar, was deconsecrated many years ago and after careful restoration is now used for concerts and exhibitions. The floor tiles are replicas of the original 14th-century ones. The glorious coffered ceiling represents a starry sky. The polychrome stuccoes and marble reliefs (1623) by Orazio Ferraro in the chapel of the titular saint are impressive, as is the monumental organ, dated 1872. Beyond is the Gothic portal of the former church of San Gerlando and the abandoned Templar hospital of Santa Margherita. Opposite are the late Gothic Palazzo Perollo-Arone and the 15th-century Torre di Pardo.

Corso Vittorio Emanuele continues into the central **Piazza Angelo Scandaliato**, shaded with trees. From here there is a view of the pastel-coloured old houses rising in terraces above the fishing harbour. The former Collegio dei Gesuiti (now the Town Hall), begun in 1613, has an elegant courtyard, the second largest in Sicily, and a fine library with many ancient incunabula.

The Corso continues to the dilapidated Piazza Duomo where the **duomo**, a basilica dedicated to Mary Magdalene, has statues by Antonino and Gian Domenico Gagini on its façade. It was rebuilt in 1656 and the vault fresco was completed in 1829. It has some good sculptures including a statue of the Madonna (1457), a marble altarpiece with reliefs by Antonino Gagini, and (on the high altar) the *Madonna del Soccorso* by Giuliano Mancino and Bartolomeo Berrettaro. In Piazza Don Minzoni, next to the duomo, is the **Museo Scaglione** (*open Mon–Fri 9–12; T: 0925 83089*), a beautiful *wunderkammer* of paintings, coins, ceramics and *objets d'art* collected by Francesco Scaglione, a local 19th-century nobleman.

The Corso continues to **Piazza Friscia**, in a pleasant part of the town, which has shady 19th-century public gardens with tropical plants. Via Agatocle leads past the new theatre to the edge of the cliff. Here the **Nuovo Stabilimento Termale** (*closed*), a pink spa building in Art Nouveau style (1928–38), offered until recently mud-baths and thermal swimming-pools with a temperature of 32°C.

THE UPPER TOWN

From Piazza Friscia, Via Valverde leads up to the gardens in front of the church of **Santa Maria delle Giummare** (or Valverde), built in 1103 by Juliet (or Judith), the daughter of Count Roger. The façade is tucked in between two crenellated Norman towers; the restored chapel in the left tower has an interesting interior. The elaborate 18th-century Rococo decoration in the main church, perhaps by Marabitti, is remarkable. The vault was frescoed by Mariano Rossi (1768). Also in the upper town is **San Nicolò La Latina** (*open 10–1 & 4–7*), a simple 12th-century church containing two remarkable painted medieval Crucifixes. Above is the **Castello Nuovo**, built in 1380, the ruined castle of the Spanish Luna family. Their feud with the Perollo clan in the 15th–16th centuries became notorious as *i casi di Sciacca* ('the Sciacca business'); it was resolved only in 1529, after half the population of the town had been decimated. It all started in the early 1400s, when a Perollo fell in love with a certain Margherita, but the king made her marry Artale de Luna instead, triggering a series of murders and reprisals which continued for 130 years. When the last Luna, Sigismondo, committed suicide by throwing himself into the Tiber, the castle was abandoned. Archaeologists are currently examining the centuries-old rubbish tip on the eastern side of the castle, with very interesting results. Apart from bones and kitchen refuse, which throw light on what the inhabitants ate and drank, fragments of bronze, iron, glass and pottery reveal that craftsmen had their workshops inside the castle, or just under the walls. Pieces of lustre ware from Spain, numerous coins, three thumb-thimbles of bronze and gold, and some tiny bells from horses' harness have also come to light.

MUSEO DEL GIOCATTOLO

In a modern district southwest of Piazza Carmine, in Via Fratelli Argento 15, is the Museo del Giocattolo (*open Mon–Sat 9–1 & 4.30–8, Sun 4.30–8; T: 335 844 4230*), a large collection of children's toys, carefully displayed according to period and materials used. Dating from 1880–1980, there are dolls, train sets, model cars, books, musical instruments and board games, all in excellent condition. There is also a gift shop.

ISOLA FERDINANDEA

Twenty-six nautical miles southwest of Sciacca, in early July 1831, a volcanic island appeared, rising through the water with fountains of black mud and clouds of ash. It was spotted by HM sloop *Rapid*, en route from Malta under the command of Captain Charles Henry Swinburne, who reported the phenomenon: 'It gradually increased in dimensions, magnificent eruptions of cinders with white vapours rising to the height of from 400 to 1,000 feet, accompanied by a noise like thunder.' By 17th July the island was 9m high, and on 11th August it was 25m with a circumference of nearly 2km. Another enterprising British captain, Commander Senhouse, passing close by the island with his ship at the beginning of August, surveyed the island, planted the Union Jack and claimed it as British territory, naming it Graham Island after the then First Lord of the Admiralty. Adventurous people started organising boat trips and picnics, one such being the novelist Sir Walter Scott in the year before his death. The claim, however, was contested by the Bourbon king Ferdinand II, who sent warships to the spot. On 17th August the island was named Isola Ferdinandea and annexed by the Kingdom of the Two Sicilies; but the victory was short-lived. By November the island was seen to be gradually sinking, and it disappeared completely on 8th December. Renamed the Graham Shoal, it remained some seven metres below the surface, until in 2002 it was announced that the capricious island was once more on the rise.

THE OUTSKIRTS OF SCIACCA

Above Sciacca (signposted) is **Monte Kronio** (or Monte San Calogero; 388m), which has caves (*closed*) with steam vapours, known since Roman times. The **sanctuary church of San Calogero** (1530–1644; *open Mon–Sat 7–12.30 & 3–7.30, T: 0925 26954*) has a statue of the saint by Giacomo Gagini. St Calogero (*see p. 245*) is said to have discovered the healing properties of the vapours, and to have provided accommodation here for the sick; he possibly lived in the largest of the caves. There is a small museum, Antiquarium Kronio (*open Mon–Fri 9–1 & 3–7; Sat–Sun 9–1; T: 0925 28989*), with a collection of vases and fragments found in the grottoes and dating from the Neolithic to the Copper Age.

On the Agrigento road (SS 115) east of Sciacca is the well-signposted 'enchanted castle', the **Castello Incantato** (*open Tues–Sun 9.30–1 & 4.30–8; T: 339 234 0174*), a park with olive and almond trees where thousands of heads were sculpted in wood and stone by a local farmer, Filippo Bentivegna (d. 1967). After being hit on the head during a robbery in the USA (where he had emigrated), Bentivegna returned home and carved heads wherever he could find space in his garden. A room is dedicated to his work at the Museum of Art Brut, Lausanne, originally Jean Dubuffet's collection of 'outsider' or pathological art.

MENFI & THE WEST

Northwest of Sciacca is **Menfi** (*map p. 571, A1*), a town laid out on a regular plan in 1638 with the houses arranged around courtyards off the main streets, many of which were made uninhabitable by the Belice earthquake of 1968. The beautiful Torre Federiciana, however, has been completely restored—it is the only remaining fragment of a Swabian castle built here by Frederick II in 1238. A new town now rises on the higher ground above. Palazzo Pignatelli, which faces Piazza Vittorio Emanuele III, was built in an area once occupied by the castle and now hosts the Museo Civico (*open Mon–Sat 9–1, Thur also 4–6; T: 0925 70217*) with an extensive and beautiful collection of seashells, molluscs and coral from all around the world, gathered by Vanna Rotolo Lombardo, a self-taught aficionado. It is one of the most interesting collections of its kind in Europe. An adjacent set of rooms contains a neat display of archaeological material excavated in and around Menfi. At the time of writing, it is hoped that the Porto Palo shipwreck will be exhibited here, once its restoration and study has been completed.

On the coast, beyond lots of condominiums and holiday villas, is the fishing village of **Porto Palo**. There are still some unspoilt stretches of coast here, adjoining the nature reserve at the mouth of the River Belice, in the province of Trapani (which extends to Marinella and Selinunte); the Menfi beaches have been awarded the European Union Blue Banner for quality.

SANTA MARGHERITA DI BELICE

Santa Margherita di Belice (*map p. 571, B1*) is home to Palazzo Filangeri di Cutò, immortalised as Donnafugata in Giuseppe Tomasi di Lampedusa's *The Leopard*. Badly damaged in the 1968 earthquake, it has now been restored and houses the **Museo del Gattopardo** (*open 9.30–1 & 3.30–6.30, closed Wed and Sun afternoons; T: 339 225 0855*), where you will find the manuscript and the first typescript of the novel, clothes worn in that historical period, a recording of the voice of Tomasi telling the story of *Lighea*, and a room with wax models of the characters in the book.

The old Matrice, now repaired, is the **Museo della Memoria** (*open 8–2, Mon and Thur also 3.30–6.30, closed Sat, Sun and holidays in winter; T: 338 747 3241*), with a collection of photographs and paintings, a moving testimony to the Belice Valley before and after the 1968 earthquake. In the **new church** the magnificent stained glass is the work of Americo Mazzotta from Florence. Santa Margherita is renowned for prickly pears and for *vastedda* sheep's milk cheese, a Slow Food niche product. From the public gardens there is a splendid view over the valley.

GIUSEPPE TOMASI DI LAMPEDUSA

Giuseppe Tomasi di Lampedusa (1896–1957), whose family were princes of Lampedusa and dukes of Palma di Montechiaro, was known to his friends simply as Peppino Palma. He wrote his famous novel *Il Gattopardo* (*The Leopard*, translated into English in 1960) at the end of his life. It was published posthumously in 1958. The book recounts the life of his great-grandfather Giulio Tomasi (1815–85; renamed Don Fabrizio Corbera, prince of Salina), who reacted with instinctive resignation to the turmoil produced by the landing of Garibaldi on the island in 1860. Set over three periods in the course of half a century, Don Fabrizio awaits the fall of his class and the ruin of his family, approving of the desire of his young nephew Tancredi Falconeri to marry the daughter of a *nouveau-riche* rogue, Calogero Sedara. Invited to join the Senate of the new Kingdom of Italy, the prince declines, proposing Sedara in his place. Disenchanted, he waits for death. The novel had enormous success, which was confirmed when it was made into a film by Luca Visconti in 1963, with Burt Lancaster and Claudia Cardinale. Tomasi di Lampedusa also wrote a collection of short stories, *I Racconti*, translated in 1962 as *Two Stories and a Memory*.

Montevago (*map p. 571, B1*), near Santa Margherita, was completely destroyed in the 1968 earthquake and rebuilt close to where it was before, leaving a poignant heap of ruins as a perpetual memory of old Montevago. This was the town with the highest number of victims. Many contemporary artists have donated works of art to Montevago, such as the stone sculpture by Giò Pomodoro of the *Deposed Sun* and the bronze group by Lorenzo Cascio of the *Embrace*. There is a spa centre, **Terme Acqua Pia** (*open 9–1 & 2–6; late closing Sat Sun and holidays; T: 0925 39026, www. termeacquapia.it*) immersed in a verdant park, with a pool into which thermal mineral waters gush constantly at a temperature of 40°C; mud baths are also available.

SAMBUCA AND MONTE ADRANONE

Sambuca di Sicilia (*map p. 571, B1*) has an old centre with the best-preserved Islamic layout in Sicily (around Piazza Navarro, with cobbled streets). Known as Sambuca Zabut until 1921, this town escaped the 1968 earthquake unscathed. The economy is based on the production of wine: the Planeta family runs a successful winery near the village of Ulmo, on the shores of nearby Lake Arancio.

The main street, Corso Umberto, leads up to the old district. On the right is the little opera house with 250 seats, Teatro L'Idea (1850; *request visit at the Antiquarium, same opening times*); to the left Via Marconi leads to the church of the Concezione, with a 14th-century portal. Back on the Corso, on the left is the church of Santa Caterina, of which the convent is an **antiquarium** (*open 9–1 & 4–7; T: 0925 940239*), housing a rich and informative collection of antiquities and works of art; a gallery is dedicated to the local artist Fra' Felice da Sambuca. In Piazza Vittoria is the Neoclassical church of the **Carmine** (or Santuario della Madonna dell'Udienza), with 19th-century stuccoes and a much-revered statue of the Madonna attributed to Antonello Gagini. Corso Umberto continues up to Palazzo degli Archi, the Town Hall, from where Via Belvedere leads to Piazza Navarro. On the left is a little street leading to the **Arab quarter**, called Vicoli Saraceni, and the Renaissance-style Palazzo Panitteri, housing the **Museo Archeologico** (*open 9–1 & 4–8, closed Mon; T: 0925 940239*), with interesting finds from the excavations on Monte Adranone (*see below*), including some beautiful sculptures, and panels describing the city of *Adranon*, its fortifications and the necropolis.

About 7km north of Sambuca, in Contrada Adragna, is the 1000m **Monte Adranone** (*open Mon–Fri 9–7, Sat–Sun 9–1; T: 0925 946083*), site of the Sican city of *Adranon*, re-founded by Selinunte in the 6th century BC and destroyed by Carthage in 408 BC. With the arrival of the Romans in 263 BC the site was abandoned. Excavations have brought to light traces of the walled city and the Iron Age necropolis, with some impressive rock-hewn tombs, including the so-called Tomba della Regina (Queen's tomb), with a suitably imposing entrance. Other remains include the walls and the South Gate, a sanctuary, and part of the acropolis to the northeast.

CALTABELLOTTA

Northeast of Sciacca, Caltabellotta (*map p. 571, B1*) is a little town in a beautiful and commanding position on a southeastern slope of its mountain, visible from vast distances around. Some historians believe this to be ancient *Kamikos*, the Sican kingdom of Kokalos, who befriended Daedalus after he came to Sicily from Crete (*see p. 225*). The Arabs erected a fortress, which they called *Qal'at al-Ballut*, or Fortress of the Oak Tree. Here the peace treaty ending the war of the Sicilian Vespers (*see p. 75*) was signed in 1302. In 1194 the **castle** sheltered Sibyl of Acerra, widow of King Tancred, her two daughters, and her infant son, who reigned for a few months as William III, shortly before they were imprisoned in Germany by the new king of Sicily, Henry VI. The little boy was never seen again; it is said that he was blinded and castrated and ended his days in a monastery. The same castle inspired Wagner, who imagined it as the dwelling of Klingsor in his *Parsifal*.

The Norman **Chiesa Madre** (*T: 0925 952783*) has Gagini statues and an isolated square bell-tower to the left, probably once a watch-tower, while in the church of San Francesco there is a splendid panel painting of the *Madonna*. The church of the **Salvatore**, below the rockface, has a late Gothic portal. From here is the narrow path and steps to the fortress, worth the climb for the marvellous views over much of Sicily.

On the western outskirts of town is the old **monastery of San Pellegrino** (17th–18th centuries; now derelict). To the left of the church are two caves, one on top of the other, used by early Christians as churches. Many prehistoric rock-hewn tombs were used as dwellings through the centuries, noticeably near the church of Santa Maria della Pietà, which is itself also partly carved into the rock.

BURGIO

Burgio (*map p. 571, B1*), across the valley of the River Verdura from Caltabellotta, is an agricultural town with a local ceramics industry founded in the 16th century, and the only remaining bell foundry in Sicily. The beautiful **carved stone portals** and doorways, of churches and palaces but also of the most humble private dwellings, are a characteristic of Burgio: there are over a hundred of them. The town has developed around the remains of a castle built by the Arabs on a spur, dominating the surroundings. In the **Chiesa Madre**, where you will find a beautifully restored 13th-century icon of the *Madonna and Child*, the third altar is dedicated to the Madonna of Trapani. Among frescoes, stuccoes and marble reliefs, there is a marble *Madonna* by Vincenzo Gagini, signed and dated 1566, and a 13th-century wooden Crucifix, much revered, and carried in procession every year to the sanctuary, 8km away, of Santa Maria di Rifesi, built in the 12th century by Ansaldo, steward of the royal household of Palermo.

The 17th-century **Convento dei Cappuccini** has recently been restored and opened to the public; during the works a painting by the Zoppo di Gangi (Giuseppe Salerno) was discovered, complete with the original early 17th-century frame, considerably the worse for wear after being exposed to the elements for several years. A small museum, called La Dimora delle Anime, the Dwelling-place of Souls, or **Museo delle Mummie** (*open every day, T: 0925 65013 to request visit, they will provide a guide*) has been created to display a collection of 49 mummies, once carefully preserved by the monks, then allowed to decay after the convent was abandoned, and now refreshed and rearranged. Mummification was once a privilege of members of the Church and wealthy citizens, and in Sicily the art of preserving bodies was almost exclusively confined to the Capuchins. Mummification was something that people planned and paid for while still in good health, even stipulating the clothes in which they should be dressed on their death. The best examples of preserved bodies can be seen at the Capuchin convent of Palermo (*see p. 70*) but there are plenty more elsewhere in Sicily, such as at Savoca near Taormina.

In Piazza Santa Maria the important **Museo della Ceramica** (*open 10–1 & 3–6, closed Mon; T: 0925 64016, www.muceb.it*), dedicated to the production of local ceramics, occupies the 16th-century former monastery of Santa Maria delle Grazie. The attractive pottery, business-like in function (floor and wall tiles, jugs, dishes and pharmacy vases) is decorated with medieval designs; particularly popular were profiles of moustachioed men wearing helmets, but suns and moons, replete with brilliantly coloured rays, are frequently found. The predominating colours are delicate yellow (the envy of rival craftsmen elsewhere in Sicily, who were never able to match it), green and cobalt blue, on a white background.

RIBERA

South of Burgio is Ribera (*map p. 571, B2*), lying in an agricultural area of groves, vineyards and strawberry fields renowned for their production of tiny strawberries, a Slow Food niche product. The first plants were brought from the forests of the Dolomites by soldiers returning after fighting in the First World War. The town was founded in 1627 by Luigi, Prince of Paternò, and named in honour of his Spanish wife, Maria de Ribera. It was the birthplace of the statesman Francesco Crispi. The beautiful coastline to the south of the town, with long sandy beaches and dunes, is still largely intact.

HERAKLEIA MINOA & THE COAST

The excavations of Herakleia Minoa (signposted 'Eraclea Minoa'; *map p. 571, B2*) are in a magnificent, isolated position at the mouth of the ancient *Halykos* (now the Platani). The road off the main coast road follows the lovely meandering river valley as it climbs the hill, passing vineyards. Beyond the turning for the seaside village an unsurfaced road continues for the last 500m. Here part of the town defences can be seen.

Above the dirt road on the left are the foundation of a circular Greek tower and a section of well-preserved wall (ending in a square Roman tower). The continuation of the walls has been lost in landslides. A splendid view extends along the wooded shore, the pearly-coloured sand, and the white limestone cliffs to Capo Bianco, beyond the river.

HISTORY OF HERAKLEIA MINOA

The name Herakleia Minoa suggests that this was originally a Minoan colony; a legend that Minos pursued Daedalus from Crete (after the Athenian inventor had helped Theseus and Ariadne escape from Knossos) and founded a city here was reiterated by Diodorus Siculus, who records that Theron of Akragas found the bones of Minos close to this spot. The Cretan king is supposed to have been murdered in his bath with boiling oil poured through a pipe in the roof by the daughters of the Sican king Kokalos. A colony was founded here by the inhabitants of Selinunte in the 6th century BC and the name Herakleia was probably added later in the century by Spartan emigrés. The town thrived during the 4th century BC when it was resettled by Timoleon, but it seems to have been abandoned at the end of the 1st century BC, perhaps because of malaria.

THE EXCAVATIONS

The archaeological area (*open 9–1hr before sunset; the main entrance is beside the ruins of Hellenistic houses; T: 0922 846005*) includes a small **antiquarium** which houses finds from the site and has plans of the area so far excavated. A path leads on through the beautifully-kept site where the visible remains date mainly from the 4th century BC. The **theatre** was built at the end of the 4th century. The soft sandstone is now protected by a Perspex cover. The site of the city is on the hillside in front of the theatre. Under cover is the so-called **Governor's House**: part of the wall decoration and mosaic floor survives. Also here is a little **sacrificial altar** (under glass). Outside excavations have revealed three levels of destruction. The second line of the walls (built when the eastern part of the town was abandoned) is visible nearby. A path (or steps) leads up to the top of the hill above the theatre and a paved path leads over the hillside to the line of walls to the northeast, with square towers, built in the 4th century BC.

THE COAST TOWARDS AGRIGENTO

The tidy little agricultural town of **Montallegro** (*map p. 571, C2*) was rebuilt in the 18th century below its abandoned predecessor on the hill, where a grotto has produced finds dating from the Early Bronze to the Copper Age. The enticing-looking ruins are in fact practically inaccessible, due to a mud slide which has obliterated the path. Between the town and the sea is a small artificial lake, **Oasi Lago Gorgo di Montallegro**, much frequented by water-birds during migration; it is protected as a nature reserve run by the LIPU, the Italian association for the protection of birds. Besides cormorants and rare ducks, there are hosts of dragonflies and butterflies, and very rare for Sicily, the terrapin, now symbol of the reserve.

Further inland, **Cattolica Eraclea** was founded in 1610, close to the Platani. Originally called Cattolica (*Kata Halykos*, 'below the Halykos'), it took the second name Eraclea in 1874, by order of Vittorio Emanuele II. The town, with its regular 17th-century street plan, is particularly attractive.

Siculiana, on a low hill between Eraclea Minoa and Agrigento, has a prominent domed church (1750–1813) and is very picturesque when seen from a distance. The castle on the top of the hill dates from 1350. A byroad leads down to the beach beside the Torre di Monterosso, where there is also a WWF nature reserve open to the public, protecting a spectacular stretch of coast with white cliffs, dunes, deep blue sea, Mediterranean maquis, and beaches where the loggerhead turtle sometimes nests: **Riserva Marina Torre Salsa** (*T: 0922 818220 or 327 774 2954, www.wwftorresalsa. com*).

Closer to Agrigento is the old city of **Realmonte**, with a salt mine whose tunnels extend for over 25km. On the outskirts, a Roman villa found while building the railway in 1907, the **Villa Romana di Durrueli** (*open 9–1; T: 349 819 4223*), dating from the 1st century AD, has been excavated. Nearby at Punta Grande is the **Scala dei Turchi**, remarkable white rocks of limestone and sandy clay which have been eroded by the sea into fantastic shapes (often used as a film set).

THE PLATANI VALLEY

This part of the province consists of peaceful countryside studded with small, sun-baked towns, a landscape defined by the River Platani, the ancient *Halykos*, 84km long, which formed the boundary between the Greek and Carthaginian territories in Sicily. Sulphur was mined in the hills here up until the mid-19th century.

ARAGONA AND ENVIRONS

Aragona (*map p. 571, C2*), c. 12km from Agrigento, was founded in 1606. It has an interesting street plan: straight, regular streets delimiting blocks of houses, which reveal a host of tiny alleys and little courtyards, Arab-style. The tiny central square, Piazza Umberto, is dominated by the 17th-century Palazzo Feudale, now the Town Hall, and the Baroque façade of the church of the Purgatorio. Close by is the

17th-century Chiesa Madre, which houses a rare 18th-century crib with large wooden statues. Four kilometres southwest of the town are the **Vulcanelli di Macalube**, tiny conical volcanoes, only 0.5–1m high, filled with salty bubbling mud, now part of a nature reserve. They fascinated Guy de Maupassant when he visited the area in the course of his journey to Malta and Sicily, in the late 19th century: *'If Satan has an abode, it is here, here in this monstrous sickness of nature, amid these pustules which in every respect resemble some loathsome suppuration of the soil, abscesses of the earth which from time to time burst noisily, spewing stones, mud and gas high into the air...'* Some of them exploded in September 2014, killing two children. At the time of writing the area was closed to the public (*Riserva Naturale Integrale Macalube di Aragona; T: 0922 699210, www.legambienteriserve.it*).

East of Aragona, on the other side of the highway, is the pretty village of **Comitini** (*map p. 571, C2*), in a panoramic hilltop position. In the central Piazza Umberto, the 16th-century Palazzo Bellacera houses a small museum with a collection of artefacts found in the area, dating from prehistory to the Arab domination, and a section dedicated to sulphur mining (*open Mon–Fri 9–1 & 4–8; T: 0922 600359*). There are numerous sulphur mines around Comitini, some of which belonged to the mother of Luigi Pirandello, providing the setting for his most poignant short story, *Ciaula Discovers the Moon*.

AROUND RAFFADALI

Raffadali (*map p. 571, C2*) has a Roman sarcophagus depicting the *Rape of Proserpine* in bas-relief, in the 16th-century Chiesa Madre. The myth of Persephone, with its themes of rebirth and resurrection, was a popular burial motif in the Classical world; worshippers believed that the goddess would bring them renewal in the afterlife. A prehistoric necropolis on the hill of Busone has yielded finds including a number of statuettes of a female divinity, each carved from a pebble, now in the archaeological museum of Agrigento. **Joppolo Giancaxio**, to the south of Raffadali, is an attractive village in a fine position with an 18th-century castle and church.

North of Raffadali, incredibly perched on a mountain-top, is **Sant'Angelo Muxaro**, in the heart of the Platani valley, surrounded by rugged farming country, another candidate as the site of the ancient *Kamikos* (*see p. 223*). Prehistoric tombs pepper the hillside. Those near the foot of the road which mounts to the village date from the 11th–9th centuries BC; the higher domed tombs were used in the 8th–5th centuries BC. The largest and most interesting, known as the 'Tomb of the Prince', has recently been cleaned and equipped with new information boards. It is located to the left of the road when driving up to Sant'Angelo, on a sharp corner. A small lay-by on the right offers parking. These tombs have revealed interesting finds, some of which are in the archaeological museum of Agrigento (a gold dish, with a pattern of animals in relief, is at the British Museum) while others are in a small archaeological museum in Palazzo Arnone in the main square of Sant'Angelo (*open Mon–Sat 9–7, Sun 9–2*). At the foot of the mountain is an interesting cave, Grotta dei Ciavoli, extending for over 1200m, with a flourishing population of bats; it is protected as a nature reserve (*Info: Legambiente; T: 0922 919669, www.legambienteriserve.it*).

Across the River Platani is **San Biagio Platani**, with white stone houses glittering in the sun; its Easter festivities, when the streets are decorated with huge arches made of palm leaves, oranges and sheaves of dates, are well worth seeing.

CASTELTERMINI & THE NORTH

To the east, above the narrow Platani valley with its odd-looking sulphurous hills, is **Casteltermini** (*map p. 571, C1*), once a sulphur-mining town. The Cozzo Disi mine, one of the largest in Europe, will soon be opened as a museum (*those interested in seeing the mine can request a visit to the mayor, email: sindaco@comune.casteltermini.ag.it*). An interesting festival takes place on the last Sunday in May known as the *Tataratà*. The name refers to the sound of the drums which accompany the colourful processions. The celebrations commemorate the miraculous discovery of an ancient Crucifix in the 17th century: a cow kept on kneeling down in a particular spot, in spite of the farmer's attempts to move her; out of curiosity, he dug a hole in the ground where she sat and revealed the Crucifix. The Cross, carbon-dated to the 1st century AD, is made of wood about 3.5m high and just over 2m wide. It is thought to be the oldest in the world and is kept in a little church 3km from the village, where the processions go on the Friday and Sunday of the last week in May. The participants wear magnificent costumes and even the horses are richly arrayed. The last procession, on Sunday evening, is a frenetic dance of hordes of 'Moors', accompanied by the drums. It is said that the Muslims in this area were miraculously converted when the Cross was discovered.

This area has been densely inhabited since the Bronze Age and material recovered from recent excavations in the vicinity is displayed in the **Antiquarium Di Pisa Guardì** (*Via Cacciatore 1, open Mon–Fri 9–1*). The contents of a hoard of bronze fragments; pottery painted with brown fishing-net designs or bearing incised patterns; a 4th-century BC jug in the shape of a boot, all accompanied by explanatory panels. One room is dedicated to the work of a local sculptor, Michele Caltagirone (1854–1928), known as the Quarantino, who specialised in modelling rather naïf terracotta figurines. Notable is his scene of *Paradise*, with a host of angel trumpeters.

CAMMARATA

Cammarata (*map p. 571, C1*) is a little medieval town on the northeastern slopes of Monte Cammarata (1578m), the highest peak of the Sicani Mountains. The town is surmounted by the ruins of its 13th-century **castle**. Many of the streets are very steep, and some of them are formed of steps, which makes the religious processions particularly exciting to watch. There are several ancient churches housing precious works of art.

The surrounding **Sicani Mountains** and their extensive forests, which abound in indigenous flora and fauna, are protected as a nature reserve (Riserva Naturale di Monte Cammarata), run by the Azienda Forestale.

SULPHUR MINING

Ancient terracotta sulphur stamp, in Agrigento Museum.

The sulphur mines in central Sicily, which were worked throughout the 19th century, gave Italy a world monopoly of the mineral by 1890. It is used, among other things, in the manufacture of sulphuric acid, electrical insulators and match heads, and in the vulcanisation of rubber. Some 32,000 miners were employed by 1860, and of the 700 or so mines in operation, steam engines were used in only four and horses in only ten; the formation of the seams of mineral allowed for nothing else. In most mines sulphur was extracted manually from an average depth of 60m, and many of the workers, known as *carusi*, were children under 14. Children were used because they were small enough to crawl through the tunnels; many of them only saw the light of day once a week. By the end of the century American sulphur was dominating the market, being much cheaper (a more economical method of refining, using steam, had been discovered, but the system was impossible to use in the Sicilian mines). The consequent decline of this part of the economy is one of the reasons for the mass emigration at the end of the 19th century from Sicily to Australia, Venezuela, Canada and the USA. In 1934 legislation was introduced forbidding employers to use women or boys under 16 in the mines that remained. The life of these people influenced many native writers, including Pirandello and Sciascia, as well as painters such as Guttuso. The last mines in the province of Agrigento were closed down in 1988, while those in the province of Caltanissetta were abandoned in the 1970s. You can see models of the mines in the Museum of Mineralogy in Caltanissetta (*see p. 249*). It may have been tough work, but the miners earned more than the peasants. The girls used to sing: *'cu surfuraru m'haju a fari zita, ca iddu lu sciallu mi lu fa di sita'*: 'I must choose a sulphur-miner for a fiancé, because he will buy me a silken shawl.'

SANTO STEFANO QUISQUINA AND BIVONA

Santo Stefano Quisquina (*map p. 571, C1*) is a sleepy town in a panoramic position, where the Chiesa Madre has a lovely altarpiece of the *Resurrection of Lazarus* by the Carracci school. Four and half kilometres east of the town, a track leads from the Cammarata road for c. 2km to an oak wood, where at 986m the 17th-century **Santuario di Santa Rosalia** (*open 10–1 & 3–5, July–Aug every day, Sept–June Sat, Sun and holidays, T: 0922 989805, www.quisquina.com*) is situated. The convent, inhabited by a small congregation of monks until the 1950s, now houses two small museums, one dedicated to monastic life and the other to farming activities in the area. There is a grotto where St Rosalia is said to have lived before she went to Mt Pellegrino near Palermo.

Bivona, where renowned peaches are cultivated, also has a number of fine churches, though most of them are in bad repair. A few years ago the beautiful carved stone portals were saved, thanks to an initiative by local schoolchildren.

LICATA & THE EAST

A plain surrounds Licata (*map p. 571, D3*), a seaside town that was once a busy port, first for the shipping of wheat and later for Sicilian sulphur, but became isolated after that industry collapsed, cut off as it is from world trade routes. Frederick of Hohenstaufen pronounced it *dilettissima* in 1234, and gave it the imperial eagle as a coat of arms. It occupies the site of *Phintias*, the Greek city founded by the eponymous tyrant from Gela, and is situated between the sea and a low hill, with the Bourbon **Castel Sant'Angelo** (*open Mon–Sat 9–1.30 & 4–7.15; T: 0922 772602*) of 1640 on the top, and the mouth of the River Salso to the east; the new section of town is on the far side of the river. Phintias was a prosperous town with a series of wells, water cisterns and aqueducts; among these, the **Pozzo della Grangela** well can still be seen, a short distance from the Town Hall. On 10th July 1943, at 2am, the beaches of Licata were the scene of the US landings of Operation Husky, a turning-point in the Second World War.

IN AND AROUND PIAZZA PROGRESSO

In the central Piazza Progresso, where the main streets of the town converge, is the Art Nouveau-style Town Hall, **Palazzo del Municipio** (1935, Ernesto Basile), housing a small collection of antique reliefs, a gorgeous early 17th-century triptych, the *Madonna with Saints*, and the white marble *Madonna della Mazza*, by Domenico Gagini (1470). The Art Nouveau opera house, Teatro Comunale Re Grillo (19th century) has recently been restored.

Corso Roma leads north, passing (left) two palaces: Palazzo Canarelli, which is decorated with grotesque heads, and Palazzo Urso-Ciarcià. To the right is the church of **San Domenico**, which has two paintings by Filippo Paladini; one is the splendid *St Anthony Abbot and Stories of his Life*, a masterpiece of *trompe l'oeil*. The kindly saint, dressed in freshly-pressed robes, appears to be stepping out from his niche, which is surrounded by little 'theatre settings', each one with a different episode to narrate. The other painting by Paladini shows the *Holy Trinity with Saints* (1611). A little further along the street is the convent and church of the **Carmine**, designed by Giovanni Biagio Amico in 1748 on 13th-century foundations, which houses ten beautifully modelled medallions with stories of the Old and New Testaments. The 16th-century cloister is interesting, with a double-lancet window and Gothic portal.

From Piazza Progresso, by taking Via Santa Maria uphill, you reach the old church of **Santa Maria La Vetere**, probably built in 580 by Benedictine monks together with their abbey. In the 16th century, it passed to Franciscan friars.

CORSO VITTORIO EMANUELE AND THE MUSEO ARCHEOLOGICO

Going towards the sea, Corso Vittorio Emanuele passes Palazzo Navarra and the church of the Purgatorio to the 16th-century church of **San Francesco**; its fine convent (now a school) was reconstructed in the 17th century and the marble façade added in 1750 by Giovanni Biagio Amico. It is also possible to see the peaceful cloister.

In the single-nave interior are a handsome 18th-century organ, elaborately carved wooden choir stalls and some interesting old tombs.

Behind the church is the favourite meeting-place of the people of Licata, **Piazza Sant'Angelo**, surrounded by imposing 18th-century buildings. The 17th-century church of Sant'Angelo has an unfinished façade and elegant cupola attributed to Angelo Italia. Inside, the 17th-century silver urn contains the bones of St Angelo, the patron saint of Licata, who was martyred in 1220. In the cloister it is planned to house a museum of the sea, with objects from shipwrecks found just offshore, including cannons and anchors, and amphorae from the Roman merchant fleet which succumbed to a storm in 249 BC. The 16th-century Cistercian abbey (*entrance from Via Dante*) houses the **Museo Archeologico della Badia**, (*open Tues, Wed, Fri 9–1, Thur, Sat 4–7.30, Sun 5–9.30, closed Mon and holidays; T: 0922 772602*), with local archaeological material from the prehistoric to the Roman periods, including a lovely display of domestic life in Hellenistic times and a treasure of gold jewellery and silver coins. The objects have been displayed following the latest and best practices: it is currently one of the finest museums in Sicily in terms of the quality and presentation of the objects.

THE CHIESA MADRE

The Corso ends at the 15th-century Chiesa Madre, or Santa Maria La Nuova. The interior, a central nave and two side aisles, has glowing 19th-century frescoes on the vault. The side aisles are adorned with several canvases by the Capuchin Fra' Felice da Sambuca. On the main altar is a 17th-century Flemish panel-painting of the *Nativity of the Virgin*. An elaborately-decorated chapel in the south transept, with a magnificent coffered ceiling, has an unusual wooden Crucifix with a black Christ, which narrowly escaped destruction at the hands of the raiding Turks in 1553. On 11th July, the notorious Anatolian corsair Dragut and a handful of pirates overpowered the garrison, crucified the chatelaine, and enslaved his two young sons and 600 citizens, but failed in their attempts to burn the Crucifix, which would not catch fire. The frustrated pirates tried to make away with some bronze church bells, but they were attacked by a swarm of bees and the bells fell into an inaccessible crevasse.

INLAND FROM LICATA

PALMA DI MONTECHIARO

On the edge of lonely countryside west of Licata, planted with almond trees, olives and vineyards, is Palma di Montechiaro (*map p. 571, D3*), founded in 1637 by the prince of Lampedusa, ancestor of novelist Giuseppe Tomasi di Lampedusa The town is surrounded by hundreds of half-constructed houses (now abandoned concrete shells), begun in the 1960s by emigrants, some of whom returned when the wine, table grapes, almonds, cherry tomatoes and especially the cantaloupe melons of the area achieved fame on the international market. The conspicuous 17th-century **Chiesa Madre**, by the Jesuit architect Angelo Italia, is a fine building with twin bell-towers and 'stocky columns of red marble', as Tomasi du Lampedusa described them, approached by a long flight of steps. To the left is the 17th-century **Palazzo Ducale** (*open Mon–Fri 9–1.30, Tues and Thur also 4–6, Sat morning on request; T: 0922 799229*), built by the Tomasi family when they gave their preceding mansion to the nuns of the Santissimo Rosario (*see below*). It has been well restored after years of abandon and is worth a visit; the ceilings are breathtaking and give an idea of the lifestyle of Sicilian aristocratic families before Unification.

In Via Amendola is the interesting church of the Collegio di Maria (1738), founded by the Tomasi family. Over the side altar is a striking painting by the local artist Domenico Provenzano of *Our Lady of Providence*, and over the main altar is a lovely depiction by Fra' Felice da Sambuca of the *Holy Trinity*. There is also a copy of the Turin Shroud, painted in 1656 and given to the Tomasi family by Princess Maria of Savoy. In a glass urn is the mummified body of St Placida.

The pastries known as *mandorlati del Gattopardo*, a favourite both with Tomasi di Lampedusa and Leonardo Sciascia, are still made by the Benedictine nuns in the **Monastero del Santissimo Rosario**, the convent where the Beata Corbera, the prince's sainted ancestor, received an enigmatic letter from the Devil. Even today the nuns are strictly cloistered; the pastries will be passed through to you on the wheel when you purchase them.

South of Palma, on a cliff overlooking the sea, looms the photogenic **Castello Chiaramontano** (1353), built to defend the town from pirate attacks.

Campobello di Licata (*map p. 571, D2–D3*) was founded in 1681. In the **Valle delle Pietre Dipinte** (Valley of the Painted Stones), a series of 110 blocks of local stone have been polished and painted by a local artist, Silvio Benedetto, with scenes from the *Divine Comedy*, creating an unusual open-air museum. The surrounding area is famed for its wine production, especially Chardonnay; harvested in August, the vines thrive on the chalky terrain.

THE SALSO IMERA RIVER

There are several Salso rivers in Sicily, so called because of their slightly salty waters. The one known as Imera (after the old city of *Himera*) enters the sea just east of Licata and is the second longest river on the island (112km). It springs from Bafurco in the Madonie Mountains, meets up with the River Gangi, and then joins the Imera Meridionale at Ponte Cinque Archi. It passes through the sulphur-rich interior, flowing north–south, neatly dividing Sicily into two parts. It once separated Sicans from Sicels. For the Arabs it defined the limits of the Val di Mazara, while for the Normans it was the dividing line between the diocese of Syracuse and that of Agrigento. It forms deep gorges as it winds its way towards the sea. Subject to frequent, abundant floods, the river was only provided with a bridge to replace the ferry in 1870. Off the mouth of the river in 256 BC the Roman consuls M. Atilius Regulus and L. Manlius Vulso defeated the Carthaginian fleet, but in 249 a convoy of Roman merchant ships intending to resupply the Roman forces besieging Lilybaeum was driven ashore by a Carthaginian fleet and broken up during a tempest shortly thereafter.

NARO

Naro (*map p. 571, D2*), which bases its economy on the production of table grapes, stands on a hilltop once defended by battlemented walls (1263), with one surviving gate of the original six, the **Porta d'Oro**, so called because it led into the Jewish quarter, renowned for its goldsmiths. Naro has a dignified Baroque aspect, almost comparable to Noto, and an assortment of crumbling old churches with wildflowers bravely growing in the cracks, ranging from the ruined Norman **duomo** (reached by 210 steep steps from Via Dante), a national monument, to early 17th-century churches. The robustly crenellated **Castello Chiaramontano** (*open 8–1 & 3.30–8 (6.30 in winter), closed Mon; T: 0922 953011*) is also a national monument and houses Vento di Donna, an interesting exhibit on women's clothes and accessories and their evolution through the 19th and 20th centuries. On the first floor, in the Sala dei Baroni, are the remains of frescoes painted by the local artist Cecco di Naro.

In the main street, Corso Vittorio Emanuele, close to Piazza Garibaldi, is the 15th-century Palazzo Giacchetto-Malfitano, which houses the **Museo della Grafica** (*open 10–1 & 3–8, until 7 in winter; entrance from Via Piave 121; T: 0922 954403*), with a display of some 250 works by artists ranging from Goya through to the Expressionism of Renato Guttuso. Some rooms are dedicated to 4,400 ancient books, incunabula and manuscripts from the library of Naro. Close by is the Baroque **church of San Francesco** (*open 9–12*), with a highly decorated, frothy façade. The single-nave interior was frescoed by Domenico Provenzano and houses a life-size silver statue of the *Immaculate Virgin* and an altarpiece of the same subject by Vito D'Anna. In the sacristy you will find beautifully carved and decorated wooden cupboards.

RACALMUTO

The little town of Racalmuto (*map p. 571, D2*), named from the Arabic *rahal-maut*, 'village in ruins', surrounded by barren, hilly countryside, is imbued with the spirit of Leonardo Sciascia (*see overleaf*), considered one of Italy's most important writers.

The quiet streets present a typically Arabian pattern, with blocks of houses facing onto narrow alleys, with stepped streets and the occasional tall palm tree. At the top of the hill is the main square, Piazza Umberto, with the 17th-century **Chiesa Madre**, or Annunziata. The interior is decorated with stuccoes, and there are five paintings by the local artist Pietro d'Asaro. Also facing onto the square are the 17th-century church of San Giuseppe and the superb 13th-century **Castello Chiaramontano** (*open 9–1 & 4–8, closed Mon; T: 0922 948820*), a national monument, with two large cylindrical towers. The ample galleries of the castle house permanent collections of works by local artists, and an exhibit of the works of Hungarian photographer Robert Capa, taken just after the Allied landings in Sicily in July 1943.

Steep steps lead up from the left of the Chiesa Madre to the former monastery of Santa Chiara, now the Town Hall; close by in Via Sciascia is the beautiful little 19th-century opera house (a miniature version of the one in Palermo), **Teatro Regina Margherita** (*1880; T: 0934 547034*). The stairs end at the sanctuary church of **Santa Maria del Monte** (1738), with a Gaginesque statue of the Virgin on the main altar; an important feast takes place here in July, attracting pilgrims from many nearby towns.

Seven kilometres north of Racalmuto is the so-called **Castelluccio** (720m), an Arab watch-tower transformed into a fortress by the Chiaramonte family. From the battlements Mount Etna is visible on a clear day.

LEONARDO SCIASCIA

Sciascia (1921–89), one of the best-known Italian novelists of the last century, was born in remote Racalmuto, and lived there for most of his life. He is commemorated by a life-size bronze statue (1997), on the pavement in the main street near the Chiesa Madre, by a local artist (the cigarette, which never left his fingers when he was alive, is repeatedly replaced by a fan). His simple white marble tomb, surrounded by jasmine, is in the little cemetery nearby. His best novels, including *Il giorno della civetta* (*The Day of the Owl*, 1961), *A ciascuno il suo* (*To Each His Own*, 1966), *Il Consiglio d'Egitto* (*The Council of Egypt*) and *Todo modo* (*One Way or Another*, both 1974), written in a particularly simple and direct style, are detective mysteries with a distinctive Sicilian flavour. In a number of essays and articles he also wrote about the problems which afflict the island and exposed political corruption and the insidious power of the Mafia long before these two evils of Italian society were widely recognised. Sciascia was very reserved and often pessimistic, but had a high standing in Italy in the 1970s as an intellectual figurehead. His 'Literary Park' (*www.regalpetra.it*) is in Racalmuto, also the foundation housing his books and papers, in the specially re-designed, elegant old Electricity Board building : *Fondazione Sciascia, 3 Viale della Vittoria; T: 0922 941993, www.fondazioneleonardosciascia.it.*

CANICATTÌ AND FAVARA

Canicattì (*map p. 571, D2*) is a market town of some importance and a railway junction. It is surrounded by vineyards, pergolas of a table grape called Italia, which can be marketed during the winter months thanks to the technique of covering the vines with thick plastic in August, when the grapes are just beginning to ripen. This blocks the ripening process indefinitely. When the farmer wants to sell his grapes, he takes off the plastic three or four days before picking. When covered with the plastic sheeting, the vineyards look like a vast sea. Peaches, nectarines and plums are also grown in this area.

In Piazza Cavour at **Favara** (*map p. 571, C2*), between Agrigento and Canicattì on the old SS 122, there is a castle of the Chiaramonte family (1275; enlarged in 1488, *open Mon–Sat 9–1 & 3.30–7.30; T: 0922 438192*). The chapel, entered from the courtyard, has a superb Gothic portal and a red Arab-Norman style dome. The town is dominated by the 18th-century church of the Rosario, a national monument, with a beautiful blue-tiled dome and a delightful interior, overflowing with Baroque stucco decoration. The original floor is of majolica tiles, and notice the coffered ceiling with paintings of saints. The heart of the old town, a close-knit series of tiny courtyards and Arab-style houses, has been successfully restored to become the **FARM Cultural Park** (*Cortile Bentivegna, open Tues ,Wed, Thur 10–10, Fri, Sat, Sun 10–midnight, closed Mon; T: 0922 34534, www.farm-culturalpark.com*), with galleries of modern art, exhibition areas, shops and residences for artists.

The pastry-shops of Favara prepare famous Easter lambs of marzipan filled with pistachio, so popular that they are now made throughout the year.

THE PELAGIAN ISLANDS

The Pelagian Islands (from the Greek *pelagos*, meaning sea) lie about 205km southwest of the Sicilian mainland and only 113km from Tunisia (*map p. 571*). Hauntingly beautiful, they lie tossed into a sea which varies in hue from pale green and lemon yellow through to turquoise and deep cobalt. There are three islands, Lampedusa, Linosa and Lampione, all quite different in character. They fell to the Allies without resistance in June 1943; Lampedusa surrendered to an English airman who landed there by accident, having run out of fuel. All three islands now enjoy protected status as a nature reserve: Lampedusa's is run by Legambiente (*www.legambienteriserve.it*), with a small museum and library on the loggerhead turtles at their headquarters in Lampedusa town (*Via Vittorio Emanuele 27, T: 0922 971611*); Linosa's and Lampione's are run by the Azienda Forestale. The collective name of the reserve is Area Marina Protetta Isole Pelagie (*www.isole-pelagie.it*).

LAMPEDUSA

Lampedusa is the largest of the three islands, some 20km square, with a population of about 6,000. On the African continental shelf, it is a flat limestone rock, similar to the Tunisian coast behind it, with crystal-clear waters and lovely sandy beaches, especially to the south, while the north coast forms a steep cliff. Once crowded with tourists, its notoriety as the main Italian landing-place for boatloads of migrants has had a negative effect. The Nobel Peace Prize has been proposed for the people of the island, in recognition of their ready, undemanding hospitality. In the village square by the port is an obelisk by Arnaldo Pomodoro, dedicated to the refugees.

Whale-watchers should come in March when the rorqual, or fin whale, passes along the south coast of Lampedusa and mates off the east coast. The **Isolotto dei Conigli**, just offshore, is a protected area because of the loggerhead turtles (*Caretta caretta*) which still lay their eggs on the beach (recently voted the most beautiful in Italy).

In Via Roma 3 is the **MARP Museo Archeologico delle Pelagie** (*open every evening 6–11; T: 0922 552611 or 0922 552516*), with a collection consisting mainly of objects salvaged from shipwrecks around the Pelagian Islands, from Phoenician to modern times. The same building incorporates the **Museo della Fiducia e del Dialogo per il Mediterraneo**, dedicated to the thousands of refugees from the war zones of Africa and the Middle East who attempt to cross the Mediterranean, only too often drowning when their makeshift boats capsize. The poignant display of humble personal effects washed ashore, items that these people treasured enough to bring with them when embarking on a voyage that did not permit luggage of any kind, is very moving. You will also find children's drawings, graphically describing the horrors they left behind them in their homelands.

LINOSA

Linosa, about 5km square in extent, 42km north of Lampedusa, is stunningly beautiful, formed of dark volcanoes, with cobalt-blue waters and tidy little houses painted in bright colours, with contrasting borders around the doors and windows, traditionally to help the fishermen recognise their home when they were far out at sea. It is quite hilly, and the most fertile of the islands. The people are not all fishermen, most of them were once cattle farmers; but they have been forced to stop this because there is no slaughter-house between here and Agrigento. They have also stopped extracting *pozzolana*, the stone formed by hardened volcanic ash (much in demand on the mainland for building), in order to preserve the landscape. The economy is now based on agriculture and tourism and the atmosphere is very peaceful. The small beaches are of black volcanic sand and there are lovely secluded rocky coves. Visitors are not permitted to bring cars, but they are not necessary as the island is so small. You can walk all the way round it in about 3hrs (strong shoes, water, sunhat, sunblock advised), or hire a motor-scooter or a bike. Sea daffodils cover the eastern slopes of Monte Nero in summer.

It has been suggested that Linosa is the lost Atlantis: offshore to the east there are great rectangular blocks of basalt on the seabed and what appears to be a primitive divinity carved in stone, now covered with seaweed. Loggerhead turtles lay their eggs on one of the beaches here (*no access*) and there is an important breeding colony of honey buzzards.

LAMPIONE

Lampione, with an area of just 1.2 km square, is uninhabited; formed of white limestone like Lampedusa and with sheer cliffs, its deep waters are frequented by scuba divers in the summer. Practically inaccessible, it is home to an important colony of Cory's shearwaters.

PRACTICAL INFORMATION

GETTING AROUND

• **By train:** From Agrigento there are services to and from Palermo, Syracuse, Catania and Caltanissetta. Cammarata, Casteltermini and Aragona are on the Agrigento–Palermo line but services are infrequent. In the eastern part of the province the nearest station for Racalmuto is Aragona (14km); Canicattì is a railway junction, from which Campobello and Licata can be reached. Sciacca can be reached from Palermo (*www.trenitalia.it*).

• **By bus:** In Agrigento small buses run by **TUA** (*T: 0922 412024*) cross the upper town along Via Atenea. Nos 1, 2 and 3 run from Piazza Marconi to the Valle dei Templi. Bus no. 1 continues to Kaos (Pirandello's house) and Porto Empedocle. Bus no. 2 to San Leone on the coast.

Inter-city buses: Tickets and information for all lines are available from **Nuova Omniabus** (*Piazza Fratelli Rosselli, T: 0922 29136; map 2*). For up-to-date bus schedules, see *www.orariautobus.it*.

ATA (*www.atabusservice.it*) to Gela, Licata, Palma di Montechiaro and Palermo.

Autolinee Licata/Sal Autolinee (*www.autolineesal.it*) runs services for Porto Empedocle, Palma di Montechiaro, Racalmuto, and Comiso airport, and three buses a day connecting Porto Empedocle (and Agrigento) with Palermo Punta Raisi Airport and vice versa, in connection with ferries to Lampedusa.

Camilleri, Argento e Lattuca (*www.camilleriargentoelattuca.it*) connects Agrigento to Aragona, Palermo and Raffadali.

Cavaleri (*www.cavaleriautolinee.it*) connects Naro with Canicattì, Licata and Palma di Montechiaro.

Cuffaro (*www.cuffaro.it*) has services for Canicattì and Palermo.

Lattuca (*www.autolineelattuca.it*) for Aragona, Comitini, Porto Empedocle and Sant'Angelo Muxaro.

Lumia (*www.autolineelumia.it*) runs services from Agrigento for Burgio, Caltabellotta, Campobello di Mazara, Castelvetrano, Cattolica Eraclea (from where you can catch another bus to Eraclea Minoa, 15mins' drive), Marsala, Mazara del Vallo, Menfi, Montallegro, Montevago, Palma di Montechiaro, Realmonte, Ribera, Sambuca, Santa Margherita di Belice, Sciacca, Siculiana, Trapani and Birgi Airport.

Panepinto (*www.panepintobus.it*) goes to Santo Stefano Quisquina.

SAIS Autolinee (*www.saisautolinee.it*) runs services for Canicattì, Caltanissetta, Catania, Enna and Messina, and an evening departure from Catania airport to Porto Empedocle (c. 3hrs) connecting with the ferry for Lampedusa and Linosa.

SAIS Trasporti (*www.saistrasporti.it*) connects Agrigento with Canicattì, Caltanissetta, Enna and Porto Empedocle.

Salemi (*www.autoservizisalemi.it*) for Caltagirone, Castelvetrano, Gela, Licata, Marsala, Mazara del Vallo, Menfi, Palma di Montechiaro, Porto Empedocle and Sciacca.

Pelagian Islands

• **By air:** Direct flights to Lampedusa from Palermo, Catania, Trapani and several mainland Italian cities are operated by Meridiana (*www.meridiana.it*), Alitalia (*www.alitalia.it*), Vueling (*www.vueling.com*), Volotea (*www.volotea.com*), Neos (*www.neosair.it*) and Blu Express (*www.blu-express.com*).

• **By sea:** For up-to-date information on shipping lines, schedules and tariffs, consult *www.traghetti.com*.

Siremar Compagnia delle Isole (*www.siremar.it*) runs car ferries from Porto Empedocle to Linosa (7hrs 30mins) and Lampedusa (9hrs) every night except Fri; visitors are not allowed to bring cars to Lampedusa in July and August, and never to Linosa.

Traghetti delle Isole (*www.traghettidelleisole.it*) runs ferries from Porto Empedocle to Lampedusa and Linosa every day except Thur and Sun.

Liberty Lines (*www.libertylines.it*) runs hydrofoils from Porto Empedocle once a day from June to Sept to Linosa (3hrs) continuing on to Lampedusa (4hrs 30mins).

Ferry and hydrofoil ticket offices:
Lampedusa: Siremar: c/o Strazzera, Lungomare Rizzo. Liberty Lines: Via L. Rizzo.
Linosa: Siremar: c/o Cavallaro, Via Principe Umberto 46. Liberty Lines: Via Re Umberto 70.
Porto Empedocle: Siremar: c/o Tricoli e Nuara, Via Molo 13. Liberty Lines: Via Molo 5.
Inter-island transport: Hydrofoil connections in summer between Lampedusa and Linosa twice a day on Sun, Tues, Thur, Fri; once a day on Mon, Wed, Sat. In winter once a day except Mon, run by Liberty Lines.

WHERE TO STAY

AGRIGENTO (*map p. 571, C2*)
€€€ **Villa Athena**. ■ Magical atmosphere, the first and the finest hotel in Agrigento, right in front of the Temple of Concord, with 27 rooms and suites, fitness centre, garden, car park and pool. *Passeggiata Archeologica 33 (Via dei Templi), T: 0922 596288, www. hotelvillaathena.it. Map 15.*
€€ **Colleverde**. Comfortable, straightforward hotel close to the town and within walking distance of the temples, with 50 rooms, beautiful garden, car park and good restaurant. *Via Panoramica dei Templi, T: 0922 29555, www.colleverdehotel.it. Map 11.*
€€ **Villa Goethe**. The villa belonging to Baron Celauro where Goethe stayed in 1787 is an elegant, central B&B with a shady hanging garden, cats, lots of stairs, and 5 lovely rooms. *Via Celauro 7 (off Via Atenea), T: 0922 816240, 349 4186915, www.villagoethe.it. Map 2.*
€€ **Camera con Vista**. This comfortable *relais* has six rooms with temple views, huge beds and bathrooms (some with jacuzzi), car park but no restaurant. *Via Porta Aurea 4, Contrada Bennici (near the hospital, just west of Porta Aurea), T: 0922 554605, www. cameraconvista.net. Beyond map 14.*
€ **B&B Monastero Santo Spirito**. The Cistercian nuns offer accommodation in their convent. Light, airy rooms, kitchen facilities available, central position, good value for money, and the breakfasts prepared by the nuns are something to write home about. *Cortile Santo Spirito 9, T: 0922 20664 or 328 737 0299, www. monasterosantospirito.com. Map 2.*
ARAGONA (*map p. 571, C2*)
€€ **Ciuci's Manor**. Country house in panoramic position close to Aragona with lake and pool. Donkeys and the local *Girgentana* goats are raised here. 5 spacious rooms, good restaurant. *Contrada Carbonia, T: 334 674 8055, www.ciucismanor.com.*
CAMMARATA (*map p. 571, C1*)
€€ **Casalicchio**. The farm has belonged to the same family since 1816. Comfortable rooms or self-catering apartments, pool, lake, tennis, sauna, good restaurant, organic food, mostly of local production. *Contrada Casalicchio, T: 0922 908144, www.casalicchio.info.*
FAVARA (*map p. 571, C2*)
€€ **Belmonte**. Central, with 9 modern rooms and a good restaurant. *Via Sottotenente Saieva 4, T: 0922 437146, www.belmontehotel.com.*
€ **Relais Garden Cactus**. ■ In the countryside 4km south of Favara, charming B&B with 5 rooms set in a garden with 3,000 different varieties of cactus. Pool, bikes, car park, delicious breakfasts. *Contrada Crocca 3, SP 3 Favara–Agrigento, T: 0922 606872 or 334 122 8051, www.bebgardencactus.it.*

LICATA (*map p 571, D3*)

€ **Antica Dimora San Girolamo**.
Delightful, colourful B&B in a
medieval house in the fishermen's
quarter; lovely breakfasts and very
comfortable accommodation. *Piazza
San Girolamo 20, T: 0922 875010, www.
dimorasangirolamo.it.*

MENFI (*map p. 571, A1*)

€€€ **Foresteria di Planeta**. Renowned
vintners offer accommodation on their
beautiful estate, with acres of well-
groomed vineyards; 14 elegant, pastel-
coloured rooms with floor tiles from
Burgio and Caltagirone, surrounded
by a garden of aromatic herbs. Good
restaurant serving the best local cuisine,
where much attention is paid to the
wine. Cookery courses organised.
*Contrada Passo di Gurra (west of Menfi,
south of the SS 115), SP 79 km 91, T: 0925
195 5460, www.planeta.it.*

€€€ **Baglio San Vincenzo**. ■ An old-
fashioned farm immersed in lovely
countryside, offering 12 comfortable
rooms, restaurant and pool, within easy
reach of Menfi town, Sciacca, Selinunte
and Castelvetrano. The farm produces
olive oil and the award-winning Lanzara
red and white wines, and both white and
pink *spumante*. *Contrada San Vincenzo,
T: 0925 75065, www.bagliosanvincenzo.
it.*

MONTALLEGRO (*map p. 571, C2*)

€€€ **Relais Briuccia**. ■ A welcoming
little hotel in what was a country
nobleman's town house (lots of stairs),
in a strategically situated village on the
road between Agrigento and Sciacca. All
7 rooms have beautiful old tiled floors,
comfortable beds, bathrooms with
jacuzzi. The restaurant, Capitolo 1, is
famous throughout Sicily. *Via Trieste 1,
T: 0922 847 755, 339 759 2176 or 334 165
0814, www.relaisbriuccia.it.*

PORTO PALO (*map p. 571, A1*)

€ **Da Vittorio**. 10 simple but functional
rooms on the lovely unspoilt beach
of Porto Palo (awarded the EU Blue
Banner); very quiet, garden and car park.
Incredible restaurant, one of the best in
Sicily, if you like fish. Closed Nov–Feb.
*Via Friuli-Venezia Giulia, T: 0925 78381,
www.ristorantevittorio.it.*

RACALMUTO (*map p. 571, D2*)

€€ **Regalpetra Hotel**. Small hotel
in the heart of town, with 9 rooms,
each dedicated to a novel by Leonardo
Sciascia; small fitness centre. No
restaurant, but good breakfasts. *Via
Garibaldi 208, T: 0922 949084 or 342
739 2295, www.regalpetrahotel.it.*

REALMONTE (*map p. 571, C2*)

€€€ **Masseria Agnello**. Just 2km north
of Realmonte, this is an old farmhouse
transformed into a *relais*, with 10 rooms,
all opening onto the garden and olive
grove. Restaurant, bar, children's play
area and pool; cookery lessons, boat
trips, mountain-biking and horse-
riding can be arranged; free shuttle to
the beach. *Contrada Fauma Caruana
6, T: 0922 24291 or 320 417 2942, www.
masseriaagnello.it.*

SANT'ANGELO MUXARO (*map p. 571,
C2*)

€ Accommodation in restored village
houses, functioning as *paese-albergo*.
Breakfast is included. Italian courses
available, walking tours and other
activities are arranged. A delightful
experience. *Val di Kam, Piazza Umberto
33, T: 0922 919670 or 339 530 989, www.
valdikam.it.*

SCIACCA (*map p. 571, B2*)

€€€ **Verdura Golf & Spa Resort**. A
Rocco Forte Collection hotel. 203 rooms
and suites, each with private terrace

and sea view. Two golf courses, infinity pool, fitness centre, good restaurants. *SS 115 km 131, T: 0925 998001, www. verduraresort.com.*

€€ **Villa Palocla**. Lovely old country house surrounded by orange groves, 9 rooms, pool, winter garden, elegant restaurant with frescoed ceilings. Note that it is a popular venue for elaborate weddings. *Contrada Raganella, T: 0925 902812 or 328 222 7962, www. villapalocla.it.*

€€ **Melqart**. ■ Small hotel on the port, the most picturesque part of Sciacca; new building with 20 rooms, nice breakfasts, garage. *Via Mulini 10, T: 0925 21828, www.melqarthotel.it.*

€€ **Jacaranda**. In a modern villa surrounded by a garden close to town, a colourful B&B with 4 comfortable rooms. Very good breakfasts, car park. *Via delle Sequoie 1, Contrada Isabella, T: 392 812 3231, www.casajacaranda.it.*

€ **Al Moro**. A 13th-century ex-watch-tower in the town centre, transformed into a tiny German-run inn with 13 rooms, patio, good breakfasts but no restaurant. Lots of stairs, both inside and out. *Via Liguori 44 (Via Licata 195 on the navigator), T: 0925 86756 or 393 946 4367, www.almoro.com.*

€ Le **Casette del Porto**. You can stay in an independent restored fisherman's house overlooking the harbour. *Lungomare Colombo 23, T: 320 832 0192, www.sciaccacase.it.*

WHERE TO STAY ON THE PELAGIAN ISLANDS

NB: Accommodation on the islands is considerably more expensive than in similar establishments on the mainland. The hotels usually demand a minimum stay of three nights or a week; many close in winter.

LAMPEDUSA

€€€ **Cala Madonna**. Elegant resort with 14 spacious rooms in stone *dammusi* (stone cottages), in a quiet position facing the sea, garden, restaurant, boat for excursions. Closed winter. *Contrada Madonna 28, T: 0922 971626, www.calamadonnaclub.it.*

€€€ **Cupola Bianca**. Very chic Moorish structure, the 23 rooms are in *dammusi*; peaceful position, lovely garden with palm trees and pool; open-air dining, tennis. Closed winter. *Contrada Madonna, T: 0922 971274 or 0922 975793, www.hotelcupolabianca.it.*

€€€ **Medusa**. Characteristic hotel on central Guitgia Bay, all 20 rooms and suites with sea view, good restaurant, private 27m gulet for excursions to Lampione and Linosa. Open year round. *Piazza Medusa 3, T: 0922 971274 or 0922 975793, www.medusahotels.it.*

€€ **Martello**. Long-standing, comfortable hotel run by the owners, 25 rooms, most with sea view, restaurant, good value for money. Open mid-March–mid-Nov. *Piazza Medusa 1, T: 0922 971479, www.hotelmartello.it.*

LINOSA

€€ **Posta**. In a good central position, occupying the old post office, B&B with 10 comfortable rooms, garden, library and rooftop terrace, kitchen available, dinghy for excursions. *Vicolo Pisa 3, T: 320 601 0556 or 339 741 0705, www. linosaresidencelaposta.it.*

€ **Linoikos**. This little hotel is also a cultural centre and organises art shows. 14 simple but comfortable rooms, decorated with flotsam, no TV, lovely terrace overlooking the sea, evening meals on request. Open June–Sept. *Via Alfieri, T: 0922 972212. From May–Oct, T: 348 423 0184 (Alessandro). www. linoikos.it.*

WHERE TO EAT

AGRIGENTO (*map p. 571, C2*)

€€ **La Posata di Federico II**. Elegant restaurant (you eat on the veranda in summer). The imaginative chef makes good use of his very fresh ingredients. Good desserts, Sicilian wines. Closed Sun. *Piazza Cavour 19 (Viale della Vittoria), T: 0922 28289 or 348 548 1497. Map 7.*

€€ **Osteria Ex Panificio**. Friendly *trattoria* in what used to be a bakery, superb Sicilian food and wines served in the garden whenever possible. *Piazza Giuseppe Sinatra 16 (Piazza Pirandello), T: 0922 595399. Map 1.*

€€ **Re di Girgenti**. The place to come for excellent fish dishes (though carnivores are well provided for too); good wine list, views over the temples. Closed Tues. *Strada Panoramica 51 (opposite the cemetery), T: 0922 401388. Map 11.*

€€ **Ruga Reali**. For a subtle mix of country cooking and marine cuisine, local wines, simple relaxed atmosphere. Open evenings only, closed Mon. *Cortile Scribani 8 (Piazza Pirandello), T: 0922 20370. Map 1.*

€ **Rosticceria Palumbo**. An ideal lunch stop, Palumbo has a vast array of Sicilian-style fast food, from delicious spit-roasted chicken to pasta or vegetable dishes and salads; also take-away. *Piazza Pirandello 25, T: 0922 29765. Map 1.*

CASTROFILIPPO (*Map p. 571, D2*)

€ **Osteria del Cacciatore**. A country inn serving good *antipasti*, local pasta or delicious thick vegetable soups in winter; grilled meat; fruit pizza for dessert, recommended by the Slow Food Foundation. Closed Wed. *Contrada Torre, SS 122 Agrigento–Caltanissetta, T: 0922 829824.*

LICATA (*map p. 571, D3*)

€€€ **La Madia**. ■ Renowned, Michelin-star chef Pino Cuttaia's restaurant offers excellent fish, meat and vegetables, well prepared to original recipes and beautifully served, accompanied by his own home-made bread and washed down with Sicilian wines. A meal here is certainly worth the trip to Licata. Closed all day Tues, Sun evening in winter, Sun lunchtime in summer. *Corso Capriata 22, T: 0922 771443.*

€€ **L'Oste e il Sacrestano**. Small restaurant where Peppe and Chiara, passionately enthusiastic about food, ensure that your meal will be a delightful experience from start to finish. Local vegetables and fish, followed by irresistible desserts. Closed Mon and Sun evenings. *Via Sant'Andrea 19, T: 0922 774736.*

MONTALLEGRO (*map p. 571, C2*)

€€€ **Capitolo Primo**. ■ This restaurant is so good it would be worth the journey to Sicily in itself: but it also happens to be in a strategic position along the route from Agrigento to Sciacca, and offers comfortable accommodation (*see p. 239*). Damiano, a chef with flair, creates dishes to delight the eye as well as the palate, using tradition and local ingredients to the best advantage, often in highly unusual ways. His cellar is stocked with the best Sicilian wines. Closed Mon. *Via Trieste 1, T: 0922 847755, 339 759 2176 or 334 165 0814.*

PORTO PALO (*map p. 571, A1*)
€€ **Da Vittorio**. ■ Family-run restaurant of long standing, on the beach, renowned for the sumptuous fish soup and seafood salads; rooms also available (*see p . 239*). Vittorio hails from the north Italian mountain town of Bergamo, but he has a real flair for cooking seafood. House wines are excellent. Closed Sun and Mon evenings in winter. *Via Friuli-Venezia Giulia 9, T: 0925 78381.*

RACALMUTO (*map p. 571, D2*)
€€ **Lo Zenzero**. ■ Close to the opera house, a historic restaurant run by the same family for many years; the home-made food prepared to traditional recipes is delicious. Pizza in the evenings. Local wines. Closed Mon. *Via Regina Margherita 22, T: 0922 949618.*

RIBERA (*map p. 571, B2*)
€ **Agorà**. Good restaurant worth a detour to Ribera. The vast menu includes local fish (fried baby cod or squid), meat (grilled pork or Florentine steak), delicious desserts made using the famous wild strawberries with lemon and orange. Also excellent pizzeria in the evenings. Closed Mon. *Via Buoni Amici 15, T: 0925 62014.*

SCIACCA (*map p. 571, B2*)
€€€ **Hostaria del Vicolo**. Local fresh fish is used to prepare some very special dishes: *spaghetti frutti di mare e finocchietto* (spaghetti with shellfish and wild fennel), *merluzzo ai fichi secchi* (cod with dried figs), or swordfish ravioli. Closed Mon. *Vicolo Samaritano 10, T: 0925 23071.*

€€€ **Porto San Paolo**. Smart restaurant overlooking the harbour, delicious seafood, local wines. Closed Wed. *Largo San Paolo 1, T: 0925 27982.*

€€ **Porta di Mare**. Tiny restaurant in the centre, a good place for memorable seafood. Don't miss the *risotto nero con i ricci* (risotto with squid ink and sea urchins) if in season. Closed Tues. *Corso Vittorio Emanuele 107, T: 0925 25846.*

WHERE TO EAT ON THE PELAGIAN ISLANDS

NB: Eating out on the islands is expensive. Dishes are often spicy and cous cous is frequently on the menu. Most restaurants are closed in winter.

LAMPEDUSA

€€€ **Gemelli**. For superb seafood crudités and sea-perch cous cous, also fish soup and local lobster; irresistible desserts. Expensive. Closed winter; booking necessary. *Via Cala Pisana 2, T: 0922 970699.*

€€ **Mille e Una Notte**. Beautiful restaurant in a large cave, excellent cuisine. Closed winter. *Lungomare Luigi Rizzo 152, T: 366 154 4903.*

€€ **Trattoria Pugliese**. A cosy and quiet *trattoria* next to the airport. The chef is from Puglia, which guarantees excellent pasta dishes. Open evenings only in summer. *Via Cala Francese 17, T: 0922 970531.*

€€ **Ciccio's**. No-frills *trattoria*, ideal for lunch or dinner; tasty snacks, seafood salad, sea-perch cous cous, nice atmosphere. Closed Thur in winter. *Via Vittorio Emanuele 30, T: 339 772 3493.*

€ **Lampegusto**. Snack bar on the main street serving typical Sicilian street food to eat on the spot or to take away. Their *polpette di gamberi* (shrimp patties) are not to be missed. Open summer only. *Via Vittorio Emanuele 19, T: 388 628 4356.*

LINOSA
€€ Errera. Close to the sea, wonderful pasta or cous cous; refreshing fruit granita for dessert. *Via Scalo Vecchio, T: 0922 972041.*

€€ Trattoria da Anna. ■ Her lentil soup is famous, or try the *pasta con gli sgombri* (pasta with mackerel). *Via Veneto 1, Belvedere, T: 0922 972048.*

LOCAL SPECIALITIES

AGRIGENTO La Badia Grande (*Via Atenea 83; map 2*) is the pastry shop of the Cistercian nuns, renowned for their unique *cous cous dolce* with pistachios and chocolate; the recipe hasn't changed for 500 years. The **Dalli Cardillo** bakery (*Piazza Pirandello 32; map 1*) makes all kinds of local bread, including the special rolls for the feast of St Calogero. **Sammartino 1961** (*Via Pirandello 24; map 2*) is a good place to buy olive oil, wines, liqueurs, cheese, anchovies with chilli pepper, swordfish pâté or the local pesto made with wild fennel. The historic coffee-house is **Infurna** (*Via Atenea 96; map 2*). Try their ice cream made with wild strawberries from Ribera.

ARAGONA Bar Europa (*Via Roma 187*) is the historic pastry shop, for excellent *cannoli di ricotta.*

BURGIO The oldest surviving bell foundry is that of **Luigi Cascio** (*Fonderia Mario Virgadamo, Piazza Roma 8*). The typical pottery can be found at **La Ceramica di Burgio** (*Via Vittorio Emanuele 19*).

CAMPOBELLO DI LICATA Sicily's finest Chardonnay comes from the **Baglio del Cristo di Campobello** estate (*Contrada Favarotta, SS 123 km 19.2; T: 0922 877709*). Fine wines are also produced by the **Azienda Agricola Milazzo**, on the Terre della Baronia estate (*SS 123 km 12.7; T: 0922 878207, www.milazzovini.com*).

FAVARA The town is famous for its marzipan Easter lambs, so good that the pastry shops now make them year-round. **Pasticceria Lombardo** (*Via Ten. Col. Russo 5*) is an excellent address.

LAMPEDUSA Cose Buone, a very up-market bakery (*Via Cavour 8*), is a good address for fresh bread and pastries. **Famularo** (*Via Roma 40*) for all kinds of local fish, smoked or in olive oil, and sponges. Lampedusa's historic coffee-house is the **Bar Dell'Amicizia** (*Via Vittorio Emanuele 60*), with a particularly congenial atmosphere.

MENFI The **Settesoli estate** (*SS 115 di Menfi; T: 0925 77111, www. cantinesettesoli.it*) produces the prize-winning Mandrarossa wine.

RACALMUTO Pasticceria Taibi (*Via Garibaldi 127*), opened over a century ago is known for its delicious *taralli racalmutesi*, delicate lemon biscuits.

RAFFADALI Pasticceria Di Stefano (*Via Murano 23*) for home-made ice cream, freshly prepared every day, including some unusual flavours such as pecorino made with sheep's milk. Their coffee is good too; try it with pistachio cream. Closed Wed.

RIBERA A small industry preparing jams and marmalades using local fruit, especially the renowned wild strawberries, is **Colle Vicario** (*Viale Garibaldi 118; T: 0925 63906, www. collevicario.com*). Very elegant packaging. Try the wild strawberry with orange blossom and pink champagne, lemon with vodka, or cherry with tequila. At the **Pasticceria Sabella** (*Via Re Federico 113*) a wide array of sweets is prepared exclusively with the local oranges; candied, crystallised, in biscuits and chocolates.

SAMBUCA The special pastries of Sambuca are called *minni di virgini* (virgin's breasts), delicate pies filled with confectioner's custard, chocolate and candied pumpkin, first made by Suor Virginia in 1725 in honour of Marquis Pietro Beccadelli and his wife Marianna; you will find them (along with numerous other delectable sweets) at **Pendola** (*Cortile Baglio Grande 42*). The **Planeta estate** at Ulmo (*request visit at least 2 days before; T: 0925 1955460, www. planeta.it/ospitalita*) produces a marvellous white wine called Cometa, a perfect accompaniment to rich fish dishes.

SCIACCA Bar Sant'Angelo (*Corso Vittorio Emanuele 66*), is an excellent choice for home-made ice cream and *granita*, this coffee-house hasn't changed at all since 1963, when it was chosen by Pietro Germi as a film set for his *Seduced and Abandoned*. Another charming Art Nouveau locale is the **Caffè Scandaglia** (*Piazza Scandagliato 5*), which opened in 1919. Pastries made according to the traditional recipes of the nuns of Sciacca (*cucchiteddi* and *ova marine*) can be found at **Pasticceria La Favola** (*Corso Vittorio Emanuele 234*). Coral is still worked in Sciacca, with excellent results, by **Conti** (*Piazza Matteotti 10, www.orodisciacca.it*), while a good address for the local pottery is **Cascio** (*Corso Vittorio Emanuele 111, www.ceramichecascio.it*).

FESTIVALS AND EVENTS

AGRIGENTO First week in February, *Sagra del mandorlo in fiore*, an international folklore festival, held at the temples (*www. sagradelmandorloinfiore.com*). First week in July, Feast of St Calogero with processions and fireworks; when the saint is carried along Via Atenea, he is pelted with decorative loaves of bread.

BURGIO Second Sun in Aug, starting at dawn, procession of the Crucifix from the Chiesa Madre to Santa Maria di Rifesi, 8km from town, where it will stay for 2 weeks.

CAMMARATA First Sun in May, unusual and picturesque feast with procession of the Cross of St Anthony called *Crocifisso di Tuvagli*. Last Sun in May, procession of the Cross of the Angels, with a cavalcade. Last Sun in August, procession of the Cross of the Rain. 19 Dec–6 Jan, Living Crib in the district of San Vito, when local people enact tableaux representing the Nativity of Christ and the Epiphany, and bring to life ancient crafts (*www. presepeviventecammarata.it*).

CASTELTERMINI Last week in May, *Tataratà* (*see p. 228; www.tatarata.net*).

LAMPEDUSA July, Lampedusainfestival, summer event which includes films, concerts and open-air theatre performances (*www. lampedusainfestival.com*).

LICATA 3–6 May, *Festa di Sant'Angelo*, including a traditional fair, parades of Sicilian carts, handicrafts, fireworks and music in honour of St Angelo, a Carmelite monk from Jerusalem martyred in the 13th century. In years of good harvest, the farmers take a mule laden with flowers into the church; in dry years the statue of the saint is taken out to sea on a boat and threatened with being thrown overboard, in the hope that he will send rain; this strategy

nvariably works (*ww.prolocolicata.it*).
PALMA DI MONTECHIARO May,
Festa della Madonna del Castello,
a procession of barefoot devotees,
accompanied by musicians and
richly-bedecked mules, accompany
the Madonna up through the steep
little streets to the castle (*www.
palmadimontechiaro.com*).
RACALMUTO Second Sun in July,
a colourful procession of riders on
festooned horses goes up the stairway to
Santa Maria del Monte.
SAN BIAGIO PLATANI Easter Sun,
Gli Archi di Pasqua (the festival of the
Easter Arches) dates back to the early

17th century; special bread is baked and
the streets are decorated with flowery
arches made of branches of palm leaves,
fruit, bread and dates, to celebrate the
meeting of the Madonna with her Risen
Son (*www.archidipane.com*).
Sciacca February, the figure of *Peppe
Nappa*, the sharp-witted Sicilian
peasant, is burnt at the end of the
Carnival processions with allegorical
floats, thought to be the oldest in Sicily
(*www.sciaccacarnevale.it*). 2 Feb and 15
Aug, two barefoot processions for the
Madonna del Soccorso.

SAN CALOGERO

This saint is the most popular in Sicily, claimed as patron by Lipari, Sciacca, Naro,
Favara, Grotte, Agrigento and Campofranco, to name just a few places; most of them
can even show relics of his body. The statues of the saint which are taken through the
city streets on his feast days are all similar: an old black man with a long white beard,
his right hand raised in blessing and a doctor's bag over his arm. He is often connected
with bread; in Campofranco enormous 'bread men' are lifted up to kiss the statue,
then broken up and distributed among the crowd in order to ensure a good crop in
the coming year, while in Agrigento, along Via Atenea, he is pelted with little loaves,
because he looked after the sick outside the town, coming in periodically to beg for
food for them. The townsfolk preferred to throw the bread at him, not wanting a
closer contact, for fear of contagion. He is often invoked against infectious diseases,
especially cholera, plague and leprosy. His name means monk in Greek, so probably
many bearded hermits, living on mountaintops and earning a reputation for healing
and wisdom, were called Calogero. An old song describes the characteristics of the
saint in his various manifestations: '*San Caloiru di Naru, li miraculi li fa pri dinaru;
San Caloiru di Girgenti, miraculi nni fa pri nenti; San Caloiru di Grutti, di miraculi
si nni futti!*' (In Naro St Calogero wants payment for his miracles, in Agrigento he
performs them for nothing, while in Grotte he couldn't care less).

Caltanissetta

The old province of Caltanissetta, between Enna and Agrigento, is neatly divided into two parts by the River Imera Meridionale (the ancient *Himera*). The town of Gela, on the south coast, dominates the southern part, while Caltanissetta, the capital, presides over the north. Particularly favourable in position for human settlement, the entire area has been inhabited since the Early Bronze Age. In the 16th century much of the land was  divided up among the more powerful aristocratic families, in order to farm it more efficiently, and many new towns were founded. The economy, after the decline of sulphur extraction, is now based on the production of wheat, fruit and vegetables, especially artichokes, table grapes, peaches and plums, and there is also an oil refinery at Gela. The famous bitter liqueur Amaro Averna is still produced near Caltanissetta, according to a secret recipe owned by the Averna family for more than 150 years. Craggy castles and beautiful beaches of golden sand are some of the prime attractions of this little-known part of Sicily.

CALTANISSETTA

The town of Caltanissetta (*map p. 572, B2*) is a small but prosperous place, built of golden-yellow sandstone. It has a charming, colourful old centre, inviting displays in the shop windows, and a lively daily fish and vegetable market.

For many years the name of the town was thought to derive from the ancient Sican city of *Nissa*, with the Arabic prefix *kal'at* (castle); but it could also come from *kal'at en-nissaat*, or 'castle of the young women'. Excavations in 1989 on Mt San Giuliano (or Redentore) yielded 7th–6th-century BC finds. The site was then abandoned until the Roman period. After its conquest by Count Roger in 1086 it was given as a feudal estate to his son Jourdain, passing subsequently into the hands of Corrado Lancia (1296) and the Moncada family (1406). The province was once the centre of the most important sulphur-mining area in the world, from the 18th century up until the early 20th century (the last mines were closed down in the 1970s).

PIAZZA GARIBALDI AND THE DUOMO

In Piazza Garibaldi is an amusing **fountain** depicting two bronze sea-monsters squirting water at a triton and a hippogryph by the local sculptor Michele Tripisciano, whose works also decorate Corso Umberto, the Town Hall and the public gardens. Dominating the square is the honey-coloured façade of the **duomo**, dedicated to Santa Maria La Nova e San Michele (1570–1622), much damaged by bombing raids in 1943. In the luminous interior, decorated with white and gold stuccoes and bright frescoes, the vault painting (1720), a brilliant, swirling triumph of *trompe l'oeil*, is thought to be the Flemish artist Willem Borremans' masterpiece. In the second south chapel is a wooden statue (covered with silver) of the Immaculate Virgin (1760). In the chapel to the right of the sanctuary is a charming polychrome wooden statue of the Archangel Michael by Stefano Li Volsi (1625), flanked by marble statues of the archangels Gabriel and Raphael by Vincenzo Vitaliano (1753). St Michael is particularly venerated in Caltanissetta, because he is thought to have saved the people from epidemics of the plague. The high altarpiece of the *Madonna with Saints* is by Borremans, and the richly painted, carved and gilded organ dates from the 17th century. In the north transept is a painting of *Our Lady of Carmel* by Filippo Paladini and in the second north chapel is a Crucifix attributed to Fra' Umile da Petralia. One of the altars is taken up by an elaborate gilded urn containing a very realistic *Dead Christ*, made by local sculptor Francesco Biangardi in 1896.

The church of **San Sebastiano**, opposite, has an unusual façade (1891), painted bright red, and a blue campanile. It is said to have been founded in the 16th century in thanksgiving to St Michael and St Sebastian, after a devastating epidemic of plague.

Another side of the piazza is occupied by a former convent which now houses the **Town Hall** (with statues by Tripisciano) and the **opera house**, Teatro Regina Margherita.

CORSO UMBERTO

Running alongside the Town Hall, Corso Umberto leads up to a **statue of Umberto I** (the second king of Italy, wearing a flamboyant hat) by Tripisciano, outside the former Jesuit collegiate church of **Sant'Agata** (1605), painted red, and preceded by an outside stairway. The Greek-cross interior is finely decorated with inlaid marble, especially the two side altars. The north altar (with a delightful frontal with birds) is surmounted by a relief of St Ignatius by Ignazio Marabitti. The high altarpiece, the *Martyrdom of St Agatha*, is by Agostino Scilla (1654). His work here is framed in black marble adorned with cherubs by Marabitti. The first north chapel has frescoes by Luigi Borremans, the son of Willem (including an *Assumption* in the vault and a *Nativity* on a side wall).

Off the right side of Corso Umberto, on Salita Matteotti, is the grand Palazzo Moncada (1635–8), now the seat of the Pro Loco tourist office, and on the first floor, the **Museo Michele Tripisciano** (*open 9.30–1 & 5–8, closed Sun and Mon; T: 0934 585890, www.museotripisciano.it*), a remarkable collection of sculptures by this unsung local artist, who lived from 1860–1914. The palace was built by Countess Luisa Moncada, when in an attempt to gain independence for the island her grandson was chosen by the Sicilians to become their king. Unfortunately the plot was discovered and the revolutionaries were executed, while Don Luigi Guglielmo (the grandson) was exiled to Madrid and his palace was never completed.

SAN DOMENICO AND THE CASTELLO DI PIETRAROSSA

A street on the left side of the duomo leads downhill to Via San Domenico, which continues to the church of **San Domenico** with a sinuously curving Baroque façade fitting an awkward site, in the oldest district of the city. The stuccoes inside have been painted bright blue while the nave is decorated in pastel shades. The fine canvas of the *Madonna of the Rosary* (1614) is by Filippo Paladini.

From here along Via Angeli, the 14th-century church of **Santa Maria degli Angeli**, the first Chiesa Madre, can be reached in ten minutes. Recently restored, the church's original west door survives. Beyond, on a rocky outcrop, stand the scattered ruins and lonely tower of the Arab-built **Castello di Pietrarossa**, so-called because of the red stone from which it was constructed.

TWO SMALL MUSEUMS

Near Villa Amedeo (the beautiful public gardens), at Viale Regina Margherita 51 (southeast of the duomo) is the seminary which houses the **Museo Diocesano** (*open Mon–Fri 9–12.30 & 4–7*), with a well-displayed collection of 17th- and 18th-century vestments and some fine paintings, including two by Luigi Borremans, who was employed in Caltanissetta as a fresco painter; also a very expressive *Martyrdom of St Flavia* by Fra' Felice da Sambuca. At Viale della Regione 73, in a school, is the **Museo Mineralogico Paleontologico e della Zolfara** (*open Mon–Sat 9–1*), an interesting collection of some 3,000 minerals, and scale models of many of the sulphur mines that once operated in the provinces of Caltanissetta and Agrigento.

ABBAZIA DI SANTO SPIRITO AND THE MUSEO ARCHEOLOGICO

The **Abbazia di Santo Spirito**, 3km north of Caltanissetta, is the oldest church in the province, founded by Count Roger and his wife Adelaide (probably between 1086 and 1093) and consecrated in 1153. It was attached to a fortified building, parts of which now form the sacristy. The church has a fine triple apse, recently restored. The charming small interior (*to request visit call priest, T: 0934 566596, or ring at the door on the right marked Abbazia*) contains a large font carved in a massive block of stone, where people were baptised by immersion, below a painted Crucifix dating from the 15th century. On the walls are three detached 15th-century frescoes. The striking 17th-century fresco of *Christ in Benediction* was repainted in 1974. On the arch of the apse is the dedication stone (1153), and nearby is a little Roman cinerary urn (1st century AD), with rams' heads, birds and a festoon.

Close by, at Via Santo Spirito 57, is the **Museo Archeologico** (*open 9–1 & 3.30–7; T: 0934 567062*). This important museum has a particularly interesting archaeological collection from pre- and post-Greek colonisation sites in the province, including objects from tombs at Gibil Gabib, Polizzello, Capodarso and Vassallaggi, and from the settlement, sanctuary and tombs at Sabucina. There are some fine kraters (many with animal illustrations), black- and red-figure vases, and figurines found on Mt San

Giuliano (on the northern outskirts of Caltanissetta) which represent the earliest portrayal of the human figure so far discovered in Sicily after the Palaeolithic graffiti in the Addaura caves near Palermo. Dating from the early Bronze Age, they are thought to have been used in a prehistoric sanctuary. Finds from the Byzantine period include splendid gold earrings from Monte Mimiani. One of the most interesting objects on display is a 6th-century BC bronze helmet from Polizzello, the cheekpiece of which is decorated with the figure of an armed warrior. It is similar to a helmet of Cretan manufacture now on display in Berlin.

ENVIRONS OF CALTANISSETTA

SABUCINA AND PONTE CAPODARSO

Off the Enna road, on the peak of Mt Sabucina, is the **site of Sabucina** (*to request visit call Sovrintendenza T: 0934 554965*). The approach road climbs up past several disused mines, and there is a view up to the right above an overgrown mine of the line of walls of Sabucina, just below the summit of the hill. After 2km the asphalted road ends beside recent excavations of a necropolis. An unsurfaced road continues downhill for another 500m to a gate by a modern house at the entrance to the site, in a splendid position with wide views. Mt Sabucina was first occupied in the Bronze Age. A thriving Iron Age village was then settled by the Greeks in the 6th century BC. The city declined after the revolt of Ducetius in 450 BC. The long line of Greek fortifications with towers and gates were built directly onto the rock. Sacred edifices can also be seen here.

In the valley below Caltanissetta to the east, the River Salso is crossed by the **Ponte Capodarso** (*map p. 572, B2*), a graceful bridge built in 1553 by Venetian engineers. A legend says that once a year the devils hold a market on the bridge; anyone lucky enough to witness it may purchase just one fruit, which next day will turn into gold. Nearby is the **archaeological area of Capodarso**, an ancient city which had disappeared by the beginning of the 3rd century BC. Part of the walls and necropolis survive. Finds from the site are kept in the archaeological museum in Caltanissetta, and the area is now part of a large nature reserve run by Italia Nostra, Monte Capodarso e Valle dell'Imera Meridionale (*44 Viale Conte Testasecca, Caltanissetta, T: 0934 541722, www.riservaimera.it*), call to book visit. There are many old mines, water-mills and caves in the reserve, some of which have thriving populations of various bat species.

GIBIL GABIB

South of Caltanissetta is the site of the ancient settlement of Gibil Gabib (*map p. 572, B3; to request visit call Sovrintendenza T: 0934 554965*). The name derives from the Arabic *Jebel Habib* (Pleasant Hill), and it was discovered in the 19th century. A necropolis here has yielded finds from three periods of occupation, in the 7th, 6th, and 4th centuries BC.

DELIA AND SOMMATINO

Some 20km southwest of Caltanissetta are two small towns, little visited and all the more authentic for that. **Delia** (*map p. 572, B3*), twinned with Vanguard in Canada

DELIA
Isolated farmstead.

(where many of its inhabitants emigrated between 1890 and 1910), was re-founded as a farming community in the early 17th century, on an older medieval settlement. The name derives from the Arabic *daliyah*, meaning vineyard. A regular street plan divides the town into rectangular blocks, which in turn present a typical Arabian network of tiny alleys, serving also as courtyards for the dwellings, often built of blocks of yellow sandstone. There are many of the old fountains where the families used to collect their water, and life is still lived largely in the open air, as in the past, in a very sociable manner. The southwest part of the town is recognisably the old centre, gathered around the Palazzo del Principe and the 16th-century Chiesa Madre, dedicated to the Madonna of Loreto. The painting of *St Rosalia of Palermo* over the altar is by Pietro d'Asaro, the 'Monocolo di Racalmuto'. Turreted ruins of the Castellazzo, the 11th-century castle of Delia, still stand, 1km from the town.

Close to Delia is **Sommatino** (*map p. 572, B3*), a bright little town founded in the 14th century as the feud of the Del Porto family, who populated it with farmers. Here too the older quarter of the town is clearly recognisable in the eastern part.

NORTH TO MARIANOPOLI

North of Caltanissetta is **Santa Caterina Villarmosa** (*map p. 572, B2*), founded in 1572 by Giulio Grimaldi, baron of Risigallo. The centre of this quiet agricultural town is Piazza Garibaldi, with the 18th-century Chiesa Madre. Many of the women are expert at embroidery and lace-making; you will see them sitting in front of their doorways in the early afternoon, hard at work.

About 2km northeast of the town, on the slopes going down to the Vaccarizzo stream, an area of particularly interesting geology is protected as a nature reserve, the **Riserva Geologica di Contrada Scaleri** (*Via Regina Margherita 28, Caltanissetta, T: 0934 534111*). Slabs of limestone have collapsed through the centuries, eroded by the streams of water; resulting in ribbed formations that are unique in Sicily.

Resuttano (*map p. 572, B2*) stands above the Imera in a northernmost pocket of the province. An Arab farming village, it was re-founded in 1625 by the Di Napoli family, to whom it belonged until feudalism came to an end here in 1812. The ruins of the Castello di Resuttano are c. 5km east of the town, on the left bank of the river. The castle, which is incorporated into a 19th-century farmhouse, can be reached by a little road which branches off to the left from the country road to Alimena. It was probably built by the Arabs (*rahsul et-tan* means fortified house, hence the name of the town) and was important during the Middle Ages because of its position on the river, controlling the southern part of the Madonie Mountains. In 1337, the last year of his reign, Frederick II of Aragon, while travelling from Palermo to Enna and Catania, stayed the night here and is supposed to have written the will that sparked off a notorious feud between the Ventimiglia and Chiaramonte families.

MARIANOPOLI AND ITS ARCHAEOLOGICAL SITES

West of Santa Caterina, along the old road to Palermo, which skirts the southern foot of Mt Chibbò (951m), is **Marianopoli** (*map p. 572, A2–B2*), founded in 1726 by Baron Della Scala, who brought a group of immigrants from Montenegro here to farm the land. The town centre is built on a chequerboard street plan around Piazza Garibaldi. On the west side is the 18th-century church of San Prospero (or Santa Maria Addolorata); the body of the saint, patron of the town, is enclosed in the main altar. The interesting Museo Archeologico is located on Via delle Regione Siciliana (*open Tues–Sun 9–1 & 3.30–7; at the time of writing signboards to the museum still pointed to a building in Piazza Garibaldi, from which it moved in 2012*), arranged across several rooms on a single floor with finds from the nearby archaeological sites of Valle Oscura, Monte Balate and Monte Castellazzo. Beginning with displays devoted to the prehistoric periods, much prominence is given to black and red figure pottery and some interesting inscriptions found at Monte Castellazzo.

East of Marianopoli is the rocky summit of **Monte Castellazzo**, where excavations (signposted) have brought to light a prehistoric necropolis with rock-hewn tombs, signs of burial in large pots, and Greek tombs. On top of the crest are the remains of a city with walls (6th–3rd centuries BC), probably the ancient *Mytistraton*, built on top of an earlier settlement, which put up fierce resistance to the Romans in the First Punic War.

Continuing south along the road, after c. 7km is a private road (right), leading to an ancient settlement on **Monte Balate**. Parts of the walls and the acropolis have been explored; the material is at the museum in Marianopoli. Still further south is a valley signposted **Valle Oscura**, where the inhabitants of an early Bronze Age village buried their dead by placing them into cracks in the rock; the same 'tombs' were used again by the Hellenistic population in the 6th century BC. These three sites are not fenced but they are of difficult access and can be dangerous; trekking boots and considerable agility required (*for advice and information call Legambiente, see below*) .

Southeast of Mt Mimiani and Marianopoli, c. 8km from the town, is a nature reserve run by Legambiente, **Lago Sfondato** (*map p. 572, B2; for information and to book visit, Legambiente,Via Rosso di San Secondo 14/A, Caltanissetta, T: 0934 564038, 329 8620594, www.legambienteriserve.it*), created to protect a very deep small lake and the surrounding area, of great beauty and scientific interest, and famous for its 31 species of dragonflies.

VILLALBA AND VALLELUNGA PRATAMENO

These villages (*map p. 572, A2*) are in a particularly spectacular part of the interior of Sicily and in another isolated northern pocket of the province. **Villalba** was a Roman colony in the 3rd century BC, and later a Muslim village, while **Vallelunga** is still an important agricultural centre.

MUSSOMELI & ITS ENVIRONS

Mussomeli (*map p. 572, A2*), a cascade of ochre houses on the southern slopes of Monte San Vito, dominates a fertile and well-watered territory. The valley was formed by the River Platani (the ancient *Halykos*), 84km long, which enters the sea near Capo Bianco. It was founded by Manfredi III Chiaramonte in the late 14th century with the name Manfreda, near a Muslim farming community. Very soon the name Manfreda was forgotten in favour of the Arabic toponym *Menzil el-emir*, the mansion of the emir.

On the north side of the central Piazza Umberto is the palace of Barone Mistretta; close by, preceded by a stairway, is the 16th-century church of San Francesco. The west side of the square gives onto the old district of Terravecchia, with quiet little streets surrounding the Chiesa Madre, which was founded by Manfredi III Chiaramonte and dedicated to St Louis of Toulouse. In the church of the **Madonna dei Miracoli** is a splendid vault fresco (1792) by Domenico Provenzano, showing heretics being flung into Hell. In the crypt is a stone with an old painting of the Madonna, found near the spot where a cripple suddenly, and miraculously, regained the use of his legs.

The **Antiquarium Archeologico Comunale** in Palazzo Sgadari (*Via della Vittoria 24; open Tues–Sat 9–1; T: 0934 961303*) displays finds from the archaeological sites at Polizzello (Prehistoric and Iron Age) and Monte Raffe (5th and 4th centuries BC), as well as Mussomeli itself, in a beautifully restored building. Note that a few of the objects exhibited are copies of pieces held in other collections (principally Caltanissetta and Palermo).

ENVIRONS OF MUSSOMELI

By taking the road for Villalba (east), after c. 2km you reach the magnificent, gravity-defying **Castello Manfredonico** (*open May–Sept 9.15–12.45 & 3.15–6.45, closed Mon; Oct–April Sat–Sun 9.15–12.45; last tickets 1hr before closing; T: 0934 992009*), a good example of medieval military architecture, and one of the most beautiful castles in Sicily; it seems to have grown out of the rock it was built upon. Manfredi built it on top of an older fortification. It is said to be haunted by the ghosts of three sisters, walled up in a small triangular room by their brother for their own safety when he went away to fight in a war. Leaving plenty of food and water, he was forced to stay away longer than expected, returning to find the corpses of his unfortunate sisters and the half-eaten soles of their shoes.

Acquaviva Platani (*map p. 572, A2*) is c. 8km west of Mussomeli. The first part of the name, meaning 'living water', is a reference to the abundant springs in the area. With panoramic views, facing north and west over the upper Platani valley towards Mt Cammarata, and of ancient origin, the town was re-founded in 1635 by Francesco Spadafora as an agricultural centre. Many years of depression and mass emigration are now giving way to new hopes for the future, thanks to the production of high-quality olive oil and wines.

SUTERA & CAMPOFRANCO

Standing in a spectacular position on the chalky-white slopes of steep Mt Paolino, **Sutera** (*map p. 572, A2*), one of Italy's 'Beautiful Villages', dominates the wide, hilly interior of the island. Its ancient castle (now completely destroyed) was once of fundamental importance for the defence of this strategic point. Probably founded by the Byzantines, the town was developed by the Muslims. The typically Arab district of Rabato is the oldest part of town, with its tiny alleys and courtyards, while the Chiesa Madre, dedicated to the Assumption, stands on the site of the mosque. In 1366 the village was assigned to Giovanni Chiaramonte, count of Caccamo, son of Manfredi III. After a period of stability, in the 16th century development ground to a halt, because many inhabitants left the town to live in the nearby settlements of Acquaviva, Campofranco and Casteltermini, where it was easier to farm the land.

Entering Sutera from the north, Via del Popolo leads to Piazza Umberto, with the Town Hall, the 15th-century church of Sant'Agata, and the monastery of Santa Maria delle Grazie. Continuing along Via Sant'Agata, you reach Piazza San Giovanni, with the church of San Giovanni; inside there are some very good stuccoes of the Serpotta school. From here, Via del Carmine leads from the Rabatello district to Rabato. From the square (Piazza Carmine), Via San Paolino leads up on the left by the church of the Carmine to the top of the hill via many flights of steps, where there is an old convent and the sanctuary church of San Paolino, built in the 14th century for Giovanni Chiaramonte in place of the old castle, with far-reaching views. Back in the village, Via del Carmine continues up to the ancient Chiesa Madre (1370).

CAMPOFRANCO

Close to Sutera is Campofranco (*map p. 572, A2*), a friendly village founded in 1573 by Baron Giovanni del Campo, which prospered during the sulphur-mining period in the

19th century. The **Chiesa Madre**, dedicated to St John the Baptist, was completed in 1575, but considerably modified in later centuries. Inside is a dramatic 17th-century canvas depicting the *Beheading of St John the Baptist*, perhaps by Pietro d'Asaro, or one of the Flemish painters active in Palermo at the time. In the central Piazza Vittorio Veneto is a magnificent bronze fountain, the **Fontana della Rinascita**, 5m in diameter and with abundant jets of water, the work of architect Vittorio Ziino and sculptor Giovanni Rosone. It was a gift from the Sicilian Regional Government in 1955, after 99 percent of the population had turned out to vote in the elections.

The statue of the patron St Calogero (*see p. 245*) is kept in the church of **San Francesco d'Assisi** and is carried around the town twice a year on the shoulders of 20 stalwarts, an honour passed down from father to son.

Frequently seen in the countryside in this area are little stone 'igloos' in the fields, some in good condition, some not. Called ***cubuli***, they were used by the peasants as emergency dwellings, for storing equipment, or to protect sick animals. Try to look inside one; you will be amazed at the clever use of space. Smaller ones were built to cover wells.

MILENA

South of Campofranco is the salty little River Gallo d'Oro, the 'Golden Cockerel', a tributary of the Platani. On the other side of the valley is Milena (*map p. 572, A3*), a farming community formed of a central village and 60 hamlets, called *robbe*, distributed on the hills around: San Martino, Vittorio Veneto, Cavour, Piave, Crispi, Roma, Monte Grappa, Cesare Battisti, Masaniello, San Miceli, Mazzini, Garibaldi and Balilla, are just some of the tiny villages, most of which are now abandoned. The area shows signs of human settlement going back to the Copper Age and even the Neolithic, and Milena itself was certainly an important Arab centre. For many centuries known as Milocca, it was donated to the monastery of San Martino delle Scale near Monreale, which held it until 1866. The monks granted the peasants perpetual lease of the land, which along with the abundant water, allowed the inhabitants to enjoy relative prosperity. In Via Napoli, in Masaniello hamlet, is a beautiful two-storey cottage, now the **Casa-Museo della Civiltà Contadina** (*open 9–12.30 & 3–6, closed Sun afternoon; T: Pro Loco 393 904 6600 or Pasquale Palumbo, 338 766 7324*), a collection of equipment used by the farmers.

In Milena town centre, on Piazza Karol Wojtyla, is the well-organised **Antiquarium Comunale Arturo Petix** (*open Mon–Fri 9.30–12.45; T: 0934 936179*), exhibiting archaeological finds from the area spanning 7,000 years, including a terracotta mould for cooling liquid sulphur stamped as the property of the emperor Commodus, and Islamic seals. The heart of the collection is a display of prehistoric material, one of the most important in Sicily, which is beautifully and informatively displayed.

The slopes of Mt Conca, running down to the Gallo d'Oro stream, are now protected as a **nature reserve**, with 17km of signposted tracks, run by the CAI, Club Alpino Italiano (*for information, T: 335 808 9759*). The river is fringed by tamarisks, a haze of pale pink in spring, and is a haven for many birds—Cetti's and fan-tailed warblers and the penduline tit, as well as kingfishers, little ringed plovers, black-winged stilts,

Bonelli's eagle, kestrels and buzzards. Two caves here are of great spelaeological interest and can be visited if you are accompanied by CAI staff.

WEST FROM CALTANISSETTA

San Cataldo (*map p. 572, B2*) is a farming community, 5km west of Caltanissetta, founded in 1607 by Baron Nicolò Galletti, who named it after St Cathald, an Irish disciple of St Patrick, who became the first bishop of Taranto. During the 19th century the economy prospered, thanks to the sulphur mines. Time stands still on the quieter back streets, where you will occasionally see women embroidering or making lace, sitting in front of their homes, working away at their threads with deft fingers.

On the road to Serradifcalco, after c. 5km a path on the right leads to the archaeological site at **Vassallaggi** (*map p. 572, B3*), five small rocky hills, where excavations have brought to light the remains of what was perhaps the Sicel town of *Motyon*, scene of a tremendous battle in 451 BC between Ducetius and his Sicels against the Greeks of Agrigento and Syracuse. So far some streets have been located, a sanctuary and a necropolis. The finds are in the archaeological museum of Caltanissetta.

Serradifalco (*map p. 572, A3*) is a neat and tidy town in a strategic position controlling the major roads, and with abundant sources of water. This too was once an important centre for sulphur mining. Not far from the town is Lake Soprano, a small, beautiful natural lake, set like a gemstone in the arid highlands. It is fed by underground springs and is protected as a nature reserve.

Across the valley of the Gallo d'Oro, **Montedoro** (*map p. 572, A3*) stands on a small plateau on the slopes of Mt Croce, overlooking the river. Founded in 1635 for agricultural purposes by Don Diego Tagliavia Cortes, Prince of Castelvetrano, the town flourished in the 19th century thanks to its sulphur and potassium-salt mines. One of these has been opened as a museum, the Museo della Zolfara (*T: 347 445 6852*), which is run as a scientific park together with an astronomical observatory and a planetarium (*to request visit, call Stargeo, T: 345 424 3223, 339 899 8391, www.stargeo. it*). Clear skies and low light interference make this one of the best places in Sicily for star-gazing. At Montedoro, and in the nearby farming village of **Bompensiere** (*map p. 572, A3*), several house-fronts have been decorated with murals illustrating the history of the communities.

GELA & THE SOUTH

Gela (*map p. 572, C4*) is an important port and the fifth largest town in Sicily. Renowned for its splendour in the past, it was the last abode of the dramatic poet Aeschylus. It is not a very beautiful city, thanks to uncontrolled building activity and the presence of an oil refinery and related industries, but these are now closing down and it is hoped that an alternative occupation for the inhabitants will be the production of allergen-free rubber from guayule, a fast-growing shrub that is flourishing on lands conceded by the oil company. Among the town's many fine qualities are the exceptional courtesy of the inhabitants; the archaeological museum; and the Greek fortifications at Capo Soprano. Recent excavations at Bosco Littorio, site of the ancient emporium and harbour, have brought to light warehouses buried under the sand, untouched since the 5th century BC.

HISTORY OF GELA

The modern city, known until 1927 as Terranova, was founded by Frederick II in 1230 on the site of *Gela*, a colony of Rhodians and Cretans established in 688 BC. Gela soon rose to importance, founding its own colony at *Akragas* (Agrigento) in 580 and contributing to the Hellenisation of the interior of the island. Under Hippocrates (498–491 BC) the city reached its greatest prosperity, but Gelon, his successor, transferred the seat of government and half the population to Syracuse in 485. Aeschylus, the great 5th-century BC playwright, died in Gela in 456, supposedly because an eagle flying above him dropped a tortoise on his bald head, mistaking it for a stone. In 405 the town was destroyed by the Carthaginians, but Timoleon refounded it in the 330s BC. The new city was larger than the earlier one and was provided with a new set of walls. In 282 BC Phintias, tyrant of Akragas, transferred its inhabitants to his new city (now Licata) at the mouth of the Imera and Gela disappeared from history.

MUSEO ARCHEOLOGICO REGIONALE

Corso Vittorio Emanuele 1. Open 9–6. Closed Sun except 1st in the month. T: 0933 912626.
At the east end of the town, this museum has one of the richest archaeological collections in Sicily, including some of the painted vases for which Gela is best known, the three famous terracotta altars found in the emporium area of the city, and a superb coin collection.

Section I: Dedicated to the acropolis area (east of the modern city), inhabited from prehistoric times up to the 5th century BC.

Section II: Later material from the acropolis (4th–3rd centuries BC) when it was an artisans' district. There is also material salvaged from an Archaic Greek ship found off the coast of Gela in 1988.

Section III: Devoted to Capo Soprano, where a residential area and public edifices were erected in the late 4th century BC; this is followed by a pottery exhibit, including some pots with dedicatory inscriptions on their bases.

Section IV: More than 50 amphorae (7th–4th centuries BC) attest to the importance of Gela's commerce with other centres in the Mediterranean.

Section V: Finds from sanctuaries found outside Gela, most of them dedicated to Demeter and Persephone.

Section VI: Prehistoric to Hellenistic finds from the surrounding territory.

Section VII: Roman and medieval material found during the restoration of the Castelluccio, together with Roman finds from Philosophiana (*see p. 262*). In front of the coin room are three **terracotta altars** with relief images, found in the emporium of the ancient city. Dating from the early 5th century BC, the two larger ones are unique for their size, artistic quality, subject matter and state of preservation. That on the left represents the Gorgon Medusa, running with her babies in her arms, Pegasus the winged horse and the warrior Chrysaor, tightening her snake belt as she goes. The smaller central altar shows a slender lioness attacking a bull in the top part, and underneath the goddess of dawn, Eos, making away with the huntsman Cephalus, husband of Procris, who in revenge seduced King Minos of Crete. The altar on the right shows three goddesses, probably Hera, Demeter (smoothing her braids) and Aphrodite. The exceptional **numismatic collection** has more than 2,000 pieces, found in or around Gela, including a magnificent hoard of some 600 silver coins, minted in Akragas, Gela, Syracuse, Messina and Athens, between 515 and 485 BC, one of the most important such collections in existence. Discovered in Gela in 1956, the coins were stolen in 1973 but most of them have been recovered.

Section VIII: The important 19th-century Navarra collection of **ancient Sicilian vases** (with a fine group of Attic black- and red-figure vases, and Corinthian ware from the 8th–6th centuries BC). Also here is the smaller Nocera collection and two cases of finds from the necropolis, including (in case F) an Attic lekythos showing Aeneas and Anchises on a white ground (460–450 BC) and (in case G) an exquisite Attic red-figure lekythos, by the Nikon Painter.

MOLINO A VENTO ACROPOLIS

Outside the museum is the entrance to the Molino a Vento Acropolis (*open 9–6, closed Sun; same ticket as museum*), overlooking the oil refinery (you may see white storks nesting on the pylons). This was part of Timoleon's city, on a terraced grid plan with shops and houses (c. 339–310 BC), above the ruins of a small sacred enclosure. In the garden on the site of the acropolis of the earliest city stands a single (re-erected) column of a temple probably dedicated to Athena (6th century BC), and the foundations of a second earlier temple also dedicated to Athena. This area had been abandoned by 282 BC.

THE ARCHAIC EMPORIUM AT BOSCO LITTORIO

A little to the south of the acropolis, in the Bosco Littorio area, is the Archaic emporium of the early Greek colony (6th–5th centuries BC). This was the commercial part of the settlement, consisting of various adjoining rooms facing onto open courtyards, in which goods from the nearby port of Gela were unloaded, stored and redistributed. The site is archaeologically important because of the excellently preserved mud-brick walls of the rooms, which are visible up to the level of the roof beams. Mud-brick is notoriously fragile and in this case it survived only because it was covered over by sand dunes. The three terracotta altars now on display in the museum were discovered here. The site was abandoned at the beginning of the 5th century due to a natural disaster (perhaps an earthquake or tsunami) and was never reoccupied (*to request visit, ask the curator, Signor Turco, T: 331 577 1462, or Sovrintendenza Caltanissetta, T: 0934 554968*).

CAPO SOPRANO AND THE COAST

The most pleasant way to reach Capo Soprano (over 3km from the museum) is along the seafront. First excavated in 1948, the remarkable **Greek fortifications** (*open 9–1hr before sunset, closed Sun except 1st in month, same ticket as museum*) have been excellently preserved after centuries beneath the sand: they extend for several hundred metres and reach a height of nearly 13m. Their state of preservation is unique for Sicily, allowing visitors to appreciate how the first courses of stone blocks were topped by multiple layers of mud brick, a building technique that was regularly used in antiquity but (as mud bricks disintegrate over time) one that can rarely be appreciated today. The walls were begun by Timoleon in 333 BC and completed under Agathocles. Their height was regularly increased to keep ahead of the encroaching sand, a danger now removed by the planting of trees. A path (right) leads past excavations of city walls to a circular medieval kiln (*under cover*). From here there is a view of the coast. The path follows walls (*partly under cover*) and foundations of the brick angle towers to the West Gate, and then descends to the most complete stretch of walls where the construction technique can best be appreciated. A small postern gate in the walls can be seen here, dating from the time of Agathocles (filled in with mud bricks soon after it was built), near a well-preserved drain. Steps lead up past a little house which contains photographs of the site.

About 500m from the fortifications (signposted 'Bagni Greci'), now engulfed by modern apartment blocks, are remains of **Greek baths** (4th century BC). The baths, including hip baths with seats, are protected by a roof, but are always open, surrounded by a garden behind railings.

THE COAST EAST AND WEST OF GELA

Behind the sand dunes, along the coast east of Gela, is a shallow coastal lake, the largest of its kind in Sicily, the **Biviere di Gela** (*map p. 572, C4; Info: LIPU, T: 0933 926051, 345 661 2743 or 345 575 5044, www.riservabiviere.it*). Now protected as a nature reserve, it is particularly interesting during bird migration periods in early spring and late summer: short-toed eagle, spoonbill, pratincole, garganey, ferruginous duck, little bittern, Audouin's and slender-billed gulls, Terek and buff-breasted sandpipers, red-necked grebe, black-tailed godwit, slender-billed curlew, purple heron, glossy ibis (symbol of the reserve), even the mute swan (very unusual for Sicily) nest or have been seen here, while the black-winged stilt nests in the marshy area nearby; another nester is the collared turtle dove, until recently, for Sicily, only found on Pantelleria and Linosa (but it now nests even in downtown Gela). Birds which winter here include the jack snipe, short-eared owl, marsh harrier, hoopoe and bluethroat; in September and October orange monarch butterflies from Africa are commonly seen.

On the coast west of Gela is **Falconara** (*map p. 572, B4*), with its well-preserved, spectacular 14th-century castle on the sea, now a hotel. There is an inviting sandy beach. Beyond are vegetable and melon fields, protected from the wind by cane fences and often covered with plastic sheeting, which gives the countryside a strange, watery aspect, like a billowing sea.

THE GELA HINTERLAND

BUTERA

Butera (*map p. 572, B4*), perched up on a flat rock in a strategic position, with fine views towards the sea, is dominated by the bell-tower of the church of San Rocco. As *Butirah* it was one of the largest cities in Arab Sicily, later becoming a Lombard centre under the Normans (for the followers of Roger's Lombard wife Adelaide). William I destroyed the town in 1161 when he suspected its baron to have taken part in a plot against his person. Later rebuilt, it became the seat of the Santapau family, Catalans who in 1563 became the first feudal lords on the island to receive the title of prince, from Philip II of Spain.

In Piazza Duomo (approached from the north) is the plain, elegant 17th-century **Chiesa Madre**, dedicated to St Thomas the Apostle, with a Latin-cross interior surmounted by a dome and decorated with stuccoes, and housing an exquisite 13th-century enamelled copper Crucifix from Limoges and a collection of paintings, including a fine canvas by Filippo Paladini of *St Mary of the Angels* (1606).

From here the main street, Via Principe di Piemonte, winds its way through to **Piazza Dante**, with a spectacular view over the hills to the Madonie Mountains and Mount Etna. Here is the interesting 15th-century triangular **Town Hall**, surmounted by a clock tower, and the 18th-century **church of San Giuseppe**, a simple façade with a large window and an unusual 16th-century painted wooden Crucifix. Via Aldo Moro leads to **Piazza della Vittoria**, where the romantic and imposing 11th-century **castle** (*open as tourist office, they will provide a guide*) was once thought to be impregnable, and the donjon is still in good condition; it now houses a collection of archaeological material found in the area

From the castle, Viale Diaz leads to the eastern crest of the hill, overlooking the plain, and the 18th-century **sanctuary church of San Rocco**, dedicated to the patron saint of Butera. The single-nave interior is richly decorated with stucco and 18th- and 19th-century canvases by local artists, representing episodes of the life of the saint, who is frequently invoked against the plague and shown pointing to an abscess on his thigh. A French nobleman, St Roch (1295–1327) was tending the sick in a plague-stricken town while on pilgrimage to Rome, before contracting the disease himself. Retiring to the forest to die, he made a miraculous recovery thanks to the devotion of a prince's dog which brought him food from its master's table. Once better, he tried to return the dog, but the prince told him to keep it, saying 'my dog knows his master'.

Important excavations of a **Bronze-Age settlement** (perhaps the Sican town of *Omphake*) have been carried out near Butera; the finds are in the Gela museum.

Southwest of Butera is an artificial reservoir (*signposted from the railway station*), **Lago Comunelli**, used as a resting-place by many species of migratory birds in spring and autumn, while the sand dunes along the coast are still intact, a wealth of typical vegetation, including the rare, sweet-scented white broom, *Lygos raetam*.

CASTELLUCCIO AND NISCEMI

On the Caltagirone road is the 13th-century **Castelluccio** (*closed; if it should be re-opened, ticket available at the archaeological museum of Gela*), a castle occupying a prominent site dominating the surrounding plain, now cultivated with artichokes. On the approach road, appropriately sited beside two pill-box defences, is a war memorial to the battle of 1943, which followed the landings of the American assault forces on the beaches in the Gulf of Gela.

There is a prehistoric necropolis on **Monte Disueri** or Dessueri (*no signs, but exactly 7.4km along the SS 190 to Mazzarino from the junction with the SS 117 bis to Gela; on the left-hand side; map p. 572, C3–C4*) with more than 2,000 rock-cut tombs, found by accident during forestry work in the 1970s. It is the most important ancient necropolis in Sicily after Pantalica (*see p. 383*) and dates from the 11th–9th centuries BC. The paths have all but disappeared and there are no explanatory information boards; trekking boots are advisable for exploring. In spring the mountain is covered with wildflowers, and bright with the song of larks.

Niscemi (*map p. 572, C4*) stands on a plateau in a panoramic position facing west over the plain. Like others in the area, the town bases its economy on artichokes, of which it grows 12 percent of the entire world production. It was completely rebuilt, following a regular street plan, after the 1693 earthquake. To the east of the rectangular central square, Piazza Vittorio Emanuele, is the 18th-century Chiesa Madre (Santa Maria dell'Itria), with a lovely portal, while opposite is the interesting octagonal church of the Addolorata (18th century, Rosario Gagliardi). Another side of the square is occupied by the elegant Neoclassical Town Hall. The highest part of Niscemi is a panoramic terrace called the Belvedere, offering wonderful views and cool breezes on summer evenings. East of the town is a residual forest of cork, kermes and holm oaks, with tree heath, officially protected as a nature reserve and occupying one third of Niscemi's territory: the **Sughereta di Niscemi**, now controversially expropriated as a USA military base for MUOS (Mobile User Object System), a series of huge parabolic antennae. At the time of writing they had not yet been activated, because of the feared negative effects on the population.

MAZZARINO

Mazzarino (*map p. 572, B3–C3*) became, in the 14th century, the seat of the Branciforte family from Piacenza, renowned for their culture, learning and magnificence. In 1507 King Ferdinand II of Aragon invested Niccolò Branciforte with the title of Count of Mazzarino. His descendant, Prince Carlo Maria Carafa Branciforte (1651–95), embellished and enlarged the town and built an enormous residence, a miniature royal palace, with its own theatre and printing shop. The prince was often sent on foreign missions by the king, but when back home he dedicated his energies to printing beautiful books (the finest published in 17th-century Sicily) and the theatre, for which he wrote several plays—and was not above acting in them himself. Parts of the building survive, though much neglected. Around the palace, convents and monasteries were built by all the major religious orders, and there were 25 churches.

The attractive main street, Corso Vittorio Emanuele, runs west to east for c. 1km, passing numerous aristocratic palaces in decay. At the west end is the 16th-century church and convent of **Santa Maria del Gesù**, containing the funerary monument of Prince Carlo Maria Carafa Branciforte. In the middle of the Corso is the Carmelite complex. The church of **Santa Maria del Carmelo** houses notable works of art, including a Branciforte funerary monument and paintings by Filippo Paladini. Another Branciforte funerary monument, by the Gagini school, is in the courtyard of the Town Hall, once the cloister of the monastery. Via Concezione runs north from the Corso to the church of **San Francesco**, or the Immacolata; on the main altar is a splendid canvas by Filippo Paladini of the *Immaculate Virgin and St Francis*, signed and dated 1606. Paladini died in Mazzarino in 1615. From here there is a view over the valley.

In Piazza Crispi, on the south side of the Corso, in front of Palazzo Branciforte, is the wide Baroque façade of the **Chiesa Madre** (Angelo Italia), dedicated to the Madonna of the Snow; inside are some paintings of the Paladini school. Close by to the east is Piazza Colajanni. In the Dominican church here is a masterpiece by Filippo Paladini, signed and dated 1608, the *Madonna of the Rosary*. Pink, white, mauve and dark green are the dominant colours; from the top corners, cherubs toss down pink roses, and in the bottom left-hand corner is the astonished-looking donor, a certain Pasquale Rondello. At the eastern extremity of the Corso is the 18th-century church of **Santa Maria del Mazzaro**; the 15th-century triptych on the main altar, showing the *Madonna with Sts Agatha and Lucy*, has been damaged by two fires, and poorly restored.

Mazzarino is dominated by the ruins of its pre-13th-century **castle**, north of the town on a hill (take Via Castelvecchio). Its round tower has given it the name of *'u Cannuni*, the cannon.

ENVIRONS OF MAZZARINO

Southeast of Mazzarino, on a ridge to the east of Mt Formaggio, are the ruins of the **castle of Grassuliato**, built to defend the vast plain of Gela and the valleys leading out of it towards the interior of the island. Close by is Mt Bubbonia, possibly the site of the ancient Sicel city of *Maktorion*. About 12km east of Mazzarino, on the SP 25, are the remains of a Byzantine village called **Philosophiana** (signposted 'Statio Philosophiana—Itinerarium Antonini'; *map p. 572, C3*), probably representing a resting point on the Roman road from Catania to Agrigento. A small bath-house has been excavated, and a Palaeo-Christian basilica.

Riesi (*map p. 572, B3*), a small town to the west of Mazzarino, where sulphur miners and farm workers have always led a hard existence, declared itself a Socialist Republic in 1893. Although short-lived, the episode remains a source of local pride.

PRACTICAL INFORMATION

GETTING AROUND

• **By train:** The station at Caltanissetta, in Piazza Roma, has services via Canicattì to Agrigento, Gela, Ragusa and Syracuse. The station of Caltanissetta Xirbi, 7km north (bus connection with the town), is on another line connecting Palermo, Enna and Catania. Gela is on the Syracuse, Ragusa, Canicattì, Agrigento line.

• **By bus:** Yellow city buses leave from Gela station for Capo Soprano and the archaeological museum; information and tickets from the booth opposite the station. Electric inter-city buses also leave from Piazza Roma (*SCAT, www.scattrasporti.com*). The bus station of Caltanissetta is in Via Rochester. For up-to-date bus schedules, see *www.orariautobus.it.*

ASTRA (*www.astraautolinee.it*) runs services to Enna, Gela, Piazza Armerina and San Cataldo.

ATA (*www.atabusservice.it*) goes to Gela, Licata, Palma di Montechiaro and Palermo.

Etna Trasporti (*www.etnatrasporti.it*) runs services to Butera, Catania, Gela and Niscemi.

SAIS Autolinee (*Via Colajanni 20/22, www.saisautolinee.it*) for Enna, with connections for Piazza Armerina, Caltagirone, Gangi, Palermo, Catania and Messina.

SAIS Trasporti (*Via Colajanni 20/22, www.saistrasporti.it, www.sais-trasporti. com*) has services for Agrigento, Canicattì, Catania, Cefalù, Milena, Palermo and Porto Empedocle; also connects Sommatino with Barrafranca,

Catania, Pietraperzia and Riesi.

SARP Trasporti (*T: 0934 597831*) connects Caltanissetta to Barrafranca, Catania, Gela, Mazzarino, Pietraperzia and Riesi.

Zuccalà (*www.zuccalabus.com*) connects Pietraperzia with Licata.

WHERE TO STAY

BUTERA (*map p. 572, B4*)
€ **Portico dei Normanni**. Panoramic old palace in the town centre with 5 comfortable rooms. Bar-restaurant-pizzeria, same ownership, on ground floor. *Via Mazzini 4, T: 0934 346146 or 328 274 7195, www. ilporticodeinormanni.it.*

CALTANISSETTA (*map p. 572, B2*)
€€€ **San Michele**. Large modern hotel just outside town, with garden, pool, restaurant, 136 rooms and suites. *Via Fasci Siciliani 6, T: 0934 553750, www. hotelsanmichelesicilia.it.*

€ **Hotel Giulia**. Charming small hotel, 18 rooms, friendly service, central and comfortable, pets welcome, car park. No restaurant, but it is next door to L'Archetto, a good restaurant and pizzeria. *Corso Umberto 85, T: 0934 542927, www.bedandbreakfastgiulia.it.*

€ **Piazza Garibaldi**. Central B&B offering 3 comfortable rooms with *trompe l'oeil* murals, panoramic terraces, helpful owners. *Piazza Garibaldi 11, T: 0934 680510, 340 379 5803, www. piazzagaribaldi11.it.*

FALCONARA (*map p. 572, B4*)
€€€ **Castello di Falconara**. Romantic crenellated castle in a quiet position over a lovely beach. Antique

furniture, park and pool; the whole castle and staff can also be rented for up to 2 weeks (9 rooms, sleeps 16). Also B&B accommodation available in 7 large rooms on the first floor. *Contrada Falconara, SS 115 km 245, T: 091 329082 or 335 770 5406, www. castellodifalconara.it.*

€€€ **Falconara Resort Eden**. Just below the castle, resort with 65 rooms and suites in two buildings, fitness centre, tennis, restaurant, large pool, pets welcome. However, the beach is small and it can be noisy due to road traffic. Closed Oct–April. *Contrada Faino, SS 115 km 243, T: 0934 196 5300, www.falconararesort.edenhotels.it.*

GELA (*map p. 572, C4*)
€ **Villa Keratea**. Charming villa surrounded by carob trees, favourably situated for exploring the area, with 12 rooms and a good restaurant. *Contrada Settefarine, SP 81 Gela, T: 0933 193 7062 or 347 800 4063, www.villakeratea.it.*

€ **Sole**. Simple, friendly hotel, all 22 rooms have sea views, car park, no restaurant. Close to the Archaeological Museum. *Via Mare 32, T: 0933 925292 or 0933 924440, www.hotelsolecl.com.*

MAZZARINO (*map p. 572, C3*)
€ **Alessi Palace**. Small modern hotel, 19 rooms, family-run, central, with restaurant. *Via Caltanissetta 20, T: 0934 381549, www.alessipalacehotel.com.*

WHERE TO EAT

CALTANISSETTA (*map p. 572, B2*)
€€ **Vicolo Duomo**. Local dishes in romantic old building in tiny alley where the snow was once stored, menu includes the authentic *farsumagru*, an appetising festive dish making use of cheap cuts of meat and cheese. Closed

all day Sun and midday Mon. *Piazza Garibaldi 3, entrance from Vicolo Neviera 1, T: 0934 582331.*

GELA (*map p. 572, C4*)
€€ **Demetra Gourmet**. Refined little restaurant specialising in superb fish dishes, a joy for the eye and the palate; delightful home-made desserts. Rather small portions. Closed Mon. *Via Giulio Siragusa 10, T: 393 794 9939.*

€€ **Osteria Miseria e Nobiltà**. Begin with the exceptionally good Sicilian *antipasti*, then try the grilled meats. Good wine list, friendly atmosphere. Booking necessary in the evenings. Closed Sun evening and Wed lunchtime. *Corso Vittorio Emanuele 291, T: 0933 914447.*

MONTEDORO (*map p. 572, A3*)
€ **Cupolette Rosse**. Country food of the Sicilian interior at its best; try home-made pasta with wild fennel dressing, or wild boar (*cinghiale*), also cooked with the aromatic local wild fennel. The restaurant also acts as the information centre for Montedoro, and they have rooms in the village if you want to stay. *Via Sacramento, T: 349 865 4614 (Pietro Petix).*

MUSSOMELI (*map p. 572, A2*)
€ **Il Giullare**. Snack bar and pastry shop, offering tasty light lunches, 'mbriulata (to be sure call the day before) and home-made ice cream. *Via Barcellona 50, T: 328 779 4790.*

NISCEMI (*map p. 572, C4*)
€€ **Cibus**. Original dishes combining exclusively local vegetables with fish or meat, making good use of the famous artichokes when in season. The *antipasti* are not to be missed; simple desserts. Closed Sun evening and Mon lunchtime. *Via Mazzini 3, T: 0933 953277 or 329 604 5024.*

SUTERA (*map p. 572, A2*)
€€ **Civiletto**. Elegant restaurant in a 12th-century convent, marvellous local dishes, good wine list. *Via San Giuseppe 7, T: 0934 954874.*

LOCAL SPECIALITIES

CALTANISSETTA Torronificio Geraci, a nougat factory opened in 1870 (*Via Canonico Pulci 10/14, www. geraci1870.it*), offers sweets in elegant packages or tins; closed Sun afternoon. **Gran Café Romano** is the historic coffee-house, renowned for ice cream and nougat (*Corso Umberto 163*), while **Calogero Garzia** (*Via Calabria 6*) is a traditional bakery with stone oven for sourdough bread.
DELIA For the *cuddrireddra* biscuits (a Slow Food niche product), try **Pasticceria del Corso** (*Corso Umberto 183*). To be found only here in Delia, they look like little golden knots of twisted dough. It is said they were invented to cheer up the noble ladies who took refuge here during the Sicilian Vespers (*see p. 75*). You can order them online from Alaimo & Strazzeri (*Viale La Verde 85/87, T: 0922 826825, www. lacuddrireddra.com*).
GELA Pasticceria Catania (*Corso Alvisio 296*) is the pastry shop for local biscuits, nougat and ice cream.
MUSSOMELI '*Mbriulata* is a tasty and filling winter snack, found in the bakeries and some coffee shops; flaky pastry encloses cheese, olives, potatoes and minced pork.

FESTIVALS AND EVENTS

BUTERA 15 Aug, '*U Sirpintazzu*, pantomime in which a man dressed as a snake must be appeased with sweets and a goose, reference to a serpent which threatened the community many centuries ago (*www.sanrocco-butera.it*).
CALTANISSETTA Holy Week, Procession of *I Misteri*, tableaux depicting the Passion of Christ (*www. lasettimanasantacl.it*). End Sept, Feast of St Michael Archangel, the patron saint; huge processions of barefoot faithful, a traditional fair, and fireworks.
CAMPOFRANCO 17 Jan, Feast of St Anthony with a traditional procession and fireworks. 11 Jan and last weekend in July, Feast of the patron St Calogero (*see p. 245*), also dedicated to bread—*Sagra dei Pupi di Pane*—almost life-size 'bread men'.
DELIA Good Friday, *La Scinnenza*, Easter procession involving almost all the inhabitants.
GELA 18–19 March, Feast of St Joseph, many families spend weeks preparing the lavish *altari di San Giuseppe*, feasts for three poor people chosen to represent the Holy Family; one 'family' for each altar.
MUSSOMELI 1–2 Sept, *Corteo Storico*, pageant in medieval costume.
NISCEMI Early April, *Sagra del Carciofo Violetto*, festivities to celebrate the artichoke harvest, with plenty of opportunities to sample the vegetable prepared in dozens of different ways, even with chocolate (*www. sagracarciofoniscemi.it*).
SUTERA Christmas–6 Jan, Living Crib in the tiny streets of the Rabato quarter (*Kamicos, 2 Via Chiesa, T: 0934 954289, www.kamicos.it*)

ENNA
Salvatore Caronia Roberti's Prefettura (1939).

Enna

E nna sits at the heart of Sicily. Its huge castle, dominating practically the whole island, was an almost impregnable stronghold for centuries. In the vicinity are some of Sicily's greatest treasures: Piazza Armerina with its Roman villa; Aidone with an array of unique antiquities in its lovely museum; Villarosa with two interesting museums, one in a train and the second a complete country hamlet; and Pergusa, a mysterious lake connected in myth to Persephone and Hades. The region is

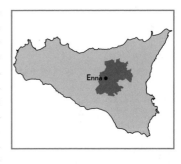

important for the production of cereals and provides a large proportion of the durum wheat used by the Italian pasta industries; the wheat-fields on the dramatically hilly landscape provide a palette of ever-changing colours.

THE TOWN OF ENNA

Enna, at 931m (*map p. 569, B2*), is the highest provincial capital in Italy, often called the Belvedere of Sicily because of its position on the top of a precipitous hill. Enna Alta, the old city, is gradually being abandoned because of the harsh climate (even in August the nights are chilly). The new districts on the southern slopes and on the plateau of Pergusa are known as Enna Bassa.

HISTORY OF ENNA

The city occupies the site of *Henna*, a Sicel stronghold subjected to Greek influences, perhaps from Gela, as early as the 7th century BC. The legendary rape of Persephone is said to have occurred here and it became a major centre of the cult of her mother Demeter (Ceres to the Romans), to whom Gelon of Syracuse erected a temple in 480 BC. Enna fell by treachery to Dionysius of Syracuse in 397. The Romans conquered it in 258 during the First Punic War. In 214, in the course of the Second Punic War, the Roman consul feared a rebellion here in support of Syracuse and ordered a large part of the population to be executed before sacking the city. In 135 the First Servile War broke out under the slave Eunus (*see p. 271*), and the town was taken in 132 by the Roman army after two years' siege. The Saracens took it in 859 AD and named it *Kasr Janni* (from the Roman name *Castrum Ennae*). It was captured by the Normans in 1087. From then on the town was known as Castrogiovanni until 1927, when on the decision of Mussolini it became the capital of a new province, in spite of the fact that Piazza Armerina had a larger population and was easier to reach.

ENNA ALTA

The centre of upper town is Piazza Vittorio Emanuele (*map 1*). On the north side is the church of **San Francesco**, with its fine 16th-century tower. The adjoining **Piazza Crispi** offers a marvellous view across the valley to Calascibetta and, on a clear day, to Etna. The bronze statue on the fountain in the middle is a copy of Bernini's celebrated *Rape of Persephone* (in the Galleria Borghese in Rome). West of the square is Piazza Cataldo with the church of **San Cataldo**, rebuilt in the 18th century on a preceding construction. The font (1473) is the work of Domenico Gagini. The vast 16th-century marble polyptych of the *Annunciation, Nativity* and *Madonna and Child with Sts Cathald and Blaise* is by an unknown sculptor. St Cathald, to whom the church is dedicated, was a 6th-century Irish missionary who preached widely in southern Italy and Sicily.

VIA ROMA
The main street of the town, Via Roma (*map 1*), leads uphill traversing a series of squares. In Piazza Umberto is the Neoclassical **Municipio** (Town Hall), which incorporates the opera house, Teatro Garibaldi. The Baroque façade of **San Benedetto** (or San Giuseppe) decorates Piazza Coppola, off which is the 15th-century **bell-tower of San Giovanni Battista**, with Gothic arches and crowned by a Moorish-style cupola.

On the north side of Via Roma the tall tower of the Rationalist-style **Prefettura** (1939) rises from Piazza Garibaldi; the building, visible from a long way around the town, was the result of Mussolini proclaiming Enna a provincial capital. Piazza Garibaldi is surrounded by faded Fascist-era buildings on three sides.

Santa Chiara, in Piazza Colajanni, functions as a war memorial and burial chapel. Two majolica scenes (1852) decorate the tiled floor, one celebrating the advent of steam navigation, and the other the triumph of Christianity over Islam. The bronze statue in the piazza outside commemorates Napoleone Colajanni (1847–1921), a statesman and social reformer born in Enna. It is the work of Ettore Ximenes. The sturdy Palazzo Pollicarini stands on the north side of the square. With its impregnable-looking stone walls and tiny windows, it retains one or two Catalan Gothic features.

Via Roma continues up towards the duomo past several narrow side streets on the left which lead to the edge of the hill, with views over the valley to Calascibetta. The house at no. 530 on the right is on the site of a building where Cicero is said to have stayed (plaque).

THE DUOMO

The duomo (*map 2*), founded in 1307 by Eleonora, wife of Frederick II of Aragon, and damaged by fire in 1446, was slowly restored in the 16th century. The façade, with a 17th-century bell-tower, covers its Gothic predecessor. The transepts and the polygonal apses survive in their original form (they can be seen from the courtyard of the Alessi Museum; *see below*). The Catalan-Gothic south door was walled up in 1447, when Pope Nicholas V, after passing though it, declared it holy and only for the use of popes.

The interior has dark grey basalt columns with splendid bases, carved with grotesques, and Corinthian capitals (1550–60), the work of various artists including Gian Domenico Gagini. The nave ceiling is by Scipione di Guido, who also carved the walnut choir stalls. On either side of the west door are 16th-century statues of the *Archangel Gabriel* and *Virgin Annunciate*. The stoups in the nave date from the 16th century and at the east end of the nave are richly-carved 16th-century organ lofts. The altarpieces on the south side (c. 1722) are by the Flemish artist Willem Borremans (the painting of *Sts Lucille and Hyacinth* on the second altar is particularly good). In the chancel are four small paintings (1613) of New Testament scenes by Filippo Paladini,

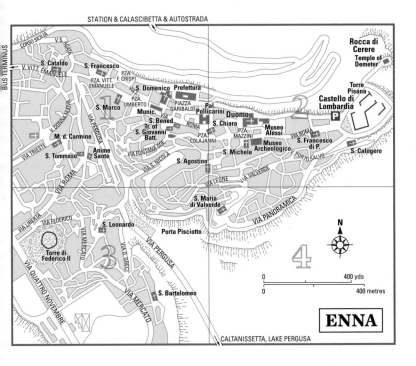

which clearly show the artist's late phase, when he had rejected his earlier Mannerism in favour of a Caravaggio-inspired style. The chapel to the right of the sanctuary has 18th-century marble decoration and a painting of the *Visitation* also attributed to Paladini. The chapel to the left has vault ribs heavily encrusted with stucco. There are more works by Borremans in the north transept and on the fourth north altar.

THE CITY MUSEUMS

The **Museo Civico Alessi** (*map 2; closed at the time of writing*) is named after Canon Giuseppe Alessi (1774–1837), a native of Enna, who left his remarkable collection to his brother intending that he should donate it to the Church. Instead, the Church was forced to buy it in 1860 and the museum was first opened to the public in 1862. The main highlights are from the cathedral treasury: splendid 16th- and 17th-century works include four reliquaries (1573) by Scipione di Blasi, a precious gold crown encrusted with precious stones and enamels, made for the statue of the *Madonna of the Visitation* by Leonardo Montalbano in 1653, and a beautiful 16th-century jewel in the form of a pelican (symbol of Christ's sacrifice). Alessi also had an important numismatic collection of Greek, Roman and Byzantine coins including many in bronze that were used in everyday transactions. A charming archaeological collection (with some of Alessi's original labels) features missiles (*glandes*) used in the Servile War. The Egyptian ushabti figurines (664–525 BC), which also formed part of the Alessi collection and were presumably found in Sicily, are also of great interest.

Across Piazza Mazzini the attractive 15th-century Palazzo Varisano, where Garibaldi made the speech in August 1863 that ended with the famous phrase '*o Roma o morte*' (Rome or death), houses the **Museo Archeologico Varisano** (*map 2; open Mon–Sat 9–6, also first Sun of month of the month, same times; T: 0935 507 6323*). The collection is housed on the first floor (*no lift*); at the top of the stairs is the marble head of a lady with an elaborate coiffure, found at the Roman Villa of Piazza Armerina. In a series of small galleries with frescoed ceilings are finds from Calascibetta and Capodarso; the prehistoric rock-tombs of Realmese; Enna (Greek, Roman and medieval ceramics, including an Attic red-figure krater); Cozzo Matrice (where the necropolis was in use from the Bronze Age up to the 5th century BC); prehistoric material from the Lake Pergusa and elsewhere, and an interesting display on fake terracotta figurines and vases from Centuripe. The numismatic collection, at the time of writing, was in preparation.

At no. 533 Via Roma is an unusual museum, the **Museo Musical Art 3M** (*corner of Via Rindone; open winter 9.30–1 & 3–6, summer 10–1.30 & 3–6, or on request; T: 338 502 3361, 339 200 2463 or 339 107 9940*) which offers the opportunity of viewing on a high-definition screen the works of Sicily's greatest painters while listening to specially-composed music to complement the subject, historical period and character of the artists, who range from Antonello da Messina to Renato Guttuso. Besides paintings, it is possible to follow on-screen the impressive religious processions of Enna.

CASTELLO DI LOMBARDIA

Map 2. Open Sept–Oct 9–6, Nov–March 9-4, April–Aug 9–8.

The 13th-century Castello di Lombardia or Cittadella was adapted as a residence by

Frederick II of Aragon. One of the best-preserved medieval castles on the island, six of its 20 towers remain. Outside is a First World War memorial by Ernesto Basile (1927) and a bronze statue of the rebel slave Eunus.

EUNUS AND THE FIRST SERVILE WAR

Eunus, originally from Syria, and a slave in Enna, organised a rebellion in 135 BC which led to the First Servile War. Sicilian slaves were notoriously badly treated. The best near-contemporary accounts we have are by Diodorus Siculus (1st century BC) and Florus, quoting Livy. They say that Eunus claimed to be acting in the name of the Syrian goddess Atargatis, the equivalent of Demeter (Ceres). He is said to have convinced his followers that the goddess spoke through him by breathing out fumes from a sulphur-filled nut secreted in his mouth, a trick that he had previously used to entertain his master and guests at dinner parties. Having persuaded his confederates to murder their Roman owners but to respect the farms, he crowned himself king (Antiochus I) and even minted coins. His forces put the majority of the citizens of Enna to the sword, sparing only the metalworkers. Joined by the ex-herdsman Cleon from Agrigento, they put together an army of some 200,000 men and took Taormina before laying siege to Messina. The revolt was only eventually suppressed by the Roman consul Publius Rupilius in 132 BC, who laid siege to Taormina and starved the rebel slaves into submission. The slaves were thrown off the cliffs of Taormina (some sources say crucified). Cleon committed suicide. Pursued by Rupilius, Eunus fled from Enna. His men turned on each other in desperation and he died in prison at Morgantina, after atrocious torture.

Steps lead up to the castle entrance. In the interior is a series of courtyards with information boards. Beyond the second court, planted with trees, the third has remains of a church and (beneath a roof) tombs carved in the rock. Here is the entrance to the **Torre Pisana**, which can be climbed by a modern flight of stairs. The view from the top encompasses Etna, Centuripe on its hill and Lake Pozzillo. In the other direction, Lake Pergusa and Calascibetta can be seen.

At the edge of the hill, beyond the castle, are the unenclosed remains of the **Rocca Cerere**, where old hewn stones mark the site of the Temple of Demeter (Ceres). Steps lead up to the summit with a view of Etna straight ahead.

ENNA BASSA

Enna Bassa, the lower town, is reached by following the branch of Via Roma which takes a sharp turn to the south below Piazza Vittorio Emanuele. On the right are the churches of **San Tommaso**, with a 15th-century tower and a marble altarpiece by Giuliano Mancino (1515), and the **Carmine** (behind San Tommaso), with another

CALASCIBETTA
The view of the hilltop town from the belvedere of Enna.

15th-century campanile and a curious stair-tower. On the left, near the southwest end of Via Roma, rises the octagonal **Torre di Federico II** (*map 3*), thought to have been built by Frederick II of Hohenstaufen in the 13th century. This tower, 24m high, is surrounded by a public garden, all that remains of Frederick's former hunting reserve.

CALASCIBETTA & ENVIRONS

Calascibetta (*map p. 569, B2*) is perched on a flat-topped hill opposite Enna. It is particularly picturesque when seen from a distance (and provides one of the most delightful views from Enna). The narrow main street leads up to the main square, with its Fascist-era monuments and the **Chiesa Madre**, built in 1310–40 for Peter II of Aragon, who replaced the castle with this church; the façade, surmounted by bells, was rebuilt after the 1693 earthquake. The spacious interior, with a central nave and two side aisles, is divided by ten magnificent columns of a local hard red stone called *di cutu*; three of them are monolithic. The bases are cube-shaped, with faces and animals carved on the corners: the fourth base in the north aisle shows Peter of Aragon, his queen, his son and the anonymous sculptor.

A one-way street leads back down to Piazza Umberto where the signposted road to Enna leads downhill past the church and convent of the **Cappuccini**, on the edge of the hill. In the church is a splendid large altarpiece of the *Epiphany* by Filippo Paladini, in the enormous original wooden frame.

REALMESE AND CONTRADA CANALOTTO

No fewer than ten archaeological areas have been located around Calascibetta, a region which has been inhabited continuously since prehistoric times. One of the easiest to visit is the **Realmese necropolis** (*unenclosed; map p. 569, B2*), c. 3km northwest of Calascibetta, well signposted; the road suddenly finishes on the brink of an old quarry, and paths lead down into the valley where some 300 rock-hewn tombs (9th–4th centuries BC) have been found (stout boots needed in winter). A short distance away (500m) in **Contrada Canalotto** is a Byzantine village, its houses and church carved into the soft sandstone rock. In summer the mountainside is covered with deep purple thyme (*satra*) and yellow mullein; there are many shrikes in this area.

VILLAROSA

Villarosa (*map p. 569, A2*), in the sulphur-rich hills west of Enna, was founded in 1762 by Placido Notarbartolo, who asked the painter Rosa Ciotti to design the town for him; the result is an octagonal central piazza onto which four main streets converge. Villarosa became quite prosperous in the 19th century, thanks to the sulphur mines. An intriguing museum devoted to the subject is housed in a train parked in a siding in the railway station: the **Museo di Arte Mineraria e Civiltà Contadina** (*open 9.30–12.30 & 4.30–7.30, closed Mon; T: 338 480 9721, www.trenomuseovillarosa.com*). One carriage is dedicated to the history of steam trains in Sicily, the others to mining activities and farming methods.

At 9km from the station of Villarosa is the intact hamlet of **Villapriolo** (*to request visit, T: 338 480 9721*), where until recently farmers and sulphur workers lived. You can visit their homes and their shops, such as the bakery and the cobbler's, besides the beautiful drinking-trough for animals carved of deep red *di cutu* stone, the water-mills for grinding wheat, and the washerwomen's sinks.

LAKE PERGUSA

Pergusa, 9km south of Enna (*map p. 569, B2*), is one of the few natural lakes in Sicily. It is said to occupy the chasm from which Hades emerged to carry Persephone down to the underworld, as mentioned by Milton in *Paradise Lost*:

...that fair field
Of Enna, where Proserpin gath'ring flow'rs
Herself a fairer Flow'r by gloomy Dis
Was gather'd, which cost Ceres all that pain
To seek her through the world...

Paradise Lost, Book IV

Today the lake has no visible inlet or outlet and is apparently disappearing, perhaps because building activity nearby has damaged its underground sources. The vegetation on the shores, as well as the bird-life, have suffered greatly since the 1950s, when it was decided to build a motor-racing track around it. Paradoxically, the lake is a nature reserve (run by the Azienda Forestale).

DEMETER AND PERSEPHONE

The goddess Demeter, patroness of the sowing of seed and the harvesting of corn, was already ancient when Homer celebrated her in his *Iliad*: 'Blonde Demeter separates fruit and chaff in the rushing of the winds'. Demeter's daughter by Zeus is Persephone or Kore; they were known as Ceres and Proserpine to the Romans. There is the legend, placed either in Eleusis in Greece or by Lake Pergusa near Enna in Sicily, that Persephone and her companions were gathering flowers in a meadow when the earth opened and Hades, the god of the underworld, charged out in his chariot and seized Persephone. The Sicilian version says that he re-entered

Gold coin with the head of Persephone.

the earth with his captive at the Fonte Ciane near Syracuse: there are records that there were drowning sacrifices at that site in ancient times, which may be linked to the myth. Demeter, after lighting a pine tree in the crater of Etna to use as a torch, wandered the earth desolate, eventually finding her daughter, but Persephone had eaten six seeds of a pomegranate Hades had offered her and had married her kidnapper. Zeus decided that Persephone should spend six months of the year with her husband (who was also Zeus' brother), and six with her mother. While Persephone is underground, Demeter is in despair and nothing can germinate or grow, her tears are the rainfall; but when she returns, everything is blissfully fragrant and colourful with flowers. This myth, of the cycle of death and rebirth, is an ancient one with echoes in many different cultures. As Sicily was an oasis of fertility compared with the home cities of the Greek colonists, it is not surprising that the legends surrounding Demeter should become so well rooted here.   C.F.

On a hill above the lake excavations (*not open to the public*) were begun in 1878 of the necropolis, city and walls of **Cozzo Matrice**, a Bronze-Age settlement. About 10km southwest of the lake in Località Gerace, a Roman villa with polychrome mosaics was discovered in 1994, but the excavations have since been covered over.

A short way southeast of Pergusa is the neat and tidy farming town of **Valguarnera Caropepe** (*map p. 569, B2*; the second part of the name, meaning 'expensive pepper', is now usually dropped). It was founded by the Valguarnera family in 1628 and reached prosperity thanks to its sulphur mines. In the countryside east of Valguarnera are the isolated ruins of the medieval **castle of Gresti** (*map p. 569, B2–B3*), on an enormous rock split in two—a very rough track for the last part of the way, but incredibly beautiful at sunset.

PIAZZA ARMERINA

The town of Piazza Armerina (*map p. 569, B3*) has a medieval character, with dark cobbled streets and interesting Baroque monuments. The inhabitants are of Lombard origin; many of them have blue eyes and blond hair and they have their own dialect.

The town is divided into four districts: Monte (on the highest point of Monte Mira, where the new town was built in 1163); Castellina (the district around the church of San Francesco d'Assisi, so-called because of a small castle which once protected it); Canali (once the Jewish Ghetto; the church of Santa Lucia was the synagogue); and Casalotto (a separate village, which was incorporated into the city only in the 16th century). Though it was once far more important and more populous than Enna (which was named capital of the province by Mussolini), it was little known to travellers before the discovery of the Roman villa nearby at Casale (*see p. 277*).

HISTORY OF PIAZZA ARMERINA

The original Sicel settlement was probably near Casale, where a luxurious Roman villa would later be built. It is a well-watered, fertile area which was conquered by the Arabs in 861 and named *Iblatasah*. The name may derive from *palatia*, a reference to the imperial villa, whose imposing ruins were visible for many centuries after its abandonment. In 1091 Count Roger gave it to his Lombard troops, who had taken it after a ferocious battle; the Lombards called their new home *Platia* or *Plutia*. The town grew, entirely covering the ruins of the Roman villa. Less than a century later, in 1161, William I (the Bad) discovered that Ruggero Sclavo of Plutia was one of the ring-leaders in a plot against him; he sent his Muslim troops to destroy the city and scatter the inhabitants (barely a hundred survived). When his son William II (the Good) came to power in 1163, the Lombards begged him to allow reconstruction; he replied that he could not disobey his father's edict, but they could build a new town 3km away, on Monte Mira (now the Monte quarter); it was called Piazza Armoria, now Piazza Armerina. The abandoned ruins of Plutia, further devastated by landslides and earthquakes, became a farming hamlet called Casale. After the Sicilian Vespers (*see p. 75*), Piazza Armerina was vocal in demanding independence for the island, and at a meeting of the Sicilian Parliament convened here in December 1295, Frederick II of Aragon was declared king. The townspeople stoutly resisted the attempts of Robert of Anjou to reclaim the island for his family. In recognition of this loyalty, King Frederick granted the town many privileges, which are listed in a manuscript, *Il Libro dei Privilegi*, still in the civic library.

THE UPPER TOWN

A number of streets converge on the central **Piazza Garibaldi**, a favourite meeting-place. Here is the 18th-century Palazzo di Città (Town Hall) next to the church of the Fundrò (or San Rocco), with a carved sandstone doorway. Between them Via Cavour leads up past the former seat of the electricity board, restored as the law courts. Further uphill is the former convent of **San Francesco**, with an elaborate Gagini balcony high up on the corner.

The road continues past the 17th-century Palazzo del Vescovado to **Piazza Duomo** at the top of the hill, with a marvellous panorama from its terrace over the district of Monte, and a statue (1905) of Baron Marco Trigona, who was responsible for financing the rebuilding of the duomo in 1627. The brick façade was added in 1719 and the copper-covered dome in 1768. The lovely bell-tower (c. 1490) survives from an earlier church. The fine brick building in the square is the large 18th-century Palazzo Trigona, which, funding permitting, is to host an archaeological museum displaying finds from the surrounding area.

The entrance to the **duomo** is by one of the side doors. The interior is decorated in white and blue and is unusually light and spacious. On the high altar is a copy of a venerated Byzantine panel painting, the *Madonna of the Victories*; the original is preserved behind it in a 17th-century silver tabernacle. The painting was given by Pope Alexander II to Count Roger in 1063, after the battle of Cerami, and entrusted to the group of Lombards who took the city from the Muslims. Three of the 17th-century paintings in the sanctuary are by the Zoppo di Gangi (Gaspare Vazano). Above the door of the chapel to the left of the sanctuary is the *Martyrdom of St Agatha* (1600) by Jacopo Ligozzi. Hanging in the nave is a Cross, painted on wood, attributed to a Provençal artist (1485).

The altarpiece of the *Coronation of the Virgin* (1612) in the north transept is by Filippo Paladini. The organ is by Donato del Piano (1760). The font is surrounded by a Gaginesque frame in mottled beige marble, decorated with monsters' heads, which survives from the earlier church. Admire the magnificent carved walnut cupboards (1612) in the sacristy. The Trigona coat of arms of the spread eagle, star and triangle, is prominent throughout. An equestrian statuette of Count Roger and a late 14th-century reliquary by Paolo d'Aversa are also among the cathedral's treasures, which may one day be exhibited in the former Bishop's Palace, the **Diocesan Museum** (*Piazza Duomo 1*), at present used for temporary exhibitions.

THE LOWER TOWN

From Piazza Duomo the picturesque Via Monte leads downhill through an attractive part of town, while Via Floresta leads down past the rear façade of Palazzo Trigona, with its Renaissance loggia, and ends in Piazza Castello. Here is the 14th-century **castle**, overgrown with ivy, and four small 17th-century palaces. From here Via Vittorio Emanuele continues down past the Jesuit Collegio on the right, now housing the **Biblioteca Comunale** (*open Mon–Fri 9–1, Mon and Wed also 3–6, T: 0935 686177*). This is one of the most important libraries in Sicily, with a small museum of antiquities including some swords, First World War shotguns, statuettes of terracotta and bronze, and the *Libro dei Privilegi*, a list of concessions granted by the kings of Sicily from 1300 to 1760.

To the east of the centre, in Piazza Umberto, is **San Giovanni dei Rodi**, the plain 13th-century chapel of the Knights of St John, with lancet windows. Nearby are the eccentric façades of Santo Stefano and the opera house, Teatro Garibaldi (1905). Downhill are the lovely public gardens, **Villa Garibaldi**, near the 16th-century church of San Pietro. On the rise to the south, the church of the **Carmine** (*open on request a few days beforehand by Domus Artis, T: 392 206 8111*) preserves a campanile and cloister of the 14th–15th centuries.

VILLA ROMANA DEL CASALE

Map p. 569, B3. Open last Sun in Oct–last Sat in March 9–5. Last tickets at 4pm; from last Sun in March–last Sat in Oct, 9–7, last tickets at 6pm. July–Aug Fri, Sat, Sun late closing at 11.30, last tickets at 11. It is possible to purchase a joint ticket with the sites of Aidone (museum and ruins of Morgantina). T: 0935 687667, www.villaromanadelcasale.it.

The celebrated Roman villa lies 5.5km southwest of Piazza Armerina in the district of Casale. The road from Piazza Armerina (signposted) leads under a high viaduct and then along a pretty valley. The complex, which has some of the most extensive and beautiful Roman mosaics known, is a UNESCO World Heritage Site and receives thousands of visitors a day.

HISTORY OF THE VILLA

Built between the 2nd and 4th centuries AD on the ruins of a 1st-century building, the villa is a single-storey structure made of rubble-and-mortar concrete faced with irregular brown stones, in some places painted to imitate marble. There is still no certainty as to its original owner. The most persuasive theories are that it was the retreat of a Roman emperor, possibly Diocletian's co-emperor Maximian, or of a powerful aristocrat, or an administrator of the imperial government. It lay in a wooded and secluded site at the foot of Monte Mangone (where the plundered tombs of the villa's necropolis have been found); the nearest Roman settlement was *Philosophiana*, 5km south, a station on the route to *Agrigentum*.

   In richness and scope the villa invites comparison with Hadrian's Villa at Tivoli or Diocletian's Palace at Split. While enough remains of the walls to give an idea of the elevation (and many of them are still covered with painted decoration, both inside and out), it is the extent of the polychrome floor mosaics (4,103 square metres, with an average of 36,000 tesserae per square metre), mostly of the Roman-African school, that makes the building unique. The owner was a person of great wealth; the variety and quality of the marble are unparalleled elsewhere; some of it was certainly reused from earlier buildings because the quarries it came from were already exhausted at the time the villa was built. Several groups of craftsmen must have worked on the floors simultaneously in order to complete the assignment within a reasonable time. The signs on some of the cupids' foreheads, 'x', 'v' or a small diamond, were perhaps the 'signatures' of the craftsmen, and sometimes appear on North African floors of the same period. It is possible that some of the floors were prefabricated in North Africa and brought here in 'panels'; the geometric designs would have been particularly suitable for this.

The villa consists of four distinct though connected parts on different levels and was perhaps inhabited for about 150 years. In Byzantine times the frigidarium, where lamps with Christian motifs have been found, was used as a church, before being partly destroyed by a flood, when much of the villa was covered with a thick layer of mud. Some rooms were reused by the Arabs or the Normans, who set up a furnace there, but after the destruction wreaked on the town by William the Bad in 1161 (*see p. 275*), the villa was completely abandoned. The buried ruins remained unexplored until 1761, when they became a source of columns for churches, and it was not until 1881 that any but spasmodic excavations took place. In 1929 Paolo Orsi brought the triclinium to light. Work continued in 1935–9 and finally, in three campaigns from 1950–4, the main structure of the building was exposed, under the direction of Vinicio Gentili. The slaves' quarters and the outbuildings are now being explored, and exciting discoveries are being made: the servants had their own bath-house, for example. Apart from the floors themselves, any archaeological evidence (such as coins or pottery) discovered during the early excavations remains unpublished. The mosaic and marble floors and the surviving murals have all been restored.

1: The original **main entrance** to the villa recalls in its massive form the Roman triumphal arch. It had two fountains on each face, probably fed from a reservoir.

2: The **atrium** is an ample polygonal courtyard with a portico of marble columns; the capitals are identical to those at Diocletian's villa near Split, coming from the same workshop, and made at the same time.

3: The villa proper is entered through the **tablinum** or reception-hall. On the mosaic floor, members of the household can be seen receiving their guests, with olive branches and torches; they are wearing garlands of flowers on their heads to indicate their joy.

4: The tablinum opens onto the **peristyle**, a quadriporticus of ten columns by eight, interrupted on the east side by an arch, and forming a garden with a pool and fountain in the centre. By studying the pollen, specialists have found that the garden was originally planted with sweetly-perfumed flowers and herbs such as roses, sage, carnations, marjoram, lavender and rosemary, and climbing roses covered the latrines.

From the raised walkway the peristyle floor can be seen, consisting of square panels with geometrical borders, in which animal heads are framed in laurel wreaths, with birds native to Sicily in the corners and a recurrent ivy-leaf motif.

5: Immediately opposite the entrance is an **aediculum**, the shrine of the household deity.

6: On the left below the walkway is the **small latrine**, the floor decorated with

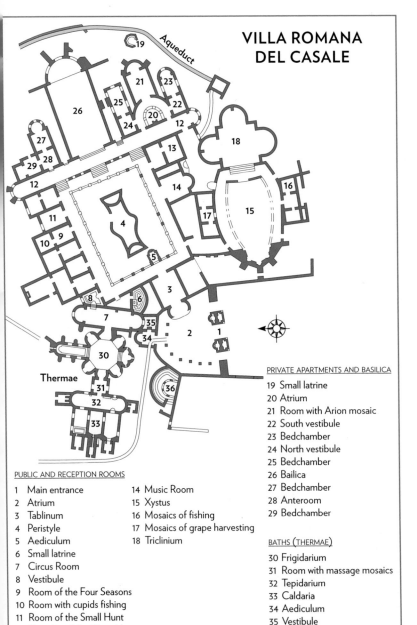

VILLA ROMANA DEL CASALE

Aqueduct

Thermae

PUBLIC AND RECEPTION ROOMS

1 Main entrance
2 Atrium
3 Tablinum
4 Peristyle
5 Aediculum
6 Small latrine
7 Circus Room
8 Vestibule
9 Room of the Four Seasons
10 Room with cupids fishing
11 Room of the Small Hunt
12 Corridor of the Great Hunt
13 Room of the Ten Girls
14 Music Room
15 Xystus
16 Mosaics of fishing
17 Mosaics of grape harvesting
18 Triclinium

PRIVATE APARTMENTS AND BASILICA

19 Small latrine
20 Atrium
21 Room with Arion mosaic
22 South vestibule
23 Bedchamber
24 North vestibule
25 Bedchamber
26 Bailica
27 Bedchamber
28 Anteroom
29 Bedchamber

BATHS (THERMAE)

30 Frigidarium
31 Room with massage mosaics
32 Tepidarium
33 Caldaria
34 Aediculum
35 Vestibule
36 Great latrine

pictures of animals, including an ocelot. Just beyond, it is possible to look down into the **Circus Room** (**7**), an exercise room intended for use before entering the baths, and so called from the scenes of the chariot races at the Roman Circus Maximus depicted on the floor; the viewpoint of the onlooker is from the emperor's box.

8: The passageway leads by a **vestibule** (this was formerly another entrance to the baths). Its mosaic, showing the lady of the house with two children and two slave girls carrying bathing necessities and clean clothing, is doubly interesting because it reveals their style of dress, and because it probably represents the owners in a family scene.

9–11: The majority of the rooms (probably for use by guests) on the north side of the peristyle have geometric mosaics, several of them damaged by Arab or Norman structural alterations. One floor shows young people dancing very vivaciously. Representations of the **Four Seasons** figure in another (**9**); yet another (**10**) shows **cupids fishing**. Of most interest is one called the **Small Hunt** (*Piccola Caccia*) (**11**), where a number of hunting scenes are depicted in great detail. On five 'levels', we see different techniques for catching and killing birds and animals, using dogs, falcons, nets, lime-sticks and double-pointed lances. Some of the dogs (upper left-hand corner) are *cirnechi*, originally imported by the Phoenicians from Cyrene in Libya, and still bred at Adrano on Mt Etna (*see p. 419*). A dangerous accident during a boar hunt is vividly portrayed in the bottom right-hand corner, while in the centre, under a red

awning, a sacrifice to Diana is being held, and slaves are emptying baskets in preparation for the picnic, while others raise their glasses to the company. Some of the characters in the scene would appear to be portraits of the owner of the house and his guests. Notice also the restless horses, the snarling dogs, and the attention to shadows. As this room could not be closed by a door, it is thought that it was a sitting-room or small dining-room.

12: The **Corridor of the Great Hunt** (*Grande Caccia*), 65.93m long, runs the width of the building to isolate the private apartments, and is closed at either end by an exedra. This is certainly the focal point of the whole building. The corridor is paved throughout with a superb series of scenes of the capture of animals (*venationes*), one of the finest Roman mosaics known. Close to the centre is a dignified figure protected by two 'bodyguards' holding shields, who appears to be the overseer; notice also the official beating a slave. It is thought that perhaps two different groups of craftsmen were working together. The left-hand part of the design is more detailed, and more colours are used, at least 25 types of stone, while for the right-hand area only 15 colours appear, in simpler compositions. In the apses are personifications of two regions, flanked by wild beasts, representing two poles of the Roman world, Africa (north, much consumed, with a leopard and a lion) and India (south, with a tiger, tusks of ivory and an elephant, and a phoenix beside her; she embraces a sandalwood tree with her right arm. The red streamers hanging on the branch over her are *formidines*, markers used during

VILLA ROMANA DEL CASALE
Detail of the floor mosaic in the Room of the Ten Girls.

Roman tiger-hunts to indicate the 'passage' along which the animal should be driven by the beaters). The landscape between contains a fish-filled sea on which large galleys sail, transporting exotic animals, and cleverly devised to show them being loaded and then disembarked at their destination. Some authorities identify Egypt in these scenes, and the departure port of Alexandria, while the arrival port could be Ostia. The scenes are remarkable for the number and detail of the species of wild animal (African elephants along the corridor, and an Indian elephant and tiger in the south apse) and for the accuracy with which they are depicted in action: the images of the leopard on the antelope's back, and the tigress attempting to rescue her cub (which she thinks she sees in the glass globe, though it is in fact her own reflection and meanwhile a horseman makes off with her offspring), are particularly skilful. Notice the mysterious griffon lifting a cage containing a man.

13: At the southeast corner of the peristyle the walkway passes above the **Room of the Ten Girls**, whose mosaic shows young women in 'bikinis', competing and performing gymnastic exercises, and receiving prizes. This is the most famous floor in the villa, though of decidedly inferior artistic quality compared with the others. In one corner is part of an earlier geometric pavement that was covered over to accommodate this one.

14: Adjacent is the **Music Room**, with a damaged mosaic representing the Orphic myth; again the animals are carefully depicted. There was a statue of Apollo here, and a fountain to cool the air.

15–17: Two entrances, one for family members (from the corridor of the Great Hunt) and one for guests (from the peristyle), lead into the **Xystus**, a large elliptical court provided with four fountains along the centre, closed at the west end by a wide exedra and at the east end by the triclinium. The six small rooms accessible from the xystus, decorated with playful scenes of cupids fishing **(16)**, wine-making and harvesting **(17)**, were bedrooms where guests could rest between courses.

18: The triconchos or **triclinium**, the ceremonial banqueting-hall, is 12m square with deep apses on three sides (hence the name). The theme of the superb central pavement is the *Labours of Hercules*, the violent episodes being combined into a single turbulent composition. Ten of the Labours can be distinguished, those missing being the man-eating Stymphalian Birds and the Girdle of Hippolyta, the Amazon Queen. In the apses you find the *Glorification of Hercules* (north), *Conquered Giants* (east) and a particularly beautiful depiction of *Lycurgus and Ambrosia* (south). The tonal shading of the figures is remarkable.

MOSAICS

The richly-tessellated floor mosaics which were such a feature of Roman villa life throughout the Empire originally developed from Greek models of the Hellenistic period (323–27 BC) when for the first time ordinary homes adopted some comfort and luxury. In Sicily the first mosaics of the 3rd century BC are crude: chips of stone placed in pavements of crushed tile and mortar. One example is the floor of Temple A at Selinunte, where the decorative motifs appear to have been copied from local Carthaginian examples. By the end of the 3rd century there is more local experimentation, as in the House of Ganymede at Morgantina, where a mixture of styles include patterned floors and figures (notably Ganymede) with shaped tesserae now in several colours. However, home-grown experiments are eclipsed in the later Hellenistic period by wider Mediterranean influences as Sicily adopted styles and motifs from the Aegean, notably Delos, and then transmitted them on to Italy. Then, in the early centuries AD, Italian styles in black and white fed back into Sicily and by the 2nd century AD there seems to have been an influx of mosaicists from the prosperous workshops of North Africa. The great period of Sicilian mosaics was the 4th century AD, above all here at the opulent villa at Piazza Armerina where a wealthy family with connections to official life in Rome flaunted their status with an amazing array of themes and subjects. It is assumed that the mosaic teams were from North Africa and there is some evidence, from the villa on the River Tellaro (*see p. 377*), for instance, that some might have settled in Sicily in order to exploit the island's prosperity. As so often in Sicily, the island becomes part of a wider Mediterranean culture, sustained in this case by the underlying stability of the Empire.   C.F.

19: Close to the line of the aqueduct is a **small latrine**, behind the private apartments. Here Pompeian-style frescoes on the wall imitate marble. The narrow doorway, in complete contrast to the sumptuous spaciousness of the villa, was for the slaves and the widening at the top was to allow the passage of whatever they were carrying on their heads.

20–21: The original approach, for the householder and his guests, was through the semi-circular **atrium** (with a mosaic of cupids fishing), divided by a tetrastyle portico into a nymphaeum and an ambulatory. On either side a vestibule leads into a bedchamber, while the centre opens into a living-room or library, with marble-covered walls (**21**); the overcrowded, *horror-vacui* mosaic shows the poet Arion riding on a dolphin, surrounded by naiads and marine creatures—sea-lions and sea-horses among them—and is the best-known representation of this myth. The inventor of dithyrambic poetry, and the toast of the court of King Periander of Corinth, Arion was rescued by a dolphin after being thrown into the sea by the mariners (who stole his prize money) on his way back to Greece after winning a musical contest in Sicily.

22–23: The **south vestibule (22)**, decorated with nursery scenes, leads into a **bedchamber (23)** in which the mosaic shows scenes of drama; the musical instruments and the indication by Greek letters of musical modes are of unusual interest.

24–25: Off the **north vestibule (24)**, with its scene showing the contest between Eros and Pan (the bearded man wearing a purple toga and the boy opposite him could be the owner and his son), is a **bedchamber (25)** with scenes of children hunting, those in the centre already amusingly routed by their quarry.

26: The **basilica** was the administrative centre of the villa, where guests and clients were received; an imposing hall, 100 Roman feet long (c. 30m). Notice the columns of red granite from Egypt at the entrance, a sign of regality, as was the disc of purple porphyry in front of the place where the throne would have stood; this rare stone was used almost exclusively for emperors. Above the throne stood a large statue of Hercules, of which the head is now at the Town Hall of Piazza Armerina. The apse and the floors are of marble in *opus sectile*, from 40 different quarries in the Mediterranean area. An enormous copper-covered semi-dome of wooden laminate has been raised over the apse, and a massive coffered ceiling over the rest of the room, the source of some controversy, because not all scholars concur with the idea that the basilica would have had a dome at all; some say that if there were one, it would have been much smaller and many point out that this is so heavy that cement has been injected into the original Roman walls in order to support its weight.

27–28: The northern group of private apartments consists of a **bedchamber (27)** with a mosaic depicting a variety of fruit, and an **ante-room (28)** with a large mosaic of *Odysseus and Polyphemus*, showing Odysseus offering wine to the unsuspecting, unusually three-eyed Cyclops.

29: The adjoining **bedchamber** has well-preserved, colourful frescoes on the walls, and a famous erotic scene in the twelve-sided centre floor panel.

30–33: The thermae. The **frigidarium (30)**, which was formerly covered with a dome, is an octagon with radiating apses of which two served as vestibules and two, larger than the rest, as plunge-baths. The mosaics show slaves helping people to dress or undress, and in the centre, marine myths (some of these show signs of having been clumsily repaired at a later date). Those in the adjoining room (**31**), show the massage of bathers by slaves, a function consistent with its position between the cold baths and the **tepidarium** (**32**) and **caldaria** (**33**), which lie beyond.

34: The **aediculum** designed for a statue of Venus, was the original entrance to the baths.

35: The **vestibule** was the entrance to the long narthex (or Circus Room). In both these the partial disappearance of the floor has exposed the hypocaust beneath.

36: Near the atrium of the villa are the remains of the **Great Latrine**, the marble seats of which are lost; the water-channel for washing and the niches for sponges can be seen.

Southwest of the villa the remains of a **12th-century village** have been found, perhaps the Lombard *Plutia* (*see p. 275*).

NORTH AND WEST OF PIAZZA ARMERINA

To the north of Piazza Armerina is the Norman **church of Sant'Andrea** (*map p. 569, B3; to request visit call Domus Artis a few days before, T: 392 206 8111*). Dating from 1096, the austere interior contains 12th–15th-century frescoes, including one of the *Crucifixion of St Andrew*, making this church particularly important for the history of Sicilian medieval art. The abbey was one of the oldest religious communities in the area. The prior was elected by the local Aleramici counts and the nomination approved by the King of Sicily. After final ratification by the pope, the appointed prior had a permanent seat in the Sicilian Parliament and was one of the most powerful men in the kingdom.

West of the town, reached from the road to Casale, a rough track climbs the Piano Marino (or Armerino; so called because from there you can sometimes see the sea) to the church of **Santa Maria di Platea**, where the Byzantine *Madonna of the Victories* was found in 1348 during an epidemic of plague, which miraculously stopped. Apparently the precious little painting, carefully packed in a cypress-wood box, had been hidden in 1161 to protect it from the Saracens. Nearby are the ruins of a castle, traditionally thought to have been founded by Count Roger. The views are delightful.

At **Montagna di Marzo**, northwest of Piazza Armerina, there was a Sicel settlement, possibly the 8th-century BC *Herbessos*, where recent excavations have revealed an extensive sanctuary of Demeter and Persephone, in use from the 6th–3rd centuries BC. Votive statuettes and coins have been found.

Due west of Piazza Armerina is **Barrafranca** (*map p. 569, A3*), a farming community of ancient origin; some historians believe it could be *Hybla Heraia*, an important Sicel town which has not yet been located with certainty. Still further west is **Pietraperzia**, a town of medieval character, especially in the old district at the foot of the photogenic Castello Barresio (*closed, sometimes open in summer for guided tours*), which was built by the Normans in 1088 on top of an existing (probably Arab) structure. The façade of the 16th-century Chiesa Madre (Santa Maria), in Piazza Vittorio Emanuele is incomplete, but inside there are some Gagini statues, the lovely marble sarcophagi of the local Barresi princes, and over the main altar is a masterpiece by Filippo Paladini, the *Madonna with Saints*. In the same square is the little opera house, where a 14th-century Catalan Gothic portal has been placed on display. Found abandoned and in very bad condition, it was restored and experts believe it comes from the castle.

MORGANTINA & AIDONE

The extensive remains of the ancient city of Morgantina (*map p. 569, B3*) lie on a high ridge surrounded by open, wooded countryside. With its superb views, the usually deserted and very peaceful site is one of the most memorable places on the island. The huge archaeological area (c. 20 hectares) occupies the long ridge of Serra Orlando to the west, once a Greek and Sicel city loyal to Hieron II of Syracuse, separated by a deep valley from the conical Cittadella hill to the east, where the original Sicel settlement had stood several centuries earlier.

HISTORY OF MORGANTINA

Here, in the centre of a rich agricultural plain near the source of the River Gornalunga, a group of Sicels called Morgetians (from the name of their leader Morges) founded a town c. 850 BC on the Cittadella hill, the site of an Early Bronze Age settlement. They probably came from the Aeolian Islands, judging by their similar pottery. Morgantina would have been an important point on the route through to Agira and southern Sicily from the north coast. Groups of Greek settlers, from both Gela and Katane (Catania), fought over the site in the 6th century BC, and rebuilt the city, which however was not abandoned by the Sicels, who continued living there, side by side with the newcomers. In 459 BC Ducetius, King of the Sicels, seeing Sicels and Greeks living peacefully together as inimical to his dream of expelling the Greeks from Sicily, sacked the city. The Cittadella was abandoned and a new city was built on Serra Orlando, which probably reached its zenith under the protection of Hieron II of Syracuse (307–215 BC; he came to power in 276 BC). Almost all of Sicily was under Roman rule when he died, but his young successor chose to side with the Carthaginians during the Second Punic War and Morgantina was sacked by the Romans in 211 BC. By the time of Augustus, Morgantina was a mere shadow of its former self and was gradually completely abandoned.

Open daily 9–7 (until 4pm Oct–March), last tickets 1hr before closing. T: 0935 87955. Combined ticket with Piazza Armerina and the archaeological museum of Aidone. NB: Bring water and a sunhat in any season. The Cittadella is a long walk from the main site.

Morgantina was first excavated by the Swedish archaeologist Erik Sjoqvist in 1955 for Princeton University; he was under the impression that the city was *Herbessos*, until coins and a wooden die carved with the initials MGT suggested that he had found Morgantina. The main excavations consist of the area of the agora, laid out in the 3rd century BC, and the residential areas on the two low hills to the east and west of it. Later excavations were carried out by Virginia University under the direction of Malcolm Bell III, and are continuing today under the direction of several separate teams.

RESIDENTIAL AREA: WEST HILL
A path leads west from the ticket office to the **Hellenistic bath-house**. Dating from the period of Hieron II, it is an interesting example of an early bathing establishment and is visibly different from the later, Roman, versions that can be seen elsewhere in Sicily.

Returning to the ticket office, a long path leads east to the main part of the site, entered from the West Hill. This was a residential district at the intersection of two streets, Plateia B and Stenopos West 4, where a number of houses have been excavated. To the right, on Plateia B, is the **House of the Tuscan Capitals**, completely rebuilt in the 2nd century BC. Part of the house has been reconstructed to protect the walls and floors.

Across the street, near a large olive tree, is the **House of the Wine-press** (or Pappalardo House, after the engineer who first discovered it in 1884). Built in the 3rd century BC, the most prosperous period for Morgantina, and paved with early mosaics, the house measures c. 500m square, and had a peristyle with twelve columns. It would have been one of the more luxurious homes in the city. In 1966, in one of the houses in this district, a pot containing 44 gold coins was found, probably buried hastily during the attack of 211 BC.

Returning to the intersection and heading northwest along Stenopos West 4, you will see the largest house in Morgantina (partly covered), the **House of the Arched Cistern**, with a cistern beneath a low arch and several mosaics. On the north side of the hill (near the approach road to the site) excavations of another house are in progress. The views from the West Hill over the agora, one of the largest public places in ancient Sicily, are incomparable.

THE AGORA
Stenopos West 4 leads down hill to join Plateia A, which brings you to what was the public heart of the city, with the **bouleuterion** on your left. This was the meeting-place of the city council, with a courtyard, a portico and originally four semicircular rows of seats that could accommodate 80 councillors. The remains of a paved street can be seen here. The **north stoa** contained the prytaneion (office of the city magistrates) in the three interconnecting easternmost rooms (rooms 19-20), one of which (room 19) contained the altar of Hestia, the symbolic hearth of the city. After 211 the prytaneion was turned into a bronze foundry and the altar was intentionally and symbolically destroyed. A number of lava millstones, used for grinding wheat, have been placed here—most of them were found in the residential quarters.

The northwest and **west stoa** were arcades of shops built into the hillside, Beyond a long terracotta **water conduit** (with holes at regular intervals provided with little lids

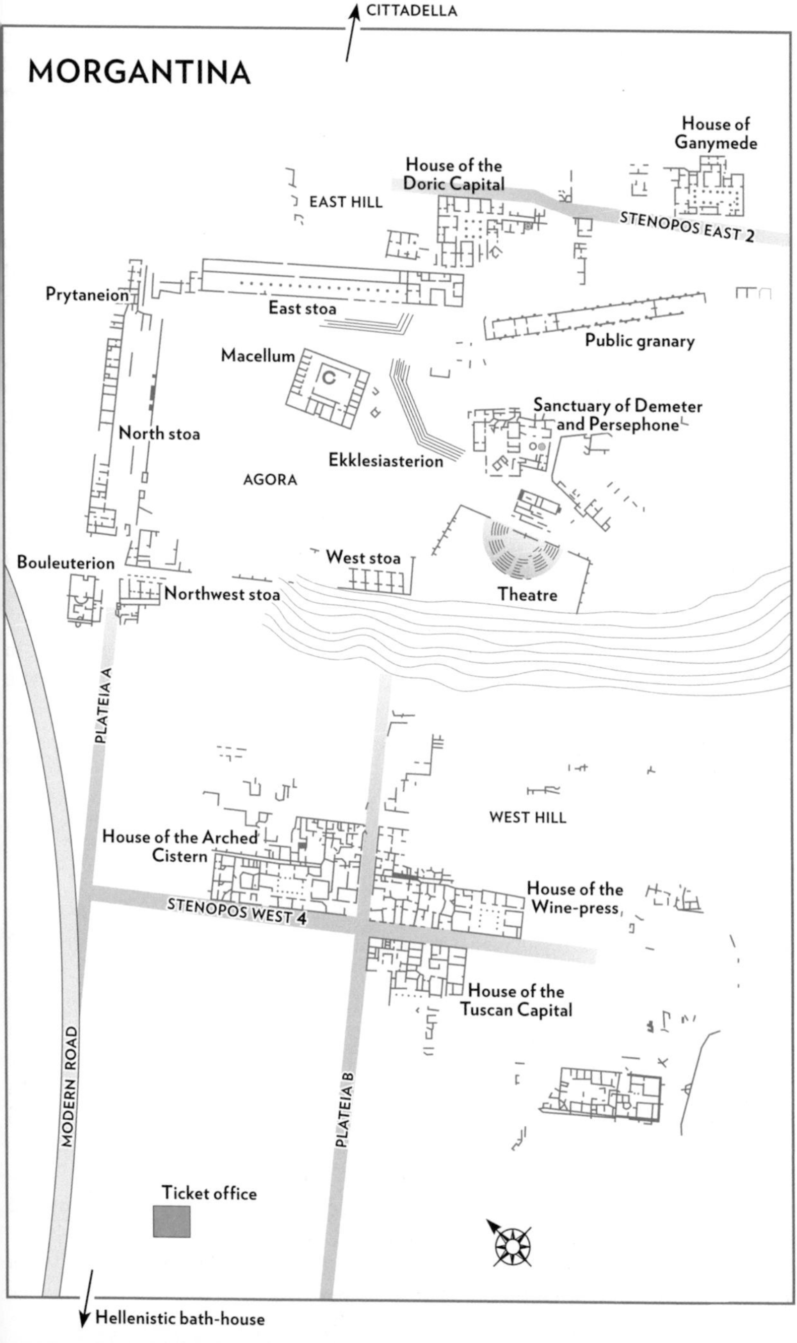

MORGANTINA

CITTADELLA

House of Ganymede

House of the Doric Capital

EAST HILL

STENOPOS EAST 2

Prytaneion

East stoa

Public granary

Macellum

C

North stoa

Sanctuary of Demeter and Persephone

Ekklesiasterion

AGORA

West stoa

Bouleuterion

Northwest stoa

Theatre

PLATEIA A

WEST HILL

House of the Arched Cistern

House of the Wine-press

STENOPOS WEST 4

House of the Tuscan Capital

PLATEIA B

MODERN ROAD

Ticket office

Hellenistic bath-house

MORGANTINA
View of the theatre.

to allow cleaning), you arrive at the **theatre**, still with appreciably good acoustics, with 14 rows of seats providing room for an audience of over 1,000. Notice the dedicatory inscription in Greek on the ninth row of the third section (counting from right to left).

In the centre of the agora is a monumental three-sided **ekklesiasterion**, a flight of steps unique in the Greek world, 55m wide, which separated the upper agora, dedicated to commerce and political meetings, from the lower, where religious functions took place. Beside the steps is a **Sanctuary of Demeter and Persephone**, with two round altars (under cover), and the pottery kilns used for manufacturing the votive offerings.

In the centre of the upper agora is the large rectangular **macellum**, a covered market with 14 shops, around an open yard in the middle of which was a circular building with thick walls for storing fresh food, and a stepped shrine built in 125 BC.

The long **east stoa** (87m) consisted of a narrow portico. A monumental fountain (under cover) with two basins has been excavated at its north end, and at its extreme south end is a large building paved in brick. The three large holes you can see carved in a stone may have been used to accommodate amphorae used for wine or water, or they may have been part of a cashier's till, with another (now lost) block placed over the holes in such a way that money could be deposited in the holes by people standing outside and scooped out by the cashier inside, who would then deposit it in a strongbox placed in the large hole in the floor. The house was also provided with an oven. Beyond this building is the huge **public granary**, a long, narrow storehouse for wheat, with a small pottery kiln (under cover), which was added later, and at the other end (by the fence), a larger kiln with elaborate ovens for tiles, bricks and storage vessels.

RESIDENTIAL AREA: EAST HILL

A stepped street zigzags up the East Hill from the end of the east stoa. Just below the summit is the elegant **House of the Doric Capital**, so-called because one was found incorporated into a wall. It has the word EYEXEI, meaning 'welcome' in Greek, inlaid into one of its floors, to the right of the entrance. A hip-bath found in the house is now in the Aidone museum.

Leaving the house on Stenopos East 2 and walking c. 50m along the summit, you reach the **House of Ganymede**, built c. 260 BC and destroyed in 211 BC, with two columns and mosaic fragments in two little huts (seen through glass doors). The **Ganymede mosaic** is particularly interesting as one of the earliest known made with cut-stone tesserae, which also incorporates natural pebbles. There is a fine view of the agora and, on a clear day, of Etna to the east. From here you can also see the original site of the settlement, the Cittadella.

THE CITTADELLA

To the east of the site can be seen the conical Cittadella hill (reached from here by a rough road, about 30 mins' strenuous walk), which was separately fortified. On the summit is a long narrow temple of the 4th century BC. Here a hut village of the Morgetians (850–750 BC) was excavated, and rock-hewn tombs of Sicel type on the slopes have yielded considerable finds of pottery. Parts of the walls (7km in circumference) of Serra Orlando, and the west gate, can be seen near the approach road to the site.

AIDONE

The little red-stone town of Aidone (*map p. 569, B3*) stands in a panoramic position in the Heraean Mountains, close to lovely woods of pines, oaks and eucalyptus, where the fallow deer has been re-introduced; part of the forest is protected as a nature reserve, the **Riserva Naturale Russomanno**, run by the Azienda Forestale. In the heart of the reserve is a photogenic group of large, mysterious stones, called the *Pietre Incantate—* the 'Enchanted Stones'. Legend says they are a petrified band of dancers.

Aidone was founded by Count Roger for the families of the Lombard troops from Monferrato, who accompanied his third wife Adelaide, mother of Roger II. In 1282 the town took a leading role in the famous uprising against the Angevins, the Sicilian Vespers (*see p. 75*). The **Chiesa Madre** is dedicated to St Lawrence, the patron saint of Aidone; the old sacristy has been transformed into a small museum of church treasures, including a 16th-century silver reliquary containing the arm of the saint. Inside the church is a magnificent 18th-century organ, recently restored and in regular use.

MUSEO ARCHEOLOGICO

In the upper part of the town, a long steep walk from the centre, in Piazza Torres Truppia, is a restored 17th-century Capuchin convent, now the Museo Archeologico (*open 9–7, last tickets 1hr before closing; possible combined ticket with Morgantina and Piazza Armerina; T: 0935 87307*), with a well-displayed collection of finds. The entrance is through a charming little church with painted wooden statues.

THE REPATRIATION OF THE MORGANTINA ANTIQUITIES

The acroliths, *Dea di Morgantina*, Head of Hades and Treasure of Eupolemos were each discovered at Morgantina between 1967 and 1980 by *tombaroli*, clandestine diggers, who sold them through a well-established antiquities smuggling chain. They found their way to the United States where they were put on display in various museums. Long recognised for what they were, many requests were made for their return but it was only in 2005 that the Italian state initiated successful international legal proceedings. They have now returned to Italy and are on permanent display in Aidone, with the exception of the Treasure of Eupolemos, which is shared with the Metropolitan Museum of New York. Each museum will display it in turn for four years, until 2050 when the treasure will return definitively to Aidone.

Ground floor: Galleries 1 and 2 are in the tiny cloister, with introductory panels and huge storage-jars or *pithoi* from Morgantina. Galleries 3 and 4 display prehistoric, Bronze- and Iron-Age finds from the Cittadella and Contrada San Francesco, including material from huts inhabited by the Morgetic colony.

The Sala degli Acroliti displays the famous **marble acroliths**: three feet, three hands and two heads, beautifully arranged by the designer Marella Ferrera, with the help of some twists of tulle, to represent two seated goddesses, believed to be Demeter and her daughter Persephone. While the hands and the faces are perfect, the feet are worn, consumed by the caresses of generations of worshippers. Notice the misshapen toe on Persephone's surviving foot; she appears to have a bunion. The features are typical of the 6th century BC, with Archaic smiles and almond-shaped eyes; scholars date them c. 530 BC. The statues themselves would have been made of humble materials such as wood, then draped in mantles of linen or wool, while the visible parts of the figures were made of stone (in this case marble from the Greek island of Thasos). Hair, diadems, earrings and other ornaments might have been made of bronze or gilded wood, and the goddesses would have been wearing veils. The position of the fingers indicates they were holding an object. The left-hand figure is slightly larger than the other. After much debate, they are believed to be both female and to represent Demeter and her daughter Persephone.

The **Dea di Morgantina** (c. 410 BC) has a room to herself. Found broken into 83 fragments, it is thought that the statue was toppled from her pedestal and smashed during the 211 attack on Morgantina, or during an earthquake. The statue is pseudo-acrolithic, carved from local limestone with head, feet and arms of Parian marble, 2.2m tall, weighing 600kg and thought by some scholars to be the work of a follower of Pheidias. Tests show that her drapery was originally painted red (faded to pink on the fragments) and blue, while her head was veiled. The goddess is striding forth, her garments rippling behind her. Scholars continue to debate which goddess she represents, Aphrodite, Demeter or Persephone.

Returned to Sicily in 2016, the terracotta **Head of Hades** (c. 400–300 BC) had been on display at the Getty Museum in Malibu since 1985. Probably

AIDONE
The *Dea di Morgantina* (5th century BC).

part of a statue, it is powerfully modelled, with a strong nose, stern mouth and almond-shaped eyes, which would originally have been fringed with metal lashes. The tight curls of the beard were made individually by the artist and applied one by one. The finished statue was then painted in bright colours, with red hair and a blue beard—in fact, in Malibu the head was affectionately known as 'Bluebeard'. It was four blue-painted curls from the beard, found among the debris left by the *tombaroli* at Morgantina, that proved beyond all doubt the provenance of the sculpture. Some scholars identify the head as Zeus, because Homer often refers to him as 'the blue-bearded one', but the proven findspot of Morgantina, where the

principal divinities were Demeter and Persephone, makes an identification of Hades much more probable.

Other galleries display examples of the architecture of Morgantina, and a remarkable collection of **objects found in the thermae**, which more than anything else give an idea of the high standard of living of the inhabitants

Gallery 9 is dedicated to the **Treasure of Eupolemos** (*on display at the Metropolitan Museum of New York until 2017; when in the US, a temporary exhibition of material from the Met is hosted here*), a group of 16 beautiful objects in gilded silver dating to the 3rd century BC and probably made in Syracuse. They may have been intended for use during temple rites; one of them is inscribed with the words 'sacred to the gods' and two others bear the embossed name of Eupolemos. The treasure consists of two large oval jars (*situlae*), each with three theatrical-mask feet; three cups with flowers and leaves in relief at the bottom; a small bowl with a fish-net pattern; a jug (*oinochoë*), a two-handled cup (*skyphos*); an offering-dish with sun-ray relief (*phiale-mesomphalos*); a miniature cylindrical altar (*bomiskos*); a pitcher (*kyathos*); two pots (*pyxides*) with lion's-foot feet and lids decorated with figures in relief, one representing a cupid with a torch and the other a female figure with a cornucopia and a child on her lap (the allegory of Peace or Justice); a wonderful medallion (probably from a missing cup) showing Scylla in the act of throwing a large stone, and two slender horns, perhaps belonging to a leather priest's mask.

First floor: Gallery 10 is on two levels, with objects illustrating the life of Morgantina during its moment of greatest splendour, in Archaic times. Corinthian and Attic ceramics, antefixes with gorgons' heads (6th century BC), a large red-figure krater by the Euthymides painter, a Corinthian krater with birds, and lekythoi. There is also a fine collection of ceramics from the agora zone of Serra Orlando (including a plate with three fish) and from the houses excavated on the west and east hills (including statues). The upper section displays household objects, cooking utensils, agricultural implements, toys and masks, all found at Morgantina.

Gallery 11 has Hellenistic and Roman finds from Serra Orlando, including fine large busts of Persephone (3rd century BC) from the three sanctuaries of Demeter and Persephone so far found there, and grave goods found in the necropoleis.

LEONFORTE & ASSORO

Leonforte ('Strong Lion'; *map p. 569, B2*) is a delightful little town founded in 1610 by the local overlord Nicolò Placido Branciforte. Seeing the potential of such a well-watered area, he founded a city, naming it after the lion on his family coat of arms. Today the town bases its economy on the production of lentils, broad beans and highly-prized late-ripening peaches.

Via Porta Palermo leads to the main street, Corso Umberto or Cassaro, just before which, below the road to the left, is the **Chiesa Madre** (17th–18th centuries), with a striking façade in a mixture of styles. It contains numerous interesting wooden statues.

A very short steep road, Via Garibaldi, can be followed on foot downhill past the church of Santo Stefano to the church of the Carmelo, beside the magnificent **Granfonte** (built in 1651 by Nicolò Branciforte), an abundant fountain of 24 jets. The water is collected in a stream which follows a picturesque lane downhill. Beside it is the gate of an overgrown botanical garden, with palms and orange trees.

Just beyond the Chiesa Madre is **Piazza Branciforte** with the impressive façade of the 17th-century Palazzo Baronale and, at the end, a stable-block for 100 horses built in 1641 (the prince of the time was a famous horse-breeder). The well-proportioned corso leads gently up through a pretty circular piazza. Beyond, a side street (left) leads to the convent and church of the **Cappuccini**. It contains an enormous canvas of the *Calling of St Matthew* by Pietro Novelli, very reminiscent of Caravaggio. On either side are niches with Gaginesque statues. A finely-carved arch (1647) precedes the Branciforte funerary chapel, with the sumptuous black marble sarcophagus (1634) of Caterina di Branciforte, supported by four lions.

Fifteen kilometres to the west of Leonforte is **Monte Altesina** (1193m), thought by the Arabs to be exactly in the centre of the island; it is said that on this spot they decided the division of Sicily into three administrative districts, the Val Demone, Val di Noto and Val di Mazara. Set in a nature reserve run by the Azienda Forestale, it is a pleasant trek through the woods to the top, where the remains of a Sicel village are to be found, and panoramic views.

ASSORO

To the east of Leonforte is Assoro (*map p. 569, B2*), a town founded by the Sicels. Ally of Syracuse until 260 BC, it changed sides, became a Roman stronghold, and was even prosperous enough to mint coins. In 72 BC the notorious Roman governor Verres (*see p. 205*) was forced by the indignant inhabitants to abandon his attempt to steal the statue of Crisa, the town's patron god, from the temple. Assoro was taken by the Arabs in 939, who fortified it, and by the Normans in 1061; during the Middle Ages, Assoro was particularly fortunate, eventually becoming the fiefdom of the Valguarnera family.

The old centre, once surrounded by walls, is medieval in character. The main street, Via Crisa, leads up to Piazza Marconi (Piazza Matrice) and the 12th-century **Chiesa Madre** (San Leone), a national monument, with a square bell-tower. It is entered by a Catalan Gothic doorway and has an unusual interior with five aisles and three apses, twisted columns and a carved and painted wooden ceiling. The gilded stucco decoration dates from the early 18th century. In the raised and vaulted presbytery is a fine marble altarpiece of the Gagini school (1515) with statues and reliefs, and two early 16th-century Valguarnera funerary monuments on the side walls. Over the nave hangs a Crucifix (late 15th-century), painted on both sides. The high altar has three Gothic statues. To the left of the presbytery is a double chapel, the first with Gothic vaulting and bosses, and the second with Baroque decoration. Here is a carved processional Crucifix attributed to Gian Domenico Gagini, and two 17th-century sarcophagi. In the nave are some particularly interesting 16th-century polychrome gilded wooden statues. The porch of the church is connected by a Gothic arch to Palazzo Valguarnera, which has a balcony supported by grotesque heads. The Baroque portal of an oratory is also in the square.

On the top of Monte Stella is the **Castello Valguarnera**, separated from the town by a steep slope, now protected as an urban park. It is only accessible from the west. Most of the visible ruins go back to the 14th century, when the Valguarnera family took over Assoro, though many of the stones used for the building may be ancient spolia.

AGIRA & THE EAST

The **River Salso**, so-called because of its slightly salty water, springs from Mt Bauda in the Madonie Mountains, and flows east, forming the lovely Lake Pozzillo (Sicily's largest), before joining the Simeto. The countryside along its course is particularly spectacular, and there are numerous interesting old towns.

AGIRA

The little town of Agira (*map p. 569, B2*) is perched on a conical hill. The ancient *Agyrion* was a Sicel settlement, important for its position between Sicel territory and that of the Sicans. It was colonised with Greeks in 339 BC by Timoleon of Corinth (the parent-city of Syracuse), who came to Sicily to oust the tyrant Dionysius II. Games were regularly organised in honour of Herakles, for whom there was a strong cult following. Traces have been found here of Roman houses with mosaic pavements, a temple on what must have been the acropolis, and necropoleis of the 4th–3rd centuries BC. The historian Diodorus Siculus (1st century BC), the first to use the chronology of the Olympic Games to date historical events, was born in Agira: in his description of Timoleon's city he declares the theatre to be the most beautiful in Sicily after that of Syracuse. The town was the scene of the miracles of the apocryphal St Philip of Syria, who is said by the local people to have imprisoned the devil in a nearby cave, where he can be heard wailing on stormy nights. Pope Leo II (682–3), who instituted the kiss of peace during High Mass, was probably born here.

The magic moment to be in Agira is just before dawn, when the town is still enveloped in the shadows of night, and the rising sun gradually outlines the profile of Mt Etna with a pink glow.

MAIN SIGHTS OF AGIRA

The highway SS 121 becomes Via Vittorio Emanuele, leading to Largo Mercato, with the church of **San Filippo** (12th and 14th centuries). The interior has a central nave and two side aisles; on the main altar is a Crucifix by Fra' Umile da Petralia. The walnut choir stalls, carved with scenes of the life of St Philip, are the work of Nicola Bagnasco (1818–22). In the left aisle are two paintings by Olivio Sozzi and three panels of a 15th-century polyptych. There is a crypt with two statues of St Philip and a relief of the Gagini school.

Piazza Garibaldi is in the centre, with the large church of **Sant'Antonio da Padova** (1549); inside there is a 16th-century polychrome wooden statue of St Sylvester, a beautiful painting on marble by Willem Borremans with a precious silver frame, and a 16th-century Flemish-school canvas of the *Deposition*.

Via Diodorea continues steeply up to Piazza Immacolata and the 13th-century church of **Santa Margherita**, the largest in the town, with 13 sumptuous altars and several paintings by Olivio Sozzi. By taking the street to the right of the church, passing under an arch and going through Largo Raccommandata, you reach Piazza Roma, with the Norman church of the **Santissimo Salvatore**; it has a beautiful bell-tower. Inside is a fine Aragonese portal from the oratory of Santa Croce (once the synagogue), a 15th-century panel painting of *St Philip of Agira* and a 13th-century bishop's mitre of red silk embroidered with coral and pearls.

By returning to Largo Raccommandata and taking via Sant'Antonio Abate, you reach the top of the hill and the romantic ruins of the **castle**. Just below it is the church of **Santa Maria Maggiore** (11th century), with an unusual interior: two asymmetric naves divided by three arches on columns, with decorated capitals; immediately in the right-hand nave is a 16th-century wooden Crucifix by Pietro Ruzzolone and a 16th-century polychrome marble statue of the *Madonna*. In the chapel at the end of the left nave is a 15th-century wooden Crucifix, painted on both sides. A short distance away is the 16th-century church of **Sant'Antonio Abate**, with a modern façade. Inside there are some remarkable works of art: a painted wooden Crucifix by Pietro Ruzzolone, 14 small 17th-century canvases of the Venetian school and a dramatic *St Andrew* by Polidoro da Caravaggio.

ENVIRONS OF AGIRA

On the road to Regalbuto, outside Agira (left; signposted) is a **Canadian Military Cemetery** (490 graves), beautifully kept in a clump of pine trees on a small hill; Canadian forces were engaged in heavy fighting here in 1943. Close to Agira is the beautiful, wooded **Lake Pozzillo**, the largest artificial lake in Sicily, measuring 6km by 1.6km, usually with cattle and sheep grazing around it. It was created in the 1950s by means of a dam on the River Salso, in order to provide water for irrigating the orange groves of the Plain of Catania.

South of Agira is a beautiful, remote valley in the central Heraean Mountains known as **Piano della Corte**, where a stream, flowing to join the River Dittaino, has created strange formations in the rock. It is protected as a nature reserve. The vegetation is typical Mediterranean maquis together with poplars, willows and tamarisks; there are rabbits, foxes, porcupines and hedgehogs, while the birds include the woodchat shrike, barn owl, buzzard and the Sicilian sub-species of the long-tailed tit.

REGALBUTO

The ancient *Ameselon*, destroyed by Hieron II of Syracuse in 270 BC, has been identified on Monte San Giorgio, near Regalbuto (*map p. 569, C2*). It was later re-founded as an Arab village, *Rahal-butah*, at the site of the modern town. The people historically feuded with the inhabitants of nearby Centuripe, who completely destroyed their town in 1261. Fortunately, the appeals of the townsfolk to King Manfred were crowned with success and Regalbuto was rebuilt the following year at his expense. The curving medieval streets, with narrow side streets and courtyards, are particularly attractive. Via Ingrassia leads north to the vast Piazza Re, with the **Chiesa Madre** dedicated to St Basil. The church has a sumptuous curving Baroque façade and a tall campanile crowned by a spire. Inside is a towering altar, 10m high, with a wooden statue of St Vitus (Giuseppe Picano, 1790). The little town also has some fine 18th-century buildings and a public garden, from whence, beyond hills flushed with ochre and crimson on the left, there is a splendid view ahead of Etna. The plain is filled with lustrous green citrus groves, many of them protected from the wind by 'walls' of olive trees, and Centuripe can be seen on its hill to the right.

CENTURIPE & CATENANUOVA

Centuripe (*map p. 569, C2*) is lonely and remote, a cascade of coloured houses surrounded by harsh countryside: an occasional prickly pear, a few almond trees. The city has grown out in five directions on the top of its ridge, like a starfish.

HISTORY OF CENTURIPE

Founded by the Sicels and known by the Greeks as *Kentoripa*, it occupies a superb commanding position facing Etna, at a height of 719m; when Garibaldi saw it in 1862 he aptly named it *'il balcone della Sicilia'*. With the advent of Greek colonisation, the city maintained good relations with the newcomers but later discovered that her true sympathies lay with Rome, an alliance that brought prosperity, wealth, power and the gratitude of Augustus, who rebuilt the town after the destruction wreaked by Sextus Pompey during the Civil War in the 1st century BC. In the early Middle Ages decadence set in, although it remained an important strategic stronghold. The people made the mistake of rebelling against Frederick II of Hohenstaufen in 1232, who got his revenge by forcibly removing the entire population to Palermo after razing Centuripe and its castle to the ground. Some people trickled back, however, and started rebuilding; but it was a forlorn effort. Crushed once more in 1268 by Charles I of Anjou, it was not until 1548 that it was re-founded by Francesco Moncada. Its capture by the Allies in 1943 caused the Germans to abandon Sicily.

The town centre is the piazza near the 18th-century pink and white **Chiesa Madre**; its attractive symmetrical façade has a clock in the middle surmounted by a bell-tower. On the edge of the cliff an avenue of pines leads to the remains of a monument on a knoll, of Roman (2nd century AD) origin, which resembles a mausoleum. Locally it is known as *Il Corradino* in allusion to a certain Corradino Capece, a Swabian who is thought to have built a castle here while supporting Conradin of Swabia against the Angevins. He surrendered after false promises had been made, was tortured and executed at Catania. There are impressive views from this point. Another 2nd-century AD Roman funerary monument, originally similar to this one and known locally as *La Dogana*, is to be found on the northern limits of the town, not far from an enigmatic Roman imperial monument known as *La Panneria*.

THE MUSEUMS OF CENTURIPE

In Via Giulio Cesare is the **Museo Regionale Archeologico** (*open 9–7, ticket includes the Anthropological Museum; T: 0935 73079, www.museocenturipe.it*), housing a display of objects discovered in the area, including a few of the famous Centuripe vases. Unfortunately, a large part of the collection was stolen while the museum was being built. The vases are unique in Sicily for their shape and decoration. The terracotta itself is a rich hazelnut colour and the ceramicists decorated the pieces further by picking out details in relief before firing, and adding brightly-coloured painted motifs afterwards. Dating to the 3rd and 2nd centuries BC, this pottery was prized right across the Mediterranean. More recently, in the 19th century and especially after the Second World War, its particular beauty gave rise to a rash of clandestine excavations for the black market. Several local craftsmen also proved to be adept at faking old vases, some of which apparently still hold pride of place in important museums of the world. Today, however, the craftsmen are limiting their activities to making souvenirs for tourists.

The museum is organised on three floors but at the time of writing the upper floors were closed and the displays had been temporarily reorganised in such a way that all of the major finds were on display on the ground floor. These include a marvellous bust of Hadrian, a rich collection of Imperial sculpture found in the Sede degli Augustali (*see below*) and material from the necropoleis.

The museum is conveniently situated in the archaeological area and the remains are all within walking distance. The local people are extremely friendly, proud of their town, and more than willing to show visitors around. In the valley (Vallone Difesa), east of the town, excavations beneath and near the church of the Crocifisso have revealed an important 2nd-century AD edifice known as the **Sede degli Augustali**. To the northwest in Vallone dei Bagni is a large **Roman thermal edifice** with five niches. Close by in Via Genova, in what used to be the slaughterhouse, is the **Anthropological Museum** (*open 9–1.30 & 3–7; T: 0935 919093*), a well-arranged collection of tools, furniture, and equipment used until quite recently by farmers, artisans and labourers.

On the road to Adrano, near the Ponte del Maccarone, a large **aqueduct** (31 arches) constructed in 1761–6 by the Prince of Biscari can be seen.

CATENANUOVA

South of Centuripe and close to the motorway is the prosperous farming community of Catenanuova (*map p. 569, C2*), overlooking the River Dittaino, and founded in the 18th century in a strategic spot on the Palermo–Catania road. Goethe stayed here during his travels in Sicily in 1787 and much appreciated the hospitality of the people. In 1714, when the Duke of Savoy (proclaimed King Vittorio Amedeo II of Sicily the year before, although forced by the Great Powers to drop the title in exchange for Sardinia) and Queen Anna were passing through Catenanuova, a local baron ordered his farm workers to pour all that day's milk into a nearby stream, thus creating for their majesties a river of milk. The royal pair were suitably impressed and the baron was made captain of the Royal Guard.

NICOSIA & THE NORTH

Founded by the Byzantines with a name meaning 'victorious', **Nicosia** (*map p. 569, BI*) became a place of some importance in the Middle Ages, and was given by Count Roger to his Lombard troops, hence the noticeable local dialect. The beautiful stone-built medieval city was damaged by a landslide in 1757, by an earthquake in 1968, and by a flood in 1972. It is known locally as the town with two cathedrals and two Christs, because for a time the churches of Santa Maria Maggiore (Byzantine rite) and San Nicola (Latin rite) took turns in being the cathedral, and therefore two processions for Good Friday were organised, with two Crucifixes and considerable rivalry between the two groups, sometimes resulting in bloodshed.

THE CATHEDRAL (SAN NICOLA)

The cathedral of San Nicola di Bari has an elegant 15th-century portico with six slender marble columns. The Arab-Norman bell-tower is one of the most important in Sicily: 40m high, it consists of three sections, in three different architectural styles. The base of the tower once formed part of a defensive structure, devised by the Arabs to protect the castle. The decorative 14th-century main door is in extremely poor repair; the entrance is through the north door.

In the Latin-cross interior, a new vault was erected in the early 19th century, unfortunately covering the 15th-century trussed and painted wooden ceiling, among the most important in Sicily. The paintings, in panels representing saints, angels and mysterious personages alternating with borders of fruits, flowers and geometric designs, have been newly restored and it is possible to see them close up from a viewing platform (*a virtual reconstruction of the panels can be seen at the Centro Civico in Palazzo Nicosia, opposite the Town Hall*). Over the second south altar is a *Martyrdom of St Placidus* by Giacinto Platania. The 16th-century pulpit is attributed to Gian Domenico Gagini.

In the right transept is a Gaginesque statue of the *Madonna of Victory*. Suspended over the crossing, in the octagonal vault, surrounded by 17th-century paintings, is an unusually large statue of St Nicholas by Giovanni Battista Li Volsi. In the chapel to the right of the high altar is a venerated wooden Crucifix by Fra' Umile da Petralia, called *Padre della Provvidenza*, one of the two carried in procession through the town on Good Friday. In the presbytery the intricately-carved walnut choir stalls (c. 1622; with a relief showing the old town of Nicosia) are by Giovanni Battista Li Volsi and his son Stefano, while the altarpiece is a *Resurrection* by Giuseppe Velasquez. In the chapel to the left of the high altar is delightful polychrome marble decoration. On the left side is a font by Antonello Gagini and, in the base of the bell-tower, the funerary monument of Alessandro Testa by Ignazio Marabitti. In the chapter house (*opened by the sacristan on request*) are some more fine paintings, including the *Madonna with Sts John and Rosalia* by Pietro Novelli, the *Martyrdom of St Sebastian* by Salvator Rosa, and the *Martyrdom of St Bartholomew* by Jusepe de Ribera.

SANTA MARIA MAGGIORE AND THE REST OF TOWN

Further uphill is the imposing **Santa Maria Maggiore**, with a handsome Baroque portal once belonging to an aristocratic palace and donated by the family when the church (founded by Count Roger, c. 1062) was being rebuilt after the 1757 landslide. The campanile collapsed in 1968 and the bells were re-hung on a low iron bracket beside the façade. The interior, a central nave and two side aisles separated by pilasters, contains a huge painted marble sculpture with scenes from the life of the Virgin by Antonello Gagini (1512), over 10m high, behind the main altar. A statue in the left transept of the *Madonna* is thought to be by Francesco Laurana. There is a view from the terrace of the modern buildings of the town and the church of San Salvatore perched on a rock. Via Carlo V and Via del Castello lead up behind Santa Maria Maggiore to the ruins of the **Norman castle**. The views from here are splendid.

From Piazza Garibaldi, Via Fratelli Testa, a narrow alley with lots of steps, leads up to a rocky outcrop at the top of the hill and the 13th-century church of **San Salvatore**, rebuilt in the 17th century, with an attractive portico and bell-tower. On the outside wall of the tower are the ***Calendari delle Rondinelle***, carved stones giving the arrival and departure dates of the house-martins, from 1737–98 and from 1837–45.

In the opposite direction Via Testa leads down past the closed churches of San Calogero (with a fine ceiling and works by Filippo Randazzo) and Sant'Antonio Abate, ending at Via Li Volsi with (left) the church of the **Carmine**, which contains statues of the *Archangel Gabriel* and *Virgin Annunciate* attributed to Antonello Gagini. At the top of Via Li Volsi, which is lined with trees, the Baroque façade of Palazzo Speciale can be seen, now propped up with concrete pillars.

In the 14th-century church of **San Michele** (just east of Nicosia) is a 16th-century font and two wooden statues by Giovanni Battista Li Volsi; the marble statue of St Michael Archangel is a youthful work by Antonello Gagini.

The landscape is particularly beautiful east of Nicosia, with frequent glimpses of Etna in the distance. In the rugged countryside at the foot of the Nebrodi mountains the fields are dotted with *pagliari*, conical huts of straw and mud, used by the shepherds as temporary refuges.

SPERLINGA

Sperlinga (*map p. 569, B1*) is the only Sicilian town which took no part in the Vespers: on an arch inside the castle are inscribed the words *Quod Siculis placuit, sola Sperlinga negavit* ('What pleased the Sicilians was shunned only by Sperlinga'). By offering refuge to the Angevins, Sperlinga earned herself a reputation for betrayal which is still remembered today. The approach road offers beautiful views over the valley. The little town is a delightful place at the foot of the conspicuous castle rock; many of the houses and all of the castle are carved into the stone. The people base their economy on raising cattle and sheep. The road enters the town past the 17th-century church of Sant'Anna and on the right you will see some **cave dwellings**, inhabited until recently and now protected by the local administration as an urban park.

Further along the main road, a road (signposted right) leads up past the large 17th-century Chiesa Madre to a car park just below the entrance to the **castle** (*open summer 9–1 & 4–7, winter 9.30–1.30 & 2.30–6.30; T: 0935 643265, www. castellodisperlinga.it*), which probably goes back to the days of the Sicels; recent archaeological surveys have found a small prehistoric sanctuary with a Mycenaean-type domed roof and a chamber with twelve niches, illuminated by the sun passing through a hole in a similar domed roof. Two grottoes are used as local ethnographic museums with agricultural implements. Steps lead up across a small bridge (on the site of the draw-bridge) through the double entrance. Stables, carved out of the rock in the Middle Ages, were later used as prisons. In one room are old photographs of Sperlinga, some taken during Operation Husky in 1943 by the great photographer Robert Capa. From a terrace a flight of high steps hewn out of the rock leads up to the battlements from which there are wonderful panoramic views.

Between Sperlinga and Gangi is an old fortified farmhouse near a **chapel dedicated to St Venera**, long the scene of country fairs in her honour; traces have now been discovered of an ancient processional route sacred to the goddess Cybele, leading to a spur with altars carved into the rock, illegible inscriptions and many tombs, one of which has the form of a perfect tholos.

TROINA AND ENVIRONS

Troina (*map p. 569, C1*), on a steep ridge, is the highest town in Sicily (1121m). Its early capture by the Normans in 1061 is recalled by Norman work (1078–80) in the Chiesa Madre, which has a 16th-century campanile and a Byzantine panel painting of the *Madonna*. Count Roger and his young bride Adelaide allegedly spent a very cold winter in the castle in 1061, with little food, sharing one blanket between them, while they were besieged by Greeks and Arabs who had improvised an alliance. Count Roger also instituted the first of his Basilian monasteries here and in 1082 made it the first diocese of the island, entrusting it to a bishop of his own choice. Nothing much remains of the castle, which must have been imposing; the Normans maintained the Royal Treasury here for many years, even after taking Palermo. Parts of the Greek walls remain and the Belvedere has a superb view.

GAGLIANO CASTELFERRATO

In a breathtaking position among the mountains, south of Troina, is Gagliano Castelferrato (*map p. 569, B2*), a picturesque village dominated by a huge rock which incorporates the castle. The numerous tombs carved into the rock show that the mountain has been inhabited continuously since the Early Bronze Age. Though the castle resisted the Arab onslaughts, the town acquired importance under their domination, and later under the Normans. The **Chiesa Madre** (1304), by the castle ruins, has a plain façade and a spire covered with brightly coloured majolica tiles, and is dedicated to the Irish saint Cathald, who preached widely in Sicily. Inside is an old organ and a lovely 16th-century carved wooden choir.

In the southern part of the village is the church of **Santa Maria di Gesù**, which contains an impressive wooden Crucifix by Fra' Umile da Petralia.

CERAMI

West of Troina, Cerami (*map p. 569, B1*) is a little medieval town on a crest, built on top of a series of earlier settlements; it was the scene in July 1063 of a decisive victory of Count Roger's Lombard troops over the Muslims. Four camels taken from the enemy were presented to Pope Alexander II. The name derives from the Greek *Keramion*, meaning terracotta. The church of the **Carmine** houses a Crucifix by Fra' Umile da Petralia, while over the main altar in the abbey-church of **San Benedetto** is a charming, recently-restored 17th-century painting on slate of the *Madonna and Child*, known to the local people as the *Madonna della Lavina* because found in a torrent (*lavina*). It is said to be miraculous and has recently been attributed to Pietro Antonio Novelli, the father of 'Il Monrealese'.

To the north of Cerami, **Lake Ancipa** or Sartori, at a height of 949m and full of fish, was formed in 1952 when the River Troina was dammed for hydroelectric works; the dam itself is 120m high. There is a nature reserve run by the Azienda Forestale, where the two peaks of the Nebrodi chain, Mt Sambuchetti (1559m) and Mt Campanito (1514m), are protected for their flourishing beech forest, the southernmost in Europe. Other trees include chestnuts, varieties of oak (including the cork oak), holly and maple; the wildlife includes the endemic form of the marsh tit, the wildcat and pine marten.

PRACTICAL INFORMATION

GETTING AROUND

• **By train**: Enna railway station is in the valley, 5km from the town centre, on the Palermo–Catania line. On the same line are Villarosa, Leonforte (Stazione di Pirato) and Centuripe (nearest station Catenanuova at 15km); *www.trenitalia. com.*

• **By bus**: The bus station in **Enna** is in Viale Diaz. Website with up-to-date bus timetables: *www.orariautobus.it*. **Troina** has a shuttle-bus leaving every 20mins, connecting Piazza Conte Ruggero and Loggiato Sant'Agostino.

ASTRA (*www.astraaurolinee.it*) has services for Gela and Caltanissetta.
Romano Autolinee (*www.romanobus. it*) runs buses to Catenanuova, Centuripe, Paternò and Catania.
ISEA Autolinee (*www.iseaviaggi.it*) for Bronte, Capizzi, Catania, Cerami, Leonforte, Misterbianco, Nicosia, Paternò and Troina.
SAIS Autolinee (*www.saisautolinee.it*) runs the bus service within Enna town, also inter-city coaches for Agrigento, Caltanissetta, Canicattì, Catania and Catania Airport and Messina.
SAIS Trasporti (*www.saistrasporti.*

it) goes to Agrigento, Caltanissetta, Canicattì, Catania and Porto Empedocle.

WHERE TO STAY

AIDONE (*map p. 569, B3*)
€ **Morgantina**. Friendly and welcoming, modern building close to the museum of Aidone with 27 simple rooms (some with views of the mountains), a restaurant, and a car park. *Vico Adelasia 43 (Piazza Cordoba), T: 0935 88088, www.hotelmorgantina.it.*

ASSORO (*map p. 569, B2*)
€ **Casa Museo Elio Romano**. 6 comfortable rooms in the fascinating country house of a local artist and anthropologist. Airport/station shuttle on request. *Contrada Morra, SP Acquanuova–Morra km 5.2, T: Francesco 338 113 7595, 328 873 7060 or 0935 669868; b&bcasamuseoelioromano@hotmail.it.*

CENTURIPE (*map p. 569, C2*)
€€ **Kento Park**. Hillside position between Centuripe and Mt Etna, elegant little hotel with 10 rooms and suites, large garden, pool, car park, panoramic restaurant, shuttle-bus for Centuripe. Note that it is popular for wedding receptions. *Contrada Tagliacasse, T: 0935 74205, www.kentoparkhotel.it.*

ENNA (*map p. 569, B2*)
€ **Grande Albergo Sicilia**. Popular, central hotel with 60 rooms, many with views, restaurant and car park. *Piazza Colajanni 7, T: 0935 500850, www.hotelsiciliaenna.it. Map 1.*

NICOSIA (*map p. 569, B1*)
€ **Umberto I**. Welcoming B&B in the heart of town; 4 comfortable rooms. *Via Umberto 34, T: 0935 638111 or 331 792 0720, www.umbertoprimonicosia.weebly.com.*

PERGUSA (*map p. 569, C2*)
€€ **Casa del Poeta**. ◾ Peaceful country house, a good choice for writers and travellers, 5 superbly designed rooms, large pool, very good breakfasts with products from their nearby farm (including goat's milk if required). *Villa Grimaldi, Contrada Parasporino, Via Diana, Pergusa, T: 328 298 8448 or 329 627 4918, www.lacasadelpoeta.it.*

PIAZZA ARMERINA (*map p. 569, B3*)
€€€ **Villa Trigona**. ◾ Just south of town, an aristocratic country house with 15 rooms furnished with antiques, pool, good food, *Contrada Bauccio, T: 0935 681896 or 333 399 9601, www.villatrigona.it.*

€€ **La Casa sulla Collina d'Oro**. Small *relais* in a panoramic position overlooking the old town, 7 comfortable rooms, excellent breakfasts, garden, car park, shuttle service to/from Catania airport or station on request. *Via Mattarella, T: 0935 684148 or 333 466 8829, www.lacasasullacollinadoro.it.*

€ **La Volpe e L'Uva**. Comfortable B&B in the centre, 3 pleasant rooms, excellent breakfasts. *Via Santa Veneranda 35, T: 0935 680752, 328 445 5062 or 329 166 1188, www.volpeuva.it.*

€ **Conte Ruggero**. Central little hotel (the oldest in town) in a medieval palace near the public gardens, 15 small, spotless rooms, nice breakfasts, no restaurant, car park. *Via Generale Ciancio 68, T: 0935 680526, www.hotelconteruggero.com.*

€ **Mosaici da Battiato**. ◾ Country inn within walking distance of the Roman Villa, car park, 23 quiet rooms, very good restaurant serving robust local cuisine; tasty grilled mutton (*castrato*). *Contrada Casale Paratore 11, T 0935 685453, www.hotelmosaici.com.*

PIETRAPERZIA (*map p. 569, A3*)
€ **Marconi**. Central, modern building with 23 rooms, breakfast but no restaurant. On request you can sleep in their Neolithic grotto. *Via Kennedy 5, T: 0934 461983, www.hotelmarconi.sicilia. it.*

VILLAROSA (*map p. 569, A2*)
€€ **San Giovannello**. 4km from Villarosa and close to the sulphur mine, the farm offers 6 comfortable rooms and an apartment, restaurant and fitness centre with sauna. The farm produces organic durum and timilia wheat and, in alternate years, vegetables and pulses; also saffron (you can buy the products and the saffron bulbs). *Contrada San Giovannello, T: 0935 31260 or 328 867 7270, www.sangiovannello.it.*

WHERE TO EAT

AIDONE (*map p. 569, B3*)
€€ **La Vecchia Aidone**. In an ancient *palazzo* with a small garden, restaurant serving simple, delicious local dishes, very well presented; open fireplace makes it cosy in winter. Closed Mon. *Via Cordova 90, T: 0935 87863.*

€ **La Piazzetta del Museo**. Delightful little bar in front of the museum, for light lunch or afternoon tea; excellent home-made *arancini* (rice balls), cakes and ice cream. *Largo Torres Trupia 5, T: 334 574 1333.*

ENNA (*map p. 569, B2*)
€€ **Bottiglieria Belvedere**. Smart little wine bar and restaurant, good assortment of cheeses, ham and salami, absolutely delicious steaks, *arancini*, risotto and pasta dishes; the menu changes every day. Closed Sun. *Via Vulturo 26, T: 0935 23396 or 348 922 8491. Map 1.*

€ **La Fortunata Caffè Belvedere**. Simple place made extraordinary by its views over the plain below and out to Calascibetta on its hilltop. Etna is visible on clear days. Pasta dishes, salads and pizza (including Pizza Euno, with garlic and anchovies, named after the rebel slave). *Piazza Crispi, T: 0935 26399. Map 1.*

LEONFORTE (*map p. 569, B2*)
€ **La Piramide**. Homely atmosphere, simple food in generous portions; excellent grilled meat, vegetables, also pizza. Local wines. Closed Mon. *Via Pirandello 26, T: 0935 902121.*

MORGANTINA (*map p. 569, B3*)
€ **Eyexei**. ■ The name means welcome in Greek (it is taken from one of the mosaics still to be seen at Morgantina, where the Greek letters of the word are picked out in white tesserae). This country restaurant close to the ruins offers a welcome break after hours of exploring. Local dishes, home-made but imaginative food, presented with their own wines; closed Mon evening. *Contrada Morgantina, T: 0935 87341 or 368 719 0257, www.ristoranteeyexei.com.*

PERGUSA (*map p. 569, B2*)
€ **Da Carlo**. Excellent grilled meats, wide assortment of *antipasti*, good choice of wines. You eat in a shady garden in summer. Also rooms if you want to stay. *Viale dei Miti 22, Pergusa, T: 0935 541030.*

PIAZZA ARMERINA
€€€ **Al Fogher**. In an old railway building at the crossroads just before reaching the town, Michelin-starred chef Angelo Treno presents an imaginative blend of tradition and new ideas. Choose ricotta mousse for dessert. Expensive but excellent. Closed Sun evening and Mon. *Contrada Bellia, T:*

0935 684123.

€ **Da Gianna**. Very simple family-run *trattoria*, with slow service because everything is cooked to order: excellent *antipasti*, good fresh fish from Licata, also meat and vegetable dishes; generous helpings. Closed Tues. *Commenda dei Cavalieri di Malta (yellow awning), T: 347 306 4581.*

€ **La Coccinella**. Situated in the modern (north) part of town, this restaurant is worth tracking down for chef Madi's excellent risotto and pasta dishes (especially when fresh fungi are in season), grilled lamb or chicken. Closed Mon. *Via Renato Guttuso 2, T: 0935 682374.*

€ **Bistrot**. Central position for this friendly locale, ideal for a fast lunch stop. Spit-roasted chicken, vegetable *caponata*, pasta, salads, very good bread, also take-away. Closed Wed afternoon. *Via Gabriele d'Annunzio 1/c, T: 342 614 2111.*

€ **Café des Amis**. Close to the Town Hall, a popular café for light lunches, with freshly-made *arancini*, pizza and *cannoli di ricotta*. *Via Marconi 22/24, T: 0935 682072.*

LOCAL SPECIALITIES

AGIRA This town is famous for delicious little pies called *cassatelle*, filled with chocolate, almonds, chick-pea flour, cinnamon and lemon zest. You will find them at **Bottega delle Cassatelle** (*Via Vittorio Emanuele 196*), freshly baked in a traditional wood-fired stone oven. Also restaurant.

CENTURIPE At **Ken Art Ceramica** (*Via Lazio 67, www.kenart.it*) you will find perfect replicas of antique pottery. For very special ice cream and confectionery, unique to Centuripe, go to **Pasticceria Centrale Leanza** (*Piazza Sciacca 11*).

ENNA The historic coffee-house is **Caffé Italia** (*Via Mastro Chiaramonte 12*), for very special coffee, breakfast pastries and granita, also lunches. **Delizia** (*Piazza Duomo 5/6*) offers ice cream in 24 flavours, besides a vast array of pastries. **Campisi** (*Via Trieste 2, Piazza Umberto 22, Via degli Astronauti 27*) runs bakeries where they still make *ciabattina*, miners' bread which lasts a week, and local biscuits.

NICOSIA A coffee-house, tea room and pastry shop offering the traditional pastries of this area is **Caprice** (*Via Nazionale 6, closed Wed*).

PIAZZA ARMERINA Pasticceria Diana (*Piazza Generale Cascino 34*) is famous for the typical local nougat, thin chewy toffee squares with nuts, cherries and candied citron, covered with white or plain chocolate.

SPERLINGA A special cake is made here called *tortone*, with durum wheat flour, olive oil, cinnamon and sugar. Try it at **Bar Li Calzi** (*Via Roma 92*).

FESTIVALS AND EVENTS

AGIRA Christmas Eve, Living Crib, the only one in Italy to take place on Christmas Night, a play and procession involving hundreds of locals, starting in the old town and finishing under the castle (*www.agira.org, www.comuneagira.gov.it*).

AIDONE Palm Sunday, *I Santuni*, procession of 12 giant figures representing the Apostles, each carrying his symbol—keys for St Peter, a fish for St Andrew, a sword for St Matthew.

CERAMI 27–28 August, Procession for St Sebastian, including a cavalcade of riders in Roman costume.

ENNA Holy Week, the religious ceremonies culminate with a Procession of the Confraternities on Good Friday; probably the eeriest of the Easter celebrations in Sicily, because it takes place in total silence. Starting in the afternoon, 2,000 hooded representatives of the 15 corporations solemnly escort the symbols of the Passion through the town, from the church of San Leonardo to the duomo, then to the Addolorata. They wear a wooden number around their necks which is passed down from father to son. First week of June until 2 July, Festivities for the Madonna della Visitazione, which are thought to go back to the ancient rites for Demeter and Persephone. The celebrations begin a month before, finishing with 124 barefoot bearers carrying the statue of the Madonna in procession, on a magnificent float called the *nave d'oro*, the golden ship, made by Scipione di Guido in 1590.

GAGLIANO CASTELFERRATO 29–31 August, Feast of the patron St Cathald, with a procession of farmers riding horses, donkeys and mules carrying branches of laurel to the church for blessing on the first day; the urn with the relics is carried through the town on the second; and finally the statue of the saint.

LEONFORTE Oct, celebrations for the unique late-ripening peaches, *Sagra delle Pesche*, with many gastronomical opportunities (*www.sagradellepesche. it*).

PIAZZA ARMERINA 19 March, Feast of San Giuseppe, with traditional banquets and ornamental loaves. 12–14 August, *Palio dei Normanni*, medieval jousting to celebrate Count Roger's victory over the Saracens. 15 August, Our Lady of the Victories procession: the banner given to Count Roger returns to the cathedral.

PIETRAPERZIA Good Friday, *'U Signuri di li Fasci*, street procession of the Crucifix mounted on top of a tall standard, to which the faithful tie strips of white linen 32m long as ex-votos. 15 August, an hour after midnight, Mass is held in a cave for the Madonna della Cava, followed by an open-air feast.

TROINA 2 January:, Feast of St Sylvester of Troina, during which the crowd is pelted with hazelnuts. This much-loved local saint is also celebrated in May, June and September.

RAGUSA IBLA
The bell-tower of Santa Maria dell'Itria.

Ragusa

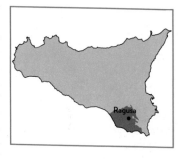

Ragusa and its environs are one of the wealthiest regions of Sicily. The hill towns of the area, devastated by earthquake in the late 17th century, were rebuilt with opulent Sicilian Baroque-style churches and palaces, a concerted architectural accomplishment that represents, in its quality and consistency, a vivid final flowering of the style in Italy. Some of them, such as Ragusa, Modica and Scicli, are now UNESCO World Heritage Sites and apart from their beauty, they enjoy a good reputation for their cuisine and hospitality. The landscape is a limestone plateau, deeply scored by its waterways, which have formed canyons and gorges luxuriant with vegetation in their depths. The uplands provide smooth green pastures, a chequerboard of tidy dry-stone walls, dotted with the intense green, almost black, of the shady carob trees, the shimmering foliage of ancient olives, and the contorted almonds which surround old stone farmhouses, low on the horizon. The limestone rises to form the Monti Iblei (Hyblaean Mountains), named after a great king of the Sicels, Hyblon.

RAGUSA SUPERIORE & RAGUSA IBLA

In the southern part of the Hyblaean mountain range, the town of Ragusa Superiore (*map p. 570, C2*) is an elegant place, laid out after the earthquake of 1693 on a spot chosen by a group of survivors as being more suitable for their new city (the others stayed where they were and rebuilt Ragusa Ibla). It occupies a ridge that runs from west to east between two deep gorges and has expanded across the river gorge to the south, where three breathtaking bridges now connect it to the modern town. On another hill just below it to the east is Ragusa Ibla, an old town of finely carved golden stone, one of the best preserved in Sicily. An intricate maze of stepped streets, it is connected to the upper town by a steep winding road. The two centres have many exceptionally fine Baroque palaces and churches, 18 of which are UNESCO World Heritage Sites.

HISTORY OF RAGUSA

Ragusa Ibla occupies the site of the Sicel *Hybla Heraia*; the Romans called it *Heresium* and the Byzantines *Reusia*; during their rule it was repeatedly attacked by Vandals, Goths and Visigoths. The Arabs refounded it as *Rakkusa*, an important centre for trade and agriculture. The county of Ragusa, created in 1091 by Count Roger for his son Godfrey, was united with that of Modica in 1296 by Manfredi Chiaramonte. The Chiaramontes were succeeded by the Cabrera family, most of whom were disliked by the people of Ragusa, resulting in a rebellion in 1448. Because of this the seat of government was transferred to Modica, which became one of the most important towns in Sicily until 1926. After the Val di Noto earthquake of 1693, which killed 60,000 people, 5,000 of whom were the inhabitants of Ragusa, the wealthy aristocracy, who were devoted to St George, decided to rebuild the town where it was (Ibla), while the equally wealthy middle class, who were devoted to St John the Baptist, decided they wanted a modern city with a rational street plan, and chose a new site to the west (Ragusa Superiore). The two groups, with the encouragement of the clergy, competed in building a large number of beautiful churches (in 1744 there were 41 churches for a population of 15,000), but considerable controversy arose over which of the two could legitimately house the cathedral. Rivalry continued for centuries and because of the friction, the upper and lower towns became separate communities from 1695 to 1703, and from 1865 to 1926, when they were united again as a new provincial capital.

The area is known for its asphalt mines. The limestone impregnated with bitumen hardens quickly in contact with the air, providing an attractive black stone which can be easily worked, while the bitumen itself has been used for paving the streets of many Italian and European cities. Oil was found here in 1953, and there used to be oil wells scattered about the upper town. Drilling now takes place offshore, and the oil is piped from Marina di Ragusa to Augusta. Numerous small farms in the area provide durum wheat, olives, fruit, vegetables, and also milk from the local breed of cattle, Modicana, used for making excellent cheese, especially the famous *caciocavallo*. Close to the sea, where the Arabs cultivated sugar cane, are market gardens, protected by plastic frames in winter and thus in production year-round.

EXPLORING RAGUSA SUPERIORE

THE CATTEDRALE

The monumental, creamy-gold **Cattedrale di San Giovanni Battista**, built after 1694 by Mario Spada of Ragusa and Rosario Boscarino of Modica, has a wide façade with a pretty campanile (*you can climb it every day from 9–12.30 & 4–6*) and spire. It dominates Piazza San Giovanni, at the centre of the well-kept upper town. The Latin-cross interior, suffused with light from the cupola, houses richly decorated chapels and many works of art: paintings, including a canvas of *St Philip Neri* by Sebastiano Conca, gilded stuccoes; marble and wooden statues; and a monumental organ.

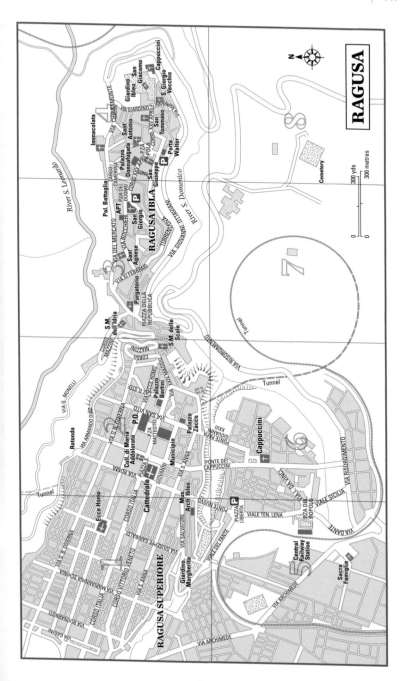

RAGUSA

Fronting the cathedral is a terrace and small garden. Next to the cathedral is the **Diocesan Museum** (*open 9–12.30 & 4–6; T: 0932 621599*), with a precious collection of works of art from the churches, many dating back to before the earthquake. Just beyond the east end of the cathedral is the elegant 18th-century Casa Canonica.

VIA ROMA AND THE MUSEO ARCHEOLOGICO IBLEO

Corso Italia is the handsome, long main street, lined with trees. Opposite the cathedral is the imposing façade of the collegiate church of Santa Maria Addolorata (1801), next to its convent. Uphill, above the cathedral, it crosses Via Roma, which to the north ends in a belvedere, **La Rotonda** (*map 2*), with a view of Ibla and the San Leonardo gorge.

Going south on Via Roma takes you towards **Ponte Nuovo** (1937), which crosses the little Santa Domenica stream high above the public gardens of Villa Margherita. From the bridge, there is a good view (left) of Ponte dei Cappuccini (1835) and Ponte Papa Giovanni XXIII (1964) beyond. Across the bridge is **Piazza Libertà** (*map 5*), with Fascist-era buildings, and the modern town.

Just before the Ponte Nuovo bridge, in a building beneath the road viaduct which also houses the Hotel Mediterraneo, is the **Museo Archeologico Ibleo** (*map 1; open Mon–Sat and 1st Sun of the month 9–7; T: 0932 622963*). The collection displays finds dating from prehistoric to Roman times. In the prehistoric section, the Bronze Age civilisation of Castelluccio is particularly well represented. Pride of place is given to a sculpture known as the *Warrior of Castiglione*, discovered by a farmer in 1999 while ploughing his field north of Ragusa. Made to fit over a door, this carved stone probably stood over the entrance to a warrior's tomb. Castiglione would have been a Sicel centre when this warrior died at the end of the 7th century BC. The relief, carved from a single block of local limestone, shows the warrior on horseback with his shield in front, at one side a bull and at the other a sphinx, probably symbolising his nobility (horse), strength (bull) and wisdom (sphinx). The carving bears an inscription with the name of the warrior, 'Pyrrinos son of Pyttikas', and is signed by the sculptor, Skyllos, very unusual for the time. Another section displays finds from Kamarina from the Archaic to the Classical period, while yet another is dedicated to the inland indigenous centres inhabited by the Sicels; in case 15 is a rare Ionic vase with an inscription in the Sicel language. Further on, a potter's workshop from Scornavacche has been reconstructed (the terracotta figurines are particularly interesting). The Roman section includes finds from Kaukana, and early Christian mosaics from Santa Croce Camerina.

TOWARDS RAGUSA IBLA

Corso Italia descends steeply from Piazza San Giovanni, passing on the right at no. 90 the 18th-century Palazzo Lupis, with ornamented balconies and corbels, to **Piazza Matteotti**. Here is the Municipio (Town Hall; 1880, enlarged 1929) opposite the monumental post office (1930), with colossal statues on the top. In the centre of the square is a large fountain with bronze dolphins.

Corso Italia next crosses Via San Vito in which, on the right, is the fine Baroque **Palazzo Zacco**, with the magnificent family coat of arms on the corner of the building and elaborate balcony corbels. Further down Corso Italia is the late 18th-century **Palazzo Bertini** (no. 35), famous for its three grotesque gargoyles known as *i Tre Potenti*. They are usually interpreted as representing Poverty, Aristocracy and Wealth.

The Corso ends at Via XXIV Maggio, with two palaces at the corner, which narrows and becomes steeper as it begins the descent to Ragusa Ibla (called *iusu* by the local people, meaning 'down'), now seen in its magnificent position on a separate spur. At the foot of an elegant Baroque palace, a small tabernacle recalls a cholera epidemic here in 1838; in front, wide steps descend to an appealing group of houses with courtyards, overlooking the valley. The road continues downhill, passing the pretty **Via Pezza** (left), which runs along the hillside, and **Via Ecce Homo**, which climbs uphill to the left. Via XXIV Maggio ends at the balcony beside the bell-tower of **Santa Maria delle Scale** (*open for Mass only, 7.30, holidays also 11*), where there is a superb bird's-eye view of Ragusa Ibla, with its beautiful expanse of tiled roofs, in various shades of terracotta, grey and gold. The large building on the top of the hill is an old military barracks occupying the site of the castle of the Chiaramonte family. Many fragments of the 15th-century structure of the church of Santa Maria delle Scale survived the 1693 earthquake. Outside, beneath the campanile, is part of a Gothic doorway and the remains of an outside pulpit. Inside is an elaborate Gothic arch decorated with sculptures and (over a side altar) a relief of the *Dormition of the Virgin* in coloured terracotta, by the Gagini school (1538).

RAGUSA IBLA

Crumbling away on its hilltop, with a maze of mysterious, inviting little stepped streets, Ragusa Ibla lends itself to exploration on foot. UNESCO recognition, a new university, and use as a location for an extremely popular Chief Inspector Montalbano TV series, have saved it from depopulation, which was becoming a problem in recent years; many old houses are being restored and there are several delightful small hotels. Ibla can be reached from Ragusa Superiore by the zigzag **Corso Mazzini** (*map 2*), or on foot by various flights of steps. By the road is a relief of the *Flight into Egypt* (15th–16th century), probably once part of a votive tabernacle. Also on the way is the delightful **Palazzo Nicastro** (or Vecchia Cancelleria), erected in 1760 and once the seat of government, with tall pilasters, a decorative doorway, and windows with large balconies.

To the left is the bell-tower and little dome decorated with blue majolica tiles of the church of **Santa Maria dell'Idria** or San Giuliano (*map 3*), built in 1626 for the Knights of Malta, and rebuilt after the earthquake: the cross of the Order can be seen over the doorway. The interior is sumptuously decorated. The Salita Commendatore (once the main street of the town, with 240 steps) continues down, passing (left) the 18th-century **Palazzo Cosentini** (*used for temporary art exhibitions*), with splendid Baroque pilasters, capitals, and more fantastic balconies, the corbels illustrating scenes from daily life, such as a group of travelling minstrels. These are considered the finest Baroque corbels in Ibla. In one corner St Francis of Paola can be seen travelling over to Sicily on his cloak. In 1464 the saint had been refused passage by the boatmen and used his cloak and staff to sail safely across the Straits of Messina with his companions. Franz Liszt composed a piece inspired by the miracle. The main façade is on Corso Mazzini, which continues right to Piazza della Repubblica at the foot of the hill.

To the left of the 17th-century church of the **Purgatorio** (*map 3*; the bell-tower was built on top of the old walls of the pre-earthquake city), Via del Mercato leads up around the left side of the hill with a view of the massive Baroque Palazzo Sortino Trono above the road. Further on it continues left past the old market building and has splendid views over the unspoilt San Leonardo valley.

Via XI Febbraio, peaceful and well paved, forks right off Via del Mercato for the centre of Ibla. On a bend there is a view (left) of the hillside traced with characteristic dry-stone walls. Via Sant'Agnese continues left, and then steps lead up to the wide Via Tenente Di Stefano near the church of Sant'Agnese. It continues uphill and soon narrows with a good view ahead of the dome of San Giorgio. On the left are the six delightful balconies of **Palazzo La Rocca**. It has an interesting double staircase in black asphalt stone, and a little garden with citrus trees.

DUOMO DI SAN GIORGIO

Via Di Stefano continues round the side of the cathedral into the charmingly asymmetrical Piazza del Duomo, planted with a row of palm trees, and then slopes up to the magnificent three-tiered golden façade of the Duomo di San Giorgio (*map 3*), designed by Rosario Gagliardi in 1744, standing above a flight of steps enclosed by a beautifully crafted 19th-century balustrade, the work of Angelo Paradiso of Acireale, a much sought-after artisan. The Neoclassical **dome** (hidden by the façade but visible from the road behind or from the extreme left side of the piazza), 43m high, was constructed in 1820 by Carmelo Cutraro, a local craftsman, who modelled his design on that of the Pantheon in Paris.

The **interior** (*entered by one of the side doors*), with a central nave and two side aisles, is lit by the impressive dome which rises above its high drum with windows between the coupled columns. The stained glass dates from 1926. In the south aisle, above the side door (and behind glass), is an equestrian statue of St George; on the third altar is *The Immaculate Virgin* by Vito D'Anna (c. 1729–69), and on the fourth altar, *Rest on the Flight into Egypt* (1864) by Dario Guerci. In the north transept is *St George and the Dragon*, also by Dario Guerci. In the sacristy is a lovely stone tabernacle with the equestrian statue of St George between Sts Hippolytus and Mercurius, with ruined reliefs below; and Rosario Gagliardi's original plans for the duomo. By the west door is a stone statue of St George by the Gagini school. The organ in the nave is by the Serassi brothers of Bergamo.

The **museum** (*open Sat and Sun 10.30–12.30 & 3–7, T: 0932 220085 or 348 101 1019*) highlights interesting works of art, vestments and Church silver.

ALONG CORSO XXV APRILE

Palazzo Arezzi Bertini forms an attractive corner of Piazza Duomo, with a wide arch passing over a side street; it has a charming secret garden. At the lower end of the piazza is a charming little fountain and the handsome Palazzo Veninata (early

DUOMO DI SAN GIORGIO

20th century). The Neoclassical **Circolo di Conversazione** (c. 1850), at Via Alloro 5, which preserves an interesting interior, houses an exclusive private members' club. The carved sphinxes over the doorways, symbolising wisdom, supposedly refer to the intelligent conversations being held within. Next to it is **Palazzo Donnafugata** with its delightful little Moorish wooden balcony, from which it was possible to watch passers-by in the street below without being seen. The palace contains a private art collection formed in the mid-19th century by Corrado Arezzo de Spuches (*see p. 331*) and a little theatre built in the late 19th century (150 seats) where public performances are sometimes held (*to request visit of the Circolo di Conversazione, the theatre of Palazzo Donnafugata, and the garden of Palazzo Arezzi Bertini, call Dottoressa Clorinda Arezzo on T: 333 750 5789 or Ragusa Infotourist on T: 0932 684780 or 0932 684781*).

The wide Corso XXV Aprile continues to **Piazza Pola** (*map 4*) with the splendid tall Baroque façade of the church of **San Giuseppe** (1590, reconstructed in the 18th century by the Carmelite monk Fra' Alberto Maria di San Giovanni Battista). In the oval domed interior there are still the raised galleries once used by the nuns. The beautiful floor is made with black asphalt, mined locally, while the unusual altars along the sides are made of shiny painted glass. In the centre of the dome is a painting of the *Glory of St Benedict* by Sebastiano Lo Monaco (1793). Above the high altar, in an elaborate frame, is the *Holy Family* by Matteo Battaglia. The side altarpieces include a *Holy Trinity* by Giuseppe Cristadoro.

Corso XXV Aprile continues to wind downhill past the closed church of the Maddalena and the high wall of the church of **San Tommaso**, which has a photogenic bell-tower. In the oval interior is an unusual font in black asphalt (1545) and a masterpiece by Vito D'Anna: *Our Lady of Carmel*.

GIARDINO IBLEO PUBLIC GARDENS

Just beyond San Tommaso, beside the church of St Vincent Ferrer (now an events hall), is the entrance to the **Giardino Ibleo** (*map 4; open 8–8*) or Villa Comunale, a public garden laid out in 1858, with a splendid palm avenue, goldfish pool, flower beds, and wide views over the Irminio Valley. It contains three small churches. Beyond the colourful campanile of St Vincent Ferrer is **San Giacomo**, founded in the 14th century with a façade of 1902. At the bottom of the garden is the 17th-century church of the **Cappuccini**, with a simple interior, and a very fine altarpiece, a triptych by Pietro Novelli of the *Madonna with Angels and Saints*, considered to be his greatest work. Pietro Novelli had fled to Ragusa after offending the court of Philip IV of Spain; the Capuchin monks, having been 'voted to poverty', were far from supportive of the monarchy and gave him refuge here. In return the artist created this masterpiece for them, including the imprisoned Sts Barbara and Agatha in his painting, perhaps reflecting his own concerns. It is still in its original minutely-carved frame. The attached convent is now the seat of a restoration laboratory; the city library occupies part of the building.

In an orchard below the balustrade are **late antique hypogea** carved into the rock. Outside the entrance to the gardens, in Via Normanni, is the 15th-century Gothic side portal of the church of **San Giorgio Vecchio** (*map 4*), with a relief of St George behind a little garden. The church, which was very large, was completely destroyed in the earthquake of 1693 but this portal has become the symbol of the town of Ibla.

NORTH OF PIAZZA POLA

From Piazza Pola, with a view of the top of the façade of San Giorgio and its dome, Via Orfanotrofio leads past the church of **Sant'Antonio** (*map 4*), with remains of a Gothic portal next to a little Baroque side doorway. Just beyond is the 18th-century Palazzo di Quattro, with a balcony along the whole length of its façade.

A road descends on the left past Santa Teresa to reach the **Immacolata**, with a fine campanile. It contains interesting works in asphalt stone. Its Gothic portal stands in Piazza Chiaramonte, in a little garden of orange trees. The narrow Via Chiaramonte leads up past the campanile to the rear side of **Palazzo Battaglia** (no. 40; *map 3*), a very original building with two completely different façades. You can see the main façade beyond the arch on the left, on Via Orfanotrofio, leading to the church of the **Annunziata**. This church houses the oldest bell in the city, dated 1501.

PORTA WALTER

A road leads out of the other side of the Piazza del Duomo, under the arch of Palazzo Arezzi Bertini, to (left) the Salita Ventimiglia (steps) which lead down to the simple façade and rich portal of the church of **Santa Maria di Gesù**. The interior has stuccoes and frescoes by Matteo Battaglia (1750).

Behind the church is the **Porta Walter** (1644), the only one of Ibla's five ancient gates to have survived the earthquake and subsequent developments. It is a Romanesque arch, about 5m high and 3m wide, with a very faded Latin inscription. The origin of the name is uncertain. Along the road outside it are some old houses carved into the rock.

MODICA

Modica (*map p. 570, C3*) is an unusual town divided into two parts, Modica Bassa (lower town) and Modica Alta (upper town), with decorative palm trees and elegant Baroque buildings, which bases its economy on the rich agriculture of its hinterland. The lower town occupies a valley at the confluence of two rivers, which were channelled and covered over in 1902 after a disastrous flood. On the steep spur between them the upper town rises in terraces above the dramatic church of San Giorgio. There is a sharp contrast between the ample main streets, built over the rivers, and the tiny alleys and courtyards of the six ancient city districts, still perfectly intact, each with its own distinctive character: Francavilla, behind the castle, a populous district reminiscent of an Arab kasbah; Cartellone, once the Jewish Ghetto, between Corso Umberto and Via Vittorio Veneto; Corpo di Terra, the district around St Peter's, with handsome houses and gardens; Malvaxia, a very poor district, also called Vignazza, on the Gigante hill opposite Porta d'Anselmo; Casale, the 'modern' district, with steep cobbled streets, behind Piazza Matteotti; and Porta d'Anselmo, a poor district under the castle, where until recently many people still lived in cave-houses.

HISTORY OF MODICA

The site of Modica was first occupied by the Sicels, then by the Greeks and the Romans; becoming an important centre in Byzantine times. Under the Normans it became a county, one of the most powerful fiefs of the Middle Ages, and passed from the Chiaramonte in 1392 to the Spanish Cabrera family. It controlled Ragusa, Comiso, Chiaramonte Gulfi, Scicli, Spaccaforno (now Ispica), Pozzallo, Vittoria, Monterosso and Giarratana, and reached its maximum splendour in the 16th century; at the end of the 17th century Modica was the fourth largest town in Sicily. It owed its prosperity to a particular custom of renting out the land to the peasants on a long-term basis, which was to prove extremely profitable both for the landowners, who were assured of a regular income, and for the farm workers themselves, who found they could make improvements and invest for the future. Like many towns in this corner of Sicily, it had to be rebuilt after the earthquake of 1693. There has always been considerable rivalry between the two churches of San Giorgio and San Pietro, both of which aspired to the role of Chiesa Madre; after the earthquake, the king expressly forbade the people to rebuild both churches, in the hope they would build only one, dedicated to both saints, but in the course of time the ban was forgotten—and so, fortunately, was the rivalry. After 1704 Modica came through Spanish connections to the seventh Duke of Berwick and Alba. For many centuries Modica was known as the 'Venice of Sicily', both for its rivers, then in use as waterways, and for the intellectual fervour of its inhabitants.

Modica was the birthplace of the Nobel prize-winning poet Salvatore Quasimodo (1901–68). Also born here was the doctor and philosopher Tommaso Campailla (1668–1740), one of a number of physicians who attempted to cure syphilis with (equally deadly) mercury. Campailla's method involved placing his patients in previously heated wooden barrels to absorb mercurial fumes. He is buried in San Giorgio.

CORSO UMBERTO

The main street of Modica Bassa is **Corso Umberto**, unusually wide because it occupies the bed of a river, covered over in 1902. Lined with handsome 18th- and 19th-century palaces, it provides a splendid view of the monumental church of San Giorgio (*see p. 318*), halfway up the hillside between the lower and upper town. On the extreme right, on top of a bare rockface, the round tower surmounted by a clock is all that remains of the castle of the counts of Modica. Secret tunnels (*not accessible*) run from the castle to the river and to the church of Santa Maria di Betlemme.

SAN PIETRO AND THE MUSEO ARCHEOLOGICO BELGIORNO

A monumental flight of steps, decorated with statues of the apostles, leads up from the Corso to the elegant flat façade of the church of **San Pietro** (*open 9–1 & 3.30–7; June and Sept 9–8, July 9–8.30, Aug 9–9; T: 0932 941074*), rebuilt after the earthquake of 1693, and provided with a balcony. The vast interior presents a central nave and two aisles separated by 14 columns with Corinthian capitals. In the south aisle is a large chapel with a splendid *Madonna of Trapani* by the Gagini school, while a little further along on the same aisle is a sculpted group by Benedetto Civiletti of *St Peter and the Paralysed Man* (1893).

To the right of the church is the inconspicuous entrance to a grotto used for many years as a storeroom. Three layers of frescoes were discovered here in 1989, the earliest of which may date from the 11th century. They decorated the ancient church of **San Nicolò Inferiore** (*open 10–1 & 4–7; T: 331 740 3045, Etnos*). The baptismal font carved into the rock is very unusual.

In front of the church, at Corso Umberto 149, in Palazzo della Cultura, is the **Museo Civico Archeologico Belgiorno** (*open winter Tues–Sun 9–1 & 3.30–7.30, summer Tues–Sun 10–1 & 5–8*), with an archaeological collection arranged in chronological order from the Neolithic onwards, with finds from Cava d'Ispica and Modica; pride of place is given to the *Ercole di Cafeo* (the 'Herakles Alexikakos', 3rd century BC), a bronze statuette found locally in 1967. The hero's hair and his lion-skin cloak are marvellously portrayed; so well, in fact, that many scholars believe that the sculptor could be Lysippus or a member of his school.

TEATRO GARIBALDI AND VIA MARCHESA TEDESCHI

By turning right along Corso Umberto after coming down the steps in front of San Pietro, you will see the Neoclassical façade of the opera house, **Teatro Garibaldi** (*open Tues–Sun 9–1 & 4–8; T: 0932 946991*), with a lovely interior, recently restored and embellished inside with paintings by Piero Guccione.

In the centre of the town, at the former confluence of the two rivers, the Corso forms a fork with the broad **Via Marchesa Tedeschi**, also on the site of a riverbed. Here is the Town Hall, the ex-convent of the 16th-century church of San Domenico (*crypt open 9–1 & 4–7, closed Sun afternoon*), once the seat of the Inquisition. At Via San Domenico 1 is a small museum dedicated to local poet Salvatore Quasimodo, the **Stanza della Poesia** (*request visit at the Casa-Museo, see below*), where you can listen to some of Quasimodo's poems. On the other side of the Corso, in Via De Leva, is a fine Arab-Norman doorway in a little garden, probably once part of a 13th-century palace. Also in Via Marchesa Tedeschi is the simple façade of a national monument, the church of **Santa Maria di Betlemme** (*open as San Pietro, see above; T: 0932 941470*), which incorporates four preceding churches including a beautiful chapel called the Cappella Palatina, built in the 15th century by the Cabrera. At the entrance is a stone with an inscription, indicating the level reached by the flood waters in 1902. The elaborate crib (1881) in the left aisle was modelled to represent Modica by Benedetto Papale, a Capuchin friar; he entrusted the task of making the 60 terracotta figurines to the well-known atelier of Vaccaro in Caltagirone.

On the other side of the Town Hall, Corso Umberto continues past **Piazza Matteotti**. Here is the 13th-century church of the **Carmine** (*open 9–12.30 & 3–7, closed Sun and holidays*) with a warm creamy façade, fine rose window and Gothic portal. The second north altar contains a superb marble group of the *Annunciation* by Antonino Gagini. Nearby is the Art Nouveau ex-Cinema Moderno, now a public hall.

MUSEUMS OF THE PALAZZO DEI MERCEDARI

Corso Umberto ends at Viale Medaglie d'Oro above which, in Via Mercè, is the majestic, but unfinished, sanctuary church of **Santa Maria delle Grazie** next to its huge former convent, the Palazzo dei Mercedari, designated to become the seat of the civic museums. On the top floor, in the lovely vaulted rooms of the old convent, is the **Museo Ibleo delle Arti e delle Tradizioni Popolari S.A. Guastella** (*entrance from Via Mercè, closed for restoration*). This fascinating ethnological collection of artisans' tools and utensils is displayed in reconstructed workshops (such as a smithy, shoemaker's shop, basketry store, chocolate laboratory, cartwright's shop, saddlery and carpenter's workroom). A typical farmhouse has also been faithfully reconstructed, and there is a collection of Sicilian carts.

MODICA ALTA

Roads and steps continue steeply uphill to the highest point of Modica Alta. The main street, **Corso Regina Margherita**, is lined with handsome 18th- and 19th-century palaces. At the highest point of the hill another monumental flight of steps leads up to its most important church, **San Giovanni Battista**, which occupies the site of a preceding church and Benedictine monastery, one of the six founded in Sicily by St Gregory in the 6th century. The top of the bell-tower represents the highest point in Modica (449m), from where it is possible to spot Malta on a clear day. The Baroque façade was erected in 1839. In another part of the upper town, in Piazza del Gesù at the end of Via Don Bosco (which can be reached by taking the alley to the right of San Giovanni), is the elaborate doorway (1478) of the church of **Santa Maria di Gesù**.

> ## MODICA CHOCOLATE
>
> During the 16th century, cocoa beans imported from Mexico by the Cabrera family were made into chocolate by the confectioners of Modica, using the ancient Aztec method of slowly grinding the beans between two stones to avoid overheating, and then adding maize. Elsewhere in Europe the method of manufacture evolved rapidly to industrialise the product, improve the flavour and lower the cost. In Modica, however, the method is still basically the same, the only difference being that sugar instead of maize is added towards the end of the grinding operation, giving a typical grainy consistency to the finished product. Natural flavourings are also added, such as cinnamon, vanilla, orange essence or chilli pepper.

SAN GIORGIO

The imposing **church of San Giorgio** (*open 9–8*), built from the 11th century–1848, is mostly the work of local stonemasons, directed later by the architect Paolo Labisi and dedicated to the patron saint of Modica Alta. It is reached from Corso Garibaldi, which runs parallel to Corso Umberto. Some 250 steps (completed in 1834) ascend to the church, built in pale honey-coloured stone. The façade is one of the most remarkable Baroque works in Italy. It has five original doorways and a very tall, central bell-tower. In the interior, with double side aisles and a central nave, the apse is filled with a large polyptych with episodes from the Gospel and the life of St George, attributed to Bernardino Niger (1573). The silver high altar was made in 1705. In the south aisle is a 16th-century painting of the *Nativity* and (on the second altar) an *Assumption* (1610) by Filippo Paladini, comparable in quality with his canvases in the cathedral at Enna. In the chapel to the right of the presbytery is a much-venerated equestrian statue of St George, while in that to the left of the presbytery is a statue of the *Madonna of the Snow* (1511) by Giuliano Mancino and Bartolomeo Berrettaro. There is a meridian on the floor of the transept, traced by the mathematician Armando Perini in 1895. The fine Serassi organ dates from 1886–8. Among the treasures of the church is a silver ark with the relics of St George, made in Venice in the 14th century. On completion in 1848, the happy parishioners placed a plaque over the main doorway with the words Mater Ecclesia (Chiesa Madre), to put an end once and for all to the rivalry with San Pietro.

Left of San Giorgio is the 18th-century **Palazzo Polara**, which houses the civic art gallery and from which there is a fine view of the lower town and the hillside beyond. Uphill behind San Giorgio, on Corso Francesco Crispi, is the Baroque **Palazzo Tomasi-Rossi**, with attractive carved balconies—the caryatids are said to be portraits of the owner.

The poet Salvatore Quasimodo (1901–68) was born at Via Posterla 84, just under the castle clock. It is possible to visit his house at no. 5, **Casa-Museo Salvatore Quasimodo** (*open Tues–Sun 10–1 & 4–7; T: 331 740 3045, Etnos*). Together with Eugenio Montale, Quasimodo is considered the most important of Italy's 'hermetic' poets. He worked for many years in northern Italy as a surveyor, where his intense homesickness for Sicily inspired many of his most beautiful poems, which are written in a characteristic lyrical style. He was awarded the Nobel Prize in 1959.

SOUTHEAST OF RAGUSA

The attractive countryside southeast of Ragusa and Modica is well cultivated, with low dry-stone walls between fields of pastureland and crops, and small farmhouses built of the local grey stone. Scicli is a bustling Baroque market town. Ispica is built on chalk, which, through the centuries, has been tunnelled for tombs and dwellings.

SCICLI

Described by Elio Vittorini, author of the lyrical anti-Fascist novel *Conversations in Sicily* (1941), as 'the most beautiful town in the world', Scicli (*map p. 570, C3*) has occupied the floor of its valley, surrounded by rocky cliffs, since the 14th century. Prosperous under the Saracens (when it was known as *Siklì*), it was taken by the Normans after a tremendous battle in which, according to legend, the Madonna herself took part. Prosperous again today thanks to its production of flowers and vegetables (especially date tomatoes), it is another of the region's charming Baroque towns rebuilt after the 1693 earthquake, now enjoying UNESCO recognition. The area known as Chiafura, around the site of the old medieval town on the hillside, dominated by the church of San Matteo (and abandoned after the 1693 earthquake), is a good place for some gentle trekking, especially in spring. There are many caves, once used as homes and the area provides a setting for theatre performances, concerts and exhibitions during the summer.

PIAZZA ITALIA

Piazza Italia, planted with trees and surrounded by Neoclassical buildings, is a favourite meeting-place for the people of Scicli. The 18th-century **duomo** (*open 8.30–12.30 & 4–9, T: 0932 931278*), dedicated to St Ignatius and to St William of Noto, who is the patron saint of the town, has a richly ornate façade. The interior, a central nave with two aisles, is bright with gilded stuccoes and frescoes by local artists. Here also you will find the brilliantly coloured *papier-mâché* statue of the *Madonna delle Milizie*, which is carried in procession in May (*see p. 341*).

Opposite is the Baroque **Palazzo Fava**, with a large entrance, flanked by elaborate columns on plinths, surmounted by Corinthian capitals crowned with cherubs. On top of the arch is a mysterious face with acanthus leaves for hair. The balconies are splendid, especially those looking out over Via San Bartolomeo, with corbels shaped into galloping horses, winged dragons and mythical creatures ridden by cherubs. The area which opens out in front of the only church in Scicli to survive the earthquake, **San Bartolomeo** (15th century; *open 10.30–1.30 & 4.30–8.30*), in front of a rockface, was created in 1824 when the San Bartolomeo stream was covered. The pastel-coloured façade, topped with a cupola, was built at the beginning of the 19th century by Salvatore Alì; the single-nave interior was decorated with stuccoes by the Gianforma, father and son. There is a monumental crib with 29 almost life-size statues by Pietro Padula (1773–5). It comes from Naples and the figures (some of them dating back to 1573; there were originally 65) are carved in limewood.

VIA NAZIONALE, VIA PENNA AND THE MUSEUMS
Via Nazionale leads uphill and on the right, at the end of a short street, is the corner of **Palazzo Beneventano**. The most famous building in Scicli, described by art historian Anthony Blunt as 'Sicily's most beautiful Baroque palace', it was designed not by an architect but by local master builders. It has elaborate balconies supported by fantastic creatures as well as the unusual addition of a richly decorated zigzag design running up one corner: on the top are two Moors and at the bottom is St Joseph.

Off the other side of Via Nazionale is the decorative central street, **Via Mormino Penna**. The relatively sombre Town Hall (1906; *the mayor's office is open 10.30–1.30 & 3.30–6.30, closed Mon*) stands next to the elegant church of **San Giovanni** (*open 10.30–1.30 & 4.30–8.30*) with a fine façade. Via Penna winds on past the oval church of **San Michele** (*open 10.30–1.30 & 4.30–8.30*), past **Palazzo Spadaro** (*entrance from Via Spadaro 25, open 10–1 & 4.30–7.30, late opening in summer*), with its splendid wrought-iron balconies and elegant carved stone window frames, which houses the delightful **Museo della Cucina Iblea**, illustrating the ingredients, equipment and techniques at the heart of the local cuisine. The palace also houses the **Museo della Bardatura** (*open 10–1 & 4.30–7.30*) dedicated to the intricate craft of weaving fresh wallflowers and wild lilies to make the beautiful coats for the horses that take part in the annual cavalcade of St Joseph (*see p. 341*). In the same building (*entrance from Via Mormino Penna 24*) is the old-fashioned chemist's shop that often features in the Montalbano series, the **Antica Farmacia Cartia** (*open 10–1 & 4.30–7.30, late opening in summer; T: 338 861 4973*), founded in 1902, with the original apothecary jars and containers, their contents still intact, the precision scales and the till. Close to Palazzo Spadaro is the interesting façade of the church of **Santa Teresa** (*open 10–1 & 4–8*), built for the nuns of St Clare and now used as a public hall; the stuccoes in the interior are remarkable.

The street continues to **Piazza Busacca**, planted with trees and flowers. In the centre is a 19th-century statue by Benedetto Civiletti of the rich local merchant and philanthropist Pietro Di Lorenzo Busacca (d. 1567). Here is the church of the **Carmine** (1751–69; *open 10.30–1.30 & 4.30–8.30*), beside its convent (1386) with a decorative balcony. **Palazzo Busacca** (1882), surmounted by a clock between two mermaids, is now used as council offices. Inside, the rooms are still decorated with wonderful frescoes and stuccoes, and 18th-century paintings. Beyond, to the right, is the elegant church of **Santa Maria della Consolazione** (*open 10.30–1.30 & 4.30–8.30*), once dedicated to St Thomas; with a wooden statue (1560) of Christ at the Column.

Still further on, surrounded by a rocky crag in an interesting part of the old town, is the large church of **Santa Maria La Nova** (15th century; *open 10.30–1.30 & 4.30–8.30*). The Neoclassical façade dates from 1816. In the stuccoed interior there is a high altarpiece of the *Birth of the Virgin* by Sebastiano Conca. The presbytery was designed by the Neoclassical architect Giuseppe Venanzio Marvuglia. Among the paintings is a particularly beautiful *Immaculate Virgin* by Vito D'Anna; there is also a Gaginesque marble statue of the Madonna. On the second north altar is a highly venerated statue of the *Madonna della Pietà*, made of cypress wood and thought to be Byzantine.

THE SICILIAN BAROQUE

Characterised by a strong sense of movement and theatrical handling of space, the Baroque was the dominant European style of architecture during the 17th and early 18th centuries. It achieved distinctive expression in southeastern Sicily after the earthquake of 11th January 1693. Within half a century more than 100 towns and villages, including some 600 churches, were rebuilt in this triumphant style, an exceptional legacy thanks to the experience and traditions of the native craftsmen, the flair of the architect and the beautiful colour of the hard local limestone. Formerly dubbed 'Sicilian Rococo', the style is now recognised as late Baroque, an idiosyncratic continuation of the mid-17th-century Italian style perfected in Rome by Bernini and Borromini. Streets and squares are arranged as theatre sets for the populace to act out their lives. Carefully detailed carvings on balcony corbels and around windows attest to the skill of the stonemasons and sculptors. Faces can be portraits of members of the family, or enigmatic monsters. Garlands of flowers and leaves, birds and animals, dragons, hippogryphs, cherubs and harpies, jostle for space, each with their own significance often carefully discussed with the owner before commencing the work. The churches have imposing façades, playing daring games with convex and concave curves, light and shade, the lines drawing our gaze up from the opulent stairways to the highest pinnacles. The dazzling interiors are decorated with gold and silver, inlaid marble, paintings, stuccoes and statues; the people of southeast Sicily certainly did their best for the saints whom they hoped would ward off further catastrophes.

FROM SCICLI TO THE SEA

Southwest of Scicli is the town's natural harbour, the simple little fishing village of **Donnalucata**. The name refers to the appearance of the Madonna one night in 1091 'bathed in light', and fully armed, to take part in Roger I's battle against the Saracens. To the east, near **Cava d'Aliga**, is a usually deserted sandy bay, perfect for swimming.

ISPICA

The small town of Ispica (*map p. 570, C3*) was rebuilt on its present site after the earthquake of 1693 destroyed the former town on the valley floor. It has fine 18th- and 19th-century buildings. Known in the Middle Ages as Spaccaforno, derived from

Ispicae Fundus, it re-adopted its old name in 1935. The chalk eminence on which it stands is pierced with tombs and cave dwellings. These can best be seen in the **Parco della Forza** at the south end of the Cava d'Ispica (*described on p. 324 but best approached from the town itself*).

THE TOWN CENTRE

In the new town centre, Piazza Regina Margherita is dominated by the elegant lines of the **Chiesa Madre** (*T: 950531*), dedicated to St Bartholomew.

Nearby is a national monument, the church of **Santa Maria Maggiore** (*T: 0932 951132*), an attractive building by Vincenzo Sinatra of Noto (or perhaps Rosario Gagliardi), with a daring semi-elliptical loggia around it inspired by the colonnaded porticoes in front of St Peter's in Rome. The startling interior is decorated with 18th-century frescoes painted by Olivio Sozzi during the last two years of his life. He included in his scheme a self-portrait in the central apse as one of the elderly Apostles admiring the Ascension. The large (40m square) fresco on the vault, with scenes from the Old and New Testaments, is considered his masterpiece, while the whole group of 26 frescoes is one of the most important in Sicily. Over the main altar is a luminous canvas of the *Madonna*, by Vito D'Anna while to the right of the altar is a panel painting of the *Madonna of the Rosary*, dated 1567, by an unknown follower of Polidoro da Caravaggio or Vincenzo da Pavia. The most venerated chapel is that dedicated to Christ at the Column, in the north transept, with a very ancient Crucifix, thought to be miraculous, and brought from the preceding church after the 1693 earthquake, which it survived. The brightly painted soldiers, made of wood and *papier mâché*, were added in 1729 by Francesco Guarino, a sculptor from Noto. Near the main door is the Casa della Cera, a room containing many of the wax figurines which it is customary to offer as ex-votos to Christ at the Column; there is also a glass case containing the body of Olivio Sozzi.

Palazzo Bruno di Belmonte, an Art Nouveau building (the finest in the province) by Ernesto Basile (1906) has been restored as the Town Hall. The most imposing building in the town is the 1704 church of the **Annunziata** (*T: 0932 951219*), with its theatrical façade; it is filled with stuccoes carried out in the mid-18th century by Giuseppe Gianforma. In the sacristy is a 17th-century painting of *St Andrew Avellino* with marked chiaroscuro. Mounted on one of the side walls is the head of a bull, supposedly the cause of a miraculous event in the 18th century: a child wearing a red cloak was attacked and carried off on the horns of this bull, which suddenly stopped and knelt down in front of the church, allowing the little boy to escape unscathed.

A little road leads 8km to the south of Ispica, to its inviting beach of golden sand at **Santa Maria di Focallo** (*map p. 570, C3*), awarded the EU Blue Banner for quality.

CAVA D'ISPICA AND PARCO DELLA FORZA

The **Cava d'Ispica** (*open April–mid-Oct daily 9–6.30; mid-Oct–March Mon–Sat and 1st Sun of the month 9–1.15; T: 0932 771667*) lies 11km east of Modica (signposted). It is a deep gorge 13km long which follows a river (now usually dry) with luxuriant

ISPICA
Assumption of the Virgin and St Michael Expelling Lucifer from Paradise:
fresco of 1763–5 by Olivio Sozzi in Santa Maria Maggiore.

vegetation (many rare terrestrial orchids in early spring). It is also an interesting place for birdwatchers, who might see sparrow hawks, buzzards, kestrels, jays and colonies of ravens. The sides of the canyon are honeycombed with prehistoric tombs, early Christian rock-hewn churches and medieval cave-dwellings; here the presence of man can be traced from the earliest times to the most recent, although the valley was greatly damaged in the earthquake of 1693.

Just below the entrance are extensive Christian catacombs known as **Larderia** (4th–5th centuries AD). They extend for some 36m inside the rock and contain 464 tombs. Across the main road is the little church of **San Nicola** (*unlocked on request*), which contains very damaged traces of late Byzantine (possibly early Norman) frescoes. A path near here leads along the dry riverbed to **Baravitalla**, with tombs dating from the Castelluccio period (1800 BC) and one with a design of pilasters on its façade.

From the entrance a gravel road (c. 400m) leads past numerous caves, including some on more than one storey, ruined by the earthquake. Outside the enclosure an overgrown path runs along the valley passing numerous **rock-tombs and dwellings** including the so-called Castello on four floors.

At the far end is the **Parco della Forza**, best approached from Ispica, along Via Cavagrande (*open as for Cava d'Ispica, see above; T: 0932 952608*). It has lush vegetation, water-cisterns, tombs and churches, all carved out of the rock, and a remarkable tunnel known as the Centoscale ('Hundred Stairs'), 60m long, formerly used by people carrying water from the river to the town. The museum displays a notable collection of finds from the site, including amphorae, pottery sherds and Bronze Age tools.

Further along the valley is the area known as **Ispicae Fundus**, with more interesting caves and churches and part of the old main street, which was paved with slabs of limestone.

POZZALLO

Pozzallo (*map p. 570, C3*) is a busy port with a prominent square tower, **Torre Cabrera** (*closed*), built by the Cabreras in the 15th century as a *palatium*, their personal residence and centre for controlling merchandise for export. It was reconstructed after 1693 and is now a national monument. The port, already well known in Roman times for the abundant springs of fresh water in the vicinity, was used in the Middle Ages as the loading point for shipping the enormous quantities of wheat grown in the county to various destinations. Now the hinterland is acquiring importance for the production of carobs, while the harbour is increasingly used both for trade and tourism—there is a daily catamaran service for Malta. The lovely beaches, awarded the EU Blue Banner, are hidden behind tree-covered dunes where cane fences control the sand. Giorgio La Pira, the *sindaco santo* (saintly mayor), who for many years was mayor of Florence, was born in Pozzallo. A great politician, he played an important role in the formulation of the Italian Constitution after the Second World War; but it was his efforts to secure conciliation between different religions and his campaigns on behalf of the poor that won him a reputation for saintliness (the Vatican is evaluating his case).

WEST OF RAGUSA

The small towns of Vittoria, Comiso and Santa Croce Camerina have fine Baroque and Art Nouveau buildings and the surrounding countryside is beautiful. Traditional ways of life have been preserved here, involving the production of wine, olive oil, vegetables and limestone for paving.

VITTORIA

Vittoria (*map p. 570, B2*) is a prosperous agricultural town and centre of the wine trade, especially for the famous Cerasuolo di Vittoria, the only Sicilian wine in the DOCG category. It was built in 1607 for, and named after, Vittoria Colonna, daughter of the viceroy Marcantonio Colonna and wife of Luigi III Enriquez, Count of Modica. Constructed according to a grid plan on a large plain overlooking the Ippari, a small river bordered by pine forests, it escaped the 1693 earthquake with little damage but a tragic death-toll: the Chiesa Madre collapsed, killing 40 children at a prayer service.

THE OPERA HOUSE AND CHIESA MADRE

In the main square, Piazza del Popolo, the elegant Neoclassical **Teatro Vittoria Colonna** (1877; *T: 0932 861517*), with 384 seats, particularly admired by Bernard Berenson, stands next to the church of the **Madonna delle Grazie**, with an attractive Baroque façade of 1754, complete with a clock. The simple interior has polychrome marble altars along the sides, with 18th-century wooden statues and canvases.

From here, the central Via Cavour, with its Art Nouveau buildings and enticing shop windows, leads to the rectangular, shady Piazza Ricca and the **Chiesa Madre**, San Giovanni Battista, dedicated to the patron saint of Vittoria, with an unusual Moorish façade and dome (18th–19th centuries). The four bells in the tower are dedicated to St John the Baptist, Our Lady of Carmel, St Rosalia and St Victoria, all of whom were thought to be suitable patron saints for the town when it was founded; the four names were placed in an urn and drawn out by a blindfolded child. John the Baptist came out three times running. The Latin-cross interior, divided into a nave and two aisles by Corinthian columns, is richly decorated with gilded stucco, marble inlay, statues and 17th–19th-century paintings. The marble floor in front of the main altar was completed with an interesting ex-voto in the 19th century. It shows two vases of grapes: the one on the right, dated 1798, is a withered vine, while that on the left, dated 1801, is flourishing, a reference to a terrible blight which destroyed the local vineyards and their miraculous recovery only three years later, thanks to the intercession of the saint. The wooden statue of St John the Baptist over the main altar is by an unknown sculptor who has depicted him as black and wearing camel skins. To the right of the main altar, under the large canvas of the *Beheading of St John the Baptist* (1600, ?Mario Minniti), is an urn with the remains of Vittoria Colonna, brought here from Spain in 1991. The magnificent organ (1748) is by Donato Del Piano.

THE MUSEUMS

The **Museo di Arte Sacra Monsignor Federico La China** (*open Mon–Fri 9–1*) at Via Cavour 51, contains a collection of material from the Chiesa Madre (stone carvings, sculptures and fragments of altars), together with fine examples of 18th-century Sicilian gold- and silverwork.

Among the Art Nouveau palaces in the town, perhaps the finest is **Palazzo Traina**, on Via Rosario Cancellieri, in the Venetian-Gothic style, a good example of the skill of the local stonemasons. The **Museo Civico**, at Piazza Enriquez 15, occupies the oldest building in town, once the castle of Vittoria Colonna. Its exhibition space was undergoing restoration at the time of writing. In the meantime it had become a temporary wine shop dedicated to local vintages.

In Via Garibaldi, the former prisoner-of-war camp, where some 20,000 Austro-Hungarian soldiers were imprisoned in 1916, the largest of such camps in Sicily, is the interesting **Museo Storico Italo-Ungherese** (*open Mon–Fri 9–1; T: 0932 865994*). The museum was prepared with the help of the Budapest Museum of Military History. In the local cemetery is a chapel dedicated to the Hungarian soldiers who died here.

The **Polimuseo Attilio Zarino**, north off the SS 115 at Viale del Tempio 10 (*open on request; T: 0932 986781*), is a small and extremely idiosyncratic collection of local material, including archaeological finds, flora, fauna, minerals and a large ethnographic collection, displayed in an only partially-completed floor of the owner's house. At the time of writing there were plans to move the collection to a more accessible location.

VILLA COMUNALE AND THE NATURE RESERVE

The **Villa Comunale**, public gardens, once the garden of the Capuchin monastery, offers a beautiful view over the Ippari valley. Along the River Ippari, between Vittoria and the sea, is a pinewood protected as a nature reserve, **Riserva Naturale Pino d'Aleppo** (*T: 0932 675526/5*). The trees are the last remaining examples of a variety of Aleppo pine, native to Sicily. Other species have benefited from the protective measures too, including typical and rare Mediterranean trees and flowers, mammals such as the hare and the garden dormouse, the tortoise, and a wide variety of birdlife.

ACATE

About 8km north of Vittoria is Acate (*map p. 570, B2*), so called because of the agate which was once abundantly found along the banks of the River Dirillo. It is surrounded by olive groves and vineyards, some of which produce excellent Chardonnay. In the central Piazza Libertà is the impressive 15th-century **Castello dei Principi di Biscari** (*open Sat 3.30–5, Sun 10–12 & 3.30–5; to visit call the Town Hall on T: 0932 877011*) flanked by the church of San Vincenzo, opposite the Chiesa Madre, rebuilt in 1859.

COMISO

On the slopes of the Hyblaean Mountains, the pretty Baroque town of Comiso (*map p. 570, B2*) is unmistakable for its skyline of church domes. The handsome paving on the streets of the old centre is made from the local stone, which has the appearance of marble. At Cozzo di Apollo are the ruins of an as-yet unidentified Greek settlement. During the Byzantine period a settlement at Comiso was known as *Jhomiso*. It became a fief of various aristocratic families until 1453, when it passed to the Naselli, who held it until 1812; Comiso flourished under their intelligent, far-seeing administration. Many inhabitants died during the 1624 plague epidemic and the 1693 earthquake destroyed much of the town. Comiso today has a strong economy based on stone quarrying and the year-round production of vegetable crops and carobs.

SANTISSIMA ANNUNZIATA TO THE CHIESA MADRE

The church of the **Santissima Annunziata** has a spectacular stairway in front and a beautiful blue dome above. It was rebuilt in 1772–93 on the ruins of the Byzantine church of St Nicholas. The plans, which can be seen in the sacristy, were drawn up by Rosario Gagliardi. The luminous interior has stucco decoration in blue, grey and white. It contains a wooden 15th-century statue of St Nicholas on the first south altar and an impressive Crucifix attributed to Fra' Umile da Petralia in the south transept. On the second north altar is a panel painting of the *Transition of the Virgin* (1605) by local artist Narciso Cidonio. The font (1913) is a fine piece in marble and bronze by Mario Rutelli. In the apse is a painting of the *Nativity and Resurrection of Christ* by native artist Salvatore Fiume.

Via Papa Giovanni XXIII leads downhill in front of the church, and Via degli Studi leads right to the central **Piazza Fonte Diana** with its amusing fountain (1937). The waters of this spring were said to refuse to mix with wine when poured by unchaste hands; in Roman days they supplied a bath-house with a mosaic of Neptune, the remains of which are visible beneath the Town Hall. Nearby, in Piazza delle Erbe, which was the old market-place, rises the imposing **Chiesa Madre**, Santa Maria delle Stelle, also with a dome. The fine 18th-century façade is attributed to Rosario Gagliardi. The interior has a wooden ceiling painted in the 17th century with scenes of the Old Testament, attributed to Antonio Alberti 'Barbalunga', and interesting altars with the statues protected by curtains.

LOCAL MUSEUMS AND THE FONDAZIONE BUFALINO

The handsome market building on Piazza delle Erbe, built in 1867, has been restored as the seat of the civic library and museums and is entered from the delightful courtyard. The collection of paintings includes 19th-century portraits. The library is officially known as the **Fondazione Bufalino** (*open Mon–Fri 9–2, Tues, Thur and Fri also 4–7; closed Sat and Sun; T: 0932 962617, www.fondazionebufalino.it*) because it houses the private collection of more than 10,000 books once belonging to the local writer Gesualdo Bufalino (1920–96), who was born in Comiso. He achieved recognition relatively late in life, at the age of 61, with his novel *Diceria dell'Untore* (1981), published in English seven years later as *The Plague Sower*. Semi-autobiographical, it is set during and immediately after the Second World War and chronicles the reflections of the sole survivor of a Sicilian TB clinic on life, death and the Christian faith. Writing in a highly literary, allusive style that critics quickly described as 'Baroque', Bufalino shared with other contemporary Italian authors a playful distrust of his own narrative. The museum also has newspaper articles written by or about Bufalino, as well as photographs and other memorabilia.

The same building houses the **Museo Civico di Storia Naturale** (*entrance from Piazza delle Erbe 13; open Tues–Sat 9.30–1, Tues and Thur also 1.30–6.30; T: 0932 748335*), with a collection dedicated to fossils of whales, dolphins and turtles and an interesting exhibit on rare creatures found washed up on the beaches of Sicily and Calabria. The sections dedicated to palaeontology and zoology are housed nearby, on the first floor of the former Art School at Via degli Studi 9.

Opposite the library is the **church of Gesù** (San Filippo Neri), with a magnificent wooden ceiling into which paintings by Olivio Sozzi have been inserted, with stories of the life of St Philip Neri.

MONUMENTS OF THE NASELLI FAMILY

From Via Giovanni XXIII, Via degli Studi leads shortly (right) to the lovely church of **San Francesco** or the Immacolata (*if locked, ring at the convent*), founded in the early 14th century and a national monument. The present church was built in 1478 and the very interesting Cappella Naselli at the east end was added (1517–55) by Gaspare Poidomani, using an imaginative pastiche of architectural styles. Arab-Norman squinches support the dome and classical details are incorporated in the decoration. It contains the marble funerary monument of Gaspare Naselli, count of Comiso, attributed to Antonello Gagini. At the west end is a 15th-century wooden choir loft. It is also worth asking to see the beautiful 15th-century cloister.

At the entrance to the town, and from a similar period, is the 14th-century **Castello Feudale** (*closed*), which until recently served as the prison. Once owned by the Naselli family, it has been much altered over the years, but parts of an octagonal tower, probably once a Byzantine baptistery, and the square 15th-century keep, are still standing.

In 1841 a Neoclassical opera house, **Teatro Naselli** (*open Mon–Fri 4–8; T: 0932 197 0010 or 338 126 6355, www.spazionaselli.com*) or Teatro Diana, which brought fame to the town and is still in use, was built on the east side of the castle.

SANTA CROCE CAMERINA

A direct descendant of the ancient settlements of *Kamarina* and *Kaukana*, Santa Croce Camerina (*map p. 570, B3*) is a little town which bases its economy on cattle-rearing and the cultivation of flowers (especially roses, tulips and gladioli) for export. Many of the buildings in the centre are in the Art Nouveau style.

In the central Piazza degli Studi is the **Museo Civico** (*closed at the time of writing; T: 0932 914169*) with interesting collections of tools and equipment used by farmers and craftsmen until the 20th century, and a section dedicated to the sea. On the coast south of the town several ruined watchtowers against pirate attacks can be seen, now surrounded by a seemingly endless rash of holiday bungalows.

The sandy headland of **Punta Secca** on Capo Scalambri has a series of coves, one of which was the site of the Byzantine settlement of *Kaukana*, a large harbour town mentioned by Procopius, where the fleet of Belisarius put in on the way to Africa and from where Roger II departed for the conquest of Malta. The remains are protected as an archaeological park run by the museum of Kamarina (*normally closed but you can request a visit at least 5 days ahead, T: 0932 826004, email: museo.camarina@regione.sicilia.it*) run by the museum of Kamarina, with three distinct groups of ruins corresponding to the different districts of the town. Among the many interesting recent archaeological discoveries is the monumental tomb (very unusually inside a house) of a young Christian mother (who was pregnant when she died) and her four-year-old daughter, dating perhaps to AD 650. In the lid of the sarcophagus is a 10cm

1ole through which wine or other offerings could be poured. Unfortunately the site, although screened with trees, has been surrounded by unattractive holiday bungalows.

MARINA DI RAGUSA

Southeast of Santa Croce, Marina di Ragusa (*map p. 570, B3*) is a crowded resort (especially in July and August) with an elegant marine promenade flanked by palm trees and a yachting harbour, which grew up in the 1950s on the site of an old Arab port. A fast *superstrada* connects it to Ragusa. The beach (awarded the EU Blue Banner) is sandy, once continuing into extensive sand dunes, many of which are now covered with holiday homes or market gardens. The well-preserved reedy sand dunes around the mouth of the River Irminio near Playa Grande are protected as a nature reserve (**Riserva Macchia Foresta dell'Irminio**, *T: 0932 675525/6, entrance c. 2km from Marina di Ragusa on the road to Donnalucata*), where black-winged stilts and avocets nest, and historical remains include a Sicel bee-farm and a Greek forge; there is even a small colony of coypu, originating from a pair accidentally freed here a few years ago.

KAMARINA

Situated on the coast is the archaeological park and museum of Kamarina (*map p. 570, B3*), an important Greek city.

HISTORY OF KAMARINA

Kamarina was a colony founded c. 598 BC by Syracusans and perhaps Corinthians, which suffered alternate sacking and repopulation by Syracuse, Gela and Carthage, because the inhabitants were of a particularly rebellious nature and tended to take sides with the Sicels. They first rose up against Syracuse only 45 years after their founding, in 552 BC, and suffered destruction in 533 and 484 BC. At the height of its splendour, about 460 BC, the city had a population of 30,000 people. It was finally taken by the Romans in 258 BC, and the inhabitants were sold as slaves, although there are signs of occupation in the Republican and Imperial eras and also of a late Arab-Norman settlement.

Kamarina was a nymph, daughter of the god Oceanus, who lived in a nearby lake and in the River Hypparis (now Ippari). She can be seen on 5th-century BC coins minted in the city (some are in the archaeological museum of Syracuse), riding on a swan and holding her dress out of the water, while fish jump around her. This was a good place to build a city: a large flat area protected by mountains and rivers and in a strong strategic position on the coast. Archaeologists have discovered traces of prehistoric settlements here and some scholars believe the Phoenicians established a trading post on this spot; the cult of Herakles, corresponding to the Phoenician Melqart, had a strong following in Kamarina. The site was first located by the historian Tommaso Fazello in the 16th century. Sporadic digs took place in the 18th and 19th centuries, followed by scientific excavations carried out by Paolo Orsi from 1896–1910. More recent excavations began in 1971.

THE MUSEO ARCHEOLOGICO AND EXCAVATIONS

The road passes several enclosures with excavations (*if closed, they are sometimes unlocked on request at the museum*) before reaching the Museo Archeologico (*open 9–2 & 3–7, closed Sun except for 1st Sun of month, last tickets 30mins before closing; T: 0932 826004*). The museum is housed in a restored 19th-century farmhouse built above the remains of the Temple of Athena. A room displays **underwater finds** made offshore where nine shipwrecks have so far been identified. These include a Greek bronze helmet (4th century BC) and objects from Punic and medieval boats. In 1991 a hoard of 1,272 bronze coins was found from the treasure-chest of a Roman cargo ship which sank offshore in AD 275. The headland by the city is surrounded by treacherously sharp rocks: an entire Roman fleet foundered here in 255 BC.

One of the most interesting exhibits shows a rare set of 3rd–2nd-century BC square **lead weights**, found under the sea in front of the acropolis in 1993, allowing experts to calculate the measuring system used by the inhabitants of this area. Outside in the courtyard, beneath a porch, are sandstone sarcophagi and a circular stone tomb. Beyond, part of the temple's sanctuary wall can be seen. Another building contains a plan of the site and explanatory diagrams, and Bronze Age finds from the area. Material from the 6th century BC includes a beautiful Corinthian black-figure vase with a hunting scene.

In another building the **foundations of the temple**, dating from the early 5th century BC, have been exposed (it was re-used as a church in the Byzantine era). A room on two floors has a splendid display of **amphorae** (mostly Corinthian and Carthaginian), around one thousand of which were found in the oldest necropolis of Kamarina, known as Rifriscolaro.

The various **excavated areas** overlooking the sea include fragments of the walls, part of the street layout and houses with three or four rooms opening onto a courtyard (built after 405 BC) and part of the agora. The necropoleis have yielded a great number of tombs, revealing different methods of burial and cremation, varying through the years: it was customary for a time, for example, to provide the corpses with pillows made of seaweed. Studies of skeletons show that the inhabitants were stocky and robust, with good teeth, but that some had serious back problems. Traces of the canal port have been found at the mouth of the River Ippari.

On the coast not far from Santa Croce Camerina is **Scoglitti** (*map p. 570, B3*), the beach resort of Vittoria. It overlooks the Gulf of Gela, a long shallow bay whose beaches provided the chief landing-place for the American assault forces on 10th July 1943, during Operation Husky.

CASTELLO DI DONNAFUGATA

Map p. 570, B3. Open mid-Sept–April 9–1, Tues, Thur and Sun also 2.45–4.30, closed Mon; May–June 9–1, Tues, Thur and Sun also 2.45–5, closed Mon; July–mid-Sept 9–7, closed Mon. T: 0932 619333

A quiet by-road (signposted Santa Croce Camerina) leads southwest from Ragusa through lovely countryside with numerous farms to the Castello di Donnafugata. On the site of a 17th-century building, the present castle was constructed by Baron Corrado Arezzo De Spuches in the 19th century. It is a large country villa, built in an eclectic style, with a Venetian-Gothic loggia. In 1893 the owner was able to have the Syracuse–Licata railway line diverted to bring his guests and himself right up to the entrance by train. Its delightful setting survives, with its farm and a large park. In the exotic **gardens**, with splendid old Morton Bay fig trees, are a stone maze entered over a miniature drawbridge guarded by a stone soldier, a coffee-house, a little Neoclassical temple above a grotto and an amusing little chapel with a *papier mâché* friar inside, which pops up to frighten people. The asphalt-stone monument to Corrado Arezzo De Spuches (2005) is the work of the Anglo-French artist Peter Briggs.

In recent years the castle has featured in the Chief Inspector Montalbano TV series, and many of its 122 rooms have been restored. The most interesting are the **Salone degli Specchi**, displaying some paintings of the Neapolitan school; the **Salone della Musica**, containing three pianos and with frescoes on the walls; and also the tiny **theatre**. In the oldest part of the building, a small chamber is indicated as the prison of Blanche of Navarre, widow of King Martin of Sicily. She was captured (in ?1410) after being chased across Sicily by Count Bernardo Cabrera who was aiming to improve his claim to the throne by forcing her into marriage. He brought her home to his domain but she thwarted his plans by steadfastly refusing to marry him. Numerous castles in Sicily have a room claiming to be her prison, even buildings (such as this one) which were built long after her death. The claims should be taken with a hefty pinch of salt but the story is still a good one.

BARON CORRADO AREZZO DE SPUCHES

Baron Corrado Arezzo De Spuches (1824–95) was several times mayor of Ragusa, member of the Sicilian parliament in 1848, and later senator of the Kingdom of Italy, besides being a farmer and editing a ferociously satirical magazine (he was nicknamed *Terremoto*, earthquake.

His family life, however, was not so fortunate. His wife, Concettina Trifiletti, gave him a daughter, Vincenzina, who at the age of 16 married a prince and herself had two daughters, before the prince absconded with another woman. Vincenzina died of a broken heart, followed soon after by her mother. De Spuches became the legal guardian of his granddaughters. The youngest, Maria, abandoned him to marry a commoner and live in Messina (where she died in the 1908 earthquake). The other, Clementina, fell in love with a Frenchman and was carried off by him on board his ship. A gardener saw them going and raised the alarm. Another ship was sent to intercept the lovers, who were brought back to Donnafugata. They were allowed to wed, in Malta to avoid scandal, yet although it was a happy marriage, Clementina was never forgiven by her grandfather, who cut her out of his will. On his death she brought a court case against distant relatives and succeeded in gaining possession of the castle. Her daughter was the last of the De Spuches line.

CHIARAMONTE GULFI & THE NORTH

Chiaramonte Gulfi (*map p. 570, B2–C2*) was founded as *Akrillai* by Syracuse in the 7th century BC. Attacked twice by the Carthaginians and then by Marcus Marcellus in 213 BC, it was annihilated by the Arabs of Ibn al-Furat in 827, who then rebuilt it, naming it *Gulfi*, or Pleasant Land. In 1299 Gulfi was destroyed by the Angevins, who killed most of the inhabitants, including the women and children, in a massacre still remembered for its ferocity. Manfredi Chiaramonte rebuilt the town for the survivors of the massacre, in a safer position at the top of the hill 4km away. Called the 'Balcony of the Hyblaean Mountains' and the 'City of Museums' (of which it has eight), Chiaramonte Gulfi is also famous today for its top-quality olive oil, as well as for excellent bread, pasta, pork, salami and cured hams.

CHURCHES OF CHIARAMONTE

In the central Piazza Duomo is the church of **Santa Maria La Nova**, its Baroque façade belying its earlier, 15th-century origins. Nearby is the 18th-century church of **San Filippo**, which houses a beautiful chapel dedicated to St Philip of Argirò, the masterpiece of Nicolò da Mineo. The stonework is very ornate; just over the doorway is a highly unusual naked mermaid, and up above, two winged sphinxes. Nicolò da Mineo, who lived until he was 83, is buried by the altar.

In the highest part of town is the Gothic **Arco dell'Annunziata**, the northwestern gateway to the castle and the only one to survive the 1693 earthquake. Through the arch is a lovely view of the simple church of **San Giovanni**, with Doric columns on either side of the portal.

CHIARAMONTE MUSEUMS

Of the eight museums in Chiaramonte, some have been set up in the Baroque Palazzo Montesano (in Via Montesano) while the others are close by in the town centre (*all museums open June–Sept every day 10–1, weekends and holidays also 3–6; Oct–May weekends and holidays 10–1 & 3–6; for information, call the Tourist Office on T: 0932 711239*).

The **Museo di Arte Sacra** (Piazza Duomo) is considered one of the finest collections of its kind in Italy. Among the rare and precious objects from the churches of the town there is a crib of 40 terracotta figures about 30cm high, dressed in the traditional 19th-century costumes of the people of Modica. The **Collezione di Cimeli Storici Militari F. Gulino** (ex-Casa del Fascio, Piazza Duomo) contains about 1,000 interesting mementoes, most of them relating to the two World Wars.

Pinacoteca Giovanni De Vita (Corso Umberto) houses about 60 paintings by this local Impressionist artist, donated by his family when he died.

The **Museo di Liberty**, in Palazzo Montesano, illustrates with photographs, paintings and furniture the fervid period between 1895 and 1913 when the Liberty, or Art Nouveau, style was fashionable in Sicily. The **Museo dell'Olio d'Oliva** (also in Palazzo Montesano) gives information about the town's most precious product, olive oil, with a complete collection of presses and tools used through the ages. Things have not changed very much; even now the excellence of this oil is due to the fact that the olives are gathered by hand and processed the same day, using only stone presses. The **Collezione Ornitologica Fratelli Azzara** (again in Palazzo Montesano) exhibits about 500 stuffed birds of Sicily and Italy (some now extinct), prepared by the Azzara brothers, expert taxidermists, while the **Collezione di Strumenti Musicali Etnici** is a beautiful arrangement in seven rooms of more than 600 rare musical instruments from all over the world.

The **Museo del Ricamo e dello Sfilato Siciliano** (Via Lauria, one of the tiny alleys off the stairway to the church of San Giovanni) has a display of beautiful embroidery and lace made by local women, together with the tools used in their craft. Many of the traditional designs can be traced back to the pottery of the Middle Ages or even further back to prehistoric art, showing fishing-nets, honeycombs, flowers, leaves, ears of wheat and birds.

AROUND CHIARAMONTE

A short walk (c. 2km east) from Chiaramonte Gulfi, in the pinewoods on the slopes of Mt Arcibessi, is the sanctuary-church of the **Madonna delle Grazie**, built in 1576 by the local population as thanksgiving for being spared a plague epidemic. The people chose this spot because a spring of water had miraculously appeared. The views towards Mt Etna from here are spectacular.

Near the site of ancient *Akrillai*, c. 4km from Chiaramonte, is the **Eremo di Gulfi** (*always open; T: 333 865 7598*), an ancient church and convent, parts of which, in a cave, go back to the earliest days of Christianity (it is said to have been visited on pilgrimage in 576 by St Gregory the Great before he became pope).

GIARRATANA

Giarratana (*map p. 570, C2*), the smallest town in former province of Ragusa, bases its economy on the production of wheat, almonds and vegetables, especially the large flat *giarratana* onions, to which a feast is dedicated every August. Rebuilt after the earthquake of 1693 on a new site, it is dominated by three Baroque churches: **Sant'Antonio Abate**, on the top of the hill, which contains gold stuccoes and a beautiful 18th-century floor of asphalt stone and bright ceramic tiles; the **Chiesa Madre**, which is similar in appearance to the cathedral of Noto; and **San Bartolomeo**, dedicated to the town's patron saint. It has a fine façade, perhaps the work of an apprentice of Gagliardi. Inside the church is a glass urn containing the mummified body of St Hilary, a Roman virgin and martyr; her body was sent here as a gift by Pope Alexander VII in 1664.

Close by, in Palazzo Barone on Via XX Settembre, is the **Museo Archeologico** (*open 9–1*), with a collection of finds from the site of Terravecchia, the pre-earthquake town, as well as from the Roman villa at Orto Mosaico (*see below*) and from another Roman dwelling in the same area.

The highest part of the town, around the ruins of the castle built in 1703, and centred on Via Galilei, forms the **Museo a Cielo Aperto** (*open Mon–Fri 9–1, Sat and Sun by prior arrangement, closed Nov–Jan; T: 0932 974307*), an open-air museum showing how the local houses once looked inside and how the tradesmen and craftsmen carried on their occupations. At Christmas time the Living Crib is et up here.

In 1988 the remains of an Imperial Roman villa dating from the 3rd–4th centuries AD were discovered close to Giarratana at **Orto Mosaico** (*not open to the public*)Its fine mosaics have been re-buried to protect them. At 10km from the town is a dam on the River Irminio, which forms the beautiful artificial **lake of Santa Rosalia**.

MONTEROSSO ALMO

North of Giarratana is Monterosso Almo (*map p. 570, C2*). At 691m it is the highest town in the former Ragusa province. It is renowned in Sicily for cherries and ricotta, both remarkably good, and for its quaint atmosphere.

In the large central Piazza San Giovanni is the church of **San Giovanni Battista** (attributed to Vincenzo Sinatra), preceded by an immense stairway. Inside there is a precious glass chandelier from Murano. Over the main altar is a 15th-century wooden statue of St John the Baptist, shown only on the first Tues of each month. On the other side of the square, in Palazzo Cocuzza, is the tiny **Museo Civico**, containing some archaeological finds from the nearby site of Monte Casasia and an ornithological collection. Via Roma leads down to the golden-brown and red neo-Gothic church of the **Assunzione**, sometimes called the Matrice, a national monument. This is the oldest parish in the diocese of Ragusa and the building suffered little damage during the 1693 earthquake. On entering, to the south you will see the original Norman baptismal font, and by the side entrance is an 11th-century holy water stoup on a 5th-century Palaeo-Christian column.

Opposite the Matrice is another national monument, surmounted by an attractive triple belfry, the church of **Sant'Antonio Abate** (15th–16th century), or Sanctuary of Our Lady of Sorrows, the patroness of Monterosso Almo. This part of town was the centre before the earthquake. Inside the church are some important works of art, including paintings by the schools of Antonello da Messina, Vito D'Anna and Caravaggio, and a poplar-wood Crucifix by Fra' Umile da Petralia.

In the **public gardens** is a small astronomical observatory, with a telescope available to the public; the clear skies and low light interference guarantee good visibility.

PRACTICAL INFORMATION

GETTING AROUND

By rail: Ragusa is on the Caltanissetta–Gela–Ragusa–Modica–Noto–Syracuse line (*www.trenitalia.it*).

By bus: For up-to-date bus schedules, see *www.orariautobus.it*. Bus companies are as follows:

AST (*www.aziendasicilianatrasporti.it*) connects Ragusa to Ragusa Ibla, also to Acate, Marina di Ragusa, Punta Secca, Scoglitti, Santa Croce Camerina and Kamarina.

Etna Trasporti/Interbus (*www.interbus.it*) goes to Catania and Catania airport, Messina and Syracuse, besides Giarratana, Marina di Ragusa, Monterosso Almo, Punta Secca, Santa Croce Camerina, Kamarina and Scoglitti.

Giamporcaro (*T: 0932 981632 or 0932 869612*) connects Vittoria with Comiso, Marina di Ragusa, Ragusa, Santa Croce Camerina and Scoglitti.

SAL (*www.autolineesal.it*) connects Ragusa to Agrigento, Comiso airport, Gela and Licata.

Tumino (*www.tuminobus.it*) runs from Ragusa railway station to Comiso airport, Marina di Ragusa, Punta Secca, Santa Croce Camerina, and in summer to Kamarina.

WHERE TO STAY

CAVA D'ISPICA (*map p. 570, C3*)
€€ **Casa al Castello**. On a spur overlooking Cava d'Ispica, a hospitable B&B, with 6 comfortable rooms, nice breakfasts, garden and pool. *Contrada Calicantone Scalepiane, T: 338 531 0229 or 347 895 1957, www.casa-al-castello.com.*

CHIARAMONTE GULFI (*map p. 570, B2–C2*)
€€ **Antica Stazione**. The old railway station on the dismantled narrow-gauge Ragusa–Vizzini–Syracuse line, which passed through Pantalica (the passengers had to get off and walk when the gradient was too steep), is now a comfortable hotel with 18 rooms, a good restaurant, garden and car park. *Contrada Santissimo (southeast of Chiaramonte), T: 0932 928083 or 334 938264, www.anticastazione.it.*

€ **Villa Nobile**. Pretty little hotel, efficient, with 22 basic rooms but splendid views, car park, friendly service, no restaurant but close to town centre. *Corso Umberto 168, T: 0932 928537, www.albergovillanobile.com.*

COMISO (*map p. 570, B2*)
€ **Cordial**. Simple but spotless, with restaurant and car park, just out of town. *SS 115 km 1 per Vittoria, T: 0932 967866/7, www.cordialhotel.com.*

€ **Balcone di Sicilia**. Perched high in the Hyblaean Mountains, a stone-built farmhouse with glorious panoramic views towards Mount Etna and the sea. 3 comfortable rooms, delicious breakfasts, children welcome. *Contrada Castiglione 16, SS 115 km 313, T: 320 0141674 or 320 775 0545, www.balconedisicilia.it.*

DONNAFUGATA (*map p. 570, B3*)
€€€ **Donnafugata Golf Resort**. Tucked away in the countryside southwest of Donnafugata, and about 20km from Ragusa, a Sheraton hotel with 202 rooms and suites, 2 restaurants, fitness centre, 2 pools and 2 18-hole golf

courses (Gary Player and Franco Piras). *Contrada Piombo, SP 19, T: 0932 914200, www.donnafugatagolfresort.com.*

DONNALUCATA (*map p. 570, B3*)

€€ **Acquamarina**. ■ Functional and rather spartan but overlooking the splendid beach, this little hotel has 22 rooms, car park, and an exceptionally good restaurant, often featured in the Chief Inspector Montalbano TV series. *Viale della Repubblica 9, T: 0932 937922, www.acqua-marina.com.*

ISPICA (*map p. 570, C3*)

€ **Corte Statella**. B&B in an old palace in town centre, with 4 palatial rooms, antique furniture, small fitness centre, garden and terrace. *Corso Umberto 411, T: 0932 793380, 333 646 0555 or 338 263 4068.*

MARINA DI RAGUSA (*map p. 570, B3*)

€€€ **La Moresca**. Charming small hotel, 15 rooms with character, patio with bougainvillea and lemons; car park, no restaurant. *Via Dandolo 63, T: 0932 239495, www.lamorescahotel.it.*

MODICA (*map p. 570, C3*)

€€€ **Palazzo Failla**. Old town house in the centre of Modica Alta with 10 individually decorated rooms. *Via Blandini 5, T: 0932 941059, www.palazzofailla.it.*

€€ **FerroHotel**. Near the railway station, modern hotel, very comfortable, 21 quiet rooms, no restaurant but good breakfasts, car park, bikes available. *Via Stazione, T: 0932 941043, www.ferrohotelmodica.it.*

€€ **Grana Barocco**. Built in 1600, tiny eco-friendly hotel in central position, 7 rooms and suites, all different, fitness centre, restaurant/pizzeria in caves under the building. *Corso Umberto 133, T: 0932 754704, www.granabarocco.it.*

€€ L**e Magnolie**. Small hotel in the heart of town, 7 comfortable rooms, panoramic terrace, good breakfasts. *Via Campailla 251, T: 0932 752552, www.lemagnoliehotel.it.*

€€ **L'Orangerie**. Superior B&B accommodation in the heart of town, with 7 beautiful rooms and a good restaurant at Vico Napolitano 14, the Fattoria delle Torri (*T: 0932 751286, closed Mon*). *Vico De Naro 5, T: 347 067 4698, www.lorangerie.it.*

€€ **Cambiocavallo Resort**. In the countryside 5km south of town, 8 bright, modern and elegant rooms, pool. *Contrada Zimmardo, SP Modica–Pozzallo km 5, T: 0932 779118 or 334 709 1959, www.cambiocavallo.it.*

POZZALLO (*map p. 570, C3*)

€ **Villa Ada**. Charming, elegant little hotel in a centrally-located 1920s building, with 22 quiet rooms, restaurant and car park, close to the beach. *Corso Vittorio Veneto 3, T: 0932 954022, www.hotelvillaada.it.*

€ **Mare Nostrum**. Simple, comfortable B&B in the centre of Pozzallo, 6 rooms named after Sicilian writers, very good breakfasts. *Via Giunta 12/14, T: 0932 958769, www.marenostrumpozzallo.it.*

RAGUSA IBLA (*map p. 570, C2*)

€€€ **San Giorgio Palace**. Group of old houses clinging to the hillside, remarkably well recuperated, lovely modern interiors. 13 rooms and suites, very good panoramic restaurant. From the ring road (*Circonvallazione Avv. Ottaviano*) a tunnel and lift take you straight up to the front desk and to the old streets of Ibla. *Via Torrenuova 50, T: 0932 686983, www.sangiorgiopalacehotel.it.Map 3.*

€€€ **Antico Convento dei Cappuccini**. This former convent in the public gardens is now an unusual and very beautiful small hotel; the 40 monastic cells have become 10 comfortable rooms with breathtaking views. Gourmet restaurant and a gastronomy school on the premises. *Viale Margherita 41, T: 0932 686750 or 347 147 2915, www. anticoconventoibla.it. Map 4.*

€ You can stay in one of the little houses of Ibla, which functions as *ospitalità diffusa*, by contacting Associazione Zuleima. *Piazza della Repubblica 3, T: 0932 061656 or 338 786 2198, www. zuleima.org.*

RAGUSA SUPERIORE (*map p. 570, C2*)

€€€ A**ntica Badia Relais**. In a beautifully restored 18th-century building; the 12 rooms and suites are all different, some with the original tiled floors. Small spa, very good restaurant, have breakfast or dinner on the rooftop in an unbelievable setting. *Corso Italia 115, T: 0932 247995, www.anticabadia. com. Map 1.*

€€€ **De Stefano Palace**. 27 elegant rooms and suites, all different, in an 18th-century palace with frescoed ceilings, fitness centre, no restaurant but breakfast is served on the patio. *Via Cavaliere De Stefano 15, T: 0932 682872, www.destefanopalacehotel.com. Map 2.*

€€€ **Villa Carlotta**. Just west of the new town, an old farm has been transformed into a comfortable, modern hotel with 26 beautiful rooms and suites, garden, pool, fitness centre, car park and Michelin-starred restaurant. *Via Ungaretti, T: 0932 604140, www. villacarlottahotel.com. Beyond map 2.*

€€ **Hotel Vittorio Veneto**. Just behind the cathedral, restored Baroque palace with 11 rooms, good service, excellent breakfasts, no restaurant. *Corso Vittorio Veneto 93, T: 0932 686119, www.*

hotelvittorioveneto.it. Map 2.

ENVIRONS OF RAGUSA

€€€ **Eremo della Giubiliana**. A restored villa with authentic antique furniture, once a convent and then a fortified farmhouse. 10 beautiful rooms and suites, fitness centre, large park, pool, very good restaurant, excellent wine list. Private airstrip, daily cruises by yacht or catamaran from Marina di Ragusa. *Contrada Giubiliana, 8km south of Ragusa, on the SP25 Ragusa–Marina di Ragusa road, T: 0932 669119, www. eremodellagiubiliana.com.*

SANTA CROCE CAMERINA/PUNTA SECCA (*map p. 570, B3*)

€€ **La Casa di Montalbano**. The house on the beach used as Chief Inspector Montalbano's home in the popular TV series is a comfortable B&B with 3 rooms (minimum 2 nights). *Via Aldo Moro 44, T: 0932 183 8967, 396 21307 or 345 062 9047, www.lacasadimontalbano. com.*

€ **Kaukana Inn**. On a lovely stretch of beach south of Santa Croce, a bright little hotel just right for families, 16 rooms, garden, pool, tennis, car park; restaurant/pizzeria close by. *Corso Mediterraneo 1, T: 0932 915673, www. kaukanainn.it.*

SCICLI (*map p. 570, C3*)

€€€ **Borgo Hedone**. Beautiful hotel created by French designers after restoring a group of crumbling old houses and caves. The 10 rooms are all different. Indoor and outdoor pools, fitness centre. Very private, no reception, restaurant or breakfast; lots of stairs. *Via Loreto 51, T: 347 359 0938, www.borgohedone.com.*

€€ **Novecento**. Elegant hotel in a tiny aristocratic palace in the heart of the Baroque town consisting of 8 (small) rooms and a suite. Linen sheets and towels, good restaurant. Unforgettable breakfasts on the flower-filled patio. *Via Duprè 11, T: 0932 843817, www.hotel900. it.*

€ **Conte Ruggero**. B&B with 5 lovely rooms in an 18th-century aristocratic palace overlooking the town's main square. *Piazza Italia 24, T: 0932 93184 or 335 821 8269, www.conteruggero.it.*

€ **Torre Camarella**. Six kilometres from Scicli towards the sea, a friendly family home in the countryside with 3 clean, simple rooms; good breakfasts with fresh milk and ricotta from the farm. *Contrada Mosca, SP 64 2km, T: 339 527 7855, www.torrecamarella.it.*

Albergo diffuso If you like, you can stay in one of 24 restored houses in the centre, from an aristocratic palace to a simple little house. *Scicli Ospitalità Diffusa, c/o Millennium, Via Mormino Penna 15, T: 0932 185 5555 or 392 820 7857, www.sciclialbergodiffuso.it.*

SCOGLITTI (*map p. 570, B3*)

€€ **Al Gabbiano**. Welcoming little hotel used as a location in the Chief Inspector Montalbano TV series, with 27 quiet rooms and a good restaurant serving local dishes accompanied by the excellent local wines, right on the beach; perfect for families with young children. *Via Messina 52, T: 0932 980179, www. hotelsulmare.it.*

VITTORIA (*map p. 570, B2*)

€€€ **Locanda Cos**. ▬ This beautiful farm 10km from Vittoria offers 6 luxurious suites and two double rooms, good restaurant, garden and pool, ideal for wine connoisseurs. Cos are one of the vintners in Sicily who use huge terracotta amphorae to ferment their wines; in this case award-winning Nero d'Avola and Cerasuolo di Vittoria DOCG.

SP Chiaramonte–Acate, T: 0932 876145, www.cosvittoria.it.

WHERE TO EAT

CHIARAMONTE GULFI (*map p. 570, B2–C2*)

€€ **Majore**. A simple restaurant, but an institution; the dining rooms were frescoed by Salvatore Fiume. Excellent local dishes, using the best ingredients Sicily can offer; pork is a speciality. Closed Mon. *Via Martiri Ungheresi 12, T: 0932 928019.*

COMISO (*map p. 570, B2*)

€ **Antica Comiso**. They are justly proud of their seafood *antipasti* in this little *trattoria*. Pizza in the evenings. Closed Tues and Sat lunchtime. *Via Di Vita 5, T: 0932 723555 or 0932 066631.*

DONNAFUGATA (*map p. 570, B3*)

€ **Al Castello**. Simple family-run *trattoria* offering Hyblaean mountain cuisine, next to the castle. Closed Mon. *Viale del Castello, T: 0932 619260 or 333 214 3959.*

MARINA DI RAGUSA (*map p. 570, B3*)

€€€ **La Anchoa**. ▬ Refined restaurant on the lovely beach, for superb fish, beef or stone-oven pizza (evenings). The menu is not extensive but every dish is especially well prepared and presented. Home-made bread using flour from rare local wheat varieties. Good wine and beer list. Closed Mon in winter. *Lungomare Andrea Doria 21, T: 0932 230561 or 335 535 1101.*

€€€ **Lido Azzurro da Serafino**. Opened in 1953, with a long-standing reputation for fish dishes, Michelin-starred. Open April–Oct. *Lungomare Andrea Doria, T: 0932 239522.*

MODICA (*map p. 570, C3*)

€€€ **Accursio**. Elegant little restaurant

where Michelin-starred chef Accursio Capraro offers inventive dishes that please the eye and the palate. Good wine list. Not to be missed. Closed Nov–mid-March. *Via Clemente Grimaldi 414, T: 0932 941689.*

€€€ **Locanda del Colonnello**. Small restaurant offering a short menu of superlative Sicilian dishes, from street food to the most refined cuisine, all prepared with exclusively local produce. Wine list of excellent Sicilian labels. Closed Wed. *Vico Biscari 6 (Modica Alta), T: 0932 752423.*

€€ **Taverna Nicastro**. An old-fashioned, award-winning *trattoria* opened in 1948, serving exceptionally good pasta and meat dishes, tasty street food, lentil or chick-pea soups in winter, good desserts; friendly and relaxed. Open evenings only, booking advisable, closed Sun and Mon. *Via Sant'Antonino 30 (Modica Alta), T: 0932 945884.*

€ **L'Arco**. Chef Grazia presents good home-made pasta or ravioli, simple desserts such as *biancomangiare*, Sicilian style. All accompanied by wine from her own vineyard. Closed Mon (July and Aug open every day). *Piazza Corrado Rizzoni 11, T: 0932 942727.*

€ **La Rusticana**. Simple *trattoria* serving local dishes with an authentic home-made flavour; generous helpings. Closed Sun evenings. *Viale Medaglie D'Oro 34, T: 0932 942950.*

POZZALLO (*map p. 570, C3*)
€€ **Ippocampo**. Large restaurant serving local fish, cooked to perfection and served in beautiful surroundings, with a sea view. Dogs welcome. Closed Wed. *SP Pozzallo–Marza (eastern outskirts), T: 0932 953658 or 334 969 1343.*

€€ **Il Delfino**. Central and on the seafront, delicious fish dishes, also pizzeria in the evening. Closed Mon. *Via delle Sirene 4, T: 0932 954732.*

RAGUSA IBLA (*map p. 570, C2*)
€€€ **Ristorante Duomo**. One of Sicily's best restaurants, presided over by famous 2-Michelin-starred chef Ciccio Sultano; excellent wine cellar; very imaginative and appetising fare. Expensive. Closed all day Mon and Sun evening in winter, all day Sun and Mon lunchtime in summer, Aug open every day. *Via Bocchieri 31, T: 0932 651265. Map 3.*

€€€ **Angelo Vini e Affini**. Tiny wine bar/restaurant near the Giardino Ibleo, offering exquisite dishes prepared exclusively with local products, served with local wines or a vast assortment of beers. Closed Wed. *Corso XXV Aprile 61, T: 0932 080109. Map 4.*

€€ **Cucina e Vino**. Friendly *trattoria* serving well-prepared typical local dishes. Good wine list, or local beer if you prefer. Closed Wed. *Via Orfanotrofio 91, T: 0932 686447. Map 4.*

€€ **I Banchi**. Latest enterprise of chef Ciccio Sultano, a delightful bistrot-style snack bar and bakery offering different kinds of Sicilian bread accompanied by mouth-watering preparations featuring cheese and vegetables; excellent desserts. Open 8.30–11pm, closed Tues. *Via Orfanotrofio 39, T: 0932 665000. Map 4.*

SCICLI (*map p. 570, C3*)
€€ **Satra**. ◼ A tiny restaurant where you can appreciate the particular local cuisine enhanced by the use of locally-grown herbs, adding just the right fillip to every dish. Local wines. Closed Tues. *Via Duca degli Abruzzi 1, T: 0932 842148 or 348 672 6875 (Rita).*

€€ **Pomodoro**. Chef Giuseppe favours

tradition with a twist, making the most of fresh local ingredients, fish, meat and cheese. Rabbit is especially good. Closed Tues. *Corso Garibaldi 46, T: 0932 931444.*

SCOGLITTI (*map p. 570, B3*)

€€€ **Sakalleo**. In the centre of the village. Fresh fish and good wine; the *antipasti* are very special; renowned for cous cous and fish soup. Closed Mon lunchtime in winter. *Piazza Cavour 12, T: 0932 871688.*

LOCAL SPECIALITIES

CHIARAMONTE GULFI For organic olive oil made with *Tonda Iblea* olives, **Pianogrillo** was voted 'Best of Sicily' in 2011. Of the 9,000 trees in their groves some are 700 years old. (*Contrada Pianogrillo, near the archaeological area of Akrillai; T: 338 819 3102, www. pianogrillo.it for online purchases*).

GIARRATANA is renowned for white nougat, made exclusively with honey and almonds. An excellent address is **Torrone Trapani** (*Via del Mercato 66*).

ISPICA Curto (*Via Galilei 4, www. curto.it*) produces Eloro Fontanelle, some of the best Nero d'Avola wine available, from very old vines which each yield only 500g of grapes; the wine is aged for 8 months in small oak casks before bottling.

MODICA Antica Dolceria Bonaiuto, founded in 1880 (*Corso Umberto 259, www.bonajuto.it*), sells delicious local sweets including *'mpanatigghi* (light pastry filled with minced beef, chocolate, and spices), *cedrata* (honey and citron rind), *cobaita* (honey and sesame seeds) and Modica chocolate. Another good address is **Casa Don Puglisi** (*Corso Umberto 267 and Largo XI Febbraio 15, www. laboratoriodonpuglisi.it*), closed Sun and Wed afternoon; it is a foundation which takes in girls in difficult situations (mostly unmarried mothers rejected by their families, thieves and repentant prostitutes), looks after them, gives them a place to live, and trains them as confectioners so they will be able to find employment once they are back on their feet.

You will find the best ice cream at the award-winning **Caffé Adamo** (*Via Marchesa Tedeschi 17*). **Casa del Formaggio** (*Via Marchesa Tedeschi 5*) has all the local cheeses, hams and salami, Modica chocolate, carob products and liqueurs.

Ottavia Failla makes unusual and decorative handbags using luxurious materials (*Via Blandini 5, www. ottaviafailla.it*).

MONTEROSSO ALMO At **Bar Terranova** (*Piazza San Giovanni*) you will find exquisite ricotta ice cream served in the little wicker *cavagne* where the cheese is prepared.

POZZALLO Gelateria Fede (*Corso Vittorio Veneto 29*) for exquisite sorbet and *granita*—chocolate *granita* was invented here.

RAGUSA IBLA Gelati DiVini (*Piazza Duomo 20*) for delicious ice cream, including novel flavours such as ginger, olive, beetroot, prickly pear or *passito di Noto*, made using only local ingredients; they also sell fine Sicilian wines and olive oil.

RAGUSA SUPERIORE The coffee house to see and be seen is **Caffè Italia** (*Piazza San Giovanni 29*), just below the cathedral; excellent sweets and breakfast pastries. **Casa del Formaggio Sant'Anna** (*Corso Italia 387; closed Wed* *afternoon*) for local cheeses, including the superb *caciocavallo ragusano*. **Panificio Maddalena** (*Via Lombardia 86*) for traditional sourdough bread, baked in a stone oven. **Di Pasquale** (*Corso Vittorio Veneto 104; closed Mon*) is one of the finest confectioners in Italy and has won many prizes. Try *testa di turco* (Turk's head), a creamy confection, or *cannoli di ricotta*.

SCICLI Excellent local pastries and biscuits are to be found at the **Pasticceria Pisana** (*Corso Mazzini 54*).

Aromatic herbs grow well in this corner of Sicily, with constant sunshine and sea breezes. Visit the Herb Garden in the suburb of Sampieri to see, touch and smell hundreds of different kinds, or practise yoga, pilates or Tai Chi on thyme lawns. *Gli Aromi, Contrada Santa Rosalia, T: 347 816 9770 (Enrico)*. You can also order online (*www.gliaromi.it*).

FESTIVALS AND EVENTS

ACATE Good Friday, *Scinnenza*, procession of the statue of Christ, accompanied by girls dressed in mourning; at sunset, representation of the Crucifixion. Third Sun after Easter, Feast of the patron St Vincent Martyr.

CHIARAMONTE GULFI Feb, *Carnevale della Contea*, including a feast of the local sausages.

COMISO 3 Feb and second Sun in July, festivities for the patron St Blaise, with fireworks and distribution of blessed loaves.

GIARRATANA 14 Aug, *Sagra della Cipolla*, harvest festival for the unique large, flat onions. 21 Aug, *Fiera di San Bartolomeo*, traditional cattle-market, followed by a festival on 24 August to celebrate St Bartholomew.

Modica Easter Sun, *La Maronna Vasa-Vasa* (the 'Kiss-Kiss Madonna'), the culmination of Easter week with the meeting of the Madonna and her Son, the two statues exchanging joyful kisses. Sun on or after 23 April, Feast of St George, patron saint of Modica Alta. End of June, Feast of St Peter, patron saint of Modica Bassa, with a fair.

POZZALLO Second Sun in Aug, *Sagra del Pesce*, in Piazza Rimembranza, fish is cooked and served using a pan 4m wide.

RAGUSA IBLA Last Sun in May, Feast of St George, procession and fireworks. October, Ibla Buskers, street artists from all over the world meet up to perform (*www.iblabuskers.it*).

RAGUSA SUPERIORE 29 Aug, Feast of St John the Baptist, the patron saint; celebrations, sweets and fireworks (*www.cattedralesangiovanni.it*).

Santa Croce Camerina 19–20 March, festivities for St Joseph, including the *tavolate*, lavish banquets featuring decorative loaves, oranges and lemons.

SCICLI Saturday after 19 March, *Cavalcata di San Giuseppe*, street-corner bonfires light the Flight into Egypt for a procession of horses caparisoned with intricately-woven blankets of fresh wallflowers (*www.cavalcatasangiuseppe. it*). Palm Sun, procession culminating in the offering of woven palm leaves to the Madonna. Easter Sun, *Festa dell'Omu Vivu*, a dramatic procession of young people carrying the statue of the Risen Christ, shouting *'Gioia! Gioia!'* (Joy! Joy!). Last Sat in May, the *Madonna delle Milizie* is celebrated in commemoration of a famous battle between the Normans and Saracens.

Syracuse

Syracuse (*Siracusa* in Italian; *map p. 570, D2*), a World Heritage Site, is the successor of the magnificent *Surakousai*, which rivalled Athens as the largest and most powerful city of the Greek world. Cicero noted that Syracuse knew no day without sun, and it does indeed enjoy a mild marine climate throughout the year. The beautiful island of Ortigia ('island of the quail', because of its shape) has many monuments of great interest. It is the heart of the city, with good restaurants and a lively atmosphere in the evenings. The principal ruins of the Greek city, including the famous theatre, are close by on the mainland.

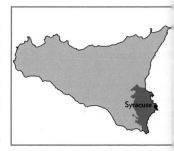

The territory of Syracuse is famed above all for its many Baroque cities, all of which were rebuilt in this style after the devastating earthquake of 1693: apart from Syracuse itself, Noto, Palazzolo Acreide, Sortino, Buccheri and Buscemi are the most noted. Other highlights include the quiet fishing villages such as Marzamemi, peaceful country towns like Avola or Floridia, the Sicel necropolis of Pantalica, and the spectacular Cassibile gorge. The wine produced in this region is famed for its quality, and fruit and vegetables are grown in abundance: strawberries from Noto or Rosolini and Pachino cherry tomatoes are known throughout Europe.

HISTORY OF SYRACUSE

The city of Syracuse was founded on Ortigia, an island so close to the mainland that it would later be joined to it by a causeway. The island had a famous freshwater spring, Arethusa (today's Fonte Aretusa; *map 5*), and it helped provide shelter for two superb harbours (the Great Harbour, 640 hectares in area, to the south and west of the island (now Porto Grande), and the Small Harbour to the north, now the Porto Piccolo, used by fishing boats; *map 1*). The city was founded in 733 BC by Corinthian settlers led by Archias, and links with Corinth remained close. The city grew fast and it soon created many sub-colonies, such as *Akrai, Kasmenai, Heloros* and *Kamarina*. Much of the new settlement on the mainland, the districts of Akradina, Tyche and Neapolis, were on the slopes of the Epipolai plateau which was to provide an outer defence line for the city.

SYRACUSE
The Fountain of Diana by Giulio Moschetti.

Landed aristocrats were the first rulers of Syracuse, and when challenged by an emerging democratic movement, they invited a strong 'tyrant' from the outside, Gelon, ruler of the city of Gela, who forcibly settled much of Gela's population in Syracuse and made it his capital in 485. In 480 he defeated the Carthaginians at Himera, thanks to an alliance with his father-in-law, Theron of Akragas (Agrigento). The Temple of Athena, built to celebrate this victory, is now the duomo. Gelon was succeeded by his brother Hieron I (478–c. 467), who married Gelon's beautiful widow Damarete and defeated an Etruscan fleet off Italy (474). He won a chariot race at the Olympics and patronised the arts, welcoming the poets Aeschylus, Pindar, Simonides and Bacchylides to his court. Much of the expansion of the city dates from this period of cultural fervour.

Following Hieron's death, the city became a democracy, with an assembly, administrative council and elected generals. Even when Dionysius I was chosen as 'general with full powers' in 405, he preserved the democratic institutions. By this time Syracuse had fought off the great Athenian invasion fleet of 415, commanded by Nikias. The Athenians had tried to close off the city with a double row of walls and blockade it but eventually, thanks to an eclipse of the moon, an omen that was misinterpreted by Nikias, their fleet was trapped inside the Great Harbour and annihilated. Dionysius I made sure that the city was made invulnerable against siege by obliging the whole population, himself included, to build a 30km-long wall around the city which would enclose also springs, pastures and gardens, starting from the heights of Epipolai. Although none of the four wars Dionysius fought against Carthage drove the Carthaginians from the island, under his rule Syracuse became a major power in Sicily and southern Italy.

It all collapsed under Dionysius' son Dionysius II, who, in spite of personal tutoring by the philosopher Plato, was dissolute and arrogant. Syracuse was forced to ask her mother city for help to restore order. The Corinthian Timoleon did have some success in confronting the Carthaginians and setting up an oligarchic government, of some 600 leading citizens, modelled on that in Corinth, but Timoleon's constitution was overthrown after his death by Agathocles who established his own tyranny in 317. Agathocles was an opportunistic adventurer who led campaigns to Africa and southern Italy and proclaimed himself king. However, he brought no long-term stability to Syracuse, which lapsed once again into anarchy after his assassination in 289. In fact, Syracuse's security was compromised by a group of his mercenaries, the Mamertines. The city had to call on the ambitious ruler of Epirus, Pyrrhus (who was already supporting Greek cities in southern Italy against the Romans), for help against both the Mamertines and a resurgent Carthage. It was from this weak position that Syracuse enjoyed an unexpected revival. When the Mamertines called for help from Rome, a new king of Syracuse, Hieron II, was persuaded of the advantages of allying with, rather than resisting, Rome and for the next 60 years he exploited his favoured position to bring about an era of prosperity. Once again trading links extended across the Mediterranean. One of the largest theatres of the Greek world, surmounted by a huge stoa, and a massive altar to Zeus, were among the magniloquent building projects of his day. Such grandeur masked the city's reliance on Rome, and when, after Hieron's death in 215, his youthful successor unwisely moved towards the Carthaginians who, under their general Hannibal, were threatening Rome from inside Italy, Rome's retaliation was inevitable. Even the genius of Archimedes (*see p. 355*) could not save Syracuse in 212, after two years of siege.

The Romans made Syracuse a provincial capital under a praetor (a magistrate elected annually in Rome) and adopted Hieron's system of a grain tax to feed Rome and her armies. Some praetors, notably the notorious Verres (*see p. 205*), used their rule to despoil the city, but evidence of Roman building—an amphitheatre, a triumphal arch and a new forum—attests to a steady prosperity. The city remained a stopping-point for any voyager coming to Italy from the east (in AD 59 the apostle Paul spent three days here on his way to Rome) and it had some status as a tourist attraction. Catacombs show the growth of Christianity (they date from a century before Constantine's Edict of Toleration of 313 and then expand rapidly after it).

After the Roman period, Syracuse's power declined rapidly, although the Byzantine Emperor Constans II resided there from 662, making it his capital until his assassination in 668. Syracuse was invaded by the Saracens in 878 but freed from Arab rule for a time by General George Maniakes (1038–40), sent by Basil II of Byzantium. The importance Syracuse regained between 1361 and 1536 by holding the quasi-independent seat of the Camera Reginale or Queen's Chamber, a kind of miniature Parliament, did not last. In 1837, having rebelled unsuccessfully against the Bourbons, it was punished by losing its role as provincial capital. After the Italian conquest of Libya the port expanded again but during the Second World War it was a target first for the Allied air forces and, after its capture on 10th July 1943, for German aircraft.

ORTIGIA

The island of Ortigia, just under 1km square, is joined to the mainland by three bridges. It forms the charming old town, best explored on foot and certainly the most pleasant place to stay in the city.

From **Ponte Umbertino** (*map 1*), the main bridge connecting the island to the mainland, numerous colourful little fishing boats that go out every night can be seen; the larger ones, moored on the Ortigia side, stay out for several days at a time. On the approach to the bridge, on the right-hand side is a 3.5m-high bronze **statue of Archimedes** (2016, Pietro Marchese and Virginia Rossello). The scientist is shown standing on his famous puzzle, the Stomachion, and is holding a compass and a burning mirror. To the left, the monumental Post Office by Francesco Fichera (1934) is now a hotel.

Soon reached from the foot of the bridge, along an avenue (with a taxi rank) of shady ficus trees, is **Piazza Pancali**. On the right, in Via XX Settembre, are the remains of the Porta Urbica, a gateway in the fortifications devised by Dionysius I.

To the left, a daily **market** for fresh fish, fruit and vegetables is held every morning except Sunday in the streets surrounding the old covered market-place, a fine turn-of-the-century building. Nearby is the district for fishermen and craftsmen, a small

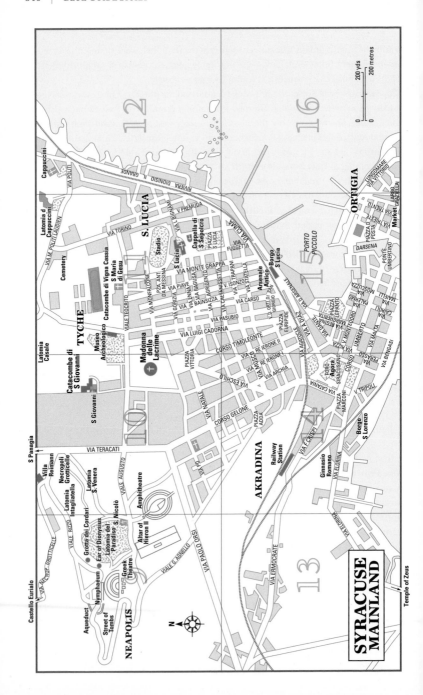

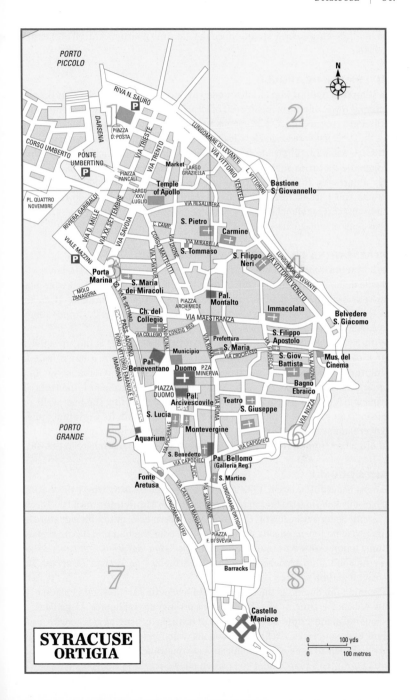

PORTO
PICCOLO

N

RIVA N. SAURO

DARSENA

P

PIAZZA
D. POSTA

CORSO UMBERTO

PONTE
UMBERTINO

P

PL. QUATTRO
NOVEMBRE

PIAZZA
PANCALI

LUNGOMARE DI LEVANTE

VIA TRIESTE

VIA TRENTO

VIA VITTORIO VENETO

L. VITTORINI

Market

Largo
GRAZIELLA

Temple
of Apollo

LARGO
XXV
LUGLIO

VIA RESALIBERA

Bastione
S. Giovannello

RIVIERA GARIBALDI

VIA D. MILLE

VIA XX SETTEMBRE

VIA SAVOIA

CORSO MATTEOTTI

VIA CAVOUR

C. CAMP

S. Pietro

VIA DIONE

Carmine

VIA MIRABELLA

S. Tommaso

S. Filippo
Neri

LUNGOMARE DI LEVANTE

VIA VITTORIO VENETO

Porta
Marina

VIA F. SETTIMO

S. Maria
dei Miracoli

PIAZZA
ARCHIMEDE

Pal.
Montalto

Immacolata

Belvedere
S. Giacomo

MOLO
ZANAGORA

VIALE MAZZINI

Ch. del
Collegio

VIA COLLEGIO

LANDOLINA

VIA CONSIG. REG.

VIA MAESTRANZA

VIA ROMA

Prefettura

S. Filippo
Apostolo

VIA GIUDECCA

VIA ALAGONA

PASS. ADORNO

FORO VITTORIO EMANUELE II

(MARINA)

Municipio

S. Maria

VIA CROCIFISSO

S. Giov.
Battista

Mus. del
Cinema

Pal.
Beneventano

Duomo

PZA
MINERVA

Bagno
Ebraico

PIAZZA
DUOMO

Pal.
Arcivescovile

Teatro

VIA ROMA

S. Giuseppe

VIA NIZZA

S. Lucia

VIA PICHERALE

Montevergine

Aquarium

VIA CAPODIECI

PORTO
GRANDE

S. Benedetto

VIA CAPODIECI

ZUCC.

Pal. Bellomo
(Galleria Reg.)

Fonte
Aretusa

S. Martino

VIA CASTELLO MANIACE

VIA SALOMONE

LUNGOMARE ORTIGIA

LUNGOMARE ALFEO

PIAZZA
F. DI SVEVIA

Barracks

Castello
Maniace

0   100 yds

0   100 metres

**SYRACUSE
ORTIGIA**

area of interesting narrow streets, once the old Arab quarter, centred on Largo della Graziella.

THE TEMPLE OF APOLLO

The Temple of Apollo (*map 3*), surrounded by lawns and papyrus plants, is the earliest peripteral Doric temple in Sicily, built of local limestone in the late 7th century BC and attributed to the architects Kleomenes and Epikleos. Some scholars have identified it with the *Artemision* recorded by Cicero, but the dedication to Apollo cut in the steps of the stereobate (still visible on the eastern side) seems conclusive. Transformed through the centuries, first into a church, then a mosque, then a Spanish prison and lastly a barracks. It was freed from overlying structures in 1938. Two monolithic columns and part of the cella walls, showing the portal of the Norman church, remain intact. Fragments of its polychrome terracotta cornice are preserved in the archaeological museum (*see p. 360*).

PORTA MARINA TO THE CHIESA DEL COLLEGIO

Porta Marina (*map 3*) is a plain 15th-century gateway to the Great Harbour, with an aedicule in the Spanish Gothic style. The long promenade by the water's edge, planted with splendid *Ficus benjamin* trees, called **Foro Vittorio Emanuele II**, is known locally as the Marina. There is a lovely view across the harbour to the wooded shore on the Maddalena headland, the ancient *Plemmyrion*.

Within the gate to the left (in the street of the same name) is the attractive little church of **Santa Maria dei Miracoli**, with a fine doorway resting on little lions, a sculptured lunette, and a worn tabernacle in the Catalan Gothic style. Straight on from the gate, Via Ruggero Settimo emerges on a terrace above the trees of the Marina and Via del Collegio leads away from the sea skirting the high walls of the imposing, Counter-Reformation **Chiesa del Collegio**, with its Corinthian pilasters and overhanging cornice (1635–87). The interior (now a temporary exhibition venue) contains altars from the former Jesuit college in Palermo, moved here in 1927–31.

PIAZZA DUOMO

The most beautiful square in the city is Piazza Duomo (*map 5*), where there are some fine Baroque buildings: to the left of the cathedral the **Municipio** (Town Hall) occupies the former Seminary begun in 1628 by Giovanni Vermexio; notice his signature lizard on the extreme left-hand side of the cornice. Under the building lie the remains of an Ionic temple known as the **Artemision** (*open Mon–Sat 10–6, Sun 10–1*). Probably never finished, and probably dedicated to Artemis (the Roman Minerva), it was discovered in 1963.

Adjoining the duomo is the **Palazzo Arcivescovile** (Archbishop's Palace; c. 1750, Louis-Alexandre Dumontier), housing the prestigious Biblioteca Alagoniana, with precious old manuscripts and incunabula. It has a shady hanging garden with oranges, lemons and palm trees. Archbishop Alagona, who founded the library in 1780, loved books so much that he excommunicated anyone caught stealing them. A doorway opening onto the square under the garden allows access to the **Ipogeo** (*open Tues–*

PALAZZO ARCIVESCOVILE AND THE DUOMO

Sun 10–1 & 6–midnight), subterranean passages under the city, some hewn out in the Byzantine era, which house an exhibition on their use as an air-raid shelter during the Allied bombing in 1943. The self-guided route through impressive dry and dripping caverns emerges at sea level on Foro Vittorio Emanuele II.

On the other side of the square, opposite the Municipio, is **Palazzo Beneventano del Bosco**, a dignified building by the local master-builder Luciano Alì (1778–88) enclosing a handsome courtyard. Next to it is the curved, pink façade of Palazzo Gaetani e Arezzo.

At the south end of the square, with a balcony on the corner, is Palazzo Impellizzeri and the church of **Santa Lucia alla Badia** (*open 11–4, closed Mon*), which has a fine Bavarian Baroque façade of 1695 by Luciano Caracciolo, who provided it with a balcony so the cloistered nuns could watch the festivities for St Lucy. Displayed over the high altar is a marvellous **painting by Caravaggio** of the *Burial of St Lucy*, carried out in 1608 after his adventurous escape from Malta, while he was the guest of his admirer Mario Minniti, and completed in less than two months. Notice the despair of Lucy's mother, who believes herself responsible for her daughter's death, and the impatience of the uncouth grave-diggers (the one on the left is perhaps a self-portrait of the artist), waiting for the priest to finish his prayer. At the time of writing discussions were in progress over whether to remove the painting to the church of Santa Lucia al Sepolcro (*see p. 357*), the church for which Caravaggio painted it.

Metal lines inserted into the paving of the piazza and the adjacent Via Minerva trace the lines of ancient structures uncovered during the various excavations carried out in this area: the path of an ancient road runs in front of the Palazzo Arcivescovile; a small archaic temple with its temenos and votive deposit (the filled circle) are picked out in front of the duomo, and the foot-print of the Artemision is indicated in Via Minerva. A map in front of the old archaeological museum, now the offices of the local archaeological authorities (opposite the Palazzo Arcivescovile) provides more information about these excavations.

Just out of the piazza is the church of **Montevergine** (*closed*) with a façade by Andrea Vermexio; the convent next door is the gallery of Modern Art, **Galleria Civica d'Arte Contemporanea Montevergini** (*open 9–12 & 4–8, T: 0931 24902*), housing temporary exhibitions by local artists.

THE DUOMO

The duomo, or Santa Maria del Piliero or delle Colonne (*open 8–7.45; T: 0931 65328*) dominates the piazza. In the 7th century Bishop Zosimus repaired the Byzantine church built from the ruins of Gelon's Temple of Athena and consecrated it as the cathedral of the city. The present façade is a powerful Sicilian Baroque composition erected in 1728–54 and designed by Andrea Palma; on the summit is a double-armed Cross, symbolising the presence of the archbishop. The marble statues of Sts Peter and Paul flanking the steps are the earliest known works of Ignazio Marabitti; he also sculpted the other statues (1754) on the façade, of Bishop Marcian, the Madonna and St Lucy.

HISTORY OF THE DUOMO

In 480 BC the victorious Gelon returned home from Himera with thousands of prisoners of war to be used as slaves. In celebration of his victory, the finest craftsmen among them were selected to build a new temple to Athena on the summit of the island of Ortigia. Work probably continued for about ten years, although some scholars suggest that it took only two years to complete. Doric peripteral and hexastyle, with 14 columns on the long sides, the temple had doors inlaid with ivory and gold. Inside, the statue of Athena, larger than life-size, was made of Parian marble, with face, hands, feet and weapons of gold. Paintings by Zeuxis lined the walls of the cella. The magnificence of the building and these works of art were famous throughout the Mediterranean. The golden shield in the tympanum, which reflected the rays of the sun, was a landmark for sailors. All these treasures were later stolen by the praetor Verres (*see p. 205*).

Under Byzantium the temple was converted into a church: arches were cut in the cella wall, the entrance was moved to the west, and the space between the columns closed by a wall. For the Arabs it was the Great Mosque. The Normans raised the height of the roof and added clerestory windows and the side chapels. The Spanish added the ceiling (of chestnut wood from Mt Etna) in 1518. Damaged by several earthquakes, it was rebuilt after 1693 when the Norman façade fell.

In Via Minerva twelve columns of the temple, with their architrave and triglyphs, punctuate the medieval north wall of the church, their cornice replaced by Muslim crenellation when the church became a mosque. Excavations beneath the cathedral carried out from 1912–17 revealed parts of an Archaic temple, demolished to make way for the later building, and, at a lower level, pre-Greek huts of the 8th century BC. More recently, while re-paving, an ancient Sicel necropolis of rock-cut tombs was discovered under the square.

SYRACUSE
View along Via Minerva with the north flank of the duomo.
The Doric columns of the Temple of Athena are clearly visible.

Interior of the duomo

Stripped of Baroque decoration between 1909 and 1927, the nave arcades were reduced to the plain massive piers formed by the eight arches opened by the Byzantine Christians in the side walls of the cella, which is the original 480 BC construction. The stained-glass windows are modern. On the internal entrance wall, two columns from the opisthodomos of the cella are preserved, and 19 columns of the peristyle are incorporated in the aisles, those on the left side being engaged. Of the temple's 36 columns, a total of 24 survive. Along both sides of the nave, more or less at the height where the roof of the temple would have been, is an inscription in Latin describing this as the oldest Christian community in Europe: *Ecclesia Syracusana prima Divi Petri filia et prima post Antiochenam Cristo dicata*: 'The church of Syracuse is the first daughter of divine Peter, and the first to be dedicated to Christ after Antioch.'

South side: The first chapel (**1**) is for baptisms. The **font** is a 3rd-century BC marble krater with a Greek inscription standing on seven miniature bronze lions (13th century). It was found in the catacombs of San Giovanni (*see p. 362*) where it had been used as a burial urn. On the wall are fragments of floor mosaics which survive from the earlier Byzantine church.

In the second chapel (**2**), with wrought-iron gates by Pietro Spagnuolo (1605), is a silver statue of St Lucy by Pietro Rizzo (1599), shown only on

SYRACUSE DUOMO

1 Baptistery
2 Second chapel
3 Third chapel
4 Cappella del Crocifisso
   (*St Zosimus* by Antonello da Messina)
5 Chancel
6 Byzantine apse (*Madonna of the Snow* by Antonello Gagini)
7 North wall

Temple pronaos

6

4

5

3

7

2

1

Temple opisthodomos

Duomo entrance

■ Temple of Athena

■ Later constructions

certain religious festivals and carried in procession in May and on 13th December. The two marble medallions are attributed to Ignazio Marabitti.

The third chapel (**3**), also with magnificent wrought-iron gates (1811), was designed in 1650–3, probably by Giovanni Vermexio. The vault frescoes are by the natural scientist and artist Agostino Scilla (1657). The altar frontal bears a beautiful relief of the *Last Supper* by Filippo Della Valle (1762).

Above is a ciborium by Luigi Vanvitelli (1752).

On the left wall of the **Cappella del Crocifisso** (**4**), is a panel painting of St Zosimus attributed to Antonello da Messina; notice the innovative three-quarters positioning, the expressive face and the varying textures of the sumptuous robes. Opposite is a damaged early 16th-century panel painting of St Marcian. In the sanctuary is a Byzantine Crucifix and 13 panels from a polyptych by the school of Antonello (or early work by Antonello himself?). Other paintings exhibited here include two works by Marco di Costanzo (*St Jerome* and the *Annunciation*).

Chancel: The bronze candelabra (**5**) date from 1513, while the main altar is the work of Giovanni Vermexio (1659), incorporating a monolith from the Temple of Athena. The altarpiece, by Agostino Scilla (1653), is the *Birth of the Virgin*. The two paintings over the choir, of *St Paul Preaching to the Christians of Syracuse* and *St Peter Sending Marcian to be Bishop of Syracuse*, were carried out by Silvio Galimberti in 1950.

North side: In the Byzantine apse (**6**) is a *Madonna of the Snow* by Antonello Gagini (1512). The end of the pronaos wall of the temple with its column can be seen here. The noticeable irregularity of the pillars on this side is due to earthquakes.

Along the north side wall (**7**) are three arresting statues in white Carrara marble: *St Lucy* by Antonello Gagini; *Madonna and Child* by Domenico Gagini; and *St Catherine of Alexandria* by the Gagini school, offering an interesting comparison in style.

FONTE ARETUSA TO CASTELLO MANIACE

From Piazza Duomo, Via Picherale passes the Hotel des Etrangers, which incorporates part of the medieval Casa Migliaccio, and leads down to a quiet terrace on the waterfront surrounding the **Fonte Aretusa** (*map 5*), one of the most famous springs of the Greek world. The spring of the nymph Arethusa was celebrated by Pindar and Ovid: when Arethusa was bathing in the River Alpheios near Olympia, the river god fell in love with her. In order to escape from him, Arethusa plunged into the Ionian sea and reappeared here. Transformed by the goddess Artemis into a spring, she was pursued here by Alpheus, who mingled his river water with that of the spring: it was believed that the river in the Peloponnese was connected, via the sea, to the fountain of Arethusa. A freshwater spring, called the Occhio della Zillica and said to be Alpheus, still occasionally wells up in the harbour. The spring of Arethusa diminished after the erection of the Spanish fortifications. Nelson stopped here before the battle of the Nile in 1798 and noted in a letter that 'surely, watering at the fountain of Arethus, we must have victory'. The fountain now flows into a pond (built in 1843), planted with papyrus, abounding in fish and inhabited by ducks, under a venerable old Morton Bay fig tree.

By the spring is the **Aquarium** (*open 10–5; T: 333 167 4461*), with some of the fish to be found in the Ionian Sea. The attractive seafront here with its shady *Ficus benjamin* trees, is a favourite spot for the *passeggiata*.

The end of the promontory, beyond Piazza Federico di Svevia, is occupied by the 13th-century **Castello Maniace** (*map 8; open Tues–Sat 8.30–1.30, Mon 2.30–6.30, closed Sun and holidays; last tickets 30mins before closing; T: 0931 450 8211*), built c. 1232 by Frederick II of Hohenstaufen but named after the Byzantine general George Maniakes, supposed (in error) to be its founder. The 51m-square keep, with cylindrical corner towers, has probably lost a third of its original height. On either side of the imposing Swabian doorway are two consoles, formerly bearing splendid 3rd-century BC bronze rams, one of which is now in the Salinas archaeological museum of Palermo.

Overlooking the harbour are the remains of a large three-light window. Beneath the castle is the so-called *Bagno della Regina*, an underground chamber once probably a reservoir.

Via Salomone and Via San Martino return past (right) the church of **San Martino** (*map 6*), founded in the 6th century, with a doorway of 1338. The interior, dating from Byzantine times, contains a fine triptych by a local 15th-century master. Opposite, at the end of the street stands the church of **San Benedetto** (*map 5*), with a huge canvas of the *Ecstasy of St Benedict* by Mario Minniti.

GALLERIA REGIONALE

Map 5–6. Open Tues–Sat 9–7, Sun 9–1. Last tickets 30mins before closing. T: 0931 69511
Palazzo Bellomo, seat of the Galleria Regionale, combines elements of its Swabian construction (c. 1234) with alterations of the 15th century. The collection includes some great masterpieces, displayed in loose historical order. Entrance is through two courtyards. In the first are stone inscriptions, including some from the Jewish cemetery. In the second courtyard are stone coats of arms and a large window allowing the view of some 18th-century state carriages. In the small rooms opening onto this courtyard are elements of medieval art: sculptures, polyptychs, and some lustre-ware bowls from Valencia. Steps lead up to the principal galleries (*lift available*).

Gallery 1: In the first room is a large wooden relief map of the city of Syracuse, made in the 18th century. High up on the wall is a painted wooden beam from the cathedral. To the left is Gallery 1, displaying the *Madonna Annunciate* by Antonello da Messina, painted for the church of the Annunziata of Palazzolo Acreide in 1474, and discovered by chance in the church in 1897. Painted on wood and much decayed, apart from the figures of the Virgin and the Angel, the fragments of colour were transferred onto canvas during a long and difficult restoration. Close by are other contemporary works of art: an illuminated book of hours, and a lustre bowl, both made in Syracuse. In the other part of the room, in front of the huge fireplace, is the *Madonna of the Goldfinch* by Domenico Gagini and the marble tombstone of Giovanni Savastida, who died in 1472, showing his effigy on one side and a *Pietà* on the other, probably the work of Francesco Laurana.

Gallery 2: A collection of crib figurines in wax and cloth, and Sicilian ceramic bowls and jugs.

Gallery 3: 17th-century paintings, mostly anonymous, and a model in wood and ivory of the city of Syracuse.

Gallery 4: Beautiful coloured marble intarsia work together with a stunning *Immaculate Virgin with Saints* by Willem Borremans. The showcases display Church silverware and embroidered vestments, and a large model ship in silver, a reliquary of St Ursula.

Gallery 5: Paintings by Giuseppe and Giovanni Reati, a *Martyrdom of St Lucy* and other paintings by Mario Minniti, and some interesting little figurines and reliquaries, examples of the skills of the local craftsmen.

Gallery 6: Large statue-reliquaries and a sketchbook belonging to Filippo

Paladini. Also a large altarpiece by Bernardino Niger of the *Adoration of the Magi*.

Gallery 7: In the middle of the room is a marvellous collection of old Byzantine icons, panel paintings of saints and a series of episodes from the Old Testament, from the *Creation* to the *Expulsion from the Garden*.

VIA ROMA AND PIAZZA ARCHIMEDE

Via Roma, the backbone of Ortigia, with charming overhanging balconies, leads away from the seafront, north past the **Teatro Comunale** (1897, Giuseppe Damiani Almeyda; *T: 333 216 7709 to request visit*). On the corner of Via Crocifisso is the church of **Santa Maria della Concezione** (1651), which has a lovely interior with a tiled floor. In the vault is a late 18th-century fresco by Sebastiano Lo Monaco, while the altarpieces on the left side and on the first right altar are by Onofrio Gabrieli, depicting the *Madonna of the Letter*, patroness of Messina, Gabrieli's home town, the *Martyrdom of St Lucy* and the *Massacre of the Innocents*.

Piazza Archimede (*map 3*) was laid out between 1872 and 1878 in the centre of Ortigia, but some palaces and courtyards preserve medieval elements. In the centre is the cement Fountain of Diana by Giulio Moschetti (1906). Off the square, reached by Via Montalto, is the Gothic façade of **Palazzo Montalto**, propped up with concrete bastions. The shell of the building, with a fine loggia, is visible from the rear.

ARCHIMEDES

The mathematical genius Archimedes may have been a close friend or relative of King Hieron II of Syracuse; certainly it was Hieron who sponsored his sojourn at the great library of Alexandria, where he was able to discuss his theories with his peers. Among the discoveries attributed to him are the cogged wheel (hence the winch); the screw pump for lifting water; the relationship between the circumference and the diameter of a circle; the lever; the displacement of liquid method for ascertaining the composition of metals (which he famously discovered while in the bath); and the calculation of the volume of a sphere contained inside a cylinder. In 240 BC he designed a luxurious cruise ship for Hieron, called the *Syrakosia*. It was a catamaran, built of timber from the forests of Etna, rope from Iberia, ivory and rosewood from Africa, was provided with marble baths and a garden, and weighed 4,000 tons. Intended to demonstrate the power of Syracuse in the Mediterranean, the ship was in fact impractical, being too large for most ports. Hieron made the generous gesture of sending it to Egypt loaded with wheat, as a gift to Ptolemy IV Philopator during a famine. During the Roman siege of Syracuse from 214–212 BC, Archimedes devised many ways of frustrating the enemy attacks: it is said he succeeded in burning some of the Roman ships by using large bronze mirrors to reflect the rays of the sun onto them. When the city fell, the Roman commander Marcus Claudius Marcellus ordered his men to take Archimedes alive but, distracted by his calculations, the inventor refused to give his name, and was killed by an impatient legionary. Marcellus himself ordered that a magnificent tomb be prepared, of which the location, searched for and found by Cicero, is now again lost.

VIA MAESTRANZA AND THE GIUDECCA

The elegant **Via Maestranza** (*map 3-4*), once seat of the wealthy city corporations leads east from Piazza Archimede towards the sea, past several Baroque palaces and the church of **San Francesco** (or Immacolata) with an attractive little convex façade It has a fine late 18th-century interior, with twelve small paintings of the Apostles in the apse. Two Gothic portals have been exposed.

Via Giudecca, to the right, recalls the Jewish district of the city. By following it south, after 150m you find on the right the tiny church of **San Filippo Apostolo**, once a synagogue. Opposite the church a little street leads to Piazza del Precursore, with the 12th-century church of San Giovanni Battista, usually known as **San Giovannello** (*to request visit of both churches, call Kairos, T: 0931 64694*), partially demolished because of earthquake damage, it still retains a fine portal and rose window. This was one of the four basilicas built in the city by the English bishop Richard Palmer in 1184, and later rebuilt under Swabian rule. Also in this district, at 33 Piazza San Giuseppe, is the award-winning puppet museum, **Museo dei Pupi** (*open March–May and Sept–Nov Mon–Sat 11–1 & 4–6, June–Aug daily 11–6, 15 Dec–15 Jan daily 11–1 & 4–6; closed 15 Aug, morning 25, 26 Dec and 1 Jan; T: 0931 465540, www.pupari.com*), with typical marionettes of Syracuse together with stage sets and posters.

Back on Via Maestranza, the last turning to the right is Via Alagona, where at no. 41 you will find Palazzo Cordaci, housing the **Museo del Cinema** (*call Remo Romeo, T: 347 831 6552 to request visit*). Besides a vast library of books about cinema and theatre, there is a collection of more than 2,600 films. Cameras and posters going back to the early days of cinema are also on view. Close by, at no. 52, is an intact medieval **Jewish mikveh**, or ablution pool, which came to light during restoration work in an ancient palace (*call Bagno Ebraico, T: 0931 22255, to book visit*).

VIA NIZZA AND VIA VITTORIO VENETO

The final crossroad of via Maestranza, before it meets the sea, leads right to Via Nizza and left to Via Vittorio Veneto. The **Museo del Papiro** at Via Nizza 14 (*open May–Sept Tues–Sat 10–7, Sun 10–2; Oct–April 9.30–2; closed 1 Jan and 25 Dec; last tickets 30mins before closing; T: 0931 22100, www.museodelpapiro.it*) contains a rich collection of material relating to the creation and use of the papyrus plant in the ancient world.

Via Vittorio Veneto, once the *Mastrarua*, the main street in Spanish times, is lined with 17th–18th-century Spanish-style palaces, and emerges on the sea by the church of **San Filippo Neri** (*map 4*), which bears the lizard signature of the architect Vermexio beside the left-hand mascaron. Next door is the fine restored Palazzo Interlandi. Via Mirabella (with Palazzo Bongiovanni on the corner) leads away from the seafront past the church of the **Carmine**, which preserves part of its 14th-century structure.

AKRADINA

The area on the mainland opposite Ortigia corresponds to the ancient district of *Akradina*, which centres on the **Foro Siracusano** (*map 14*), a large and busy square with a Fascist-era war memorial (1936) and fine trees. Here are some remains of the ancient **agora**; recent excavations have revealed other parts of the agora near Corso Umberto and Corso Gelone, where dwellings of the late 8th century BC have also come to light, the earliest of the Greek period so far found in Syracuse.

GINNASIO ROMANO

From Piazza Marconi, Via Crispi forks right to the railway station, while Via Elorina (left) leads to the so-called Ginnasio Romano (*map 14; closed*), a small group of ruins surrounded by lawns and palm trees, with a portico on three sides, an altar, a temple and a small theatre. The portico on the north side, and part of the high temple podium remain. The theatre's orchestra is now under water but a few of the lower steps of the cavea are visible. The buildings, all of Imperial date, probably formed part of a serapeum, a Roman sanctuary dedicated to the Egyptian god Serapis.

ARSENALE ANTICO

From the Foro Siracusano, Viale Diaz leads towards Borgo Santa Lucia (*map 15*). On the left are two excavated sites: the first (straddled by a modern condominium) includes a small **bath-house** of Roman origin, possibly the Baths of Daphne in which Emperor Constans II was assassinated in 668; the second, just beyond, behind railings, marks the **Arsenale Antico**, where the foundations of the mechanism used by the Greeks to drag their ships into dry dock can be seen. In a simple house at no. 11 in Via Orti di San Giorgio, a plaster image of the Virgin is supposed to have wept in 1953. A plaque in Piazza Euripide commemorates this. The sanctuary of the Madonna delle Lacrime (*described on p. 362*) was built in honour of the miracle.

SANTA LUCIA AL SEPOLCRO

The church of Santa Lucia al Sepolcro (*map 11*) faces a large shady square. It was begun in 1629 to a plan by Giovanni Vermexio and completed in the 18th century (perhaps by Rosario Gagliardi), on the spot where St Lucy, patron saint of Syracuse (*see overleaf*), was buried. The portal, apses and base of the campanile are Norman work and the rose window is of the 14th century. Inside the church, in the sacristy, is a copy of Caravaggio's *Kiss of Judas* (the original is in Dublin). The church's other Caravaggio the *Burial of St Lucy*, together with two medieval Crucifixes, have been transferred to the church of Santa Lucia alla Badia in Ortigia (*see p. 349*).

A tunnel from the church leads past the entrance to the **catacombs of St Lucy** (*open 9–12.30, T: Kairos 0931 64694 to request visit*). These are the oldest catacombs in Sicily and the most extensive in existence after those in Rome. Caverns in the limestone existed here before the Christian era; there are Christian remains of the 2nd century and fragmentary Byzantine paintings. The tunnel emerges in **Santo Sepolcro**, a domed octagonal chapel by Giovanni Vermexio, partly below ground. This was the burial-place of St Lucy (her empty tomb remains behind the altar) and it was from here that her body was taken to Constantinople in 1038. It was later seized as booty by the Venetians and taken to Venice, where it can still be seen in the church of San Geremia. The 17th-century statue of the saint is by Gregorio Tedeschi.

ST LUCY OF SYRACUSE

According to the Vatican files, Lucy of Syracuse would have been about 24 years old when she was martyred in 304, during the persecution of Diocletian. She had accompanied her wealthy, ailing mother to Catania to pray at the tomb of St Agatha. Having obtained a miraculous recovery, the two women returned to Syracuse, where they proceeded to donate all their possessions to the poor, as testimony of the miracle. Lucy was denounced by her betrothed for practising Christianity, and imprisoned. As punishment for her refusal to make sacrifices to the gods, the consul Pascasius sentenced her to be taken to the brothel, stripped and raped. The soldiers, however, could not move her; she seemed rooted to the ground. Not even a team of oxen was sufficient. By now the people of the city were rejoicing and calling out her name. Pascasius told the soldiers to pile logs of wood around her to burn her, but even with the help of generous quantities of oil, the pyre would not catch. She was finally killed by a soldier who thrust his dagger into her neck. Portrayals of Lucy show the saint with her eyes in a dish or cup, about which the Vatican says nothing, but she is constantly invoked by people with eye problems, and also by the Swedish, to whom light is so important. Swedish girls traditionally take part in her procession in Syracuse on 13th December, once thought to be the shortest day in the year, harbinger of spring. The name Lucy derives from the Latin word *lux*, 'light', and the goddess Artemis, bringer of light, was once an important divinity in Syracuse.

MUSEO ARCHEOLOGICO REGIONALE PAOLO ORSI

Map 11. Open Tues–Sat 9–7, Sun and holidays 9–2. Last tickets 1hr before closing. T: 0931 489511.

This museum, dedicated to the great archaeologist Paolo Orsi, superintendent of antiquities from 1895–1934, has one of the most interesting archaeological collections in Italy, especially representative of the eastern half of Sicily. The material from excavations made by Orsi himself is outstanding. The collections are displayed in an unusual, low-level functional building in the shape of a broken triangle designed by Franco Minissi in 1967 and opened to the public in 1988.

The approach is through the garden of Villa Landolina, with splendid trees and some antique remains, which was once used as a Protestant cemetery. Among the 19th-century British and American tombstones (reached by the upper path which encircles the garden) is that of the Classicist German poet and scholar August von Platen (1796–1835).

Beyond the entrance hall the centre of the building has a display on the history of the museum and the organisation of the exhibits, which are arranged chronologically and begin on the ground floor. At the time of writing the section on the territory of Syracuse during the Early Middle Ages was still in preparation. In the basement is the Medagliere, the numismatic collection.

Section A (Ground floor): Geology, Palaeontology and Prehistory

Prehistory: The geology and the palaeontology of Sicily, with models of the famous dwarf elephants, the skulls of which, when unearthed in the past, gave rise to the legend of the Cyclops.

Neolithic Period: Represented by the Stentinello culture, characterised by villages protected by ditches and the use of incised and impressed pottery.

Early Bronze Age: Display relating to the site of Castelluccio (between Noto Antica and Palazzolo Acreide), with objects recovered by Paolo Orsi, including brown painted pottery and carved stone doors from rock-cut tombs, each presenting spirals and what appear to be male-female motifs, presumably symbolising death, rebirth and eternity.

Middle Bronze Age: Material from Thapsos, an emporium of the Mycenaean world, with inhabitants from various parts of the Mediterranean. The necropolis was excavated by Paolo Orsi but the inhabited area (1500–900 BC) has only recently been examined. Finds include imported pottery (from Mycenae, Cyprus and Malta) and some splendid large storage jars made using the 'coil of clay' method (some of these had been recycled as tombs). There are also some fascinating lebetes (water-bowls) with a pedestal underneath, and strangely-modelled upright backs, with what could be eyes and ears, or nipples and upheld arms, perhaps recalling a divinity who protected water. They had handles behind, so they could be carried from one place to another, perhaps for ritual use. High stemmed vessels were also for serving food, with diners seated on the floor.

Late Bronze Age: A display is dedicated to Pantalica, the most important Late Bronze Age site in Sicily (*see p. 383*). There are many of the handsome, characteristic red vases, turned on the wheel, and in some cases (the heart-shaped jugs for carrying water) reminiscent of Mycenaean ware.

Nearby are some of the numerous bronze artefacts found at Pantalica. Interesting reconstructed tombs, illustrating different burial methods, and a fine hoard of bronze fragments from Mendolito near Adrano, complete this part of the museum.

Section B (Ground floor): Greek colonies in Eastern Sicily

Greek colonisation: This period began in the mid-8th century BC, when settlers from Naxos, Corinth and Chalcis arrived on the island. Among the finds is a superb kouros (late 6th century BC) from Leontinoi, the head of which is in the Museo Civico in Catania. Ample space is dedicated to **Megara Hyblaea** (*see p. 386*). The most interesting sculptures include a marble statue of a young man (c. 560–550 BC), thought to be a funerary monument, with an inscription on the leg naming him as the physician Sambrotidas, son of Mandrocles, and a headless statue of painted local limestone of a seated mother goddess suckling twins (550 BC). When found in the 1950s it was smashed into more than 900 pieces by workers building the oil refineries for fear of losing their employment; the head was never found, probably pulverised when the statue was thrown over a cliff. **Syracuse**: Finds from Ortigia are arranged topographically, giving an idea of the continuous habitation of the island. Akradina is represented by material from excavations in Piazza della Vittoria, where a sanctuary of Demeter and Persephone of the 5th–4th centuries BC was found, with hundreds of votive statuettes and an exceptional polychrome terracotta bust of Artemis. The necropoleis of the city have revealed much of interest, arranged in chronological order and displayed as they were found. Items include an exquisite proto-Corinthian lion-shaped perfume vase (725–700 BC, Case 190) and a fine bronze 8th-century BC Geometric-style statuette of a horse, now the symbol of the museum (Case 188). Models of the temples of Apollo and Athena and terracotta fragments from them are exhibited. The frieze of seven lion-faced gargoyles comes from the Temple of Athena. The stunning polychrome marble relief of the running Gorgon with Pegasus, the earliest-known representation (7th century BC) of the unfortunate lady, was part of the older temple on the same site, replaced by Gelon's magnificent new building in 478 BC.

Section C (Ground floor): Sub-colonies and Hellenised centres

Heloros, Akrai and Kasmenai are represented by a high-relief in limestone (570–560 BC) of Persephone holding a dove, and weapons left as ex-votos. **Kamarina**: Finds include a large terracotta horse and rider (6th century BC), perhaps one of the Dioscuri, used as part of the roof decoration of a temple. **Grammichele**: A fine marble torso by a Greek artist (c. 500 BC) and a terracotta goddess enthroned (late 6th century BC). **Francavilla di Sicilia**: A remarkable series of pinakes, little terracotta pictures in relief (470–460 BC), which previously had only been found at the sanctuary of Persephone at Locri, in Calabria. **Centuripe**: A miniature clay altar bears a relief from the 6th century BC showing a lion attacking a bull. **Adrano**: The bronze statuette known as the *Ephebe of Mendolito* dates from c. 460 BC. The last section on the ground floor is devoted to Paolo Orsi's work in **Gela and Agrigento**. The vases from Gela include a krater signed by Polygnotus (440 BC); part of a cup signed by Chachyrylion (520–510 BC); a lekythos with a Nike, signed by Douris (470–460 BC), and a bronze dish with a relief of horses (7th century BC). Also a fragment by the Panaitos Painter, and fine bronze kraters. The finds from Agrigento include three rare wooden statuettes of Archaic type dating from the late 7th century BC, found by a sacred spring at Palma di Montechiaro (Case 309).

Section D (Upper floor): Hellenistic and Roman statuary

Two colossal heads of Asklepios, one found in the Syracuse amphitheatre and the other found on the isthmus of Ortigia, a delicate statuette of Asklepios, a marvellous figure in marble of an old fisherman (a Roman copy of a Greek original). The highlight, however, is the famous **Venus Anadyomene**, 'emerging from the water', an Imperial-Roman work inspired by Praxiteles' famous Cnidian Aphrodite of the 4th century BC. Found in Syracuse in 1804 by the aristocrat and amateur archaeologist Saverio Landolina, she was greatly admired by Guy de Maupassant, who came purposely to see her in 1885 and left a vivid description of his emotions when he saw her: 'It is not woman poeticised, idealised, divine or majestic like the Venus de Milo; it is woman as she is, as she is loved, desired and should be embraced.'

Section F (Upper floor): Late Antique Syracuse

This section is devoted to a somewhat shadowy period in the history of the city. Christianity is no longer a forbidden cult but times are difficult, epidemics and pirate raids are frequent, and the economy suffers accordingly. The highlight of the collection is the Sarcophagus of Adelphia, a white marble coffin carved in high relief with episodes from the Bible, including the *Nativity*, *Flight into Egypt* and *Massacre of the Innocents*, surrounding the central medallion with the magistrate Valerius and his wife Adelphia. Notice also the beautifully crafted bronze liturgical vessels recovered from the seabed off the Plemmyrion headland, where the ship that was transporting them from Constantinople to Syracuse sank during a storm. The display is called *Il Relitto del Plemmyrion*.

Medagliere (Basement)

The exceptional numismatic collection (*open Tues–Sat 9.30–1.30, Wed 9.30–5.30, closed Sun and Mon*) includes coins from the Greek cities of Sicily and southern Italy, together with Roman, Byzantine and Islamic coins, the first coins minted by the Normans, followed by Swabian, Aragonese and Spanish examples. The first coins issued on the island are from Naxos, showing Dionysus or Silenus and bunches of grapes; the earliest go back to about 525 BC. Beautiful examples were also made in ancient Katane (Catania); see the splendid tetradrachm with the head of Apollo, made by Herakleidas at the end of the 5th century BC. Coins from Gela show Zeus as a human-headed bull. Ancient Syracuse was famed for the beauty of its coins minted from the late 5th to the early 4th century BC, and some of the finest of these can be seen in Case 16, mostly in silver, but you will also find a gold coin showing Herakles strangling a lion. Among the rarities from the famous Floristella collection is a small gold coin of Messana (Messina) showing a hare on the obverse and a chariot drawn by mules on the reverse. There are also interesting examples of the art of Sicilian goldsmiths, from prehistory to modern times, with lovely seal-rings from Sant'Angelo Muxaro, rings and Byzantine earrings from Pantalica, and necklaces.

TYCHE

MADONNA DELLE LACRIME

The vast tepee-shaped sanctuary of the Madonna delle Lacrime, Our Lady of Tears (*map 10; open 7–8, until 9 on Sun and holidays; T: 0931 21446 or 0931 22102*) was begun in 1970 to enshrine a small mass-produced plaster image of the Madonna, and inaugurated in 1994. The figure is supposed to have wept for four days in 1953 in a nearby house. The sanctuary (by Michel Andrault and Pierre Parat) incorporates a late Roman tomb and numerous ex-votos in the crypt. The huge conical spire (98m high, including the statue) towers incongruously above the city.

Adjoining it to the south, in Piazza della Vittoria, extensive excavations begun in 1973 during the construction of the sanctuary have revealed a group of Hellenistic and Roman houses, a sanctuary of Demeter and Persephone (late 5th or early 4th century BC) and a monumental 5th-century BC fountain. Five thousand terracotta votive statuettes were found here, some of which are now exhibited in the archaeological museum.

THE CHURCH AND CATACOMBS OF SAN GIOVANNI

Open 10–12.30 & 2.30–4 (6 in summer). Guided tours every 30mins. Call Kairos, T: 0931 64694, to request visit, www.kairos-web.com.

The ruined church and catacombs of San Giovanni lie amidst modern buildings. The church façade is preceded by three arches constructed of medieval fragments. To the right is the main entrance and ticket office, beyond which are the entrances (right) to the catacombs and (left) to the ruined church and crypt.

The catacombs

The catacombs are the remains of an early Christian burial ground, probably in use from the 3rd century to the end of the 6th. They are among the most interesting and extensive in Italy outside Rome, preserving examples of different types of burial, loculi, arcosolia and tombs cut into the rock floor. From the decumanus maximus, or principal gallery, adapted from a disused Greek aqueduct, smaller passages lead to five domed circular chapels, one with the rock-cut tombs said to be of seven nuns, members of one of the first religious houses established after the persecutions in Syracuse. One of the niches contains a sarcophagus bearing a Greek inscription.

The church and crypt

On the left of the main entrance, a garden now occupies the site of the roofless **church** which was built into the western portion of an old basilica, once the cathedral of the city, perhaps destroyed by the Arabs in 878. It was reconstructed by the Normans in 1200 (some of the visible remains date from that period) and in the early 17th century was remodelled on a smaller scale. The earthquake of 1693 finally reduced it to the ruins from which it has never subsequently risen. A fine 14th-century cusped rose window survives, as well as the 7th-century apse.

The **crypt** is in the form of a Greek cross, with three apses. Once a part of the ancient Greek quarries, it is according to local legend the site of the martyrdom of St Marcian, first bishop of Syracuse, sometime in the 1st century. The visible remains, which include faded frescoes, date from the Norman reconstruction. The fine Byzantine capitals, with symbols of the Evangelists, are thought to have been reused from the earlier basilica. In one apse are traces of 4th- and 5th-century frescoes from a hypogeum. The column against which the saint was flogged to death, and his tomb, surrounded by some of the earliest catacombs, can be seen. An altar is said to mark the site of St Paul's preaching in Syracuse.

To the east of the archaeological museum is the **Vigna Cassia** (*map 11; may be closed; call Kairos T: 0931 64694 to request visit*), a particularly photogenic ancient quarry with 3rd-century catacombs.

LATOMIA DEI CAPPUCCINI

Close to the former Capuchin convent, the Latomia dei Cappuccini (*map 11; open 9.30–1, closed Sat, Sun and holidays*) is one of the most extensive of the twelve ancient quarries that surrounded the city. It is now a pleasantly bosky limestone canyon. Adjacent is **Villa Politi**, the hotel where Winston Churchill stayed on his painting holidays in Syracuse. From Piazza dei Cappuccini, in front of the 17th-century church, is a panoramic view of Ortigia.

NEAPOLIS: THE ARCHAEOLOGICAL PARK

Map 9–10. Entrance on Viale Augusto. Open summer 8.30–7 (Mon 8.30–1.30), last tickets 1hr before closing; winter 8.30–3.30 (Sun, Mon and holidays 8.30–1). NB: Call first to be sure of closing time. A visit can take at least 2hrs. A single entrance gives access to the Latomia del Paradiso, the Greek Theatre and Roman Amphitheatre. Combined tickets with the Paolo Orsi Archaeological Museum are available. T: 0931 66206. The ticket office, preceded by shops, cafés and toilets, is on the opposite side of the road from the park entrance.

Beside a splendid giant magnolia and a group of ficus trees is the little Norman church of **San Nicolò dei Cordari** (*to request visit, call Kairos, T: 0931 64694, www.kairos-web.com*). The funeral service of Jourdain de Hauteville, illegitimate but favourite son of Count Roger, was held here in 1093. Below it, part of an aisled Roman piscina can be seen, a reservoir to provide water for the amphitheatre, to which it is connected by a channel.

THE ROMAN AMPHITHEATRE

The Roman Amphitheatre is an imposing building, probably of the 1st century AD, partly hollowed out of the hillside. In external dimensions (140m by 119m) it is only a little inferior to the one in Verona. Beneath the high parapet encircling the arena runs a corridor with entrances for the gladiators and wild beasts; the marble blocks on the parapet have inscriptions (3rd century AD) recording the ownership of the seats. In the centre is a rectangular depression, probably for the machinery used in the spectacles. The original entrance was at the south end, outside which a large area has been exposed, including an enclosure thought to have been for the animals, and a large fountain. Excavations here have revealed the old road, mentioned by Cicero, and the base of an Augustan-era triumphal arch directly to the east of the amphitheatre. The stone sarcophagi laid out here were found in the necropoleis of Syracuse and Megara Hyblaea and brought here by Paolo Orsi.

THE ALTAR OF HIERON II

From the amphitheatre the path continues to the huge Ara di Ierone (may be viewed from above), hewn out of the rock. The altar, built between 241 and 217 BC, was used for public sacrifices to Zeus, when as many as 450 bulls could be killed in one day. It was 198m long and 22.8m wide (the largest altar known) and was destroyed by the Spanish in 1526 in order to use the stone for harbour fortifications. The altar was presumably about 15m high and elaborately decorated; the sacred area in front of it contained a rectangular pool for ablutions and was delimited by a colonnade, more or less where the cypress trees stand today.

THE GREEK THEATRE

On the right-hand side of the road, opposite the altar, is a gate which leads (follow the path to the left) to the Greek Theatre, the most celebrated of all the ruins of Syracuse and the largest Greek theatre in Sicily (138m in diameter). Archaeological evidence confirms the existence on this spot of a wooden theatre as early as the 6th century BC, and here it was that Epicharmos (c. 540–450 BC) worked as a comic poet. In c. 478 BC Gelon excavated a small stone theatre, engaging the architect Damokopos of Athens. It was inaugurated by Aeschylus in 476 BC with the first production of *Women of Aetna*; his *Persian Women* was performed shortly afterwards. The theatre was enlarged in the 4th century BC, under Timoleon, by excavating deeper into the hillside; it was again enlarged under Hieron II (c. 230 BC) by extending the cavea upwards, using blocks of stone. It could thus hold an audience of 15,000; some scholars think even more.

Under the Romans the scena was altered several times, eventually to make it suitable for gladiator battles. The Romans probably also cut the trapezoidal lines around the orchestra, when creating a *kolymbethra*, an ornamental fish pool, but it was abandoned in the 1st century AD in favour of the elegant new amphitheatre.

The existing cavea, with 42 rows of seats in nine wedges, is almost entirely hewn out of the rock. This is now believed to represent Hieron II's auditorium of 59 rows, less the upward extension, the stone of which has been removed. The extent of Timoleon's theatre before Hieron's excavations is marked by the drainage trench at the sixth row, above the larger gangway. Around the gangway runs a very worn frieze bearing, in large Greek characters, the names of Hieron (II), Philistis (his queen), Nereis (his daughter-in-law, wife of Gelon II), and Zeus Olympius, which served to distinguish the blocks of seats. The foundations of the scena remain, but successive alterations make it difficult to identify their function. The little house which dominates the cavea is a medieval watch tower against pirates.

Steps at the far end of the Greek Theatre, or a path near the entrance (which passes behind the medieval watch-tower) lead up to the rock wall behind the theatre. Here there are recesses for votive pinakes and a **nymphaeum** or grotto in which the Galermi aqueduct ends after traversing Epipolai bringing water from the River Bottigliera near Pantalica, 33km away. Two porticoes once stood at right angles on this platform, traces of which can be made out on the rock floor. At the left-hand end of the wall the **Via dei Sepolcri** (Street of Tombs) begins, rising in a curve 146m long. The wheel-ruts in the limestone were made in the 16th century by carts serving the mills which at that time occupied the cavea of the theatre. The Byzantine tombs and Hellenistic niches in its rock walls were all rifled long ago. Its upper end (*no admission*) crosses the rock-hewn Acquedotto Galermi.

A set of steps to the east of the grotto leads up to another platform (no access) on which the foundation cuttings for a pi-shaped trio of stoas have been found, part of a sanctuary that would have overlooked the theatre and enjoyed magnificent views of the Great Harbour. To the west of the theatre a sanctuary of Apollo Temenites has been discovered. A smaller, and probably older theatre lies to the southwest, the Teatro Lineare, with seats arranged in straight lines.

THE LATOMIA DEL PARADISO AND EAR OF DIONYSIUS

From the gate opposite the altar steps lead down to a beautiful garden with lemons, oleanders and pomegranates, the **Latomia del Paradiso**, the largest and most famous of the twelve quarries excavated in ancient times, and since then one of the great sights of the city. The size of the quarries testifies to the colossal amount of building stone used for the Greek city and for Dionysius' famous fortifications. Following the northern limit of Akradina from here to the Cappuccini near the sea they also served as a defensive barrier. They were sometimes used as concentration camps and according to Thucydides some 7,000 Athenians were incarcerated in one of them in 413 BC.

By following the path you will see a tall isolated column of rock, the only surviving support for the roof of the enormous cave which the stone-cutters had formed, both to reach the fine-quality limestone deep under the surface, and to shelter themselves from sun and rain. The great blocks of stone fell when the vault collapsed during the 1193 earthquake. The path continues to the **Ear of Dionysius** (Orecchio di Dionisio), a sinuous artificial cavern, 65m long, 5–11m wide, and 23m high, in section like a rough Gothic arch. Its name was given to it by Caravaggio in 1608. Because of the strange acoustic properties of the cavern, it has given rise to the legend that Dionysius used the place as a prison and, from a small hole in the roof at the far end, heard the whispers of his captives. Before Caravaggio, local people called the cave the 'grotto of the noises'. It amplifies every sound and has an interesting echo, which only repeats each sound once. Now it is filled with the strange echoes of noises made by the pigeons which nest here. Once your eyes get accustomed to the dark you can walk to the far wall. The entire surface bears the marks of the slaves' chisels and you can see the regular size of the blocks they were cutting: exactly one square cubit.

To the right of the Ear of Dionysius is the **Grotta dei Cordari**, named after the rope-makers who worked here for centuries. The vault of this picturesque cavern is supported by huge pillars and the walls are covered with maidenhair ferns and coloured lichens. Access, unfortunately, is prohibited because of its perilous state.

A short way to the north of the church of San Nicolò is the beautiful, verdant **Latomia di Santa Venera** (*may be closed*), the walls honeycombed with niches for votive tablets. At the far end is the **Necropoli Grotticelle**, a group of Hellenistic and Byzantine tombs, one of which, with a triangle over the entrance, is arbitrarily known as the Tomb of Archimedes. The 20th-century excavations here can be seen from the fence along the main road, Via Teracati.

VILLA REIMANN
Map 10. Via Necropoli Grotticelle 14. To visit the park, T: 0931 411939 or 0931 33777.
Overlooking the Latomia di Santa Venera and the Necropoli Grottticelle, Villa Reimann is a handsome Art Nouveau villa of 1881 bequeathed to the city by Christiane Reimann (1888–1979), a Danish scientist and pioneer in the nursing profession. The building is now used by the University. The splendid park consists of a citrus grove and botanical garden containing 160 different kinds of trees and plants, culminating in a picturesque wooden belvedere, offering views over the port; everything was planted by Reimann herself.

ENVIRONS OF SYRACUSE

CASTELLO EURIALO
Beyond map 9. Open Mon–Sat 9–1. Last tickets 1hr before closing. Sometimes closed in winter or at other times for lack of custodians. It is always advisable to phone ahead to check. T: 0931 711773.
At the western limit of the ancient city, on the open, barren plateau of Epipolai, is Castello Eurialo. The approach road crosses the great Walls of Dionysius, which defended the Epipolai ridge. Begun by Dionysius the Elder (Dionysius I; *see p. 368*) in 402 BC, they were finished by 397 and were 30km long. Just before the main road to Belvedere crosses the walls, a path (50m) leads right to the **Latomia del Filosofo** (or Bufalaro). The famous Greek dithyrambic poet Philoxenos of Kythera was supposedly confined here for expressing too candid an opinion of the verses of Dionysius. His friends pleaded for his freedom and when he returned to court, Dionysius offered him a second opportunity to judge his work. Philoxenos turned to the guards, saying 'Take me to the Latomia!' The tyrant was amused by his wit and let him be (*Diodorus Siculus 15:6*). This quarry supplied stone for the walls and the castle. The main road winds up towards the town of Belvedere; just after the signpost for the town, a narrow road (signposted) leads right for the Castello Eurialo.

Three ditches precede the west front: the **outermost** is near the custodian's house. Between the second and the third are the ruins of an outwork, the walls of which have partly collapsed into the second ditch. On the left, steps lead down into the **inner ditch**, the principal defence of the fortress, which gave access to a labyrinth of casemates and passages. To the south the three piers of the **drawbridge** are prominent. There are eleven entrances from this main ditch to the gallery parallel with it; from here three passages lead east; the longest, on the north (174m long, *may be closed*) connects with

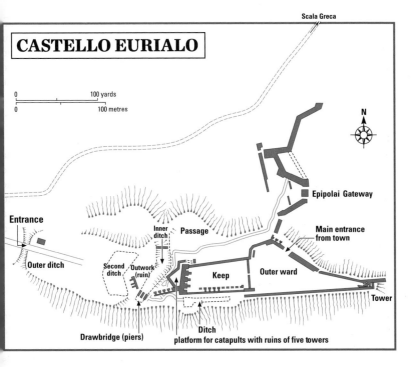

CASTELLO EURIALO

0 — 100 yards
0 — 100 metres

N

Scala Greca

Epipolai Gateway

Main entrance
from town

Entrance

Inner
ditch

Passage

Outer ditch

Second
ditch

Outwork
(ruin)

Keep

Outer ward

Tower

Drawbridge (piers)

Ditch
platform for catapults with ruins of five towers

the Epipolai gateway (*see below*). Prominent in this part of the castle are the remains of **five towers**, originally 15m high, and surmounted by catapults.

The two southernmost passages lead to a ditch outside the south wall of the castle. At the end, steps (which were concealed from the enemy) lead up to the outer ward of the castle proper, which consisted of a **keep** with an irregularly-shaped **outer ward** on the east. The barracks and cisterns were located in these parts of the castle. On the northeast side of the outer ward was the **main entrance from the town**; on the southeast rose a **tower** connected with the south wall of Dionysius. From here there is a good view of the **Epipolai Gateway** below, a 'pincer' type defence work on the spur of the north wall of Dionysius, which can be seen, broken at intervals by towers and posterns, stretching towards the sea. It was united to the keep by a complicated system of underground works, notable for their ingenious provisions for shelter and defence.

An arch leads back towards the entrance into the keep. Once inside, the remains of the five towers are visible directly in front of you, and a series of rooms (possible barracks or officers' quarters or storage rooms) hug the southern wall. To the left of the southernmost tower a few steps lead down to a path which follows the edge of the site back to the entrance.

There are plans to re-open the **antiquarium**, with its interesting collection of maps, plans and artefacts found during the excavations, but at time of writing no firm date had been given.

DIONYSIUS THE ELDER

Dionysius I (c. 432–367 BC) was one of the most remarkable rulers of his day. In 405 BC he exploited tensions in his native Syracuse after the failure of a campaign against the Carthaginians in order to seize control of the city and declare himself 'general with full powers'. The people supported his claim when it was reported that he had been seen with a swarm of bees clinging to the mane of his horse while crossing a river in full spate, a sign of the favour of the gods. Dionysius became a legend in his own lifetime, as the tyrant who forced Damocles to sit under the heavy sword suspended by a horsehair, who imprisoned Plato and tried to sell him into slavery (fortunately he was purchased by his students in Athens) and who consummated two marriages on the same night. Intelligent and pragmatic, he has been credited with the invention of the use of mercenary troops, siege towers, nocturnal attacks and catapults; whether true or not, he certainly made good use of all of them.

While his chief ambition to rid Sicily of the Carthaginians and to bring it all under the control of Syracuse was never achieved, he came to control much of the island and extended his rule to the Greek cities of the mainland, even founding the city of Ancona and thus controlling trade routes to Dalmatia. His capture of the Carthaginian stronghold of Mozia in 397 BC was a major achievement, but failed to follow through after every battle which might have given him a decisive victory. The oracle at Delphi had told him that he would succumb when he had defeated his superiors, and perhaps he believed that his 'superiors' could only be the Carthaginians.

Sure of his talent as a dramatist, in 367 BC he presented his play *The Ransom of Hector* at the annual drama festival at Athens, and was awarded the laurel crown; he died suddenly during the ensuing banquet. Perhaps he had been allowed to win for political reasons, and his superiors were his fellow playwrights. We shall never know, because the play did not survive. Today the extensive fortifications at Syracuse, culminating in Castello Eurialo, are his most visible legacy.

THE TEMPLE OF ZEUS

The ruins of the Temple of Zeus or Olympieion (*beyond map 13; may be closed*) are on the right bank of the Ciane. Built in the 6th century, just after the Temple of Apollo on Ortigia, it was the second Doric temple in Sicily, hexastyle and peripteral with 42 monolithic columns, two of which remain standing on part of the stylobate. On the approach, the two columns can be seen among trees on the skyline of a low hill, the *Polichne*, a point of great strategic importance, invariably occupied by the besiegers of Syracuse. About 1km after the bridge over the Ciane, at the top of the rise, a road (right; signposted) leads in less than 1km (keep right) to the temple in a cypress grove. There is a superb view from here of the island of Ortigia.

FONTE CIANE

The Fonte Ciane, source of the river and now a nature reserve (*map p. 570, D2*), is reached by a turning off the Canicattini Bagni road, SP 14. After crossing the Anapo, a byroad (left; signposted) leads for 3km through a fertile valley with orange and lemon groves and magnificent old olive trees. Beyond a tributary of the Ciane, a road

FONTE CIANE
Papyrus plants at the famous blue pool.

(signposted) continues left to end in a grove of eucalyptus and cypress trees beside the romantic spring (the ancient *Cyane*), overgrown with reeds and thick clumps of papyrus. This plant grows only here and along the River Fiumefreddo in Sicily, and in no other part of Europe. The name of the spring (meaning blue in Greek) describes the colour of its waters, but a myth relates how the nymph Cyane, who tried to prevent Hades from carrying off Persephone, was changed into a spring and condemned to weep forever. Beyond the bridge a path follows a fence along the reeds to the large pool, inhabited by numerous waterfowl. Both springs, the Testa della Pisma and the smaller Pismotta, have pools with papyrus.

PLEMMYRION AND THE COAST TO THE SOUTH

The ancient district of Plemmyrion, now known as the **Maddalena peninsula** (*map p. 570, D2*), was on the headland opposite Ortigia on Syracuse's Great Harbour. The headquarters of Nikias were established here after his defeat on Epipolai by Gylippus, in the famous war between Athens and Syracuse in 415–413 BC. Although disfigured by concrete villas and holiday apartment blocks, the coast is still intact and is protected as a marine nature reserve (*T: 0931 449310, www.plemmirio.it*), one of six such reserves around the coast of Sicily. You can book a guide to do some seawatching, or you can birdwatch along the 7km of protected coastline. The many interesting birds include kingfishers, here adapted to fishing in the sea.

Neolithic settlements have been found further south on the offshore islet of **Ognina**, where Neolithic and Early Bronze Age pottery finds suggest that it may have been a

Maltese trading outpost. There is a little port here and sea bathing at Capo Sparano just to the north.

The bay to the south, **Fontane Bianche**, is the crowded bathing resort of Syracuse Nearby is **Cassibile**, where a huge Bronze Age necropolis and hut village yielded extremely interesting finds, now in the archaeological museum in Syracuse. In an olive grove near the bridge over the river, close to the road, on the afternoon of 3rd September 1943, Generals Bedell Smith and Castellano signed the military terms of surrender of the Italian army to the Allies. Several pill-boxes survive along the road and on the river bed. At the mouth of the Cassibile, the ancient *Kakyparis*, the Athenian general Demosthenes, covering the rear of Nikias' forces during the retreat from Syracuse, was cut off and forced to surrender. The countryside here is particularly lovely, with old olive trees, carobs, almonds and citrus groves.

NOTO

Noto (*map p. 570, C2–D2*) is perhaps the most interesting of the 18th-century Baroque towns of Sicily. It was built after the earthquake of 1693 when the former town (now known as Noto Antica) was abandoned. An excellent example of 18th-century town planning, the local limestone has been burnt gold by the sun. The inhabitants call their city *il giardino di pietra*, the garden of stone. The surrounding vineyards produce an exquisite dessert wine, Moscato di Noto, also rich gold in colour. Made from white Muscat grapes, the wine comes in three varieties: *naturale*, *spumante* and *liquoroso*.

HISTORY OF NOTO

This was ancient *Neas*, founded in 448 BC by Ducetius. It enjoyed several privileges under the Romans, who called it *Netum*, and was chosen by the Arabs in 903 to be the capital of the Val di Noto, one of the three administrative areas of the island. The economy flourished, thanks to the introduction of citrus, mulberry trees, almonds, rice, sugar cane and cotton; there were wool mills and tanneries. Trade was encouraged and there was a flourishing Jewish community.

In 1693, when the great earthquake struck, the town on Monte Alveria was so severely damaged that a new site about 14km away was chosen by the Spanish government, against the wishes of the Church and the majority of the inhabitants, making reconstruction slow. Only in 1702 was the old town abandoned for the rational new city, planned and built by some of the greatest engineers, architects and master-builders of the time.

In 1817 Syracuse was preferred by the Bourbons as provincial capital (briefly returned to Noto from 1837–65) and the economy languished. A further blow was the governmental decision in 1866 to expropriate the monasteries and convents; Noto, seat of a bishopric, had always had a very strong ecclesiastical community, which had a considerable influence on the life of the city. People began to abandon Noto in favour of new districts to the south. Because of neglect, buildings started to crumble; in the mid-1980s many of the most beautiful were propped up with scaffolding. A serious earthquake in 1990 did further damage and in 1996 the dome of the cathedral collapsed. Now a World Heritage Site, much of the reconstruction has now been completed.

NB: It is possible to a buy a combined ticket for all Noto's monuments and museums.

PORTA REALE AND THE EAST

At the east end of the main street of Noto is a bronze statue of the patron saint, San Corrado Confalonieri (*see p. 374*) by Mario Ferretti (1955), near the luxuriant public gardens (Giardino Pubblico; *map 4*), where the thick evergreen *Ficus benjamin* trees form an impenetrable roof over the road. To the south is the Neoclassical church of Ecce Homo or **Pantheon** (*open for Mass Sun morning at 8 and 10.30*), now a sanctuary dedicated to local soldiers who died in the Second World War.

Porta Reale, surmounted by the three symbols of the people of Noto, a tower for strength, dog for loyalty, and pelican for self-sacrifice, was erected for the visit of Ferdinand II of Bourbon in 1838. It leads into Corso Vittorio Emanuele, along which the town rises to the right and falls away to the left. By skilful use of open spaces and monumental flights of steps, this straight and level street, 1km long, has been given a lively skyline and provides successive glimpses of the countryside. The main streets are paved with blocks of stone, while the side streets are cobbled. On the right, a grandiose flight of steps leads up to **San Francesco all'Immacolata** (*map 4*; 1704–8), by Vincenzo Sinatra, with a decorative façade and an interior of lavish white stucco by Giuseppe Gianforma; there are two canvases here by Olivio Sozzi: over the first left altar; *The Ecstasy of St Francis*, and opposite, *St Anthony Preaching to the Fish*. Facing the left flank of San Francesco across the street is the former convent of San Salvatore (now a school), with a fine, long 18th-century façade and attractive tower possibly designed by Rosario Gagliardi).

Across the Corso from San Salvatore is the church of **Santa Chiara** (*open for Mass 8.30*), with an oval interior by Gagliardi (1730–48) and a *Madonna* by Antonello Gagini, from Noto Antica. The convent now houses the civic museums (*open 10.30–1 & 2.30–4*), including the **Galleria di Arte Moderna**, a collection of sculptures and drawings by the local artist Giuseppe Pirrone, responsible for the impressive bronze doors of the duomo. The **Museo delle Carte** (*open on request, T: 335 743 4549*) is an interesting museum dedicated to paper and its various uses.

AROUND THE DUOMO

At the heart of the town, the immense façade of the **duomo** (*map 3*), rising above a dramatic stairway, looks down on Piazza Municipio with its symmetrical horseshoe hedges of ficus. The Cattedrale San Nicola (18th century, Rosario Gagliardi and Vincenzo Sinatra) is newly repaired, including the dome. To the right of the duomo is the Neoclassical Bishop's Palace and beyond it, also with a flight of approach steps, is the church of **San Salvatore**. It has a façade was designed by Andrea Giganti of Trapani and probably built by Antonio Mazza (1791). The polychrome interior, with a vault painting by Antonio Mazza, contains 18th-century paintings by Giuseppe Velasquez.

To the left of the duomo is **Palazzo Sant'Alfano Landolina**, once the residence of the only local family to have a palace on the main street and to be allowed to offer hospitality to visiting royalty.

On the south side of the piazza, facing the cathedral, is the Town Hall, **Palazzo Ducezio** (*the Sala degli Specchi, Hall of Mirrors, is open 10.30–1 & 2.30–4*), a splendid building of 1746 by Vincenzo Sinatra. The upper floor was added in 1951. The **Chiesa del Collegio** (*open 10–1 & 3.30–7*), with a curved façade probably by Gagliardi (1730, restored by Vincenzo Sinatra in 1776), has a luminous interior with frescoes in the vault. It is possible to climb up the bell-tower, for a view over the rooftops.

PIAZZA XVI MAGGIO AND VIA DUCEZIO

The long façade of the former Collegio dei Gesuiti (now a school) stretches as far as Piazza San Domenico (or Piazza XVI Maggio, *map 3*), with the opera house, **Teatro Vittorio Emanuele** (*open 10.30–1 & 2.30–4*), a perfectly preserved building of 1861 with a beautiful interior and 330 seats. In front of the building, in a little garden, is a 17th-century Baroque fountain from Noto Antica with a statue of Hercules, thought to be Roman. In the pavilion behind is the Tourist Information office. Above to the left is the soaring, glorious golden façade of **San Domenico** (1737–56; *may be closed*) by Gagliardi, perhaps his most successful building in the town. In Via Bovio above is the former convent of the **Casa dei Crociferi** by Paolo Labisi (1750), finished by Vincenzo Sinatra. It has been restored for use as the law courts.

From Piazza XVI Maggio, Corso Vittorio Emanuele continues to the rather severe **Palazzo Zappata**. To the left Via Ruggero Settimo leads past an aristocratic palace to the pretty Via Ducezio, which runs parallel to the Corso to the south. It is closed at the west end by the fine concave Baroque façade (with Rococo details) of **Santa Maria del Carmine** (or Carmelo), a late work by Gagliardi, with an unusual elliptical interior. At the east end of the street, on Via Vicerè Speciale, is the church of **Santa Maria dell'Arco** (1730; *map 3–4*), also by Gagliardi, with an elegant portal and a decorative stucco interior with two stoups from Noto Antica; the organ is dated 1778 and the wooden Crucifix over the altar is 14th century. Nearby is an attractive Art Nouveau house. Via Aurispa parallel to Via Ducezio on the south, is another pretty street with simpler buildings and the church of **Santa Maria Rotonda**, which has a Baroque façade.

VIA NICOLACI AND VIA CAVOUR

From Santa Maria dell'Arco, Via Vicerè Speciale leads up to the splendid rear façade of the Municipio. To the left is **Palazzo Rau della Ferla**, which has a handsome front and a courtyard covered with jasmine. Part of the palace houses the Costanzo pastry shop. At the end the impressive wall of the Collegio dei Gesuiti can be seen, which a road now follows uphill back to the Corso, straight across which Via Corrado Nicolaci continues uphill, overlooked by the delightful Baroque balconies of **Palazzo Nicolaci**

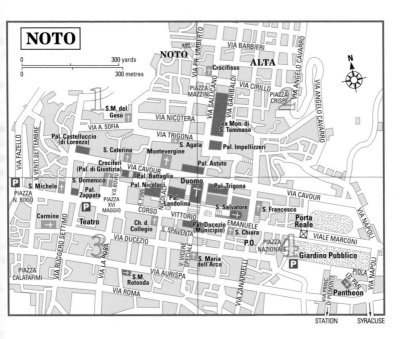

Villadorata (*map 3; open 10–1 & 3–5; for guided tour, T: 338 742 7022 or 320 113 2936*), built between 1737 and 1765, once the residence of Don Giacomo Nicolaci, a patron of the arts. He donated part of his collection of books to the City Library, housed here.

The façade of the church of **Montevergine** (*map 1*) is attributed to Vincenzo Sinatra. Deconsecrated, it has a magnificent 18th-century floor of majolica tiles from Caltagirone, and paintings by Costantino Carasi. The church is on the handsome Via Cavour, an 18th-century street, with views of the countryside at either end. It leads west past **Palazzo Battaglia** (1735), on the corner of Via Rocco Pirri, in which a charming little market-place, with a loggia supported on iron pillars surrounding a fountain, has been restored and is used for open-air concerts in the summer. Via Cavour continues west past the former Oratorio di San Filippo Neri (1750) and the church of Santa Caterina (right; attached to the oratory, on Via Fratelli Ragusa). Beyond, near the end of Via Cavour, is the large Neoclassical **Palazzo di Lorenzo** (**Castelluccio**) built for the Knights of Malta.

At the other end of Via Cavour, to the east of Montevergine, is the beautiful **Palazzo Astuto** (late 18th century; Vincenzo Sinatra or Paolo Labisi; *map 1–2*). Further on, on the right, is **Palazzo Trigona** (1781), part of it renovated as an events space.

NOTO ALTA

The simpler, upper part of the town was laid out facing north and south, on a different plan and orientation from the lower monumental area. There is a view of the battlemented former Convento di Sant'Antonio di Padova on the top of the hill.

Palazzo Impellizzeri San Giacomo (1752; *map 2*) has a balcony along the whole length of the first floor. Part of the palace is used to house the city archives,and is often used for exhibitions. In one room there is a splendid 18th-century crystal chandelier. The corner and bell-tower of the former Ospedale Trigona are visible here. Via Trigona leads past the former convent to the deconsecrated church of **Sant'Agata** (*map 1*) attributed to Gagliardi and completed by Paolo Labisi. It contains stuccoes by Labisi and paintings by Costantino Carasi. Opposite is the **Santissima Annunziata e Badia**, another church dating from 1720. Just beyond, approached by a double stairway, is **Santa Maria del Gesù**, next to its convent.

Via Trigona leads back to the impressive former **Monastero di San Tommaso** (1720; *map 2*), with an attractive façade and double stairway. It is now used as a prison. On the summit of the hill, at the centre of Noto Alta, is the enormous church of the **Crocifisso** (1715, Gagliardi; *map 2*), which contains a number of works of art from Noto Antica, including (in the right transept) a beautiful statue of the *Madonna della Neve* (Our Lady of the Snows) signed by Francesco Laurana (1471) and two Romanesque lions. The Cappella Landolina contains paintings by the school of Costantino Carasi. On the high altar is an 18th-century reliquary designed by Gagliardi which contains part of a venerated Crucifix from Noto Antica. A relic of the Holy Thorn also belongs to the church (only shown on Good Friday).

ENVIRONS OF NOTO

The most beautiful road from Noto to Noto Antica (12km, signposted for Palazzolo Acreide) leads uphill to the left from the public gardens, crossing Noto Alta and passing through the village of **San Corrado di Fuori** (*map p. 570, D2*), with attractive early 20th-century houses. Outside the town is the verdant Valle dei Miracoli, home to the hermitage of San Corrado Confalonieri, who lived here in the 14th century. The 18th-century sanctuary contains a painting of the saint by Sebastiano Conca.

SAN CORRADO CONFALONIERI

Corrado Confalonieri was born an aristocrat in Piacenza in 1284. While out hunting a white deer, he set fire to the forest to flush out the animal, but the ensuing blaze did a great deal of damage to the nearby crops and villages. A vagabond was blamed, who confessed after torture. On the point of the man's execution by hanging, Corrado saved his life by admitting his responsibility. All Corrado's possessions were confiscated to make good the damage, but he saw in this episode a sign that he should change his way of life. He told his young wife to enter a nunnery, while he himself joined the Franciscans. After a few years he came down to Sicily, where he lived as a hermit in the hills between Noto and Avola, gaining a reputation for wisdom and sanctity. It is said that he could conjure loaves of bread from the air whenever he was hungry. On his death, on 19th February 1351, his body was hotly contested by the two towns, so it was placed on an ox-cart with no driver, allowing Corrado to choose the place of his burial. He ended up in Noto, and is portrayed with a flame on his right hand, and a white deer by his side.

NOTO ANTICA

The road north from San Corrado continues across a beautiful upland plain with old olive trees. It then descends to cross a bridge decorated with four obelisks. The byroad (left) for Noto Antica is lined with early 20th-century Stations of the Cross on the approach to the large sanctuary of **Santa Maria della Scala** (*open 9.30–12.30 & 3–6 in winter, 4–7 in summer*), next to a seminary with an elegant façade (1708) surmounted by three statues and a balcony.

The road now descends to cross another bridge over a ravine before reaching **Noto Antica** (*map p. 570, C2*), abandoned since the earthquake of 1693 and now utterly deserted. The scant ruins, reduced to rubble and overgrown, are very romantic, and provide inspiration for artists, photographers and writers. The settlement here long antedates its legendary foundation by the Sicel chief Ducetius in 448 BC, and was the only Sicilian town to resist the depredations of Verres (*see p. 205*). The entrance is through the monumental Porta della Montagna, with remains of the high walls on either side. A rough road leads up past a round tower and along the ridge of the hill. The conspicuous wall on the left (the highest one to survive) belonged to the Chiesa Madre. After 1km, beside a little monument, the right fork continues (and the road deteriorates) to end beside the Eremo della Madonna, a small deserted chapel, with a good view of the surrounding countryside.

Some distance to the west is the remote prehistoric village of **Castelluccio** (c. 18th–14th centuries BC), which has given its name to the most important Early Bronze Age culture of southeast Sicily. The rock tombs had carved portal-slabs (now in the archaeological museum at Syracuse).

CAVA GRANDE DEL CASSIBILE AND AVOLA ANTICA

The **Cava Grande**, formed over the centuries by the River Cassibile, where centuries-old plane trees and colourful oleanders grow, is a nature reserve run by the Azienda Forestale. (*Map p. 570, D2. Open Oct–March 8–4, April–Sept 8–7; closed during bad weather. Wear stout shoes (they won't let you enter with sandals), bring water, no dogs or other pets. No mobile coverage. You may be required to sign a responsibility waiver. T: 0931 67450, www.cavagrandedelcassibile.it. NB: At the time of writing the gorge was closed because a fire badly damaged the paths, which are awaiting repair. The only possible access was the Carrubella path from the Belvedere, which passes alongside the gorge without going down inside it.*) A spectacular gorge nearly 10km long, it reaches a depth of 300m, and is the deepest canyon in Europe, containing a series of rock pools, waterfalls, and ancient cave-homes. The river was the first in Sicily to be exploited to produce hydroelectric energy, in 1910. Thousands of tombs (11th–9th centuries BC) have been identified here (finds in the archaeological museum of Syracuse). The easiest approach is normally through **Villa Vela**, a little village with some Art Nouveau villas on the road between Noto and Palazzolo Acreide. The gorge can also be entered from the **Belvedere** (where you will find a restaurant and an Azienda Forestale information kiosk) at the end of the very winding road to Avola Antica. The path down into the gorge (about 40mins) is steep and overgrown but it is the most impressive approach and brings you right to the lakes. Birds that may be heard or spotted include dippers, ravens, kingfishers, Cetti's warblers, blue rock thrushes, spotless starlings, shrikes nightingales and owls; but the Cava Grande is particularly important for the resident populations of different bat species.

Avola Antica is the site of the pre-earthquake town. Its deserted and desolate streets, overgrown with vegetation, can be explored.

AVOLA

Avola (*map p. 570, D2*) is a prosperous agricultural town and an important centre for almond cultivation. It has expanded in a disorderly way around its centre, which retains the hexagonal plan on which it was designed after 1693 by Angelo Italia. The central square is Piazza Umberto, where the **Chiesa Madre**, dedicated to St Nicholas and St Sebastian, is situated. The interior houses two splendid canvases, the *Madonna of the Rosary* by Sebastiano Conca and the *Marriage of the Virgin* by Olivio Sozzi. In the choir is an 18th-century organ by Donato Del Piano, while the Chapel of the Sacrament is richly decorated with stuccoes in Rococo style. Near the church is one of Sicily's most famous cafés, the **Caffè Finocchiaro**.

Four smaller squares open off the outer edge of the hexagon, one of which, **Piazza Vittorio Veneto**, has an early 20th-century fountain with three lions stooping to drink, by Gaetano Vinci. The 18th-century churches include **Sant'Antonio Abate** in Piazza Regina Elena, which houses a wooden statue of *Christ at the Column* from Avola Antica, and, in Via Manzoni, the **Santissima Annunziata** (with a façade by Giuseppe Alessi), which is a national monument. There are a number of **Art Nouveau buildings**, evidence of the flourishing economy in the early 20th century.

The 16th-century church of the **Cappuccini**, outside the hexagonal centre, in Piazza Francesco Crispi, has a lovely 17th-century altarpiece, a painting by an unknown artist of *The Invention of the Cross*.

THE GULF OF NOTO

Noto Marina (or **Lido di Noto**; *map p. 570, D3*) is a little resort with some of the best beaches on the east coast of the island. The beautiful landscape has huge old olive, carob, almond and citrus trees. The River Asinaro, which reaches the sea near **Calabernardo**, a fishing village and popular spot for bathing, is the ancient *Assinaros*, where the Athenian general Nikias' forces, trying to reach Heloros, were overtaken while drinking at the river and killed after the great battle between Syracuse and Athens in 413 BC.

ANCIENT *HELOROS*

Near the mouth of the Tellaro river, on a low hill in peaceful countryside, are the remains of *Heloros* (Eloro; *map p. 570, D3, to request visit at least ten days before, call the Soprintendenza, T: 0931 450 1258*), the first sub-colony to be founded by Syracuse, probably at the beginning of the 7th century BC. The excavations are in a lonely, deserted position by the sea and there is a good view inland of the Pizzuta column (*see below*), with Noto seen beyond green rolling hills.

The road passes the foundations of a **temple of Asklepios**. To the right of the road, in a large fenced enclosure sloping down to the canal, is the **Sanctuary of Demeter**, consisting of a larger temple and a monumental stoa. A theatre has been partially excavated nearby. To the left, beyond the custodian's house, is another enclosure of recent excavations. An ancient road continues to the **walls and north gate**. Outside the walls another later (Hellenistic) **Temple of Demeter and Persephone** has been found.

The **Pizzuta** or Torre di Vendicari, a column over 10m high, can be reached by returning to the approach road beyond the railway bridge. It is a funerary monument of the 3rd century BC. Paolo Orsi found the burial-chamber underneath it, with three stone funerary couches complete with skeletons.

VILLA DEL TELLARO

From the main road (SS 115), just by the bridge across the river, a road leads inland towards a farmhouse (conspicuous to the right of the road) in the locality of Caddeddi, less than 1km from the main road. Beneath it, discovered in 1972, lies a Roman villa of the mid-4th century AD, known as the Villa del Tellaro (*open Oct–March 9–5, April–Sept 9–7; last tickets 30mins before closing; T: 0931 573883*). The villa was destroyed by fire in the mid-5th century. Its mosaic floors have been restored and replaced *in situ*. Those in the portico and the rooms on the north side of the peristyle courtyard are the best preserved. In the first (east) room is a fragmentary scene representing the *Ransom of Hector*, with the corpse of Hector on one of the pans of a large set of scales, balanced by his weight in gold on the other; to the left stand Odysseus, Achilles and Diomedes, and to the right are the Trojans and Priam; the features of all are remarkably well defined. The floor of the room to the west of this, the Room of the Kraters, has a decoration of festoons of leaves and flowers sprouting from kraters in the corners, which divide the floor into four areas, each with a representation of a satyr and a maenad. In the large Room of the Hunt are vivid scenes of a day's hunting. At the top (badly damaged), animals are being directed into a cage. In the centre an allegorical figure, perhaps representing Africa, watches over the proceedings. Above her, a lion is about to be killed; to her right, an elderly bearded huntsman has fallen and is protecting himself with his shield from the assault of an angry tigress. At the bottom, a banquet is taking place in the woods; the six protagonists, reclining on a long bolster around the *stibadium* or barbecue, are having their hands washed by a slave, while another pours wine. Their horses are tied to a group of trees in the bottom right-hand corner, and in the opposite corner, a servant brings flaming coals, while the dogs try to reach a deer hanging from a tree while the cook skins and disembowels it.

Although similar to the mosaics at Piazza Armerina, these are different in style and use of materials. They were probably the work of prestigious North African ateliers, perhaps two, because the stones used in the Room of the Kraters are of different geographical origin from the materials used in the other rooms.

THE VENDICARI NATURE RESERVE AND MARZAMEMI

The eight-kilometre stretch of coast south of the mouth of the River Tellaro is the **Oasi Faunistica di Vendicari**, run by the Azienda Forestale (*map p. 570, D3; open*

9–dusk, www.riserva-vendicari.it; further information and guides are available at the entrance). This beautiful wetland, of interest for its wildlife, has been protected since 1984 after the construction of a vast tourist village was successfully halted. More than 250 species of birds have been recorded, some nesting (including black-winged stilts), some migratory (including flamingoes). From the main road, beyond the railway, a track closed to cars continues to the entrance for c. 1km through lemon groves. At the south end is the 18th-century farmhouse of San Lorenzo Lo Vecchio, with remains of a Hellenistic temple transformed into a Byzantine church. On the edge of the shore are ruins of a Norman tower and an old tuna fishery.

The landscape from here to the southern tip of the island is less striking. In the shallow bay by the charming fishing village of **Marzamemi** (*map p. 570, D3*; the name derives from the Arabic *marsa el-hamaam*, Bay of the Pigeons), a wonderful place for diving, excavations have brought to light 14 ancient shipwrecks (four Greek, five Roman and five Byzantine) as well as more modern wrecks such as the *Chillingham*, a British cargo ship that sank in the 19th century; a Hurricane fighter plane which came down in 1943; and a submarine, the *Sebastiano Veniero*, which sank in 1925 after colliding with a merchant ship. On the waterfront is the sturdy Palazzo Nicolaci next to an old tuna-fishing establishment (one of the sources of wealth for the Nicolaci princes of Noto). Close to the shore is a tiny island, almost entirely occupied by a pink house, once the home of writer Vitaliano Brancati (1907–54).

PACHINO AND PORTOPALO

Pachino (*map p. 570, D3*) is known for its wine production and in recent years has also acquired fame for cantaloupe melons and, especially, for cherry tomatoes.

Beyond almond and olive trees and an inland lagoon is the fishing port and tiny municipality of **Portopalo di Capo Passero**. An imposing early 17th-century fortress stands on the eastern end of the island of Capo Passero, the ancient *Pachynus*, the southeast horn of Sicily. Overshadowing the fortress is a bronze statue of the Madonna in her guise as guardian of the sea of Sicily (1959, Mario Ferretti), 5m tall on a pedestal of 20m. A Roman necropolis has been excavated on the island, which until recently was joined to the mainland by an isthmus, and is of interest to naturalists for its exceptional endemic vegetation, and for the migratory passage of birds.

The southernmost point of Sicily is the little **Isolotto delle Correnti**, with a lighthouse. West of Pachino, several marshy areas now form a nature reserve for the protection of migrating birds, known as the Pantani Cuba e Longarini.

ROSOLINI

Rosolini (*map p. 570, C3*) is a town of very ancient origin, re-founded in 1713 by Francesco Moncada. In the spacious central Piazza Garibaldi is the elegant Town Hall, surmounted by a clock, and the sturdy Chiesa Madre, which dominates all the buildings around it. Begun in 1720 on the orders of Moncada, it was only finished in the late 19th century, thanks to the town's carters, who transported the blocks of stone from the quarry free of charge. A rock-hewn Palaeo-Christian basilica lies beneath the Castello del Principe (1668) amid extensive catacombs (now used as a garage).

PALAZZOLO ACREIDE

Successor to the Greek city of *Akrai*, of which the impressive remains can be seen on the outskirts, Palazzolo Acreide (*map p. 570, C2*) is a charming town with a good climate. Akrai was a sub-colony founded by Syracuse in 663 BC, in a strategic point for dominating southeast Sicily and the route to the interior. In a treaty between Rome and Hieron II in 263 BC, Akrai was assigned to Syracuse. Its period of greatest splendour followed, and its main monuments, including the theatre, were built at this time. Under Byzantium it had a conspicuous and vocal Christian community, which probably caused its destruction in the 9th century by the Arabs. Count Roger assigned the town to his son Godfrey and from 1374 it was governed for two centuries by the Alagona family. Its finest buildings were erected after the earthquake in 1693, in Baroque style, for which the town is a UNESCO World Heritage Site.

LOWER TOWN

The **Chiesa Madre** (San Niccolò), of the 13th century with an 18th-century façade by Vincenzo Sinatra, is in the central Piazza Moro. Inside there are two late 19th-century carved thrones used for transporting the 16th-century statue of St Nicholas in procession. The charming sacristy with its painted vault dates from 1778 and retains its original furniture. Opposite is the elegant church of **San Paolo** (18th century, Vincenzo Sinatra). The interior is richly decorated with stucco.

From San Paolo a road leads down to Piazza Umberto and the red 18th-century **Palazzo Zocco**, with a decorative long balcony supported by grotesque heads, all different. Via Annunziata leads down towards the edge of town and one of its oldest churches, the unfinished **Annunziata**, with a lovely 18th-century portal decorated with four twisted columns and vines and festoons of fruit. In the luminous interior, covered with stuccoes, is a fine high altar in marble. Antonello da Messina's *Annunciation*, now in Palazzo Bellomo in Syracuse, was commissioned for this church in 1474.

From Piazza Moro, Via Garibaldi leads uphill past **Palazzo Caruso** (or Judica-Cafici) at no. 127, with monsters' heads beneath its long Baroque balconies. Further uphill, after a flight of steps, is **Palazzo Ferla** (no. 115) with four graceful balconies. Close by, at Via Gaetano Italia 36, is the Art Nouveau Palazzo Cappellani which houses the **Museo Archeologico** (*open Sun, Mon and holidays 2–6.30, Tues–Sat 9–6.30; T: 0931 876602*), a rich and varied collection of antiquities formed by the local historian Baron Gabriele Judica, who from 1809–24 was the first to excavate the monuments of Akrai.

UPPER TOWN

The centre of the busier upper town is **Piazza del Popolo**. Here is the 18th-century church of San Sebastiano, approached by a flight of steps and with a splendid façade and portal by Paolo Labisi. In the interior are a painting of *St Margaret of Cortona* by Vito D'Anna (fourth north altar) and a pre-earthquake statue of St Sebastian. The handsome Town Hall dates from 1808. In Corso Vittorio Emanuele the 19th-century Palazzo Judica has an imaginative façade and vases on the roof.

Just off the piazza, at 19 Via Macchiavelli, entered through a courtyard, is the **Casa-Museo Antonino Uccello** (*open 9–6.30, ring the bell; T: 0931 881499, www. casamuseo.it*), a fascinating local ethnographic museum created by schoolteacher and anthropologist Antonino Uccello (1922–79) and displayed in his 17th-century home. The material from the provinces of Syracuse and Ragusa includes farming utensils, household objects, puppets and terracotta statuettes; recently some of the rooms lived in by the aristocratic family who owned the rest of the building have been included in the museum itinerary.

An old 17th-century convent later transformed into an aristocratic dwelling, Palazzo Vaccaro at Via Maestranza 5, now houses the **Museo dei Viaggiatori in Sicilia** (*open 9–1 & 3–7, closed Mon; T: 0931 883880, www.museoviaggiatori.it*), dedicated to travellers in Sicily over the last few centuries. Paintings and sketches by Grand Tourists are contrasted with photographs showing the present appearance of the places depicted.

At the top of the road, Via Acre continues uphill to Piano Acre and the church of the **Immacolata**. Its convex façade is difficult to see as the church is now entered through the courtyard at the east end (*ring at the central door, at the house of the custodian of a school*). It contains a very fine statue of the Madonna by Francesco Laurana.

THE RUINS OF *AKRAI*

Beyond the Immacolata a road continues westwards up to the entrance to the remains of ancient Greek *Akrai* (*open Oct–March 8.30–3.30, April–Sept 8.30–7.30; last tickets 1hr before closing; T: 0931 876602*). It is a well-kept site, with signposted pathways offering splendid views over the area and its surroundings. The path from the ticket booth leads past a long stretch of the **decumanus** (on the right), the main street, constructed in basalt and later altered by the Romans. A gap in the dry-stone wall to the left takes you to the small **theatre** (seating for 600), built in the late 3rd century BC, which is well preserved and now used regularly in spring for Greek drama presented by school students. The scena was altered in Roman times, and in AD 600 a mill with round silos was built over the ruins. Nearby is a small round altar for sacrifices. To the right of the theatre when facing it is the tiny **bouleuterion**, which is connected to the theatre by a passageway now closed for safety reasons. To the left of the theatre various paths lead to two stone quarries with traces of a heroic cult and of later Christian occupation. The path furthest from the theatre leads to the small site **antiquarium** (site plan, architectural fragments, toilets), across from which niches can be seen in the quarry face (they were formerly closed with commemorative plaques carved with reliefs and inscriptions) and an interesting **funerary bas-relief** of c. 200 BC, showing a complicated scene in which a warrior is making a sacrifice and two adults recline on a couch. Further on from the relief are extensive Byzantine catacombs (*currently locked*) carved into the rock, some of which were adapted by the Arabs as dwellings. The larger family chapels are decorated with unusual lattice-work transennae.

The path closest to the theatre leads into a quarry in which a smaller network of **Byzantine catacombs** can be visited, (care should be taken as the rock is slippery underfoot and a torch is necessary). The middle path curves up to the highest point of the site, from which the views are magnificent. A fenced-off area contains the foundations of a peristyle **temple of Aphrodite** (6th century BC) and the foundations of a number of cult buildings, possibly from an adjacent sanctuary of Demeter. From here, another path drops down towards the entrance, passing on the left a second sanctuary (probably dedicated to Persephone), of 3rd-century date. It contained a circular temple covered by a cupola with a circular opening in the centre, supported on girders of terracotta (no longer *in situ*, but preserved); the holes for them are visible in the walls, and the pavement survives.

Leaving Akrai, the road from the theatre goes down the hill to the Ragusa road, off which a paved byroad (left) ends beside a gate. Here, on a cliffside, you can see the **Santoni** (*request visit at the Akrai ticket office; accessible May–Sept 10.30 & 4.30; closed Sun and holidays; impossible in bad weather; the custodian will go with you in your car*), a series of twelve very worn but interesting reliefs of Cybele, carved in a rockface, probably in the 3rd century BC. Her role as the mother-goddess is sometimes conflated with that of Demeter, because in some of the carvings she is seen together with Persephone. Most of the carvings show the goddess enthroned, with two lions at her feet. The path once led to a sacred spring and a small sanctuary (*no access*).

ENVIRONS OF PALAZZOLO ACREIDE

East of Palazzolo Acreide, on the fast road to Syracuse, is **Canicattini Bagni** (*map p. 570, C2*), surrounded by new buildings. Founded in 1678, it is noted for its early 20th-century houses decorated in the local stone in Art Nouveau style, and a beautiful 18th-century bridge, known as Ponte di Sant'Alfano, over the Cava Cardinale stream. Known as *La Città della Musica* (city of music) because of its award-winning brass band, founded 150 years ago, Canicattini also has an unusual museum at Via XX Settembre 132, the Museo del Tessuto e dell'Emigrante (*to request visit, T: 0931 945620, www.galleriadelricamo. com*), dedicated to mainly locally-made textiles and embroidery, very well displayed, and with some rare pieces. An evocative gallery explores the reasons behind emigration, which has so much affected Sicily over the last 150 years. Poignant testimonies include house keys left behind by people who knew they would never return.

Near Canicattini is the **Grotta Perciata**, the largest cave so far discovered in Sicily, where prehistoric artefacts have been found.

BUSCEMI

Across the Anapo valley north of Palazzolo Acreide is the attractive little town of Buscemi (*map p. 570, C2*), rebuilt after 1693. The main road runs uphill past its four impressive churches. **Sant'Antonio di Padova** has an 18th-century façade which incorporates ten splendid large columns on its curving front (with three bells hung across the top). Higher up is **San Sebastiano**, preceded by a stairway, and then the elliptical 19th-century church of **San Giacomo**, high up on a terrace. At the top of the town is the 18th-century **Chiesa Madre**, which houses a wooden statue of *Our Lady of Sorrows* by Filippo Quattrocchi (1732).

BUCCHERI

On the barren Piana di Buccheri, with views to Mt Lauro (986m), the highest point of the Hyblaean Mountains, and of Etna to the north, pinewoods have recently been planted. Buccheri (*map p. 570, C2*) was destroyed in the 1693 earthquake and rebuilt in Baroque style. Corso Vittorio Emanuele passes the 18th-century church of **Santa Maria Maddalena**, which contains a statue of Mary Magdalene by Antonello Gagini (1508). From Piazza Toselli a steep flight of steps rises to the towering façade of the church of **Sant'Antonio Abate**; the rich interior is decorated with stuccoes by Giuseppe Gianforma (1760) and houses two signed and dated (1728) paintings by Willem Borremans: *Sts Vitus, Modestus and Crescenza* in the right aisle and *Ecstasy of St Anthony the Abbot* over the main altar.

To the south of Buccheri, on the road to Giarratana, a few kilometres south of Mt Lauro, is a vast archaeological site that is almost certainly ancient ***Kasmenai***, the second colony founded by Syracuse. The views from here are stunning, but the site is unfortunately closed.

THE ANAPO VALLEY

The plateau above the Anapo valley to the south is beautiful open countryside, with characteristic old farmhouses and low dry-stone walls. Dark carob trees provide welcome shade and the olive groves are renowned for the high quality of their oil (in 2015 the production of three farms was voted best in the world). Shepherds pasture their flocks and small herds of cattle wander around apparently untended; the sound of their neck-bells lingers after their passage. Byzantine tombs and caves in the area show evidence of Neolithic and Bronze Age occupation.

Near the picturesque village of **Cassaro**, famous for olive oil from the Tonda Iblea variety, is the **Valle dell'Anapo** (*open 8–1hr before sunset*), a beautiful deep limestone gorge run by the Azienda Forestale. A map of the paths is available at the entrance. No private cars (or any pet animals) are allowed: a van takes visitors for 8km along a rough road on the course of the disused narrow-gauge railway (and its tunnels) which runs along the valley floor, once the Syracuse–Vizzini line. The vegetation here includes ilexes, pines, figs, olives, citrus trees and poplars; wildlife includes birds of prey such as the peregrine falcon and Bonelli's eagle, also the porcupine and the pine marten. The only buildings to be seen are those once used by the railway company. Horses are bred here and picnic places are provided with tables. In the centre of the valley there is a good view of the tombs of Pantalica (*see below*) high up at the top of the rockface. There is another entrance to the valley from the Sortino road, where maps are also available.

On the Ferla road is the site of the destroyed town of Cassaro, which was moved after the 1693 earthquake up to the top of the cliff face (seen above the road). Orange trees, prickly pear and pomegranates have been allowed to grow wild on the approach to **Ferla** itself (*map p. 570, C2*). A small stone-built town, it is traversed by one long main street climbing steeply uphill past four Baroque churches with imposing facades, lined with interesting early 20th-century houses, and makes the best approach to Pantalica.

PANTALICA

A lonely road leads from Ferla for 12km along a ridge through beautiful remote pastureland and pinewoods to the extraordinary prehistoric necropolis of Pantalica (*map p. 570, C2*), in deserted countryside, now a UNESCO World Heritage Site and a nature and archaeological reserve run by the Azienda Forestale (*www.parks.it/riserva. pantalica*). All around rock tombs carved in the cliffs can be seen. The deep limestone gorges of the Anapo and Cava Grande rivers almost encircle the plateau. It seems as though the inhabitants of nearby coastal settlements such as Thapsos settled in this naturally defended site in the 13th century BC. The cliffs of the vast necropolis, one of the largest and most important in Europe, are honeycombed with many hundreds of tombs of varying shapes and sizes.

There is a visitors' centre just off the road into Pantalica, about 5km before the end of the asphalt road, equipped with toilets, a picnic area and a large car park. The wardens can provide you with a map, and on request will show a 30-min film about Pantalica. Mountain bikes are available free of charge, for which you must produce a valid ID document. For those who wish, it is possible to drive beyond the visitors' centre and park closer to the tombs of the Anaktoron.

THE PANTALICA NECROPOLIS

About a hundred burials have been recovered from the thousand tombs cut into the limestone rocks of Pantalica and there is some sign in the early ones (13th century BC onwards) of Mycenaean influence in the way that the tombs have been cut, with corridors embellished with masonry leading to the grave entrance, while some of the pottery is either directly imported from Mycenaean Greece or copied from Mycenaean models. Although the size and importance of graves vary, women are given some status and one of the wealthier tombs of c. 1200 BC contained a female body with an array of golden goods. A common feature is a basin placed on a large pedestal, evidence of some kind of feasting rite at the time of burial, with the basin left after the sealing of the tomb. In the Late Bronze Age (1200–900 BC) a few larger tombs connected by corridors suggest a stratified society at Pantalica based on strong kinship groups. Clearly the local Sicel community was an effective and self-supporting one with some limited contact in earlier times with the Mycenaeans. However, with the coming of Greek settlement in the 8th century the community was dispersed and burials at Pantalica cease. Some of the tombs were converted into cave-dwellings at the time of the fall of the Western Roman Empire, and later inhabited by Christians. The objects discovered in the course of official archaeological excavations are displayed in the archaeological museum in Syracuse.

An easy footpath (signposted 'Villaggio Bizantino') at the beginning of the road leads to a tiny Byzantine oratory carved in the rock (with traces of frescoes) known as **San**

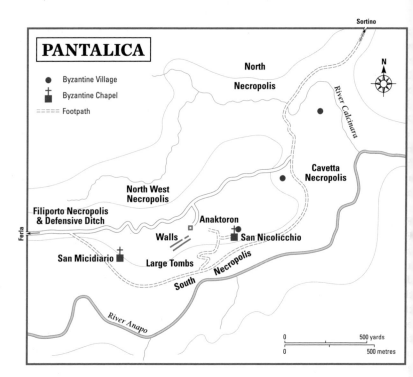

Micidiario, and the **South Necropolis**. Off the road, further on, a track leads up to the top of the hill and the so-called **Anaktoron**, or Palace of the Prince, a megalithic building dating from the Late Bronze Age, only the foundations of which survive (35m by 11m); it was the only stone construction in the settlement. Nearby are short sections of wall and a defensive ditch, the only remains of the city, recently identified with the legendary *Hybla*, whose king, Hyblon, allowed the Megarian colonists to found Megara Hyblaea in 728 BC. Far below, the Anapo Valley can be seen, with a white track following the line of the old railway. Further on, downhill, near the end of the road, a signpost indicates the **Cavetta Necropolis** (9th–7th centuries BC), and another Byzantine village.

A path leads towards the **North Necropolis**, beyond the stream in the valley. The road ends abruptly here and the road from Sortino, which will now never be completed, can be seen across the valley. There is a view of Sortino in the distance. In the early months of the year, flocks of ravens can sometimes be seen here, performing a mysterious mating flight, almost like a joyous dance, during which they fly upside down and link feet for a moment.

SORTINO

Reached from Solarino, on the main road between Ferla and Syracuse, Sortino (*map p. 570, C1*) is well known for the production of honey and oranges, and for its traditional puppet theatre. The town developed at the foot of an Arab watch-tower (*a shortin*) but was destroyed by the earthquake of 1693 and rebuilt close by. In the old Franciscan convent, at Piazza San Francesco 9, is the **Museo dei Pupi** (*to request visit, T: Marco Cannata, 392 077 9920*), a collection of puppets, posters and scenery accumulated by the Puglisi family, illustrious *pupari*. At Via Gioberti 5 is a museum dedicated to the production of honey, the **Museo dell'Apicoltura Casa d'o Fascitraru** (*T: 0931 952992, www.museoapicoltura.beepworld.it*), which explains all the secrets of this fascinating craft. Hyblaean honey was celebrated in antiquity. In 1848 James Leigh Hunt published a popular volume of Sicilian *divertimenti* simply entitled *A Jar of Honey from Mount Hybla*. Hyblaean honey can still be purchased, in different varieties according to the flora of the season: *satra* honey is derived from wild thyme; *zagara* honey from citrus blossom.

FLORIDIA

Floridia (*map p. 570, D2*) was a Sicel stronghold (in 1909 Paolo Orsi found a Mycenaean vase in a necropolis here, indicating Bronze Age trading activity), re-founded in 1628 and rebuilt after 1693. About 3km from Floridia is the beautiful and little-known **Cava di Spampinato**, one of the deepest gorges in the area. The road leaving town from the south, signposted Canicattini Bagni, immediately crosses the gorge and goes to the right. At the first crossroad, where the road curves left, take the byroad right (it becomes a track after 800m) to reach the entrance. There are many caves here, and tombs carved into the rock. It was through this gorge that the defeated Athenians, in 413 BC, tried to retreat inland, but they were blocked by Syracusan forces; they eventually reached the Assinaros, where they were defeated.

THAPSOS & THE GULF OF AUGUSTA

Capo Santa Panagia, the headland north of Syracuse, has been identified with ancient *Trogilus*. Fossils are found in the limestone caves, and in the overlying clays are remains of Neolithic habitation.

The flat peninsula of Magnisi, a little further north along the coast, was the ancient **Thapsos** (*map p. 570, D1*), under whose northern shore the Athenian fleet anchored before the siege of Syracuse. It is almost an island (2km long and 700m wide), connected to the mainland by a sandy isthmus 2.5km long and little more than 100m wide at one point. The fleet of Marcellus also moored near here during the Roman siege of Syracuse. Finds from the settlement and its vast necropolis have given the name to a Bronze Age culture and interesting domed rock-tombs line the shore west of the lighthouse.

The excavations at Thapsos show three periods of occupation: c. 1500–1400 BC, characterised by round huts; c. 1300–1200 BC, where the square houses are of the Mycenaean type (a bronze bar with figures of a dog and fox, unique in prehistoric Sicily, and thought to be of Aegean origin, was found here); and a final period c. 1100–900 BC, with finds of remarkable large terracotta vases (now in the archaeological museum in Syracuse).

The old salt pans close by are protected as a very attractive nature reserve run by LIPU, the Italian association for the protection of birds (*www.salinepriolo.it*). The coastal wetland is an ideal resting-place for migrating birds, especially ducks and herons, and flamingoes regularly nest; about 215 different species have been spotted including some rarities: marsh harrier, glossy ibis, avocet, black-winged stilt, greater sand plover (the only sighting for Italy), shoveler, ferruginous duck and Caspian tern.

MEGARA HYBLAEA

Near the port of Priolo, a fast road signposted Zona Industriale and Catania Via Litorale (the old SS 115 coast road to Catania) branches off towards the sea. Yellow signposts indicate the way to the excavations of the ancient city of Megara Hyblaea (*map p. 570, D1*).

HISTORY OF MEGARA HYBLAEA

The city was founded by Lamis of Megara in 728 BC. Having delayed their departure because of his illness, his settlers found no land available for them in the area, beaten to it by the Corinthians of Syracuse and the Chalcidian sub-colony of Leontinoi. After uncomfortable sojourns at Leontinoi and then at Thapsos, where Lamis died, King Hyblon of the Sicels magnanimously donated a small but choice stretch of land still under his control, at the mouth of the River Cantera; the grateful people remembered this when choosing a name for their new home, Megara Hyblaea.

A century later, wanting to found a sub-colony of their own, they found themselves forced to go to southwestern Sicily in order to found Selinunte. Megara Hyblaea was destroyed by Gelon in 483. A second city was founded here by Timoleon in 340, which in its turn was obliterated by the Romans in 214, after which the site was abandoned. Excavations were begun by the French School in Rome in 1949. In spite of the industries all around and a general air of neglect, the site is enchanting in spring, when wild chrysanthemums (*fiori di maggio*) carpet the surrounding countryside.

The lonely, overgrown excavations (*open 9–1hr before sunset; last tickets 1hr before closing, T: 0931 512364*) are approached by a byroad which runs alongside a citrus grove behind a line of cypresses. The road continues right (signposted 'Scavi') and here in a group of pines is a stretch of **Archaic walls** (6th century BC) with four semicircular towers (a fifth has been destroyed). The walls can be followed on foot for some 250m as far as the **West Gate**. A number of tombs have been placed near the walls, salvaged from excavations of the two necropoleis which are now covered by industrial plants. The third necropolis was located in the vicinity of these walls. Further on, below ground level, is an oblong construction with seven bases for columns. Excavated in

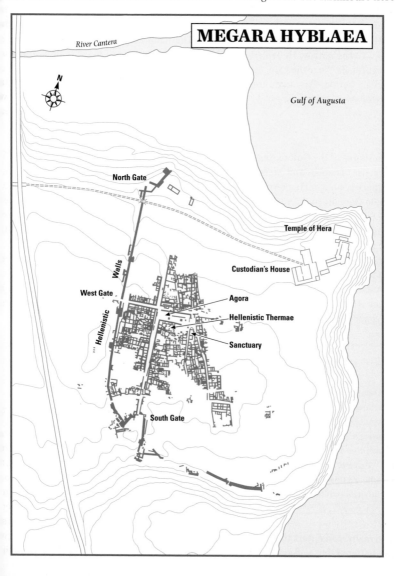

1880, it is of uncertain significance. Just before the little bridge over the railway is a car park; cars can continue over the narrow bridge along a rough road past some abandoned farmhouses. The road passes over the second line of **Hellenistic walls** built around the Hellenistic town (they follow a line of cypresses). To the left of the road here, the Hellenistic **North Gate** has been identified near the remains of Archaic walls. The road ends at the custodian's house in a little garden. The farmhouse here

MEGARA HYBLAEA

River Cantera

N

Gulf of Augusta

North Gate

Temple of Hera

Custodian's House

Walls

West Gate

Agora

Hellenistic

Hellenistic Thermae

Sanctuary

South Gate

will be used as an antiquarium to house the finds, including a tomb with a decorative frieze, although the most important Archaic sculptures are now in the archaeological museum in Syracuse.

A path leads across a field to the main area of excavations: the complicated remains include buildings from both the Archaic and Hellenistic periods (the red iron posts indicate the Archaic areas, and the green posts the Hellenistic buildings). At the intersection of the two main roads is the **agora**, near which are a sanctuary, interesting Hellenistic **thermae** with intact floors, and a poorly-preserved small **Doric temple** of the 4th century (protected by a roof). The main east–west road leads from the agora to the narrow Hellenistic **West Gate** (with two square towers) along the line of cypresses. Near the gate, on a lower level to the south, are kilns and houses of the Archaic period. The main north–south road ends at the Hellenistic **South Gate**, a 'pincer'-type defence work.

AUGUSTA

The shores of the Gulf of Augusta (*map p. 570, D1*), once lined by the ancient cities of Syracuse, Thapsos and Megara Hyblaea, are now hidden by a maze of factories and refineries, while oil tankers anchor offshore. The industrial zone extends from here to Priolo Gargallo and Augusta, and has a large concentration of chemical plants. After the Second World War, the industrialisation of the area seemed the answer to many peasants' prayers and the population of Syracuse rocketed from 44,000 to 135,000, the newcomers attracted by the possibility of employment. More recently, problems deriving from pollution have revealed the shortcomings of what was once considered the solution to the economic woes of southeastern Sicily.

Augusta itself is the most important oil and military port in Italy. It stands on a rocky islet connected to the mainland by a long bridge. To the east and west are two capacious harbours, the Porto Xifonio, and the Porto Megarese with two old forts.

HISTORY OF AUGUSTA

Augusta was founded by Frederick II in 1232 as a refuge for the inhabitants of Montalbano, which he himself had destroyed. In 1269 it was sacked by Philip and Guy de Montfort. It was taken by the French in 1676 after Admiral Duquesne defeated a Dutch fleet commanded by De Ruyter in the bay. De Ruyter was mortally wounded in the action and died a few days later at Syracuse, where he still lies.

The city was completely destroyed by the earthquake of 1693, and the modern town suffered severe damage from air raids in the Second World War. Another earthquake hit the town in 1990, leaving 13,000 people homeless.

The main road enters the town through the old Spanish bastions (1681); on the left is the battered, but still imposing **Castello Svevo**, built by Frederick of Hohenstaufen in 1232–42 and surrounded by a double circle of walls. Until recently it was used as a prison but there are plans to restore it for use as a museum and a library. Further ahead on the left are the public gardens. From here Via Principe Umberto leads south through the city. It crosses Via Garibaldi, with some fine churches and convents. Via Umberto continues to **Piazza Duomo**, with the severely damaged Chiesa Madre (Santa Maria Assunta, 1644). The north side of the square is taken up by the Municipio (1699), with a long balcony and the Swabian eagle under the cornice. The sundial was erected to record a total eclipse of the sun in 1870. On the first floor is the opera house (1730).

On the coast to the north is the ruined **castle of Brucoli**, erected by Giovanni Bastida in 1468 near a beautiful little fjord used by fishing boats. *Trotilon*, one of the oldest Greek settlements in Sicily, probably stood on the bay, which now has a large holiday village.

MELILLI

Clearly visible on the hill to the right when approaching Syracuse from Augusta, is Melilli (*map p. 570, D1*), destroyed and rebuilt after the 1693 earthquake and famous in the past for its production of wild thyme honey, highly prized by both Greeks and Romans. The town has suffered from the proximity of the industrial area, which has also affected the health of the population.

In the centre is the **Chiesa Madre**, dedicated to St Nicholas, with a beautiful wooden ceiling set with paintings by Olivio Sozzi representing the *Triumph of Faith*. In the lower part of town, to the east, is the church of **San Sebastiano** (1751, Louis-Alexandre Dumontier), approached by a large square with a portico where country fairs used to be held. The church has a remarkable series of frescoes by Olivio Sozzi, carried out between 1759 and 1763. The priest will show you on request the tiny statue of St Sebastian, reported to be miraculous, and usually only shown on his feast days.

Tombs along the nearby rivers Mulinello and Marcellino (the ancient *Mylas*) have revealed interesting archaeological remains (now in Syracuse) showing that trade with the Greeks existed before the mid-8th century BC colonisation. Melilli also has some beautiful **caves** in the district of Villasmundo (signposted from Villasmundo village, c. 12km north of Melilli, on the Carlentini road); they are protected as a nature reserve run by the University of Catania (*to visit two of the caves a few days ahead call Dr Petruzzello, T: 333 700 7305, office hours or check www.cutgana.unict.it*). The caves extend for almost 3km (the longest in Sicily), with magnificent stalactites and stalagmites, underground streams and a small lake. At the Town Hall of Melilli (Piazza Crescimanno; *T: 0931 552111*) is a museum with information about the caves and some fossils found there.

LENTINI AND ENVIRONS

Set in a dip between verdant hills, the sudden cliffs around Lentini (*map p. 570, C1*) were caused by seismic subsidence. Now a busy agricultural centre, famous for its oranges, Lentini was destroyed in the earthquake of 1693 and the modern town was again badly shaken in 1990. The atttractive **Chiesa Madre** (*open 8–12 & 3–8; T:*

095 941734 or 328 459 9945) was built over a 3rd-century Christian hypogeum. It preserves a 9th-century icon of the Madonna covered with silver. The church of San Luca, in Via Settembrini, has an anonymous but very beautiful *St Francis in Prayer* in the north aisle. In Piazza Dante is the church of the **Trinità**, with a vault fresco of the *Glory of the Holy Trinity with Sts Francis, Clare and Marcian* by Sebastiano Lo Monaco. On the second south altar is a polyptych attributed to Vincenzo da Pavia and on the high altar is a 15th-century panel painting of *St Anthony*.

The **Museo Archeologico** (*Via del Museo 1, open 9–6; closed Mon, last tickets 30mins before closing; T: 095 783 2962*) houses a collection of local finds dating from the Bronze Age to the 2nd century BC, including three fine kalyx kraters and a reconstruction of the South Gate of ancient Leontinoi. There are also two cases devoted to underwater finds recovered from Punta Castelluccio

On the top of Lentini's highest hill stand the ruins of the **Castellaccio** (*open Sat-Sun 9.30–12.30; to request a professional guided tour (fee) of the Castellaccio park, the rock-hewn churches and the 3rd-century Roman prison, possible any day, email or call in advance, T: 393 992 6088, giorditalo@yahoo.com*), a Swabian castle built on top of a Greek stronghold. Now an archaeological park, there are views over the sparse remains of the fascinating and complex fortification system of Leontinoi, built in four distinct periods, its necropolis, and the hill where the Sicel village stood. On the hill and on those nearby are several rock-hewn Byzantine churches and monasteries, some with conspicuous frescoes. To the southeast is the clifftop town of **Carlentini**, named after Charles V and founded in 1551 by the Spanish viceroy.

ANCIENT *LEONTINOI*

The ancient Greek city of *Leontinoi* in Contrada San Mauro (*map p. 570, C1; open Tues Thur, Sun 6 holidays 9–1.30*) was founded by the Chalcidians of Naxos in 729 BC, on the site of an earlier Sicel settlement, on two hills, the Metapiccola and the San Mauro, probably in order to control the fertile plain of Catania. In spite of being situated about 10km from the coast, the city flourished thanks to its commerce. The River San Leonardo (the ancient *Terias*) was navigable at that time, and barges loaded with merchandise came and went from the heart of the town to the coast. In the 6th century BC Panaetius set himself up as tyrant of Leontinoi, the first such ruler in Sicily. In the early 5th century BC it was taken by Hippocrates of Gela, and soon afterwards succumbed to the Syracusans. In 427 BC the city sent the orator Gorgias (480–c. 380) to invoke the assistance of Athens against her tyrants. Hieronymus, the last native tyrant of Syracuse, grandson of Hieron II and barely 14 years old, was assassinated at Leontinoi in 215 BC, a month or so after coming to power, during which time he had declared allegiance to Hannibal and the Carthaginians. The Roman general Marcus Marcellus captured Leontinoi in the same year.

A path leads down from the entrance to the elaborate South Gate. Across the valley steps lead up to a path which follows the walls to the top of the hill, from which there is a fine view of the site and the surrounding hills. The area of the prehistoric settlement, with a necropolis (6th–4th century BC), and hut village, is not at present open to the public, but most parts of interest can be viewed over the low enclosure fence.

LAGO DI LENTINI

Northwest of Lentini is a large artificial lake, the Biviere or Lago di Lentini (*no admission, you have to view through the fence*), a vast wetland thought to have been created by the Templars in the Middle Ages, which was drained in the 1950s, with disastrous effects on the climate, so it was filled again in the late '90s. Potentially, this is the most important area in Sicily for waders and water-birds, both as a resting-place during migration, and as a nesting site; but the level of the water in the lake varies constantly, as water is siphoned off for agriculture and for nearby industries, and this damages plant life, and sometimes nests. However, there is an important colony of white storks, which seem to be doing well.

FRANCOFONTE

Southwest of Lentini is the hill town of Francofonte (*map p. 570, C1*), whose Town Hall occupies the 18th-century Palazzo Palagonia adjoining the medieval castle. Local orange groves produce the *Tarocco di Francofonte*, voted by an international jury as the finest orange in the world. Quite large, it peels easily and the flesh is tinged with red. The flavour is reminiscent of strawberries. Opera lovers will remember that in *Cavalleria Rusticana*, Francofonte is the place where Alfio the carter came to get his wine.

PRACTICAL INFORMATION

GETTING AROUND

• **By rail**: Trains run from Syracuse north to Lentini, Melilli and Augusta on the Syracuse–Catania line, and southwest to Noto on the Syracuse–Gela line. A new line connects Syracuse and Palermo. For details, *www.trenitalia.it*.
• **By bus**: For up-to-date information on bus schedules see *www.orariautobus.it*. **AST** (*www.aziendasicilianatrasporti. it*) runs bus services within the city. The main terminus is in Corso Umberto, near the railway station. Shuttle buses run to Ortigia and around the city, and from the main car park at Molo Sant'Antonio to Ortigia and back. AST also runs inter-city services from Syracuse railway station in Corso Umberto to Augusta, Avola, Buccheri, Buscemi, Caltagirone, Canicattini, Cassaro, Cassibile, Carlentini, Catania, Comiso, Ferla, Floridia, Francofonte, Gela, Grammichele, Ispica, Lentini, Melilli, Modica, Noto, Palazzolo Acreide, Pozzallo, Priolo, Ragusa, Rosolini, Solarino, Sortino, Vittoria and Vizzini. **SAIS/Interbus** (*www.saisautolinee. it, www.interbus.it*) leave from Corso Umberto 194 to Acireale, Catania (and airport), Messina, Pachino, Palermo, Piazza Armerina, Portopalo di Capo Passero, Ragusa, Taormina and Trapani.

WHERE TO STAY

AUGUSTA (*map p. 570, D1*)
€€€ **Palazzo Zuppello**. Augusta's only

hotel, smart and modern, in an old *palazzo*. 20 rooms and suites (no lift), restaurant (in summer meals are served on the terrace, with a view over the bay). *Via Epicarmo 72/74, T: 0931 995633, www.palazzozuppellohotel.it.*

CASTELLO EURIALO (*map p. 570, D2*)

€ **Villa Mater Dei**. Nuns at this monastery in Belvedere, west of the castle, offer 25 rooms with private bath, restaurant and large park. Very good value. *Via delle Carmelitane 77, Contrada Sinerchia, SP 77, T: 0931 744044, www.villamaterdei.it.*

LENTINI (*map p. 570, C1*)

€ **Il Giardino dei Cavalieri**. Central B&B, an ex-convent with garden, next to the old Templar church of San Francesco di Paola. 5 comfortable rooms, each with separate entrance. Breakfast is served in the charming old-fashioned kitchen. Car park on request. *Salita Pisano 13, T: 095 945307 or 347 806 2801, www.algiardinodeicavalieri. com.*

NOTO (*map p. 570, C2–D2*)

€€€ **La Dépendance**. Tiny boutique hotel in the centre, 9 lovely rooms and suites, excellent restaurant, 'A Mastra. *Via Rocco Pirri 57, T: 0931 838831, www. ladependancehotel.com. Map 3.*

€€ **Flora**. Small hotel in an ideal position overlooking the public gardens, close to the bus stop, 11 rooms and suites, restaurant close by, friendly proprietor. *Via Piola 1, T: 0931 573052, www.hotelfloranoto.com. Map 4.*

€€€ **Seven Rooms Villadorata**. 7 rooms of the prince's palace have been transformed into an elegant guesthouse; 2 nights minimum stay. *Via Nicolaci 18, T: 0931 835575 or 338 509 56434, www.7roomsvilladorata.it. Map 3.*

€€ **Casuzza di Noto**. *Albergo diffuso*, little old houses in the heart of the town, beautifully restored and decorated, with air conditioning and washing machines. Award-winning service. Call Pietro Viola. *T: 366 197 8087, www.casuzza.it.*

€ **Masseria degli Ulivi**. 18 comfortable rooms in a beautiful farmhouse set in a centuries-old olive grove, good restaurant; pool, tennis. *Contrada Porcari, SS 287 Noto–Palazzolo Acreide, T: 0931 813019, www.masseriadegliulivi. com.*

€ **Borgo Alveria**. Old farmhouse at Noto Antica with 12 rooms, garden, pool, restaurant, peaceful atmosphere. *T: 0931 810003, www.borgoalveria.com.*

NOTO LIDO (*map p. 570, D3*)

€€ **La Corte del Sole**. Country house in a point overlooking the Vendicari nature reserve, once an olive mill; 34 rooms, restaurant, large garden and pool. *Contrada Bucachemi, Eloro, T: 0931 820210, www.lacortedelsole.it.*

PACHINO (*map p. 570, D3*)

€€ **Camporeale**. Country house in a quiet position, 5 bright rooms, all different. Very nice breakfasts; car park. *Contrada Camporeale, T: 0931 846543 or 339 606 1872, www.camporealerooms.it.*

PALAZZOLO ACREIDE (*map p. 570, C2*)

€€€ **Colle Acre**. A small wine farm just outside the town producing DOC wines from locally-grown grapes. 15 comfortable rooms, car park, restaurant serving marvellous food. *Via Giuseppe Campailla (northeast outskirts), T: 0931 040001 or 0931 881058, www. hotelcolleacre.it.*

€€€ **Feudo Bauly**. Restored hamlet in an isolated position 5km southeast of Palazzolo, once belonging to the amateur archaeologist Baron Judica.

25 beautiful rooms each with little sitting-room. Pool, fitness centre (expert massage) and wonderful restaurant. Feudo Bauly is run by the renowned confectioner Corsino; be aware that it is often used as the setting for wedding receptions. Mountain bikes and horse-riding in the nearby forest available. *Contrada Bauly, T: 0931 882088 or 0931 881568, www.feudobauly.com.*

PORTOPALO DI CAPO PASSERO (*map p. 570, D3*)

€€ **La Rosa dei Venti**. Isolated and panoramic, to the west of Portopalo, 10 rooms and suites, with splendid views over the sea. Car park, no restaurant. Good value. *Contrada Corridore Campana, T: 0931 844343, www. hotellarosadeiventi.it.*

SYRACUSE (*map p. 570, D2*)

€€€ **Livingston**. ◼ Small hotel on the seafront of Ortigia, with a tiny beach. 17 beautiful rooms, luxurious bathrooms, good rooftop restaurant, fitness centre with indoor pool and whirlpool in a cave. *Via Nizza 17, T: 0931 463830, www. livingstonhotel.it. Map 6.*

€€€ **Henry's House**. On Ortigia, facing the harbour. Two houses have been joined together to form this charming hotel, with 12 rooms furnished with Sicilian antiques and modern paintings by the local artist Fiore. Very good home-made breakfasts. *Via Castello Maniace 68, T: 0931 21361, www. hotelhenryshouse.com. Map 7.*

€€€ **Musciara Resort**. A tuna fishery transformed into a small hotel with a quiet, relaxing atmosphere. 12 rooms and suites, all with views of Ortigia, private sandy beach. Breakfast is provided, other meals on request. *Riviera Dionisio il Grande 42, T: 0931 463613, www.siracusaresort.it. Map 12.*

€€€ **Roma**. Pink Art Nouveau hotel built in 1880, right next to the cathedral, with restaurant and private beach. *Via Minerva 10, T: 0931 465630, www. hotelromasiracusa.it. Map 5.*

€€€ **Des Etrangers**. Beautiful 19th-century hotel, comfortable, overlooking the harbour, good service. 76 rooms and suites, restaurant, sauna, indoor pool. *Passeggio Adorno 10–12, T: 0931 319100, www.desetrangers.com. Map 3.*

€€€ **Villa Politi**. Charming old hotel built in 1862 as an artist's retreat (Winston Churchill came here). 100 comfortable rooms and suites, car park, restaurant, garden and pool. *Via Politi Laudien 2, T: 0931 412121, www. villapoliti.com. Map 11.*

€€ **Gutkowski**. ◼ On the north side of Ortigia, a small hotel of 26 rooms; nice breakfasts and evening bistro; cosy fireplace in winter. *Lungomare Vittorini 26, T: 0931 465830, www.guthotel.it. Map 2.*

€€ **Posta**. In a pleasant quiet part of Ortigia near the bridge and market, good value, 17 comfortable rooms, no restaurant. *Via Trieste 33, T: 0931 21819 or 0931 452177, www.hotelpostasiracusa. it. Map 1.*

€€ **Palazzo Gilistro**. B&B in the heart of Ortigia, carefully restored palace offering 8 modern rooms with soundproofed windows. Airport shuttle on request. *Via dell'Amalfitania 12, T: 331 865 0835, www.palazzogilistro.it. Map 3.*

WHERE TO EAT

AUGUSTA (*map p. 570, D1*)
€€ **Osteria della Mattonella**. The oldest inn of Augusta, for a blend

of Tuscan-Sicilian traditional fare, including (in season) snails, salt cod, thick vegetable soups. In summer you eat outside. Good house wine. Closed Tues and Aug. *Via Garibaldi 88, T: 0931 976466.*

AVOLA (*map p. 570, D2*)

€ **Cava Grande**. This little restaurant is an ideal lunch stop: simple, appetising dishes, also pizza in the evenings. They have a couple of rooms if you want to stay overnight. Closed Mon; in winter open weekends only. *Piazzale Laghetti di Cava Grande, T: 0931 811220 or 347 350 2342.*

BUCCHERI (*map p. 570, C2*)

€€ **'U Locale**. ■ Award-winning *trattoria* serving very good country food; *macco* (broad-bean potage), *cinghiale* (boar), spaghetti with mint and lemon, pig's trotters, tripe; *cannoli di ricotta* for dessert. Closed Tues. *Via Dusmet 14, T: 0931 873923.*

FRANCOFONTE (*map p. 570, C1*)

€ **Antica Hostaria Le Streghe**. This characteristic trattoria/pizzeria is situated in the stables of the Cruyllas castle, near Piazza Garibaldi. Vast array of vegetable *antipasti*, excellent pasta, simple desserts, Sicilian wines; also pizza in the evenings. Closed Mon. *Via Verdi 5, T: 095 784 3493.*

LENTINI (*map p. 570, C1*)

€ **A Maidda**. Owner-chef Salvo Bordonaro really cares about Sicilian food and wine; his restaurant (worth a detour) is recommended by the Slow Food Foundation and has a lovely shady garden. Unusual, inventive dishes. Closed Wed and Sun lunchtime. *Via Alfieri 2 (corner of Via Alaimo), T: 095 941537 or 339 776 0134.*

MARZAMEMI (*map p. 570, D3*)

€€ **La Cialoma**. *Cialoma* is the Sicilian word for sea shanty and chef Lina Campisi comes from a family of fishermen. Start with smoked tuna and swordfish; you eat outside in the square. Lunch only; Fri and Sat also dinner. *Piazza Regina Margherita, T: 0931 841772.*

NOTO (*map p. 570, C2–D2*)

€€€ **Meliora**. Nice little restaurant tucked away in the back streets, where the owner will present each dish and suggest the right wine. Very good *antipasti*, selection of fish or meat, good wine list, delicious desserts. Closed Tues. *Vico Milazzo 9, T: 0931 892161. Map 1.*

€€ **Trattoria del Crocifisso**. Wide assortment of vegetable *antipasti* and selection of local cheeses, home-made spaghetti with sardines, but the star dish is *coniglio alla stimpirata*, rabbit cooked the Sicilian way. Closed Wed. *Via Principe Umberto 46/48, T: 0931 571151. Map 1.*

€ **Trattoria del Carmine**. With a superb view of the church of the Carmine, this simple restaurant serves pizza in the evenings and sandwiches (*panini*) during the day, if you prefer these to a plate of delicious pasta. Closed Mon. *Via Ducezio 1, T: 0931 838705. Map 3.*

PALAZZOLO ACREIDE (*map p. 570, C2*)

€€ **Andrea**. ■ Interesting dishes using ingredients from the local mountains, including black or white truffles. Very good desserts, excellent wine list. Closed Tues. *Corso Vittorio Emanuele 4, T: 0931 881488 or 338 851 9092.*

PORTOPALO DI CAPO PASSERO (*map p. 570, D3*)

€€ **La Giara alla Tavernetta del Porto**. On the dockside, this delightful restaurant serves excellent fresh fish. Try the *brezza marina* (sea breeze), spaghetti with 8 different kinds of fish; a meal in itself, or the appetising *fritto misto di paranza*, mixed fried fish. Closed Mon. *Porto, T: 0931 843217.*

SYRACUSE (map p. 570, D2)

€€€ **Don Camillo**. In 2015 voted one of Sicily's best restaurants. This is one of the few restaurants where you will find (when in season) *zuppa di mucco*, soup of tiny new-born fish; definitely worth a visit. Excellent wine cellar. Closed Sun. *Via Maestranza 106, T: 0931 67133. Map 4.*

€€€ **La Foglia**. Unusual restaurant, principally vegetarian, run by an artist; the experience is rather like eating in someone's front room, where nothing matches—all odd crockery, tablecloths and cutlery. Superb grilled vegetables and famous soups; it should not be missed. *Via Capodieci 29, T: 0931 66233. Map 5.*

€€€ **Macallè**. Charming '50s-style restaurant serving dishes prepared exclusively with local produce. Good local wines. Closed Mon. *Via dei Santi Coronati 42, T: 392 297 4875. Map 4.*

€€ **La Volpe e l'Uva**. Lovely setting in front of the duomo, good for salads or grills, also pizza in the evening. *Piazza Duomo 20 (Palazzo Beneventano), T: 0931 66029. Map 5.*

€€ **Osteria da Mariano**. Tiny restaurant specialising in Hyblaean mountain food; the simple dessert consists of home-made almond brittle and a piece of crystallised ginger, or *cannoli di ricotta*. Closed Tues (except summer evenings) and 1–16 July. *Vicolo Zuccalà 9, T: 0931 67444. Map 5.*

€ **Bistrot Notre Dame**. Friendly French-style bistrot serving light, appetising Sicilian food with considerable flair. Closed Wed evenings. *Via Maestranza 58/60, T: 388 563 2105. Map 3.*

€ **Antica Salumeria**. ▪ Old-fashioned grocery where Lino prepares delectable, imaginative sandwiches to order, using the array of local produce he has on his counter, and several kinds of local bread. He also sells water and soft drinks. Closed Sun. *Via Cavour 1 (corner of Via dell'Amalfitania), T: 347 005 0877. Map 3.*

LOCAL SPECIALITIES

AVOLA The historic **Caffè Finocchiaro** (*Piazza Umberto, closed Tues*) is renowned throughout Italy for the excellent ice cream, granita and the unique almond nougat covered with chocolate. Try **Sebastiano Munafò**, (*Via Monte Grappa 13, T: 0931 833252*), for the local *pizzuta d'Avola* almonds.

FLORIDIA The picturesque **Bar Centrale** (*Piazza Umberto 17*) is the oldest café in town, with a very good reputation. Try the *crèpe al gelato*, ice cream in a pancake, or the *gelato al torrone*. A good savoury snack is the *strudel salato*.

LENTINI Lentini's historic (1912) café and pastry shop is **Navarria** (*Via Conte Alaimo 8–12*), close to the cathedral, for tasty snacks and ice cream. There is a bustling **farmers' market** in Piazza Duomo on Sat mornings. Get someone to help you find **Lucinda Nocita**'s tiny bakery (*Via De Pinedo 22*) in a little back street, for delicious sourdough bread baked in a stone oven using almond shells as fuel.

MARZAMEMI Campisi (*Via Marzamemi 12, www.*

specialitadelmediterraneo.it) is an irresistible shop stocking locally-prepared canned, bottled or smoked tuna, swordfish, mackerel, sardines and anchovies; also vegetables from Pachino, olives, artichokes, sun-dried tomatoes; you can shop online. If you are looking for the local DOC wines, **Feudo Ramaddini** (*Contrada Lettiera, www.feudoramaddini.com*) produces Al Hamen, a delectable Moscato Passito di Noto that has won many awards.

NOTO **Market** day is Mon morning. There is a country fair on the first and third Tues of every month, and a flea market (public gardens) every third Sun of the month. **Corrado Costanzo** (*Via Silvio Spaventa 7–9; map 3*) is a famous old-fashioned confectioner's; of more recent foundation is **Mandolfiore** (*Via Ducezio 2; map 3*), which also sells very good cakes, biscuits and ice cream; try tangerine sorbet or *dessert di carruba* made only with carobs; *cubbaita* nougat (sesame seeds and honey) is available all year round. The **Caffè Sicilia** (*Corso Vittorio Emanuele 125, closed Mon; map 3*) is among the best in Italy for unusual home-made jams and ice cream. At **Tenuta dei Fossi** (*Contrada San Lorenzo, www.tenutadeifossi.it*), wines are aged the ancient way in cement tanks instead of wooden barrels or stainless-steel vats. Try their DOC Eloro Pachino and Moscato di Noto.

PACHINO For some DOC Moscato di Noto or Eloro Pachino, try **Cantine Rudinì** (*Contrada Camporeale, www. vinirudini.it*).

PALAZZOLO ACREIDE **Cose a Caso** (*Via Antonino Uccello 11, open afternoons only*) has beautiful bedspreads, tablecloths, curtains and cushions, inspired by local Baroque

and Art Nouveau motifs. **Corsino** (*Via Nazionale 2/Piazza Pretura, www. corsino.it*), opened in 1889, is famous for excellent sweets, especially the nougat (*torrone*), but the fried rice balls (*arancini*) and other savoury snacks are superb too. For traditional *pignuccata* and *giuggiulena* made with local thyme honey, try **Caprice** (*Via Iudica 1*).

SYRACUSE A daily **market** (not Sun) is held in the morning in Ortigia on the streets near the Temple of Apollo, around the former market building. Fresh fish, fruit and vegetables are sold here. A **farmers' market** is held on Sat afternoon near the Marriott Hotel on Ortigia (Ortea Palace, by the bridge).

There are many places in where craftsmen make paper by hand, using papyrus which grows in the River Ciane. **L'Angolo del Papiro** (*Viale Giuseppe Agnello 11, www.angolodelpapiro.com; map 9*), sells papyrus stationery and business cards. Go to **Fish House** (*Via Cavour 29–31, www.fishhouseart.it; map 3*) for ceramics inspired by the sea.

Reoro (*Via Landolina 17; map 3*) is where Massimo Sinatra creates stunning jewellery in gold and precious stones, including the rare amber from the River Simeto. Another goldsmith is the internationally famous **Massimo Izzo** (*Piazza Archimede 25, www. massimoizzo.com; map 3*), who draws his inspiration from the sea, preferring coral, diamonds and aquamarines; yet another is **Zappalà** (*Via Po 11; map 10*), who creates unique pieces, using gold, coral, pearls and turquoise. **Bazar delle Cose Vecchie** (*Via Consiglio Reginale 7; map 3*) sells interesting curios, antique jewellery and puppets.

Marciante (*Via Landolina 9; map 3*) makes excellent pastries and marzipan;

suppliers of *cassata di ricotta* to the late Queen Mother, who was very partial to it. **Café Apollo** (*Piazza Pancali; map 1*) is a good place for coffee, ice cream or snacks.

For Moscato di Siracusa DOC wine, the **Fausta Mansio farm** (*Via Nausicaa 10, T: 0931 744508, www.faustamansio. com*) produces this rare 'condensed sunlight' using organic methods; you can shop online.

FESTIVALS AND EVENTS

AVOLA Feb, Carnival, famous for the processions of sumptuous allegorical floats.

FRANCOFORTE March, the *Sagra del Tarocco*, celebrations for the harvest of the famous blood oranges. Tasting opportunities, guided tours, concerts.

MARZAMEMI July, *Festival del Cinema di Frontiera*, open-air screenings of films dealing with adventure, explorations and heroism—the 'frontier' can be geographical, mental or cultural.

MELILLI 20 Jan and 3–11 May, Feast of St Sebastian, with a procession, a fair, and fireworks; many thousands of pilgrims arrive from all over the world.

NOTO 19 Feb, the last Sun in Aug, and the first Sun in Sept: festivities in honour of San Corrado. Easter: the Procession of the Holy Thorn takes place on Good Friday, and other religious ceremonies during the week. 3rd Sun in May, the *Infiorata*, when Via Nicolaci is carpeted with fresh flowers.

NOTO ANTICA 4th Sun in May, *Festa dell'Alveria*, when the inhabitants of Noto go for a stroll through the streets of the earthquake-destroyed town, accompanied by expert guides. Nostalgic and fun at the same time.

PACHINO May, *Inverdurata*, to celebrate the rich and varied local production, the road surface of central Pachino from Via Roma to Piazza Vittorio Emanuele is decorated with fruits and vegetables, forming intricate designs. Free sampling. *www. inverduratapachino.it*.

PALAZZOLO ACREIDE Jan, the great feast for St Sebastian, *Festa di San Sebastiano*, attracts thousands of enthusiastic worshippers (*www. sansebastiano.org*). Feb, Carnival is unusual in this town because the allegorical floats are miniature. Live music every night in Piazza del Popolo (*www.comune.palazzoloacreide.sr.it*). Aug, the dramatic, moving celebrations for St Paul are concluded by a firework display (*www.sanpaolopalazzolo.it*).

SOLARINO 7 Nov, procession of tractors and other farm machinery to the church of Madonna delle Lacrime at Via Matteotti 97 for a solemn Thanksgiving. On the way people give them fruit, flowers, cakes, bread, meat etc., which are later distributed among the poor.

SORTINO 1st weekend in Oct, a celebration of the area's famous thyme or orange-blossom honey.

SYRACUSE First and second Sun in May, *Santa Lucia delle Quaglie*, commemorating a miracle of the saint which took place here in 1642, procession and fireworks. May–June, *Rappresentazioni Classiche*, the Greek plays presented yearly in the Greek theatre (*www.indafondazione.org*). 8 Dec, *Immacolata*, a procession for the Madonna. 13 Dec, *Santa Lucia*, procession from the cathedral to the church of Santa Lucia.

Catania

The city of Catania (*map p. 573, C2*) is one of the liveliest and most interesting in Sicily, though it is often bypassed by tourists on their way from Syracuse to Taormina. It is a stimulating place, the second largest city on the island after Palermo. It has been destroyed nine times in the course of its history, variously by earthquakes, bombardments and lava flows, yet has been rebuilt each time on exactly the same spot. Noisy and untidy, it is also generous and fun; a city of enormous cultural 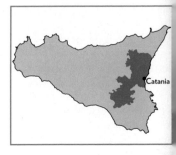 fervour, of many theatres and occasions to listen to music. The city enjoys a love–hate relationship with the volcano at whose foot it stands; the people never call Etna by its name, preferring instead to refer to it simply as '*a muntagna*, 'the mountain'.

The harmonious appearance of the centre, a UNESCO World Heritage Site, with long straight streets of imposing Baroque churches and palaces, dates from the reconstruction which followed the earthquake of 1693. The colour scheme of the city-centre buildings is black and dark grey, relieved with white limestone details around the doors and windows. The dark colour is provided by the lava sand used in the plaster but he effect is rarely sombre: Catania is one of the sunniest cities in Europe and can well afford to use the glittering black '*azzolu* on its house fronts. The result is extremely elegant. Blocks of basalt have also been used for paving the streets.

Once the most prosperous city on the island, Catania was known in the 1960s as the Milan of the South. Its fortunes dwindled drastically in the 1990s but now it is re-emerging from that chaotic period. Large quantities of fruit, vegetables, wheat, wine and raw materials of many kinds are brought to Catania to be sorted, graded, packed and shipped.

The hinterland of Catania and the nearby coast includes Mount Etna, one of the world's most active volcanoes and the largest in Europe, besides interesting old cities such as Acireale, Randazzo, Mineo, Adrano, Militello and Caltagirone, famous for its ceramics. Historic castles include those of Calatabiano and Aci Castello, while the Simeto, Sicily's most important river, which springs in the Nebrodi mountains, flows through the territory of Catania for most of its 88km.

HISTORY OF CATANIA

Catania was perhaps a Sicel trading-post when the first Greek colony (from Chalcis) established itself here in 729 BC. As *Katane*, it soon rose to importance. Hieron I of Syracuse took the city in 476 and exiled the inhabitants to Leontinoi, re-founding Katane as *Aetna*, with celebrations for which Aeschylus wrote his *Women of Aetna*. The exiles returned and drove out Hieron's Doric colonists in 461 and in 415 it was the base of the Athenian operations against Syracuse—but it fell to Dionysius in 403 and the citizens were sold as slaves. After the defeat of the Syracusan fleet by Mago the Carthaginian, it was occupied by Himilco. Catania opened its gates to Timoleon in 339 and to Pyrrhus in 278, and was one of the first Sicilian towns to surrender to the Romans (263). Its greatest prosperity dated from the time of Augustus, who rewarded it for taking his part against Sextus Pompey. It flourished under the Antonine emperors too, when the theatre and amphitheatre were rebuilt and a number of other major civic works completed.

In the early Christian period Catania was the scene of the martyrdom of St Agatha (238–251, *see p. 409*). In the Middle Ages it was wrecked by an earthquake (1169), sacked by Henry VI (1194) and again by Frederick II (1232), who built the castle to guard the harbour and hold his rebellious subjects in check. Constance of Aragon, his beloved empress, died here on 23rd June 1222. The 17th century saw the calamities of 1669 and 1693, the former the most terrible eruption of Etna in history, the latter a violent earthquake. The lava flows which reached the town in 1669 can still be seen from the ring road. In 1943 Catania was bombarded from the air and from the sea, receiving more bomb attacks than Naples.

EXPLORING CATANIA

NB: Visitors can purchase a CATANIA PASS card (www.cataniapass.it), allowing unlimited free use of the public transport system (buses, Alibus for the airport, and metropolitana), free or discounted entrances to the civic museums and the botanical garden, and discounts in shops and restaurants displaying the sign. You will find the card at the Tourist Info points and at museums.

PIAZZA DUOMO

The old centre of Catania is the well-proportioned Piazza Duomo (*map 11*). In the centre stands a fountain supporting an antique lava-stone elephant, the symbol of Catania. On the elephant's back perches an Egyptian obelisk (perhaps once a turning-post in the Roman circus or part of a sanctuary of Isis and Serapis), erected here in 1736 by Giovanni Battista Vaccarini, who was responsible for much of the look of the square. The fountain is modelled on the monument by Bernini in Piazza Minerva in Rome. The people refer to the elephant as *Liotru*, after Heliodorus, a Byzantine necromancer who is supposed to have used it as a 'Jumbo Jet' to fly between Catania and Constantinople in the 6th century AD. The square is surrounded by 18th-century buildings, many by Vaccarini, and dominated by the superb duomo on the east side.

To the right of the duomo is the **Diocesan Museum** (*open Mon–Fri 9–2, Tues and Thur also 3–6, Sat 9–1; last tickets 30mins before closing; closed Sun and holidays; T: 095 281635, www.museodiocesicatania.com*), which displays the cathedral treasure, fine artworks and objects relating to the cult of St Agatha (*see p. 409*). From the terrace there is an interesting view over the old city centre and you can walk along a short stretch of the city walls. From just outside the museum it is possible to go down some narrow steps to the Roman baths under the square, **Terme Achilliane** (*open Mon–Sat 9–1, Sun 10–1*), used as an air-raid shelter in 1943 and since then closed due to flooding and other problems; they are well worth a visit. Jean Houel succeeded in descending into the subterranean tunnels in the 19th century; he thought he had found a temple of Bacchus.

The **Municipio** (Town Hall), begun in 1695, was finished by Vaccarini in 1741. Two state carriages are on view in the entrance passage. The south side of Piazza Duomo is closed by the fine **Porta Uzeda** (1696), which leads to the public garden called **Villa Pacini**, often busy with pensioners playing cards and talking, and beyond to the harbour. The streets behind the striking 19th-century white marble **Amenano Fountain** (an underground river which emerges at this point) are lined with a colourful daily **food market**, *'a Pescheria*, where fish, meat, cheese and vegetables are sold.

THE DUOMO

Map 11. Open Mon–Sat 7–12 & 4–7, Sun 7.30–12 & 4.30–7. No visits during services. T: 095 320044.

Dedicated to St Agatha, the duomo was founded by Count Roger in 1094. Consecrated on 15th May, the following day it was declared to be the cathedral, taking the place of the old Sant'Agata la Vetere, which had acted as such for 800 years. It was rebuilt after the earthquakes of 1169 and 1693. The granite columns on the lower storey of the Baroque façade (Vaccarini, 1736–58) come from the Roman theatre. The cupola, by Battaglia, dates from 1804. The north door, with three statuettes, is attributed to Gian Domenico Mazzola (1577). The structure of the mighty 11th-century black lava-stone apses can be seen from no. 159 Via Vittorio Emanuele.

The spacious simplicity of the interior, with its wide nave and aisles separated by sturdy pilasters, is relieved by the side altars with their elegant 18th-century gilded picture-frames, forming a remarkable collection. During restoration work in the 1950s, the foundations of the Norman basilica were revealed beneath the nave, and vague traces of a large Roman temple, probably dedicated to Jupiter. On the right, against the second pier, is the **tomb of the composer Vincenzo Bellini** (1801–35), by Giovanni Battista Tassara (1876). The second and third altarpieces are by Borremans. Under the last altar is the body of the **Blessed Giuseppe Benedetto Dusmet** (1816–94), the face covered by a silver mask. Still revered today, he was a sympathetic cardinal and archbishop during difficult times, known for his devotion to the poor and needy.

The fine antique columns (of late Imperial and Byzantine date) in the transepts and three apses formed part of Count Roger's construction. In the south transept, a doorway by Giovanni Battista Mazzola (1545) leads into the Cappella della Madonna which preserves a Roman sarcophagus, with the figures (very worn) finely carved in the round. It contains the remains of Frederick II (d. 1337), Louis (d. 1355), Frederick III (d. 1377)

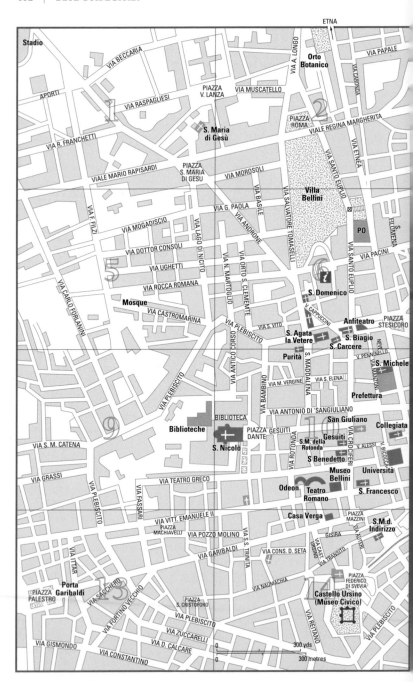

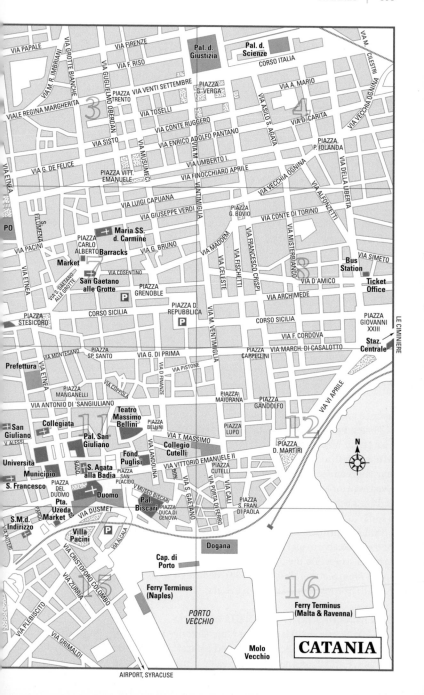

and other illustrious members of the House of Aragon. Opposite is the beautiful **tomb of Queen Constance of Aragon** (d. 1363), wife of Frederick III, with contemporary scenes of Catania. The sculptured fragment above the door dates from the 15th century.

The chapel to the right of the high altar is the **Cappella di Sant'Agata**, seen through a magnificent wrought-iron gate. The chapel contains a marble altarpiece (*Coronation of the Saint*); the tomb (right) of the Viceroy Fernández d'Acuña (d. 1494), a kneeling figure attended by a page, by Antonello Freri of Messina; and (left) the treasury protected by seven doors, with the relics of St Agatha, including her reliquary bust by Giovanni di Bartolo (1376). These are displayed only for the saint's feast days (3rd–5th Feb, 17th Aug, and, in procession, on 4th and 5th Feb). The walnut choir stalls, finely sculpted by Scipione di Guido (1588), represent the life and martyrdom of St Agatha.

In the north transept, the Norman Cappella del Crocifisso is approached through an arch designed by Gian Domenico Mazzola (1563). In the sacristy is a fresco showing the destruction of Catania by the lava flow from Etna in 1669, painted in 1675 by Giacinto Platania, an eye-witness; the painting has proved of great interest to volcanologists.

SAN FRANCESCO AND THE MUSEO BELLINI

From Piazza del Duomo the handsome, long, straight Via Vittorio Emanuele leads west. In Piazza San Francesco (*map 11*), a large votive deposit of 6th-century BC pottery came to light in 1959, indicating the presence here of an important sanctuary, probably dedicated to Demeter. Dominating the little square, which in the Middle Ages was the grain market, is an uninspiring monument (1935) to the cardinal and archbishop Giuseppe Benedetto Dusmet (*see p. 401*). The medallions at its foot represent some of his acts of charity. The majestic church of **San Francesco** (*open 8.30–12 & 5–7; T: 095 312103*) houses two of the *candelore*, the impressive candlesticks representing the city corporations used during the processions for St Agatha (*see p. 409*). Each one weighs about a ton and is borne by eight stalwarts chosen from the corporation represented.

Facing the scenographic façade of San Francesco is a palace containing a small apartment (across the courtyard to the left and up an old flight of steps) housing the **Museo Bellini** (*map 10; open Mon–Sat 9–1; T: 095 715 0535*). This delightful little museum commemorates the great composer Vincenzo Bellini, who was born here and lived here for 16 years. Known as the 'Swan of Catania', he died in Paris and was buried in Père Lachaise, before being returned to Catania in 1876, where a state funeral and a tomb in the duomo awaited him. The rooms have retained their character and are crowded with mementoes, including his harpsichord (in the alcove where he is thought to have been born) and his death mask. The music library (*open to students*) preserves original scores. On the opposite side of the same palace is the **Museo Emilio Greco** (*open Mon–Sat 9–1; T: 095 317654*), dedicated to the graphic works of the sculptor Emilio Greco, who was also born in Catania.

SAN BENEDETTO AND SAN GIULIANO

Via Crociferi (*map 10*) is the most representative 18th-century street in Catania, lined with Baroque churches, convents and palaces, many of them approached by flights of steps. Excavations here have revealed remains of Roman houses. On the left, the church of **San Benedetto** (*open 10–7, closed Thur; bookshop; T: 095 715 2207 or 345 308 7645, www.benedettineviacrociferi.it*) has an elegant façade and vestibule of 1762. The pastel-coloured interior has an elaborate nuns' choir, a frescoed barrel vault by Giovanni Tuccari (1725) and a beautiful floor. You are also shown the *parlatorio*, the parlour where the cloistered nuns (there were 23 at the time of writing) can speak to their relatives through bronze grilles. The same ticket allows access to the remains of a Roman *domus* and to the MACS, **Museo d'Arte Contemporanea della Sicilia** (*open 10–7, closed Thur; T: 095 715 2207, www.museomacs.it*), which displays modern sculptures and paintings in small wing of the monastery on the opposite side of Via Crociferi, connected to the main building by the arch over the street. Under the arch, at no. 16, is the **Herborarium** (*open 10–1 & 5–7.30, mornings only on Sat and Sun, closed Mon; tea room and shop; tickets for San Benedetto can be purchased here at a discounted price; T: 349 539 7736, www.herborarium.com*), dedicated to tea, with a curious collection of equipment for its preparation. Special blends are prepared here, using Oriental teas mixed with Sicilian herbs and flowers.

Across Via Alessi (its steps to the right are a popular gathering-place in the evenings), the former church of **San Francesco Borgia** or Gesuiti (*open Mon–Sat and 1st Sun of month 9–7, Sun 9–1; T: 095 747 2304*), reconstructed after the 1693 earthquake, is now an exhibition venue. Both the church and the large Jesuit college next door are the work of Vaccarini and Angelo Italia (1754). On the fourth north altar is a relief of St Ignatius by Marabitti and on the third is a wooden reliquary Cross (1760), with skulls dimly visible behind glass. The cherry-wood pulpit is the work of a local artist. The dome was frescoed by Olivio Sozzi.

Across the street, on the right, **San Giuliano** (*sometimes open for services; T: 095 715 9360*) was begun in 1739 and continued by Vaccarini, who was responsible for the façade. In the fine elliptical interior is a 14th-century painted Crucifix.

SAN NICOLÒ L'ARENA

Via Antonio di Sangiuliano, a handsome street lined with oleanders, leads uphill to the church of **San Nicolò l'Arena** (*map 10; open 9–12.30; T: 095 715 9912*). It faces a little crescent of houses designed by Stefano Ittar. This is the largest church in Sicily (105m long, transepts 42m wide), begun in 1687 by Giovanni Battista Contini and rebuilt in 1735 by Francesco Battaglia, probably to the design of Antonino Amato. The dome was designed by Stefano Ittar. The striking façade, with its gigantic columns, was left incomplete in 1796.

The simplicity of the interior emphasizes its good proportions. The complex meridian line, 39m long, on the floor of the transept dates from 1841. The 18th-century choir stalls were intricately carved by craftsmen from Naples. The huge organ was intended to be played by three organists at once. Its builder, Donato Del Piano (d. 1775), lies buried beneath. Goethe alluded to its wonderful sound when he heard it in 1787, and it was played by Vincenzo Bellini when he was still a child—being so small, he got his friends to move the pedals for him while he was at one of the keyboards. The chapels at the east end have been made into war memorials. The roof is accessible and there is a superb view.

To the left of the church façade (surrounded by railings) are some remains of a **Roman bath complex**, well below ground level. The building in front is the remarkable **convent** (*guided tours 9–5, Aug 11–6; bookshop; T: 095 710 2767 or 334 924 2464, www.monasterodeibenedettini.it*), the largest in Europe after that of Mafra in Portugal. When the traveller Patrick Brydone saw it in 1770 he thought it was a royal palace, only to discover it 'was nothing else than a convent of fat Benedictine monks, who wanted to assure themselves a paradise in this world, if not in the other'. It was almost entirely rebuilt after 1693 to the design of Antonino Amato and his son Andrea; the rich detail of its Baroque ornamentation combines well with its simplicity of line. The first court is overlooked by the splendid façade with delightful windows and balconies, completed in the early 18th century and decorated with an exuberant display of grotesque masks, cupids, fruits and flowers. Excavations here have revealed prehistoric traces as well as Greek and Roman remains, including a lava-stone road. In one of the cloisters there is a beautiful enclosed garden with trees and a neo-Gothic majolica tabernacle. Another cloister has a graceful arcaded portico. The monumental Neoclassical staircase (1794) was designed by Antonio Battaglia. The impressive long corridors have fine vaults. The huge building is now used by the University.

To the right of the church façade, an iron gate leads into another courtyard past the department of Archaeology. An iron staircase leads to the **Biblioteche Civica e Ursino Recupero** (*open Mon–Fri 9–1, Sat 9–11.30; T: 095 316883*), including the recently restored monastic library, with thousands of ancient manuscripts held in their original 18th-century bookcases, a UNESCO World Heritage site. The beautiful majolica floor is of 1700 (the tiles are from Vietri). Close by, in Via Biblioteca 4, is **Palazzo Ingrassia**, which houses the University's archaeological collection (*open Mon, Wed, Fri 9.30–1; T: 095 710 2761 or 334 924 2464*). The finds date from prehistory to the Middle Ages. Of particular interest is the last section, dedicated to 78 fake Centuripe vases, so skilfully forged that they have deceived many experts.

THE PARCO ARCHEOLOGICO

Via Gesuiti, with herringbone paving in large blocks of basalt (typical of the side streets of the city), descends from San Nicolò and Piazza Dante past modest houses. Via Rotonda branches off to the right. Remains of a Roman bath complex are visible here, under the primitive domed church of **Santa Maria della Rotonda** (*map 10; open Wed and Sun 9–1; request joint ticket at the Teatro Romano; see below*). Once considered to be the oldest church in Catania, founded AD 44, it was only in the 18th century that it was identified as an Imperial-era bath complex that had been transformed into a church in the Middle Ages. The baths were in use from the 1st–6th centuries AD and their rooms were richly decorated. When they fell out of use, the area was used as a cemetery. Many of the adjacent houses have been converted from another bath-house.

Via Sant'Agostino continues down to Via Vittorio Emanuele past the Odeon (*see below*). This old part of the city corresponds approximately to the area occupied by the Greek *Katane* and is now protected as an archaeological park, **Parco Archeologico Greco-Romano di Catania**, the offices of which are at the Teatro Romano (*NB: The Roman theatre is always open but a shortage of custodians may mean that other* *monuments are closed. To be sure, request your visit a few days ahead indicating the places you want to see: T: 095 715 0508, museo.catania@regione.sicilia.it).*

At Via Vittorio Emanuele 266 is the inconspicuous entrance to the Roman theatre, **Teatro Romano** (*open 9–7; last tickets 30mins before closing; joint ticket valid also for Santa Maria della Rotonda; NB: lots of steep steps; T: 095 715 0508*). This is the latest of three Roman theatres, one on top of the other, on the site of the preceding 5th-century BC Greek theatre where it is said Alcibiades harangued the people of Catania to win them to the cause of Athens (415 BC) and to join him in the battle against Syracuse, in the final phase of the long war against Sparta. Elements of the underlying Greek structure have recently come to light, including some limestone blocks inscribed with Greek letters. The building is of basalt, practically all of the marble facing having disappeared. The underground passageways which gave access to the cavea, which has nine wedges of seats in two main tiers, are very well preserved. The diameter of the cavea was 98m and the seating capacity was c. 7,000. The orchestra is often flooded since the underground River Amenano tends to come to the surface here at certain times of the year. Until the 1960s the theatre was almost completely covered with houses, which have been gradually expropriated and demolished. Some of the houses, however, have been spared and serve as a museum (Casa Liberti) with an archaeological collection and an area for exhibitions and cultural events (Casa dell'Androne), showcasing a collection of old prints, maps and photographs.

From the top of the cavea a path leads round to the small **Odeon**, a semicircular building used for rehearsals and competitions, which could accommodate 1,500 spectators. It was probably provided with a roof. The stage is covered by a modern building that has not yet been demolished. Close to the exit is the last remaining fragment of Via delle Grotte, Street of the Caves, a road built in the Middle Ages which led from the top of the hill and over the theatre to the sea. Before leaving the theatre, look up at Casa Liberti above the right-hand side of the cavea; the four holes in the wall over the last east window are pigeon-holes, allowing access to the roof where the birds were kept. The way out passes through a small antiquarium, with some of the decorative marble elements from the theatre. Note the dolphin that was probably an arm-rest of a seat of honour.

CASA VERGA

On the second floor of Via Sant'Anna 8, is **Casa Verga** (*map 14; open Mon–Sat 9–1; T: 095 715 0598*), the simple apartment of the parents of the writer Giovanni Verga (*see p. 413*), who lived and died here. Some of the original furnishings have been preserved in his study, library and bedroom. The museum contains the personal libraries of Verga, Federico De Roberto and Luigi Capuana.

AROUND CASTELLO URSINO

At the far west end of the busy Via Garibaldi stands the Baroque Porta Ferdinandea, or **Porta Garibaldi** (1768; *map 13*). In Via Consolato della Seta (*map 14*) is the handsome church of **Santa Maria dell'Aiuto** (*open Mon, Wed, Fri 9–11, or daily for Mass at 8*), with a Baroque façade by Antonio Battaglia, in golden limestone with antique columns.

It preserves a full-size replica of the Holy House of Loreto in the Marche, reproduced here by order of the prelate Lauria, who had visited Loreto in 1730.

Piazza Mazzini (*map 14*) is charmingly arcaded with 32 columns from a Roman building which stood close to the Odeon, perhaps on the ancient forum. This was done to provide a portico for the fruit and vegetable vendors, who held their daily market here. Via Auteri, in a dilapidated district of the city, leads south to Piazza Federico di Svevia, where low houses surround the **Castello Ursino** (*map 14; open Mon–Fri 9–7, Sun 9–1.30; last tickets 30mins before closing; T: 095 345830*), built by Richard of Lentini for Frederick II of Hohenstaufen. It was partly destroyed by the lava of 1669, which completely surrounded it, but restored after 1837 to house the **Museo Civico**. Material from the monastery of San Nicolò was augmented by archaeological finds collected by the Prince of Biscari in the 18th century. The ground floor is devoted to ancient vases and sculpture, while the upper floor displays paintings. A fine courtyard contains sculptural fragments and sarcophagi. Archaeological excavations around the castle have revealed long sections of the Norman fortifications.

Near the submerged railway line just outside the square is the simple little church of **Santa Maria dell'Indirizzo**. Behind it, in the courtyard of a school are the remains of late Roman baths called **Terme dell'Indirizzo** (*to request visit, T: 095 715 0508*) and a tiny domed Greek-cross building in black lava stone. This site has recently been studied and restored and will hopefully soon be open to the public.

SANT'AGATA ALLA BADIA AND PALAZZO BISCARI

The eye-catching little church of **Sant'Agata alla Badia** (*map 11; open Tues–Sun 9–12, Fri and Sat also 5–8, Sun also 7–8.30; T: 348 796 7711*), its dome harmoniously setting off that of the cathedral, when viewed from Piazza Duomo, is another work by Vaccarini (1735–67). The interior was completed after his death, but notice the side altars in yellow marble from Castronovo (a stone he also used also for the royal palace of Caserta; the quarry was thus exhausted) and the magnificent floor with an intricate design in white and grey marble. Under the Crucifix (1696) is the grille where novices would kneel to make their vows on entering the Benedictine Order. Exactly in the centre hangs a beautiful crystal chandelier, recently restored. You can climb up to the dome and walk around it, for some marvellous views.

Beyond, in a little square on the right, is the church of **San Placido** (Stefano Ittar; *usually closed*) with a façade of 1769 and a pretty interior. The vast convent behind it, Palazzo Platamone (*open Mon–Sat 9–7, Sun 9–1; T: 095 742 8038 or 095 742 8034*), is now a cultural centre. Opposite the church is the workshop of a chandler, skilled in making the enormous wax candles for the feast of St Agatha.

Via Museo Biscari is named after the **Palazzo Biscari** (*to request visit, T: 095 321818 or 320 211 4802*). The most impressive private palace in Catania, said to have 600 rooms, it was an obligatory stop on the Grand Tour. The best view of the magnificent exterior, by Antonino Amato, is from Via Dusmet. Here, in the 18th century, Ignazio Paternò Castello, Prince of Biscari, catalogued *objets d'art* for his famous collection, part of which is preserved in the Museo Civico (*see above*). Concerts are occasionally held in the lovely Rococo Salone della Musica, and part of the building, entered from no. 16, houses **Museum & Fashion** (*open Tues–Sun 10–7; T: 095 250 3188*), created by the designer Marella Ferrera, who was born in Catania. It displays items from her most famous collections, temporary exhibitions and her atelier.

ST AGATHA OF CATANIA

The Feast of St Agatha (Sant' Agata) in Catania is one of the most lavish in the Roman Catholic world. It galvanises the city during the first week of February and again on 17th August. An early Christian martyr, Agatha was only thirteen when she was arrested for her religious beliefs. In spite of blandishments and then threats, she would not recant. On 4th February 251 she underwent terrible torture, including the mutilation of her breasts. Miraculously recovering during the night after seeing a vision of St Peter, she survived being burned the next day in the amphitheatre, on the orders of Quintianus, Roman governor of Catania. The flames would not touch her and a sudden earthquake caused the Romans to flee the town leaving Agatha unscathed. She asked to be taken to her prison cell, where she died. Her body, still intact, was taken to Constantinople in 1040 by the Byzantine general George Maniakes as a gift for Basil II, but on 17th August 1126 it was brought back to Catania by two soldiers of the Imperial Guard, who had cut it into pieces in order to smuggle it home.

St Agatha is the patron saint both of women who have undergone mastectomy and also of firemen. The processions in her honour are impressive and richly Baroque, sometimes continuing for 24 hours. The huge, 20-ton float, bearing the silver chest that contains parts of her body and the jewel-bedecked 14th-century reliquary bust with her torso and head, is dragged through the streets by thousands of *divoti* wearing traditional white robes and black caps, preceded by the *candelore*, enormous highly-decorated candlesticks representing the corporations of the city. The celebrations are concluded with spectacular fireworks. The event is regularly attended by crowds of some 300,000 and has been declared a UNESCO World Heritage Tradition.

TEATRO MASSIMO BELLINI AND VIA VITTORIO EMANUELE

The splendid opera house, **Teatro Massimo Bellini** (*map 11; to request visit, T: 095 250 2961*), by Carlo Sada, was inaugurated on 31st May 1890 with the première of Bellini's *Norma*. During construction the architect had been heavily criticised by local opera lovers and city administrators who thought it would be ugly, to the point that he was forced to buy his own ticket for the opening night. When the audience heard the marvellous acoustic effects, however, there was an ovation. Sada stood up, bowed, and left the theatre. The tenor Beniamino Gigli pronounced this theatre to have the finest acoustics he had ever encountered. The narrow streets in this area, once a run-down part of the city, are now full of life; many pubs and open-air cafés open in the evening, giving rise to the so-called '*movida*': live music for all tastes, especially in the summer.

Via Vittorio Emanuele leads east towards the sea, passing on the right Via Bonajuto with the **Cappella Bonajuto** (*open Tues–Sun 9–1; to book visit, T: 095 836 1194*), a Byzantine chapel built between the 6th and the 9th centuries. The elegant Palazzo Valle at no. 122, designed by Vaccarini and until recently on the verge of collapse, was purchased, restored and returned to the city by a benefactor as a stylish showcase for exhibitions of modern art, the **Fondazione Puglisi Cosentino** (*open Tues–Sun 10–1 & 4–7.30, late closing Sat 9.30pm; bookshop; T: 095 715 2118, www fondazionepuglisicosentino.it*). At the end of the street, **Piazza dei Martiri** has a statue depicting *St Agatha Trampling the Plague*, on top of a column removed from the ancient theatre; the monument was erected by the city senate in 1743 when a plague epidemic miraculously spared Catania. Here a wide terrace, *'u Passiaturi*, popular in the 19th century for afternoon strolls and often mentioned by Verga in his novels, overlooks the harbour and leads to the **Stazione Centrale**, in front of which is a large cement fountain representing the Rape of Persephone (Giulio Moschetti, 1904).

VIA ETNEA TO PIAZZA STESICORO

On the north side of Piazza Duomo is the handsome **Via Etnea** (*map 11*), nearly 3km long, the main street of the city. It is lined with elegant shops (especially for clothes and books) and cafés, and its wide lava-stone pavements are always crowded. It rises to a splendid view of the peak of Mount Etna in the distance.

Beyond the Town Hall (Municipio) is the distinguished **Piazza Università**, laid out by Vaccarini. The University, known as Siculorum Gymnasium, was founded in 1434 by Alfonso V of Aragon (the Magnanimous) as the first in Sicily, and rebuilt after the earthquake of 1693; the lovely courtyard was begun by Andrea Amato and finished in 1752 by Vaccarini; the shady portico with its loggia was designed to allow students to walk in the open air while repeating their lessons.

Just beyond is the **Collegiata** (*open Tues–Sun 9–12 & 5–7; T: 095 313447*), a royal chapel of c. 1768 by Stefano Ittar, with a dazzling Baroque interior, much in demand for weddings; the vaults were frescoed on the theme of the Glorification of the Virgin by Giuseppe Sciuti. The canvases are by the little-known local artist Francesco Gramignani (1770), while the splendid painting by Olivio Sozzi over the first south altar represents St Apollonia. The main altarpiece is a copy made after the 1693 earthquake of a Russian icon, destroyed in the disaster.

Still further north, at no. 85, is the imposing church of **San Michele Arcangelo ai Minoriti** (*map 10; open 8.30–12 & 4.30–8; T: 095 316974*), built by Francesco Battaglia in 1771. The circular interior is striking for its huge dome. In the third north chapel is a beautiful Crucifix by Agostino Penna, and opposite, a fine *Annunciation* by Willem Borremans, painted in 1720. The monumental organ is the work of the famous Serassi brothers of Bergamo.

SAN BIAGIO, THE AMPHITHEATRE AND VIA MANZONI

Piazza Stesicoro (*map 6 and 7*) is the heart of modern Catania, with a monument to **Vincenzo Bellini** by Giulio Monteverde (1882). The figures at the feet of the composer, who sits relaxed in an armchair with pigeons all over him, represent the protagonists of his four most famous operas, *Norma, Il Pirata, I Puritani* and *La Sonnambula*. Dominating the square from the west is the 18th-century church of **San Biagio** (*open Mon–Sat 9–12 & 3–7, Sun 9–1; T: 095 715 9360*), said to stand on the spot where the Romans tried to burn St Agatha in a furnace and known locally as *Sant'Agata alla Carcarella*, 'St Agatha on the Hot Coals' (the mouth of the furnace can be seen in the interior on the right). In the centre of the square are the scant ruins of the **Roman amphitheatre** in black lava stone, thought to date from the 2nd century AD (*open Tues–Sat 9–1.30 & 2.30–5; NB: often closed for lack of staff, to be sure call a day or so ahead specifying 'Anfiteatro'; T: 095 715 0508*). The external circumference was 389m and the arena was one of the largest after the Colosseum in Rome. There were 56 entrance arches and 32 rows of seats, and it could hold 16,000 spectators. The visible remains include a corridor, part of the exterior wall and fragments of the cavea supported on vaults. Beneath the surrounding buildings, the rest of the structure still partly exists, with labyrinthine tunnels which have given rise over the centuries to legends of citizens mysteriously vanishing. Its destruction had already begun under Theodoric, when it was used as a quarry. Totila made use of the stone in building the city walls in 530 and Count Roger stole its decorative elements to embellish his cathedral in 1091. In 1693 the area was used as a dump for rubble left by the earthquake.

Via Manzoni (*map 10*), which leads out of the south side of the square parallel to Via Etnea, is interesting for its numerous well-stocked haberdashery shops and old-fashioned clothes shops for children; once it was the site of the *niviere*, pits where snow from Mt Etna was stored. A little way along on the right is a small section of the first and second *ordine* of the amphitheatre, in Via dell'Anfiteatro.

SANTO CARCERE AND SANT'AGATA LA VETERE

The **church of the Santo Carcere** (*map 6; open daily 5–7; T: 327 663 5963*) is flanked by a strong defence wall. Incorporated into the Baroque façade is a beautiful doorway with grotesque animal heads (1236), formerly in the façade of the duomo. In the interior (*shown by the custodian on request*) is St Agatha's prison, with a Roman barrel vault; the magnificent altarpiece representing her martyrdom is by Bernardino Niger.

Via Cappuccini leads uphill to Via Maddalena, where the church of **Sant'Agata la Vetere** (*open Mon–Sat 8.30–1 & 3–7; T: 095 321902 or 340 213 1794*), probably built only a few years after the martyrdom of the saint in the 3rd century, stands opposite the church of the Purità (or the Visitazione), with a curving façade by Battaglia (1775) next to its handsome convent. Sant'Agata la Vetere was once Catania's cathedral; inside is the Roman marble sarcophagus that was the first tomb of the martyr. The lid is a substitute, the original was used for many centuries as the altar in the cathedral.

A little to the north is the church of **San Domenico** (*open before 9.30 and 5–6.30; T: 095 321616 or 095 296 2357*). It contains a beautiful *Madonna of the Snow* by Antonello Gagini (1526), a painting of *St Vincent Ferrer* by Olivio Sozzi (1757), and the central fragment of a painting representing the head of the Virgin (c. 1518) by Cesare da Sesto Calende, a pupil of Leonardo da Vinci. On the second south altar is a *Madonna del Rosario*, attributed to Innocenzo da Imola (1531).

NORTH OF PIAZZA STESICORO

Via San Gaetano alle Grotte with its daily market, leads to the little church of **San Gaetano alle Grotte** (*map 7*), which dates from 1700. The former church, built into a volcanic cavern beneath in 1262, is now usually closed but is sometimes open for Mass.

The cave itself probably represents the oldest Christian place of worship in the city and perhaps the first burial place of St Agatha.

The main **market** for produce and textiles, known as *'a Fera d'o Luni*, the Monday Fair, occupies Piazza Carlo Alberto. The piazza is overlooked by the massive sanctuary church of the **Carmine** (*open Mon–Fri 7.30–12 & 4–7, Sun 8–12.30 & 5.30–7; T. 095 836 4013*), one of the largest in the city. Inside you will find a collection of thousands of ex-votos. To the right is a fine 18th-century palace occupied by a military barracks, in the courtyard of which is an ancient tomb traditionally (and erroneously) held to be that of the poet Stesichorus of Himera (d. c. 540 BC).

The **Villa Bellini** (*map 6; open daily summer 6am–11pm, spring and autumn 6am–10pm, winter 6am–9pm*) is a fine public garden laid out c. 1870, incorporating an 18th-century 'labyrinth-garden' belonging to the Prince of Biscari. There are many shady walks, magnificent old trees, flower-beds, two hills, fountains and a pond, besides busts of famous citizens (all without noses, thanks to local vandals). At the north end of the garden a gate leads out to Viale Regina Margherita, part of the modern east–west artery of the city, c. 5km long and lined with fine old villas.

Further north is the **Orto Botanico**, the University's important botanical garden (*map 2; open Mon–Fri 9–6.30, Sat 9–12.30, closed Sun and holidays; bookshop; T: 095 430901, www.dipbot.unict.it*), founded in 1858. The main gate is on Via Etnea but the usual entrance is on Via Longo. It is particularly famous for its cactus plants and trees from all over the world, but the Orto Siculo contains rare plants from Sicily, grown in specially-prepared beds reproducing as closely as possible their natural habitat. Via Etnea ends at Parco Gioeni, on a lava flow, an attractive and unusual public park (*open summer 6am–11pm, spring and autumn 6am–10pm, winter 6am–9pm*).

About 500m west of the Orto Botanico, surrounded by tall, modern apartment blocks, is the church of **Santa Maria di Gesù** (*map 1*; 1465). On its north side is the pretty exterior of the Cappella Paternò, which survived the earthquake of 1693. It is entered from the north aisle of the church through a doorway by Antonello Gagini (1519) with a *Pietà* in the lunette above. On the altar is a fresco (transferred to wood) of the *Madonna with Sts Agatha and Catherine* by the otherwise unknown Angelo de Chirico or d'Errico, signed and dated 1525. Above the main altar is a Crucifix by Fra' Umile da Petralia, and on the second north altar a *Madonna with Two Angels in Adoration* by Antonello Gagini (1498).

PIAZZA VERGA AND CORSO ITALIA

Piazza Giovanni Verga (*map 4*), a large square dominated by the Palazzo di Giustizia (1952), is the focus of the post-war Catania. The fountain in the centre, by local sculptor Carmelo Mendola (1975),is a monument to Giovanni Verga and represents the tragic moment in his masterpiece, *The House by the Medlar Tree*, when the Malavoglia family lose their fishing-boat, symbolically named *Provvidenza*.

Further east, at Corso Italia 55, the **Palazzo delle Scienze** (1942; *to request visit, possible Mon–Fri 9–1, email russo@unict.it, T: 095 719 5767, www.museoscienzeterract. it*) houses a superb museum with the University's geological and volcanological collections. The Corso ends at the sea in Piazza Europa, with a watch-tower on top of a mound of lava, and under the trees a marble statue of a girl by Francesco Messina.

GIOVANNI VERGA

One of Sicily's best-known writers, Giovanni Verga (1840–1922) is famous for his naturalistic style which gives a dramatic picture of the social conditions of everyday Sicilian life. His first great success was *Storia di una Capinera* ('Story of a Black-cap', 1871), which was adapted for the screen by Franco Zeffirelli as *Sparrow* in 1993. His masterpieces include *Vita dei campi* (a collection of short stories, including *Cavalleria Rusticana*), *I Malavoglia* ('The House by the Medlar Tree') and *Mastro-don Gesualdo*. Both these last were first translated by D.H. Lawrence, who was much influenced by Verga. By 1884 he was acclaimed as the greatest living Italian writer. He made contact with Emile Zola and remained a life-long friend of the writer Luigi Capuana, also born in the province of Catania. Both writers were fiercely proud of their Sicilian roots and both made frequent use of the local idiom. Although Verga's fame diminished towards the end of his life, his 80th birthday was publicly celebrated in Catania with Luigi Pirandello as orator, and he was nominated senator in the same year. His influence remained strong on Italian novelists long after the Second World War.

LE CIMINIERE CULTURAL CENTRE

Beyond the railway station, Viale Africa leads north to **Le Ciminiere** (*beyond map 8; open June–Sept Tues–Sun 10–6, Oct–May Tues–Sun 9–5; last tickets 1hr before closing*), built in the 19th century as a sulphur refinery and named after its tall chimneys. It has been restored as a cultural centre and houses several museums: the museum of the 1943 Allied landings in Sicily, **Museo Storico Sbarco in Sicilia 1943** (*T: 095 401 1929*) documents the invasion code-named Operation Husky; the **Museo del Cinema** (*T: 095 401 1928*) offers an interesting excursion into the world of films made in Sicily, ; the **Mostra Radio d'Epoca** (*T: 095 401 3058*) is a large collection of beautiful old radio sets together with an interesting description of the pioneer work of Marconi; while the **Mostra Collezione 'La Gumina'** (*T: 095 401 3072*) is an exhibition of old maps and atlases of Sicily. The **Museo del Giocattolo** has a fascinating collection of toys (*to book visit, T: 095 539073 or 348 233 3597*).

THE SIMETO RIVER NATURE RESERVE

Map p. 573, C3. When arriving from Catania on the SS 114, you will see the entrance and car park on the left just before reaching the old bridge over the Simeto, Ponte Primosole.

The Riserva Naturale Oasi del Simeto occupies the mouth of the River Simeto, a few kilometres south of Catania. Although many holiday villas were built here illegally from the 1960s onwards, it was first protected in 1975 and became a nature reserve in 1984, thanks mainly to the efforts of Wendy Hennessy Mazza, a British local resident and representative of the Lega Italiana Protezione Uccelli (LIPU), the Italian society for bird protection. In 1989, 54 of the houses erected without building permits were demolished, but hundreds still remain. The marshes and brackish lakes offer protection to numerous birds, both nesting and migratory, including rare ducks, great white heron, flamingo, black-winged stilt, godwit, cattle egret, glossy ibis, avocet and spoonbill. The purple gallinule has been successfully reintroduced and on the nearby electricity pylons white storks now nest. Amber can sometimes be found on the shore here, the fossilised resin of almond trees which grew about 60 million years ago. The colour is rich chestnut brown, giving green or blue reflections in artificial light; sometimes there are insects or fragments of leaves trapped inside.

On the right bank of the Simeto, close to the bridge where you can see a low hill, stood the ancient Sicel town of *Symaethus*, whose necropolis survives on the Turrazza estate. The River Simeto, 88km long, is the most important river in Sicily; it springs from Serra del Re in the Nebrodi mountains and picks up some important tributaries on its way to the sea: the Salso, Troina, Dittaino and Gornalunga. In the course of time it formed the immense alluvial Plain of Catania. Its marshy delta was drained in the 1930s under Mussolini to create farmland and eliminate malaria, but this illness continued to be a problem until 1943, when Allied troops eradicated it with DDT.

MOUNT ETNA

Mount Etna, a UNESCO World Heritage Site, is the highest volcano in Europe (c. 3350m) and one of the largest and most active in the world. Its regional park protects 59,000 hectares of unique geology, flora and fauna, villages and farms, and traditional methods of forestry, bee-keeping, winemaking, stonework and carpentry. The ascent is easy and an experience which should not be missed, not only for the volcanic phenomena but also for the views. The extent of a visit is always subject to volcanic activity, and visibility is determined by cloud conditions (which tend to build up in the course of the day) and the direction of the smoke from the main craters. There are splendid views of the lava fields on the approach roads to Rifugio Sapienza and Piano Provenzana, the two starting-points for the ascent. Higher up it is often possible to see smoking and gaseous fissures, and explosions from the main craters, of which there are five—it is not permitted to approach these. There may be a strong smell of sulphur, and here and there the mountainside is covered by yellow sulphurous patches. The view, beyond the mountain's hundreds of subsidiary cones and craters, can extend across the whole of Sicily, the Aeolian Islands and Calabria. The spectacle is unique owing to the enormous difference in height between Etna and the surrounding hills.

ETNA STATISTICS

Etna's circular cone is 45km in diameter at the base. From a distance it appears almost perfectly regular in shape and the great width of its base detracts from its height. The terminal cone, with its five open summit craters, rises from a truncated cone 2801m high, on the sides of which are about 300 side craters. The smaller craters are often arranged along a regular line of fracture and are known as 'button formations'.

On the northeast side is the Valle del Bove, an immense caldera 19km in circumference, bounded on three sides by sheer walls of tufa and lava, in places 900m high; it formed about 20,000 years ago when the crater known as Trifoglietto subsided.

During recent eruptions the lava has been flowing into this huge natural reservoir, thus sparing the towns on the southeast slopes.

HISTORY OF MOUNT ETNA

Etna, called *Aetna* in ancient times and Mongibello (from *monte* and *jebel*, Italian and Arabic for mountain) by the Sicilians (often simply *'a muntagna*), probably originated from a submarine eruption which took place in the gulf now occupied by the Plain of Catania. In ancient Greece the volcano was held to be the forge of Hephaistos or of the Cyclopes, or the mountain from beneath which the Titan Enceladus, imprisoned by Zeus, forever struggled to free himself. The 5th-century BC philosopher Empedocles (*see p. 217*) is said to have thrown himself into the crater to obtain complete knowledge. Among early eruptions, that of 475 BC was described by Pindar and Aeschylus while that of 396 BC, whose lava reached the sea, is said to have prevented the Carthaginian general Himilco from marching on Syracuse. The eruption of 122 BC covered the city of Catania and the surrounding countryside in a thick layer of sand, disastrous enough for the senate in Rome to exempt the inhabitants from tax for ten years. Hadrian climbed Etna to see the sunrise and the conical shape of the mountain reflected on the island. In 1169, 1329 and 1381 the lava again reached the sea, twice near Acireale, the third time at Catania. The largest eruption ever recorded took place in 1669 when an open cleft extended from the summit to Nicolosi and part of Catania was overwhelmed. The resulting crater, which appears double, is called Monti Rossi.

Since 1800 there have been over 130 eruptions, the one in 1928 being the most destructive, obliterating the town of Mascali. In 1908 a huge pit of lava opened in the Valle del Bove. The eruption of 1947 threatened Passopisciaro and that of 1950–1 menaced Rinazzo and Fornazzo before the lava halted. The 1971 eruption destroyed the observatory and the second stage of the cableway on the summit, as well as vineyards and some houses near Fornazzo. In 1978–9 four new cones erupted and the lava flowed into the Valle del Bove; the town of Fornazzo was again threatened. Nine British tourists were killed by an explosion on the rim of the main crater itself in 1979. In the spring of 1983 activity started up on the opposite side of the mountain above Nicolosi and Belpasso, forming the southeast crater, which has since been the most active of the summit cones. In 1984 an earthquake damaged the town of Fleri. In 1991–2 eruptions took place over four months, threatening Zafferana Etnea. The eruption of summer 2001 started just below the Montagnola at 2800m, on 18th July, and within a few days 18 temporary craters had opened up all over the top of the volcano, providing spectacular displays at night. The lava was successfully prevented from doing too much damage, by the use of bulldozers to form enormous dykes to contain and direct the flow. 2002 saw another eruption, which took the same path as that of the previous year, and an earthquake at Santa Venerina; since then there have been several explosive and eruptive phases. In 2007 a new crater opened up on the side of the southeast crater and has grown very fast, now equalling the others; it is known as NCSE (New Southeast Crater).

VEGETATION AND WILDLIFE

The soil at the foot of Etna is extraordinarily fertile because the volcanic ash is rich in nutrients. In the cultivated zone (*pedemontana*) oranges, lemons and tangerines are grown behind low black basalt dry-stone walls. The higher slopes of the mountain were forested up until the 19th century but are now planted with olives, apples, pears, pistachios, hazelnuts and vines. The apparently delicate, willowy, pale green indigenous Etna broom, *Genista aetnensis*, flourishes on many of the lava flows; it is an important 'pioneer plant', helping to break up the rock and turn it into soil, a process which takes about 400 years. At 1300m forest trees grow, especially oaks, chestnuts, pines and beeches. This is the southernmost point in Europe where the beech tree can be found, and it is also here that it reaches its highest altitude, growing up to 2250m. It is also the extreme southern limit for the silver birch, which is found in its endemic form, *Betula aetnensis*. From 2000 to 3000m the black lava is colonised by tough little plants, most of them found only on this volcano, such as the Etna holy thorn (*Astragalus aetnensis*) or the Etna violet (*Viola aetnensis*), creating a wonderful carpet of flowers in spring and early summer. Botanists should not miss the 'Nuova Gussonea' Alpine Garden (*to request visit, T: 095 234310*), run by the University of Catania. It is in Contrada Carpinteri, not far from the Grande Albergo, and can be reached from the Nicolosi–Rifugio Sapienza road.

Since the creation of the park the golden eagle has returned, and nests regularly. Etna is the only place in Sicily where the long-eared owl can be found. Wolves and boars no longer roam the forests, but there are plenty of foxes and rabbits, hares, porcupines, wildcats, hedgehogs, the garden and the edible dormouse, many species of bat, five snakes (of which only the viper is venomous), the tortoise and two kinds of toad. There are plans to reduce access to the area of maximum protection (*Zona A*) to allow nature to take over again, and to reintroduce some long-absent species, such as the roe deer and griffon vulture.

Pot-holers or spelaeologists will find the numerous lava tubes on Mount Etna fascinating, but exploration should not be attempted without expert help. For information, contact the park offices (*T: 095 821111, www.parcoetna.it*).

The heat of the rocks and the hot vapours from the terminal cones cause the snow to partially melt, even in winter, but in some depressions with a northern aspect the snow was covered with a layer of volcanic ash to keep it fresh throughout the summer. It was transported on mule-back down to the towns as necessary, and used for refrigeration.

EXPLORING MOUNT ETNA

The summit can be visited from either the southern or the northern side of the mountain. There are organised excursions from Rifugio Sapienza on the southern slopes (Etna Sud) and also from Piano Provenzana on the northern slopes (Etna Nord). Both can be reached easily by car, but only Rifugio Sapienza can be reached by bus. The upper part of the volcano can also be explored on foot from both these points and there are some spectacular walks which are signposted on the lower slopes of the mountain. Near the top there is almost always a very strong wind and the temperature

MOUNT ETNA
View of the Crateri Silvestri, near the Rifugio Sapienza.

an be many degrees below freezing: a warm jacket, sturdy shoes and a close-fitting
at are in order (boots and jackets can be hired at the cableway station near Rifugio
apienza). The five summit craters are strictly off limits.

THE SOUTHERN APPROACH: ETNA SUD

The *Strada dell'Etna* was opened in 1934 by Vittorio Emanuele III. It is well signposted
beyond **Nicolosi** (*map p. 573, C2*), which is one of the best centres for visiting Etna. At
Via Cesare Battisti 28 is the **Museo Vulcanologico Etneo** (*open Tues–Sun 9.30–12.30,
Tues and Thur also 3.30–5.30; T: 095 791 4589*), an informative display about Etna and
its phenomena, together with a collection of various types of lava and minerals and a
diorama of the volcano and its territory. To the west of Nicolosi are the twin hills of the
Monti Rossi (949m), which represent one of the most important subsidiary groups of
craters (over 3km round), formed in 1669 by the biggest eruption ever recorded.

Beyond Nicolosi the road climbs through lava fields and some woods, crossing
lava flows from 1886 and 1910; the names of the craters on either side of the road are
indicated. Walks off this road are also signposted. The main road continues to the Casa
Cantoniera at 1910m and ends at the 2001 lava stream beside the **Rifugio Sapienza**.
Here there are souvenir shops, an information office, first-aid point, cafés, restaurants,
and honey vendors. In the desert of hardened volcanic lava nearby, several extinct
craters can be explored easily on foot, and the 400 metre-wide 2001 lava flow is
impressive, superimposed with the lava from 2002.

A cableway ascends from here up the slopes of the **Montagnola** (2507m), a crater of 1763, through a desert of lapilli with splendid views of the sea and port of Catania. It takes about 15mins to reach the site of the Piccolo Rifugio, destroyed during the 2001 eruption. Although at present you are not allowed any nearer to the main crater, from this distance you can usually see (and hear) volcanic activity. A road has been cut through the 2001 and 2002 lava streams, making it possible to reach the **Crater Silvestri**, formed during the eruption of 1892, and continue down the thickly-wooded eastern slopes of the mountain and across the 1992 lava to Zafferana Etnea.

GETTING TO THE SUMMIT

Organised excursions to the summit leave from the Rifugio Sapienza and take about 2hrs. Tickets can be bought at the cableway station near the refuge. If weather conditions are adverse, 4WD vehicles are used to reach a height of about 2800m, from where guides take people on foot to the more interesting areas. From the Rifugio Sapienza, guides also take walking tours to the 2001 crater. Before undertaking the climb independently, advice about weather conditions should be obtained from the SITAS offices at the cableway station (*T: 095 914141*) or at Nicolosi, where guides are available to accompany walkers. The easiest and most usual approach from Sapienza follows the track used by the 4WD vans. About 4hrs should be allowed for the return trip on foot from Sapienza. The most spectacular time for the ascent is before dawn. It cannot be stressed too frequently that the rim of the summit craters must never be approached.

THE NORTHERN APPROACH: ETNA NORD

Linguaglossa (*map p. 573, C1*) is a peaceful little town, surrounded by pinewoods and hazel groves and with a number of late 19th- and early 20th-century houses. The doorways and windows of the 18th-century church are decorated with lava stone and elaborate 19th-century lamps ornament the façade. Close by, in Piazza Annunziata 1, is the **Museo Francesco Messina** (*open Wed–Sun 9–1 & 4–8; T: 095 643874*) dedicated to the sculptor Francesco Messina (1900–95), who was born here, and to Salvatore Incorpora (1920–2010), a painter, sculptor and poet who was born in Calabria but lived and worked in Linguaglossa.

Linguaglossa is the best centre for excursions on the northern slopes of Etna (though unfortunately there is no public transport to the town). The mountain road known as the **Mareneve**, which climbs towards the summit of Etna, begins here. It leads up for 12km through the **Pineta Ragabo**, ancient pinewoods, to the ski fields of **Piano Provenzana** (1800m). The refuge and the restaurants were completely destroyed by the earthquakes and lava in the 2002 eruption, and had not yet been rebuilt at time of writing. Excursions by 4WD vans are organised to the most interesting and panoramic craters (STAR; *T: 095 643180 or 347 495 7091*) . It is also possible to walk up the cone from here in c. 3hrs: it is a splendid trek through the forest, with dramatic views over the Straits of Messina, the Ionian and the Tyrrhenian seas, and the Aeolian Islands.

Another mountain road descends from Piano Provenzana following the eastern slope of the mountain passing beneath the Rifugio Citelli at 1741m, to Fornazzo.

THE SOUTHERN FOOTHILLS OF ETNA

ADRANO

Adrano (*map p. 573, B2*) was the ancient *Hadranon*, founded by Dionysius I close to the site of a Sicel temple to the god Hadranon, said to have been guarded by hundreds of dogs called *cirnechi* (from Cyrenaica), originally purchased from Phoenician merchants and still raised in the area today. Of medium size, with upright ears, a long, thin straight tail, ginger in colour with a pinkish nose, they are extremely intelligent and highly prized (the breed is the oldest registered with the Italian Kennel Club).

Overlooking the public gardens, **Giardino della Vittoria** (with superb trees), is the enormous former monastery of Santa Lucia, now a school, flanked by the towering façade (1775) of its church, which has a pretty oval interior. The imposing black lava-stone **castle** (*open Mon–Sat 9–7, Sun and holidays 9–1.30; ticket includes Mura Dionigiane; T: 095 760 2608 or 095 769 2660*) was built in 1070 by Count Roger on the site of Greek, Roman and Arab fortifications. The interior houses an interesting local museum and art gallery. The archaeological section includes prehistoric material from the Stentinello and Castelluccio cultures, later finds from Mendolito including a hanging askos and a bronze figurine of a banqueter, dated 530 BC, and a Greek bronze helmet (490–480 BC) found nearby.

Next to the castle is the **Chiesa Madre**, of Norman origin. The interior incorporates 16 basalt columns, possibly from the ancient temple of Hadranon. High up above the west door is a fine polyptych by the 16th-century Messina school in its original frame. The painted 15th-century Crucifix was damaged by restoration work in 1924. In the transepts are four panels (two saints and the *Annunciation*) by Girolamo Alibrandi. In the pretty sacristy is a fine painting of the *Last Supper* by Pier Paolo Vasta.

The opera house, **Teatro Bellini** (*T: 095 760 6111*), built in 1845 to replace an earlier theatre of 1742, has been restored and is now in regular use; its Art Nouveau façade was added in the early 20th century.

South of the town, in Contrada Difesa dei Mulini, a long stretch of the lava-stone walls that protected the city of Hadranon and some of the houses have been brought to light. The remains of the city are contained in an archaeological park, **Mura Dionigiane** (*open Mon–Sat 9–1*), with interesting explanatory panels.

PONTE DEI SARACENI

Off a byroad leading c. 8km northwest of Adrano (signposted 'Strada per il Ponte dei Saraceni'), a rough road between low lava-stone walls leads (in c. 1.5km) past citrus plantations and old farmhouses to the Simeto river, spanned by the lovely 9th-century **Ponte dei Saraceni**. Of Arab construction over a preceding Roman bridge (and much restored), it has four asymmetric arches decorated with black lava stone; the path over the top is still passable. The road it served was an important link between Troina and Catania. In this peaceful spot there is a view of Etna and the rapids on the rocky river bed. Nearby (*not signposted and unfortunately closed*) are a few remains of the walls and south gate of an ancient Sicel town in Contrada Mendolito. The gate was surmounted by an inscription in the Sicel language, now in the archaeological museum in Syracuse. Recent archaeological work suggests that this was a rich farming community, perhaps *Piakos*, inhabited until the 5th century BC, when the people were transferred by Dionysius to Hadranon. Curiously, the inhabitants did not bury young babies in the necropolis, but interred them in terracotta jars under the floors of their houses.

EAST FROM ADRANO

Southeast of Adrano is **Biancavilla** (*map p. 573, B2*), where excellent oranges and clementines are grown; beside the extensive citrus plantations are olive groves and hedges of prickly pear. At **Paternò**, another important centre for orange-growing, the town sprawls at the base of an 11th-century castle (*open Tues–Sun 9.30–12.30, Thur also 3.30–5.30; T: 095 7970304*). The austere tower of volcanic rock commands the wide Simeto valley. Inside there is a fine hall and frescoed chapel. The churches of San Francesco and Santa Maria della Valle di Giosafat retain Gothic elements.

From Paternò the road continues to **Motta Sant'Anastasia**, perched on an extremely interesting rock formation, a 'neck' of lava (visible close-up from Via Montalto and Via Vittorio Veneto), with a fine 12th-century Norman castle (*open Mon–Sun 9.30–1.30, Sat–Sun also 3.30–7.30; T: 095 309202*) which preserves its crenellations. The unusual name of **Misterbianco**, a town now swallowed up by Catania, with an industrial area and several hypermarkets, comes from a Benedictine monastery, the *monastero bianco*, which was destroyed along with the town in the eruption of 1669.

A secondary road from Paternò leads up the volcano to **Belpasso**. Once known as Malpasso, it was covered by lava in 1669 and rebuilt with the name Fenicia Moncada; destroyed once again in the 1693 earthquake, it was again rebuilt, this time with the more optimistic name, which it still holds. The black and white Art Nouveau theatre (1890) is dedicated to the popular local comic playwright Nino Martoglio (1870–1921).

The road continues to Nicolosi, Pedara and **Trecastagni** (*map p. 573, C2*) where the Chiesa Madre is a pure Renaissance building thought to be the work of Antonello Gagini. The Chiesa del Bianco has an elegant 15th-century campanile. The town is renowned for the production of wine, especially Etna Rosso.

Zafferana Etnea is the main town on the east side of Etna. Its name derives from the saffron which once formed the base of the economy, though today it is an important honey-producing area, renowned for its *miele di zagara* or citrus-blossom honey. The area was damaged by an earthquake in 1984, and in 1992 a lava flow reached the outskirts of the town (this can now be visited, at the end of a signposted road, where a statue was set up as a thanksgiving to the Madonna). Climbs towards the Valle del Bove can be made from here.

A road leads north from Zafferana through the vineyards of Milo to **Sant'Alfio** (*map p. 573, C2*), north of which is a famous giant chestnut tree, known as the Castagno dei Cento Cavalli (signposted) because during a storm a queen and her 100 horsemen found shelter under its branches. It has a circumference of over 22m and is between two and four thousand years old. The area was once a forest of chestnuts, nowadays largely coppiced for timber. The fruit from the orchards in the district is sold on the streets in the autumn, together with chestnuts and wild fungi.

THE NORTHERN FOOTHILLS OF ETNA

RANDAZZO

Above the Alcantara valley, Randazzo (*map p. 573, B1*) is a lava-built town of great antiquity, which has never suffered volcanic destruction. Its medieval history resolves itself into a rivalry between the three churches of Santa Maria, San Nicolò and San Martino, each of which served as the cathedral for alternate periods of three years. The parishioners of each church (of Greek, Latin and Lombard origin) spoke different dialects until the 16th century. The town was damaged during Allied bombing in August 1943, when the Germans made it the strong point of their last resistance on the island.

Close to the northern entrance to the town, in Largo San Giuliano, is the **Museo dell'Opra dei Pupi** (*open 10–1, often also 3–7, closed Mon; T: 095 921615*), which houses a magnificent collection of puppets and backdrops dating from the 18th–19th centuries. By taking the main street, Via Umberto, you reach the present **cathedral**, Santa Maria, a 13th-century church with fine black lava-stone apses and a three-storey south portal (approached by two flights of steps) in the Catalan Gothic style of the 15th century. The dome is attributed to Venanzio Marvuglia. The black and white tower was restored in 1863. The terrace, with another fine doorway, looks out over the Alcantara Valley. The interior (1594) has fine black columns and capitals, one of which serves as an altar. Over the south door is a small painting with a view of the town attributed to Girolamo Alibrandi (15th century); over the north door is a fresco fragment of the *Madonna and Child* (13th century). The church contains six paintings by Giuseppe Velasquez (first north altar, fourth and fifth altars in the north and south aisles, and south wall of the sanctuary). The Crucifix in the chapel to the right of the sanctuary is by Fra' Umile da Petralia. The second north and south altarpieces are by Onofrio Gabrieli. The third south altarpiece is by Jan van Houbraken. Outside, the south side shows beautiful windows of the original structure and a magnificent Catalan Gothic doorway with a tiny marble relief of the Madonna over it, probably from Pisa.

Via Umberto leads past the southern flank of Santa Maria past the **Museo delle Scienze Naturali** (*open 10–1, often also 3–7, closed Mon; T: 095 921615*), with an ornithological section, a display of local mammals and a collection of shells, to Piazza Municipio where the Town Hall occupies a 14th-century convent reconstructed in 1610. The lovely cloister has columns of lava stone.

From here the narrow, pretty Via degli Archi leads beneath four arches to the church of **San Nicoló**, which dates mainly from the 16th–17th centuries (damaged in 1943), though the apse is 13th century. In the north transept is a seated statue of St Nicholas (with two small reliefs below) by Antonello Gagini, signed and dated 1523. In the south transept is a 16th-century painted Crucifix and four delicately carved bas-reliefs of the Passion by Giacomo Gagini. Outside, there is an 18th-century copy replacing the original, destroyed in 1943, of a curious antique statue of a man, thought to symbolise the union of the three parishes (*see above*). Known as Old Randazzo or *Piracmone*, the eagle represents the regality of the Latins, the snake the wisdom of the Greeks, and the lion the strength of the Lombards. Nearby is Palazzo Clarentano (1509), where a medieval arch tunnels beneath houses back towards the Corso.

Via Umberto (at no. 197 is the information office) continues to the district of San Martino, with evidence of Second World War shelling. The damaged church of **San Martino** still has its fine 14th-century campanile. On the top is a charming iron weather vane in the form of a cherub. The façade has 15th-century reliefs of saints and martyrs. In the interior are black lava-stone columns and in the south transept a statue of the *Madonna and Child* by the Gagini school (which retains part of its polychrome decoration). In the north aisle is a triptych by a local painter influenced by Antonello da Messina. Here also is a *mistura* **Crucifix**, recently restored, the work of Giovannello Matinati, signed and dated 1540. The marble font was made in 1447.

In front of the church is the 13th-century Swabian castle, rebuilt in 1645 and used as a prison until 1973. It is now the **Vagliasindi Museum** (*open 10–1, often also 3–7, closed Mon; T: 095 921861*). The collection includes some fine vases from a neighbouring Greek necropolis, including a 5th-century red-figure oinochoe, as well as coins and jewellery. There is a lovely view of the church of San Martino from the uppermost tower. Just beyond is Porta San Martino (1753) in the walls.

BRONTE

Bronte (*map p. 573, B1*) is an important centre for the cultivation of pistachios (90 percent of the pistachios produced in Italy are grown here). The trees are small and grey, with long contorted branches which almost reach the ground. The fruit is harvested every two years at the end of August and early Sept. Pistachios are used in local cuisine for pasta dishes, sweets and ice creams, and exported to northern Italy for flavouring mortadella.

In a little wooded valley to the north of Bronte, on the Saraceno, a tributary of the Simeto, is the **Castello Maniace** or **Castello Nelson** (*open daily April–Sept 9–1 & 2.30–7, Oct–March 9–1 & 2.30–5; T: 095 690018*). A convent was founded here in 1173 by Margaret of Navarre, mother of William II, on the spot where the Byzantine general George Maniakes defeated the Saracens in 1040 with the help of the Russian Varangian Guard and Norman mercenaries, among whom may have been the Scandinavian hero Harold Hardrada. The house and estate were presented to Admiral Horatio Nelson in 1799 by Ferdinand IV (later King Ferdinand I of the Two Sicilies). The duchy of Bronte was bestowed on Nelson in gratitude for his help the year before when the king had fled from Naples on Nelson's flagship during the Napoleonic invasion. Nelson himself apparently never managed to visit Maniace, but the title and estate passed, by the marriage of Nelson's niece, to the family of Viscount Bridport who sold the property in 1981 to the Bronte town council. Patrick Brunty from Ulster, who had a living as a country parson in Yorkshire and who was a great admirer of Nelson, changed his name to Brontë in celebration of his hero's success. He went on to father the Brontë sisters.

In the courtyard is a stone cross memorial to Nelson. The 13th-century **chapel**, with the original portal, has a Byzantine icon of the *Madonna and Child*, two charming primitive reliefs of the *Annunciation*, and two 15th-century paintings. In the **barn** there are walkways above excavations of an older church. The **house** retains its appearance from the days when it was the residence of Alexander Hood, who lived here from 1873 until just before the Second World War: it has majolica tiled floors and English wallpaper.

The delightful **gardens**, also designed by Hood (with palm trees, planted in 1912, magnolias, cypresses and box hedges), can also be visited. The Scottish writer William Sharp, who was once considered a father of the Celtic Renaissance and published under the pseudonym Fiona Macleod, died here in 1905 aged 55. He is buried beneath an Iona cross in the cemetery (*shown on request*).

Between Bronte and Randazzo the landscape is barren, with numerous wide streams of hardened lava. The countryside, studded with little farmhouses, is used for grazing and the cultivation of vineyards. There is a large lava stream of 1832 near **Maletto**, whose sandstone cliff, called Pizzo Filicia (1140m), is the highest sedimentary rock on Etna (views). The vineyards in this region produce excellent red and white wines (Etna Rosso and Etna Bianco); the vines are grown close to the ground (known as the *alberello* method) for climatic reasons.

EAST OF RANDAZZO

To the east of Randazzo is the town of **Passopisciaro** (*map p. 573, C1*). Beyond, near a massive lava flow (1981), oaks and chestnuts are being replaced by vineyards and olive trees. Some of the prettiest scenery in the foothills of Etna can be seen here, with numerous handsome old russet-coloured houses (many of them now abandoned), excellent views of the volcano and, to the north, the wooded mountains beyond the Alcantara.

Francavilla di Sicilia, with its ruined Norman castle, stands in a dominant position overlooking the road. Above the cemetery on the outskirts is the well-signposted **Convento dei Cappuccini** (17th century), where the church has a beautiful 15th-century *Madonna and Child* attributed to the school of Antonello da Messina, and the 17th-century funerary monument of the Ruffo family. The friars will show you their interesting little monastic museum. A Greek sanctuary dedicated to Demeter and Persephone was excavated in the town in 1979–84 (perhaps this was the ancient *Kallipolis*). It is believed that some of the survivors of Dionysius' destruction of Naxos in 403 BC took refuge here. Material found here is displayed in a small **antiquarium** at Via Liguria 30 (*open mornings by request; T: 0942 682752*). Among the objects discovered are *pinakes*, pictures made of terracotta with reliefs relating to the cult of Persephone, of a type previously found only at the sanctuary at Locri in Calabria. Worshippers would hang the pictures on trees in the sacred grove around the sanctuary, and periodically the priests would smash them, placing the fragments in the bothros, or sacred pit. In Piazza San Francesco, the 18th-century **Palazzo Cagnone** (*open Tues–Sun 9–4; T: 0942 682752*), restored by the municipality, hosts several small collections and cultural events. It is hoped that the archaeological collection will be transferred here at some point in the future.

Castiglione di Sicilia is a quiet little town in a stunning position perched on a crag. Founded by the survivors of the destruction of Naxos, wreaked by Dionysius of Syracuse in 403 BC, it was once a stronghold of Roger of Lauria, inveterate opponent of Frederick II of Aragon. Frederick II of Hohenstaufen loved the town. He called it *animosa* for the courage of its population and conceded it the privilege of minting its own coins. Its many churches are mostly kept closed—a great pity because they contain remarkable works of art. The **Chiesa Madre** (San Pietro) however, whose magnificent apse of 1105 is visible from outside, opens for Mass (*8 every day, also 10 on Sun*). Inside is an interesting meridian line traced by Temistocle Zona in 1882. Below it in a charming little piazza is the **church of Sant'Antonio** (*key at wine shop in front*) with an ingenious façade and campanile. Inside it preserves delightful marble inlay work (1700) and four octagonal paintings by Giovanni Tuccari. In the sanctuary is an elaborate wooden confessional supporting a pulpit and a simple painted organ loft.

The Rocca del Leone, Castello Lauria or **Castel Leone** (*open daily April–June and Sept–Oct 9.30–1.30 & 3.30–6.30, July–Aug 10–1 & 3.30–7.30; to request visit at other times, T: 0942 980348*), which gives its name to the town, is perched on an enormous spur of rock. Extremely interesting and of great antiquity, its highest, ruined rampart the Castelluzzo, is said to have been constructed in 750 BC by a Greek commander called Leon, even before the creation of the first colony at Naxos. The old stones are haunted by jackdaws and there are peerless views over the rooftops to Mount Etna, the Alcantara Valley and the Peloritan Mountains. Castiglione is magical, especially on winter mornings when the air is crisp and clear, Etna is covered with snow, and the scent of woodsmoke lingers in the air; or on hot summer evenings, when the sky is like a deep blue bowl and swifts screech and whirl untiringly among the steeples.

Below the town, off the Randazzo road (well signposted for the *Cuba Bizantina*), is an abandoned Byzantine-Arab building surrounded by vineyards, usually called the **church of Santa Domenica**. It is approached along a narrow country road beyond a railway line. Built of lava stone, probably in the late 8th century, it has an interesting plan and although very ruined, the vault survives.

ACIREALE

Famous for exquisite almond confectionery, the sound of church bells and the stubbornness of its people, Acireale (*map p. 573, C2*) is a beautiful and atmospheric little city, perched between Etna and the sea on a cliff of lava, verdant with lemon trees and Mediterranean maquis, called the Timpa, now a nature reserve. The maze of tiny jasmine-scented streets in the centre is often used as a film set. The surroundings are rich in mineral-water springs which have been exploited since Roman times. The city is particularly interesting for its Baroque buildings, erected after the earthquake of 1693. In 1642, a grateful Philip IV of Spain declared it a royal city, thanks to which Acireale gained considerable prestige. Acireale and nine other neighbouring towns and villages derive their name from the Aci, a mythical underground river which came into being on the death of Acis, the shepherd beloved by Galatea and killed by the Cyclops Polyphemus.

CENTRAL ACIREALE

The main Via Vittorio Emanuele leads up to Piazza Vigo. Here the church of **San Sebastiano** has a 17th-century façade in Spanish Baroque style with numerous statues and a delightful frieze of cherubs with garlands, considered by some to be the loveliest in Sicily. The balustrade and statues are by Giovanni Battista Marino (1754). Entered by the side door, the Museo Basilica San Sebastiano (*open 9–1, closed Mon; T: 095 601313*) houses (partly in the old crypt) a collection of paintings, statues and embroidered priests' robes.

On the other side of the Piazza Vigo, with two charming little kiosks, is the large Neoclassical **Palazzo Pennisi di Floristella**, belonging to the foremost aristocratic family of the city (it now offers accommodation; *see p. 437*). Beyond, the main streets of the town meet at the elegant Piazza Duomo. Here is the 17th-century Town Hall, with splendid balconies supported by grotesque figures. It houses a collection of military uniforms: the **Museo degli Uniformi Militari** (*open daily 9.30–12.30 & 4.30–7.30; T: 095 895256*). The west side of the square is occupied by the basilica of **Santi Pietro e Paolo**, with an asymmetrical early 18th-century façade and just one bell-tower instead of the two which were originally planned. The 17th-century **cattedrale** (Acireale has been a diocese since 1844) has a neo-Gothic façade, added in the late 19th century by Giovanni Battista Basile, and an interesting early 19th-century meridian line in the transept. It is dedicated both to the Madonna and the patron St Venera, a Roman martyr. At the east end are 18th-century frescoes by Pier Paolo Vasta, although the best place to admire the work of this much-loved local artist is at the church of **Santa Maria del Suffragio** in Via Romeo, where a dazzling series of frescoes carried out in 1750 can be seen. There are more of his frescoes at the church of **San Camillo** in Via Galatea, called the 'church of the women' because the theme chosen by Vasta for the paintings was women of the Old Testament.

Opposite the cathedral, Via Cavour leads west. Via Alessi, a turning to the left, houses at no. 5 the puppet theatre and a museum of local marionettes and backdrops, the **Museo Opera dei Pupi** (*open 9.30–12.30 & 4.30–7.30; T: 095 768 5611*). At the end of Via Cavour is the church of San Domenico, close to the large 17th-century Palazzo Musmeci with an unusual curving façade and pretty windows. At Via Marchese di San Giuliano 15 is the **Accademia Zelantea** (*picture gallery open Tues–Sat 10–1, library also 3.30–6.30; T: 095 763 4516, www.zelantea.it*), a handsome building of 1915. The Academy was founded in 1671 and the library in 1716. It possesses a fine collection of artworks. Notice in particular the Roman marble portrait bust found at Capomulini in the 17th century and thought to represent Julius Caesar.

OUTSKIRTS OF ACIREALE

A surprising and lovely walk follows Via Romeo from the cattedrale down to the perilous main road, which can be crossed by means of a footbridge, then down the many steps of the picturesque Strada delle Chiazzette through the Timpa nature reserve to **Santa Maria la Scala**, a tiny fishing village. There are many springs of fresh water down here at sea level: the fishermen's wives were washerwomen, using the steps to carry their baskets of laundry up and down.

The sulphur baths of **Santa Venera** are at the south end of town in a park overlooking the Timpa; water and volcanic mud are used for treatments. The spa building is of 1873 and was visited by Wagner. Just south of Acireale, in the district of Reitana, a Roman spa, Santa Venera al Pozzo (*closed; T: 095 877169*) has been brought to light (with a small antiquarium), and at Capomulini the remains of a **Roman podium temple**, perhaps dedicated to Venus, can just be made out behind a locked gate.

THE COAST SOUTH OF ACIREALE

South of Acireale is **Acitrezza** (*map p. 573, C2*), a fishing-village described by Giovanni Verga in his masterpiece, *I Malavoglia* (*The House by the Medlar Tree*). In the sea in front of the tiny harbour, with its boats in various stages of construction or repair, are seven lava-stone rocks called the **Faraglioni del Ciclope**, now protected as a marine nature reserve run by the University of Catania. According to legend, the rocks are those thrown by the Cyclops Polyphemus at Odysseus, who had just blinded him. They are the result of an ancient lateral eruption of Mt Etna and represent the fragmentary rim of a crater. On one of the rocks, Isola Lachea, is a small house used by the University of Catania. The rocks have surprisingly varied fauna (as does the sea around them), including a tiny population of an indigenous lizard, found only here, *Lacerta situla faraglionensis*, recognisable by its red throat.

Aci Castello is a large village on the coast close to Catania, which retains a small quay with colourful fishing boats beneath the castle (*open July–Aug 9–1 & 4.30–8, spring 9–1 & 3–7, winter 9–1 & 3–5; T: 095 737 3421 or 320 433 9691*) on a splendid basalt rock which rises sharply out of the sea, with interesting formations of 'pillow lava'. The town was covered with lava in the eruption of 1169. It was rebuilt (1297) by Roger of Lauria, the rebel admiral of Frederick II of Aragon. Frederick succeeded in capturing it by building a wooden siege tower of equal height alongside. A long flight of steps built in the lava leads up to the entrance to the small museum, with mineralogical, palaeontological and archaeological material, including underwater finds. According to Giovanni Verga, the castle is haunted by the ghost of an unfortunate lady, Donna Violante. From the terrace there is a fine view of the Faraglioni del Ciclope in front of Acitrezza. Further south, on a cove, is Ognina, now a suburb of Catania. The bay, originally much bigger, was half-filled with lava in the 14th century.

THE LEMON RIVIERA

To the north of Acireale the beautiful, fertile coastline is known as the Riviera dei Limoni; lemon groves are planted along the coast all the way to Taormina. The main road runs through **Giarre** (*map p. 573, C2*), where ceramics and Sicilian folk art are sold. The town has unexpectedly grand eclectic buildings and the huge church of Sant'Isidoro Agricola (1794), the patron saint, with an impressive dome and two bell-towers. Giarre was a suburb of Mascali until 1815; the name derives from *giare*, the terracotta storage jars where the tenth part of the entire agricultural production of Mascali was stored, before being sent to the bishop of Catania, by ancient right also the baron of Mascali. This meant enormous quantities of wine, olive oil and wheat. Giarre may have been the site of the ancient *Kallipolis*.

Separated from Giarre by the railway line, on the sea, with an elegant yachting harbour and another imposing church, is **Riposto**, eternal rival of Giarre. The harbour was once used for shipping the baron of Mascali's wine to Catania; the local craftsmen are still able boat-builders. **Mascali** itself was completely rebuilt after being covered by the lava-stream during the November 1928 eruption of Etna.

Fiumefreddo (*map p. 573, C1*) takes its name (cold river) from the short river (only 1800m long) close by, with abundant, but icy-cold, waters, which enters the sea at Marina di Cottone, a lovely beach awarded the EU Blue Banner for quality. The area is a nature reserve run by the province, protected since 1984 because of the papyrus which grows along its course. This is one of only two rivers in Europe where the plant can be found growing spontaneously; the other is the River Ciane near Syracuse.

CALATABIANO

North of Fiumefreddo the dramatic ruins of the castle of Calatabiano come into view, on a hilltop dominating the Alcantara Valley, close to the mouth of the river. The **Castello Cruyllas** (*open Oct–March Tues–Fri 9–5, Sat–Sun 9–8, April–Sept daily 9am–10pm, always closed Mon; last tickets 30mins before closing; bookshop and restaurant; T: 095 640450, www.castellocruyllas.com*) is easily accessible by the mountainside lift (a tremendous eyesore, however convenient). Because of its Arabic name (Calatabiano translates as 'Castle of Bian'), it was previously thought to date back to the Arab domination, but archaeological surveys have revealed that the fortification was first built by the Greeks in the 4th century BC and was rebuilt or repaired as necessary over the centuries, providing—together with the castles of Taormina and Castelmola—a defensive system to protect the vulnerable Alcantara Valley, a highway towards the interior of the island. A settlement grew up at the foot of the castle, but it was destroyed during the 1693 earthquake and the survivors moved to the present position lower down the hillside. The 360° panorama from the battlements is superb, encompassing Etna and the coast as far as Syracuse, Taormina and the Peloritan Mountains, the Straits of Messina and the coast of Calabria.

Just below the castle on the south side, you can see the winding path leading up from the village of Calatabiano (c. 30mins' walk), and the two pretty churches of the Carmelo (the lower one) and **San Filippo** or the Crocifisso (1484; *closed except for the feast*), with its resident colony of jackdaws in the belfry. Inside is the statue of the patron St Philip, weighing over two tons, which is raced down the mountainside and through the town for his feast in May (*see p. 444*).

PARCO FLUVIALE DELL'ALCANTARA

From Giardini Naxos a road signposted Francavilla leads inland along the Alcantara Valley (*el-qantara*, meaning barrage-bridge in Arabic), which is verdant with lemon groves. The river, 50km long, springs from Mt Soro in the Nebrodi Mountains. Just before reaching the turning for Motta Camastra (c. 15km from Giardini Naxos), a sign on the left indicates the **Gole dell'Alcantara** (Alcantara Gorge; *Via Nazionale 5 Motta Camastra, T: 0942 985010*). Beside the car park is a lift which descends into the unexpectedly deep gorge of basalt prisms. It was originally formed when a lava flow from nearby Mt Moio (a side crater) was eroded by the cold waters of the river, forming a narrow passage through the still hot basalt. Waders can be hired to explore the gorge. By the lift are a restaurant and coffee-bar and a shop selling organic produce from the nearby farm. The whole river valley is protected as a regional park (Parco Fluviale dell'Alcantara; *www.parcoalcantara.it*). Along the river the vegetation is luxuriant, including willow, beech, oleander, birch, elm, and prickly pear. Mammals include the pine marten, porcupine and wildcat; among the birds to be spotted are the golden eagle, red kite, dipper, blue rock thrush, kingfisher, bittern and glossy ibis.

CALTAGIRONE

The old town of Caltagirone (*map p. 573, A3*), with dark, weathered buildings, is built on three hills, to which it owes its irregular plan and narrow streets, and its medieval name *Regina dei Monti*, 'Queen of the Mountains'. Traces of one or more Bronze- and Iron-Age settlements have been found in the area. During the Greek colonisation, the town came under the influence of Gela. The present name is of Arabic origin (*kal'at*, castle and *jerun*, caves). The town was conquered by Genoa in 1030, retaken by the Arabs and destroyed in the 1693 earthquake. The old centre, with its Baroque architecture, is a UNESCO World Heritage Site. It has always also been renowned for ceramic ware thanks to a rich vein of high-quality clay in the area. The Arabs opened many potteries here, introducing new techniques, colours and designs, and today there are numerous artisans' workshops and a prestigious School of Ceramics. The use of majolica tiles and terracotta finials is a characteristic of the local architecture.

PIAZZA UMBERTO AND PIAZZA DEL MUNICIPIO

In the central Piazza Umberto a bank occupies the Neoclassical Monte delle Prestanze, erected by Natale Bonaiuto in 1783. The **duomo**, dedicated to St Julian, was completely transformed in 1920. In the south aisle are altarpieces by the Vaccaro, a 19th-century family of local painters, and in the south transept an unusual carved Crucifix attributed to Giovannello Matinati (1500). Beyond is the **Corte Capitaniale**, a delightful one-storey building decorated in the 16th–17th centuries by Antonuzzo and Gian Domenico Gagini. In **Piazza del Municipio** is the Neoclassical façade of the former opera house, which serves as an entrance to the Galleria Luigi Sturzo, a monumental building inaugurated in 1959. The Town Hall has a fine façade of 1895.

From Piazza del Municipio, Via Principe Amedeo returns to Piazza Umberto past (left) the **Chiesa del Collegio**, with a lovely façade decorated with statues, visible below the road. Built at the end of the 16th century, it contains a painting of the *Annunciation* by Antonio Catalano and a *Pietà* by Filippo Paladini.

Adjacent to Piazza del Municipio rises the impressive long flight of 142 steps known as the **Scala Santa Maria del Monte**. It has colourful majolica risers, predominantly yellow, green and blue on a white ground. They were designed and completed in 1606 and altered in the 19th century. It is a climb (past numerous little ceramic workshops) up to **Santa Maria del Monte**, once the Chiesa Madre. The Baroque façade is by Francesco Battaglia and Natale Bonaiuto. The campanile, by Venanzio Marvuglia, is one of the very few bell-towers which can be climbed in Sicily. A little spiral staircase, which gets narrower and lower as it reaches the top, leads to the bell-chamber, from which there is a fine view. In the church is displayed a statue of the *Madonna* attributed to the workshop of Domenico Gagini. Further up the hill is the attractive former church of San Nicola, in a maze of medieval streets.

VIA LUIGI STURZO

From near the foot of the steps, Via Luigi Sturzo leads past the church of Santa Maria degli Angeli with a 19th-century façade, behind which the façade of **Santa Chiara** can be seen, by Rosario Gagliardi (1743–8), which contains majolica decorations. Further uphill is Palazzo della Magnolia (no. 76), an elaborate Art Nouveau house.

Just beyond, the 19th-century façade of San Domenico faces that of **San Salvatore**, by Natale Bonaiuto (1794). It has a pretty white and gold octagonal interior with a Gaginesque *Madonna*. A modern chapel contains the tomb of Luigi Sturzo (1871–1959), priest and politician and a much-honoured native of the town. He advocated local autonomy and improved social conditions here while he was mayor. A founder of the national Partito Popolare in 1919, he remained its secretary until 1923. It was the first Catholic political party, a forerunner of the Christian Democrat Party (which came into being in 1942) and remained at the centre of Italian political life for much of the 20th century.

Via Sturzo continues uphill past the former Ospedale delle Donne at no. 167, an attractive building, now the **MACC Museo di Arte Contemporanea** (*entrance from Viale Regina Elena 19, open 9.30–1.30, closed Wed and Sun; T: 0933 21083*), an interesting collection of contemporary art, mostly by local artists; there is also an itinerary for the blind. The road ends at **San Giorgio**, rebuilt in 1699, which contains a beautiful little altarpiece, the *Mystery of the Trinity*, attributed to Rogier van der Weyden. From the terrace (left) there is a fine view of the countryside.

SAN GIACOMO

From Piazza del Municipio the handsome Corso Vittorio Emanuele passes several fine palaces and the Art Nouveau post office, on the way to the basilica of San Giacomo, rebuilt in 1708; at the side a pretty flight of steps ascends through the base of the campanile. In the interior, above the west door, the marble coat of arms of the city is by Gian Domenico Gagini. In the left aisle is a blue and brown portal (formerly belonging to the baptistery) and a blue and gold arch in the Cappella del Sacramento by Antonuzzo Gagini. In the left transept is the charming little Portale delle Reliquie, also by Antonuzzo, with bronze doors by Agostino Sarzana. In the chapel to the left of the sanctuary (behind glass doors) is a silver urn (*illuminated on request*), the masterpiece of Nibilio Gagini (signed 1604). In the sanctuary is a processional statue of St James by Vincenzo Archifel (1518) protected by a bronze canopy of 1964 (the original gilded throne is kept in the Museo Civico). This and the urn are carried through the streets of the town in a procession on 25th July.

MUSEO CIVICO AND VIA ROMA

To the south of Piazza Umberto, at Via Roma 10, is the **Museo Civico** (*open 9.30–1.30, Sun 9.30–12.30; Tues, Fri Sat and Sun also 4–7; closed Mon; T: 0933 31590*), housed in a massive building with an interior courtyard and double columns, originally a prison (Carcere Borbonico), built in 1782 by Natale Bonaiuto. On the stairs are architectural fragments and on the landing, four 19th-century terracotta vases by Bongiovanni Vaccaro. Beyond a room with modern local ceramics, another room contains the gilded Throne of St James (16th century, by Scipione di Guido; the statue is kept in the church of San Giacomo), a 19th-century bishop's sedan chair and a Christmas crib. There is a room dedicated to paintings and ceramics by the local artists Giuseppe, Francesco and Mario Vaccaro. There are also some 16th–17th-century paintings (including *Christ in the Garden* by Epifano Rossi) and two terracotta cherubs by Bongiovanni Vaccaro, as well as a small archaeological collection. On the top floor are modern works. Beside the museum is the fine façade, also by Bonaiuto, of Sant'Agata (*closed*).

Via Roma continues south from Piazza Umberto to **Ponte San Francesco**, an 18th-century viaduct, which has pretty majolica decoration and a good view of Palazzo Sant'Elia below the bridge. The road continues past the piazza in front of the simple church of **San Francesco d'Assisi**, founded in 1226 but rebuilt after 1693. It contains paintings by Francesco and Giuseppe Vaccaro and a Gothic sacristy. Behind the church (reached by Via Sant'Antonio and Via Mure Antiche) is **San Pietro**, with a 19th-century neo-Gothic majolica façade.

The street continues past the Tondo Vecchio, an exedra built by Francesco Battaglia in 1766. Beside the church of San Francesco di Paola, a road leads up past the **Teatro Politeama Ingrassia**, with interesting Art Nouveau details, to the entrance gate of the delightful **public gardens**, laid out in 1846 by Giovanni Battista Basile. The exotic trees include palms, cedars, ficus and huge pines. There is a long balustrade on Via Roma decorated with pretty ceramics from the workshop of Enrico Vella, and throughout the gardens are copies of terracotta vases and figures by Giuseppe Vaccaro and Giacomo Bongiovanni. There is also a 17th-century fountain by Camillo Camilliani and a decorative bandstand. The palace of Benedetto Ventimiglia, also on Via Roma, is preceded by a colourful ceramic terrace.

MUSEO DELLA CERAMICA

The Museo della Ceramica (*open 9–6.30, last tickets at 6; T: 0933 58418*) is situated in the gardens, entered through the elaborate Teatrino (1792) by Natale Bonaiuto. From the top of the steps there is a good view beyond a war memorial and some palm trees to the hills (with the town on the left). The museum contains a fine collection of Sicilian ceramics from the prehistoric era to the 19th century. In the corridor to the right are 17th- and 19th-century ceramics from Caltagirone. Beyond a room with 18th- and

19th-century works, the archaeological material is displayed, including Hellenistic and Roman terracotta heads and figurines. Prehistoric pottery from San Mauro and Castelluccio is also exhibited. In Case 26 is a krater depicting a potter at his wheel protected by Athena (5th century BC). Case 27 contains the Russo Perez collection, including 5th-century BC red- and black-figure vases. In the courtyard, bases used in various potteries from the 11th–13th centuries are exhibited. In the large room on the left are Arab-Norman stuccoes from San Giuliano, 10th–12th-century Arab–Norman pottery, and medieval works.

On a lower level is a large hall with 17th–19th-century ceramics from Palermo, Trapani, Caltagirone and Sciacca, including blue enamelled vases and pharmacy jars. The fine collection of terracotta figures includes works by Giuseppe Bongiovanni and Giacomo Vaccaro. The hall is also used for exhibitions.

MUSEO DEI FRATI CAPPUCCINI

On the east side of the town, at Via dei Cappuccini 138, is the Museo dei Frati Cappuccini (*open Mon–Sat 9–12 & 3.30–7, Sun 10.30–12 & 3.30–7; Christmas Day, New Year's Day and Easter Sunday 5–7; T: 0933 21753*). On the ground floor is a gallery of 17th–18th-century paintings by Filippo Paladini, Mario Minniti and many others; notice in particular the masterpiece by Pietro Novelli, *St Francis of Assisi Comforted by an Angel with a Violin*: the light coming from the left creates a dramatic diagonal effect, from the tip of the angel's right wing to his left leg. There is an interesting collection of 18th-century leather processional banners and a copy of the Turin Shroud, painted on silk and given by Prince Maurice of Savoy to the Capuchin father Innocenzo da Caltagirone in 1649. On the first floor, Church treasures are displayed, including vestments of embroidered silk and damask, gold and silver chalices and monstrances, statuettes in alabaster, wood and wax, and a fine collection of 16th–17th-century jewellery, donated as ex-votos. In the crypt of the church next door is a permanently-displayed Christmas crib, with terracotta statuettes made by the local workshops.

Via Santa Maria di Gesù leads south from the public gardens to (10mins) the church of **Santa Maria di Gesù** (1422), with a charming *Madonna* by Antonello Gagini, while on the opposite side of the city, at Viale Principessa Maria José 7/9, is the photography museum, **Museo della Fotografia Storica e Contemporanea** (*open Nov–May 9–5, June–Oct 10–6; always closed Mon; T: 0933 54567*), with a collection of cameras and photographic equipment and a selection of interesting photographs and posters, all beautifully displayed. There is also a collection of terracotta whistles, for the manufacture of which Caltagirone was renowned.

ENVIRONS OF CALTAGIRONE

North of Caltagirone is the clean and tidy **Mirabella Imbaccari** (*map p. 573, A3*) famous for the lace and embroidery still made here. You can see the work at the Mostra del Ricamo e del Tombolo (*open 9.30–12.30 & 3.30–7.30, closed Mon; T: 328 025 4791*), in the central Via Alcide De Gasperi 13.

GRAMMICHELE

Grammichele (*map p. 573, A3*), 15km east of Caltagirone, was founded by Carlo Maria Carafa Branciforte, Prince of Butera, to house the people of Occhiolà, destroyed in 1693. The ruins of the old town, on a ridge c. 2km away, are now a very interesting **archaeological park** (*usually open 9–5; if closed to request visit T: 340 294 6826, www. fondazioneterravecchia.it*).

The new town was built to a concentric hexagonal plan around the spacious, central, six-sided Piazza Carafa, with an array of honey-coloured palaces between the six roads. Here the weather-worn, unfinished **Chiesa Madre**, begun in 1723 by Andrea Amato and dedicated to St Michael Archangel, who protects against earthquakes, stands next to the elegant red and gold Town Hall, Palazzo Comunale (Carlo Sada, 1896), which is home to the **Museo Civico** (*open 9–1, closed Mon; T: 0933 941536*) with a well-arranged collection of finds from excavations in the district, begun in 1891 by Paolo Orsi, who identified a pre-Greek settlement at Terravecchia. Exhibits include prehistoric bronzes and Bronze Age ceramics, three large pots used for female burials, vases found in tombs (6th century BC), terracotta votive statuettes and 15th–16th-century majolica from Occhiolà.

In front of the Town Hall is the Art Deco **Teatro Intelisano** (1940s), the balconies supported by ledges reproducing the faces of great personalities of the past, including Rossini and Leonardo da Vinci.

THE SOUTH OF THE PROVINCE

VIZZINI

Vizzini (*map p. 573, B4*) nestles among the Hyblaean Mountains. On the summit of two hills, it occupies the site of ancient *Bidis*, recorded by Cicero. In the central Piazza Umberto is a stairway (1996) decorated with majolica tiles like the one in Caltagirone, leading up to the church of Sant'Agata (14th and 18th centuries). In the square is **Palazzo Verga**, an unfinished 18th-century palace which used to be owned by Giovanni Verga's family: the great writer (*see p. 413*) was born in Vizzini and most of his works, such as *Cavalleria Rusticana*, are set here or in the vicinity. Close by, in the 18th-century Palazzo Costa, at Salita Vespucci 5, is the **Museo Immaginario Verghiano** (*open 9–1 & 3.30–7.30, morning only on Sun, closed Mon; T: 0933 966323*), dedicated to the writer, with a collection of his photographs (he was a keen amateur photographer), interesting pictures of the Sicilian locations used for the films based on his books, and various memorabilia.

From Piazza Umberto, Via San Gregorio Magno winds its way up to the **Chiesa Madre**, dedicated to St Gregory the Great, patron saint of Vizzini. His statue stands on a column by the side entrance to the church, which still retains some pre-earthquake elements, such as the splendid 15th-century Catalan Gothic portal on the right side. The interior is decorated with Baroque stuccoes; in the south aisle are two paintings by Filippo Paladini: the *Martyrdom of St Lawrence* (second altar) and the *Madonna of Mercy* (fourth altar).

Vizzini is a prosperous farming community, renowned for its excellent sheep's milk cheese, ricotta, olive oil, prickly pears and durum wheat, and in the past leather was tanned along the little River Dirillo just outside the town. Now the workshops and the vats, many carved out of the rock, and the homes of the workers, all long since abandoned, are being repaired and transformed into a cultural centre called 'a Cunziria (the Tannery). The mountains around Vizzini are ancient spent volcanoes, now rich pastures or wheat fields, where flocks of ravens fly.

LICODIA EUBEA

Situated on a crest overlooking the River Dirillo, Licodia Eubea (*map p. 573, B4*) was probably founded in the 7th century BC as a sub-colony of *Leontinoi* (Lentini). In the Middle Ages it had a formidable castle, of which few traces remain today—it was destroyed in the 1693 earthquake. In the 15th century the town and castle became the property of the Catalan Santapau family. In recent years there has been considerable archaeological research in the area; the finds are displayed in the Museo Civico Antonino Di Vita (*open Tues and Thur 9–12.30, Wed 3–6, Sat–Sun 10–12.30; T: 0933 963460*) at Corso Umberto 208, where besides the objects of Greek origin, there are interesting traces of the preceding Sicel settlement.

MILITELLO IN VAL DI CATANIA

Thanks to the munificence of its prince, Don Francesco Branciforte, Militello in Val di Catania (*map p. 573, B3*) is a splendid little town with remarkable Baroque buildings, designated a UNESCO World Heritage Site. Don Francesco and his wife Donna Johanna of Austria wanted their town to be the cultural centre of this part of Sicily in the early 17th century, and poured money into public works, sponsored religious communities and invited artists, architects and writers to their court. The 22 lovely churches here contain paintings by Vito D'Anna, Olivio Sozzi, Pietro Ruzzolone and others.

The main square, Piazza Municipio, houses the great abbey and church of **San Benedetto**, now the Town Hall, modelled on the Benedictine monastery of San Nicolò in Catania (*see p. 405*). Inside the church, the 18th-century carved walnut choir stalls are of particular interest.

At Via Umberto 67, in the crypt of the Chiesa Madre di San Nicola, is the **Museo di San Nicola** (*open Wed–Sun 10–12; T: 095 811251*). The subterranean chamber was discovered accidentally in 1981 during repairs. The museum houses 17th- and 18th-century works, including vestments, Church silver, sculpture and paintings. In the treasury of the imposing Baroque church of **Santa Maria della Stella** (*to request visit, T: 095 655329*) there is an altarpiece in enamelled terracotta by Andrea Della Robbia (1487) with the *Nativity, Annunciation to the Shepherds*, and (in the predella) a *Pietà* and the *Twelve Apostles*. Another altarpiece, the *Retablo di San Pietro*, is thought to be the work of Antonello da Messina. For centuries these two churches, both said to have been founded before the 9th-century Arab invasion, one of Greek rite (San Nicola) and the other of Latin tradition (Santa Maria), were rivals for the title of Chiesa Madre and for dedication to the patron saint; the question was resolved only in 1966, when the pope was forced to intervene. Now Mary is the patron saint, and the Mother Church is that of St Nicholas.

Another interesting museum has been opened near the Branciforte Castle, in Largo Majorana, the **Polo Museale Sebastiano Guzzone** (*open Mon–Sat 9–1; T: 095 655202*), housing a collection of paintings, medieval books and the city archives. The half-ruined **Santa Maria la Vetere**, to the south of the historic centre, has a porch supported by lions and a magnificent doorway of 1506.

Not far from Militello is **Scordia** (*map p. 573, B3*), noted for its blood oranges. In the central Piazza Umberto stands the church and convent of Sant'Antonio di Padova (1644). Inside is an exceptional 18th-century floor of coloured tiles from Caltagirone, now rather fragmentary, showing a pelican in its piety. The wooden Crucifix is the work of Fra' Umile da Petralia.

MINEO

A small town on an ancient settlement founded by Ducetius, king of the Sicels, in the 5th-century BC, Mineo (*map p. 573, B3*) was later occupied by the Greeks and Romans. High-quality olive oil, wheat and oranges are produced here. The church of Sant'Agrippina, patron saint of the town, and that of the Collegio both have fine 18th-century stuccoes. Behind the church of San Pietro (which houses an organ by Donato del Piano), at Piazza Buglio 40, is the house of the writer Luigi Capuana (1835–1915), now a museum: the **Biblioteca-Museo Luigi Capuana** (*open June–Sep. Mon–Fri 10–1, Tues and Thur also 5.30–7.30; Oct–May Mon and Fri 2.30–7.30, Tues, Wed, Thur 10–12.30; T: 0933 983056*). A close friend of Giovanni Verga, Capuana wrote various works both in Italian and Sicilian, including tales for children. The museum holds his books, manuscripts and photographs, and the library of the Capuchin monastery, with 16th- and 17th-century volumes.

On the outskirts of the town, at Viale della Rimembranza 8, is the **Museo Civico Corrado Tamburino Merlini** (*open Tues–Thur 10–1, Thur also 4–6; T: 0933 989059*), with a wide variety of finds (from Palaeolithic flint tools to Greek and Latin inscriptions) from archaeological sites in the area. The medieval **castle**, on the summit of one of the two hills of Mineo, is now a romantically crumbling ruin.

Three kilometres southeast of the town, on a hillside, are two rectangular, man-made caves called **Grotte di Caratabia** (pron. ca-ra-ta-BEE-a; *the site is unenclosed, but you may need a guide, request visit Municipio di Mineo a day or so ahead; NB: steep path slippery in wet weather; T: 0933 980008*), where some Sicel graffiti of the 5th century BC have been found. The designs represent a procession with horses, a scene with hunters and their servants, and deer; although barely discernible, the artistic quality is high. Some scholars retain that they were originally painted.

PALAGONIA

Palagonia (*map p. 573, B3*) stands on the edge of the fertile Plain of Catania, known to the Greeks as the Laestrygonian Fields, the home of the cannibal Laestrygones. Its vast groves are watered by the Simeto and its tributaries, the Dittaino and the Gornalunga.

Today the district is well known for its oranges and tangerines. Five kilometres east of the town, reached from the road to Militello, is an area with many rock-hewn Sicel tombs later used as dwellings. Among these (signposted) is the 7th-century Byzantine **Eremo di Santa Febronia**, carved into the rock, with abundant 14th-century frescoes. Reached by stairs is an upper floor, once a large tholos tomb, where the monks had their cells. More stairs lead down under the church to a T-shaped cave probably used as a crypt.

By taking the road from the cemetery of Palagonia towards the River Catalfano, you reach, after c. 1.5km, the ruined **Basilica di San Giovanni**, surrounded by orange groves, probably built in the 7th century. The apse and parts of the nave arcades survive.

The old Sicel town of *Paliké* is close to Palagonia, at a sacred lake with two small geysers emitting gases (no longer visible), said to be the Palikes, gods who dispensed justice; the spot became a sanctuary for runaway slaves. The archaeological site of **Rocchicella-Paliké** (reached from the SS 181; *open Tues–Sat 9–1.30, Wed 9–4.30 (5.30 from March–Oct); T: 331 577 1468*), is an ancient volcano with a characteristic shape and a cave at the base. The antiquarium on the site contains material found during archaeological excavations, and explanatory panels. The earliest traces of human activity date back to the Palaeo-Mesolithic period, but it is only in the 6th century BC that the site indisputably became the principal religious sanctuary of the area. The most impressive structure is the hestiaterion, a ritual banqueting hall of the 5th century BC, perhaps built by Ducetius. The four larger rooms would have held seven couches for dining, and the three smaller rooms were probably used as service areas.

RAMACCA AND RADDUSA

Ramacca (*map p. 573, A3–B3*) is an elegant little country town, founded by Prince Ottavio Gravina in the early 18th century and often called 'City of Jesus' because its street layout resembles a Crucifix. It is famous for its delectable violet artichokes. The Museo Civico Archeologico (*open daily 9–1 & 3.30–6; T: 095 793 0227*) at Via Marconi 2, displays archaeological material from settlements in the vicinity, including some grave goods (in particular a pair of Attic black-figure skyphoi) from 6th–5th-century BC necropoleis. The museum staff are willing to give guided tours of the local archaeological park La Montagna if asked a day or two in advance.

Raddusa (*map p. 573, A2–A3*) has an interesting tea museum, La Casa del Te, at Via Garibaldi 45 (*to request visit T: 095 662193 or 339 205 3677 (Salvo Pellegrino), www.lacasadelte.it*), well worth a detour. You can visit the tea plantation and sample some of the 600 different kinds of tea in Dr Pellegrino's collection, including varieties belonging to Berber, Bedouin, Chinese, Japanese, Ethiopian, Iranian, English, French, Singalese and Burmese tradition, prepared with appropriate ceremony. He has discovered that tea was first cultivated in Sicily by the Arabs, from c. 950, for an emir who was fond of the beverage. There is also an interesting museum dedicated to wheat, Raddusa's most famous product, at Via Tenente Sollima 41, the Museo del Grano (*open 9–1 & 3–7; closed Sun and Mon, T: 095 293 3181*).

PRACTICAL INFORMATION

GETTING AROUND

• **By air**: Catania Fontanarossa airport (*www.aeroporto.catania.it*) has flights connecting the major Italian cities and many European destinations. All major car-hire companies have booths at the airport. Taxis are available, reaching Catania centre in c. 30 mins. ALIBUS no. 457 runs every 20mins from 5am–midnight, connecting the airport to various points in Catania, including the railway station and port. Other bus companies offer services to destinations around the island.

• **By train**: Catania railway station is at Piazza Papa Giovanni XXIII, (*map 8; www.trenitalia.com*), for all services on the line to Palermo via Enna and on the coastal line between Syracuse and Messina. All trains stop at Acireale and Taormina, which are on the main line. Caltagirone (station in Piazza della Repubblica) is on the Catania–Caltanissetta line. It has services to Catania in c. 2hrs. Several towns around Caltagirone are served by rail, but sometimes (Vizzini, Mineo, Licodia, Militello) the stations are a long way from the towns.

• **By bus**: In Catania an efficient network of yellow city buses is run by **AMT** (*www.amt.ct.it*). **KATANE LIVE** (*www.katanelive.it*) runs sightseeing tours in open-top buses with a multi-lingual audio-guide departing hourly 9–7 from the duomo.

Inter-city services: (*NB: For up-to-date schedules consult www.orariautobus.it.*) **AST** (*www.aziendasicilianatrasporti. it*) runs services from Piazza Giovanni

XXIII (*map 8*) to many places including Acireale, Avola, Caltagirone, Ispica, Lentini, Modica, Nicolosi, Noto, Palazzolo Acreide, Piazza Armerina, Syracuse, Scicli, Vizzini and Zafferana Etnea. AST also runs a daily bus (in c. 2hrs) to the Rifugio Sapienza on Mt Etna, departing early morning. An extra service runs in July and Aug, leaving Piazza Giovanni XXIII in the later morning for Nicolosi, where a connecting bus continues to the Rifugio Sapienza. A bus returns to Catania in the afternoon.

Buda (*www.autolineebuda.it*) runs infrequent services from Piazza Giovanni XXIII to Giarre, Fiumefreddo and Calatabiano.

Etna Trasporti-Interbus (*www. etnatrasporti.it, www.interbus.it*) from Via Archimede (*map 8*) to a wide variety of destinations, including Acireale, Aidone, Avola, Gela, Giardini Naxos, Licata, Noto, Piazza Armerina, Ragusa, Santa Croce Camerina, Syracuse, and Taormina.

FCE Metropolitana (*www.circumetnea. it*) leaving from the entrance to the port of Catania, for Catania Borgo, Adrano, Biancavilla, Bronte, Castiglione di Sicilia, Fiumefreddo, Giarre, Linguaglossa, Maletto, Mascali, Randazzo, Riposto, and Santa Maria di Licodia.

Giamporcaro (*www.saistrasporti.it*) links Catania Piazza Giovanni XXIII to Catania airport, Comiso airport, Comiso and Vittoria.

Giuntabus (*www.giuntabus.it*) connects Catania airport to Milazzo port (for the Aeolian Islands) from April–Sept.

ISEA (*www.iseaviaggi.it*) leaves from Catania (Piazza Repubblica; *map 7*) to Bronte, Capizzi, Cerami, Cesarò, Enna, Leonforte, Nicosia, Paternò and Troina.

Romano (*www.romanobus.it*) leaves from Catania (Via VI Aprile near the railway station) to Centuripe, Paternò, Catenanuova and Enna.

SAIS Autolinee (*www.saisautolinee.it*) from Piazza Giovanni XXIII run coaches about every hour via the motorway to Palermo (2hrs 40mins) and Messina (1hr 30mins); less frequently via the motorway to Enna (1hr 30mins), Caltanissetta and Gela. Most also stop at the airport.

SAIS Trasporti (*www.saistrasporti.it*) has services to Agrigento, Caltanissetta and Canicattì.

SARP Trasporti (*www.saistrasporti. it*) connects Catania (Via D'Amico, off Via Libertà; *map 8*) to Sommatino, Riesi, Barrafranca, Mazzarino, Caltanissetta and Pietraperzia.

• By sea: Boats from Catania serve the Italian mainland, Greece and Malta. For the Sicilian islands, ferries leave from Trapani, Palermo, Cefalù, Porto Empedocle, Messina and Milazzo (*see the relevant chapters*).

WHERE TO STAY

ACIREALE (*map p. 573, C2*)
€€€ **Santa Caterina**. Breathtaking position on the cliffside for this charming hotel, 23 comfortable rooms, good restaurant, car park, pool and garden. *Via Santa Caterina 42/b, T: 095 763 3735, www.santacaterinahotel.com.*
€€ **Maugeri**. 59 spacious rooms, some with Jacuzzi, in a 1950s building, restaurant, very central. Car park. *Piazza Garibaldi 27, T: 095 608666,*

www.hotel-maugeri.it.
€€ **Ibis Styles**. Modern hotel just outside town on the cliff edge, with 66 comfortable rooms, garden, pool, personal car park. No restaurant, but good breakfasts. *Via Madonna delle Grazie 98 a/b, T: 095 763 4275, www. dimsiway.it.*
€€ **Palazzo Pennisi di Floristella**. Smart B&B in a prince's palace offering two large rooms with private bath and a delightful little penthouse apartment. Roof garden where breakfast is served in summer, using products from the family farm. *Piazza Lionardo Vigo 16, T: 095 763 3079, www. palazzopennisidifloristella.com.*
€ **Palazzo Leonardi**. B&B in a 19th-century house with garden, car park, 5 well-appointed rooms, hospitable owners. *Corso Savoia 241, T: 095 891501, www.palazzoleonardi.it.*

CALATABIANO (*map p. 573, C1*)
€€€ **Castello San Marco**. Close to the sea under the mountain of Calatabiano, a romantic castle built by an eccentric millionaire is now a comfortable hotel, 30 rooms all leading into the beautiful gardens. Pool and restaurant. *Via San Marco 40, T: 095 641181, www. castellosanmarco.it.*

CALTAGIRONE (*map p. 573, A3*)
€€€ **Villa Tasca**. Stylish accommodation in this splendid old aristocratic villa 3km from town, with 10 rooms. Pool, gardens, sauna, cycling track, horse-riding. *Contrada Fontana Pietra, SP 37 km 11, T: 0933 22760, www. villatasca.it.*
€€ **Vecchia Masseria**. Old country house in the heart of the woods in a convenient position for touring Caltagirone, Piazza Armerina, Niscemi, Butera and Gela, with 20 luxurious

rooms and suites. Forms part of the Charme & Relax chain. Helicopter tours, boat trips and horse-riding are organised. Good food (you can purchase their products, including wine). *Contrada Cutuminello, SS 117bis km68, T: 0935 684003 or 333 873 5573, www. vecchiamasseria.com.*

€ **Tre Metri Sopra il Cielo**. Comfortable B&B in a breathtaking position on the central stairway; 10 rooms, good breakfasts. *Via Bongiovanni 72, T: 0933 193 5106 or 331 530 3926, www.bbtremetrisoprailcielo.it.*

CASTIGLIONE DI SICILIA (*map p. 573, C1*)

€€ **Federico II**. In a 14th-century building right in the town centre, a charming hotel run by the owners with 9 rooms, garden, good restaurant serving Sicilian dishes accompanied by wines from Etna. *Via Baracca 2, T: 0942 980368, www.hotelfedericosecondo.com.*

€ **Borgo Santa Caterina**. *Albergo diffuso* in the old Jewish quarter, where several houses are available. Good breakfasts and evening meal on request. *Via Sottotenente Mazza 10, T: 347 441 7473, www.borgosantacaterina.com.*

CATANIA (*map p. 573, C2*)

€€€ **Una Hotel Palace**. Prestigious 19th-century hotel with 94 luxurious rooms, fitness centre with sauna and Turkish bath, roof garden, good restaurant, garage, courteous staff. *Via Etnea 218, T: 095 250 5111, www. unahotels.it. Map 6.*

€€€ **Liberty Hotel**. Beautifully restored in perfect Art Nouveau style, the bathrooms are gorgeous; some of the 18 rooms and suites have frescoed ceilings. No restaurant. Car park. *Via San Vito 40, T: 095 311651, www. libertyhotel.it. Map 6.*

€€€ **Katane Palace**. Elegant 19th-century building, central, with 135 rooms, Michelin-recommended restaurant, garage parking. Cooking courses organised. *Via Finocchiaro Aprile 110, T: 095 7470702, www. katanepalace.it. Map 4.*

€€€ **Il Principe**. This hotel in the Baroque heart of Catania, has 12 very comfortable rooms and suites and a fitness centre with Turkish bath. No restaurant. It can be noisy; the steps of Via Alessi are a popular meeting-place for young people on weekend evenings. *Via Alessi 24, T: 095 250 0345, www. ilprincipehotel.com. Map 11.*

€€ **Novecento**. Art Nouveau elegance, just behind the Opera House. 18 comfortable rooms, no restaurant. *Via Ventimiglia 35, T: 095 310488, www. hotelnovecentocatania.com. Map 12.*

€ **Centrale Europa**. Old-fashioned little hotel, very central, offering 17 well-appointed rooms, most with view over Piazza Duomo. No restaurant. *Via Vittorio Emanuele 167, T: 095 311309, www.hotelcentraleuropa.it. Map 11.*

€ **Catania Bedda**. Opposite the Orto Botanico, comfortable B&B with 3 rooms, wonderful breakfasts, helpful polyglot owners. *Via Etnea 502, T: 095 2866417, 348 655468, www. cataniabeddabb.com. Map 2.*

€ **La Foresteria**. Quiet B&B with 2 comfortable rooms, nice breakfasts, car park. Good if you want to be self-sufficient. But it is a long way from the centre. *Via Ammiraglio Toscano 6, T: 095 7167929 or 337 888850, www. laforesteriacatania.com. Stadio area. Beyond map 1.*

€ **Bed and Breakfast Stesicoro**. In an aristocratic palace overlooking the Roman amphitheatre, entered from the little alley where snow was once stocked. 5 welcoming rooms, evening meals and airport shuttle on request. *Via Neve 7, T: 095 311178 or 393 919 3342, www. bbstesicoro.it. Map 6..*

GIARRE (*map p. 573, C2*)

€€€ **Zash**. Boutique hotel in the countryside 3km south of Giarre, with 9 luxurious rooms, garden, pool, spa, and Michelin-recommended restaurant. *SP 2 no. 60, Contrada Archi, T: 095 7828932, www.zash.it.*

€€ **Etna**. Historic villa with garden, pool, panoramic views of Etna, 18 well-equipped and comfortable rooms, no restaurant but lovely breakfasts. Bikes available. Car park. Shuttle service to/from Catania airport on request. *Via Continella 10, T: 095 934070, www. etnahotel.it.*

RAMACCA (*map p. 573, B3*)

€€€ **Contea di Wagner**. Named after its most famous guest (Wagner's eldest daughter married Count Gravina, owner of the farm, and while staying here it is said that he found inspiration for his *Parsifal*), this old-fashioned country house offers luxurious accommodation in 35 rooms, delicious food. Well-placed for Catania airport. *SS 288 km 12, Contrada Mendolo, T: 095 653134, 330 847823, www.conteadiwagner.com.*

€ **Paradiso della Zagara**. Good-value, basic hotel in pretty Art Nouveau building, family-run, 10 simple but comfortable rooms, good restaurant (closed Mon) specialising in local dishes, including artichokes when in season. *Piazza Sottotenente Di Fazio 8, T: 095 653279, www.paradisodellazagara.it.*

RANDAZZO (*map p. 573, B1*)

€€ **Scrivano**. Comfortable modern hotel in town centre, no frills, family-run, 30 rooms, good restaurant. *Via*

Bonaventura 2, T: 095 921433, www. hotelscrivano.com.

€€ **Nebrodi Monte Colla**. An out-of-the-way country house with 13 beautiful rooms, horses are raised, very peaceful, within the boundaries of the Nebrodi Mountains Park at 1460m, reached by a rough track (transfer to/from Randazzo on request), good food. *Frazione Monte Colla, T: 338 2376569, 333 6666960, www.hotelnebrodi.it.*

€ **Parco Statella**. Gorgeous 18th-century villa surrounded by a park. The 10 comfortable rooms furnished with delightful antiques were once the farm buildings. Very kind owners. *Via Montelaguardia 2/s, Località Montelaguardia, T: 095 924036, www. parcostatella.com.*

RIPOSTO (*map p. 573, C2*)

€€€ **Donna Carmela**. Old winery producing award-winning Etna Rosso and also ornamental plants, beautifully restored farmhouse with 18 comfortable rooms, all different and subtly colourful, pool surrounded by centuries-old olive trees, good restaurant. *Contrada Grotte 5, Carruba di Riposto, T: 095 809383, www.donnacarmela.com.*

SAN GIOVANNI LA PUNTA (*map p. 573, C2*)

€€ **Paradiso dell'Etna**. Pretty 1920s-style hotel, with 34 elegant rooms and suites, garden, pool, and excellent restaurant. *Via Viagrande 37, T: 095 751 2409, www.paradisoetna.it.*

SAN MICHELE DI GANZARIA (*map p. 573, A3*)

€€ **Baglio Gigliotto**. A very beautiful large farm, with olive groves and vineyards, cereals and prickly pears, conveniently situated for Morgantina and Piazza Armerina. The farm buildings comprise the original

14th-century farmhouse and an ancient monastery. 14 comfortable rooms furnished with antiques, restaurant serves good home-made food using local organic products. *SS 117bis km 60, Contrada Gigliotto, T: 0933 970898 or 0933 979092, www.gigliotto.com.*

€ **Pomara**. ◼ An efficient, family-run hotel in an excellent position for touring central Sicily, with car park and pool, 40 welcoming rooms. The restaurant serves marvellous local dishes, Sicilians come here from miles around, just for the food. *Via Vittorio Veneto 84, T: 0933 976976, www.hotelpomara.com.*

VIZZINI (*map p. 573, B4*)
€ **'A Cunziria**. Some of the workers' cottages of this old tannery have been recuperated and transformed into comfortable accommodation for a peaceful holiday. Plenty of activities are organised. *Contrada Masera, T: 0933 965507, www.agriturismocunziria.com.*

ZAFFERANA ETNEA (*map p. 573, C2*)
€€€ **Monaci delle Terre Nere**. A few kilometres south of Zafferana, an aristocratic country house surrounded by organically farmed groves, vineyards and vegetable gardens. 20 stunning rooms, park, infinity pool, and excellent restaurant recommended by the Slow Food Foundation. *Via Monaci, Contrada Pisano, T: 095 708 3638, www. monacidelleterrenere.it.*

WHERE TO EAT

ACIREALE (*map p. 573, C2*)
€€ **Il Tocco**. You go through a tunnel to reach this pizzeria, perched on the edge of the cliff, offering stupendous views. All the dishes are good, but Il Tocco bases its claim to fame on its pizzas, which are varied and superb. Open

evenings only, closed Mon in winter. *Viale dello Ionio 38, T: 095 764 8819.*
€ **Al Ficodindia**. ◼ Excellent pizza, antipasto, pasta and seafood, in a beautiful setting. Closed Tues. *Piazza San Domenico 1, T: 095 7637024.*

ACITREZZA (*map p. 573, C2*)
€€ **da Federico** (*Piazza Verga/Via Provinciale 115, T: 095 276364*. Closed Mon) and €€ **Verga da Gaetano** (*Piazza Verga/Via Provinciale 119, T: 095 276342*. Closed Thur). These two restaurants in front of the little harbour are both renowned for long, leisurely fish dinners; up-market clientèle. Crowded at weekends, booking necessary.

BRONTE-MANIACE (*map p. 573, B1*)
€ **Don Ciccio**. A delightfully simple restaurant near Castello Maniace, serving country food and local wine. *Contrada Serra, T: 095 772 2916.* Another good restaurant not far from the castle is € **Fiorentino**, closed Sun evening and all day Mon. *Contrada Serra, T: 095 691800.*

CALTAGIRONE (*map p. 573, A3*)
€€€ **Coria**. Central, refined Michelin-starred restaurant, with a open kitchen so you can watch Francesco and Domenico at work. A marvellous starter is the platter of assorted raw fish. Home-made bread. Good wine list. Closed Sun evening and all day Mon in winter, all day Sun and Mon lunchtime in summer. *Via Infermeria 24, T: 0933 26596.*
€€ **Il Locandiere**. Tiny family-run *trattoria* serving only seafood, to very high standards. Try the fish cous cous or the *ravioli di ricotta con bottarga* (tuna roe). Good wine list, obliging service. Closed Mon. *Via Sturzo 55, T: 0933 58292.*
€ **La Piazzetta**. Besides pasta, meat,

or pizza, wonderful vegetarian dishes. Closed Thur. *Via Vespri 20/a, T: 0933 24178.*

CASTIGLIONE DI SICILIA (*map p. 573, C1*)

€ La Dispensa dell'Etna. Simple local dishes, beautifully cooked, accompanied by their local wines (which they also sell). Closed Fri in winter. *Piazza Sant'Antonio 2, T: 0942 984258.*

€ President. Welcoming restaurant/caffetteria, ideal lunch stop, delicious local dishes and home-made ice cream. *Via Regina Margherita 174, T: 0942 984142.*

CATANIA (*map p. 573, C2*)

€€€ Km.0. Zero kilometres, meaning low-mileage. A little gourmet restaurant run by young brothers Marco and Fabio. Their inspiration does sometimes come from thousands of kilometres away, though, as do a few of the ingredients. Booking advised a few days ahead. Closed Sun evening and all day Mon. *Via Antonino Longo 26 (opposite the Orto Botanico), T: 347 732 7788. Map 2.*

€€€ Il Sale Art Café. Dishes made using fresh, exclusively Sicilian ingredients accompanied by local wines. Congenial and elegant. Evenings only. Booking essential, especially at weekends. *Via Santa Filomena 10, T: 095 316888. Map 7.*

€€ Da Nuccio. ■ A family-run *trattoria* in the heart of the city, Nuccio in the dining room and his wife and daughter in the kitchen. Superlative fish dishes. Old-fashioned and completely authentic. Closed Mon. *Via Penninello, T: 095 322461. Map 10.*

€€ Mm!! Trattoria. Rather simple restaurant in the fish market, for seriously excellent fish. Home-made bread from locally-grown wheat, organic

wines. Closed Sun. *Piazza Pardo 34, T: 095 348897. Map 15.*

€€ La Canonica. ■ Warm and friendly atmosphere in this little *trattoria* next to Sant'Agata alla Badia, where the speciality is cous cous with fish, meat or vegetables. Sicilian wines. Closed Wed evenings. *Via Raddusa 7, T: 095 316428 or 347 061 1619. Map 11.*

€€ I Cutilisci. The name means 'pebbles', because this little restaurant is perched on the stones surrounding a fishing harbour miraculously enclosed by the great city. Ideal for summer evening dinners. Home-made bread from locally-grown wheat, organic ingredients, tasty fish dishes and pizza. Closed Tues lunchtime. *Via San Giovanni Li Cuti 69, T: 095 372558. Off the Lungomare (beyond map 4).*

€€ Blanc à Manger. Sleek, minimalist bakery-café for delicious, highly original sandwiches, pasta and cakes. They bake their own bread. Also take-away. Closed Mon morning. *Via Santa Filomena 55, T: 095 320719. Map 7.*

€ Prestipino. ■ In front of the duomo, close to the elephant fountain, an ideal spot for light lunch, snacks or ice cream. *Piazza Duomo 9, T: 095 320840. Map 11.*

MILITELLO (*map p. 573, B3*)

€ 'U Trappitu. Delicious recipes typical of the interior of Sicily, served in a transformed oil press. Closed Mon. *Via Principe Branciforte 125, T: 095 811447.*

NICOLOSI (*map p. 573, C2*)

€ Antico Orto dei Limoni. Old wine press, wonderful atmosphere, delicious food, closed Tues. *Via Grotte 4, T: 095 910808.*

€ Café Esagonal. ■ At the Rifugio Sapienza, right in front of the cableway station. Nunzio and Dominique serve good coffee and hot chocolate, and

salads, snacks or pasta (as well as all the latest information on the volcano's activity). Gift shop too. *T: 095 780 7868.*
RANDAZZO (*map p. 573, B1*)
€ **San Giorgio e il Drago**. Close to the old walls, in the cellars of the convent of St George. The home-made pasta is particularly inviting. Closed Tues. *Piazza San Giorgio 20, T: 095 923972.*
RIPOSTO (*map p. 573, C2*)
€€ **Bistrot del Porto**. In the yachting harbour, an elegant café/restaurant/pizzeria open all day. The pizza and the ice cream are particularly recommended. Closed Tues. *Via Duca del Mare, T: 095 779 3561.*
SANTA MARIA LA SCALA
€€ **Al Molino**. Fish dishes in the tiny village of Santa Maria La Scala under the Timpa on the eastern edge of Acireale, prepared the moment the boats land. Closed Wed. *Via Molino 106, T: 095 764 8116.*
€€ **La Grotta**. This restaurant in a cave is legendary, and gourmets try to keep the secret to themselves. Fantastic fish; raw anchovy salad, fish soup, fried shrimps, seafood antipasto, and lots more, always superb. Closed Tues. *Via Scalo Grande 46, T: 095 764 8153.*
ZAFFERANA ETNEA (*map p. 573, C2*)
€€ **Parco dei Principi**. Very elegant, member of the Buon Ricordo chain. Closed Tues. *Via delle Ginestre 1, T: 095 708 2335.*
€ **La Capannina**. ■ By the Silvestri Craters on top of Mt Etna, this little inn was almost swallowed up by lava in 2001. Very good *arancini* (fried rice balls), barbequed sausages, *cannoli* and pistachio cake. Honey, local wine and other souvenirs are sold. *T: 095 780 8427 or 349 758 4751.*

LOCAL SPECIALITIES

ACIREALE Try **Condorelli** (*Via Sciont 26*), for the best granita, almond pastries and home-made nougat; their unique breakfast pastry is called *senzanome alla ricotta* ('no-name with ricotta').
Pasticceria Bella (*Corso Umberto 66*), which opened in 1914, is the place to buy home-made candied and crystallised fruit. **Chiarenza** (*Via Vittorio Emanuele 86/88*) is a sculptor (included in the UNESCO list of traditional craftsmen), with a fascinating souvenir shop.
Ask him to show you his *magazzini*, storerooms packed with dismantled carts, puppets, furniture and curiosities.
ADRANO The historic café and pastry-shop is **Spitaleri** (*Piazza Umberto 68*) near the castle.
BELPASSO Bar Condorelli (*Via Vittorio Emanuele 542, www.condorelli. it*) for the world-famous *torroncini*, soft nougat covered with chocolate.
BRONTE Caffetteria Luca (*Via Messina 273*) is the historic confectioner's for pistachio ice cream, cakes and pastries. For pistachio delicacies also **Gino** (*Viale Regina Margherita 46*) and **Conti** (*Corso Umberto 275*). To simply buy pistachios, go to **Marullo** (*Via Baracca 59/a, www. fmarullo.com*),or order some online.
For the renowned local olive oil, **Oleificio Costa** (*Via Palermo 132, www. oleificiocosta.com*).
CALTAGIRONE There are some 150 ceramic workshops in town. Many of them are around Piazza Umberto and on the Scala. Albanian **Harizaj Besnik** (*Via Gueli 1, www.besnik-harizi.it*), makes replicas of the antique pottery in the museum. Caltagirone's puppet theatre was renowned in the past: **Teatro**

Stabile dei Pupi Siciliani (*Discesa Verdumai 4, open daily 10–12.30 & 3.30–7*) displays 200 marionettes, backdrops and costumes, and will put on a show on request.

CASTIGLIONE DI SICILIA **Tenuta di Fessina** (*Via Nazionale SS120, km22, Contrada Rovittello, www.tenutadifessina.com*) is an ancient vineyard of Nerello Mascalese grapes, where Silvia, Roberto and Federico produce excellent Etna Rosso DOC wine. **Torrepalino Patria** (*Via Nazionale SS120, km194, Contrada Solicchiata, www.vinipatria.it*) is another well-known producer with beautiful vineyards and cellars.

CATANIA **Markets** are open mornings only, 7.30–1. A large daily food market (antiques on Sun) is held in Piazza Carlo Alberto (*map 7*), called *'a Fera d'o Luni*, and a general market in the surrounding streets (including Via San Gaetano alle Grotte), now largely taken over by Chinese. In the streets to the southwest of Piazza Duomo and Via Garibaldi (including Via Gisira; *map 14*) there is another vast and colourful daily food market called *'A Pescheria*, where fresh fish, meat and other foodstuffs are sold.

Fecarotta (*Via Etnea 162; map 7*), for jewellery made with amber from the River Simeto. A good traditional pastry shop is **I Dolci di Nonna Vincenza** (*Piazza San Placido 7, www.dolcinonnavincenza.it; map 11*). They also have an outlet at Catania Airport and you can order online. **Mantegna** (*Via Etnea 350; map 2*), is a historic coffee-house which opened more than 100 years ago. **Scardaci** (*Via Santa Maddalena 84; map 10*) also has an excellent reputation; about midnight people start to line up here for fresh breakfast pastries, the famous *cornetti*. At **Sa di Sapone** (*Via Coppola 58, www.sadisapone.it; map 11*) you will find handmade soap and cosmetics with olive oil, local herbs, fruits and spices, and lava from Mt Etna.

GIARRE **Fabbrica Finocchiaro** (*Corso Italia 199/203*) is a historic Art Nouveau coffee-house and chocolate factory which opened in 1914.

LINGUAGLOSSA **Azienda Agricola Gambino** (*Contrada Petto Dragone, www.vinigambino.it*) is a high-altitude (800m) vineyard where you can taste wine. Their Cantari white, made with Nerello Mascalese grapes, is delightful, so is the red Alicante. Also good Etna Rosso and Bianco DOCs, both named Tifeo. Another good winery is **Vivera** (*www.vivera.it*).

MILITELLO VAL DI CATANIA **Snack Poker Bar** (*Via Umberto 97*) for Militello's celebrated pastries, the *cassatelline, infasciatelli, totò* and *'nzulli*. This is an address for those in the know; you would pass by this humble little bar otherwise. They have been making these pastries to their own secret recipes for generations.

MILO One of the oldest and most prestigious wineries of Etna is that of the **Barone di Villagrande** (*Via del Bosco 25, www.villagrande.it*), where the vineyards on the sunny eastern slopes have been carefully groomed since 1727 to produce award-winning DOCs, Etna Rosso and Etna Bianco Superiore.

PASSOPISCIARO This village is in the heart of the Etna Rosso district. **Antichi Vinai** (*Via Castiglione 49, www.antichivinai.it*) for very good local wines, all the Etna DOCs, and their own *spumante*. Their vineyards have been in the family for four generations, since

1877. You will find excellent award-winning Etna Rosso also at **Girolamo Russo**'s vineyards (*Via Regina Margherita 78, www.girolamorusso.it*) or **Graci** (*Contrada Arcuria, www.graci. eu*), who has vineyards at an altitude of 600, 1000 and 1100m, producing Etna Rosso and Bianco, and their own red Quota 600, using only Nerello Mascalese grapes.

PIEDIMONTE ETNEO Caffè Calì (*Via Vittorio Emanuele 19, www. pasticceriacaffecali.it*) is a historic coffee-house famous for *granita*, but also for the superb pastries; ask for their almond cake, *torta di mandorla*.

RANDAZZO Musumeci (*Piazza Santa Maria 5*), for *biscotti della nonna* (grandma's biscuits), *croccantini alla nocciola* (hazelnut crunchies), *paste di mandorla aromatizzate* (almond biscuits flavoured with lemon, orange or tangerine), and excellent pistachio cakes. They make prize-winning ice cream and *granita*: try lemon and basil, the two flavours go well together. **Arturo** (*Via Umberto 73*), is the historic coffee-house with a stunning Art Nouveau interior, for fragrant breakfast pastries with fresh ricotta.

SANTA VENERINA Russo (*Via Vittorio Emanuele 105, www.dolcirusso. it*), founded in 1880, for an excellent Sicilian breakfast of *granita*, *cornetti al miele* (honey pastries), or hot chocolate in winter. Traditional Sicilian pastries, on request packed in practical tins.

VIZZINI La Spiga D'Oro Terlato (*Via Roma 169*) is the best place for bread, biscuits, cakes and snacks; always crowded.

ZAFFERANA ETNEA is renowned for its crunchy paper-thin cookies made with hazelnuts, pistachios or almonds, called *foglie da té* (tea-leaves). You will find them at **Salemi** (*Via Eusebio Longo 30, www.dolceriasalemi.com*) or **Donna Peppina** (*Via Roma 220*).

FESTIVALS AND EVENTS

ACIREALE 20 Jan, colourful processions and fireworks for St Sebastian; the saint is rushed out of the church and down the steps into the crowds of worshippers. Later in the day he is slowly taken back (you will see people in tears as their saint leaves them for another year). Feb, Carnival, one of the most famous in Italy. (*T: 095 893134, www.carnevaleacireale.com*). 26 July, Feast of the patron St Venera, including the procession of the *candelore*, Baroque candlesticks up to 5m high, and a magnificent firework display.

ACITREZZA 24 June, *'U Pisci a Mari*, on the feast day of St John the Baptist, the fishermen enact a pantomime from their boats to ensure a good catch for the following year; the most agile swims around the boats pretending to be a swordfish, until someone 'catches' him and 'spears' him to death (*www. festasangiovanni.it*).

ADRANO Easter Sun, the *Diavolata*, in the main square, a play celebrating the victory of Christianity over the Devils. Great fun (*www.comune.adrano.ct.it*).

BRONTE Late Sept, *Expo del Pistacchio di Bronte DOP* (pistachio festival; *www. siciliainfesta.com*).

CALATABIANO 3rd weekend in May, Feast of St Philip of Syria (*San Filippo Siriaco*), when the statue of the saint is carried down a steep path from his church and then around the town; very exciting, because he has to race down at breakneck speed.

CALTAGIRONE Easter, Procession of the Dead Christ, followed on Easter Sunday afternoon with *'A Giunta,* when an enormous *papier-mâché* St Peter endeavours to contrive the meeting of the Madonna with her Son; the Santa Maria del Monte stairway is illuminated with coloured paper lamps, and there is a also a ceramics fair. Last week of May, Feast of the Madonna of Conadomini with a procession of Sicilian carts and decorated tractors, *'A Russedda,* to assure a good harvest. The Santa Maria del Monte stairway is completely decorated with vases of flowers, forming a design. 24–25 July, procession of San Giacomo (St James), when the stairway is again illuminated with paper lamps. Christmas–Epiphany, *La Città del Presepe*, exhibitions of terracotta Christmas cribs. Every 3rd Sun of the month in winter, *'a Truvatura* (the treasure hunt), with puppet shows, concerts and antiques fairs (*www. comune.caltagirone.ct.it*).

CATANIA 3–5 Feb and 17 Aug, the Feast of St Agatha (Sant'Agata) is celebrated with traditional processions and magnificent fireworks.

MILITELLO Last week in Aug, *Settimana del Barocco*, a celebration of Baroque art; second Sun in Oct, prickly pear festival.

MINEO Christmas, *Natale nei Vicoli,* a series of displays and tableaux in the streets of the old centre.

MOTTA SANT'ANASTASIA 23–25 Aug, fFeast of the patron St Anastasia, with much flag-tossing and fireworks, to celebrate the victory of Count Roger over the Saracens; also pageants in medieval costume to evoke the story of Queen Blanche of Navarre and her would-be lover, Count Bernardo Cabrera.

RADDUSA Mid-Sept, Festa del Grano, celebrating wheat, with parades of traditional wooden carts, Sicilian music and dancing, free tasting of bread and pasta (*www.festadelgrano.it*).

RAMACCA April, the town celebrates its famous artichokes, *violetto di Ramacca,* with opportunities for tasting them prepared in many different ways (*T: 335 1531605, www.carciofofest.it*).

RANDAZZO 15 Aug, Festival of the Madonna.

SANT'ALFIO 10 May, Feast of the patron saint, Alfio.

TRECASTAGNI Early May, feast of the three patron saints—*i tre casti agni*—Alfio, Cirino and Filadelfo, culminating on Sun closest to 10 May with parades and fireworks and Sicily's largest garlic market.

VIZZINI June, *Sagra della Ricotta*, celebrations in honour of the local sheep's milk ricotta (*www. sagradellaricotta.it*).

ZAFFERANA ETNEA Sundays in Oct, the *Ottobrata*, with local specialities (especially honey) sold in the square, and craftsmen demonstrating their skills along the main street.

Messina

Messina (*map p. 568, D2*), on the western shore of the Straits bearing its name, extends along the lowest slopes of the Peloritan Mountains above a splendid harbour, one of the deepest and safest in the Mediterranean. With its fine port and ideal position between Europe and Africa, the Straits of Gibraltar and the Bosphorus, Messina was long an important city, a key trading post from the Bronze Age until the discovery of America, and for some time afterwards. Today the port is always busy with ferries and hydrofoils travelling to and from the mainland; plans for a controversial bridge over the Straits have been shelved. The third largest city in Sicily, Messina was destroyed by an earthquake followed by a tsunami in 1908, when 84,000 people died out of a population of 120,000. It was soon rebuilt with broad streets planted with trees, and low buildings to minimise the danger from future tremors. The centre of Messina now combines sea, sky and hills in a pleasant, open townscape. The prevailing wind is the *maestrale*, which blows from the northwest, making it one of the breeziest places in Sicily.

The former province of Messina encompasses two meandering mountain ranges, the Peloritans and the Nebrodi; also here are the famous hilltop town of Taormina; the ancient sanctuary of the Black Madonna of Tindari; and the tiny UNESCO World Heritage Aeolian Islands, all of volcanic origin, yet each with its own particular character. In several towns where Queen Adelaide settled her Norman followers in the 1090s (San Fratello, Acquedolci, Novara di Sicilia) the people still use their Gallic dialect.

HISTORY OF MESSINA

Zancle, as Messina was called by the Greeks, in allusion to the sickle-shaped peninsula enclosing its harbour, was probably a settlement of the Sicels before being occupied by a colony from Chalcis. In 493 BC it was captured by Anaxilas, tyrant of Rhegium, and renamed Messana, in honour of his native country of Messenia in the Peloponnese. It took part in local wars against Syracuse and then against Athens, and was destroyed by the Carthaginian general Himilco. Rebuilt by Syracuse, it was occupied by the Campanian

VOS ET IPSAM CIVITATEM
BENEDICIMUS

MESSINA
View of the harbour entrance with the statue of the *Madonna della Lettera* (see p. 451).

mercenaries of Agathocles, who called themselves Mamertines. These obtained the alliance of Rome against the Carthaginians and Messina prospered with the fortunes of Rome. Under Byzantium, and later under the Arabs, the surrounding hills were planted with groves of mulberry trees to support the burgeoning silk industry, which brought fame and fortune until the late 19th century when business came to a standstill because of a parasite which attacked the silkworms.

Under the Normans the town was renowned for monastic learning and was important as a Crusader port. In September 1190 Richard Coeur de Lion and Philip Augustus of France arrived to spend the winter here before leaving for their Crusade in March 1191. Philip behaved politely, but Richard ensconced himself and his troops in the revered Basilian monastery of San Salvatore and proceeded to ransack the city in redress for perceived offences to his sister Joan, widow of William II. The Holy Roman Emperor Henry VI died of dysentery at Messina in 1197. After a successful resistance to Charles of Anjou in 1282, the city flourished until losing privileges for rebelling against Spanish misrule in 1674.

Much of the city's history has been disastrous: plague in 1743, an earthquake in 1783, naval bombardment in 1848, cholera in 1854 and another earthquake in 1894, culminating in the catastrophe of 1908, 7.24 on the Richter scale. The first shock, at 5.20 in the morning of 28th December, lasted only 37 seconds but destroyed almost the entire city, causing the shore to sink more than half a metre. The subsidence caused a violent tsunami which swept the coast, rising to a height of 8m, drowning many as they escaped from their ruined homes. A series of lesser shocks continued almost daily for two months. Reconstruction, though assisted by liberal contributions from all over the world, was by no means complete when the city was again devastated in 1943 by aerial bombardment. In 1955 a preliminary agreement to found the European Union (EU) was signed by 'the six' in Messina.

EXPLORING MESSINA

THE ORION FOUNTAIN

In the centre of the city, Piazza Duomo (*map 3–4*) was spaciously laid out in the 18th century. Beside the duomo is a free-standing bell-tower (1933) and in front of them, the Orion Fountain, the masterpiece of Giovanni Angelo Montorsoli (1553), described by Berenson as the most beautiful Renaissance fountain in Europe. In white marble and black lava stone, it was commissioned to celebrate the construction of an aqueduct from the nearby River Camaro, which made running water available to a large part of the city for the first time. Although the people had wanted Michelangelo to design the fountain, the commission went instead to his pupil, the friar Montorsoli, who enjoyed his stay in Messina enough to delay his return to Tuscany for more than ten years, and then only on the orders of the pope. The figures around the fountain represent the Nile, Tiber, Ebro and Camaro and are shown looking in the direction of their respective rivers. On the top is Orion, mythical founder of the city, with his faithful dog Sirius.

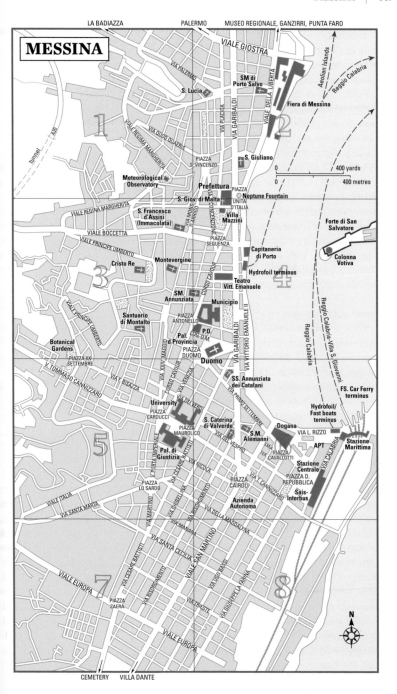

THE DUOMO

Despite successive reconstructions, the duomo (*map 4; open 7.30–12.30 & 4–8; T: 090 774895*) retains much of the appearance of the original medieval church. First built by Count Roger, the cathedral was one of the major Norman churches in Sicily. It was consecrated in 1197 in the presence of Emperor Henry VI and Queen Constance, and was first destroyed in 1254 by a fire which broke out during a funeral service for Conrad IV, son of Frederick II, because the mourners had lit too many candles. The new building was shattered by earthquakes in 1783 and 1908 and in 1943 was hit by an incendiary bomb aimed at the port. The fire raged for three days and many treasures were destroyed, including the mosaics and the frescoes, the royal tombs and choir stalls. Everything that could be salvaged was carefully replaced in the reconstructed church. A surviving column can be seen outside the building on the north side, with a carved fragment from the church on top, erected in 1958 as a monument to the 50th anniversary of the earthquake. The lower part of the façade preserves much of the original sculpted decoration, including panels in relief with *naif* farming scenes, and three fine doorways by 14th-, 15th- and 16th-century artists. The beautiful central doorway has a tympanum by Pietro da Bonitate (1468). On the south side is a doorway by Polidoro da Caravaggio, and a wall, still intact, with fine Catalan Gothic windows.

Interior of the duomo

The majestic basilican interior, in pink and grey tones, was well restored after the fire. The side altars (replicas of those made by Montorsoli), the columns (made of cement), the marble floor and the painted wooden roof are all copies of the originals. On the first south altar is a statue of St John the Baptist by Antonello Gagini (1525). At the end of the aisle is the so-called 'tomb of five archbishops' (14th century), with five Gothic trilobed arches. On the nave pillar in the transept is the fragmented Byzantine-style tomb slab of Archbishop Palmer (d. 1195).

From the south aisle is the entrance to the **treasury** (*open April–Oct Mon–Sat 9.30–1, Tues 9–3.30; Nov–March Mon–Sat 11–1*). Arranged in four rooms and on two floors, it is particularly rich in 17th- and 18th-century artefacts, including Church silver made in Messina. Among the most important pieces are a 10th-century lamp in rock crystal altered in 1250, and a very fine reliquary of the arm of St Martianus, commissioned by Richard Palmer (as the inscription states) when he was bishop of Syracuse. Brought with him when he became archbishop of Messina around 1182, it shows the influence of Islamic and Byzantine goldsmiths' art. The most precious piece in the treasury collection is the golden *manta*, used on important ceremonial occasions to cover the *Madonna della Lettera* (*see below*). It was made by a 17th-century Florentine goldsmith. Other works of particular interest include a 13th-century processional Cross, a large, brightly-coloured 17th-century silk embroidery, and a pair of silver candlesticks made in 1701.

Outside the south apse chapel, elaborately decorated in marble, is the damaged tomb of Archbishop De Tabiatis by Goro di Gregorio (1333). The high altar bears a copy of the venerated Byzantine ***Madonna della Lettera*** which was destroyed in 1943. The canopy, the stalls, and the bishop's throne have all been reconstructed and the mosaic n the central apse has been recomposed. In the north apse chapel is the only original mosaic to have survived *in situ* from the 14th century, showing the *Madonna and Child*. The monument to Bishop Angelo Paino (1870–1967), who rebuilt the cathedral after the last war, is to the left of the apse.

THE MADONNA OF THE LETTER

In front of the high altar of the duomo of Messina is a lower altar enclosing a silver frontal attributed to the local silversmith Francesco Juvarra (late 17th or early 18th century). It depicts the Madonna in the act of consigning a letter to the ambassadors of Messina after hearing of the citizens' conversion by St Paul. The dedication of the duomo dates to 1638 and the foundation of the 'Congregation of the Slaves of the Madonna of the Letter', whose seat was the crypt of the church. In fact, the Madonna has been protecting Messina since 3rd June 42, when delegates from the city received from her hand a letter bound with a lock of her hair. The text of the letter, written in Hebrew and giving Jerusalem as the address, is said to have been as follows: Humble servant of God, Mother of Christ crucified, of David's line, greets all the people of Messina. With the blessing of God, our Almighty Father, we see by your letter that all of you, with great faith, have sent us legates and ambassadors confessing that our Son, generated by God, is God and Man and that after his resurrection He rose to Heaven. And you have learned the path of Truth by means of the sermon of Paul, the Apostle Elect. Thanks to which, we bless you and your city, which we want to protect in perpetuity. The important words 'we bless you and your city' are inscribed (in Latin) on the base of the monument known as the Madonnina, which heralds the entrance to the harbour, greeting newcomers and bidding farewell to those who leave. The gilded bronze statue, by the local sculptor Tore Calabrò, was inaugurated by Pius XI on 3rd June 1934 directly from Castel Gandolfo, thanks to a device invented by Guglielmo Marconi. At the touch of a switch, the statue and the base were illuminated.

n the two transepts part of the organ can be seen, manufactured by Tamburini of Crema in 1948; with its 16,000 pipes and 127 registers it is the largest in Italy and one of the biggest in Europe. In the north transept the tomb effigy of Bishop Antonio La Lignamine is surrounded by twelve fine small panels of the *Passion* sculpted by the Gagini school. Nearby is a 17th-century bust of Archbishop Proto, and part of the tomb of Archbishop Bellorado by Giovanni Battista Mazzola (1513). In the north aisle, beside the doorway, is a 16th-century relief of *St Jerome* (the exterior of the 15th-century north doorway can be seen here).

The campanile

The campanile (*open April–Oct daily 9.30–1, Tues 9.30–3.30; Nov–March Sun 10.30–, last entry 30mins before closing*) was designed by Francesco Valenti to house a remarkable astronomical clock, the largest of its kind in the world, built by the Strasbourg firm of Josef Ungerer in 1933. At noon the chimes herald an elaborate and very noisy movement of mechanical figures (Dina and Clarenza, the 13th-century heroines who ring the bells, are 3m tall), representing episodes in the city's history, religious festivals, the phases of life and the days of the week, accompanied by the *Ave Maria*. On the right side of the tower are the quadrants showing the planetarium, the phases of the moon and a perpetual calendar.

SOUTH FROM PIAZZA DUOMO

South along Corso Cavour is the **University** (1927; *map 5*), whose library dates from the institution's foundation in 1548. It faces the Palazzo di Giustizia (1928) the monumental Neoclassical Law Courts building in ochre stone surmounted by a Roman chariot representing the victorious course of Justice.

Via I Settembre (a stone on the corner records the outbreak of the Sicilian revolt against the Bourbons in 1847) leads southeast from Piazza Duomo towards the railway station. It passes two Baroque corner fountains, which survived the earthquake, near (left) the church of **Santissima Annunziata dei Catalani** (*map 6; Via Garibaldi 111 open 9–12; T: 090 53874*), with its remarkable exterior, a 12th-century Norman church altered under the Swabians. The apse, transepts and cupola, with beautiful arcading date from the 12th century, while the three doors at the west end were added in the 13th century. The interior has a brick apse and dome in yellow and white stone, and tall dark grey columns with Corinthian capitals. The windows and nave arches are decorated with red and white stone. The large stoup is made up of two capitals. In Piazza Catalani is a statue of Don Juan of Austria by Andrea Calamech (1572), which was erected to celebrate the commander's victory over the Turks at Lepanto in 1571 On the morning after the battle, the general personally congratulated the wounded Miguel Cervantes on his devotion to duty.

Just off Via Garibaldi, the long broad thoroughfare which crosses Via I Settembre are the ruins of **Santa Maria degli Alemanni** (c. 1220), founded by the Teutonic Order of knights, damaged by the 1783 earthquake and since restored. It is one of the few Gothic churches in Sicily and is thought to have been built by German craftsmen hence the name 'Alemanni'. On the opposite side of the street, the church of **Santa Caterina di Valverde** contains a beautiful 16th-century painting of *Madonna dell'Itria between Sts Peter and Paul* by the local artist Antonello Riccio.

Via Garibaldi ends in **Piazza Cairoli**, the centre of the modern town and the most popular scene of the *passeggiata*. Thanks to its fountains and magnificent ficus trees it is always cool and shady.

VIALE SAN MARTINO

Viale San Martino (*map 7–8*), one of the main shopping streets, with the tram running through the middle, traverses an area of attractive Art Nouveau-style houses. The avenue itself is the most beautiful in Messina. It ends at the public gardens of **Villa Dante** beside the monumental cemetery, designed in 1872 by Leone Savoja. The luxuriant garden, built in terraces on the slopes of the hill, has a lovely view of Calabria The Famedio, or Pantheon, was damaged by the 1908 earthquake but almost all the smaller family tombs were left intact. In 1940 the British cemetery, founded during the Napoleonic wars, was transferred here (reached by a path on the extreme left side of the cemetery), when its original site near the harbour was needed for defence works

NORTH FROM PIAZZA DUOMO

A short way north of the duomo is the circular **Piazza Antonello** (*map 3*), dedicated to the famous local painter Antonello da Messina and laid out in 1914–29 with a group of monumental buildings: the Post Office (1915), the administrative seat of the province (1918); the Town Hall (1924; it faces Via Garibaldi); and an arcade (1929) with a café, offices and shops.

In **Via XXIV Maggio** (*map 3*) are the remains of the 18th-century Monte di Pietà (pawnshop), with a beautiful flight of steps, and the **church of Montevergine** with a lovely Baroque interior.

Via Garibaldi runs north–south, parallel to Corso Vittorio Emanuele and the waterfront, with a view of the busy harbour and the sickle-shaped tongue of land protecting it that ends at the Forte di San Salvatore, erected by the Spanish in 1546. On the point of the sickle, at the entrance to the port, can be seen the **Colonna Votiva** (*map 4*), a white pillar topped by a 7m golden statue of the Madonna, patroness of Messina (*see p. 451*).

The opera house, **Teatro Vittorio Emanuele** (*map 4; T: 090 896 6215, www. teatrodimessina.it*), on Via Garibaldi, built in 1842, was re-opened in 1985 after repairs; strangely, the earthquake had spared the perimeter walls and only the interior was ruined.

The two parallel streets passing a statue of Ferdinand II, end in Piazza Unità d'Italia, with the **Neptune Fountain** by Montorsoli (*map 2*; 1557; the figures of Neptune and Scylla are 19th-century copies, the originals being kept in the Museo Regionale). Behind is the huge 1920s Prefettura and nearby the little church of **San Giovanni di Malta** (c. 1590; Camillo Camilliani). Here, in the Cappella Palatina, an exhibition of sacred art has been arranged (*open 9.30–5.30; closed Sun and holidays*), displaying embroidered silk vestments, Church silver and paintings. Also facing the piazza is Palazzo Carrozza, built in the 1930s in an eclectic style. There is a garden with pines and ficus trees facing the waterfront and, behind, the public gardens of **Villa Mazzini**, with beautiful trees.

Viale Boccetta, which was a watercourse before the earthquake, leads inland from Piazza Sequenza on Via Cavour to the church of San Francesco d'Assisi, better known by the inhabitants as the **Immacolata** (*map 3*). Built in 1252, with a large convent in Sicilian-Gothic style, it stood outside the city walls, as was usual with Franciscan foundations. The church can be identified in some of Antonello da Messina's works, as can the Straits of Messina, which often appear in the background.

ALONG THE NORTHERN WATERFRONT

Viale della Libertà (*map 2*), which follows the shore in full view of the Calabrian coastline, passes the *passeggiata a mare*, opposite which is the church of **San Giuliano**, with red domes in eclectic style.

The road runs along the coast passing the church of **Gesù e Maria del Buonviaggio**, known as the church of Ringo (an old fishing village close by). Built in 1598 and dedicated to seamen, its façade is adorned with a fine portal, Corinthian capitals and two niches with statues of Christ and Mary: both statues have one hand pierced to hold oil lamps to guide passing boats. From here, Viale della Libertà leads to the Museo Regionale (c. 3km from Piazza Duomo; *described below*).

MUSEO REGIONALE

Housed in an old silk mill since the 1908 earthquake, the important Museo Regionale (*beyond map 2; open Tues–Sat 9–7, Sun and holidays 9–1, last tickets 30mins before closing; T: 090 361292*) was at the time of writing in the process of moving into a new purpose-built construction next door, on three floors, thus allowing much more space for the exhibits; the old museum will be used for exhibitions.

The large painted wooden Crucifix (Spanish, early 15th century) portraying a *Christus Dolens* close to Renaissance style, was found on a donkey-cart after the 1908 earthquake and the church it came from is still unknown. Some splendid paintings by **Antonello da Messina** and his school, together with Flemish and Spanish artists represent the late 15th century. A remarkable work is the luminous polyptych of the *Madonna with Sts Gregory and Benedict* (oil on panel), an ideal synthesis of Flemish and Italian Renaissance styles, painted by Antonello in 1473 and bearing his signature. Painted for the monastery of St Gregory and much damaged in the earthquake, it has since been restored. Also here is a recent acquisition, a tiny panel by Antonello painted on both sides, and among other works, a striking *Pietà and Symbols of the Passion* by an unknown Flemish painter.

The early 16th century is represented by Girolamo Alibrandi, a native artist who admired the work of Leonardo and Raphael, whose influence can be seen in the two panel paintings of the *Circumcision* and the *Presentation in the Temple* (1519); this latter work is considered his finest. Recovered after the earthquake in more than 300 fragments, it has been extensively restored. The *Adoration of the Shepherds* (1533) by Polidoro da Caravaggio also shows the influence of Raphael, with whom Polidoro studied. Works of the 16th–17th centuries follow, in the Sicilian Mannerist style.

The highlights of the museum are **two masterpieces by Caravaggio**, both dramatic late works painted during his stay in Messina in 1608–9: the *Nativity* (commissioned by the Senate of Messina for the Capuchin church) and the *Raising of Lazarus* commissioned by the De Lazzari family for their private chapel in the church of San Camillo (demolished in 1880 and rebuilt on Viale Principe Umberto).

CRISTO RE AND THE BOTANICAL GARDENS

On the slopes of the hillside above the town stands the church of **Cristo Re** (Christ the King, 1939; *map 3*), which dominates the city with its huge dome. It was designed to be a collective memorial to the victims of the 1908 earthquake and all those killed in war. To one side stands an old tower called the Torre Guelfonia (part of the old city fortifications) with a great bell (diameter 3m) made from the melted-down enemy guns of the First World War. The interior of the church is richly decorated with fine marble and stuccoes; in the crypt is a sarcophagus on which lies the symbolic marble image of a soldier.

From here Viale Principe Umberto runs south, passing Torre Vittoria and the ruins of the 16th-century Spanish walls, and the striking **Santuario di Montalto** (rebuilt in

930; *map 3*). Its twin bell-towers are a city landmark. The lush **Botanical Gardens** are in Piazza XX Settembre (*map 3–5; open Mon–Fri 8–12; T: 090 391940, www. ortobotanico.messina.it*).

OUTSKIRTS OF MESSINA: PUNTA FARO AND LA BADIAZZA

Punta Faro at Cape Peloro (14km north; *beyond map 2*), the extreme northeastern tip of the island and the nearest point to Calabria, can be reached by the old road lined with a modest row of houses along the seafront, which traverses the ambitiously-named suburbs of Paradiso, Contemplazione, Pace (and Sant'Agata). It is at the mouth of the Straits of Messina, the *Fretum Siculum* of the Romans. This is the site of the legendary whirlpools called Scylla and Charybdis, greatly feared by sailors in ancient times. The name of Cape Peloro recalls Pelorus, Hannibal's navigator, who was unjustly condemned to be thrown into the sea for misleading the fleet. Further south the Calabrian coast is sometimes, in certain weather conditions, strangely magnified and distorted by a **Fata Morgana mirage**, a phenomenon anciently attributed to King Arthur's half-sister, Morgan le Fay, whose enchanted city of Avalon appears to float on the water in the middle of the Straits.

Just short of the cape is the fishing village of **Ganzirri**, on two little lagoons (Pantano Grande and Pantano Piccolo), separated from the sea by a dune barrier and fed by artesian water. It is famous for mussels and other shellfish.

The twin pylons, over 150m high, at **Punta Faro** (*map p. 568, D1–D2*) are an impressive landmark, standing at the proposed site of the contested bridge between Sicily and the mainland. Sword-fishing has taken place off the coast here since ancient times; it was for many years considered one of the sights of Messina. The traditional method of harpooning the fish from characteristic small boats (*luntri*) with tall look-out masts, is still carried out, but most fishermen nowadays use modern equipment and motor-boats called *felucche*.

WEST TO THE BADIAZZA AND THE PELORITAN MOUNTAINS

The road is well signposted from the centre of Messina (Colle San Rizzo, Portella Castanea, Santa Maria Dinnamare and Badiazza). Off the SS 113, a very poor road on the river bed (almost impassable in places) leads right (signposted) past Sant'Andrea, a little church built in 1929, and poor houses to the head of the valley. Here, in a group of pine trees, is **La Badiazza** (also called Santa Maria della Scala or Santa Maria della Valle; *map p. 568, D2*). This fine 13th-century church (*although recently restored, it is officially closed*) belonged to a ruined fortified Cistercian convent and has an interesting exterior with lava-stone decoration.

The main road continues uphill to enter all that remains of the forest which once covered these slopes of the Peloritan Mountains. Thick pinewoods survive here. The road sign indicating Palermo (250km) is a reminder that this was the main road to the capital before the motorway was built. At **Colle San Rizzo** (460m) is a crossroads. From here a spectacular road (signposted 'Santuario di Maria Santissima di Dinnamare') leads for 9km along the crest of the Peloritan range to a height of 1130m.

The first stretch is extremely narrow and dangerous but further on the road improves. The views on either side are breathtaking: on the right Milazzo can be seen and on the left the toe of Italy. The church of **Maria Santissima di Dinnamare**, built in the 18th century, was rebuilt in 1899. The superb panorama, one of the most exceptional in Italy, takes in the whole of Calabria, the port of Messina and the tip of Punta Faro. On the other side the Aeolian Islands, including Stromboli (beyond Milazzo), and Mount Etna, can be seen.

From the Colle San Rizzo crossroads the road signposted to Castanea leads through fine pinewoods, with wide views down over the port of Messina to the right, and to the left the Aeolian Islands and the motorway snaking through the hills. In spring Mt Ciccia (609m) is on the migratory route from Africa to central Europe for thousands of birds of prey, especially honey buzzards.

A winding road leads to the village of **Castanea delle Furie** (*map p. 568, D2*). Castanea, despite its menacing name, has a typical medieval town plan and some lovely old churches. The road continues down to Spartà past olives and pines. As the road nears the sea there is a wonderful view of Stromboli.

TAORMINA & ENVIRONS

Taormina (204m; *map p. 568, C3*) is renowned for its magnificent position above the sea on a spur of Mt Taurus (so-called for its resemblance to a bull when seen from the south), commanding a celebrated view of Etna. Being a particularly deep and solid wedge of limestone, Mt Taurus is not subject to earthquakes, thus preserving the medieval buildings of the little town. With a delightful winter climate, it became a fashionable international resort at the end of the 19th century, and during the 20th century was the most famous holiday destination on the island. The small town, with its elegant Corso off which lead intriguing little stepped streets, is now virtually given over to tourism and can be very crowded from Easter to September. Many of the villas and hotels, built in mock Gothic or eclectic styles at the beginning of the 20th century, are surrounded with verdant gardens. Too much building has been allowed on the hillsides of Taormina in recent years, although the medieval churches and palaces, the tiny streets and Roman remains, have lost none of their magic.

There are two large car parks, one close to the south gate, Porta Catania. The other, called Lumbi, is convenient for Porta Messina, the north gate. Both, thanks to a tunnel which goes through the mountain, are easily accessible from the motorway exit.

HISTORY OF TAORMINA

Andromachos, father of the historian Timaeus, officially founded this as a new city in 358 BC, to be known as *Tauromenion*, for the refugees of Naxos, whose town on the coast below had been destroyed by Dionysius of Syracuse in 403 BC. It was favoured by Rome during the early days of occupation and suffered in the First Servile War (134–132) when the castle was held by slaves for several months, but forfeited its rights as an allied city (now called *Tauromenium*) by taking sides with Sextus Pompey against Octavian. In 902 it was the last Christian centre to fall to the Arabs but this did not save it from being attacked by the Tunisian Caliph al-Muez in 965, when the theatre (which was by then a city district) was destroyed. The caliph, who later founded modern Cairo, rebuilt the town, modestly renaming it Almoezia, which name it retained until Count Roger conquered it in 1078. Here the Sicilian Parliament assembled in 1410 to choose a king on the extinction of the line of Peter of Aragon.

Taormina was visited and described by numerous travellers through the centuries, and the famous view of Etna from the theatre was painted countless times. John Dryden came here in 1701. John Henry (later Cardinal) Newman stayed in the town as a young man in 1833. In 1847 Edward Lear spent four or five days in what he described as 'Taormina the Magnificent'. Sibelius, Wagner and Brahms all found inspiration here. Taormina was first connected to Messina by railway in 1866 and a year later the line to Catania was inaugurated. In 1864 the first hotel, the Timeo, was opened in the town, and it became internationally known as a winter resort soon after the first visit of the Kaiser (Wilhelm II) in 1896. The Kaiser returned in 1904 and 1905 with a large retinue, and set the fashion for royal visitors, some of whom came here incognito, using false names. In 1906 Edward VII wintered at the San Domenico Hotel and George V made a private visit in 1924. Before the First World War the town had a considerable Anglo-American, German and Scandinavian colony, including the impoverished Baron Wilhelm von Gloeden (1896–1931), who opened a photographic studio specialising in mildly erotic child portraits; his atelier became one of the sights of the town. The painter Robert Kitson built a villa for himself here, where he lived from 1905 onwards. Kitson was concerned about the poverty of the local inhabitants and encouraged Mabel Hill, another English resident, to set up a lace-making school. The Scottish writer Robert Hitchens arrived by car in Taormina in the winter of 1910, the first time a car had reached the town. D.H. Lawrence and his wife Frieda lived here from 1920–3; local tradition asserts that her amorous encounter with a young peasant during a heavy rainstorm provided the inspiration for *Lady Chatterley's Lover* (though many other people and places claim the same distinction).

The town attracted the attention of Allied aircraft in July 1943, when it temporarily became Field-Marshal Kesselring's headquarters. In the '50s and '60s, King Gustav of Sweden regularly spent a winter month in Taormina, delighting in the climate and indulging his passion for archaeology. But what saved Taormina from the post-war economic crisis was its re-invention as a bathing resort, and above all, in 1954, the institution of the June film festival. Famous visitors in this period include Truman Capote—who wrote *Breakfast at Tiffany's* while here—Cecil Beaton, Jean Cocteau, Osbert Sitwell, Salvador Dalí, Winston Churchill, Sibelius, Orson Welles, John Steinbeck, Tennessee Williams, Rita Hayworth, Marlene Dietrich, Greta Garbo and Cary Grant. Elizabeth Taylor and Richard Burton spent at least part of both of their honeymoons in Taormina.

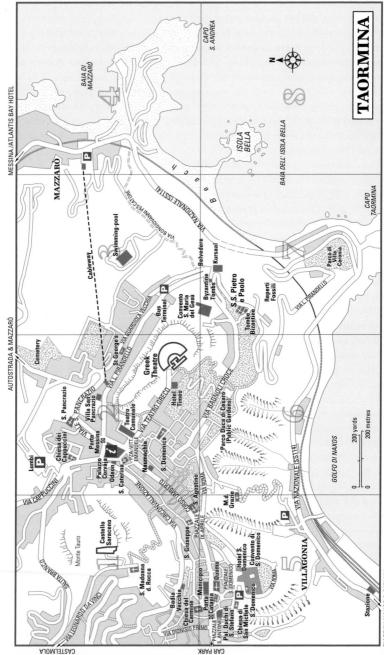

TAORMINA

EXPLORING TAORMINA

The main street, Corso Umberto, runs south–north from Porta Catania to Porta Messina, connecting three squares, Piazza Duomo, Piazza IX Aprile and Piazza Vittorio Emanuele. Side streets lead to the Greek Theatre and to the public gardens, and steps and a road go up to the Saracen Fort, the church of the Madonna della Rocca, and Castelmola.

PORTA CATANIA

Porta Catania or Porta del Tocco (1440; *map 5*) has the Aragon family emblem on the outside. The Jewish Ghetto was located by the walls here (Jews were forced to leave Sicily and all the Spanish possessions in 1492), with narrow alleys and the interesting old **Palazzo Duchi di Santo Stefano** (*open summer 9.30–12.30 & 4.30–7.30, winter 9.30–12.30 & 3–6; T: 0942 620129*). Built in the 14th–15th centuries, the palace formed part of the second ring of city walls, and with its decorative stonework in contrasting colours of black and white, is a masterpiece of Sicilian Gothic architecture. The garden and upper floors have a permanent display of works by the sculptor Giuseppe Mazzullo, born in Graniti, a village near Taormina, while the lower floor (with four cross-vaults) is used for exhibitions and civil-rite weddings. South of the gate, the little 14th-century **church of Sant'Antonio** (Gothic portal) was damaged in an air raid in 1943. The church contains a crib made in 1953, which is modelled on the town. To the left of the gate, in Piazza San Francesco di Paola, reached from Via Dionisio Primo (*map 1*), stands the old church of St Francis of Paola, which now houses the **Museo Siciliano di Arte e Tradizioni Popolari** (*open 4–8*), a collection donated by local antique dealer and antiquarian Giovanni Panarello, offering a synthesis of Sicilian handicrafts from the 16th–20th centuries. In the first section are pieces of decorated Sicilian carts, puppets, and puppet-show posters, along with a section dedicated to shepherding in the Peloritan Mountains and Calabria: items made of wood and horn (collars for cows and sheep, spoons, bowls, flasks, kegs, walking-sticks and spindles). Engraved with geometric and fertility symbols, the decorations were also the proud stamp of property. The collars of animals never went with their sale. The spindles are usually decorated with a female figure. These, and decorated whalebones for corsets, were love-tokens from the shepherds to their women. There is also a good collection of anthropomorphic pottery from Caltagirone, Collesano, Patti and Seminara (Calabria), especially cache-pots representing human faces. In the second section is a collection of traditional Christmas cribs made of ivory, coral and mother of pearl. At the time of writing the prolonged closure of the Museo Badia Vecchia archaeological museum had led to some of archaeological finds being temporarily exhibited here. Principally Roman sculpture and fragmentary wall frescoes, they give a small but interesting insight into the wealth of the ancient city.

THE DUOMO AND DISTRICT

At the south end of Corso Umberto, close to Porta Catania, is the attractive square facing the **duomo** (St Nicholas of Bari; *open summer 8.30–7, winter 8.30–6; map 5*), founded in the 13th century, with battlements and two lovely side-portals (15th and 16th century). The façade has a late rose window and portal of 1636. The interior has six monolithic antique pink marble columns. In the south aisle is a painting of the *Visitation* by Antonino Giuffrè (1463) and a polyptych, some say the work of Antonello da Messina, others say by Antonello de Saliba (1504), from the former church of San Giovanni. In the chapel at the end of the aisle is a delicate tabernacle dated 1648 and an early 16th-century *Madonna and Child* in marble. On the first north altar is a 16th-century panel painting of the *Madonna Enthroned with Saints*, on the second, a 16th-century statue of *St Agatha* and on the third, an *Adoration of the Magi*.

In the piazza is a charming **fountain** of 1635, a symbol of Taormina. The bizarre figure on the top would appear to be the bust of an angel on the body of a bull (adapted here as a pregnant female centaur with only two legs). Said to have been found in the ruins of the Greek theatre, it is probably a Baroque pastiche.

From Piazza Duomo steps ascend past a small black-and-white Roman mosaic (right; within an enclosure) and (left) the rebuilt church of the **Carmine** (*map 1*) with a pretty campanile. More steps lead up to (left) the Porta Cuseni (or Saraceni), the name given to the district just outside the walls. Outside the gate steps (the Salita Castelmola) continue up to Via Dionisio I which leads right to the **Badia Vecchia**, with its large crenellated tower with fine mullioned windows and black and white intarsias. From here Via Leonardo da Vinci leads past a wall in front of cypresses, bougainvillea and plumbago to **Casa Cuseni** (no. 7; *garden open daily 9–sunset, house open 11.30–1; booking necessary for both; T: 0942 28222, www.casacuseni.com*). The villa (which now styles itself Museo del Grand Tour) was built by the painter Robert Kitson in 1907. You can admire his work on the walls of the dining room, painted in *trompe l'oeil*. It later became a *pensione*, run by his niece, Daphne Phelps, author of *A House in Sicily*. She had some eccentric guests, including Truman Capote, Roald Dahl and Bertrand Russell. Today the guest rooms are named after famous former tenants.

On the opposite side of Piazza Duomo, a street descends to the **Hotel San Domenico** (an ex-convent, first opened as a hotel in 1894), which has a late 16th-century cloister. Field-Marshal Kesselring set up his headquarters here in July 1943, and many of his staff were killed by an Allied air raid which destroyed the church.

ALONG CORSO UMBERTO

Corso Umberto is lined with shops and boutiques. The buildings have medieval doorways and flower-filled balconies, and stepped alleyways lead off the street. Facing the west wall of the cathedral is the pink 18th-century **Municipio** with its Star of David, perhaps on the site of a Jewish merchant's house. This south stretch of the Corso, called Borgo Medioevale, is lined with small medieval palaces, where Arab influences seem to linger among the 15th-century Catalan Gothic details. Near no. 209 a wide flight of steps leads up to **Palazzo Ciampoli** (1412). At no. 185 is the former church of **San Giovanni** (1533), which is now a club for war veterans and is full of trophies and photographs. The glorious old **Hotel Metropol** at no.154 has two columns from the Roman theatre.

Halfway along its length, Corso Umberto passes through the **Clock Tower** (?12th century, using blocks of stone cut by the Greeks; notice the beautiful modern mosaic of the Madonna; the gate was restored (1679) and opens into **Piazza IX Aprile** (often called Piazza Panoramica; *map 1–5*), where there is a superb view south across to the sea and Etna. The date refers to 9th April 1860, when the people of Taormina rebelled against the authority of the Bourbons during the Risorgimento; they were among the first in Sicily to do so. Several cafés here have tables outside, including the Mocambo, once one of the most celebrated in the town, once notorious for scandalous brawls and assignations among the rich and famous and now with a mildly decadent atmosphere. Churchill's favourite was the Wunderbar.

On the north side is the former church of **Sant'Agostino** (1448), now the public library, with a Gothic doorway, and to the west, approached by a pretty flight of steps, stands the 17th-century church of **San Giuseppe**, with a heavily decorated Rococo stucco interior, much in demand for fashionable weddings and often used as a film set. Eight paintings of scenes from the life of the Virgin (*Nativity of Christ, Visitation, Annunciation, Marriage of the Virgin, Assumption, Rest on the Flight into Egypt, Presentation in the Temple* and *Adoration of the Magi*), painted for this church by an unknown Flemish artist in the late 17th century, have recently been returned after careful restoration. In many of the scenes the city of Taormina appears in the background, seen from several viewpoints. Steps to the left of the church lead up to the Castello Saraceno (*see p. 463*) and Castelmola (*see p. 466*).

Between nos. 133 and 135 is **Vicolo Stretto**, only 52cm wide, one of the narrowest streets in Italy. Near no. 100, steps (Via Naumachia) lead down to the so-called **Naumachia**, a long brick wall (122m) with niches (formerly decorated with statues) standing on a stone stylobate. The stylobate belongs to a portico or stoa of the late Hellenistic period, which would have overlooked a gymnasium or lower agora. The brick wall and niches date to the late Roman period, when it was converted into a nymphaeum. Behind it is a huge cistern (*no admission*). Corso Umberto, after passing at no. 42 the pretty doorway and tiny rose window of the deconsecrated church of Santa Maria del Piliere, reaches Piazza Vittorio Emanuele.

PIAZZA VITTORIO EMANUELE

Often called Piazza Badia, and the site of the ancient agora and the Roman forum, Piazza Vittorio Emanuele (*map 2*) is now a popular meeting-place, with shady *Ficus benjamin* trees and a taxi-stand. The two coffee-bars are ideal for people-watching and good for breakfast, ice cream, hot chocolate or aperitifs. The Shaker Bar was the favourite of Tennessee Williams, who was in the habit of ordering a glass of whisky which he replenished from a hip flask filled at a cheap wine store in the back streets, and sitting for hours here, reading or talking.

The west side of the square is occupied by **Palazzo Corvaja** (early 15th century; the central tower is a 10th-century Arab structure), with mullioned windows and a 15th-century side portal in Catalan Gothic form. The limestone ornamentation with black lava-stone inlay is characteristic of Taormina. Inside the courtyard is a staircase with a very worn relief of *Adam and Eve*. The building houses the tourist information office, where you will find a collection of authentic 19th-century marionettes and two

Sicilian carts. The great hall on the first floor, meeting-place in 1410 of the Sicilian Parliament, is now used for art exhibitions.

The 17th-century church of **Santa Caterina** has three large white stucco Baroque altars and a panel painting on the high altar of the *Martyrdom of St Catherine* (16th century) by the native artist Jacopo Vignerio. In the floor of the nave, parts of a Hellenistic building have been revealed. A lovely 15th-century marble statue of St Catherine stands on a plinth with stories of her life and martyrdom. Behind the church are the scant remains of the **Odeon** or Teatrino Romano, incorporating part of the preceding Hellenistic structure. Built in the 1st century AD, it could hold 200 people. Excavations nearby have revealed public baths of the Imperial Roman period and traces of the forum.

THE GREEK THEATRE

From Piazza Vittorio Emanuele, Via Teatro Greco leads east past the congress hall and (on the right) **Villa Papale** (no. 41), once Palazzo Cacciola and the residence of Florence Trevelyan (*see below*). The street ends at a group of cypresses covered with bougainvillea beside the historic **Hotel Timeo**, with a pergola, the first hotel to be opened in the town in 1864. In 1850 the painter W.H. Bartlett had complained that 'anywhere but in Sicily a place like Taormina would be a fortune to the innkeepers, but here is not a single place where a traveller can linger to explore the spot'. Illustrious guests of the hotel have included Kaiser Wilhelm, King George V, Winston Churchill, the writers Thomas Mann, Oscar Wilde, Somerset Maugham, André Gide and Tennessee Williams (who wrote *A Streetcar named Desire* and *Cat on a Hot Tin Roof* here), Rudolph Nureyev, Bob Dylan and Elton John.

Here is the entrance to the magnificent **Greek Theatre** (*map 2; open 9–1hr before sunset; T: 0942 23220 or 0942 51001*), famous for its panoramic position and acclaimed for its acoustics. First erected in the Hellenistic period (4th century BC), it was almost entirely rebuilt under the Romans when it was considerably altered (1st–3rd centuries AD). This is the largest ancient theatre in Sicily after that of Syracuse (109m in diameter; orchestra 35m across). The cavea, as was usual, was dug out of the hillside; above the nine wedge-shaped blocks of seats, a portico (partially restored in 1955) ran around the top (a few stumps of the 45 columns in front survive). The scena is well preserved; it must have had a double order of columns, the four now visible were erected during restoration carried out in the 19th century. The outer brick wall is pierced by three arched gates; the inner wall was once cased with marble. The foundations of the proscenium, or stage, remain, together with the parascenia, or wings, and traces of porticoes at the back. The superb view from the top of the cavea inspired Gustav Klimt, Paul Klee and many other artists, including the Hungarian colorist Tivadar Csontváry. Goethe, visiting in 1787, exclaimed: 'Never did any audience, in any theatre, have before it such a spectacle!' On a clear day Etna is seen at its most majestic. In the other direction the Aspromonte Mountains of Calabria extend to the northern horizon, and inland the Peloritans stretch behind Castelmola. A small building at the southeastern end of the top of the cavea, the 'Casina degli Inglesi', now serves as the antiquarium for the site. The first room hosts temporary art exhibitions and a Roman mosaic, while the second contains 20 Greek and Latin inscriptions from Taormina (embedded in the walls so that only their inscribed surfaces are visible) and two statue heads, one of which was found in the orchestra of the theatre, one of which is presumed to have come from there. The inscriptions, sadly untranslated on the accompanying information panels, contain an enormous amount of detailed information about the finances and political institutions of the city.

THE PUBLIC GARDENS

By continuing down the steps after the Naumachia, you reach Via Bagnoli Croce and the beautiful public gardens, Parco Duca di Cesarò, among the loveliest in Italy (*map 6; open summer 8–midnight, winter 8–sunset*). The gardens are colourful at all times of the year, with many different varieties of flowering plants and a vast array of Mediterranean and exotic trees. They were created in 1899 by Florence Trevelyan Cacciola (1852–1907), whose bust (a copy of her funerary monument) has been placed just inside the main entrance on Via Bagnoli Croce. The daughter of Lord Edward Spencer Trevelyan (cousin of the historian), Florence was lady-in-waiting to Queen Victoria but she fell from favour and came to Taormina in 1881 with her four dogs, married the wealthy local doctor Salvatore Cacciola in 1890, and dedicated herself to charitable works among the poor of the town and to her favourite hobbies: landscape gardening and birdwatching. In the heart of the garden, near her monument, is a group of mock Renaissance ruins, delightful Victorian follies which were used by Lady Florence as bird-feeders, with a maze of wooden terraces, antique fragments and lava-stone decoration. In Florence Trevelyan's day the gardens were known, after this construction, as 'The Beehives'. Outside the west entrance, a narrow road with steps descends to the Monte Tauro Hotel past a plaque which records the work of Mabel Hill (*see p. 457*).

MADONNA DELLA ROCCA AND THE CASTELLO SARACENO

Above the town, from the Circonvallazione, a path (signposted) leads up through trees to the tiny church of the **Madonna della Rocca** (*map 1*), carved into the rock. The Crucifix in front of it, which dominates all Taormina, was erected in 1743 by the grateful population when an epidemic of plague passed them by. Here, at a height of 398m, is the so-called **Castello Saraceno** (*closed*), from which there are wonderful views. The castle stands on the remains of the Greek acropolis and shows signs of construction dating from Byzantine, Arab, Norman and Spanish times; forming part of a defensive system completed by the castles of Castelmola and Calatabiano, it was never captured by the enemy, although rebellious slaves held it for several months during the First Servile War, enduring a Roman siege so harsh that they were reduced to cannibalism before being deceived into surrender. The slaves (some say 6,000) were tortured and thrown from the cliffs. The return can be made by the 738 steps that link the serpentine loops of the Castelmola road.

OUTSIDE THE CENTRE AND DOWN TO MAZZARÒ

Outside Porta Messina, at the lower end of a busy, downward-sloping square, by the beautiful Ashbee Hotel, is the church of **San Pancrazio** (*map 2*) dedicated to the patron saint of Taormina and built on the ruins of a 4th-century BC Greek temple to Isis, Zeus and Serapis, still partly visible; the remains of Roman houses can be seen in the middle of the square. Continuing downhill, you reach the Lumbi car park and then the motorway entrance and the beach of Spisone. By turning right on exiting Porta Messina you are on the old Via Pirandello, which winds down the hill past lovely gardens to Cape Taormina. You soon reach on the left the glass cableway station, and then, again on the left, (no. 24), surrounded by a little garden, the Anglican **St George's church**, built by the British community in 1922, with lava-stone decoration on the exterior. It contains British and American funerary monuments and memorials to the victims of the two World Wars. Now on the right you will find the bus terminal. Via Pirandello proceeds down by a little belvedere with a fine view of Isola Bella and Mazzarò, and then a series of **Byzantine tomb-recesses** in the wall below the former convent of Santa Caterina, and the attractive 1920s Villa Carlotta Hotel. It then passes the tiny 15th-century church of Santi Pietro e Paolo (*open only for services*) and the ruins of the unfinished Kursaal. On the right-hand side of the road, by a sharp bend at no. 107, is the entrance to **Villa Caronia** (*map 7; open Tues–Sat 9.30–1.30; T: 0942 52579*), known locally as the 'Casa Rossa' because of the presumed Russian origin of its owner, Baron Karl Stempel (1862-1951), who was in fact German. The splendid Mediterranean garden created by the baron, with its frangipani trees, is now open to the public. It was a lodestone for the foreign colony at the turn of the last century, when it was considered the ideal point for sketching the bay and Mt Etna. The garden borders that of Villa Falconara, built for Alexander Nelson Hood, Viscount Bridport and Duke of Bronte. By turning left on arriving at Capo Taormina, you reach the beach of Mazzarò at the bottom of the cableway.

MAZZARÒ

The fishing village of Mazzarò (*map 4*) by Capo Sant'Andrea (St Andrew is patron saint of fishermen), with its sandy beach, is well supplied with hotels. A narrow isthmus leads to **Isola Bella** (*map 8; open Tues–Sun 9–1hr before sunset; NB: you might have to wade to reach the island, which is inaccessible in bad weather; only 15 visitors at a time are allowed*), of great natural beauty, a famous symbol of Taormina and now an open-air museum. In the 19th century the government sold the island to Florence Trevelyan for 5,000 lire. She built a house on it and later it came into the hands of the Bosurgi family, and was finally acquired by the Sicilian region in 1987. The whole bay enjoys protected status as a nature reserve. To the south are the sheer limestone cliffs of **Capo Taormina**, where 35 Roman columns lie submerged: they are unworked quarried stone, probably destined for a temple or the portico of a villa, which must have been lost in a shipwreck. This point is the wide part of the funnel formed by the straits; the toe of the boot of Italy is 17 kilometres away. The beautiful cove just inside the promontory, at the foot of the northern slopes of the mountain of Taormina, looking out over the Straits of Messina, is the fashionable little **Spisone beach**, with white sand and turquoise water, the most exclusive place for bathing.

GIARDINI NAXOS

Four kilometres south of Cape Taormina, Giardini Naxos (*map p. 568, C3*) was founded by a group of settlers led by Theocles of Naxos in 734 BC, and was the first Greek colony on Sicily, closely followed by Syracuse and Leontinoi. It flourished, thanks to the strategic position dominating the straits. In 403 BC Dionysius of Syracuse had to suppress a revolt in his city. After restoring order, he pronounced himself *archon* (monarch) of eastern Sicily, and moving with a huge army of mercenaries, he proceeded to destroy the Chalcidian colonies thought to be hostile to his rule, starting with Naxos. According to Diodorus Siculus, most of the inhabitants were sold into slavery. Some trickled up to the Sicel village on the top of the hill, while others moved inland and founded an important settlement at Francavilla di Sicilia. In the Middle Ages it became a town of fishermen and lemon-growers (*giardini* means citrus groves in Sicilian). From this bay, Garibaldi, with two steamboats and 4,200 men, set out on his victorious campaign against the 30,000 Bourbon troops on the Aspromonte in Calabria (19th August 1860). This place, with a long main street parallel to the sea, was developed in the 1960s into a holiday resort. The wide bay is now lined with hotels, apartments and restaurants from Cape Schisò as far as the railway station of Taormina-Giardini, and new buildings have been erected wherever possible. The point of Cape Schisò, where the Greeks presumably made their landfall, was formed by an ancient lava flow which can still be clearly seen at the water's edge, by the harbour. From the seafront there is a view of Monte Tauro, with Taormina and Castelmola, and south, a splendid view of Mount Etna. Overlooking the bay and built on the lava flow, is the ponderous grey mass of the **Castello di Schisò** (*www.castellodischiso.it*), planned to be open to the public. Built in the 13th century to protect the bay from pirate attacks, it was rebuilt by the Spanish in the 16th century to incorporate a sugar refinery, and modified in later centuries to make it more suitable as a dwelling for the local baron.

MUSEO ARCHEOLOGICO

By the modern harbour wall is the entrance to the excavations of Naxos and the Museo Archeologico (*site and museum open daily 9–1 hour before sunset; T: 0942 51001, www.parconaxostaormina.it*). The entrance is through a pretty garden, in which an ancient lava-stream is still visible. The collection is displayed chronologically on two floors and is well labelled. Recent finds on the site include pottery of the 8th century BC from the island of Naxos in the Aegean Sea, the first tangible proof that at least some of the first settlers came from there and gave the name to this first Greek colony on Sicily.

Ground floor: Neolithic and Bronze Age finds from the Cape including Stentinello ware. A Neolithic village site near Syracuse, Stentinello has given its name to a type of impressed ware which usually takes the form of round-based dishes with carefully stamped designs, occasionally decorated to suggest human features, dating from c. 5600–4400 BC. Also here are Iron Age finds from the necropolis of Mola, including Geometric-style pottery.

First floor: The main part of the

museum displays terracottas and architectural fragments from a sanctuary at Santa Venera (6th century BC) and finds from a nearby tomb of the 3rd century BC, including four pretty vases for perfume and a glass bowl; material found in the area of the ancient city including a fine antefix with polychrome decoration, and Attic pottery; a little altar dating from around 540 BC decorated with sphinxes in relief; a statuette of a goddess (late 5th century BC); a rare marble lamp from the Cyclades found in the sea (late 7th century BC); and some exceptionally fine Greek coins, dating from 410–360 BC, many of them bearing the head of Marsyas. After losing a musical contest to which he had incautiously challenged Apollo, he was tied by the god to a tree and skinned alive.

Garden: Beyond the lava flow a collection of underwater finds has been arranged in a small Bourbon fort. It includes anchors (7th–4th century BC) and amphorae dating from various periods.

THE EXCAVATIONS

The interesting excavations (well signposted) in the fields to the south are reached from the garden. A path, lined with bougainvillea, leads through the peaceful site of the ancient city. Excavations, which are ongoing, were first carried out here in 1953.

On the right a path leads through a lemon grove to a stretch of Greek walls. The main area of excavation is about 10mins' walk from the museum in a beautiful orchard planted with a wide variety of exotic trees, including lemons, palms, olives, oranges, eucalyptus and Japanese medlars (loquats), above flowering bougainvillea, hibiscus and jasmine. Prickly pear, agave and oleander plants also flourish here.

There is an impressive stretch of city walls in black lava stone (c 500m) parallel to a line of eucalyptus trees. The West Gate is raised on two circular terraces. A path leads to the original entrance of the *area sacra*, and other remains from the 7th and 6th centuries, including part of the walls (which were 8m high, of mud-brick on a foundation of stone), an altar and a temenos of Aphrodite. A simple temple constructed towards the end of the 7th century, had a larger temple built over it at the end of the 6th century. Under cover, two kilns are preserved, a circular one for water jars, and a rectangular one for tiles; both were in use during the late 6th and 5th centuries BC. Beyond is the Sea Gate with a fine polygonal lava-stone wall. The military port was enclosed within the city walls, but the merchant ships were docked outside near the modern town. The naval arsenal has recently been brought to light, with the dry docks where the famous trireme warships were laid up when they were not at sea. The high wall to the east, behind a row of cypresses, which blocks the view of the sea, was built during excavation work.

CASTELMOLA

Of probable Sicel origin, now a tiny town with a dwindling population, Castelmola (529m; *map p. 568, C3*) sits on top of a rock with a ruined Byzantine castle, high above Taormina; it forms part of the association of Italy's most beautiful villages. In the iny square, with a view from the terrace of Etna and the bay of Naxos, the **Caffè San Giorgio** was founded in 1907 and has a famous collection of autographs in dozens of visitors' books, totalling many thousands of signatures. Castelmola is well known for its almond wine, which was invented here at the San Giorgio. Another picturesque café is in Piazza Duomo, the **Caffè Turrisi**, with an interesting collection of another sort, phalluses in every shape, form and material. The façade of the parish church of San Giorgio, reconstructed in Gothic style, opens onto a terrace with another wonderful panorama. The view is still better from Mt Venere or Veneretta (884m), reached by a long footpath from the cemetery of Castelmola.

THE PELORITAN MOUNTAINS

The Peloritan Mountains, of which the highest peak is the Montagna Grande (1374m), were once thickly forested, but now most of the slopes are carpeted with wildflowers in the spring and barren for the rest of the year. Conspicuous features of the landscape are the *fiumare*—wide, flat-bottomed torrent beds filled with gravel and usually waterless. With the autumn rain storms the water descends these channels in spate, carrying a considerable quantity of alluvial matter and sometimes washing away roads, bridges and even villages.

Although the mountains are for the most part inaccessible, there are a number of remote little upland villages that can be reached by steep roads from the coast between Taormina and Messina.

Just north of Taormina, above the thriving holiday resort of **Letojanni**, with its sandy beach, bars and restaurants, are **Mongiuffi** and **Melia** (*map p. 568, C3*), characteristic of the hill villages on the southern slopes of the Peloritans. Pilgrimages are organised in summer to several sanctuaries of the Madonna here, following an ancient tradition.

FORZA D'AGRÒ

Forza d'Agrò (*map p. 568, D3*) is a charming little medieval town, overlooking the privately-owned Arab-Norman **castle** on a spur of red Dolomitic limestone at Capo Sant'Alessio, from which the views extend along the straight coastline towards Messina, across the straits to Calabria and south to Taormina. Above the piazza a lane leads up to circular steps which ascend through a 15th-century Catalan Gothic archway, **Arco Durazzesco**, in front of the church of the **Santa Trinità**, with a 15th-century façade and campanile. It stands next to the former 15th-century Augustinian convent, which houses a museum dedicated to chocolate, **Cioccolart Sicily** (*open April–Oct daily 10–2.30 & 3.30–7.30, Nov–March Sat–Sun 10–5; T: 339 225 9998*). It presents the art, monuments and history of Sicily reproduced as large chocolate models by master confectioners. A wide view of the coast can be had from the terrace behind the church. From the other side of the piazza, a narrow road leads through the village past the Baroque Chiesa Madre, with a lovely 16th-century façade, used as a setting in Francis

Ford Coppola's *Godfather 2*. Opposite is a charming abandoned old house with pretty balconies. The road continues past old houses covered with flowering plants to the castle which was strengthened at the end of the 16th century by a double circle of walls and which was used for many years as the cemetery.

SAVOCA

From the coastal town of Santa Teresa Riva, a byroad runs inland to Savoca (303m, *map p. 568, D3*), a village on a saddle between two hills, belonging to the association of Italy's most beautiful villages. In the Middle Ages this was a city, the most important in the province, controlling more territory and with a larger population than Messina and rich because of its silk production. The numerous reliefs in terracotta and ceramic attest the artistic tendencies of the population. In an old house in Piazza Fossia, at the entrance to the village, is the **Bar Vitelli**, with a flowery veranda, a collection of local artisans' tools, and photographs taken when Francis Ford Coppola shot some scenes of *The Godfather* here in July 1971. Facing the Bar Vitelli is a profile in stainless steel representing Coppola, by the local artist Nino Ucchino (more sculptures by this interesting artist can be seen along the seafront of Santa Teresa di Riva).

Walk up the street, keeping left at the junction (fabulous **view** over mountains and valleys, studded with tiny villages, to Mt Etna), then through the old Porta della Città to the 15th-century church of **San Michele** (small exhibition of photographs regarding the local cult of St Lucy) with its two portals dating from the early 16th century. Near here is the **Museo Comunale Città di Savoca** (*open 9–1 & 5–10, mornings only in winter; T: 0942 761125*), displaying a collection of furniture, household equipment, folk-medicine charms against illness and the Evil Eye, and information on the local aristocracy.

Beyond the church of San Nicolò, usually known as **Santa Lucia** (with a 16th-century bust of St Lucy above the portal), the road continues up to the **Chiesa Madre**, built in the 12th century and restored in the 15th. From here the remains of the 17th-century church of the **Immacolata** and the ruins of the Arab castle, Pentefur, can be seen. The street continues round the mountain, bringing you back to the Bar Vitelli.

Outside the town in the church of the **Cappuccini** are catacombs (*open April–Sep 9–1 & 3–8, Oct–March 9.30–1.30; T: 0942 798769*) which display the mummified bodies, fully dressed, of citizens who lived here in the 18th century.

CASALVECCHIO SICULO

Casalvecchio Siculo (*map p. 568, D3*) is charmingly situated on the slopes of a hill. This was the Byzantine *Palachorion*, meaning 'ancient outpost'. Next to the 16th-century **Chiesa Madre** (which has a beautiful wooden Baroque ceiling), in the central Piazza Crisafulli, is an interesting little **Museo di Arte Sacra** (*to request visit, T: 0942 761122*), with religious paintings and other works of art, also tools used by farmers and craftsmen dating from the 12th–20th centuries.

The narrow Via Sant'Onofrio continues through the village; beyond, after c. 700m a very narrow road (in places single-track) leads left and descends through lovely countryside for c. 3km to one of the most complex and interesting Norman constructions n Sicily, the abbey-church of **Santissimi Pietro e Paolo d'Agrò** (*open summer 9–1 & 3–6, mornings only in winter; T: 340 398 9939*). On the site of a Basilian monastery built during the Byzantine domination in the 6th century, this imposing and elegant church occupies a beautiful, lonely spot near the Agrò torrent. Begun in 1116, it is extremely well preserved both inside and out. An inscription over the door relates how Gerardo il Franco dedicated it to Sts Peter and Paul for the Basilian monks in 1172; having suffered intense damage from earthquakes and Arab incursions, it was probably also restored at this time. Built of brick and black lava stone, the exterior has splendid polychrome decoration. The Byzantine interior also shows Arab influence in the stalactite vaulting and the tiny domes in the apse and nave. The stucco was removed from the walls in the 20th century to reveal the attractive brickwork. The columns made from Sardinian granite appear to be Roman in origin. It is possible to return to the coast road from here along a very rough road on the gravel bed of the wide torrent (*fiumara*).

ALONG THE COAST TO MESSINA

Back on the coast road, a byroad leads inland to **Fiumedinisi** (*map p. 568, D2*), where the duomo, probably of Norman origin, has an interesting interior with monolithic columns made of local marble and an unusual raised transept. Here, over the north altar, is a Byzantine-style fresco of the *Madonna and Child*. The Fiumedinisi torrent is one of the most important of these mountains; much of its water is channelled off to supply the needs of Messina. The bed of the torrent is rich in silver ore, exploited until the 18th century for minting coins.

Famous for its thermal baths and mineral-water springs, **Alì Terme** (*map p. 568, D3*) has been visited since the 18th century for the treatment of various ailments. From here the Calabrian coastline is in full view. A winding road leads up to the picturesque village of Alì, sadly suffering from depopulation. It is formed of two distinct parts, an Islamic settlement on the southern slopes of Mt Santa Lena, and a 16th-century enlargement on the eastern hill, with the Chiesa Madre (1582) dedicated to the patron St Agatha.

Itala (*map p. 568, D2*) is built on the side of a valley with lush vegetation. Above the village a road (very narrow in places) continues uphill and then left past ancient olive trees and lemon groves to the well-preserved church of Sts Peter and Paul (*open for Mass Sun morning 10.30*). It is preceded by a delightful little courtyard with a garden and palm trees. The church was built in 1092 by Count Roger in thanksgiving for the Norman victory over the Arabs and has a handsome exterior with blind arcading and a little dome; the interior also presents a raised transept, like that of the church of Fiumedinisi; among the works of art is a 16th-century painted Crucifix and a 16th-century panel-painting of the *Madonna with Two Saints*. The bell-tower is modern, as are the columns in the interior.

Scaletta Zanclea has a long narrow main street (still the main coast road); fishing-boats are kept in the alleyways which lead down to the sea under the railway line. The street is particularly busy in the mornings when fresh fish is sold from stalls here. In the upper town the remains of the 13th-century Castello Ruffo lie beneath Mt Poverello (1279m), one of the highest peaks of the Peloritans.

Mili San Pietro (*map p. 568, D2*) is in a pretty wooded valley with terraced vineyards and orange groves. On the outskirts of the village (by the school) is the little Norman church of Santa Maria di Mili (*closed*), dating from 1092 and founded together with a convent of Basilian monks by Count Roger, as a burial place for his favourite son Jourdain, killed in battle at Syracuse. It can be seen just below the road to the left. Steps descend to the ruins of a house, from which the church can be reached under the arch to the left. The monks made wine and raised silkworms in the lower part of the long-abandoned abbey; their cells were on the top floor.

THE NORTHERN PELORITANS

The northern coast road follows almost exactly the same route as the Roman consular road, Via Valeria, which once joined Messina to Syracuse (south) and Lilybaeum (north). At sea off Venetico, Agrippa defeated the fleet of Sextus Pompey at the Battle of Naulochos (36 BC). Close to Venetico is the attractive coastal town of **Spadafora** (*map p. 568, D2*), famous since Roman times for its bricks. In the centre is the 15th-century Castello Samonà (*open 9–7, closed Sun and holidays; T: 090 368 94435*) said to be connected by secret underground passages to the nearby ruined fortress of Venetico. From Spadafora a road climbs the mountains to **Roccavaldina**, with the imposing palace of its feudal baron in the central Piazza Umberto. On the corner, at Via Umberto 1, is the famous 16th-century Farmacia (*open Mon–Fri 9.30–1; T: 090 997 7741*). Inside are 256 16th-century decorated majolica pharmacy jars from the Patanazzi workshop of Urbino, perfectly preserved on their original shelves.

SANTA LUCIA DEL MELA

A narrow road leads up to Santa Lucia del Mela (*map p. 568, C2*), clinging to the hillside crowned by the ruins of the Arab-Norman castle. The fine **cathedral** in the central square is of medieval origin with a 15th-century portal and a font dated 1485. In the south aisle, the first altarpiece of the *Martyrdom of St Sebastian* (in poor condition) is by Giuseppe Salerno, a Zoppo di Gangi; on the second altar is a painting of *St Mark the Evangelist* by Deodato Guinaccia (1581) and a statuette of the *Ecce Homo* attributed to Ignazio Marabitti. In the south transept is a painting of *St Blaise* by Pietro Novelli. In the chapel to the right of the sanctuary there is a marble statue of St Lucy (1512). The high altarpiece of the *Assumption* is by Fra' Felice da Palermo (1771). In the chapel to the left of the sanctuary is an unusual little sculpted *Last Supper* in the frontal of the altar attributed to Valerio Villareale. The altarpiece in the north transept is by Filippo Iannelli (1676), and on the third north altar is an 18th-century Crucifix.

Next to the cathedral is the Palazzo Vescovile housing the **Museo Dioecsano 'Prelatura Nullius'** (*open Mon–Fri 9–1; T 090 935004*), with a fine collection of works of art from local churches. Other churches of interest (*open only for services*) include the Santissima Annunziata with a campanile of 1461 and a painting of the *Madonna and Child* of c. 1400, and **Santa Maria di Gesù** (or Sacro Cuore) with a Crucifix by Fra' Umile da Petralia. The road leads up to the **castle**, first built by the Arabs, then restructured by the Normans and by Frederick II of Aragon when he repopulated the town with a colony of Lombards in 1322. All that remains of the old fortress is a triangular-plan tower and a round keep. Now it houses the seminary and the sanctuary of the Madonna della Neve (1673) with a *Madonna and Child* by Antonello Gagini.

THE SCIFO FOREST AND BARCELLONA POZZO DI GOTTO

A narrow mountain road snakes along a crest into the Peloritan Mountains, from Santa Lucia del Mela as far as Pizzo Croce (1214 m). The beautiful **Scifo Forest** here (*map p. 568, D2*), with chestnuts, turkey oaks and ash trees, has recently been preserved with the help of the local division of the WWF, and you may spot pine martens, especially in spring when they are less shy.

Barcellona Pozzo di Gotto (*map p. 568, C2*) is a busy agricultural centre, famous for its nurseries of ornamental and flowering plants and fruit trees, mostly citrus. Founded in the 17th century, it has some interesting churches, such as the Chiesa Madre, and the church of San Giovanni, and at the eastern extremity of the town, at Contrada Manno 10, a well-kept museum of farming traditions, the Museo Etno-Anthropologico 'Nello Cassata' (*open daily summer 9–1 & 3.30–7.30, winter 9–1 & 4–8; T: 090 976 1883*), the largest and most complete of its kind in Sicily. Nello Cassata was a 19th-century collector and keen local historian. Allow at least an hour to browse among the 13,000 artefacts, including old vehicles, wine- and olive presses, looms, old clocks and sundials. There is a coffee shop on the premises.

From Barcellona a steep and narrow road leads up to the thickly-forested **Parco Jalari** (*open Jan–March and Oct–Dec Sat, Sun and holidays 9.30–1 & 3–sunset; April–June and Sept Tues–Sun 9.30–1, Sat, Sun and holidays also 3–6; July–Aug 9.30–1 & 4–8; last tickets 1hr before closing;T: 090 974 6245*), where the theme is water and stone. There are sculptures, pretty stone buildings and fountains, and from the park there is a fine view of Castroreale.

CASTROREALE

Perched on a mountain crag like an eagle's nest, Castroreale (394m; *map p. 568, C2*) was once a favourite residence of Frederick II of Aragon, from whose castle it gets its name. The **Chiesa Madre** contains a *St Catherine* by Antonello Gagini (1534) and a magnificent organ dated 1612, recently restored and in regular use. From Piazza dell'Aquila there is a fine view of the fertile plain. The Corso leads to the 15th-century church of the **Candelora**, with a Moorish dome and a 17th-century carved and gilded wooden high altarpiece.

In Via Guglielmo Siracusa is the old church of **Santa Maria degli Angeli** (*open on prior request, T: 090 974 6514*), probably built over the synagogue, which contains a gallery with interesting paintings and two sculptures (*St John the Baptist* by Andrea Calamech, 1568; and a *Madonna* by Antonello Freri, 1510) and a rich collection of Church silver and vestments. Further on, at Via Siracusa 31, is the interesting **Museo Civico** (*open Mon–Fri 9–1, Tues also 3–6; T: 090 974 6444*), housed in the restored former oratory of San Filippo Neri, with a charming balcony decorated with prancing horses and lions above the doorway. The collection of sculpture and paintings comes from local churches. On the ground floor are Crucifixes (including a painted one dating from the mid-15th century), Antonello da Saliba's *Madonna and Child Enthroned with Angels* (a panel from a dismembered polyptych), and a sarcophagus with the effigy of Geronimo Rosso by Antonello Gagini (1507). On the first floor are vestments, precious books, ceramic tiles and 18th-century paintings, including works by Fra' Felice da Sambuca. An 18th–19th-century silver Cross is from the Chiesa Madre.

At the end of the street is the church of **Sant'Agata**, with a charming *Annunciation* by Antonello Gagini, dated 1519. At the top of the town a circular tower survives from the ruined **castle**, founded by Frederick II of Aragon in 1324.

TERME VIGLIATORE TO MONTALBANO ELICONA

Back on the coast road, just short of **Terme Vigliatore** (a thermal resort with a spring called Fonte di Venere, used for the treatment of gastrointestinal and liver ailments) at **San Biagio** (Via Nazionale 3; *map p. 568, C2*), are the remains of a large Roman villa (*open 9–7, closed Sun and holidays; last tickets 30mins before closing; T: 090 97- 0488*). Dating from the 1st century AD, a large peristyle and part of the baths can be seen. Several rooms, protected by a plastic roof, have black and white mosaics, mostly geometric, and one floor is decorated with a lively fishing scene: dolphins, swordfish and other fish still found off the coast here can be made out. The main hall has a fine *opus sectile* pavement.

Inland near the long-drawn-out settlement of **Rodì** and **Milici**, overlooking the Patti river valley, is the site of ancient *Longane*, a Sicel town of some importance which was no longer inhabited by the 5th century BC. Traces of the walls survive and the foundations of a sacred building.

From Terme Vigliatore a road (SS 185) runs inland across the western side of the Peloritans (rising to a height of 1100m at Sella Mandrazzi), connecting the Tyrrhenian coast with the Ionian Sea at Giardini Naxos, passing through Francavilla di Sicilia. This quiet and exceptionally scenic road follows the wide Mazzarrà and Novara valleys with their extensive citrus-fruit plantations.

Novara di Sicilia (*map p. 568, C3*), the ancient *Noae*, refounded by the Normans who populated it with Lombards, is now a quiet little town below the main road; it forms part of the association of Italy's most beautiful villages. From Largo Bertolami with a 19th-century bronze statue of *David*, Via Duomo leads down to the 16th-century duomo. In the south aisle is a wooden statue of the *Assumption* by Filippo Colicci. In Via Bellini there is a beautiful little 19th-century opera house. The fantastic bare lion-shaped **Rocca Novara** (1340m) dominates the town of Novara.

Another very winding minor road, the SP 110, leads southwest from Terme Vigliatore to **Montalbano Elicona** (*map p. 568, C2–C3*), a hill town in a fine position surrounded by woods, dominated by the spectacular Castello (*open April–Oct Tues–Sun 9.30–1.30 & 3–7; Nov–March Sat, Sun mornings only; T: 0941 670081*), formed of two parts. The highest, now in ruins, was probably Norman, while the other was built by Frederick II of Aragon in 1302 as his summer residence. During restoration work in the 1980s the battlements were irrevocably damaged when the original Ghibelline swallowtail crenellation was replaced with the plain rectangular Guelph type. In 2015 Montalbano Elicona was voted Italy's most beautiful village.

ARGIMUSCO
The 'Woman at Prayer' megalith, resembling a female statue with veiled head and clasped hands. The human figure on top of the rock gives a sense of the scale.

On a barren, blustery hilltop 6km to the southeast of Montalbano, a plateau (1200m) emerges from the turkey-oak woods of the Bosco di Malabotta nature reserve. Take the SP 110 from the village (signposted 'Megaliti del Argimusco', and after c. 5km turn right on the SP 115. At c. 1.5km you will see a large gate on the left, with a faded map, labelled 'Bosco di Malabotta'. Park here and follow the bed of the stream—hopefully dry—to the top of the hill. Here stands the little-known **Argimusco**, a group of huge megaliths (some are 40m high) that are almost certainly natural formations although the tantalising idea that they might be man-made has its adherents. Some believe that they can discern in the rocks the deliberate forms of an eagle, a man, a praying woman, menhirs and a collapsed dolmen. No archaeology has been carried out here as yet. The panorama, however, is indescribable. To the north the twin volcanoes of Salina emerge through an azure haze, while below you to the east stretches the Malabotta forest as far as the bare sphinx-like rock of Novara. Mt Etna looms, immense, to the south, and Mt Cuculo and Mt Guardiola of the Nebrodi chain can be seen to the west.

Following the SP 115 north for c. 13km (but it can also be reached from Terme

Vigliatore on the coast), you arrive at **Tripi** (*map p. 568, C2*). Along the way you will see horses, cattle and even black pigs roaming freely in the woods. The Azienda Forestale encourages grazing in the forest, because it lessens the risk of summer wildfires. Tripi is a picturesque cluster of toffee-coloured houses nestling in the lap of a steep mountain crowned with an Arab-Norman castle. Sadly depopulated, it is hard to believe that this charming village was once *Abakainon*, an important Sicel centre, perhaps founded c. 1100 BC; it stood at the foot of the hill where Tripi now stands. During the Greek colonisation it maintained its independence thanks to trade and was rich enough to mint its own coins. After surrendering to Rome in 263 BC, it became a *municipium* but was destroyed by Octavian in 36 BC because the people could not—or would not—feed his troops. After a long period of abandon the town gradually recovered, but the Arabs moved it to its present position, changing its name to *Tarbulah*. After prospering thanks to its production of cheese, silk and products from the forest, Tripi gradually declined, from the 19th century to the present day. There is an interesting and well laid-out museum, the **MAST Museo Archeologico Santi Furnari di Tripi** (*to request a visit including the archaeological area, T: Municipio 0941 82014, Donata Aveni*), displaying the finds from excavations carried out in the Hellenistic-era necropolis (4th–2nd centuries BC), where some of the tombs have a monumental character. Among the numerous objects brought to light are containers for cosmetics, coins, bronze mirrors, painted vases and fine gold jewellery, attesting to the wealth of ancient Abakainon.

MILAZZO

The main port for ferries and hydrofoils to the Aeolian Islands, Milazzo (*map p. 568, C2*) stands on the isthmus of a narrow peninsula on the northeast coast of the island. It is an old city with considerable charm, marred by an oil refinery and power station on the outskirts. Milazzo was the ancient *Mylae*, founded as a sub-colony by Greeks from Zancle (Messina) in 716 BC. Here Gaius Duilius defeated the Carthaginians of Hannibal Gisco in their first major sea battle between Rome and Carthage (260 BC), and here in 1860 Garibaldi successfully assaulted the castle, garrisoned by Bourbon troops, promoting J.W. Peard, a Cornish volunteer, to the rank of colonel on the field. The castle, with its successive and extensive modifications, demonstrates the town's former strategic importance. Milazzo is divided into four areas: the lower-lying, more modern district of Città Bassa, which is now the centre; the older, higher district of Borgo Antico; Piana, the rural suburb; and Capo Milazzo, the peninsula.

CITTÀ BASSA

The road for the centre passes the port where the boats and hydrofoils for the Aeolian Islands dock. In Via Crispi is the late 19th-century Neoclassical **Municipio**. On the other side of the building (reached through the courtyard) is Piazza Caio Duilio. Here is the harmonious red façade of the former convent of the Carmelitani (16th century;

restored). The building houses the Tourist Office and the **Museo della Tonnara** (*open Mon–Fri 9–1 & 3–6, Sat 9–1; T: 090 922 2865*), a display on Milazzo's old tuna fishery, once the mainstay of the economy. Next to it is the Baroque façade of the Carmine (1574; rebuilt in 1726–52) and, on the other side of the square, Palazzo Proto, Garibaldi's headquarters for a time in 1860. In Via Pescheria, behind the post office, fresh fish is sold in the mornings from stalls in the street.

The marine parade (Lungomare Garibaldi), planted with trees, is a continuation of Via Crispi along the seafront. The 18th-century church of San Giacomo is well-sited at a fork in the road which leads to the **Duomo Nuovo** (1937–52), which contains paintings by Antonello de Saliba and Antonio Giuffrè, and sculptures attributed to the Gagini school. Further on, Via Colombo leads away from the sea past two little Art Nouveau villas, Villino Greco and Villa Vaccarino, now surrounded by unattractive buildings.

BORGO ANTICO

From Piazza Roma, Via Impallomeni leads up towards the castle past the Baroque 18th-century church of **San Francesco di Paola** (*open Mon–Fri 8.30–11 & 4.30–8; T: 090 928 1337, www.sanfrancescomilazzo.it*), which contains six paintings of miracles of the saint by Letterio Paladino. Nearby, in the old Spanish military barracks, is the **Antiquarium Domenico Ryolo** (*open Mon 9–2, Tues and Sat 9–7.30, Sun 2–7; T: 090 922 3471*), which houses a large collection of material found in the ancient inhabited areas and the necropoleis surrounding the city, arranged in chronological order. In three sections, devoted to pre- and early history, Greece and Byzantine Rome, the various burials shed interesting light on life and death in the area from c. 5000 BC to the 7th century AD, and show the evolution of Greek and Roman influence on the population. Terracotta vases were widely used for burying the dead, who were interred in the foetal position, or cremated. The presence of pottery from all over the Mediterranean demonstrates the role of ancient Mylae, an important harbour at the centre of trade routes.

At no. 49, a former women's prison built in 1816 and abandoned around 1960, the **ICAN-Itinerario Culturale Archeologico Naturalistico** (*open Mon and Wed 5–7, Fri 6.30–8.30, Sat 3.30–6.30, Sun 9.30–12.30; T: 388 119 3095*) displays in six rooms an ethnographic collection illustrating the work of peasants, fishermen and craftsmen, and local flora and fauna.

Picturesque low houses and open-air cafés (in summer) surround the double walls of the **castle** (*open winter 8.30–1.30 & 3.30–6.30, summer 8.30–1 & 4–10, closed Mon; T: 090 922 1291 or 320 794 7874*). Built by the Arabs in the 10th–11th centuries on the site of the Greek acropolis, it was enlarged by Frederick II in 1239, by the Aragonese in the 14th century and by Charles V in the 16th century, and then restored in the 17th century. The Spanish walls date from the 16th century and enclose a large area used for theatre performances and concerts in summer. Here are the remains of the Palazzo dei Giurati, used as a prison in the 19th century, and the **Duomo Antico**, an interesting late 17th-century building attributed to Camillo Camilliani or possibly Natale Masuccio. It was abandoned when the new cathedral was begun in 1937. In the same area a Gothic doorway leads to the oldest structures of the castle: the imposing Arab-Norman keep and a great hall known as the Sala del Parlamento. From the castle a flight of steps leads to the church of the Rosario, built in the 16th century and restored in the 18th. The convent by the church housed the Inquisition.

CAPO MILAZZO

The narrow peninsula of Capo Milazzo is simply called *il Capo* by the local people. The road threads its way through olive groves and prickly pears to a point where steps go down to the sanctuary of St Anthony of Padua, a little church (1575) built in a cave where the saint took refuge after a shipwreck in January 1221. A path continues to a lighthouse and down to a stony beach and the crystal-clear sea. It is a beautiful spot but crowded with bathers on summer weekends. From the cape the view (on a clear day) encompasses all the Aeolian Islands, and also Mount Etna.

CAPO TINDARI TO CAPO D'ORLANDO

On the headland of **Capo Tindari** (*map p. 568, C2*) stands a conspicuous church near the excavations of the ancient city of *Tyndaris*, founded in the 4th century BC. The road leads to a car park below the church, a modern sanctuary built in 1957–79 to house a seated Byzantine-style statue of the **Black Madonna**, greatly venerated since the 10th century (pilgrimage on 8th Sept) when it was found in a wooden chest on the beach under the cliff, apparently abandoned by pirates. The life-size statue of the Madonna, her Child and her throne is made of a single large block of painted cedarwood and was probably made in the 7th or 8th century, although it is not known where. The well-preserved red and blue colours symbolise divinity and humanity. The structure of the new, very ornate church (*open Mon–Sat 6.45–12.30 & 2.30–7 (8 in July–Aug), Sun and holidays 6.45–12.45 & 2.30–8; T: 0941 369003 or 0941 369260*) encloses the old 16th-century sanctuary, on the seaward side (*open Mon–Sat 11–12 & 3–4, Sun and holidays 2.30–4*), with a portal of 1598 and an interesting reproduction of the Black Madonna, allowing a closer look. From the terrace in front of the church there are splendid views of the Aeolian Islands. The shifting currents in the shallows at the foot of the cliffs produce beautiful formations of sand and gravel and areas of temporary marshland that are of great interest to naturalists.

THE RUINS OF *TYNDARIS*

From the car park a path and steps take you up to the road which leads to the entrance to the impressive ruins of *Tyndaris* (*map p. 568, C2; open 9–7; last tickets 30mins before closing; possible joint ticket with the Roman Villa at Patti; T: 0941 369023*). The ancient city was founded in 396 BC after the victory of Dionysius of Syracuse over the Carthaginians, when he transferred a number of Greek Messenians from Messina to this spot (*Diodorus Siculus 14:78*). Tyndaris remained an ally of Syracuse until taken by the Romans in 254. A large part of the city slipped into the sea during an earthquake aused by the eruption of Vesuvius in AD 79, and then by another earthquake in AD 365. Excavations begun in 1812 by Robert Fagan, then British Consul, were resumed from 1949–64 and are still in progress.

A path leads down through a little garden to the excavations in a grove of olives and pines planted with bougainvillea and prickly pear. The beautiful, peaceful site overlooks fields with olive trees on a cliff directly above the sea. To the right, along the **decumanus maximus**, are the remains of Roman buildings, including a series of tabernae, two private houses (with peristyle and mosaics), and a bath-house with black and white mosaics. At the end of the decumanus is the **Basilica** (1st century AD), once called the Gymnasium but now thought to have been the Magistrates' Court or a monumental entrance to the agora (which is thought to lie under the square in front of the church). It is an unusual building with barrel vaulting across the main road of the city. The façade, which collapsed in Byzantine times, was restored in 1956.

To the left of the entrance is the large **theatre**, a Greek building adapted by the Romans for use by gladiators. A long stretch of the nicely paved decumanus has recently been excavated near the theatre, and the front steps of an extremely large public building have been revealed on the south side. To the north of the decumanus, at the far western end of the site is a large early Imperial brick-built **funerary monument**. The **Greek walls** (3rd century BC), obscured by vegetation on the seaward side, survive in a good state of preservation to the south (beside the approach road below the sanctuary), extending, with interval towers, for several hundred metres on either side of the main gate, which takes the form of a dipylon with a barbican.

The **antiquarium** has a reconstruction of the theatre's monumental stage and backdrop, and finds from the site, including a colossal head of the emperor Augustus (1st century).

PATTI

Some 7km west of Tindari, Patti (*map p. 568, C2*) is an important agricultural town on a hill, renowned for its colourful ceramics; as the proverb has it: 'If you want a tasty dish, cook it in a pot from Patti'. Founded in 1094 as a Benedictine monastery by Count Roger, the first king of Sicily, the town grew and flourished, especially when it became the seat of a bishopric. It was looted and burned by the pirate Kheir ed-Din Barbarossa in 1554, and more recently, in 1978 the town was severely damaged by an earthquake. The **cathedral**, consecrated on 6th March 1094 and dedicated to the patron saints Bartholomew and Febronia, dominates the city. In the south transept is the Renaissance tomb of Queen Adelaide (d. 1118), third wife of Count Roger and mother of Roger II. She died of leprosy in the local Benedictine monastery, where she had withdrawn after the annulment of her marriage to Baldwin of Jerusalem. He had sought her hand because of the rich dowry she would bring as Count Roger's widow, and once he had secured it, he declared their nuptials to be null and void. There are some fine paintings over the side altars, including a *Madonna and Child Enthroned* (1531) by Antonello de Saliba and the *Adoration of the Shepherds* by Willem Borremans.

Next to the cathedral is the **Diocesan Museum** (*Via Cattedrale 7, open on prior request, T: 0941 246318 or 0941 240866, www.diocesipatti.it*), with a rich collection of bishop's vestments, missals, silverware, paintings and marble reliefs from local churches. Close by, in Via Cappellini, is the old convent of San Francesco, which now houses the **Museo dell'Antica Ceramica** (*open Tues–Fri 9–1, other days on request, T: 347 864 4204*). A collection of the famous local pottery is displayed here, including cooking pots, serving dishes, jugs and large bowls for washing clothes.

MARINA DI PATTI AND THE ROMAN VILLA

During the construction of the motorway from Messina in 1973, at Marina di Patti (*map p. 568, C2*), part of a large **Roman villa** was uncovered (*follow the signs for Marina di Patti and the motorway: the entrance to the site is beneath the motorway viaduct; open 9–7; possible joint ticket with Tindari, T: 0941 361593*). The villa (4th century AD; c. 20,000m square) was made up of three main structures with three different orientations. On the western side there are the remains of walls relating to rooms. The main structures centre on a large peristyle with a pillared portico; on the northeast side part of a bath-house has been brought to light. The villa also contains a few polychrome mosaics with geometric and floral designs as well as hunting scenes. There is a small antiquarium on the site with objects found during the excavation, including coins, carved reliefs, fragments of sculpture and pottery. Although the villa was destroyed by an earthquake, perhaps in the 5th century, the area was inhabited continuously at least until the 10th century, and the remains of tombs have also been found.

GIOIOSA MAREA AND BROLO

A seaside resort, **Gioiosa Marea** (*map p. 568, B2*) was built in the 18th century after an earthquake destroyed the old town of Gioiosa Guardia (or Gioiosa Vecchia). The alluring ruins of the abandoned city survive high up (828m) on a hill beyond the motorway. A winding road leads up to them, from where there is a wonderful view of the coast and the Aeolian Islands. Vulcano is only 19km offshore.

Midway between Gioiosa and Capo d'Orlando is the charming medieval village of **Brolo**, with a maze of narrow cobbled streets leading up to the well-kept, photogenic castle (*open April–May Sat ,Sun and holidays 9–1 & 4–8; June daily 9–1 & 4–8, July–15 Sept 9–1 & 4–midnight; Oct–March open on request a few days beforehand; T: 0941 562600, www.castellodibrolo.com*), which houses several interesting exhibits on punishment and torture, weapons, coastal defences and watchtowers.

CAPO D'ORLANDO

According to legend, the peaceful resort of Capo d'Orlando (*map p. 568, B2*) with a rocky promontory (noted for its sudden storms) and sandy beaches, was founded by one of the sons of the wind god Aeolus and known as *Agathyrnum*. Punished by the Roman governor in 210 BC with the deportation of 4,000 inhabitants, accused of banditry, the town declined until the days of Charlemagne, who refounded it with the name of Orlando, his favourite knight. Frederick II of Aragon was defeated off the headland in 1299 by Roger of Lauria, commanding the allied fleets of Catalonia and Anjou. The promontory is crowned by the ruins of the 14th-century **Castello d'Orlando** and the

6th-century sanctuary church of **Maria Santissima**, the patron saint. A modern building at Via del Fanciullo 2 (entrance from Via Mancari) houses the **Antiquarium** (*open Tues–Sat 8–8; T: 0941 911392*), housing archaeological material found in the vicinity, recently returned from the principal museums of the island. On the first floor is the **Pinacoteca Tono Zancanaro** (*open Tues–Fri 8.30–2 & 3–7; T: 0941 912946*), a collection of paintings depicting Capo d'Orlando, winning entries in a competition once held annually. Over 200 artists from all over the world are represented, including Giuseppe Migneco, who first organised the event in 1955.

In Borgo Malvicino, Contrada Piscittina, east of the SS 113 and reached by the SP 149, is the charming 17th-century **Castello Bastione** (signposted; *open 9–1 & 3–7*). Until recently the home of an English lady, Mary Johnson, it now houses the new Museo dell'Etnostoria, with exhibits illustrating the cultivation and processing of sugar cane and lemons, once the linchpin of the local economy. Sections are planned on fishing and silk.

To the east, at **Lido di San Gregorio**, there is a beautiful sandy beach and a little fishing harbour. Nearby is the Villa Bagnoli (signposted 'Scavi Archeologici' from the SS 113; *open 9–7.30, last entrance 6.30; T: 0941 955401*), excavations of a luxurious Roman villa built in the late 4th or early 5th century AD, surrounded by a little garden. Eight rooms, some with coloured mosaic floors, have been unearthed, as well as the bath-house. The villa was covered by a landslide during an earthquake.

THE NEBRODI MOUNTAINS

The Parco dei Nebrodi (*www.parcodeinebrodi.it*) is a protected area of great natural beauty, stretching from the Peloritans in the east to the Madonie Mountains in the west. The mountains have an average height of 1200–1500m and are the largest forested area to survive on the island. The remarkable landscape changes constantly. The wide variety of trees includes turkey oak, elm, beech, holm oak, cork and yew, and is especially fine in the Caronia forest. The forests are home to the porcupine, the wildcat and the pine marten; the last wolves disappeared in the 1920s. At Rocche del Crasto, one of the highest peaks of the park near Alcara Li Fusi, there are golden eagles and griffon vultures, besides the lanner and the peregrine falcons. These mountains have abundant water, with many streams, small lakes and springs. The upland plains provide pastureland for numerous farm animals which roam free, including cows, sheep, goats and black pigs, a breed native to Sicily. The San Fratello breed of horses (identified by their characteristic rounded noses) are now protected and allowed to run free in the forest. Renowned ricotta, cheeses and salted hams are made by the local farmers.

Monte Soro (1847m) is the highest peak of the Nebrodi. The Biviere di Cesarò (1200m) is a beautiful natural lake with interesting birdlife (including herons, black-winged stilts and great white herons on migration), and a spectacular view of Etna. Nearby Lago Maulazzo is an artificial lake constructed in the 1980s for irrigation but never put into operation. In this area are numerous turkey oaks, maple trees, beech woods, and wild fungi (especially the delicious penny bun or cep mushroom, known locally as *porcino*, 'little pig'). In spring beautiful wild flowers bloom and the hillsides are covered with broom. The colours in autumn are also spectacular. The small towns and villages each have something particular to offer.

THE EASTERN NEBRODI

An old road leads from Capo d'Orlando across the eastern Nebrodi Mountains to Randazzo below Etna. It passes picturesque **Naso** (*map p. 568, B2*), which has 15th–17th-century tombs in the church of Santa Maria del Gesù. The church contains a monument to Artale Cardona (d. 1477) in Gothic-Renaissance style; the Cardona family were once lords of Naso. Other churches in Naso are the church of the Santissimo Salvatore, the Chiesa Madre and the church of San Cono, which has a 17th-century chapel with inlaid marble walls and the reliquary of St Conus, the patron saint. The catacombs under the church house the **Museo di Arte Sacro** (*open Mon–Sat 9.30–1 & 3.30–7; T: 0941 961 0060*), with a well-arranged collection of items from local churches. The highlight is an early 16th-century painting of the *Madonna with the Sleeping Child*, attributed to the Flemish artist Joos van Cleve. The tiny panel, thought to have been a cupboard door, shows a young, sweet-faced Madonna wearing a mantle of crimson damask, but her hands are those of a peasant girl. In the 19th century the town was prosperous enough to build an elegant theatre, the Teatro Alfieri.

AROUND TORTORICI AND FRAZZANÒ

After about 20km a narrow road branches off to the west, reaching **Tortorici** (*map p. 568, B3*), famous for the medieval painted ceilings in its churches, in particular that of San Francesco d'Assisi. The town was also renowned for its bell foundries. Bells from Tortorici are still ringing in many Italian churches. The road continues back towards the coast, passing **San Salvatore di Fitalia** (*map p. 568, B2*), a tiny village where the old Franciscan convent in Piazza San Calogero is now a cultural centre, housing the interesting Museo delle Tradizioni Religiose (*open Mon–Fri 9–1; to request visit other days, T: 0941 486278 or 329 409 5425*) dedicated to ex-votos left in sanctuaries of the Madonna or other saints (especially San Calogero; *see p. 245*) in thanksgiving for recovery from illness or delivery from danger. The offerings take the form of *naïf* pictures, sometimes painted on glass, and wax effigies of the anatomical parts which were healed; some of these go back to the 17th century and are extremely rare.

Floresta (*map p. 568, B3*), with its lovely houses of pale grey stone, slow pace and women embroidering in front of their doors, is the highest municipality in Sicily (1275m), with winter sports facilities. The road reaches a summit level of 1280m before descending in full view of Etna to Randazzo.

From the coastal highway a road climbs from Rocca di Caprileone to the old town of **Capri Leone** and to **Frazzanò** (*map p. 568, B2*), 2km from where in 1090 Count Roger built the Basilian monastery and church of San Filippo di Fragalà (*open daily 9.30–12.30; T: 346 572 2241*), a national monument, with three high apses, a large transept nd a polychrome exterior of red brick and local stone. The interior still bears traces of yzantine frescoes and has a lovely floor of 18th-century majolica tiles made in Naso. seat of learning, the monastery had an important library that was dispersed in 1866. mong the few remnants saved and now in Palermo, is the oldest document yet found 1 Europe written on paper, an edict sent by Queen Adelaide to the abbot in 1099.

From here the road continues up to the ancient centres of **Longi** and **Galati 1amertino** which has some notable works of art, including two marble statues of the *Madonna* attributed to the Gagini school in the Chiesa Madre, and a Crucifix by Fra' *'*mile di Petralia, thought by some to be his finest, in the church of Santa Caterina.

AN MARCO D'ALUNZIO

it San Marco d'Alunzio (*map p. 568, B2*), ancient *Haluntium*, Robert Guiscard built he first Norman castle in Sicily in 1061 (it survives in ruins at the top of the hill). The iteresting little hill town has 22 churches built of a distinctive local red marble (called *osso di San Marco*). At the entrance to the town, on a spectacular site overlooking the ea, is the **Temple of Herakles**, dating from the Hellenistic era: on the red marble asement a Norman church (now roofless) was built. Later a Baroque portal and vindows were added. Above the road on the right is the **church of the Aracoeli**, vith a Baroque portal. The interior, including the columns, has local red marble ecorations. In the south aisle a marble altar has a gilded wooden statue of St Michael rchangel, and another chapel has a fine red marble altarpiece. Via Aluntia continues ast (left) the deconsecrated 12th-century church of Santa Maria dei Poveri (used or exhibitions) and then descends past the Town Hall and a fountain. On the left is he **Chiesa Madre** (San Nicolò), built in 1584. It has a very unusual triumphal arch vith large marble sculptures and an 18th-century organ. In the north aisle, the fourth hapel has a 16th-century painting of the *Madonna of the Rosary* in a fine frame, and he fifth chapel a wooden 16th-century processional statue of the *Immaculate Virgin*.

A road leads uphill to the left past the tiny church of San Giovanni and then down o the side of the hill where the deconsecrated church of San Giuseppe has a lovely ortal. There is a fine view of the sea from here. On the left of the façade is the entrance o the **Museo Parrocchiale di Arte Sacra** (*open Sat & Sun 10–1 & 4–7; bookshop; T: 'ircolo Anspi Demenna, 329 608 4536*). In the vestibule are the original capitals from he portal of the church, as well as vestments and statues. The rest of the collection s arranged in the church which has a lovely red, grey and blue floor and decorative tuccoes. The collection of miscellaneous objects includes a sculpture of the *Madonna ell' Odigitria* by Giuseppe Li Volsi (1616), statues, reliquaries and church furniture.

Higher up in the town is the tiny church of **Maria Santissima delle Grazie** with delightful carved high altar with a statue of the *Madonna and Child with the Young t John*, and, on either side, two imposing tombs of the Filangieri family, one with n effigy (1481) and the other in red marble (1600). Opposite, built on the rock, is the hurch of San Basilio.

A short distance south of San Marco d'Alunzio, by the Byzantine church of San eodoro, with interesting remains of frescoes, is the ex-Benedictine monastery r Badia Nica (Via Ferrarolo 96), housing the **Museo della Cultura e delle Arti**

Figurative Bizantine e Normanne (*open daily 9–1 & 3.30–7.30; T: 0941 797719*). rich collection of antiquities found in the surrounding area and frescoes removed from the many churches of the town are displayed with admirable clarity over two floors.

SANT'AGATA DI MILITELLO AND THE NEBRODI PARK

A seaside resort from which climbing expeditions may be made in the Nebrod Mountains Park, **Sant'Agata di Militello** (*map p. 568, B2*) also has a fine castle a Piazza Francesco Crispi 211, the Castello Gallega (*open 8.30–12.30 & 4–8, closed Mon* Originally built in the 14th century and accessed by a drawbridge, it was rebuilt in th 18th century as an aristocratic mansion. The ground floor houses a collection devote to life in the Nebrodi Mountains, divided into three sections: the role of womer sheep- and cattle-herders; and traditions and religious customs.

Alcara Li Fusi (*map p. 568, B3*) is a little mountain village beneath the Rocche de Crasto mountain (1315m). In the old Benedictine monastery at Via Vittorio Emanuel 56 is the Museo di Arte Sacra (*open Mon–Fri 9–12, Sat 9–1, Sun 3–7; bookshop; T 0941 793055 (priest) or call the Municipio, T: 0941 793010*). Paintings, silverware and vestments from local churches are on display, together with a collection of rare book and incunabula.

Excursions into the Nebrodi Park can easily be organised from here. The mountain where golden eagles still nest, can be explored on foot to see the **Grotta del Laur** (1060m), one of the most interesting caves in Sicily, with impressive stalagmites and stalagtites, an important bat population, and where traces of prehistoric habitatio have been found. On one of the mountain peaks, Rocca Traora, is a flourishing colon of griffon vultures, successfully re-introduced after their accidental extermination i 1966.

A picturesque road leads south from Sant'Agata di Militello through the Nebrod Mountains past **San Fratello**, a Lombard colony founded by Adelaide, wife of Coun Roger; the people still use their ancient Gallic dialect. The old town is built of dar brown stone, with mellow, mossy roof-tiles. Recent archaeological surveys on nearb Mt San Fratello, called Monte Vecchio by the local people, show that the town is c prehistoric origin. It was later the ancient *Apollonia* and was moved to its presen position by order of the queen. On Monte Vecchio is the 12th-century Norma sanctuary church of three brothers, Sts Alfio, Cirino and Filadelfo, all martyred i AD 253. San Fratello is surrounded by forests; close by are two lakes: Maulazzo and Biviere, of great interest to bird-watchers and botanists.

Back on the coast, **Acquedolci** is a coastal resort whose name means sweet waters a reference to the sugar industry founded here by the Arabs, which brought prosperit to the whole area. It also had a tuna fishery and a port for exporting wheat from th interior; now its fortunes are declining. A path leads south up the slopes of Mt Pizz Castellano (c. 30mins) to the Grotta di San Teodoro (*9–1, 3–6, closed Sun*), wher important Palaeolithic burials have been found, including one of a woman, about 3 years old and 1.65m tall, who has been named Thea. Numerous fossils near the cav attest the presence of dwarf hippos here 150,000 years ago, when there was a vast lak which has since disappeared. The Antiquarium Comunale (*Via Crispi; open Mon–Sa*

–12.30, Mon and Thur also 3–7; T: 327 068 3408) has a collection of fossils, some of hem mounted.

THE WESTERN NEBRODI

Caronia (*map p. 568, A3*) lies in a beautiful forest of the same name, Sicily's largest. The picturesque town preserves a privately-owned and still-inhabited Norman castle on the top of the hill, traces of its 14th-century fortifications, and an intact Roman bridge spanning the Caronia torrent. On the outskirts, the site of ancient *Kale Akte* has been identified, founded by Ducetius of the Sicels (*see p. 10*) on his return from exile in 447 BC.

A mountain road leads south across the Nebrodi from here to the hill town of Capizzi (1100m), one of the highest villages in Sicily. The road joins the beautiful SS 120 south of the Nebrodi from Nicosia to Randazzo. East of Troina the road traverses rugged country with a superb view of Etna, passing below remote **Cesarò** (*map p. 568, B3*), where the remains of its castle can be seen.

On the coast, at the western end of the Nebrodi, is **Santo Stefano di Camastra** (*map p. 568, A3*), once situated further inland on a rise, and destroyed by a landslide in 1682. It is noted for fine ceramics, which are made and sold in potteries on the outskirts (most of which are east of the town on the road towards Messina), and for building materials. Local ware is also sold in numerous shops in the town. In the heart of the attractively designed town (the work of Giuseppe Lanza, Duke of Camastra, in 1693), at Via Palazzo 1, is Palazzo Trabia, seat of the very fine Museo della Ceramica (*open Sept–May 9–1 & 3.30–7.30, June–Aug 9–1 & 4–8, closed Mon; T: 349 298 7908*). with collections of the local pottery, with its bright colours and typical designs, illustrating its evolution through the centuries. The upper floor displays the famous floor-tiles, and a section is devoted to the work of contemporary artists. Some of the huge oil jars, a speciality of the town, are shown, together with a typical old Sicilian kitchen.

A pretty road leads inland through the Nebrodi via **Mistretta**, an attractive old town with some beautiful Baroque and Rococo buildings, on the site of the ancient *Amestratus*. At the entrance to the town is the 16th-century church of San Giovanni with a fine flight of steps and a portal carved in 1534. The 17th-century Chiesa Madre (St Lucy) has a magnificent carved wooden choir, a carved marble transept, some beautiful statues of the Gagini school and two interesting side portals carved in the 14th and 15th centuries respectively. The carved south portal has been ascribed to Giorgio da Milano (1493). At Via Libertà 184 is the Museo delle Tradizioni Silvo-Pastorali (*open Tues–Sat 9–1, also 1st Sun of month 9–1*), a collection illustrating the life and activities of the local shepherds and foresters. At Mistretta they make unique biscuits of white marzipan called *pasta reale*, which are baked until pale gold in colour.

From Mistretta a magnificent old mountain road goes south to Nicosia, in Enna province. No less than nine spectacular **waterfalls** in the Nebrodi Mountains park can easily be reached from the town, about 4km away (*for information or a guide T: 328 662 1215, www.cascatedimistretta.it*).

TUSA AND ANCIENT *HALAESA*

A road leads inland above the wide torrent bed of the River Tusa, 21 km long and now usually dry, the ancient *Halaesus*, to the pretty little hill town of **Tusa** (*map p. 568, A3*) which has interesting medieval sculptures in the Chiesa Madre. Modern sculptures works by well-known contemporary artists including Pietro Consagra, Tano Festa and Hidetoshi Nagasawa, have been erected on the riverbed, from the shore to the village of Castel Di Lucio. Called **Fiumara d'Arte**, this constitutes an interesting walk, and although the local people were hostile at first, in the 1980s, and there were attempt to have the works demolished by court order, the sculptures are now appreciated and enjoyed. The latest addition is a dramatic three-sided pyramid of red steel, 30m high called *Pyramid–38° Parallel*, by Mauro Staccioli; its hollow interior can be visited only one day a year, for the summer solstice on 21st June. The sides of the pyramid are aligned with the three points of Trinacria, the ancient name of Sicily. The sponsor of this artistic initiative, Antonio Presti, runs the Hotel Atelier sul Mare (*see p. 498*) where the same artists and several others have designed 20 rooms. The sandy beach of Tusa has been awarded the Blue Banner for its quality.

Off the road to Tusa, in Contrada Santa Maria delle Palate, is the **site of *Halaesa Arconidea*** (*open 9–1hr before sunset, closed Mon; 1st Sun of month open 9–6.30*) on a hill. A road leads up from the gate on the byroad to the car park beside the restored convent and church and custodian's house. The attractive site, with ancient olive and almond trees, commands a fine view of the pretty Tusa valley, and on a clear day the Aeolian Islands. Halaesa was founded in 403 BC by Archonides, dynastic ruler of Herbita, who claimed to be the direct descendant of Ducetius. In recent years stretch of the paved Hellenistic street leading to the agora has been uncovered. The agora itself (partly protected by a roof) preserves part of its marble wall panelling and brick paving on the west side. The city walls (a stretch further uphill is strengthened by buttresses) are well preserved, and the Roman necropolis near the entrance to the site consists of an early Imperial columbarium and several further tombs. The excellent Giacomo Scibona antiquarium displays some of the objects found at Halaesa including two bronze inscriptions in the form of a temple façade honouring the local resident Nemenios, several statues and some other inscriptions.

THE AEOLIAN ISLANDS

Lipari, Salina, Vulcano, Stromboli, Filicudi, Alicudi and Panarea, together with some rocky islets, form the archipelago known as the Aeolian Islands (*map p. 568*). Wild and unspoiled, the islands are very small but each has its own identity and its own particular beauty. Their name derives from *Aeolus*, the mythical guardian of the winds who inhabited the largest island, Lipari. This volcanic area marks the point where the African plate meets the European, folding over and forcing itself under the opposing plate, in the process of subduction. Two of the islands, Vulcano and Stromboli, are still active. All are protected as a nature reserve, and Lipari's tiny beaches of black volcanic and have been awarded the EU Blue Banner for quality. On Stromboli the slopes on the opposite side to the lava flows are fertile and cultivated with vineyards. Vulcano smells strongly of sulphur and there is little cultivated land, but it is a magical place where shepherds pasture their sheep and goats. In spring, when the yellow broom is in flower, it is breathtakingly beautiful. Alicudi and Filicudi still show signs of the patient terracing carried out many centuries to preserve the tiniest drop of water. Salina, with its two extinct volcanic cones, is the greenest and the most fertile of the group, with extensive vineyards and forests where every effort is made to prevent summer wildfires. Lipari, the largest of the islands, has many ancient tracks, ideal for gentle trekking. Panarea is a tiny island full of wildflowers, with pretty houses set in the vegetation. The local style of architecture is perfect for the islands: small cube-like homes made of blocks of lava, plastered on the outside with white pumice, with characteristic little round windows like portholes; a flat roof for drying grapes, figs, pumpkins or tomatoes; a veranda (*'u bagghiu*) in front, which is the main living area, under a pergola supported by white columns (*'e pulera*); an open-air oven for baking bread, and a cistern underneath the house for storing rainwater. Several prehistoric sites have been excavated on the islands and the archaeological museum in the citadel of Lipari is one of the most important of its kind in Europe.

Capers grow everywhere on the islands, even on sheer rockfaces. Birds on their migratory flights frequently stop to rest on the Aeolians. Some of the rocky islets around the larger islands are important nesting spots for Eleonora's falcon (*Falco eleonorae*), a small, dark bird of prey, now extremely rare, which lays its eggs late in the spring so that its young can prey on the flocks of migrating birds flying south in late summer. Among the mammals, there are plenty of bats of various species, and rabbits. Fish are abundant and varied. Flying fish can often be seen in the summer, and also groups of dolphins, playing together close to shore. The whole archipelago is a UNESCO World Heritage Site.

It is worth noting that it gets very crowded on Lipari, Panarea and Vulcano in July and August, with day trippers from Calabria and Sicily. By nightfall, though, peace returns.

HISTORY OF THE AEOLIAN ISLANDS

The islands were important in ancient times because of the abundance of obsidian, a hard volcanic glass used for making tools and exported throughout the Mediterranean. The earliest traces of settlement belong to the Stentinello culture of the Neolithic Age. In the Middle Bronze Age the islands were on the main trade routes between the Aegean Islands and the Western Mediterranean. The Greeks colonised Lipari in c. 600 BC, and in the following centuries the islands were attacked by the Athenians and the Carthaginians. They fell to Rome in 252 BC. The population dropped in later centuries, because of an increase in the activity of the volcanoes, especially on Lipari. In 836 the islands were raided by the Arabs, who destroyed the towns and burnt them, carrying off the inhabitants as slaves and scattering the remains of St Bartholomew. A stone sarcophagus containing the mummified body of a man who had been flayed alive, thought to be Bartholomew, had drifted onto a Lipari beach in the 5th century. From that time nobody returned to live on the islands until Count Roger sent a group of Benedictine monks there in 1083. In spite of the concession of various privileges, it was not easy to attract people to settle on the islands, because of the threat of raids, until an enterprising monk declared that he had miraculously traced all the remains of St Bartholomew, who would again protect the islands. Notwithstanding the good saint, piracy remained a constant threat; when the fearsome pirate Kheir ed-Din Barbarossa attacked Lipari in 1544, burning the city and carrying off the population, there was pessimism about the islands ever being inhabited again. But the viceroy Peter of Toledo immediately sent aid, rebuilt the fortifications, confirmed the old privileges and allowed so many new ones that large groups of settlers came from Campania and Calabria. In the 19th century the citadel of Lipari was transformed into a prison and in 1926 it became a place of isolation for political opponents of the Fascist regime. Only in 1950 was it opened again to visitors. A heavy blow to the economy came in the late 19th century, when thousands of people emigrated (mostly to Australia), after phylloxera destroyed the grape vines.

LIPARI

Lipari (37km square), ancient *Meligunis*, the largest island of the group, 40km from Milazzo, is formed of twelve dormant volcanoes. Its small beaches have been awarded the Blue Banner for quality. About half of the island's 11,000 inhabitants are concentrated in the lively and attractive little town of Lipari, with its low houses and maze of narrow streets. The citadel or acropolis, of deep red lava rock, called *Castello*, commands the shore above the town, and separates the two harbours. On the north side of it is the port used by hydrofoils and ferries, Marina Lunga or Porto Sottomonastero.

The main road of the town is Corso Vittorio Emanuele. On the far (west) side is the **Palazzo Vescovile** (*map 3*), eventually to be restored as the seat of a Diocesan Museum. Beside it is the **archaeological area of Contrada Diana** where two Roman hypogea were found and where excavations revealed part of the Greek walls (5th–4th centuries BC) and Roman houses. It is no longer open regularly to the public.

Near Porto Sottomonastero is **Piazza Mazzini** (*map 2–4*), with a garden and some charming houses beside the neo-Gothic Town Hall (Municipio). The 18th-century church of Sant'Antonio (or San Francesco) has pretty marble altars. Steps lead down to the crypt which was the burial place for the islanders before the cemetery (which can be seen nearby) was opened. The route from Piazza Mazzini to the citadel leads through impressive 16th-century Spanish fortifications, with double gates and an entrance tunnel which incorporate Classical fragments.

On the south side of the citadel, at **Marina Corta** (*map 8*), the fishing-boats dock beside the picturesque church of the Anime del Purgatorio. Another attractive church

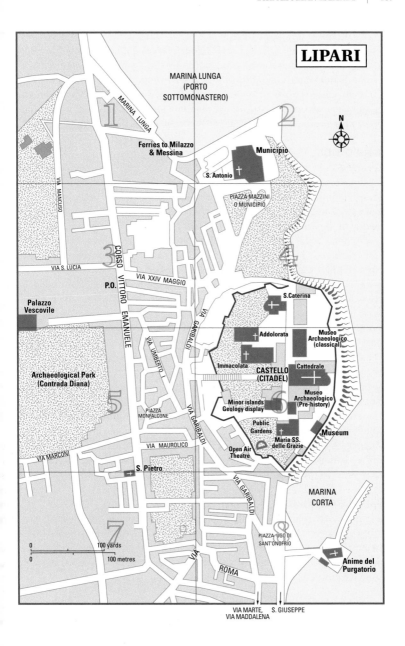

LIPARI

MARINA LUNGA
(PORTO
SOTTOMONASTERO)

N

Ferries to Milazzo
& Messina

Municipio

S. Antonio

PIAZZA MAZZINI
O MUNICIPIO

MARINA LUNGA

VIA MANCUSO

CORSO VITTORO EMANUELE

VIA S. LUCIA

VIA XXIV MAGGIO

P.O.

VIA GARIBALDI

S.Caterina

Palazzo
Vescovile

Addolorata

Museo
Archaeologico
(classical)

VIA UMBERTO I

Immacolata

CASTELLO
(CITADEL)

Cattedrale

Archaeological Park
(Contrada Diana)

PIAZZA
MONFALCONE

Minor islands
Geology display

Museo
Archaeologico
(Pre-history)

Public
Gardens

Museum

VIA MAUROLICO

VIA GARIBALDI

Maria SS.
delle Grazie

Open Air
Theatre

VIA MARCONI

S. Pietro

MARINA
CORTA

0   100 yards

0   100 metres

VIA GARIBALDI

PIAZZA UGO DI
SANT'ONOFRIO

VIA ROMA

Anime del
Purgatorio

VIA MARTE,   S. GIUSEPPE
VIA MADDALENA

close by is San Giuseppe, at the top of a ramp. Outside the church, fishermen are often at work mending their nets, their colourful boats pulled up on the quay beside a solitary palm tree, watched over by the statue of the patron St Bartholomew.

Via Garibaldi winds uphill through the town from Marina Corta. It passes a wide scenic flight of steps constructed at the beginning of the 20th century up to the citadel framing the façade of the cathedral at the top. The hill itself is a very peaceful spot, verdant with oleanders, prickly pear and ivy.

THE CITADEL

The **cattedrale** (*map 6; open 10–12, until 1 in summer*) is more easily reached by using the street from Porto Sottomonastero rather than the long flight of steps from Via Garibaldi. It is dedicated to the patron saint Bartholomew and was first built on this site by Count Roger (c. 1084). Seat of the bishop, it enjoys the same status as the cathedral of Messina. Admire the bronze doors with reliefs describing the arrival of Bartholomew's body on a beach of Lipari, and some of the miracles he has accomplished for the islanders. The pretty interior, hung with chandeliers, has a marvellous cross-vaulted ceiling frescoed in 1700 with scenes from the Old Testament. On the side altars of polychrome marble are 18th-century reliquary busts in gilded wood. In the north transept is a *Madonna of the Rosary*, attributed to Girolamo Alibrandi, and a silver statue of St Bartholomew which dates from 1728. The statue, together with an elaborate silver reliquary of a boat, is carried in procession through the streets on 24th August, 16th Nov, 13th Feb and 5th March. The Benedictine cloister, reached from the south aisle, has been restored. Dating from 1131, with later additions, it has vaulted walks, and columns of different shapes and sizes (some of them Doric, and some re-used from Roman buildings). Several primitive capitals are decorated with animals and birds.

The church of **Maria Santissima delle Grazie**, with a fine restored façade, is reached down a few steps in a little garden. On the other side of the road are public gardens (with fine views) which have a large number of Greek and Roman sarcophagi. These were found in the necropolis of Contrada Diana (late 5th and 4th centuries BC) (now covered by the modern town). There is also an open-air theatre, built in 1978.

MUSEO ARCHEOLOGICO REGIONALE

The Museo Archeologico Regionale Bernabò Brea (*map 6; open 9–7.30, Sun and holidays 9–1.30, last tickets 1hr before closing; T: 090 988 0174*) is arranged in several separate buildings. The superb collections, beautifully displayed in chronological sequence (with labels also in English), contain finds from Lipari and other islands in the Aeolian group, as well as from Milazzo and southern Italy.

Prehistory section

Beside the cathedral is the former Bishop's Palace (early 18th century), with an attractive portal and balconies, which houses the first section dedicated to Prehistory. A tour begins on the first floor with Neolithic finds from Lipari, including painted vases, Serra d'Alto-style pottery (resembling southern Italian forms), and red pottery

Ancient coin of Lipari in the collection of the Museo Mandralisca in Cefalù.

of the Diana style, so called because it was discovered in the area known as Contrada Diana. Objects found on the citadel hill belonging to the Capo Graziano (1800–1400 BC) and Milazzese (c. 1400–1250 BC) cultures are displayed, showing Greek influences. Notable are the vessels on tall pedestals.

The ground floor is dedicated to the Ausonian culture (from southern Italy) and to finds made on the citadel. Many show the influence of the Italian mainland: the vessels have a great variety of strangely-shaped handles. There are also the remains of a small cooking device, and a large terracotta pot, the repository of almost 100kg of bronze objects from the 9th century BC. There are signs of a violent destruction of Lipari at that time, and the island appears to have remained uninhabited for the next three centuries. The Greek and Roman period on Lipari is covered in Room 10. The large restored Attic vase, used for mixing water and wine, has exquisite black-figure decoration on the rim showing the *Labours of Herakles* and (inside) a frieze of ships. The couchant lion (c. 575 BC) carved from volcanic rock probably guarded a votive deposit to the wind god Aeolus. Also here are a Roman statue of a girl of the 2nd century AD, found in the Bishop's Palace, and a statuette of Asklepios (4th century BC).

A door leads out to the garden which contains sarcophagi from Contrada Diana and the Epigraphic Pavilion (*not always open*), which contains funerary inscriptions of 5th–1st centuries BC.

Prehistory of the minor islands and Geological sections

Two further sections of the museum are housed in the buildings opposite the former Bishop's Palace.

The Prehistory section has state-of-the-art displays (beginning to the left of the entrance and following a circular route around the building) that treat each prehistoric period in turn, drawing together material from across the minor islands to illustrate the phases of human settlement. The plentiful finds are accompanied by maps, diagrams, photographs, chronological tables, reconstructions and descriptions of all the principal archaeological sites. If you are planning a visit to Panarea, Filicudi or Salina and would like to see the archaeological sites there, it is highly recommended that you visit this part of the museum before doing so.

The building next door houses a geological display on three floors with diagrams, maps, reliefs and models illustrating volcanic activity and the formation of the Aeolian Islands. In the courtyard between them is a small collection of inscriptions.

Classical section

On the other side of the cathedral is the building devoted to the Classical period. The displays begin on the ground floor with three sets of rooms leading off from the entrance hall. Those to the left display finds from Milazzo in chronological sequence from the Middle Bronze Age to the 3rd century BC; a reconstruction of a burial site shows the burial pots in the position in which they were found. The room to the right contains a superb collection of terracotta and stone sarcophagi from Lipari, including a perfectly-preserved stone example found in Contrada Diana. It is thought to have been made by a sculptor in the 2nd or 1st century BC as his own tomb. Another reconstruction, of the Piazza Monfalcone necropolis in Lipari (1125–1050 BC), is in the following room. The rooms straight ahead of the entrance display finds discovered on the seabeds around the islands, dating from 2000 BC to the 5th century BC, discovered near Capistello (Lipari), and near Filicudi and Panarea, including a magnificent display of amphorae. There are also finds from the wreck of a 17th-century Spanish warship.

On the upper floors are Attic red-figure kraters of the 5th century BC and early Sicilian and Campanian red-figure vases (4th century BC), including a splendid krater with columns by the Painter of Adrasto (c. 450 BC). Grave goods from a similar period, and white-ground Attic pottery, are followed by a superb display of theatrical figurines in terracotta (early 4th–mid-3rd centuries BC) found on Lipari. Especially striking are the statuettes of dancers, and Andromeda with her child. A fascinating and unique collection of tragic masks and theatrical terracottas can also be seen, along with some very fine gold jewellery. Further rooms contain brightly-coloured vases by the Lipari Painter, a master who depicted exclusively female figures and who enjoyed working with different colours, and southern Italian vases including a krater with Dionysos watching a nude acrobat and two actors, and a bronze hydra with a female bust (early 5th century BC). Hellenistic gold jewellery includes a ring of the 4th century BC with a female nude.

The top floor displays the latest finds from the hill showing evidence of the destruction of Lipari in 252 BC, and sporadic finds from the Roman and Norman periods, as well as medieval and Renaissance ceramics.

THE EXCAVATIONS

Close to the church of Santa Caterina, extensive excavations were begun in 1950 by Luigi Bernabò Brea (*see www.luigibernabobrea.it for more information on this exceptional archaeologist*). They have revealed a sequence of levels of occupation dating from the Neolithic Age when the islands were first inhabited. Because the prevailing winds have consistently brought volcanic dust and sand to settle here, cuttings reveal the history of habitation in remarkable detail. The unique pottery strata (reaching a depth of 9m) make the citadel the key dating-site for the central Mediterranean. The different levels are well labelled and explained by diagrams.

AROUND THE ISLAND

A road (26.5km) encircles the island. It leads north from Lipari town via the stony beach of Canneto to traverse magnificent white cliffs of pumice, with deep gallery-quarries. The loading jetties protrude into the sea, a brilliant turquoise blue because of the pumice on the seabed. Beyond Porticello, the road crosses remarkable red and black veins of obsidian, some of which reach the sea. The beaches are covered with pumice and obsidian, and some of the paths in the villages are cut out of obsidian. A road connects Acquacalda (where there are hot springs in the sea) with Quattropani. At Piano Conte lava-stone axes and Bronze Age weapons have been found. Near the coast (reached by a byroad) are the hot springs of San Calogero, with remains of Roman baths. The road returns to Lipari past the viewpoint of Quattrocchi, literally 'four eyes', the number needed presumably to encompass the vast panorama. Monte Sant'Angelo (594m), in the centre of the island, is an extinct stratified volcano of unusual form (superb views).

ALICUDI AND FILICUDI

The most westerly island is **Alicudi**, with a particularly far-away, lonely character, one-and-a-half hours' hydrofoil journey from Lipari. Here five square kilometres support a dwindling population of 105. It is a particularly beautiful island, with terraces and attractive local architecture. There are no roads, only steep tracks and steps over the hills, and no public illumination (it has only had electricity since 1990). Several houses can be rented, but it should be borne in mind that there is only one small shop selling basic necessities. Visitors should bring everything else with them, including a torch for getting around after dark, and spare batteries. The tiny schoolhouse, now bereft of pupils, houses a poignant display of photographs showing the islands from the point of view of the children; an award-winning collection gathered together by the last schoolmistress.

FILICUDI

The remote and picturesque island of Filicudi (9.5km square; population 235) lies 19km west of Salina. Anciently called *Phoenicoesa*, it has comfortable accommodation and is a peaceful place to spend a holiday.

The hydrofoils dock in **Filicudi Porto**, a small settlement with a few houses, a restaurant/bar, and a small museum on the waterfront near the jetty (*if closed, ask at da Nino sul Mare for the current keyholder*). An ethnographic collection consisting of farming equipment, mill-stones and ship models has been laid out on the ground floor, while the upper floor is divided into four rooms in which a small archaeological collection is displayed: a few inscriptions, column capitals, pottery and some underwater finds, many of which have been recovered by sport divers, together with some information panels about the sites on the island.

Two prehistoric villages have been excavated on Capo Graziano in the southeast of the island, a short walk from Filicudi Porto. The earliest, **Filo Braccio**, is located by the sea on the southern shore. Only two of the oval-shaped huts that were excavated are still visible, the remainder having been covered over when the excavations were concluded. The abandonment of this settlement in c.1700 BC coincided with the foundation of another just a short walk away at **Montagnola**, on a natural terrace of the steep hillside that constitutes the cape proper. This site is reached by a short but steep climb from the main road that runs from Filicudi Porto to Pecorini, and was well signposted at the time of writing. The view from the site is superb, and well worth the climb. The many huts that were excavated here are nearly all visible, and date to two consecutive periods that lasted from 1700–1300 BC. Layers of ash and charcoal coinciding with their final abandonment suggest that it may not have been an entirely peaceful process. Off the cape in 1975 a hoard of Bronze Age pottery was found on the site of a shipwreck (nine Greek, Roman and modern ships foundered here). The coast here is now a marine park, run by the Filicudi Wildlife Conservation group (*Pecorini; T. 349 440 2021, www.filicudiconservation.com*); they will take you trekking, snorkelling or sea-watching for whales, dolphins and turtles.

The picturesque little fishing-harbour of **Pecorini**, where the ferry from Naples docks, is popular with the rich and famous in the summer. The offshore stacks are a haven for birds, especially Eleonora's falcon.

PANAREA

Panarea (3.5km square; population 241) lies to the northeast (15km from Lipari) towards Stromboli. Its natural beauty and the style of the local architecture have been carefully preserved, although the hotels and restaurants, popular with wealthy Italians, are more expensive than those on the other islands. Electricity was only brought to the island in 1982. Near the fishing harbour, hot spring water mixes with the sea.

A signposted path (c. 30mins) leads from the harbour to **Punto Milazzese**, a naturally defended promontory on the southern tip of the island. A Bronze Age village thrived here between the 15th and 13th centuries BC, the inhabitants of which were clearly concerned for their safety when they chose such a secure location, with steep cliffs dropping into the sea and just a tiny corridor of land connecting it to the rest of the island, across which they constructed a wall. Excavations have shown that the inhabitants had strong links to Sicily and to the area of Thapsos in particular, while the Mycenaean ceramics found here indicate long-distance trading contacts with the Aegean world (now on display in the archaeological museum on Lipari). Only the central part of the settlement is visible today (erosion at the cliff edges having damaged much of the remainder). Twenty-two huts were excavated, 21 of which were oval in shape; the one rectangular hut is thought to have been either a sanctuary, a communal meeting place, or the house of the ruler.

A small **archaeological museum** below the church of San Pietro in the harbour (*open 9.30–1.30 & 3–in summer, otherwise by appointment with the archaeological museum in Lipari; see p. 488*) contains finds from many excavations on the island representing the broad sweep of its history from the 4th millennium BC to the 4th century AD.

At the opposite end of the island, near the last houses on the coast, a path descends to the shore at **Calcara** where the fumaroles emit sulphurous gases. Nearby are traces of Neolithic pits made from boulders and volcanic clay, probably used for offerings. Three ancient shipwrecks have so far been found in the seas around Panarea, the most recent of which (a 3rd century BC cargo vessel that sank while travelling from southern Italy to Sicily) was explored in 2014. Finds from these wrecks are on display in the Lipari museum and in the small collection on Panarea itself.

In the sea near the island the beautifully coloured rocks of **Lisca Bianca** and **Basiluzzo** (with many traces of Roman occupation) provide a foreground to the ever-changing view of Stromboli.

SALINA

Salina (27km square; population 2,600), 4km northwest of Lipari, is the highest of the islands (962m) and is formed of two twin volcanic cones and the saddle between them. The shape of Monte dei Porri is one of the most perfect mountain cones in the world. It has been identified with *Anthemoessa*, Homer's island of the Sirens who tempted Odysseus, and was anciently called *Didyme*. Its population lives in three municipalities, each formed of several picturesque villages: Santa Marina, Malfa and Leni. The public library of Malfa, **Biblioteca Comunale** (*Via Fontana 2, open weekdays 8.30–13, Tues and Thur also 4–7; T: 090 984 4372*), houses an interesting and poignant museum on the emigration of the islanders to America and Australia, and a section dedicated to the flora of the Aeolians.

The island is exceptionally green and very pleasant walks can be taken on the two mountains, the Monte dei Porri (mountain of leeks) and the Fossa delle Felci (glen of the ferns). The latter is partly covered in woods of chestnut. The attractive old houses and the fine scenery have been carefully protected for many years.

MALVASIA OF SALINA

This exquisite wine was once so much in demand that almost all the available land on the Aeolian Islands, including the tiny islet of Basiluzzo, was dedicated to its production. The industry supported a population (in 1880) of over 32,000 people, while today there are only 15,000 inhabitants in the archipelago. Most of the wine was exported, some of it to England where it was called Malmsey. In 1889 the phylloxera blight hit the islands and destroyed almost all the vines; at least 20,000 islanders emigrated, mostly to America and Australia.

New incentives for Malvasia came in the 1960s, when a young architect, Carlo Hauner, was invited to spend a few days painting on Salina, and he decided to take up the challenge of re-introducing the production of Malvasia to the island. Hauner is still the best-known name when buying this delectable drink; the winery is now run by his son. Made from white Malvasia grapes (95 percent) and black Corinth (5 percent), after harvesting the bunches are left to wither in the sun on wicker trays for 10 days before being pressed. Sweet but not cloying, it is best drunk chilled as an aperitif or to accompany dessert. It is thought that the Greeks first planted vines here in the 5th century BC.

A Middle Bronze Age settlement has been excavated at **Portella** on the east coast on the road between Santa Marina and Capo Faro. It has recently been landscaped to provide easier visitor access (*no ticket or gate; open throughout the year*) but it is a very steep climb up a stepped path to the top, from which the views are magnificent. The settlement was inhabited between the 15th and 13th centuries BC, and 25 huts have been excavated to date, in an exceptional state of preservation. This rich archaeological bounty is sadly not readily apparent to the visitor today, but alongside the scant remains of the huts it is possible to see a few of the pithoi that were used in the site (25 have so far been found) for water storage. Some of the finds are on display in the Lipari museum, and the **archaeological museum in Lingua** (*Via Pantano, usually open 10–8 in summer; if closed, or to visit at other times of the year, contact the Comune di Santa Marina, T: 090 984 3021*) also contains much interesting material from Portella, in wonderful new display cases, together with some finds from the Roman site at Contrada Barone (near Santa Marina). The **Museo Civico di Lingua** (*open as archaeological museum*), in an 18th-century house opposite the archaeological museum, has an interesting collection of farming equipment, the interior of a reconstructed island house, and paintings, drawings and equipment related to the recent maritime endeavours of the islanders. After the Arab conquest of the Aeolian Islands in 838, the island remained virtually uninhabited until the 16th century. It was the setting for the Oscar-winning film *Il Postino*, which describes an episode in the life of Pablo Neruda. Among the interesting varieties of bird life that can be spotted on a visit to Salina are flamingoes. They usually pause to rest during their migratory flights on the salt pan of Salina, at Lingua. The kestrel, sparrowhawk and buzzard are birds of prey present as nesting species, both here and on the other islands.

STROMBOLI

Stromboli (12.5km square; population 542), c. 28km from Lipari, is the best-known island of the archipelago because of its continual volcanic activity. It consists of a single cone (924m); the present active crater is 200m below the summit. It has been abandoned several times after severe eruptions, but is now again increasing in population and is popular with tourists. Strong activity in December 2002 caused a tsunami and considerable damage. The inhabitants were evacuated for several days. The inhabitants never refer to their volcano by name, calling it simply *Iddu*, 'Him'.

The main village of Stromboli, **San Vincenzo**, is on the northeast side; ferries and hydrofoils dock at the harbour of Scauri. The boats also call at **Ginostra**, an attractive small group of houses on a rocky headland on the southwest tip of the island, completely isolated from the rest. A small dock for the ferries and hydrofoils has been built here, in spite of opposition. Ginostra has about 30 permanent inhabitants, of whom ten are originally from Germany. All the villages of the island, including Ginostra, now have electricity, but not along the paths and tracks (a torch is indispensable) because the inhabitants decided that they prefer to see the stars.

Eruptions occur on the northwest side of the **volcano** and are not visible from the villages. The cone should be ascended with a guide (c. 3hrs) because trekking on the volcano is dangerous, but an easy footpath from San Vincenzo ascends as far as the Semaforo (c. 1hr 30mins), from which point the explosions can usually be seen. Small eruptions normally occur at frequent intervals; on days of unusual violence the spectacle (best seen at night from the sea) of the volcanic matter rushing down the Sciara del Fuoco into the sea is particularly impressive. Climbs on the volcano (very strenuous and particularly exhilarating at night; possible from March–Oct) can be booked (well ahead, places are limited) with Magmatrek (*Via Vittorio Emanuele, T: 090 986 5768; www.magmatrek.it*); take a torch, chocolate and water with you.

The schoolhouse of San Vincenzo, in the centre of the village, houses the **Museo del Cinema di Stromboli e Ginostra** (*Via Vittorio Emanuele; open weekdays 8.30–12; www.museodistromboli.blogspot.it*), with collections of photographs and newspaper articles, and a viewing-room for showing films and videos. The island provided the setting for a landmark film of Italian cinema history, *Stromboli* (1949), by Roberto Rossellini, starring his new lover Ingrid Bergman (his discarded lover, Anna Magnani, immediately sought redress by convincing Otto Dieterle to star her in *Volcano* (1950), which did not enjoy the same box-office success). The islands became a popular location for movie-makers. Significant films include *Islands of Fire* (1956) by Vittorio De Seta, *The Adventure* (1960) by Michelangelo Antonioni, *Kaos* (1984) by the Taviani brothers, and *Dear Diary* (1991) by Nanni Moretti.

Off the northeast coast is the striking isolated rock of **Strombolicchio**, a steep volcanic neck of basalt (43m) looking like a cathedral in the sea.

VULCANO

Vulcano (21km square; population 715) is the most southerly of the isles (separated from the southern tip of Lipari by a channel less than a kilometre wide) and easily reached from the Sicilian mainland or by frequent hydrofoil services from Lipari (and by local boat excursions). It is of outstanding interest because of its geological structure and the spectacular volcanic landscape with black lava rocks on the sea and beaches of black sand. Formed of four volcanoes, the last volcanic eruption of Fossa Grande took place from 1888–90. It has simple houses, mostly built in the 20th century in a disorderly way. Deserted out of season, it becomes very crowded in summer. Many northern Italians have their summer houses here. A characteristic of Vulcano is the strong smell of sulphur, especially in the area around the port. The easily accessible deposits of sulphur, alum, boric acid and other minerals, were first exploited industrially in the early 19th century; after 1860 the deposits were purchased for extraction by a certain Mr Stevenson, a Scot who had fallen in love with the island. He also planted vineyards and fruit orchards, dug wells, and tried to improve the lot of the islanders. The eruption of 1888 put a violent end to his dreams. His house, near the mud pools, can still be seen and is now a restaurant.

The boats dock at **Porto di Levante** near the quay used by the hydrofoils. A road with simple shops and a few cafés leads to **Porto di Ponente** with mud pools on the beach fed by hot springs. The fine black lava-sand beach nearby has a number of hotels.

Caution is advised while swimming, because there are scalding hot springs in the sea quite close to the shore.

In the other direction from the port a straight road leads across the plain at the foot of the volcano. A narrow path (signposted; about 1km from the port) leads up across the fine volcanic soil and rocks to the top of the crater (391m), called **Fossa Grande**, in about 2hrs. The route can be damaged and almost impassable after heavy rain, but is normally quite easy (although sturdy shoes are necessary). There is a remarkable view of the inside of the crater and the rim steams constantly with sulphurous vapours. On a clear day all of the Aeolian Islands can be seen from here. The path can be followed right around the rim in about one hour.

Most of the islanders live on the upland plain of the island known as **Piano**, 7km from the port (reached by a few buses every day). There is a bar, a shop, a church, a couple of restaurants and a school: most of the farms have now been abandoned and some of the houses are only used in summer. The Piano road passes close to the volcano and at the top of the hill, by the first house on the corner, a byroad leads left. Another turn left leads to the edge of a cliff with a number of caves and a view of the coast. The road continues gently uphill past a road on the left for **Gelso**, with some restaurants open in summer and good sea bathing. Another byroad leads to **Capo Grillo**, which has the best panorama on the island. The Piano road ends in front of the parish church destroyed by an earthquake in 1978 and rebuilt in 1988.

On the northern tip of the island is **Vulcanello**, a volcanic cone which rose out of the sea in 183 BC. Near the Faraglione della Fabbrica, a high rock with alum quarries, are the hot springs of Acqua Bollente and Acqua del Bagno. Between Vulcano and Lipari are some dramatically tall stacks emerging from the sea,, including the Pietralunga, a 72-metre-high obelisk of basalt.

PRACTICAL INFORMATION

GETTING AROUND

• **By air**: There are helicopter services run by **Air Panarea** (*T: 090 983 4428 or 340 366 7214, www.airpanarea. it*), **Icarus Elicotteri** (*T: 0968 53737, www.elicotteri-icarus.it*) and **Dedalus Elicotteri** (*T: 090 983333, www.elieolie. it*) connecting the Aeolian Islands with some airports, and offering air-taxi services.

• **By train**: Messina, Giardini and Taormina are on the main line which runs along the coast from Syracuse via Catania to Messina. Milazzo is on the Messina–Palermo line.

• **By bus**: NB: for up-to-date bus schedules see *www.orariautobus.it*. **ATM** (*www.atmmessina.it*) runs town buses and trams. Useful services are no. 79 from the station—Via I Settembre—Duomo—Corso Cavour and via Garibaldi to the Regional Museum (continuing to Ganzirri and Punta Faro), no. 28 (velocittà) from Piazza Cairoli and Via Garibaldi, no. 29 from Piazza Cairoli to he cemetery, and the tram that runs hrough Messina from the cemetery in he south to the regional museum in the 1orth.

Giuntabus (*www.giuntabus.com*) rom Via Terranova 8 (at the junction vith Viale San Martino; *map 6*) run ervices from Messina to Milazzo in 50mins (connecting with hydrofoils to he Aeolian Islands), also services to/ rom Catania Airport and Milazzo from April–Sept. **INTERBUS** (*www.interbus. t*) to Taormina (via SS 114) in 90mins, lso to Alì Terme, Barcellona, Forza D'Agrò, Giardini Naxos, Santa Teresa li Riva, Scaletta Zanclea and Terme Vigliatore. **Jonica Trasporti** (*www. onicatrasporti.it*) serves the southern Peloritans, from Messina to Taormina nd Roccafiorita. **SAIS Autolinee** (*www. aisautolinee.it*), terminal by the railway tation in Piazza della Repubblica (*map 5*), run coaches from Messina to Castel li Tusa and Palermo in 2½hrs, and Catania (direct via the motorway) in 90mins (continuing to Catania airport). **TAI** and **Magistro** (*www. utolineemagistro.it*), departing from n front of the Chamber of Commerce n Via Santa Maria Alemanna (*map 6*), un weekday-only services to towns in he northern Peloritan and Nebrodi Mountains, including Brolo, Capo l'Orlando, Falcone, Galati Mamertino, Longi, Mirto, Naso, Olivarella, Rocca di Caprileone, Tindari and Tortorici.

From **Taormina** (bus station in Via Pirandello; *map 3*) there are buses to Mazzarò, Castelmola, the Alcantara Gorge and the towns on the foothills of Etna, as well as services to Catania (and Catania airport) and Messina.

Aeolian Islands On Lipari buses un by Urso (*www.ursobus.it*), from Marina Lunga to Canneto and to the pumice quarries and Acquacalda; to Quattrocchi, Pianoconte, and Quattropani; also tours of the island in summer. There are a few buses a day from the port on Vulcano to Piano. On Salina buses run by CITIS (*www. trasportisalina.it*), from Santa Marina Salina and Rinella to Leni, Pollara, Malfa and Lingua.

• **By car**: Cars are allowed (not July and August) on Lipari, Vulcano, Filicudi and Salina. However, visitors are not advised to take a car as distances are short and local transport good. It is a good idea to garage your car at Milazzo; the attendant will pick it up for you on the dockside and then bring it back on your return. A reliable company is Garage delle Isole, English spoken (*T: 090 928 8585 or 090 928 6986, www. garagedelleisole.it*. On request they can provide shuttle service to/from Catania, Palermo and Trapani airports. Some car-hire services operate on Lipari, Vulcano and Salina. On the other islands small electric vehicles are used to transport luggage, and on Alicudi and Stromboli, mules and donkeys. On Lipari and Vulcano, vespas and bicycles can also be hired.

• **By sea**: Throughout the year ferries, hydrofoils and catamarans run to the Aeolian Islands. The most convenient starting-point is Milazzo.

N.G.I. (Milazzo; *www.ngi-spa.it*), runs car-ferries to Vulcano, Lipari, Salina, Panarea and Stromboli.

Liberty Lines (*www.libertylines.it*) run car ferries from Milazzo taking 1hr 45mins to Vulcano, 2hrs to Lipari. Also an overnight ferry to the islands from Naples. There are hydrofoils from Milazzo (*Agenzia Catalano,Via dei*

Mille 32) to the Aeolian Islands, taking 45mins to Vulcano, 1hr to Lipari. **Ferry and hydrofoil ticket offices on the islands**: Some ticket offices on the islands open only 30mins before sailing. All the islands are connected by ferry and hydrofoil services; the ferries are slower, cheaper, more reliable and often less direct. Fishing boats may be hired on all the islands, and the trip around the coast of the islands is strongly recommended.

WHERE TO STAY

ACQUEDOLCI (*map p. 568, A2–B2*)
€€ **Villa Nicetta**. Sleeps 15 people in a series of strange but comfortable rooms, in a very old fortified farmhouse (once the hunting-lodge of Prince Pignatelli) with its own church, close to Acquedolci. Many activities on offer, including horse-riding and trekking in the Nebrodi Mountains park, watching harvesting, sheep-milking, etc. Slow Food-recommended restaurant. Pets welcome. Landing-strip close by. *Contrada Nicetta, T: 0941 726142, www. villanicetta.it.*
ALÌ TERME (*map p. 568, D3*)
€ **Liberty B&B**. The roads in this area are a bit hectic, especially in summer, but the town is friendly and the wide beach (shale and sand) is clean.. This B&B, in a pretty building in the town centre (opposite the railway station), has 5 welcoming rooms and the breakfasts are very good. *Via Federico 1, T: 0942 701009, www.libertybeb.com.*
CAPO D'ORLANDO (*map p. 568, B2*)
€€€ **Sant'Andrea**. New structure just out of town with 25 rooms, good restaurant, car park, pool. *Via Torrente Forno 67/b, T: 0941 911111, www.*

hotelsantandrea.eu.
€€ **Il Mulino**. A good hotel on the seafront with 85 rooms and suites, private beach, reputable restaurant. *Via Andrea Doria 46, T: 0941 902431, www. hotelilmulino.it.*
€ **Nuovo Hotel Faro**. Good value for money at this little place on the sea front, 20 clean rooms, close to centre, no restaurant, pets welcome. *Via Libertà 7, T: 0941 902466, www.nuovohotelfaro. com.*
CASTEL DI TUSA (*map p. 568, A3*)
€€€ **Atelier sul Mare**. Close to the sea, 20 of the 40 rooms have been 'created' by famous contemporary artists so you can literally sleep in a work of art. *Via Cesare Battisti 4, T: 0921 334295, www. ateliersulmare.com.*
CASTELMOLA (*map p. 568, C3*)
€€€ **Villa Sonia**. Superb position on the mountaintop, just beneath the castle, for this old villa. Lovely rooms, most with panoramic balcony. Pool, garden, sauna, gymnasium, tennis. The hotel has an exceptionally good restaurant, worth a visit in its own right. *Via Porta Mola 9, T: 0942 28082, www.hotelvillasonia.com.*
CASTROREALE (*map p. 568, C2*)
€€€ **Green Manors**. Luxurious old country house surrounded by olive groves, 10 beautiful rooms, all different, pool, good restaurant. *Via Porticato 70, T: 090 974 6515, www.greenmanors.it.*
GANZIRRI (*map p. 568, D2*)
€€ **Villa Morgana**. A luxurious 1970s villa on one of the Ganzirri lakes, now a lovely small hotel surrounded by a garden, good fitness centre, pool, the 15 rooms are all different. *Via Consolare Pompea 1965, T: 090 325575, www. villamorgana.it.*
GIARDINI NAXOS (*map p. 568, C3*)
€€€ **Hellenia Yachting**. Refined

atmosphere, restaurant, private beach and pool. *Via Jannuzzo 41, Località Recanati, T: 0942 51737, www. hotelhellenia.com.*

€€ **Palladio**. Colourful, comfortable small hotel in good position on the seafront, from April–Sept also restaurant on the veranda overlooking the bay. *Via Umberto 470, T: 0942 52267, www.hotelpalladiogiardini.com.*

LONGI (*map p. 568, B3*)

€ **Nebrodi Albergo Diffuso**. The village of Longi is the ideal base for nature-lovers and especially birdwatchers. The *Albergo Diffuso* organisation can provide several houses in the heart of this village or others in the surroundings, with comfortable rooms and marvellous Sicilian breakfasts. If you choose Il Vignale, you will be staying in an old silk mill in the heart of the forest, near the Rocche del Crasto and the Catafurco waterfall. It is isolated, though, 4km from Longi. *T: 366 989 2762, www. nebrodialbergodiffuso.it.*

MESSINA (*map p. 568, D2*)

€€ **Messenion**. Modern central hotel with 18 rooms, near the University, no restaurant. *Via Faranda 7, T: 090 712674, www.hotelmessenia.it. Map 5.*

€ **Sant'Elia**. Small, friendly, old-fashioned, central hotel with 15 rooms, no restaurant. *Via I Settembre 67, T: 090 678 3570, www.hotelsantelia.com. Map 5.*

MILAZZO (*map p. 568, C2*)

NB: The following hotels will provide a good breakfast but they do not have restaurants.

€€ **Cassisi**. Aristocratic residence transformed into a charming hotel, 17 comfortable modern rooms. *Via Cassisi 5, T: 090 922 9099, www.cassisihotel. com.*

€€ **Petit Hotel**. Close to the pier for ferries to the islands, this hotel is built entirely to eco-friendly standards (it has ceiling fans, no air conditioning). 9 rooms, good beds, a spectacular terrace and very good organic breakfasts. *Via dei Mille 37, T: 090 928 6784, www. petithotel.it.*

€€ **Garibaldi**. Charming little hotel in the fishermen's quarter, 28 rooms (some with extra-large beds) or apartments, nice buffet breakfasts, car park, shuttle to/from port or railway station on request. *Lungomare Garibaldi 160, T: 090 924 0189, www.hotelgaribaldi.net.*

MONTALBANO ELICONA

€ **Albergo Diffuso**. Ask at the tourist office (*Via Roma, T: 0941 678019, www. comune.montalbanoelicona.me.it*), if you would like to stay in one of the little medieval houses of this beautiful village.

PATTI (*map p. 568, C2*)

€ **Hotel Sacra Famiglia**. In the high part of the town, ex-monastery recently restored and run by the Diocese, with its own church; clean simple rooms, restaurant. Intended for pilgrims to Tindari—but it represents excellent value for money for everyone. *Via Dante Alighieri 1, T: 0941 241622, www. sacrafamiglia.it.*

SAVOCA (*map p. 568, D3*)

€€€ **Borgo San Rocco**. ■ Old houses of the fishermen's quarter in this hilltop village, meticulously restored and transformed into a delightful hotel, with 21 rooms and suites, fitness centre, gardens, pool and an excellent restaurant. *Via San Rocco, T: 0942 761234, www.borgosanrocco.com.*

TAORMINA (*map p. 568, C3*)

€€€ **Grand Hotel Timeo**. The first hotel to open in Sicily; 70 rooms and suites (some in Villa Flora on the other side of the street) with spacious bathrooms; pool, glorious views, good restaurant. *Via Teatro Greco 59, T: 0942 627 0200, www.belmond.com. Map 2.*

€€€ **San Domenico**. One of Sicily's oldest hotels, a converted 15th-century convent; ambassadors, royalty and film stars of yesteryear stay here. 105 rooms with varying levels of luxury, 3 restaurants, one of which, 'Principe di Cerami' (closed Mon), has 2 Michelin stars. Beautiful gardens, pool. *Piazza San Domenico 5, T: 0942 613111, www. amthotels.it. Map 5.*

€€€ **The Ashbee**. ■ Another historic hotel in a panoramic position just outside Porta Messina, with 25 cool, spacious rooms, good bathrooms, beautiful terraced garden, restaurant. Designed in 1907 for Colonel Shaw-Hellier by Charles Ashbee, exponent of William Morris's Arts and Crafts movement. *Viale San Pancrazio 46, T: 0942 23537, www.theashbeehotel.com. Map 2.*

€€€ **NH Collection (ex-Imperiale)**. Close to the heart of town, 138 beautiful rooms, pool, fitness centre and good restaurant. *Via Circonvallazione 11, T: 0942 625202, www.nh-collection.com. Map 2.*

€€€ **Villa Angela**. The home of Jim Kerr (Simple Minds); way up above Taormina, on the road to Castelmola, 43 nice rooms, stunning views, pool, tennis. Restaurant open for lunch, car park. *Via Leonardo da Vinci 71/e, T: 0942 28513, www.hotelvillaangela.com. Map 1.*

€€ **Villa Schuler**. ■ One of the best small hotels in town, opened in 1905, with 51 rooms and suites, garden, garage, no restaurant. *Piazzetta Bastione, Via Roma 16, T: 0942 23481, www. hotelvillaschuler.com. Map 6.*

€€ **Piccolo Giardino**. Tiny hotel with 25 comfortable rooms, good restaurant 'Nettuno da Siciliano'(cookery courses organised), a roof garden, fitness centre and panoramic pool, in the town centre, just above Corso Umberto. *Salita Lucio Denti 4, T: 0942 23463, www. ilpiccologiardino.it. Map 2.*

TAORMINA (Mazzarò)

€€€ **Atlantis Bay**. Built for the Hollywood stars arriving for the film festival in the 1950s, a luxurious, delightfully kitsch hotel with a series of terraces descending to sea level at the Bay of the Mermaids, with 85 rooms and suites, fitness centre, seawater pool and a good restaurant. Excellent breakfasts. *Via Nazionale 161, T: 0942 618011, www. atlantisbay.it. Beyond map 4.*

TERME VIGLIATORE (*map p. 568, C2*)

€ **Grand Hotel Terme Parco Augusto**. For a relaxing break, 90 comfortable rooms, restaurant, spa and a Maurice Mességué fitness and beauty centre. The baths, first exploited by the Romans, were conceded to the city by Philip III of Spain in 1643. *Viale delle Terme 85, T: 090 978 1078, www.parcoaugusto.com.*

TORTORICI (*map p. 568, B3*)

€ **Casa Zia Maria Antonina**. 6 comfortable rooms in the oldest part of Tortorici, some with shared bathrooms. No breakfast but there are plenty of coffee bars close by, excellent value. *Via Roma 54, T: 0941 421028 or 339 220 1027, www.casaziamariantonina.org.*

TRIPI (*map p. 568, C2*)

€€ **Rosa dei Venti**. In a hamlet at the foot of the hill of Tripi, ideally situated for exploring the lovely coast, the Malabotta forest and the Argimusco, this hotel (closed Jan) has 22 comfortable rooms, garden, pool and restaurant. *Via*

Garibaldi 1, Campogrande di Tripi, T: 0941 801020, www.larosadeiventihotel. com.

WHERE TO STAY ON THE AEOLIAN ISLANDS

NB: Many hotels on the islands close in winter.

ALICUDI

€€ Ericusa. The only hotel on the island, charmingly rustic, on the beach, with 21 air-conditioned rooms. Good restaurant and coffee bar. *Via Regina Elena, T: 090 988 9902, www. alicudihotel.it.*

€ Casa Mulino. Typical Aeolian house overlooking the harbour offering self-catering accommodation. *Via Regina Elena, T: 090 988 9681, www. alicudicasamulino.it.*

FILICUDI

€€ La Sirena. 4 comfortable rooms with old-fashioned furniture, balconies overlooking the sea a stone's throw away. Excellent restaurant, or self-catering on request. Pets welcome. *Via Pecorini Mare, T: 090 988 9997, www. pensionelasirena.it.*

€€ Villa La Rosa. The 3 rooms open onto personal verandas, Aeolian-style. Renowned restaurant where the bread is freshly baked every day in a wood-fired oven. Shuttle service to/from the port. *Via Rosa, Contrada Rocca di Ciauli, T: 090 988 9965, www.villalarosa.it.*

€ La Canna. In a beautiful panoramic position, with 14 rooms, open all year, good restaurant, panoramic pool, car park. *Via Rosa 43, Contrada Rocca di Ciauli, T: 090 988 9956 or 336 926560, www.lacannahotel.it.*

LIPARI

€€€ Villa Meligunis. Right in the heart of the old city, 43 beautiful rooms, atmosphere, and a rooftop terrace with pool. Good restaurant. Free shuttle service to/from the port or Canneto beach. *Via Marte 7 (two blocks south of Via Roma), T: 090 981 2426, www. villameligunis.it. Beyond map 8.*

€€ Villa Liberty. 12 comfortable rooms, all different, in a pretty Art Nouveau villa surrounded by a lush garden, no restaurant. Open year round. *Via Conti Vainicher 20, T: 090 981 4270, www. libertyresort.it. Beyond map 5.*

€€ Gattopardo. A 19th-century villa in a beautiful sub-tropical garden, with 47 rooms in little Aeolian cottages, pool, good restaurant. Free shuttle to/from the port or Canneto beach. *Via Diana 67, T: 090 981 1035/6, www. gattopardoparkhotel.it. Beyond map 5.*

€€ Giardino sul Mare. 46 rooms in cottages, beautiful gardens going down to the sea; pool. *Via Maddalena 65, T: 090 981 1004, www.giardinosulmare.it. Beyond map 8.*

€€ Casajanca. Interesting, comfortable little hotel in Canneto village, with 10 rooms, verdant patio, small thermal pool, close to the sea. Pets welcome. *Marina Garibaldi 115, Canneto, T: 090 988 0222, www.casajanca.it.*

€ Oriente. Comfortable hotel, albeit rather bizarre, 30 rooms, little garden, no restaurant; free port shuttle. *Via Marconi 35, T: 090 981 1493, www. hotelorientelipari.com. Map 5.*

€ Enzo il Negro. ■ Near Marina Corta, a spotlessly clean *pensione* with 8 rooms, all with private bath and air conditioning; there is a beautiful rooftop terrace for breakfasts. Enzo is a fisherman who knows the islands like the back of his hand. His children and grandchildren now help with the running of the *pensione* and can give you plenty of help for organising your trip. *Via Garibaldi 29, T: 090 981 3163, www. enzoilnegro.com. Map 8.*

PANAREA

€€€ **Raya**. Perched on a hill dominating the port; exclusive clientèle, very expensive. 30 peaceful rooms, all with sea view, beautiful thermal pool and fitness centre, good restaurant serving only organic food. *Via San Pietro, Località Costa Galletta, T: 090 983013, www.hotelraya.it.*

€€€ **Hycesia**. Small hotel with 11 rooms, surrounded by a garden, with a wine bar and good restaurant. *Via San Pietro, T: 090 983041 or 090 983226, www. hycesia.it.*

€€ **Cincotta**. Right on the brink of the cliff, this was the first hotel to open on the island. Garden, saltwater pool, restaurant, close to harbour. Closed winter. *Via San Pietro, T: 090 983014, www.hotelcincotta.it.*

€€ **Lisca Bianca**. Small hotel in a panoramic position in front of harbour, all 28 rooms and suites with terrace or patio in true Aeolian Islands style; restaurant, lush garden. A place for night owls: dancing on the terrace until 2am in the summer. *Via Lani 1, T: 090 983004/5, www.liscabianca.it.*

SALINA

€€€ **Capofaro Malvasia**. Splendid hotel consisting of 20 Aeolian cottages immersed in the vineyards belonging to the Tasca d'Almerita family, for a really relaxing holiday. Good restaurant, excellent breakfasts, pool. *Via Faro 3, T: 090 984 4330, www.capofaro.it.*

€€€ **Santa Isabel**. Small hotel in a lovely clifftop position, accommodation in 10 comfortable suites, gourmet restaurant (cookery courses available), *Via Scalo 12, Malfa, T: 090 984 4018, www.santaisabel.it.*

€€€ **Signum**. ■ A restructured hamlet, Aeolian-style architecture for the 30 cool and welcoming rooms, peaceful position surrounded by vineyards, fitness centre, pool, Michelin-starred restaurant. *Via Scalo 15, Malfa; T: 090 984 4222, www.hotelsignum.it.*

€€ **Locanda del Postino**. At the tiny village of Pollara (70 inhabitants), in the house used as a set for Michael Radford's 1994 Oscar-winning film *Il Postino*. 10 quiet rooms and a restaurant. Open May–Oct. *Via Picone 10, T: 090 984 3958, www.lalocandadelpostino.it.*

STROMBOLI

€€€ **La Sirenetta**. One of the oldest hotels, many say it is still the best. 50 rooms, pool, scuba-diving centre, tennis, water-skiing, windsurfing, sailing. *Via Marina 33, Ficogrande, T: 090 986025, www.lasirenetta.it.*

€€ **Ossidiana**. In the fishermen's quarter of Scari, a short walk from the harbour, all rooms offer panoramic views. Thermal pool and Turkish bath. *Via Marina, T: 090 986006, www. hotelossidiana.it.*

STROMBOLI (Ginostra)

NB: Ginostra is totally isolated from the rest of the island and can only be reached by boat, the streets are steep steps, donkeys provide the only means of transport. Bring a torch. A small general store supplies food and other necessities, meat is seldom available in this village.

€ **Locanda L'Incontro**. Tiny inn with comfortable rooms run by Immacolata Petrusa, a famous cook. She can also assist in finding rooms or apartments to rent close by. *Via Sopra Pertuso, T:*

090 981 2305 or 338 141 4620, www.
vinostraincontro.it.

VULCANO

€€€ **Therasia Resort**. The ex-Hotel
Arcipelago, in a quiet position on
Vulcanello, with a magnificent view
embracing all seven islands. Very
comfortable, 97 spacious rooms, 2
seawater infinity pools and whirlpool,
fitness centre with sauna and Turkish
bath, three restaurants, one of which,
'Il Cappero', is Michelin-starred.
Vulcanello, T: 090 985 2555, www.
therasiaresort.it.

€€€ **Les Sables Noirs**. One of the
oldest and most prestigious hotels on
Vulcano. 45 comfortable rooms, garden,
pool, private beach, restaurant on a
panoramic terrace. Porto Ponente, T:
090. 9850, www.framon-hotels.com.

€€€ **Eros**. Small hotel near the hot
water springs, 26 rather tiny rooms,
pool with whirlpool, garden and private
beach. Via Porto Levante 64, T: 090 985
3265, www.eroshotel.it.

WHERE TO EAT

CAPO D'ORLANDO (map p. 568, B2)
€ **Pasticceria Giulio**. The historic
pastry-shop of Capo d'Orlando, a good
place for a light lunch and superb
home-made ice cream. Closed Tues. Via
Amendola 25, T: 0941 912546.

CAPRI LEONE (map p. 568, B2)
€€€ **Antica Filanda**. Family-run,
with a long tradition for excellent and
inventive food, making much use of local
ham, lamb, kid, various cheeses, and
wild fungi from the Nebrodi Mountains.
Excellent desserts. Ample wine list. In
summer you eat on the terrace looking
out towards the Aeolian Islands. Closed
Mon. Also guesthouse with pool.

Contrada Raviola, T: 0941 919704, www.
anticafilanda.net.

GANZIRRI-TORRE FARO (map p. 568,
D2)
€€€ **Bellavista**. An elegant, special-
occasions restaurant near the lighthouse
on the northeastern tip of Sicily, offering
a wonderful panorama over the Straits.
Particularly lovely on full-moon nights.
The food is a match for the occasion:
seafood of course. Try the tuna or the
local shrimps, and finish with a cannolo
di ricotta and a glass of rum—they have
12 different kinds. Closed Mon and Jan.
Via Circuito 126, Torre Faro, T: 090
326682.

GIARDINI NAXOS (map p. 568, C3)
€€€ **Garden da Nino**. Eat right next to
the sea, very good seafood (especially
the antipasti), good wine list. Just let
Salvatore take you by the hand. Via
Tysandros 74, T: 0942 51502.

€€ **'A Putia**. Old-fashioned tavern,
delightful atmosphere, well-presented
Sicilian dishes brought up-to-date
with flair, good wine list. For dessert,
cinnamon or tangerine jelly. Closed Sun.
Via Umberto 456, T: 0942 52755.

MESSINA (map p. 568, D2)
€€€ **L'Ossidiana**. Elegant place
near the port offering excellent
Mediterranean fare, delightfully
presented. Good wine list. Closed Mon.
Via dei Verdi 7, T: 090 675899. Map 6.

€€ **Amici Miei Ristoria**. Comfortable
but tiny restaurant, the place to
come for authentic Messina cuisine.
Exceptionally good seafood risotto.
Closed Sun. Via Cesare Battisti 124, T:
090 674393. Map 5.

€ **Past'Ovo**. Fresh home-made pasta,
grilled chicken or meat, interesting
vegetables, also take-away. Closed Sun.
Piazza Catalani 1, T: 090 774979. Map 4.

€ **Porta Messina**. Self-service restaurant and bar, also a pizzeria in the evenings, serving freshly-cooked food (generous portions) and delicious desserts. Close to the railway station. Closed Sat. *Via Calabria 16, T: 090 673831. Map 6.*

€ **Il Cappero**. Excellent lunch stop, for tasty Sicilian 'fast food' and *focacce*, soft bread rolls with various fillings; also take-away. Closed evenings. *Via Manara 85, T: 090 669693. Map 8.*

MILAZZO (*map p. 568, C2*)

€€€ **The Loft**. Small, elegant restaurant in the heart of town, offering well-prepared dishes, all cooked to order. Closed Tues. *Via Migliavacca 44, T: 090 907 3733 or 340 404 8016.*

€€€ **Doppio Gusto**. Fish is the speciality of this restaurant, which has a veranda providing a view of the port. Very nice hot and cold *antipasti*; crudités, spaghetti with lobster or shrimp ragout, home-made desserts, Sicilian wines, all well presented. Closed Mon. *Via Rizzo 44, T: 090 924 0045.*

€€ **La Casalinga**. In a tiny alley, friendly, relaxed atmosphere, generous portions. *Via D'Amico 13, T: 090 922 2697.*

TAORMINA (*map p. 568, C3*)

€€€ **Andreas**. In front of the public gardens, a refined restaurant with a flowery patio offering high-standard cuisine that aims to please the eye as well as the palate. Michelin-starred Andreas, an Austrian who fell in love with Sicily many years ago, uses his prime ingredients with flair. Apple strudel with vanilla ice cream is the perfect dessert. Good service, extensive wine list. Closed lunchtime Mon and Tues. *Via Bagnoli Croci, 88, T: 0942 24011. Map 6.*

€€€ **La Capinera**. Just outside Taormina at Mazzarò. Michelin-starred chef Pietro D'Agostino prepares fabulous dishes inspired by tradition, but with an innovative twist. Everything is prepared fresh in his kitchen, from the bread to the after-dinner chocolates, and served on the terrace overlooking the sea. Good wine list, also lists for mineral water and beer. Closed Mon. Expensive. *Via Nazionale 177, T: 0942 626247. Beyond map 4.*

€€€ **Osteria Nero D'Avola**. Michelin-listed restaurant opposite the San Domenico hotel. Offers well-presented Sicilian fare accompanied by the best Sicilian wines. Booking advisable. Open evenings only, closed Mon. *Piazza San Domenico 2, T: 0942 628874. Map 5.*

€€€ **Osteria Rossodivino**. Near Porta Catania, *trattoria* with a little garden, where seafood reigns supreme. The *antipasto* includes very fresh fish crudités, followed by home-made pasta, perhaps with tuna ragout. Meat dishes are also good, and the desserts are delicious. Strictly Sicilian wines. Closed Tues. *Vico De Spuches 8, T: 0942 628653. Map 5.*

€€ **La Botte**. Congenial *trattoria* frequented by artists performing at the Greek Theatre, or 'locals' such as Jim Kerr and Mick Hucknall. Good Sicilian *antipasti. Piazza Santa Domenica 4, T: 0942 24198. Map 2.*

€€ **La Griglia**. Romantic restaurant famous for fish dishes (and the exclusive clientèle). Closed Tues. *Corso Umberto 54, T: 0942 23980. Map 1.*

€€ **Il Borghetto**. Corrado's little *trattoria* in a pretty square near Porta Catania. Good pasta, salads and meat dishes. Closed Mon. *Piazzale Sant'Antonio 14, T: 0942 628846 or 347*

290 1091. *Map 5.*

€€ **Sapori di Mare**. Just outside Porta Messina, a small restaurant specialising in seafood; good desserts, good service. *Viale San Pancrazio 26, T: 0942 24743. Map 2.*

€€ **Il Barcaiolo**. ■ On the northern headland of the bay of Mazzarò. Tiny family-run restaurant for delicious fish, especially the local red shrimps caught just a few yards away, accompanied by Sicilian wines. From the road opposite Hotel Villa Esperia you go down 120 steps to the beach. Very romantic in the evening, but bring midge repellent in the summer. Booking advisable. *Via Castelluccio 43, T: 0942 625633. Map 4.*

TINDARI (*map p. 568, C2*)

€ **Pane e Vino**. In the village at the foot of the sanctuary of the Black Madonna, a simple *trattoria*. No menu, Nino will bring you an array of *antipasti*; salami and ham, olives, *caponata* and cheeses accompanied by jams and local honey. These are followed by mixed grilled meat, all from local farms, and salad. His house wine is good. *Via Manzoni 82, T: 330 559933.*

WHERE TO EAT ON THE AEOLIAN ISLANDS

ALICUDI

€€ **L'Airone**. Overlooking the sea, romantic but simple, for memorable seafood feasts. Alicudi is particularly famous for tattlers, a type of squid. *Via Perciato, T: 090 988 9808 or 338 497 8277.*

FILICUDI

€€ **Da Nino sul Mare**. A terrace overlooking the sea for this *trattoria/café*/newsagent; good seafood *antipasti* and grilled fish. He also has comfortable rooms if you want to stay. Closed winter. *Via Porto, T: 090 988 9984.*

LIPARI

€€€ **Filippino**. Opened in 1910 and still in business. Dishes include *ravioli di cernia* (grouper or sea-perch ravioli), borlotti-bean soup with fresh sardines and wild fennel, or Aeolian sushi. Good wine cellar. Closed Mon in winter. *Piazza Mazzini, T: 090 981 1002.*

€€€ **Kasbah Café**. Delightful restaurant with a quiet garden, good seafood and pizza, delicious desserts. Closed winter. *Vico Selinunte 43, T: 090 981 1075.*

€€ **'E Pulera**. Beautiful setting in a lemon grove for this elegant restaurant with a long-standing reputation for excellence. Open evenings only April–Oct. *Via Vainicher Conti, T: 090 981 1158.*

€€ **Caffè La Vela**. ■ This is what island life is all about, people-watching on the harbour at breakfast while lingering over your mulberry *granita*. Lunch is good too: choose an award-winning Aeolian salad, deceptively simple, and worth the trip to Lipari. *Piazza Sant'Onofrio 2 (Marina Corta), T: 090 981 2800.*

€ **Mancia e Fui**. 'Eat and run' is how the name translates: excellent Sicilian fast food, from *arancini* to pizza, cooked in front of you. *Via Vittorio Emanuele 94, T: 090 981 3505.*

PANAREA

€€€ **Da Pina**. This place has become an institution, known for superb, innovative Aeolian cuisine. Pina's *gnocchi di patate e melanzane* (aubergine dumplings) are unique. *Via San Pietro 3, T: 090 983032.*

€€€ **Antonio il Macellaio**. Grilled meat from Antonio 'the Butcher', for carnivores who have surfeited on fish.

Also a pizzeria. Open March–Oct. *Via San Pietro 20, T: 090 983258.*

SALINA

€€€ **Il Delfino**. Hotel/restaurant on the seafront run by three sisters, talented chefs. You will find perfect grilled fish. Closed winter. *Via Marina Garibaldi 5, Lingua,T: 090 984 3024.*

€€€ **Porto Bello**. Famous for *spaghetti al fuoco* (fiery spaghetti) and a dessert of fresh ricotta with honey, pistachios and currants. Meals are served on the terrace overlooking the harbour. *Via Lungomare 2, Santa Marina, T: 090 984 3125.*

€€€ **Signum**. The Michelin-starred restaurant in this reconstructed hamlet is the best place to eat on Salina (*for contact details, see p. 502*). W€€ **Da Franco**. Franco is very proud of his spaghetti with sea urchins, or the unique caper salad. Also a guest house. *Via Belvedere 8, Santa Marina, T: 090 984 3287.*

€ **Il Gambero**. For shrimps and grilled squid, or try the *pane cunzato* for lunch. Also guest house. Closed winter. *Via Marina Garibaldi 3, Lingua, T: 090 984 3049.*

STROMBOLI

€€€ **Da Zurro**. Try his *pietre*, black ravioli filled with fish and ricotta. *Via Crivelli 5, T: 340 772 0689.*

€€€ **Punta Lena**. On a panoramic terrace overlooking Strombolicchio; excellent grilled vegetables, sardines with onions, fish is cooked on a hot slab of lava. Closed mid-Oct–April. *Via Marina 8, Ficogrande, T: 090 986204.*

€€ **Ai Gechi**. A firm favourite with local people, for creative Aeolian cuisine; beautiful panoramic terrace. Open evenings only, closed Nov–March. *Vico Salina 12, T: 338 357 7559.*

€ **L'Osservatorio**. On the slopes of the volcano 2km from the village, uncomfortable to reach on foot, but the pizza, the house wine, and the views of the eruptions are excellent. *Via Salvatore di Losa, T: 338 109 7830.*

VULCANO

€€ **Cantine Stevenson**. Modern, pleasant atmosphere; interesting cuisine and good list of wines and beers. *Via Porto Levante, T: 090 985 3247.*

€€ **Vincenzino**. Restaurant in a good position, with a long-standing reputation (though it has its ups and downs). Spaghetti *'alla Vincenzina'* (with shrimps and capers) is excellent. Closed winter. *Via Porto Levante, T: 090 985 2016.*

€€ **Maria Tindara**. At Piano, in the heart of the island, Maria Tindara specialises in home-made pasta, grilled meat (chicken, kid or rabbit), freshly-caught fish and salads. Call and she will arrange transport at no extra charge. She also has comfortable rooms. *Via Provinciale 38, T: 090 985 3004.*

€ **Trattoria Pina Maniaci**. On the tiny, isolated beach of Gelso (best reached by boat), for the freshest possible fish. Open May–Oct. *Strada Provinciale 179, Gelso, T: 368 668555.*

LOCAL SPECIALITIES

FILICUDI Be sure to visit the cave-house/studio of artist **Marina Klemente** (*Via Zucco Grande, www. marinaklemente.com*), who makes interesting lamps and sculptures from sun-bleached flotsam and jetsam.

LETOJANNI Niny Bar (*Via Vittorio Emanuele 213, corner of Piazza Durante*), run by the same family for three generations. Their speciality is *granita arcobaleno* (rainbow), with alternating layers of fresh fruit granita—lemon, peach, mulberry, strawberry and pineapple—in a glass. Top it with whipped cream.

LIPARI For *cassata* and *cannoli* made with fresh local ricotta, visit **Pasticceria Subba** (*Via Vittorio Emanuele 92; map 5*). The best place for ice cream is **Giovanni D'Ambra** (*Via Morfeo 50, a back street*). **I Gioielli del Mare** (*Via Garibaldi 8, Marina Corta, www. gioiellidelmare.com; map 8*) is where Francesco Berté creates striking jewels inspired by the sea, using shells, semi-precious stones and obsidian, the black glass-like volcanic stone. Closed Fri–Sun in winter. **Da Giulio** (*Via Garibaldi 153, T: 090 981 2457; map 4*) is a browser's paradise, with antiques, nautical curios and odd bric-à-brac.

MESSINA **Irrera** (*Piazza Cairoli 12; map 6*), founded in 1910, is one of the most famous historic pastry shops in Sicily. Renowned for its *pignolata messinese*, a confection formed of small pastry balls individually iced with lemon and chocolate, and piled up on a tray to form a cake. **Salumeria Francesco Doddis** (*Via Garibaldi 317; map 2*) for cheese, salami and ham from the Nebrodi Mountains. Salvatore Geraci of the **Azienda Agricola Palari** (*Contrada Barna, Santo Stefano di Briga, T: 090 630194*), on the hills overlooking Messina, produces the wonderful DOC Faro, mentioned by Homer, and several other excellent wines,

MISTRETTA **Antonino Testa** (*Via Monte 2*), for the local almond marzipan biscuits called *pasta reale*.

NOVARA DI SICILIA **Cucinotta** (*Via Benigno Salvo 1*) is a bakery where you will find the large, round, fragrant loaves of bread for which Novara is famous. The cafés in Novara serve **gelato di cedro**, made with large knobbly lemons with very thick peel and practically no flesh inside. The zest is particularly aromatic so the candied peel is used in many Sicilian confectionery recipes.

SALINA Try **Carlo Hauner** (*Via Umberto, Lingua, www.hauner.it*) for excellent Malvasia wines or some capers. **Fenech** (*Via Fratelli Mirabito 41, Malfa, www.fenech.it*) produces good Malvasia wines and olive oil. **Caravaglio** also has superb dry Malvasia (Occhio di Terra, an excellent white, is aged in terracotta amphorae) and capers (*www. caravaglio.it*). **Giuseppe Di Lorenzo** (*Via Leni 10, Pollara, T: 090 984 3951*) cultivates capers and makes pickles and spicy sauces. At Lingua, **Da Alfredo** (*Piazza Marina Garibaldi, opposite the pier, T: 090 984 3075, closed winter*) is a good place for scrumptious fresh-fruit granita: watermelon, mulberry, prickly pear, peach or fig. **Cosi Duci** (*Via San Lorenzo 9, Malfa, T: 090 984 4358; open every day; if closed in winter, they will open if you phone*) is an institution on Salina. They sell sweets, honey and jams made with local wild fruits such as pomegranates, mulberries, prickly pear, sorb apples and arbutus.

SAN MARCO D'ALUNZIO **La Tela di Penelope** (*Via Aluntina 48, T: 0941 797734, www.teladipenelope.it*) is a delightful shop offering traditional hand-woven linen articles, decorated with embroidery, lace, macramé or drawn-thread work.

SANTA LUCIA DEL MELA **Vasari** (*Contrada Casale, T: 090 935 9956, www. biovinivasari.it*) produces Mamertino DOC, a wine once much appreciated by Julius Caesar.

SANTO STEFANO DI CAMASTRA
La Maga (*Via Nazionale 114, T: 0921 331286*) for irresistible pottery and tiles, all hand-made using traditional colours and designs.

TAORMINA Gladys Art (*Corso Umberto 6, near Porta Messina; map 2*), sells paintings of local scenes by local artists. They make good souvenirs.

Gelatomania (*Corso Umberto 7; map 2*) for award-winning ice cream; try their delectable Ferrero Rocher, or in summer, mango flavour, prepared with locally-grown fruit. **C&G** (*Piazzale Sant'Antonio 7, near Porta Catania; map 5*) for good hot chocolate, coffee or ice cream, on their panoramic terrace.

TORTORICI For the exquisite *pasta reale* pastries made with hazelnuts, a good address is **Ciancio** (*Piazza Mazzini 2*).

FESTIVALS AND EVENTS

ACQUEDOLCI 14 May, the *Fiera del Bestiame* was the occasion when local farmers met to trade cattle, horses, pigs and sheep; no animals are traded nowadays, but a popular country fair is held.

ALCARA LI FUSI 24 June, *Festa del Muzzuni*—the summer solstice is celebrated. The *muzzuni* is a large glass bottle, or earthenware jar, one for each of the town districts. On the evening of the 23rd June, the jars are richly decorated with silk scarves, gold jewellery and ears of wheat, and carried to roadside altars by young unmarried girls. The altars are draped with brightly coloured *pezzare*, hand-woven rugs. The statue of St John the Baptist is carried in procession through the streets to bless the *muzzuni*, thus guaranteeing prosperity and fertility to every part of the town. The custom probably goes back to pre-Christian fertility rituals (*www.comune.alcaralifusi.me.it*).

CAPO D'ORLANDO July, Internationa Blues Festival, at the stadium (*www.capodorlandoblues.it*).

CASTROREALE 23–25 Aug, the *Cristo Lungo*, a Crucifix on a pole 12m high is carried in perilous procession along the steep streets from the church of Sant'Agata to the Matrice.

LIPARI 18 July, Our Lady of Portosalvo, a fishermen's celebration. 24 Aug, feast of San Bartolomeo, the patron saint of the islands. July–Aug, *Efesto D'Oro*, screening of films which have been inspired by, or made on, the islands, followed by a prize-giving ceremony.

MESSINA 30 March, St Eustochia, preceded by a week of concerts and debates. Good Friday, *Le Varette*, traditional religious procession. 3 June, *'A Matri 'a Littra'*, festivities for the feast of the Madonna of the Letter, the patron saint. June, Corpus Domini procession including a ship, the *Vascelluzzo*. 13–14 August, traditional processions of the *Giganti* (Giants). 15 August, the *Vara* (float with tableau) for the feast of the Assumption.

NOVARA DI SICILIA Carnival, *Gara del maiorchino* is a competition between teams of three who each roll a truckle of *maiorchino* cheese down the steep streets (*www.comunedinovaradisicilia. me.it*).

SALINA 23 July *Madonna del Terzito*, held at Leni, a very colourful and heartfelt occasion; mid-July, music festival (*www.salinafestival.it*). 20–25 Sept, festivities celebrating local products plus a festival of documentary films: Salina DOC Fest (*www.salinadocfest.it*).

SAN FRATELLO Wed, Thurs and Good Friday, the ancient *Festa dei Giudei* is celebrated; colourfully dressed Judaeans', provided with tails, chains and trumpets, perform acrobatics and fanfares to celebrate the trial and the Crucifixion of Christ. 10 May, *Cavalcata*, a procession on horseback to the sanctuary church (national monument) on the nearby mountain where the three patron saints, Alfio, Cirino and Filadelfo, stopped on their way to martyrdom at Trecastagni or Lentini (c. AD 350). Sept or Oct, *Mercato-Concorso del Cavallo di San Fratello*, traditional parade and market of the famous San Fratello horses, still living wild in their native habitat (*www.comunedisanfratello.it*). 17 Sept, Feast of St Benedict the Moor, with a procession and fireworks.

TAORMINA June–Sept, *Taormina Arte*, a series of events, starting with the Film Festival, including drama, concerts, and ballet, with top performers (*www.taormina-arte.com*). 20 Sept, feast dedicated to the Madonna della Rocca, when roast kid and lamb is offered to pilgrims on their way down from the church; almost certainly a tradition going back to the times when the cave-church was the sanctuary of an earth goddess, perhaps Demeter or Cybele.

TINDARI May–July, the old theatre and the Roman villa at Patti are used for presenting concerts, plays and operas (*www.teatrodeiduemari.it*).

TORTORICI 20 Jan, the annual feast of St Sebastian (here known as *Sammastianuzzu*) involves a dramatic procession of barefooted faithful who carry the heavy stone statue of the saint across the river.

PRACTICAL INFORMATION

Planning your Trip

WHEN TO GO

Travelling in Sicily is enjoyable year round, though autumn rainstorms can be very heavy. Winters are mild, but there can be some very cold days. It is usually very hot in July and August (sometimes 40° or more). The dreaded *scirocco*, the hot, suffocating wind from Africa, can blow at any time of the year. The best time for wildflowers is February–March and February is also Carnival time. Easter is celebrated with impressive traditional processions in many towns, but in March, April and May school groups descend on historic sites and museums. The best time to visit places such as the Roman villa at Piazza Armerina or the Greek theatre in Taormina, for example, is at lunchtime. The *maestrale*, the prevailing wind around Messina and the Aeolian Islands, blows from the northwest and is very strong in winter, often making it difficult for the hydrofoils; sometimes even the ferryboats have problems and the islands can be cut off for several days. Strong winds can also affect communications between Trapani and the Aegadian Islands and between Porto Empedocle and the Pelagian Islands. In winter, although the days are shorter, there are no crowds, the weather is usually mild with cloudless skies, and there is the incomparable sight of Mt Etna covered in snow. At the end of October and early November there is much preparation for one of the island's most popular celebrations, the *Festa dei Morti*, All Souls Day (2 Nov), when everyone takes sheaves of chrysanthemums to the cemeteries and children receive toys and special sweets, ostensibly from their dead ancestors.

MAPS

These are still a necessary supplement even to the best GPS system. The best are published by the Touring Club Italiano (*www.touringclub.it*). Their *Grande Carta Stradale d'Italia*, on a scale of 1:200,000, is divided into 15 maps covering the regions of Italy, including Sicily (sheet 14). They are also published in a three-volume atlas called the *Atlante Stradale d'Italia*. The one entitled *Sud* covers Sicily. Individual city, province and island maps are available in most local bookshops, along with some detailed walking maps for regions of specific interest, such as Etna.

HEALTH AND INSURANCE

EU citizens are entitled to receive health care in Italy if they have the free European Health Insurance Card (EHIC). Otherwise you are advised to take out insurance before travelling. Remember to keep all receipts (*ricevute*) and medical reports (*cartella clinica*) to give to your insurer if you need to make a claim. Thefts or damage to property must be reported immediately at the local police station; a copy of the report (*denuncia*) will be needed to claim your insurance.

DISABLED TRAVELLERS

Sicily is not good for disabled travellers, who will need all their resources of patience and adaptability in order to get around. Although legislation obliges public buildings to provide access and facilities, it will be many years before Sicily catches up with mainland Italy or the rest of Europe. Many churches have imposing flights of steps as their only means of access, and many towns and villages are filled with stepped streets and alleys. Toilets in coffee bars or restaurants are often on the first floor, and lifts are rare. In the annual accommodation list published by the local tourist offices, establishments which can offer hospitality to the disabled are indicated. Airports and railway stations now provide assistance and certain trains are equipped to transport wheelchairs. Access for cars with disabled people is allowed to town centres usually closed to traffic, where parking places are reserved for them. For more information, contact the local tourist offices.

USEFUL WEBSITES

General: *www.regione.sicilia.it/turismo*; *www.visitingsicily.it*; *www.bestofsicily.com*; *www.sicilia.indettaglio.it*; *www.borghitalia.it* (beautiful villages).

Agrigento: *www.valleyofthetemples.com*.

Etna: *www.funiviaetna.com* (Italian only, but useful webcam of the summit area).

Offshore islands: *www.egadi.com* (Aegadians); *www.welcometolipari.it* (Aeolians); *www.orcadivingustica.com* (Ustica).

Palermo: *www.visitpalermo.it*.

News: *www.balarm.it* (informative but in Italian only).

Coach timetables: *www.orariautobus.it*.

Events: *www.regione.sicilia.it/eventiturismo*.

Food and wine: *www.slowfood.com*; *www.justsicilia.it* (to order food products, wine and other articles online); *www.movimentoturismovino.it*.

Gardens: *www.grandigiardini.it*.

Museums, archaeological sites and galleries: *www.regione.sicilia.it/beniculturali*.

Nature: *www.siciliaparchi.com*; *www.parks.it*; *www.legambientesicilia.it*; *www.lipu.it*.

Personalised tours: *www.closertosicily.com*; *www.sicilydriverandguide.com*.

Renting a house: *www.dicasainsicilia.it*; *www.solosicily.com*; *www.travelsicilia.com*.

Getting Around

BY AIR

Palermo (Falcone Borsellino Airport, *www.gesap.it*), Catania (Fontanarossa Airport, *www.aeroportocatania.it*), Comiso (Pio La Torre Airport, *www.aeroportodicomiso.it*) and Trapani (Vincenzo Florio Airport, *www.aeroportotrapani.com*) are served by national and international flights. In addition, Trapani connects Pantelleria and Lampedusa to Sicily and the mainland. Besides direct international flights, several companies offer one-stop flights via Rome or Milan. Most Italian mainland cities, and Sardinia, have frequent flights to Sicily.

BY SEA

Car ferries on the Straits of Messina operate to and from Villa San Giovanni on the mainland (24hrs a day, no booking necessary), taking about 20mins to reach Messina. There are often queues and delays in the summer. Less frequent ferries and hydrofoils leave from Reggio Calabria, taking 40mins. Details of ferry and hydrofoil services to the offshore islands are given at the end of each relevant chapter.

BY RAIL

Rail services in Sicily lag behind those on the mainland. Rolling stock is outdated while most lines are single track and in some cases are those laid in the 19th century. Recent cutbacks mean that intercity services within the island have been slashed. It is wise to check the frequency of connections before you plan to travel by rail.

The Italian Railway Company, Trenitalia (*www.trenitalia.com*) runs various categories of trains: ES (Eurostar) are international express trains between major cities with first- and second-class carriages (obligatory seat reservation); EC and IC are international and national express trains; Espressi are long-distance trains (both classes), not as fast as the Intercity trains; Diretti, although not stopping at every station, are slower than Espressi; and Inter-regionali and Regionali are local trains stopping at all stations, mostly with second-class carriages only. Many stations are now unmanned: tickets can be purchased in the nearest coffee bar, tobacconist or newsagent. Valid for two months after the day sold, they must be bought before the journey, and date-stamped in the machines you find on the platforms, otherwise the ticket-collector will exact a stiff fine. In Italy fares are still much lower than in many other parts of Europe. Children under the age of four travel free, and between the ages of four and 12 travel half price. If you are planning lengthy journey through Europe starting in Italy, then a Eurorail pass (*www.eurorailways.com*) is useful, with a voucher for each country you intend to visit. Also for journeys starting in Italy, the Carta Verde (under 26) and Carta Argento (over 60) and Railplus allow discounts on tickets.

BY BUS

Inter-city and inter-village services in Sicily are widespread, punctual (although perhaps infrequent) and fairly comfortable. Services tend to finish in the early evening. Information of the bus companies, with websites, are in each chapter listing. Tickets can sometimes be purchased on board, sometimes at the nearest coffee bar or tobacconist; unfortunately there is no standard system.

BY CAR

The quality of the roads is on the whole quite good. In large towns, traffic is chaotic, streets are congested and parking is difficult. Signposting is erratic and you will often have to stop to ask directions. Motorways (*autostrade*) have green signs, normal roads blue signs. At the entrance to motorways, the two directions are indicated by the name of the town at the end of the road, not by that of the nearest town. They are a fast and convenient way of travelling around, crossing difficult terrain by means of viaducts and tunnels, and in places they are spectacularly beautiful. Most stretches are toll free.

NB: always lock your car when parked, and never leave anything of value inside it. If purchasing fuel or oil at a motorway service station, always check that you have been given the right quantity, that the seal on the oil can is intact, and that you have been given the correct change.

General Information

ACCOMMODATION

A few places to stay have been suggested at the end of each chapter, chosen either for character, historical interest, location, value for money or comfort. They range from luxurious 5-star hotels, to *relais de charme*, simple inns or B&Bs. They are classified as €€€ (200 euros or over), €€ (100–200 euros) or € (under 100 euros). Prices vary widely according to season and location.

NB: Continental breakfast is usually included in the room price: by law it is an optional extra. Hotels are now also obliged (for tax purposes) to issue a receipt: in theory guests can be fined for leaving the premises without one.

There is a wide choice of B&B accommodation in Sicily, both in the towns and in the countryside; legislation in Italy has been relaxed, making it much easier for people to offer rooms to paying guests, who are in turn likely to achieve a much better understanding of the places they visit. Sicilians are extremely hospitable, and their homes are comfortable. Throughout Sicily this type of accommodation is mostly classified according to the star system: one star means you will have to share the bathroom with the family; three-star establishments can be as good as luxurious small hotels.

There are now hundreds of working farms in Sicily which offer rooms (*agriturismo*), highly recommended for travellers with their own transport and for families with young children. Terms vary from B&B to full board or self-contained flats; some farms require a stay of a minimum number of days. Cultural or recreational activities such as horse-riding are sometimes provided and on some farms you can help with the work on a voluntary basis: milking sheep, gathering olives or fruit, harvesting wheat and so forth. Again, most places use the star system to classify the *agriturismi*.

Country houses are simply houses in the country without a working farm; some of them are aristocratic villas, others are quite basic. They can be recommended to independent travellers who enjoy the countryside.

There is a wide range of rooms and apartments to rent, including villas, farmhouses, beach bungalows and city-centre apartments, readily available for short-term rental. In some towns where the old centres are being abandoned, civic administrations are helping home-owners to restore their properties in order to provide accommodation for tourists in *paese-albergo* or *albergo diffuso*. The owners usually live elsewhere. It is an adventurous (and inexpensive) solution for those who want to get a 'feel' for a town. The neighbours will certainly be welcoming. Information is available from town councils or tourist offices.

Many convents and monasteries have rooms available for visitors. These are usually very basic, but always with private bath or shower. Sometimes meals can be taken in the refectory. It is not required of guests to be Roman Catholic. This always represents a very good value for money option.

CRIME AND PERSONAL SECURITY

Pickpocketing is a widespread problem in Sicily: it is always advisable not to carry valuables and to take special care of handbags or shoulder bags. Snatch thefts, especially by passing scooters, are common. Crimes should be reported immediately to the police or local *carabinieri* office. Emergency numbers are as follows:

Police: 113 (Polizia di Stato) or 112 (Carabinieri).

Fire and Rescue: 115.

Ambulance and First Aid: 118.

OPENING TIMES

Opening times for museums, churches and archaeological sites are given in the text, but they are subject to frequent change and should always be checked prior to your visit. What appears in the text should be taken as a guideline only. Telephone numbers have been supplied where possible and were correct at the time of going to press. Churches usually close in the middle of the day, opening again around 4pm. Visitors are expected to dress suitably (no miniskirts, shorts or bare shoulders) and to avoid eating, drinking, talking loudly or using mobile phones. Photography is always forbidden when Mass is in progress. In Holy Week most of the images are covered and are on no account shown. Many museums and archaeological sites are suffering from staff shortages and are ever more likely to close in the afternoons and on public holidays. If some of the rooms are closed, try asking one of the guards to open them. If they can, they are often happy to help and may be able to arrange for the room to be opened especially for you if you can wait for just a few minutes. Thank them profusely if they are able to arrange this, as it is often done on their own initiative and at their own risk. Local tourist offices are supposed to have up-to-date information, but this is often not the case. If there is something you are travelling all the way to Sicily purposely to see, it is worth contacting the site or the museum about ten days ahead to find out if it will be open; efforts will be made to arrange a custodian for you.

TELEPHONES AND THE INTERNET

For all calls in Italy, local and long-distance, dial the city code (for instance, 091 for Palermo) followed by the phone number. For international and intercontinental calls dial 00 plus the country code, then the city code (for numbers in the UK drop the initial zero) and number. To call Sicily from abroad (not USA) dial 0039, then the city code and number. To call Sicily from the USA dial 011 39, then the city code and number.

Mobile phone coverage has very few gaps on Sicily and the offshore islands; often it is sufficient to move a few metres to get the line back. Most hotels, and many restaurants and coffee bars, offer wifi. If you have problems, you will find plenty of people ready to help.

Food & Drink

A selected choice of restaurants for all pockets is given at the end of each chapter. The choices reflect pleasant personal experience and a desire to introduce travellers to the very best local dishes and wines. They are categorised according to the approximate cost of a meal without drinks:

€€€ means a fine-dining restaurant, over €40 per head (sometimes well over);
€€ means a good restaurant, €25–35 per head;
€ means a simple *trattoria* where you will pay €15–30 per head.

MEALTIMES AND TIPPING

Mealtimes are later than elsewhere in Italy: lunch usually about 1.30pm; dinner at 8.30 or later. Service charges are included in the bill unless otherwise stated (some places also add a cover charge), so tipping is not an obligation but is always much appreciated. The main meal of the day is lunch, almost invariably consisting of pasta; soup rarely appears on the menu. Restaurant meals are the occasion for dressing up, to look and be looked at, in the comfortable knowledge that each dish you have chosen will be specially prepared and not warmed up in the microwave. Sicilians rarely ask for the menu, they prefer to accept the advice of the waiter, the cook or the restaurant owner, who will describe the delicacies found at the market that morning and how they will be prepared, eventually suggesting the best wine to accompany each course, or the whole meal.

SICILIAN FOOD

That food, its preparation and consumption, should be of such absorbing interest for Sicilians is not surprising; their cuisine is the sum of successive episodes of foreign domination, each one of which introduced new ingredients and cooking techniques. Sicilian cooks are good. Often slightly bizarre, they have an inborn sense of colour and design, a strong natural talent allied to inventiveness, and they all stubbornly refuse to use anything but the freshest ingredients available; qualities for which they are known and appreciated everywhere. The earliest surviving cookery book in the world was written in the 4th century BC by Archestratus of Gela. Entitled the *Hedypatheia* or *On Good Taste*, it takes the form of a long poem listing various foods and drinks, how they should be prepared, and how they should be enjoyed. He enthuses about the flavour of lobsters from Lipari, gilt-head bream from Syracuse, swordfish from Messina, tuna from Tindari, bread, wine and hares, and advises cooks to keep condiments to a minimum. His book was translated into Latin and even became the object of a satire by Horace. Some of the recipes were included by the famous gourmet Apicius (1st century ad), in his book *De Re Coquinaria*, or *The Art of Cooking*.

Sicilians have known and used saffron since prehistory. They were the first people in Italy to cultivate artichokes and the first to use rice. The Arabs, in fact, in the 9th century, created rice paddies in the meadows south of Catania, between the Simeto and the San Leonardo rivers, and also introduced citrus, dates, sugar cane, aubergines, pistachios, a taste for cinnamon, and the use of terracing and irrigation. Pasta, in the form of vermicelli, was already being made at Trabia near Palermo in the 12th century, according to Roger II's geographer el-Edrisi, long before Marco Polo brought some back from China, and it was almost certainly the Sicilians who invented sun-dried tomatoes. Tomatoes, together with chilli pepper and chocolate, had arrived with the Spanish in the 17th century. A hundred years later, the Kingdom of the Two Sicilies, based in Naples, ushered in the demand for the expensive, capricious but indispensable *monzù*, the French cook that the aristocratic families of the island deemed a status symbo. With him came butter, cream and refined sauces and soups.

Many local writers have described the symphony of colours, aromas and flavours which can be achieved in Sicily. Federico De Roberto, in his *I Viceré*, opens for us the monastic kitchens of San Benedetto in Catania. Giuseppe Tomasi di Lampedusa in *The Leopard* conjures up the magnificent banquets prepared by the prince's French *monzù*, and Andrea Camilleri, his mouth probably watering, evokes Chief Inspector Montalbano's *arancine*, golden-brown rice balls, or his favourite grilled red mullet and baby octopus. (NB: In western Sicily the rice balls are called *arancine*, little oranges, because they are round. In Eastern Sicily, where they are cone-shaped, they are called *arancini*. There are heated debates about which should be the correct term.)

BLUE GUIDES RECOMMENDED

Hotels and restaurants that are particularly good choices in their category—in terms of excellence, location, charm, value for money or the quality of the experience they provide—carry the Blue Guides Recommended sign: ■. All these establishments have been visited and selected by our authors, editors or contributors as places they have particularly enjoyed and would be happy to recommend to others. To keep our entries up to date, reader feedback is essential: please do not hesitate to contact us (*www. blueguides.com*) with any views, corrections or suggestions.

SICILIAN SPECIALITIES

BREAD

It was the wheat fields of Ramacca, in the province of Catania, that inspired Wagner's *Harvesters' Hymn*; the wheat fields which were the gift of Demeter herself. Sicilian bread varies enormously in shape, size, colour and flavour. There are 72 different specialities. Each family eats an average of almost 100kg of bread a year, which is more than most other Italians (all great bread eaters) and they treat it with almost religious reverence. It is always placed face up on the table and is kissed if it falls on the ground. Often made using the sourdough method and topped with sesame seeds, it is preferably cooked in stone ovens, which are heated by burning olive, almond, oak, lemon or orange wood, or even almond shells, depending on whatever fuel is more abundant. Some bakers can trace the origin of their sourdough back over 200 years. The basic ingredient is durum-wheat flour, usually a blend of different varieties. At Castelvetrano, for example, the coffee-coloured loaves owe their aroma and rich flavour to the addition of *tumminia* flour, which grows only in a very small area and is thought to have been first cultivated by the people of Selinunte, while in Lentini they add a little *timilia* wheat. Other localities renowned for the quality of the bread are Monreale, Favara, Novara di Sicilia, Montalbano Elicona and San Giuseppe Jato. Bread is at the centre of several religious festivities over the course of the year, some probably of pagan origin. At Campofranco, for example, for the feast of St Calogero, huge 'bread-men', almost life-size, are paraded around the town with the saint, before offering him a farewell kiss and being broken up by the priest and divided among the onlookers. In Agrigento the same saint is pelted with tiny loaves thrown from the balconies as he makes his progress through the streets. St Joseph's Day, 19th March, is the occasion for baking particularly fancy loaves to place on the altars set up in the streets of many towns, together with hundreds of different foods which will be presented to the poor; but nowhere is this art expressed better than in Salemi, where the loaves are worked with such intricacy they look like delicate carvings in old ivory.

OLIVE OIL

Sicilian olive oil is excellent. So many different soil types, plus slight local variations in climate, mean that several different varieties of olive tree can be cultivated, some of which can be traced back thousands of years and may be native to the island. Sicily provides only ten percent of the entire national production of oil but by far the largest quantity of olives for salting and curing, both black and green. The finest groves are probably those of the province of Trapani, around Castelvetrano. Here the trees are pruned to stay very small, almost bonsai size, and the olives are picked by hand, resulting in perfect oil and sublime pickles. Oil to rhapsodise over is also produced at Caronia (Messina), Ragalna, Bronte and Mineo (Catania), Syracuse and Chiaramonte Gulfi (Ragusa), where the precious liquid is the linchpin of the economy (there is even an olive-oil museum). All Sicilian olive oil is protected by the IGP seal and the most outstanding varieties are distinguished by the DOP label, a guarantee of quality similar to that offered to the finest wines.

CONFECTIONERY

Sicilian confectionery is a delectable riot of colours, aromas and flavours: there are the simple, fragrant breakfast pastries; crystallised and candied fruits; fruits made of marzipan; nougat; biscuits made with almonds, pistachios or hazelnuts; crunchy *cannoli* filled with sweet ricotta cheese; the elaborate Baroque complexities of the magnificent *cassata siciliana*, filled with ricotta; and the light and delicate *paste di mandorla*, the almond pastries of Acireale. Every town or village has its own speciality and different sweets are prepared for the main feasts of the year. The abundance of local nuts and fruits, and the introduction of sugar by the Arabs, are at the base of the Sicilian tradition, perfected through the centuries first by the Arab women in their harems, preparing sweet delights to offer to guests, and later by the cloistered nuns in many Sicilian convents. They achieved such excellence that their exquisite confections were always much in demand, especially at Easter time: the nuns in fact were kept so busy that the bishops were forced to intervene, warning the sisters to abstain from baking, at least during Holy Week, and to dedicate their energies to prayer instead.

ICE CREAM

Italians eat a lot of ice cream (apparently only the Americans and Australians eat more) but Sicilians like it so much that they even have it for breakfast. It is quite possible that ice cream was invented in Sicily: we know that the Romans brought down snow from Mount Etna during the winter. They stored it in *niviere*, pits dug in cool cellars, covering it with a thick layer of straw or sawdust to keep it fresh until summer. It was then unpacked and mixed with wine, honey and spices, and sold as a great luxury to those who could afford it. The Arabs in Sicily adapted the process, using sugar instead of honey and fruit juice instead of wine. They called their confection *sharbat* (hence sherbet; sorbet). But the first confectioner to have the brainwave of adding cream to the mixture was a young late-17th-century Sicilian, Procopio de' Coltelli of Acitrezza. He took his discovery to Paris, to delight Louis XIV and the king gave him the exclusive rights of manufacture. He opened the Café Procope, still in existence, which claims to be the world's first coffee-house, frequented by Voltaire, Benjamin Franklin and much of Parisian society.

In Sicily the manufacture of ice cream is still a point of honour, and there are plenty of pastry shops and coffee bars where you will find ice cream made on the premises (a list of ingredients by the counter is a very good sign). The coveted annual Procopio de' Coltelli award goes to the best ice-cream maker on the island. *Gelato* is ice cream made with eggs and milk or cream. *Granita* is fruit juice (or coffee, chocolate, ground almonds or pistachios) frozen together with sugar. The secret is to obtain a very fine-grained, thick but not too thick consistency. *Cremolata* and *sorbetto* are variations on the theme, which sometimes see the addition of egg whites.

In Sicilian towns from April until October, the ice cream vendors take up their stands in the early morning and blow a whistle or ring a bell to announce breakfast. People sometimes come down into the street in their pyjamas. Ice cream is usually served in a soft brioche bun, like a sandwich. Granita comes in a plastic cup, into which pieces of brioche are dunked. You can have several flavours at the same time, and even add a dollop of whipped cream. In city centres people will have their ice-cream breakfast at the coffee bar. Wherever it takes place, it is the first moment of social aggregation of the day.

SOFT DRINKS

The thirsty Sicilian asks for *latte di mandorla* (almond milk), made with crushed almonds and sugar diluted with water and chilled (the best will be found in Catania and Modica). Very sweet, it is surprisingly refreshing. In town centres, kiosks serve other inexpensive thirst-quenchers: freshly-squeezed lemon juice with soda water and a pinch of salt is one of the most popular (*selz, limone e sale*). Kiosk owners often make their own fluorescent fruit syrups, which are then diluted with soda water. Cheap and popular fizzy drinks, which have been around for generations, are *spuma*, *gazzosa* and *chinotto*.

UNIQUE CULINARY DELIGHTS, PROVINCE BY PROVINCE

The geography of Sicily varies dramatically and it is only natural that different regions should have different specialities. The international Slow Food Foundation has a strong following here and has nominated about 40 different Sicilian food products as worthy of inclusion in the Ark of Taste. Several risked disappearing altogether, due to globalisation and tough EU laws (the use of time-honoured equipment and ancient farming methods are not always compatible with strict modern hygiene standards). Special regional decrees have had to be issued for many of them, underlining their incalculable traditional value, to save them from oblivion.

PALERMO
The people of Palermo love to eat simple, cheap snacks in the street, such as boiled octopus, chick-pea fritters or beef spleen sandwiched in crunchy bread rolls, and intestines of sheep or kid wound around a piece of cane and grilled. They are also the acknowledged masters in the preparation of *pasta con le sarde*, macaroni served with a rich sauce of wild fennel, anchovies, onion, fresh sardines, pine nuts, currants, saffron, almonds, and sometimes tomatoes (an addition which is frequently hotly disputed). Pollina and Castelbuono in the Madonie Mountains are the only places in the world where the manna-ash trunks are incised (like maple trees) to collect the *manna*, white syrupy sap, which is dried and used for making medicines and sweeteners. Also from the Madonie Mountains comes *provola*, sweet-flavoured sheep's milk cheese. Each one weighs about 1kg and has a little 'neck' to hang it from while it ripens. On the island of Ustica, tiny dark brown lentils are grown, completely without herbicides or fertilisers; donkeys dragging stones are still used for threshing. They are soft, tender and quick to cook. Late-ripening tangerines can be found at Ciaculli, in the Conca d'Oro behind Palermo.

TRAPANI
The salt pans of Trapani (now a UNESCO World Heritage Site), so jealously husbanded by Phoenicians and Romans and profitably used by the Florio family in the 19th century, meant that Trapani's fabulous bluefin tuna could be salted, preserved and exported widely; likewise the island's sardines and anchovies. Red garlic is grown in the salt marshes around Nubia. It has small corms, red skin, and an intense flavour. The island of Pantelleria is famous for its capers: very small and strong-flavoured, they are the flower buds of the plant, gathered just before blossoming. Black bread is baked

in stone ovens in Castelvetrano, using the sourdough method, and a mixture of two different kinds of durum wheat. The crust is very dark brown, almost black, the crumb is golden and the flavour is sublime. *Vastedda* cheeses from the Belice Valley are the small round cheeses mentioned by Homer. Formed in a soup-plate (the meaning of the name in Sicilian), they are made only from local sheep's milk, which is kneaded and pulled. Slightly elastic, it has a vague aroma of vanilla. The production is very small (only 15 people make it), and the cheese must be eaten fresh. The winter melons from Trapani are bright yellow, very sweet, and stay good until Christmas. The cooks of Trapani are acknowledged masters in the art of preparing durum-wheat cous cous served with a rich fish broth. There is even an annual Cous Cous Fest at San Vito Lo Capo, an eagerly-awaited event, when chefs from Trapani, the Middle East and Africa (where cous cous is usually served with meat and vegetables) compete for the coveted award.

AGRIGENTO

Girgentana goats from Agrigento are a highly-prized breed. These attractive animals, with their long horns and silky hair, are exploited for their milk and their skins. Wild strawberries from Ribera are derived from seedlings brought back to Sicily from the Alps by soldiers who had fought in the First World War. The island of Lampedusa is famous for its *cernia* (sea-perch or grouper).

CALTANISSETTA AND ENNA

The inland regions are the realm of sheep's cheeses: *tuma*, *primosale* and *pecorino*, often with the addition of black peppercorns or coriander seeds. In the province of Enna you will even find wild saffron, gathered in spring from the hillside crocuses. Here too are the finest beans and pulses, essential ingredients in dishes such as *zuppa di ceci* (chick-pea potage) or *maccu di fave* (a hash of broad beans seasoned with wild fennel). Late peaches from Leonforte are succulent: these strong-flavoured, yellow peaches ripen from September to November; each fruit is protected in its own little bag, from birds, insects and hail.

RAGUSA AND SYRACUSE

Modicana cattle from Ragusa and Modica graze in the open air, indifferent to the hot climate. The meat is tough but good; the excellent milk is used for making several different local cheeses, such as *caciocavallo*. It is pressed into long rectangular shapes and then hung two by two over a beam to mature. The town of Modica has the reputation for producing the best food on the island, both in the restaurants and at home; chocolate is still prepared according to the Aztec tradition (*see p. 318*). Almond trees are grown everywhere in Sicily and probably form part of the native flora, but those from Noto and Avola—*pizzuta d'Avola*—have the finest flavour of all.

CATANIA

Though the soil is fertile in central Sicily, no area can compare with the hinterland of Catania, where rich volcanic earth and sunshine give an intensity to the fruits and perfumes of its orchards and gardens. This is the secret of the huge success of its ices and sorbets, and its citrus summer salads. In fact, a healthful simplicity informs the food of this area, so much of which is based upon the household bread-oven: golden pies called *scacciate*, richly-filled *focacce*, vegetables grilled over charcoal, and fish and seafood wrapped in fig or citrus leaves and then roasted over the coals. Sheep's milk ricotta from Vizzini is as rich as double cream. Pistachios from Bronte were introduced by the Arabs and the nuts now grown on Mount Etna have a superb flavour and are deep emerald green in colour. Snuff-box peaches from Mount Etna (*pesche tabacchiera*) are small, flat and intensely aromatic. Sicilian blood oranges are protected by the IGP seal (*Indicazione Geografica di Produzione*). There are several different varieties, all limited to the area of Mount Etna and the Plain of Catania, the only place in the world where the colour of the flesh is so intense, almost purple. From the Gulf of Catania come anchovies, *masculini di magghia*, so good that they can be eaten raw; the *magghia* is the fine-meshed net with which they are caught, from small boats. Catania's special pasta dish is *pasta ca' Norma*, spaghetti with a topping of fresh tomato, basil leaves, tasty slices of fried aubergine, and salted ricotta, invented to celebrate Bellini's triumphal inauguration of the Teatro Massimo Bellini opera house with the première of his masterpiece, *Norma*.

MESSINA

The tiny, offshore Aeolian Islands base their cuisine on the intense flavours of capers (those from Salina are protected) and wild herbs such as oregano, thyme, wild fennel and *nepitella* (calamint); the currants and Malvasia grapes which they produce; tasty cheese and ricotta from the goats; and the cactus fruits and miniature lentils which survive in the dry and rocky environment. The islands and the coastal cities have obviously always prized their abundance of fish: in Messina this particularly means swordfish, caught in consistent numbers during the migratory season. *Impanata di pesce spada* is a magnificent envelope of delicate pastry containing the swordfish and its accompaniments of tiny *pireddu* tomatoes, which have been hung up in the kitchen until they wither like raisins, olives, capers, currants, pine nuts and bits of ripe caciocavallo cheese. In the Nebrodi Mountains an ancient breed of black pigs (seen in medieval paintings and probably introduced by the Normans) are allowed to live wild in the woods, eating acorns and beech-nuts. The result is excellent sausage, salami, ham and bacon. In Novara di Sicilia they make *maiorchino*, a round, flat, well-matured sheep's milk cheese with a dark brown rind; the truckles are even used at Carnival time for a race, rolling them down the main street. Unfortunately, maiorchino is becoming increasingly rare, as its manufacture is very time-consuming.

WINE

Archaeologists confirm the ancient origin of wine production on Sicily, where the first vines were certainly autochthonous. The Greeks introduced the trick of cultivating the vine *ad alberello*, close to the ground, increasing the sugar-content and alcohol level.

The Romans introduced new grape varieties and new techniques of manufacture. The famous wine of ancient Sicily was *Mamertine*, said to have been the favourite of Julius Caesar. Even the Arabs, who as Muslims could not drink wine, carefully cultivated and improved the vines in order to use the grapes as table fruit and for drying as raisins and sultanas. The heyday of Sicilian winemaking began in the 13th century and lasted some 200 years, a period when Sicilian wines were exported to Rome, Liguria, Venice and Tuscany, playing an important role in shaping European palates. Real innovation began in the late 18th century, when the British wine merchant John Woodhouse introduced Spanish and Portuguese methods of manufacture to Marsala, with great success. The late 19th-century phylloxera blight, which destroyed the vineyards, was a setback, followed after the Second World War by a total neglect of quality—the only thing that mattered at the time was quantity.

Thankfully those days are receding and we are now seeing the dawn of some energetic and exciting new winemaking. Local and foreign investors in Sicilian viticulture are drawing out the virtues of the island's terroir. Although traditional winemaking methods are largely giving way to modern vinification technology, the focus is firmly on getting the best out of indigenous grape varieties. A new generation of producers, in the tradition of Vincenzo Florio's famous Marsala and Duke Alliata di Salaparuta's Corvo, are experimenting with new techniques, new varieties and new blends, while at the same time nurturing the native vines. The results are more than satisfactory: they are winning major international awards.

Noble grape varieties such as Chardonnay, Sauvignon Blanc, Cabernet Sauvignon and Merlot also flourish in the hot, dry, sulphurous soil or in the richness of the black lava. Syrah and Sangiovese do well too; even German varieties from the Rhine Valley thrive in Sicily. The Sicilian grape harvest begins early, often in August. In one or two places the grapes are gathered in the time-honoured way, at night, when the fruit is cool, so that it doesn't start fermenting too soon, a technique that goes back to the days of the Greeks.

There are at present 23 DOC wine appellations in Sicily (*Denominazione d'Origine Controllata*), and one DOCG (*Denominazione d'Origine Controllata e Garantita*. Such a long list means that the island is one of the most important oenological areas in Italy (in fact the province of Trapani comes second only to Bordeaux as the largest wine-producing district in Europe). The most recent DOC is 'Sicilia, used for all wine produced exclusively in Sicily and thus not limited to a specific grape or wine type. The other 22 areas are as follows:

Alcamo from the gentle hills between Trapani and Palermo
Contessa Entellina
Delia Nivolelli from the banks of the River Delia ('vineyard' in Arabic), in the territory of Mazara del Vallo, Marsala, Petrosino and Salemi
Eloro, from the area of Noto, Pachino, Portopalo di Capo Passero, Rosolini and Ispica
Erice
Etna, the first to receive the DOC seal in 1968
Faro from the hillsides behind Messina

Malvasia delle Lipari from the Aeolian Islands
Mamertino di Milazzo from the foothills of the Madonie and Nebrodi Mountains
Marsala, DOC since 1984, producing aged wines of three types, according to colour: Oro (gold), Ambra (amber), and Rubino (ruby). Fine is aged one year, Superiore for two years, Superiore Riserva for four years, Vergine or Soleras for five years. Also, Vergine or Soleras can be Stravecchio or Riserva, aged for ten years.
Menfi
Monreale
Moscato di Noto, the *pollium* mentioned by Pliny, produced in the territory of Noto, Rosolini, Pachino and Avola
Moscato di Pantelleria, produced exclusively on the island
Moscato di Siracusa, produced exclusively from the vineyards surrounding Syracuse; the flavour is subtly different from that of Noto
Riesi
Salaparuta
Sambuca
Santa Margherita di Belice
Sclafani
Sciacca
Vittoria, for its Cerasuolo di Vittoria, the only Sicilian DOCG, a characteristically cherry-red wine, pleasantly dry and vaguely aromatic of fruits and flowers.

Glossary of Sicilian Artists

Mainly Sicilian artists are listed here, or lesser-known figures from elsewhere who were active in Sicily or had an influence on Sicilian art.

Alberti, Antonio ('Il Barbalunga', Messina, 1600–49), painter who introduced a new and original style to Sicilian art. He studied in Rome with Domenichino, who greatly influenced him. His opus consists of numerous altarpieces carried out for the churches of Rome, Messina and Palermo.

Alessi, Giuseppe (Avola, early 18C), priest and architect, he worked on the reconstruction of Avola and the surrounding towns after the 1693 earthquake.

Alì, Luciano (Syracuse, 1736–1820), architect, much in demand in Syracuse and its province after the 1693 earthquake. His masterpiece is Palazzo Beneventano del Bosco in Syracuse, with its lovely courtyard. He was often assisted by his brothers **Antonino** and **Saverio**, master-builders, and by his son **Salvatore** (1767–?1820), friar, architect and civil engineer, a follower of the teachings of Vitruvius and Palladio, who designed a new façade for the church of San Bartolomeo at Scicli.

Alibrandi, Girolamo (Messina, 1470–1524), painter sometimes called the 'Raphael of Messina', follower of Antonello da Messina. He died of plague after completing relatively few paintings, most of which are in Messina.

Almeyda, Giuseppe Damiani (Capua, 1834–1911), architect employed as civil engineer by the municipality of Palermo, he received many private commissions to design architectural works but was sometimes hindered by his Neapolitan origins and the final choice often went to his Palermitan rival, Ernesto Basile. Fortunately he could count on the friendship of Ignazio Florio, for whom he designed the villa of Favignana. Almeyda's projects are less monumental in character than those of Basile, but they give a particular flavour to *fin de siècle* Palermo, with their elegant, Pompeian-style ornamentation.

Amato, Antonino (Messina, fl. 1697–1717), architect and sculptor; he was often assisted in his projects by his son **Andrea** (Messina, fl. 1720–35). His most important project was the Catania palace of the Prince of Biscari, while his son Andrea was engaged on the construction of the huge Benedictine monastery of San Nicolò l'Arena.

Amato, Giacomo (Palermo, 1643–1732), friar and gifted architect who studied in Rome with Carlo Rainaldi. Back in Palermo, he applied the techniques of his maestro combined with elements he had garnered from Carlo Fontana.

Amico, Giovanni Biagio (Trapani, 1684–1754), theologian and self-taught architect who designed many sacred and secular buildings for his city. In 1726 he wrote the influential treatise *L'Architetto Prattico*.

Andrea da Salerno (Andrea Sabatini, Salerno, 1480–1530), one of the finest Renaissance painters of southern Italy.

Antonello da Messina (Messina, c. 1430–79), painter, noted for his superb portraits and sense of perspective. One of the first Italian artists to perfect the technique of oil painting, he exerted considerable influence on Giovanni Bellini. His son **Jacobello** and his nephew **Antonello da Saliba** were also painters.

Archifel, **Arcifer** or **Arichitofel, Vincenzo** (?Naples, fl. 1486–1533), goldsmith and sculptor. Arriving in Catania aged 25, he married a local girl and opened his workshop at the Pescheria. The archbishop invited him to make the splendid reliquaries for the body of St Agatha and he spent the rest of his life completing them, together with the huge silver catafalque used for her processions, but also finding the time to carve statues for several churches in Caltagirone, Mineo and Vizzini. On his death he was honoured by being buried in the church of the Carmine. His son **Antonio** continued his trade, completing all his unfinished works.

Bagnasco, Nicola or **Nicolò** (Palermo, 18–19C), sculptor and wood-carver, exponent of a highly acclaimed family of craftsmen who carried out commissions for many towns in Sicily.

Baragli, Giacomo (Palermo, 1934–89), sculptor and medal-engraver.

Barisano da Trani (Bari, fl. 1175–90), sculptor and metal worker who made three very beautiful bronze doors, for the cathedrals of Ravello and Trani in south Italy and Monreale in Sicily; the two latter are signed.

Basile, Ernesto (Palermo, 1857–1932), the most famous *fin de siècle* architect in Palermo, a major exponent of international Modernism and Art Nouveau, and the eternal rival of Almeyda. Basile was particularly influenced by the Arab-Norman architecture of the city in developing his style. He started his career in the studio of his father, **Giovanni Battista Filippo** (Palermo, 1825–91), later inheriting his university post, and he completed the Teatro Massimo opera house, where his long collaboration with the painter Ettore De Maria Bergler and furniture designer Vittorio Ducrot began. His outstanding works in Palermo include the Villino Florio (one of the first examples of Art Nouveau to appear in Italy), and Villa Igiea. He designed several buildings for Messina during the post-earthquake reconstruction, while for Rome he created Palazzo Montecitorio, the seat of Parliament.

Battaglia, Francesco (Catania, 1701–88), architect and sculptor, son-in-law of Andrea Amato, for whom he continued work on the monastery of San Nicolò l'Arena until one of the piers supporting the dome collapsed due to an underground cavity, and the monks terminated his contract. An industrious and prolific worker, one of his most striking projects was the mother church of Aci San Filippo near Acireale, visible from a vast distance. He was the father of Antonino or **Antonio**, architect and Jesuit priest.

Battaglia, Matteo (Ragusa, 18C), gifted, self-taught painter who worked exclusively in the city of Ragusa.

Benefial, Marco (Rome, 1684–1764), painter who followed the classical tradition of the Bologna artists such as Guercino or Ludovico Carracci.

Berrettaro or **Berrettari** or **Birrittaro, Bartolomeo** (Carrara, fl. 1499–1524), sculptor whose first commissions in Sicily were in Alcamo, where he met (or invited) a fellow-citizen and sculptor from Carrara, **Giuliano Mancino**. Their atelier flourished and they created sculptures for many towns in Sicily.

Besio, Fra' Giacomo (Genoa, 1612–45), architect, a lay brother of the Theatine Order, whose rule obliged its members to have 'a poor cell, plain food and rich churches'. He succeeded in blending the Baroque of his native Genoa with elements of the Roman style, expressing in Palermo a new, elegant form of his own.

Bonaiuto, Natale (Syracuse, fl. 1781–94), architect and stucco-moulder who appears to have worked exclusively in his own area.

Bonaiuto da Pisa or **Bonaiuto Pisano** (Pisa, 14C), sculptor who probably found his way to Sicily together with merchants from his native city, which enjoyed excellent trade relations with Palermo.

Bonaiuto Vincenzo (17C), silversmith who worked in one of the most renowned ateliers of Trapani, mainly embroidering Church vestments with silver thread.

Bongiovanni, Giacomo (Caltagirone, 1772–1859), sculptor and ceramics-moulder, founder together with his nephew **Giuseppe Vaccaro** (Caltagirone, ?1808–99) of the famous Bongiovanni-Vaccaro atelier which specialised in creating terracotta statuettes for Christmas cribs.

Borremans, Willem (Antwerp, 1672–1744), fresco painter who learned his art in the atelier of Rubens. On arriving in Palermo in 1714 his first commission was to create a series of frescoes dedicated to the life of St Benedict for the Martorana church.

He soon became fashionable, and besides working in churches, he decorated many villas for the aristocracy. In his later years he was assisted by his son **Luigi** (Palermo, early 18C), about whom little is known.

Boscarino, Rosario (Modica, fl. 1693–1706), master-builder who often worked together with Mario Spada. After completing the church of San Pietro in Modica in 1697, they designed and built the new cathedral of San Giovanni Battista in Ragusa.

Calamech or **Calamecca, Andrea** (Carrara, 1524–89), sculptor and architect from a family of artists and marble-traders. He learned his art in Florence, where he perfected his Michelangelesque-Mannerist style. While delivering marble to Messina for Montorsoli, he was invited to superintend the sculptures for the cathedral.

Camilliani, Camillo (Florence, d. 1603), sculptor, son of **Francesco Camilliani** or **Della Camilla** (Florence, 1530–76), sculptor, a follower of Baccio Bandinelli, Michelangelo's arch rival. He appears to have settled in Sicily, where he carried out several works and was asked by the Spanish government to carry out a survey of the watch-towers and coastal defences of the island. Of the 144 towers which were repaired or rebuilt, 103 were his work.

Canzoneri, Michele (Palermo, b. 1944), abstract sculptor, happiest working with glass.

Caracciolo, Luciano (Syracuse, late 17C–early 18C), little-known architect or master-builder who was engaged in the reconstruction of the city after the 1693 earthquake.

Carasi, Costantino (Noto, early 18C), artist who painted numerous frescoes and altarpieces for the churches of Noto and many other towns in southeastern Sicily.

Carnelivari or **Carnilivari, Matteo** (Noto, fl. late 15C–1506), architect who probably began his activity in Noto and Syracuse. He went to Palermo in 1486 to obtain the acquittal of his son Antonio, who had committed murder, and remained in the city thereafter. His masterpieces are Palazzo Ajutamicristo and Palazzo Abatellis.

Caronia Roberti, Salvatore (Palermo, 1887–1970), architect. He worked as Ernesto Basile's assistant for several years, until he became Professor of Architecture at the University. Many of the Art Nouveau villas at Mondello were designed by him, but in the 1920s he took up the new Rationalist style, of which he is considered the finest Sicilian exponent.

Carreca or **Carrera, Andrea** (Trapani, 1592–1677), painter, initially inspired by Novelli, Caravaggio, the Venetian school and Flemish art but who soon developed an inclination for Roman Baroque and Pietro Cortona.

Carrera, Giuseppe (Trapani, fl. 1608–30), painter, whose elder brother **Vito** (Trapani, 1552–1622) was Novelli's maestro. On Vito's death, Giuseppe completed on his behalf a series of paintings for Palazzo dei Normanni in Palermo, commissioned by the viceroy. He worked for some time in Alcamo.

Caruso, Bruno (Palermo, b. 1927), painter who lives and works in Rome, first taught by his father, who made him copy the works of old masters.

Cascio, Lorenzo (Sciacca, b. 1940, www.cascio.it), painter and sculptor who started modelling clay as a child. He lives and works in Portofino and is noted for his delicate bronze statuettes and large paintings with bold designs and jewel-like colours.

Castello, Bernardo (Genoa, 1557–1629), Late Mannerist painter , a friend of Torquato Tasso, for whom he illustrated the first two editions of *Gerusalemme Liberata.*

Catalano, Antonio ('Il Giovane', Messina, 1585–1666), painter, the son of another painter by the same name called 'L'Antico' or '**Il Vecchio**', who had studied with Barocci. Il Giovane painted frescoes and canvases, but of his vast output very little remains, principally in the Regional Museum of Messina.

Catti, Michele (Palermo, 1855–1914), painter inspired by De Nittis, who after a long period of sunny landscapes fell into depression, thereafter preferring to depict Palermo in rainy, cold weather.

Cecco di Naro (Naro, nr. Agrigento, fl. 1377–80), fresco painter. After carrying out the frescoes for the church of St Catherine and the castle of the Chiaramonte family, he was invited to decorate their home in Palermo, Palazzo Steri, together with Simone da Corleone and Pellegrino Dareno.

Civiletti, Benedetto (Palermo, 1845–99), sculptor whose true-to-life renditions of popular subjects were much in demand. Besides small marble statues, he made many large monuments in bronze, including the figure representing *Tragedy* on the right-hand side of the stairway in front of Palermo's Teatro Massimo.

Conca, Sebastiano ('Il Cavaliere', Gaeta, 1680–1764), painter, one of the most successful artists in Rome during the early 18th century, with a distinctive style that introduced elements of academic Classicism into the grandeur of Late Baroque. He achieved fame for his frescoes. In Rome he opened an art school in Piazza Farnese, where many young Sicilian artists learnt how to paint.

Consagra, Pietro (Mazara del Vallo,

1920–2005), one of Italy's leading abstract sculptors, he dedicated much of his activity to Gibellina and the post-earthquake reconstruction.

Crescenzio, Antonello ('Antonello da Palermo', Palermo, 1467–1542), painter whose style changed so abruptly halfway through his career that several critics believe there were two artists of the same name, father and son. If he was indeed one person, his first period reveals Spanish and Flemish influences, while the second phase shows the effect of Vincenzo da Pavia and Andrea da Salerno. Existing documents show that he collaborated with Antonello Gagini.

Cristadoro or **Crestadoro, Giuseppe** (Palermo, 1711–1808), painter, the son of a goldsmith, who learned his art in the studio of Vito D'Anna, where he was able to examine drawings by Carlo Maratta, Sebastiano Conca and Corrado Giaquinto, and where he made friends with Olivio Sozzi and Pier Paolo Vasta, often collaborating with them.

D'Anna, Vito (Palermo, 1718–69), painter, probably the greatest Sicilian artist of his time. After training as an apprentice with Pier Paolo Vasta in Acireale, he married the daughter of Olivio Sozzi and used her dowry to go to Rome, where he studied with Corrado Giaquinto. Once back in Palermo, he was soon caught up in a vast number of projects, painting frescoes for important villas and palaces, and splendid altarpieces for many churches in Sicily.

D'Antoni, Andrea (Palermo, 1811–68), painter and excellent portraitist, a pupil of the Neoclassicist artist Giuseppe Patania. Sensitive to social problems, and politically involved, he took part in the 1848 riots, after which his paintings are exhortations to withstand the bitterness of exile.

D'Asaro, Pietro ('Il Monocolo di Racalmuto', Racalmuto, 1591–1647), Late Mannerist painter, his nickname derives from the fact that he had only one eye. It is uncertain where he studied, but his work shows touches of Caravaggio, Filippo Paladino and the two Zoppi di Gangi.

De Lisi, Benedetto (Palermo, 1830–75), sculptor from a family of sculptors. He was often invited to sculpt monuments and portrait busts of illustrious citizens.

De Maria Bergler, Ettore (Naples, 1850–1938), the acknowledged master of Art Nouveau interior decoration and also one of the finest landscape artists of his generation, as well as a superb portraitist.

Del Piano, Donato (Naples, 1704–85), organ manufacturer who spent most of his life in Sicily, where he arrived together with his brother Giuseppe in 1722. Invited to make a great organ for the church of San Nicolò l'Arena in Catania, the finished instrument could be played by three organists at once. Donato continued adding to it for the rest of his life and asked to be buried beneath it on his death.

Dufourny, Léon (Paris, 1754–1818), architect active in Sicily from 1788–93, during the French Revolution. On his return to Paris, he became curator of the Louvre.

Felice da Sambuca, Fra' (Sambuca, 1733–1805), painter and Capuchin monk. He worked with Olivio Sozzi in Palermo, and also with Vito D'Anna. His intensely devotional works adorn many Capuchin convents in Sicily.

Ferraro, Antonino (Giuliana, fl. 1552–98), painter, sculptor and stucco-moulder, talented Mannerist artist. He was often assisted in his work by his son **Orazio** (Giuliana, fl. 1573–1650) and grandson, also **Antonino** (Giuliana, fl. 1651–60), both accomplished in the same arts.

Ferretti, Mario (Livorno, 1915–74), artist who often designed stained-glass windows, but was happiest sculpting in bronze, as two works of his in Sicily, in and near Noto, attest.

Fiume, Salvatore (Comiso, 1915–97), painter, poet, playwright and novelist, noted for his characteristic Metaphysical-style paintings with scenes formed of bright patches of colour, and his bronze statues, often of a humourous nature. He also ventured into the realm of Land Art.

Franzese, Gaetano (Naples, 18C), renowned wood-carver called to Catania in 1766 by the organ manufacturer Donato del Piano to decorate the case of the organ he was completing for the church of San Nicolò l'Arena.

Freri, Antonello (Messina, fl. 1479–1513), sculptor who seems to have followed the Lombard school, with a decorative touch of his own. Most of his surviving works are in the cathedral of Catania and in the Regional Museum of Messina.

Fuga, Ferdinando (Florence, 1699–1782), architect who studied in Rome with Alessandro Specchi and Filippo Juvarra. In Sicily he is remembered for his disastrous interventions in the cathedral of Palermo, which King Ferdinand III of Bourbon had asked him to re-design in 1767. Among other things, he replaced the columns with piers, moved the royal tombs and opened them, dismantled the enormous marble altarpiece (the Gagini's masterpiece) and surmounted the roof with an ungainly dome and a series of small pepper-pot cupolas, in order to change it from a Norman basilica into a Latin-cross building with side aisles and long transepts. But some say it was not entirely his fault; perhaps the king should have let well alone?

Fumagalli, Gaspare (Rome, fl. 1735–85), painter who probably arrived in Sicily in 1730, where he worked with Borremans at the archbishop's palace in Palermo. After a sojourn in Rome, where he admired Maratta's frescoes, he returned to Sicily, working mainly in Gangi and Palermo, sometimes assisted by his three sons, **Eugenio**, **Ermenegildo** and **Epifanio**.

Furetto, Orazio (Palermo, 1714–85), architect chiefly remembered for his design for the charitable institution in Palermo known as the Albergo delle Povere (1746–72).

Gabrieli or **Gabrielli, Onofrio** ('Onofrio da Messina', Messina, 1616–1706), painter; as a boy, after having shown little aptitude for literary or legal studies, he was sent to the atelier of Antonio Alberti, the Barbalunga. Later he went to Rome, where he met Poussin and Pietro Cortona, then to Venice and Padua, where he became art tutor to the children of Count Antonio Maria Borromeo. On returning to Messina in 1650, he began a period of intense activity, painting for many towns and villages and also working as a civil engineer. His style is reminiscent both of Alberti and Cortona, but the tenderness of his paintings is all his own.

Gagini family Although originally from Bissone on Lake Lugano, they were prominent in Italy as sculptors, metalworkers and also architects (but never officially acknowledged as such), who managed their workshops along medieval lines, frequently collaborating on different tasks. They were active in several parts of Italy from the 15th century until well into the 1800s. Examples of their work can be found in almost every town of any size in Sicily, as well as in many villages. **Domenico** (c. 1420–92) was the most outstanding of the early artists, possibly a disciple of Brunelleschi. Born in Bissone (Switzerland), he worked for a time in Genoa, notably in the cathedral, and in Naples. In 1460 he brought his skills to Palermo. Called by the governor Pietro Speciale to carve the tomb of his son Antonio, who had died tragically the day before his wedding, he carried out several commissions on his behalf. Soon he was being called by many towns in Sicily to carve statues for their churches. In Palermo he founded the association of marble-workers in 1478, and in the city his son, **Antonello** (1478–1536) was born. Trained in his father's workshops, Antonello became the head of the family in Sicily. He was probably briefly an assistant to Michelangelo in Rome. His best-known works, carefully composed statues of the Madonna, also show the influence of Francesco Laurana. Less well documented is his work as an architect. Antonello's son **Antonino** (fl. 1537–81), although with less confident artistic talent, continued to maintain the family's virtual monopoly on decorative religious art commissions in Sicily. One of Antonello's younger brothers, **Gian Domenico** (c. 1503–67), was also a sculptor of note, and his son **Antonuzzo** (fl. 1576–c.1606) went on to collaborate with his own offspring, also named **Gian Domenico**, who was probably born in Caltagirone, where Antonuzzo died. **Nibilio** Gagini (fl. 1583–1607) was raised in Palermo and became a much sought-after goldsmith and medal-engraver, a craft also practised around the same time by **Giuseppe** (fl. 1575–1610).

Gagliardi, Rosario (Syracuse, ?1690–1762), architect who played a prominent part in the reconstruction of the city of Noto, where the characteristic layout of the new town and many of the churches and convents were to his design. He is one of the finest exponents of Sicilian Baroque architecture, on a par with Vaccarini.

Gambara, Antonio (?Palermo, 15C), sculptor and master-builder, responsible for the magnificent south portal of the cathedral of Palermo, partly inspired by the 14th-century west doorway.

Gaspare da Pesaro (?Palermo, 15C), painter and engraver, active mainly in Palermo, where he was the preferred artist of the Catalan community resident in the city. He has been suggested as the author of the *Triumph of Death* fresco in Palazzo Abatellis. He had two sons, both artists: **Guglielmo** (Palermo, b. 1430), who might have painted the wooden Crucifix in the cathedral of Cefalù, and **Benedetto**.

Gianforma, Giuseppe (Palermo, fl. 1740–70), stucco-moulder. His two sons **Gioacchino** and **Giovanni** were also stucco-moulders. Giovanni was a greater talent than his father; his work recalls that of Giacomo Serpotta.

Giganti or **Gigante, Andrea** (Trapani, 1731–87), priest and architect originally inspired by the work of Giovanni Biagio Amico. Arriving in Palermo after his studies, he soon found himself at the centre of attention for the excellence of his work; he proved himself capable of running large building sites with smooth efficiency, and finishing constructions down to the last tiny decorative detail, on occasion working also as civil engineer. Many sumptuous villas and palaces, such as Villa Valguarnera Gangi in Palermo and Villa Galletti at Bagheria, and numerous fine churches, were designed and completed by Giganti.

Giordano, Luca (Naples, 1634–1705), painter, such a fast worker that he was nicknamed 'Luca fa presto' (Luca works fast) by his contemporaries; he completed over 3,000 paintings in the course of his career. He was apprenticed to Jusepe de Ribera for nine years and frequented the atelier of Pietro da Cortona, before going to Parma to see the works of Correggio and Veronese.

Giorgio da Milano (Milan, 15C), sculptor who left his native Lombardy to work in Sicily, one of the first artists to introduce the early Renaissance style to the island.

Giorgio di Faccio (Turin, 16C), Mannerist architect summoned to Palermo by the Genoese community to design their new church of San Giorgio dei Genovesi at La Loggia (1576).

Giovanni di Bartolo (Siena, 14C), sculptor and goldsmith invited to Catania in 1372 to make the reliquary bust of St Agatha.

Goro di Gregorio (Siena, 1275–1334), sculptor whose father was the assistant of Nicola Pisano. He was summoned to Messina in 1333 to make the tomb of Archbishop Guidotto de' Tabiati in the cathedral.

Graffeo, Nicolò and **Giacomo** (Termini Imerese, late 15C), painters and miniaturists, brothers, they usually worked together.

Gramignani, Francesco (Palermo, 18C), type-setter and engraver, a student of Olivio Sozzi.

Grano, Antonino or **Antonio** (Palermo, 1660–1718), painter and engraver. His first task as an apprentice was to restore the frescoes by Pietro Novelli in the church of Casa Professa in Palermo. In 1680 he went to Rome, where he worked with artists following in the tradition of Carlo Maratta. On returning to Palermo, he found that his conservative style was out of favour.

Greco, Emilio (Catania, 1913–95), sculptor of figurative works mainly in bronze or marble and initially inspired by the medieval master Francesco Laurana. Angered by the indifference with which he

was always treated in his home town, he left Catania nothing in his will.

Greco, Ignazio (Palermo, 1830–?1910), architect best known for his collaboration with the Whitaker family, for whom he designed Villa Malfitano in Palermo.

Guarino, Francesco (Noto, 18C), modeller of processional statues in *mistura* and stucco.

Guccione, Pietro (Scicli, b. 1935, www.pieroguccione.it), painter, fascinated by the sea and its myriad colours, his depictions of waves and the water are very impressive.

Guerci, Dario (Ragusa, 19C), painter; from 1856–66 he painted some canvases for the duomo at Ibla, including the memorable *St George Killing the Dragon*.

Guercio, Gaspare (Palermo, 1611–79), architect and sculptor who worked occasionally with Gaspare Serpotta and designed and built numerous monumental tombs for aristocratic families.

Guttuso, Renato (Bagheria, 1912–87), committed Communist and controversial painter noted for his bold brush strokes and use of colour. His most famous painting is of the Vucciria street-market in Palermo.

Houbraken, Jan van (Flanders, fl. 1636–65), artist versed in the tradition of Flemish still-life painting, who travelled to Messina after a sojourn in Naples, where he appreciated the effect that Caravaggio had on local painters. Nothing survives of the work of his son **Ettore**, who fled Messina for Livorno in 1674 because of the anti-Spanish uprisings, together with his son **Nicola** (Messina, 1660–1732), who became a great still-life painter.

Italia, Angelo (Licata, 1628–1700), Jesuit architect who started his career in his home town and in Palma di Montechiaro, where he worked for the Tomasi di

Lampedusa family. In 1670 he went to Palermo to design the cupola and the stuccoes for the church of the Carmine; in Monreale he designed the sumptuous Cappella del Crocifisso for Archbishop Roano.

Ittar, Stefano (Ovruch, present-day Ukraine, 1724–90), architect who carried out various projects in Catania, including Porta Ferdinandea. His son **Sebastiano** (Catania, 1768–1847), a skilled draughtsman, showed a strong interest in ancient monuments. In 1800 Lord Elgin took him to Greece to draw the ancient monuments for him (his drawings are now in the British Museum).

La Valle, Raffaele (Palermo, 16C) and his son **Antonino** (?Cefalù, 1572–1645), organ manufacturers. Their instruments had an unmistakable sound and were beautiful to look at. Five of the superb organs built by Antonino still survive.

Labisi, Paolo (Noto, fl. 1731–90), architect, exponent of the Sicilian Baroque style. A student of Rosario Gagliardi, he worked almost exclusively in Noto, where his greatest achievement was Palazzo Nicolaci Villadorata.

Laurana, Francesco (Vrana, Dalmatia, fl. 1458–1500), sculptor, architect and medal-engraver, who absorbed a variety of influences in France and Naples as well as Sicily, where he worked in the late 1460s and early '70s. In his most famous works, often quiet and austere portraits of women, there is a pursuit of abstract formal perfection that has led to comparisons with Piero della Francesca.

Leto, Antonino (Monreale, 1844–1913), painter, noted for his landscapes blazing with sunlight. He considered his most important painting to be *La Mattanza*, a study of the tuna-fishing that he witnessed in the Florio fishery at Favignana.

Li Volsi family, sculptors, wood-carvers and stucco-moulders, the sons and descendants of **Giuseppe** (?Nicosia, fl. 1607) include **Francesco** (Tusa, fl. 1621–30) and his brother **Giovanni Battista** (Nicosia, fl. 1622–86), who often worked together with his son **Stefano**. Another brother was **Scipione** (Tusa, fl. 1621–30), an excellent sculptor; although he never achieved great fame, his work bears comparison to the best production of the Serpotta and Gagini families.

Lojacono, Francesco (Palermo, 1838–1915) influential painter, called the 'thief of the sun' by his contemporaries for the inimitable way he illuminates his landscapes. He was in Florence from 1861–5, where he developed a taste for painting in the open air.

Lo Monaco, Sebastiano (Catania, 1730–75), fresco-painter who studied under Olivio Sozzi. His most notable work is the frescoed vault of the church of the Holy Trinity in Lentini.

Lo Verde Giacomo (Trapani, fl. 1619–45), painter, he studied together with his friend Andrea Carreca under Pietro Novelli.

Mancini, Antonio (Rome, 1852–1930), painter, inspired by the poor of Naples, to whom he dedicated almost his entire production. Invited to Paris, he did not enjoy the experience, which ruined his health; afterwards, he had to spend four years in a clinic. He lived his last years in Rome, happily experimenting with colours, which he enriched by adding bits of tinsel, glass, mirror and mother-of-pearl.

Mancini or **Mancino, Giacomo** (?, 16C), sculptor, probably Sicilian.

Mancino, Andrea (Lombardy, fl. 1480–1500), sculptor brought to Sicily by Domenico Gagini, and about whom very little is known.

Mancino, Giuliano *see Berrettaro.*

Manno, Antonio or **Antonino** (Palermo, 1739–1810) **Vincenzo** and **Francesco** (Palermo, 1752–1831), all painters, were brothers who often worked together. Antonio was a student of Vito D'Anna.

Manzù, Giacomo (Giacomo Manzoni; Bergamo, 1908–91), sculptor and painter. Self-taught, he admired Gothic and Romanesque art, Donatello and Picasso. Bronze and wax were his preferred materials. His lifelong friend was Renato Guttuso, whose tomb he made at Bagheria.

Marabitti, Ignazio (Palermo, 1719–97), sculptor who studied in Rome under Filippo Della Valle. A prolific worker, he prepared statues for several Sicilian towns, especially Palermo, where his most notable works are his graceful fountains.

Mariani, Giuseppe (Pistoia, 1681–1731), architect and painter. In 1700 he went to Rome where he probably worked together with Giacomo Amato, a fellow monk and a Sicilian, who invited him to Palermo. He designed Villa Aragona Cutò in Bagheria, inspired by the 16th-century palaces and villas of Rome.

Martorana, Gioacchino (Palermo, 1735–79), painter, draughtsman and portraitist. In Palermo he had a successful career painting canvases, altarpieces and frescoes for churches and palaces. He died very young of pneumonia, leaving his atelier to two of his sons, **Ermenegildo** (who worked in Syracuse, Piazza Armerina and Palermo) and **Pietro**, expert in watercolour, who married the daughter of Vito D'Anna.

Marvuglia, Giuseppe Venanzio (Palermo, 1729–1814), Neoclassical architect often assisted in his projects (for example the royal hunting-lodge at Ficuzza) by his son **Alessandro Emanuele** (Palermo, 1769–

1845) and his brother **Salvatore** (Palermo, 1735–1802), a priest who worked with him on the Palazzina Cinese in the Favorita park.

Master of the Trapani Polyptych (?, 14–15C), painter with a superb technique and an original style who would appear to have carefully studied the works of Tuscan masters. Bright colours, elegant figures and symmetrical settings characterise his work.

Masuccio, Natale (Messina, 1568–1619), Jesuit architect who exclusively designed churches for his Order. He travelled frequently to Rome and Malta, and in 1599 was kidnapped by pirates, who released him without demanding a ransom, interpreted by Masuccio as divine intervention. Bad-tempered and arrogant, after several heated arguments with his superiors he left the Order in 1616.

Matera, Giovanni (Trapani, 1653–1718), wood-carver and clay-modeller, famous for his skill in carving figurines for Christmas cribs. Accused of murder, he found refuge in the convent of Sant'Antonino in Palermo, where he spent the rest of his life.

Matinati, Giovannello ('Giovanni Antonio', Messina, fl. 1509–48), sculptor and engraver renowned for his Crucifixes, sculpted in wood and painted, showing Christ wearing a gold-trimmed loincloth.

Mazza, Antonio (Noto, 1761–1825), architect and painter who designed and decorated several buildings in his native Noto and also in Scicli.

Mazzola or **Mazzolo, Gian Domenico** (Carrara, fl. 1544–77), sculptor who arrived in Messina in 1513 with his father **Giovan Battista** (fl. 1513–50) to complete the cathedral sculptures left unfinished on the death of Antonello Gagini. Later Gian Domenico carried out some work for the cathedral of St Agatha in Catania, notably the north door.

Mazzullo, Giuseppe (Graniti, nr. Taormina, 1913–88, www.fondazionemazzullo.it), sculptor, son of a building-site foreman. He was apprenticed to a tailor, where he took an interest in art. His father helped him go to Rome and Perugia, where he studied at the Academy of Fine Arts. In 1939 he opened a studio in Rome, which soon became the haunt of intellectuals and the artistic élite. His taste evolved towards sculpture in stone, preferably granite, while his inspiration derived from the humble lives of fishermen and peasants. In 1980 he settled in Taormina, creating a foundation in his name, for which the city conceded the palace of the dukes of Santo Stefano.

Mendola, Carmelo (Catania, 1895–1976, www.carmelomendola.com), self-taught sculptor whose preferred medium was bronze. His sculptures have the lightness and delicacy of a bird on the wing.

Messina, Francesco (Linguaglossa, nr. Catania, 1900–95), sculptor. His bronze studies of young girls and dancers are unmistakeable for their graceful abandon; he also liked to portray horses. In 2002 his study of a fallen stallion caused an outcry in Catania (it now stands in the central garden of Piazza Galatea) and the council blacksmith was ordered to provide the animal with a pair of iron knickers to avoid embarrassing the ladies. The story was featured on CNN and the ridiculous 'panties' were immediately removed.

Messina, Vincenzo (Sambuca di Sicilia, 1670–1757), painter and stucco-moulder, admirer of Giacomo Serpotta. He usually carried out work to the design of other artists. His sons **Giacomo**, **Giovanni** and **Gabriele** also worked in his atelier.

Migneco, Giuseppe (Messina, 1908–97),

expressionist painter whose works are full of life and colour. As a sculptor, he preferred working in bronze.

Minniti, Mario (Syracuse, 1577–1640), painter who went to Rome to seek his fortune, soon becoming a friend and follower of Caravaggio, for whom he also acted as model. When Caravaggio escaped to Sicily from Malta, he was the guest of Minniti.

Montalbano, Leonardo (Sambuca, fl. 1606–53), silversmith who made at least two masterpieces, the *Sfera d'Oro* (Palazzo Abatellis, Palermo) and the *Corona della Visitazione* for the statue of the Madonna in Enna, now in the Alessi museum.

Montorsoli, **Fra' Giovanni Angelo** (Montorsoli, nr. Florence, 1507–63), sculptor, engraver and architect, who learnt his art in the atelier of Michelangelo. In 1547 he was called to Messina by the city senate to design a fountain in order to celebrate a rational new water-supply system; the resulting Fountain of Orion is considered one of the loveliest in Italy.

Moschetti, Giulio (Ascoli Piceno, 1847–1909), sculptor who settled in Catania when he was invited to make the fountain in front of the railway station. He also carried out some of the sculptures of great musicians on the façade of the opera house, and the Fountain of Diana in Syracuse. Cement was his favourite material. Because he had nine children, it was always difficult for him to make ends meet, and he died in poverty. His son **Mario** (Rome, 1879–1960), also a sculptor, helped his father with some of his later projects.

Musarra, Giuliano (Palermo, fl. 1591), craftsman who specialised in making bronze gates for chapels.

Napoli, Tommaso Maria (Palermo, 1655–

1723), Dominican friar, mathematician and architect, an expert in fortifications and military architecture. He designed Palermo's first Baroque square, Piazza San Domenico, and two of the most elegant houses in Bagheria, Villa Valguarnera and Villa Palagonia, with its famous grotesque statues.

Nicolò da Mineo (Mineo, 1542–1625), sculptor who worked almost exclusively with the Gagini family.

Nicolò da Pettineo (Pettineo, 15–16C), painter who excelled in frescoes and panel paintings.

Niger or **Nigro, Bernardino** (Modica, fl. 1513–88), painter. The fact that he always signed and dated his paintings helps trace his artistic career through the provinces of Ragusa and Catania. His later work clearly shows the influence of Polidoro da Caravaggio.

Nolfo, Antonio (Trapani, 1696–1784), sculptor and modeller of statuary groups for the procession of the *Misteri*, in particular that of the Confraternity of Bakers, representing *The Coronation with the Crown of Thorns*. His three sons **Domenico**, **Francesco** and **Antonio** continued the work of his atelier.

Novelli, Antonio ('Pietro Antonio', Monreale, 1568–1625), a gifted painter, well known and much sought-after in his day. His fame has been overshadowed by that of his far greater son Pietro (*see below*). Between 1614 and 1616 he was commissioned to paint 40 altarpieces on slate, showing the Madonna and Child. Similar yet not quite identical, five of these paintings survive, at Piana degli Albanesi, Sclafani Bagni, Caltanissetta, Cerami and Licata.

Novelli, Pietro ('Il Monrealese'; Monreale, 1603–47), painter and architect; one of Sicily's finest artists, who perfected his chiaroscuro in Naples under Jusepe de Ribera and was fascinated by Van Dyck during that artist's visit to Palermo. Recognisable by his stylish beard and moustache, he often appears in his own works. He eventually became court painter to Philip IV of Spain, but he offended the king and fled to Ragusa in Sicily, where the monks gave him refuge. Pietro's daughter **Rosalia** (Palermo, 1628–?88) was a gifted artist, two of whose works can be seen in the Casa Professa church in Palermo: *St Agatha Professing her Faith before Quintianus*, and the *Immaculate Virgin with St Francesco Borgia*. Novelli died of the wounds inflicted on him by the rabble during the revolt against the Spanish in 1647.

Padula, Pietro (Naples, fl. 1773–6), sculptor and wood-carver, famed for his Christmas cribs peopled with realistic shepherds, craftsmen, washerwomen and peasants.

Paladini, Filippo ('Il Paladino'; Casi, nr. Rufina, 1544–1615), Mannerist painter; he arrived in Sicily from Malta in 1601, at the invitation of Counter-Reformation religious orders, after serving a sentence as a galley-slave. His cool, elegant colour schemes and careful positioning of figures owes much to his Tuscan origins. He was tutor to the two Zoppi di Gangi, and his later works show the influence of Caravaggio.

Palma, Andrea (Trapani, 1644–1730), architect and painter who helped introduce the Neoclassical style to Palermo. His grandson **Nicolò** (Trapani, 1694–1779) was also a successful architect, who designed many aristocratic palaces in the city of Palermo as well as the Villa Giulia public gardens.

Pampillonia, Giuseppe or **Baldassarre** (Palermo, 1646–1741), sculptor particularly skilled in inlaid marble decoration. He worked for Angelo Italia at the cathedral of Monreale. One of his finest achievements is the altar of the Madonna in the sanctuary-church of Gibilmanna.

Paradiso, Angelo (Acireale, 19–20C), blacksmith renowned for his beautiful iron gates; he was considered to be the finest craftsman in a city famous for its wrought-iron work.

Patania, Giuseppe (Palermo, 1780–1852), versatile painter related to the Sozzi and the D'Anna families. As a boy he studied under Velasquez until they quarrelled. He opened his own studio aged 15, and concentrated on historical and mythological subjects until he developed his own style. He became especially noted for his expressive portraits.

Patricolo, Giuseppe (Palermo, 1834–1905), architect and painter, member of an illustrious family of artists.

Pennino, Giacomo (Palermo, 18C), sculptor, a student of Giacomo Serpotta; it is reported that he died at the age of 104. His son **Filippo** (Palermo, 1733–94), also a sculptor, studied with Marabitti.

Piero or **Pietro da Bonitate** (Bonate Sotto, nr. Bergamo, fl. 1466–1501), sculptor who served his apprenticeship with Francesco Laurana, becoming his partner until Laurana went to Naples in 1471. They opened an atelier in Sciacca but were forced to close it because of local hostility. In Palermo they made the arch for the Mastrantonio Chapel in the church of San Francesco, thus introducing the Renaissance into Sicilian sculpture and architecture.

Pirandello, Fausto (Rome, 1899–1975), painter. Son of the famous writer, he lived from an early age in Paris, with a circle of friends including Picasso, Severini, Tozzi, De Chirico and De Pisis; he was also strongly influenced by Modigliani, Marini, Manzù and Moore.

Platania, Giacinto (Acireale, 1612–97), one of the greatest painters of his age. He liked to include realistic details in his paintings, and to use the city of Acireale or its surroundings as a backdrop. He worked almost exclusively for the religious authorities and his canvases and frescoes can be found in many churches of Acireale and eastern Sicily. Something of an engineer, during the massive eruption of Mt Etna in 1669, together with some friends he tried to divert the lava stream (it was the first ever attempt to do this) that was heading for Catania, by building dykes. His efforts were unsuccessful because various landowners objected to having their vineyards and orange groves submerged with rock.

Poidomani, Gaspare (Comiso, fl. 1517), architect or master-builder responsible for the construction of the splendid apse of the church of San Francesco in Comiso.

Polidoro da Caravaggio (Polidoro Caldara, Caravaggio, nr. Bergamo, ?1495–1546), painter who found employment in Raphael's atelier. After the Sack of Rome in 1527, he worked in Naples and Messina, where he was murdered by his servant on the eve of his planned return to Rome.

Provenzano, Domenico (Palma di Montechiaro, 1736–94), fresco-painter. The son of a carpenter, he trained in Palermo under arch-rivals Gaspare Serenario and Vito D'Anna, eventually showing more of the influence of the latter.

Quartararo, Riccardo (Sciacca, 1443–1506), painter with a complex personality who worked in Naples, central Italy, and perhaps Valencia, areas that strongly influenced his art, which also shows Flemish touches.

Quattrocchi, Filippo (Gangi, 1734–1818), sculptor in wood. Although he served his apprenticeship in Palermo, he returned to Gangi where he spent the rest of his life, sculpting groups for the churches of his home town and other villages of the Madonie. His son **Francesco** (Palermo, 1779–1861) followed in his father's footsteps, although he used marble and stucco for his sculptures, besides wood.

Ragusa, Giovanni Battista (Palermo, fl 1713–97), sculptor; at the start of his career he divided his time between Palermo and Rome, where he had fallen under the spell of Bernini. He spent most of the rest of his life carving statues for the cathedral and several other churches in Palermo.

Ragusa, Vincenzo (Palermo, 1841–1927), sculptor and painter of humble origins (his parents were servants in an aristocratic household). Something of a firebrand, he signed up with the 'Thousand' for the Battle of Milazzo. Aged 24 he commenced his artistic career. For many years he was director of the department of sculpture at the Academy of Fine Arts of Palermo, and in 1892 he won the competition for the bronze monument to Giuseppe Garibaldi which now stands in Via Libertà.

Randazzo, Filippo ('Il Monocolo di Nicosia', Nicosia, 1695–1748), painter with only one eye, who after an apprenticeship in Palermo was sent to study at the school of Sebastiano Conca in Rome. His style was found pleasing, and he had a long and successful career painting frescoes and altarpieces for many towns in Sicily. His son **Mariano** was also a minor painter.

Ribera, Jusepe de ('Lo Spagnoletto'; Játiva, Spain, 1588–1652), painter and etcher. He went to Naples as court painter for the Spanish viceroy. Impressed by Caravaggio, he in his turn influenced the great Sicilian painter Pietro Novelli.

Ricca, Michele (Palermo, 1590–1654), silversmith, a prestigious exponent of the Palermitan Baroque.

Riccio, Antonello (Messina, 16C), painter, perhaps a disciple of Polidoro da Caravaggio, and son of **Mariano** (Messina, 1510–?), with whom he is often confused. Mariano was a fine artist from an aristocratic family whose works are distinguished by skilful draughtsmanship.

Riolo, Vincenzo (Palermo, 1772–1837), Neoclassical painter who studied with Antonio Manno before going to Rome. Returning to Palermo in 1799, his popularity soon eclipsed that of his contemporaries, for example Giuseppe Velasco (Velasquez), and he was much in demand by the élite to decorate their palaces and villas. He died together with his eldest son Antonio during the 1837 cholera epidemic.

Rizzo, Pietro (Palermo, fl. 1590–1628), silversmith who probably learnt his craft in the atelier of Nibilio Gagini. He soon attained the highest levels of the art and was invited to make the silver reliquary statue of St Lucy for the duomo of Syracuse, before working almost exclusively for the Benedictine monastery of San Martino delle Scale, near Monreale.

Rizzo, Pippo or **Filippo** (Corleone, 1897–1964), painter, the most important Sicilian exponent of Futurism.

Roberto di Oderisio (Naples, c. 1335–82), painter, one of the greatest exponents of Neapolitan art, often called the Giotto of Naples.

Rosa, Salvator (Naples, 1615–73), Baroque painter, etcher, musician and poet, one of the most unconventional and rebellious artists of his city. He studied under Jusepe de Ribera. Orphaned at 17, with his mother and five siblings to support, he apprenticed himself to Aniello Falcone, working with him on enormous battle scenes. After a spell in Rome he returned to Naples, painting romantic landscapes full of wild rocks and vegetation, peopled with bandits, seamen, shepherds and peasants, his finest work.

Rossi, Epifanio (?Caltagirone, 17C), elegant painter who appears to have worked exclusively in Caltagirone.

Rossi, Mariano (Mariano Russo, Sciacca, 1731–1807), painter described by Berenson as anti-Baroque. Much in favour with the Bourbons, he followed them from Naples to Sicily in 1798 when they were fleeing the Napoleonic troops, but refused to join them in Caserta in 1806, preferring to stay in Rome, where he died in solitude after refusing to paint for the new masters, the French.

Rutelli, Mario (Palermo, 1859–1941), exponent of a family of talented sculptors, wood- and stone-carvers and stucco-moulders.

Ruzzolone, Pietro (Palermo, fl. 1484–1526), highly esteemed painter, sometimes compared with Raphael, noted for his remarkable Crucifixes.

Sada, Carlo (Bellagio, nr. Como, 1809–73), architect. After completing with success the Massimo Bellini opera house in Catania, he spent the rest of his life in the city as the most fashionable architect in town.

Salerno, Giuseppe *see Zoppo di Gangi.*

Sarzana, Nicolò (Palermo, 1700–86), ceramist who made floors of majolica tiles for palaces and churches, possibly including that of San Benedetto in Caccamo.

Savoja, Leone (Messina, 1814–85), architect. His most remarkable achievement is Messina's monumental

cemetery, in a splendid position overlooking the Straits.

Scilla, Agostino (Messina, 1629–1700), painter; in 1670 he published a controversial argument for the organic origin of fossils, an important contribution to palaeontology.

Scipione di Blasi (Naples, 16C), silversmith who brought a new Mannerism to Sicily, influencing a generation of the Gagini family.

Scipione di Guido (Naples, fl. 1587–1604), wood-carver who was invited to Catania to decorate the choir stalls in the cathedral. Before returning to Naples he carried out work in Caltagirone and Enna.

Sciuti, Giuseppe (Zafferana Etnea, nr. Catania, 1834–1911), painter who loved portraying historical events by using huge canvases, a rich colour palette, an eye for drama, and careful attention to detail. His liking for large surfaces led to him being invited to paint frescoes in many churches and villas. His dramatic works have been compared to blockbuster films *à la* Cecil B. De Mille, and undoubtedly, if he had been born a few years later, he would have found in Hollywood the fame which eluded him all his life.

Serassi (Bergamo, 1720–1895), as **Fratelli Serassi**, organ manufacturers, the family dominated their field for six generations.

Serenario or **Serenari, Gaspare** or **Gasparo** (Palermo, 1694 or 1707–59), painter who worked for a time in the atelier of Borremans (the artist who would appear to have most strongly influenced him), before going to Rome in 1730 to join the circle of Sebastiano Conca. On his return to Palermo he worked there with amazing energy.

Serpotta, Giacomo (Palermo, 1656–1732), sculptor and stucco-moulder, son of **Gaspare** (Palermo, d. 1669). Giacomo took the art of moulding to its highest levels; he is credited with ushering in the Rococo style. The name Serpotta means snake or lizard; the sculptor often included either reptile in his works as a trademark. He was sometimes assisted by his brother **Giuseppe** (Palermo, 1653–1719) and his talented son **Procopio** (Palermo, 1679–1755). Serpotta's secret, by means of which his stuccoes acquired the glossy appearance of carved stone, was to add marble dust to his paste.

Simone da Corleone (Corleone, nr. Palermo, fl. 1377–88), painter whose only known surviving work is the ceiling of the Steri palace in Palermo, which he decorated with Arab motifs together with Cecco di Naro and Pellegrino Dareno.

Sinatra, Vincenzo (Noto, 1707–65), master-builder and architect who began his career as a stonemason. He married the niece of Rosario Gagliardi and took over the atelier when Gagliardi was paralysed by a stroke.

Siragusa, Federico (?Milazzo, fl. 18C–early 19C), sculptor. Little is known about him. He was the teacher of the sculptor Nunzio Morello.

Smiriglio, Mariano (Palermo, 1561–1636), architect and painter, his maestro was Paladini. Chief Architect for the senate, he also worked for the theatre as set designer and planned religious processions.

Sogliani, Giovanni Antonio (Florence, 1492–1544), a painter who learned his art in the atelier of Lorenzo di Credi. His restrained Mannerist style, free of formal exaggerations, delighted those religious orders voted to poverty and earned him many commissions from monasteries and confraternities.

Sozzi, Olivio (Catania, 1690–1765), painter; after marrying a wealthy woman, he used her dowry to put himself through his studies, working in Rome under Sebastiano Conca and the fresco painter Corrado Giaquinto. His son-in-law Vito D'Anna would later follow a similar path. Sozzi's style is largely Roman Classicist. On returning to Sicily he worked in Catania and Palermo. His body is preserved in a glass case in the church of Santa Maria Maggiore at Ispica, where you can also admire some of his finest frescoes.

Spada or **Spata, Mario** *see Rosario Boscarino*.

Stom, Matthias (or Stomer; Amersfoort, Holland, c. 1600–?50), painter. He began his career in Rome, about 1630, probably attracted there by the works of Caravaggio. After a long stay in Naples, in 1641 he came to Sicily and lived in Palermo for the rest of his life. Theatrical and unconventional, most of his vast production of paintings were carried out for wealthy private families rather than for churches and convents.

Tancredi, Filippo (Messina, 1655–1722), influential painter who studied with Maratta in Rome. In 1674, to escape the revolutionaries, he hid in Rome's Ruffo Gallery and copied all the paintings there. He is noted for his precise draughtsmanship and skilful colouring technique, and was much influenced by Pietro Novelli.

Tartaglio, Giacomo (Trapani, fl. 1729), sculptor, one of a group of artists that modelled many of the figures for the annual Easter procession of the *Misteri* in his city.

Tassara, Giovanni Battista (Genoa, 1841–1916), sculptor born into a family of fishermen. As a soldier for Garibaldi, he took part in the 1860 expedition of the 'Thousand' at Marsala. He made his way to Florence where he befriended Giovanni Dupré and perfected his technique as a sculptor. In 1876 he won the competition for the tomb of Vincenzo Bellini in the cathedral of Catania, and in 1890 Ernesto Basile asked him to carve the bronze reliefs for the monument to the Thousand at Pianto Romano near Calatafimi. During the First World War he served as a nurse in the military hospital of Genoa, where he died in 1916.

Tedeschi, Gregorio (Florence, fl. 1609–50), sculptor who lived most of his life in Sicily. He created some of the allegorical figures (1629) for Piazza Vigliena in Palermo, where he also carved the statue of St Rosalia sleeping (1650) for her sanctuary on Monte Pellegrino, which fascinated Goethe.

Tipa, Andrea (Trapani, fl. 1725–76), sculptor, the best-known member of a family of sculptors who brought new life to the art in Trapani in the mid-18th century.

Tomaselli, Onofrio (Bagheria, 1886–1956), painter particularly sensitive to the plight of the poor, especially the children working in the sulphur mines. Renato Guttuso decided to become a painter after seeing one of his canvases, the *Carusi nelle Zolfare* (now in Palermo's GAM, Gallery of Modern Art).

Tommaso de Vigilia (?Palermo, fl. 1444–97), painter, particularly active in western Sicily. He was possibly an assistant of Gaspare da Pesaro. Most of his surviving works are in Palermo.

Tuccari, Giovanni (Messina, 1667–1743), Baroque-style painter who used a restricted palette enlivened by sudden flashes of colour.

Umile da Petralia, Fra' (Giovanni Francesco Pintorno; Petralia Soprana, c. 1580–1639), wood-carver. To escape an arranged marriage, he became a Franciscan friar and from then on devoted his life to fasting, prayer and carving and painting Crucifixes, 32 of which are still extant. He always shows Christ with a thick crown of thorns, one of which is piercing His left eyebrow (the artist suffered all his life from a similar pain). The face of Christ has three expressions, depending from which angle it is viewed: suffering, smiling, and dying.

Vaccarini, Giovambattista or **Giovanni Battista** (Palermo, 1702–67), the greatest 18th-century Sicilian architect. Born to a poor family, his parents asked the priest who christened him to act as his godfather, which he did with zeal: the boy became a priest himself before his 23rd birthday. An earthquake in 1726 called to action all the priests who could design to assist in rebuilding, and Giovambattista's talents were revealed. Self-taught, he was inspired by the Renaissance and Baroque art that he encountered in books and drawings. Having followed his godfather to Catania, where the former had been appointed archbishop, Vaccarini took part in the massive reconstruction of the city after the earthquake of 1693. After completing a difficult commission for King Charles of Bourbon, the grateful king awarded Vaccarini a generous pension; he lived the remaining ten years of his life as a wealthy abbot.

Vaccaro, Giuseppe, Francesco and **Mario** (Caltagirone, 19C), brothers, painters, ceramists and moulders, famous for their terracotta Christmas-crib statuettes.

Vasta, Pier Paolo (Acireale, 1697–1760), painter, noted for his soft pastel colours. He was particularly happy when painting women and Biblical episodes featuring heroines.

Vazano or **Bazano, Gaspare** *see Zoppo di Gangi*.

Velasquez or **Velasco, Giuseppe** (Palermo, 1750–1827), very popular painter; after following the taste for Baroque art, he developed Neoclassical tendencies.

Vermexio, Andrea (Spain, fl. 1594–1643), architect and master-builder who settled in Syracuse, where he carried out several commissions in Late Renaissance style, including the archbishop's palace with its hanging garden. His two sons **Giovanni** (Syracuse, fl. 1618–48), who designed the city hall, and **Francesco** were also architects. They often added a carved lizard (the meaning of their name) as a signature on the façades of their buildings.

Villareale, Valerio (Palermo, 1773–1854), Neoclassical sculptor who studied in Rome from 1797 at the school created by Antonio Canova. Several works of art in Sicily previously attributed to a youthful Canova are now thought to be by Villareale. His particular skill was in carving portrait busts and celebratory reliefs.

Vincenzo da Pavia or **Vincenzo degli Azani da Pavia** (Pavia, fl. 1495–1557), painter who spent the last part of his life in Palermo and was one of the principal exponents in Sicily of the style of Raphael and Perugino.

Vitaliano, Gioacchino (Palermo, 1669–1739), sculptor who liked working to the design of other artists, such as Antonio Grano or Paolo Amato, with whom he created his masterpiece, the Garraffo Fountain in Piazza Marina, Palermo. He married Teresa, sister of Giacomo Serpotta. His brother **Giacomo** and his son **Vincenzo** (Palermo, fl. 1743–53) were also sculptors.

Ximenes, Ettore (Palermo, 1855–1926) eclectic sculptor who studied with Nunzio Morello before going to Naples in order to attend the Academy of Fine Arts. He became famous abroad, especially after winning the competition organised by the city of Kiev for a new monument to Tsar Alexander II, to replace that destroyed during the Russian Revolution.

Zoppo di Gangi two painters went under the name of Zoppo di Gangi ('Cripple of Gangi'): **Giuseppe Salerno** (1570–1632) and **Gaspare Vazano** or **Bazano** (1555–1630). Both were born in the town of Gangi and though they are known to have been friends and colleagues, their working relationship remains obscure. It is possible that they were both prepared to adopt the same signature, common practice among the decorators of the time. Gaspare Vazano, the elder of the pair, is less widely known and seems to have preferred working in fresco. The majority of works attributed to the Zoppo di Gangi are by the hand of Giuseppe Salerno, the younger and perhaps the more talented of the two. His work demonstrates the influence of Raphael and also, very markedly—and typically for the time—that of Spanish art. His masterpiece, the *Last Judgement*, can be seen in the church of St Nicholas of Bari in Gangi. Closely based on Michelangelo's work of the same name in the Sistine Chapel, the painting also includes, as does Michelangelo's original, a possible self-portrait of the artist on St Bartholomew's flayed skin. Such direct quotation from the master's work in Rome would not at the time have been seen as plagiarism: on the contrary, it would have lent authority to the painting, and this kind of direct 'borrowing' was not unusual in the 17th century. Works by both Zoppi can be seen in many of the small towns and villages of the former province of Palermo, especially in Isnello and Polizzi Generosa, besides Gangi itself.

Glossary of Special Terms

Abacus, flat stone in the upper part of a capital

Acrolith, extremity of a statue (hand, foot, head) made of stone, while the body of the statue would have been of wood

Acroterion, ornamental feature on the corner or highest point of a pediment

Adyton, inner sanctum of a temple, with no natural light

Aedicule, small opening framed by two columns and a pediment, originally used in classical architecture

Agora, public square or market-place

Ambo (pl. *ambones*), pulpit in a Christian basilica; two pulpits on opposite sides of a church, from which the gospel and epistle were read

Amphiprostyle, temple with colonnades at both ends

Amphora, antique vase, usually of large dimensions, for oil and other liquids

Antefix, ornament placed at the lower corner of the tiled roof of a temple to conceal the space between the tiles and the cornice

Antis, in *antis* describes the portico of a temple when the side walls are prolonged to end in a pilaster flush with the columns of the portico

Architrave, lowest part of the entablature, horizontal frame above a door

Archivolt, moulded architrave carried round an arch

Arcosolium (pl. *arcosolia*), tomb where the sarcophagus is in an arched recess

Atlantes, (or telamones) male figures used as supporting columns

Atrium, forecourt, usually of a Byzantine church or a classical Roman house

Badia, (*abbazia*) abbey

Baglio (pl. *bagli*), from the medieval word *ballium* meaning a large fortified building. It is now used to describe the main buildings and cellars of a wine estate

Baldachin, canopy supported by columns, usually over an altar

Basilica, originally a Roman building used for public administration; in Christian architecture, an aisled church with a clerestory and apse, and no transepts

Bouleuterion, council chamber or meeting place

Caldarium, room for hot or steam baths in a Roman bath

Campanile, bell-tower, often detached from the building to which it belongs

Capital, the top of a column

Cardo, (pl. *cardines*), the main north–south street of a Roman town, at right-angles to the decumanus

Caryatid, female figure used as a supporting column

Cavea, the part of a theatre or amphitheatre occupied by the rows of seats

Cella, sanctuary of a temple, usually in the centre of the building

Chiaroscuro, distribution of light and shade, apart from colour, in a painting

Chiesa Matrice (or Chiesa Madre), the principal church in a town or village

Chryselephantine, of gold and ivory

Chthonic, dwelling in or under the ground

Ciborium, casket or tabernacle containing the Host

Cipollino, onion-marble; a greyish marble with streaks of white or green

Cippus, sepulchral monument in the form of an altar

Cista, casket, usually of bronze and cylindrical in shape, to hold jewels, toilet articles, etc., and decorated with mythological subjects

Columbarium, a building (often subterranean) with niches in the walls to hold urns containing the ashes of the dead

Console, ornamental bracket

Crenellations, battlements

Cuneus, wedge-shaped block of seats in an antique theatre

Cyclopean, the term applied to unmortared masonry walls of huge stones, older than the Etruscan civilisation, and attributed by the ancients to the giant Cyclopes

Decumanus, major east–west street of a Roman town

Diorite, a type of greenish-coloured rock, of volcanic origin

Dioscuri, Castor and Pollux, twin sons of Zeus

Dipteral, temple surrounded by a double peristyle

Diptych, painting or ivory tablet in two sections

Dipylon, monumental gateway between two supporting piers or pylons

Distyle, of a temple with two columns in front

Dithyrambic, pertaining to an ecstatic hymn of ancient Greece, especially one dedicated to Dionysus

Duomo, cathedral

Ekklesiasterion, council house for the citizens' assembly

Emporium, commercial centre of an ancient city, where imported goods were traded

Entablature, the part above the capital (consisting of architrave, frieze and cornice) of a classical building

Entasis, the difference in the diameter of a column at its top, middle and base

Ephebe, Greek youth under training (military or university)

Epigraph, inscription, especially on coins or sculpture

Exedra, semicircular recess

Ex-voto, tablet, wax model or small painting expressing gratitude to a saint

Fiumara, wide flat-bottomed torrent-bed filled with gravel, usually waterless

Forum, open space in a town serving as a market or meeting-place

Frigidarium, room for cold plunge-baths in a Roman bath-suite

Fumarole, volcanic spurt of vapour (usually sulphurous) emerging from the ground

Gigantomachia, contest of giants, a popular motif for relief carvings on temple exteriors

Graffiti, design on a wall made with an iron tool on a prepared surface, the design showing in white, also used loosely to describe scratched designs or words on walls

Greek cross, cross with arms of equal length

Hellenistic, the period from Alexander the Great to Augustus (c. 325–31 BC)

Herm, (pl. *hermae*) quadrangular pillar decreasing in girth towards the ground, surmounted by a bust

Hexastyle, temple with a portico of six columns at the end

Hypogeum, subterranean excavation for the interment of the dead

Intarsia, inlay of wood, marble or metal

Kore, maiden, usually used for Persephone

Kouros (pl. *kouroi*), boy; in statuary, an Archaic male standing figure

Krater, antique wine-bowl, conical in shape with rounded base

Kylix, wide shallow vase with two handles and short stem

Latomiae, the limestone quarries of Syracuse, later used as prisons and now lush gardens

Lekythos (pl. *lekythoi*), small slender jug for storing oil or perfume

Loculus (pl. *loculi*), burial cavity in a wall, as in a catacomb

Lunette, semicircular space in a vault or ceiling, often decorated with a painting or a relief

Mandorla, in art, an almond-shaped aureole around a holy figure

Marmi mischi, inlay decoration of various polychrome marbles and coloured stone, used in church interiors in the 17th and 18th centuries

Mascaron, caricatured human face or mask used as architectural decoration

Megalith, a huge stone (often used as a monument)

Megaron, an oblong hall (usually in a Mycenaean palace)

Metope, decorated panel between two triglyphs on the frieze of a temple

Misteri, wood and/or stucco sculptures representing the episodes of the Passion of Christ which are processed around the towns and cities on floats during Holy Week

Mistura, mixture used by sculptors, especially in the late 15th and early 16th centuries, to make processional statues lighter, and also because the Vatican approved the use of humble materials, such as straw, cloth, glue, *papier mâché*, wood, cork and plaster, used in varying proportions

Monolith, single stone (usually a column)

Muqarna, in Islamic architecture, a squinch (qv) subdivided into decorative divisions resulting in vaulting with a honeycomb or stalactite effect

Narthex, vestibule of a Christian basilica

Naumachia, mock naval combat for which the arena of an amphitheatre was flooded

Nymphaeum, a sort of summer-house with pool in the gardens of bath-houses and palaces, decorated with statues of the Nymphs

Octastyle, a portico with eight columns

Odeon, a concert hall, usually in the shape of a Greek theatre, but much smaller

Ogee (arch), arch shaped in a double curve, convex above and concave below

Oinochoe, wine-jug usually of elongated shape for dipping wine out of a krater

Opisthodomos, the enclosed rear part of a temple

Opus sectile, mosaic or paving of thin slabs of coloured marble cut in geometrical shapes

Ossuary, deposit of or receptacle for the bones of the dead

Palazzo, a dignified and important building in a town or city

Pantocrator, designating Christ in his guise as Almighty or All-Powerful

Pax, sacred object used by a priest for the blessing of peace, and offered for the kiss of the faithful, usually circular, engraved, enamelled or painted in a rich gold or silver frame

Pediment, gable above the portico of a classical building

Pendentive, concave spandrel beneath a dome

Peripteral, temple surrounded by a colonnade

Peristyle, a columned portico surrounding a court or garden

Pietà, group of the Virgin mourning the dead Christ

Piscina, Roman tank; a basin for an officiating priest to wash his hands before Mass

Pithos, large pottery vessel

Podium, a continuous base or plinth supporting columns, and the lowest row of seats in the cavea of a theatre or amphitheatre

Polyptych, painting or tablet in more than three sections

Predella, small painting attached below a large altarpiece

Presepio, literally, crib or manger. A group of statuary of which the central subject is the Infant Jesus in the manger

Pronaos, porch in front of the cella of a temple

Propylon, propylaea. Entrance gate to a *temenos*; in plural form when there is more than one door

Prostyle, edifice with columns on the front only

Punic, pertaining to the Carthaginians

Putto, figure of a child sculpted or painted, usually nude

Quadriga, four-horsed chariot

Quadriporticus, courtyard surrounded on each side by a portico

Reredos, decorated screen rising behind an altar

Rhyton, drinking-horn usually ending in an animal's head

Sinopia, reddish-brown pigment used to draw the first outline of a fresco

Squinch, arched space at the angle of a tower

Stamnos, a squat vase with two small handles at the sides, closed by a lid

Stele (pl. *stelae*), upright stone bearing a monumental inscription

Stereobate, basement of a temple or other building

Stilted arch, round arch that rises vertically before it springs

Stoa, a covered, free-standing colonnaded porch or portico

Stoup, vessel for Holy Water, usually near the entrance door of a church

Stucco, plasterwork

Stylobate, basement of a columned temple or other building

Taberna (pl. *tabernae*), shop in a Roman town

Tablinum, reception room in a Roman house with one side opening onto the central courtyard

Telamon (pl. *telamones*), see Atlantes

Temenos, a sacred enclosure

Tepidarium, room for warm baths in a Roman bath-suite

Tessera, a small cube of stone, terracotta, marble, glass, etc., used in mosaic work

Tetrastyle, having four columns at the end

Thermae, originally simply baths, later elaborate buildings fitted with libraries, assembly rooms, gymnasia, circuses, etc

Tholos, a circular building

Tondo, round painting or bas-relief

Transenna, open grille or screen, usually of marble, in an early Christian church

Triclinium, dining-room and reception room of a Roman house

Triglyph, blocks with two vertical grooves on either side of a metope on the frieze of a temple

Trinacria, literally "three feet", the ancient name for Sicily derived from its triangular shape

Triptych, painting or tablet in three sections

Tympanum, area above a doorway or the space enclosed by a pediment

Tyrant, in ancient times, the head of a city state, who ruled autocratically (though not necessarily tyrannically)

Villa, country house with its garden; in Sicily also public gardens in a town

Xystus, an exercise court; in a Roman villa the open court in front of the triclinium

POTTERY SHAPES

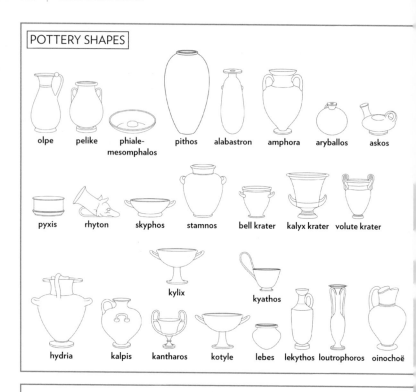

olpe pelike phiale-mesomphalos pithos alabastron amphora aryballos askos

pyxis rhyton skyphos stamnos bell krater kalyx krater volute krater

kylix kyathos

hydria kalpis kantharos kotyle lebes lekythos loutrophoros oinochoë

TEMPLE DESIGN

Early temple. This example is distyle in antis, meaning that the entrance has two columns nestling between the projecting piers (antae) of the side walls. The inner chamber (naos) is preceded by an antechamber (pronaos).

More complex temple design, again with two columns in antis, but this time also amphiprostyle, meaning that each end has a colonnaded porch (prostyle). The temple and its porches are built onto a crepidoma, a stepped platform.

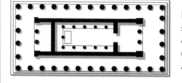

Peripteral temple, with peristyle (colonnade surrounding the naos). Access to the inner chamber (the naos) is through the pronaos (antechamber). The room at the back (with no access to the naos) is the opisthodomos.

THE CLASSICAL ORDERS

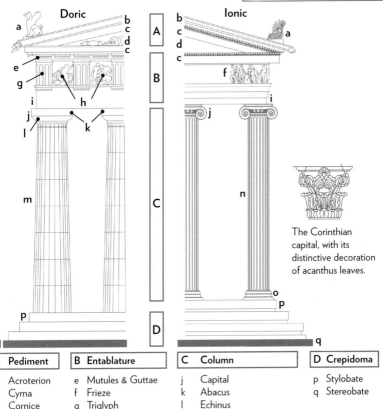

The Corinthian capital, with its distinctive decoration of acanthus leaves.

A	Pediment	B	Entablature	C	Column	D	Crepidoma
a	Acroterion	e	Mutules & Guttae	j	Capital	p	Stylobate
b	Cyma	f	Frieze	k	Abacus	q	Stereobate
c	Cornice	g	Triglyph	l	Echinus		
d	Tympanum	h	Metopes	m/n	Shaft: (m) flutes meet in sharp ridges (arrises); (n) flutes lie between flat ridges (fillets)		
		i	Architrave	o	Base		

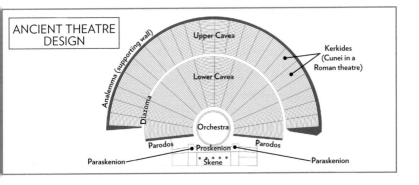

ANCIENT THEATRE DESIGN

Index

Explanatory or more detailed references (where there are many), or references to places where an artist's work is best represented, are given in bold. Numbers in italics are picture references. Dates are given for all artists, architects and sculptors with works referenced in this guide. Ancient names are rendered in italics, as are works of art.

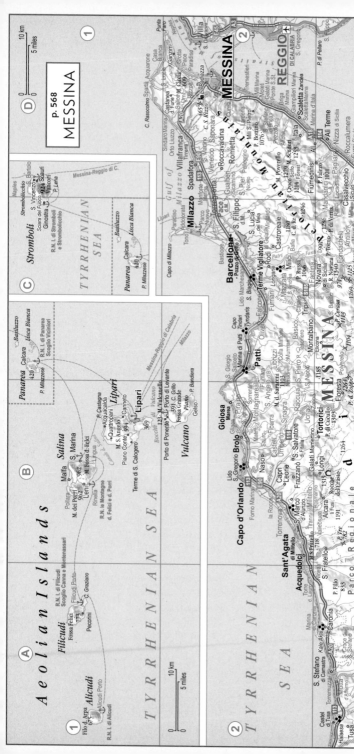

p. 568
MESSINA

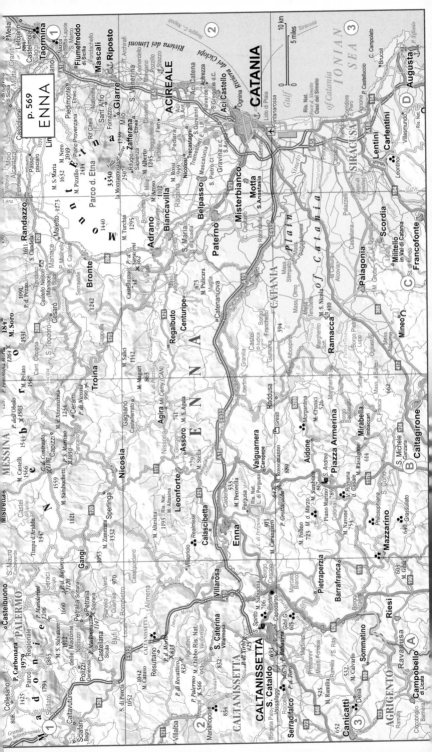

RAGUSA & SYRACUSE

p. 570

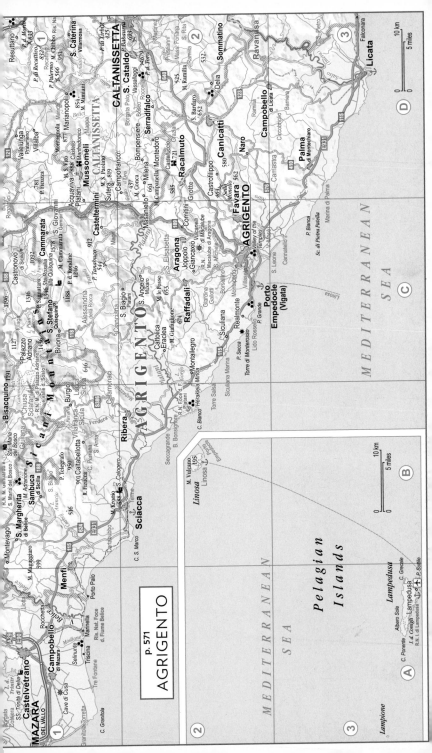

AGRIGENTO

p. 571

p. 572

CALTANISSETTA

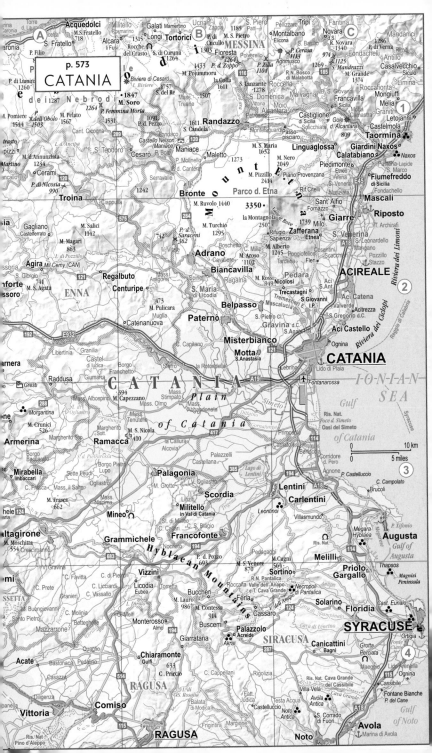

Torre
di Lauro
Caronia
P. di Lumini
1260
A. Pomiere
1544
M. d'Obolo
1505
trasto
pizzi
Martino
ancalo
Gagliano
Castelferrato
M. S. Agata
711
sfore
ssoro
ENNA
arnera
ne
Armerina
rele 124
Itagirone
M. Moschitta
554 Creacimanno
mi
Ragusa
Acate
SSETTA
Vittoria

Acquedolci
M.S.Fratello
S. Fratello
718
Alcara
il Fusi
P. Filio
Rocche
del Crasto
S. di Curuna
1264
Militello
Rosmarino
Longi
Galati Mamertino
Tortorici
P. di
Cuiculo
1303
Floresta
Ucria
Zappa
1185
M.S. Pietro
S. Piero
Patti
Montalbano
Elicona
Pellizzara
Tripi
Fantina
Novara
Fondachelli
P. d. Zoppo
1264
P. Zilla
1104
R.N. Bosco
di Malabotta
S. Basilio
Francavilla
di Sicilia

Biviere di Cesaro
il Biviere
S. del Re
Mass.
Treane
1847
M. Soro
P. Femmina Morta
1264
1091.
P. d. Pezzo
Castello Nelson
(Maniace)
Maniace
P. Molinello
d. Cantera

Nebrodi
1287
dei
M. Pelato
1567
1531
Cant. Cicogna
289
S. Teodoro
Cesaro
Serravalle
1242

M. Pojummoru
la Colla
1611
1433
S. Lanzarite
1278
S. Domenica
Vittoria
Moio
Alcantara
Petrosino
Castiglione
di Sicilia
Solicchiata
S. Giovanni

Randazzo
S. Candela
120
Maletto
M. S. Maria
1652
Piedimonte
Etneo
Gole
d. Alcantara
Motta
Camastra
809

Linguaglossa
Montelaguardo
Roccella
Malvagna
B. S. Giacomo
Graniti
Calatabiano
Fiumefreddo
di Sicilia
Fondachello

Mandanici
Antillo
Casalvecchio
Siculo
Limina
Roccafiorita
Mongiuffi
Melia
Letojanni
Taormina
Naxos
Giardini Naxos
Pastena-Lapide
d. Sicilia

M. Nero
2049
M. Pizzillo
2414
Piano Provenzana
Rif. Citelli
Sant' Alfio
Fornazzo
Mascali
Riposto

Troina
Ciappulla
575
284
P. d.
Saraceni
362
M. Turchio
1295
M. Ruvolo 1440
la Montagnola
2507
3350
Val le del Bove
1739
Milo
Rif. Sapienza
Zafferana
Etnea
Giarre
S. Venerina
T. Archirafi
Riviera dei Limoni

Regalbuto
Centuripe
121
Mass.
Aragona
Spinelli
Adrano
Biancavilla
S. Maria
di Licodia
Ragalna
Boschetto
C. Milia
M. Alberto
1245
M. Aroso
1102
Cavaliere
Pedara
Nicolosi
M. Rossi
949
Poggiofelice
Tardaria
Fleri
Cosentini
Scacchieri
Pozzillo
Stazzo
ACIREALE

473
M. Pulicara
Catenanuova
Libertinia
Paternò
Belpasso
S. Pietro Cl.
Gravina
S. Agata li B.
Trecastagni
S.Giovanni
Tremestieri E. L.P.
Mascalucia
Valverde
S. Gregorio d.C.
Aci
S. Ant.
Aci Catena
Acitrezza

192
E932
Castel
di Iudica
Borgo
Franchetto
Sferro
la Rotondella
Misterbianco
Motta
S.Anastasia
Lido di Plaia
Ognina
Aci Castello
Riviera dei Ciclopi
Reggio di Calabria

Granila
Raddusa
288
Morgantina
M. Crunici
526
Borgo
Baccarato
Margherito
Sop.
M.S. Nicola
410
Ramacca
Alcovia
Primosole
Bicocca
Corridore
d. Pero
Ris. Nat.
Foce d. Simeto
Oasi del Simeto
of Catania
C. Pastelluccio

C A T A N I A
Plain
of Catania
Fontanarossa
Gulf
of Catania

CATANIA

I-O-N-I-A-N
SEA
Syracusa

M. Frasca
662
Mass.
Niscima
Sette Feudi
Borgo Pietro
Lupo
Oglastro
Palagonia
M. Grotte
Scordia
Linzity
Militello
in Val di Catania
S. di Mineo
C. Callari
C. S. Biagio
385
Lago di
Lentini
194
Lentini
Carlentini
Villasmundo
Agnone
Brucoli
Megara
Hyblaea
P. Xifonio
Augusta
Gulf of
Augusta

Mirabella
Imbaccari
C. Frasca
Mass. il Salto
Mineo
Leontinoi
Ris. Nat.

Francofonte
Grammichele
Nocchiero
194
Castle
683
Palazzelli
Castellana
Pedagaghi
M. S. Venere
870
M.Cugni
Melilli
Priolo
Gargallo
Thapsos
Magnisi
Peninsula

Vizzini
C. di Pietro
V. Gravina
C. Favitta
C. Prete
Licodia
Eubea
Torretta
Buccheri
M. Lauro
986
P. d. Pozzo
693
M. Contessa
914
564
Sortino
Solarino
Floridia
Cast. Eurialo

mi
Granieri
C. Licciardi
C. Vassallo
L. Dirillo
Feria
Cassaro
R.N. Pantalica
Valle dell'Anapo
e T. Cava Grande
Necropoli
di Pantalica
Roccafia
Canicattini
Bagni
V. dell'Anapo
124
Grotta
Perciata

M. Buongiovanni
Santo Pietro
C. Molinia
Botteghelle
Monterosso
Almo
194
Buscemi
Palazzolo
Acreide
Akrai
Anapo
SYRACUSE
Ortigia
115
Ognina
Cassibile
Fonte
Ciane

Mazzarrone
Quaglio
Giarratana
Chiaramonte
Gulfi
633
C. Priccio
C. Cappellani
Rigolizia
SIRACUSA
Cava Grande
Maggiore
Lido Arenella

Bastonaca
Pedalino
Casazza
Diligenza
P. d.
S. Rosalia
Balata
di Modica
514
RAGUSA
Fatt.
Judica
Castelluccio
Testa Acqua
Noto
Antica
Villa Vela
Ris. Nat. Cava Grande
del Cassibile
Avola
Antica
S. Corrado
di Fuori
A18
Fontane Bianche
P. del Cane
Gulf
of Noto

Pino d'Aleppo
Ris. Nat
Comiso
115
RAGUSA
Frigintini
Margione
NOTO
Avola
Marina di Avola

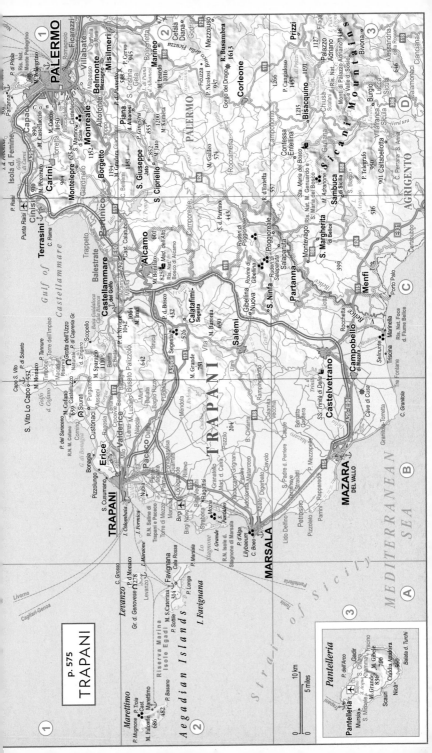

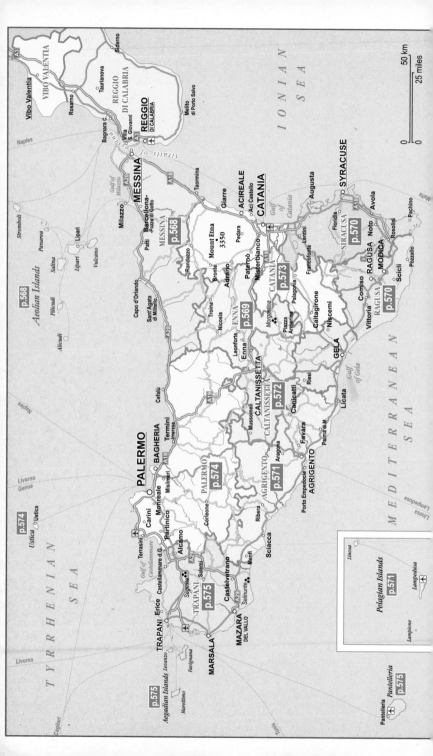